MATHEMATICS FOR ECONOMISTS

An introductory textbook

Malcolm Pemberton and Nicholas Rau

Department of Economics, University College London

Manchester University Press

Manchester and New York

Distributed exclusively in the USA by Palgrave

Published by Manchester University Press
Oxford Road, Manchester M13 9NR, UK
and Room 400, 175 Fifth Avenue, New York, NY 10010, USA
http://www.manchesteruniversitypress.co.uk

Distributed exclusively in the USA by
Palgrave, 175 Fifth Avenue, New York,
NY 10010, USA

Distributed exclusively in Canada by
UBC Press, University of British Columbia, 2029 West Mall,
Vancouver, BC, Canada V6T 1Z2

British Library Cataloguing-in-Publication Data
A catalogue record for this book is available from the British Library

Library of Congress Cataloging-in-Publication Data applied for

ISBN 0 7190 3340 3 *hardback*
　　 0 7190 3341 1 *paperback*

First published 2001

10 09 08 07 06 05 04 03 02 01   10 9 8 7 6 5 4 3 2 1

Printed in Great Britain
by Biddles Ltd, Guildford and King's Lynn

Contents

Preface   **x**

1 LINEAR EQUATIONS   **1**
- 1.1 Straight line graphs 1
- 1.2 Simultaneous equations 9
- 1.3 Input-output analysis 15
- Problems on Chapter 1 18

2 LINEAR INEQUALITIES   **19**
- 2.1 Inequalities 19
- 2.2 Economic applications 24
- 2.3 Linear programming 28
- Problems on Chapter 2 33

3 SETS AND FUNCTIONS   **35**
- 3.1 Sets and numbers 35
- 3.2 Functions 41
- 3.3 Mappings 49
- Problems on Chapter 3 51

4 QUADRATICS, INDICES AND LOGARITHMS   **53**
- 4.1 Quadratic functions 53
- 4.2 Indices 61
- 4.3 Logarithms 65
- Problems on Chapter 4 68

5 SEQUENCES AND SERIES   **69**
- 5.1 Sequences 69
- 5.2 Series 74
- 5.3 Geometric progressions in economics 78
- Problems on Chapter 5 84

6 INTRODUCTION TO DIFFERENTIATION   86
6.1 The derivative 87
6.2 Linear approximations and differentiability 91
6.3 Two useful rules 96
6.4 Derivatives in economics 99
Problems on Chapter 6 102
Appendix to Chapter 6 104

7 METHODS OF DIFFERENTIATION   107
7.1 The product and quotient rules 107
7.2 The composite function rule 110
7.3 Monotonic functions and inverse functions 113
Problems on Chapter 7 117
Appendix to Chapter 7 119

8 MAXIMA AND MINIMA   121
8.1 Critical points 121
8.2 The second derivative 126
8.3 Optimisation 130
8.4 Convexity and concavity 138
Problems on Chapter 8 145

9 EXPONENTIAL AND LOGARITHMIC FUNCTIONS   147
9.1 The exponential function 147
9.2 Natural logarithms 153
9.3 Time in economics 157
Problems on Chapter 9 160
Appendix to Chapter 9 163

10 APPROXIMATIONS   165
10.1 Linear approximations 166
10.2 The mean value theorem 170
10.3 Higher derivatives and Taylor's theorem 174
10.4 Taylor series 177
Problems on Chapter 10 180
Appendix to Chapter 10 182

11 MATRIX ALGEBRA   184
11.1 Vectors 185
11.2 Matrices 189
11.3 Matrix multiplication 193
11.4 Square matrices 198

Problems on Chapter 11 200

12 SYSTEMS OF LINEAR EQUATIONS — 203
12.1 Echelon matrices 204
12.2 More on Gaussian elimination 207
12.3 Inverting a matrix 213
12.4 Linear dependence and rank 219
Problems on Chapter 12 222

13 DETERMINANTS AND QUADRATIC FORMS — 224
13.1 Determinants 225
13.2 Transposition 230
13.3 Inner products and quadratic forms 235
Problems on Chapter 13 242
Appendix to Chapter 13 244

14 FUNCTIONS OF SEVERAL VARIABLES — 245
14.1 Partial derivatives 245
14.2 Approximations and the chain rule 252
14.3 Production functions 257
14.4 Homogeneous functions 261
Problems on Chapter 14 266
Appendix to Chapter 14 268

15 IMPLICIT RELATIONS — 271
15.1 Implicit differentiation 271
15.2 Comparative statics 279
15.3 Generalising to higher dimensions 285
Problems on Chapter 15 289
Appendix to Chapter 15 292

16 OPTIMISATION WITH SEVERAL VARIABLES — 294
16.1 Critical points and their classification 294
16.2 Global optima, concavity and convexity 302
16.3 Non-negativity constraints 309
Problems on Chapter 16 313
Appendix to Chapter 16 315

17 PRINCIPLES OF CONSTRAINED OPTIMISATION — 318
17.1 Lagrange multipliers 318
17.2 Extensions and warnings 325
17.3 Economic applications 329

17.4 Quasi-concave functions 338
Problems on Chapter 17 344

18 FURTHER TOPICS IN CONSTRAINED OPTIMISATION 347
18.1 The meaning of the multipliers 347
18.2 Envelope theorems 351
18.3 Inequality constraints 357
Problems on Chapter 18 367

19 INTEGRATION 370
19.1 Areas and integrals 370
19.2 Rules of integration 377
19.3 Integration in economics 384
19.4 Numerical integration 387
Problems on Chapter 19 394
Appendix to Chapter 19 396

20 ASPECTS OF INTEGRAL CALCULUS 398
20.1 Methods of integration 398
20.2 Infinite integrals 404
20.3 Differentiation under the integral sign 408
Problems on Chapter 20 413

21 INTRODUCTION TO DYNAMICS 415
21.1 Differential equations 416
21.2 Linear equations with constant
coefficients 420
21.3 Harder first-order equations 426
21.4 Difference equations 432
Problems on Chapter 21 440

22 THE CIRCULAR FUNCTIONS 442
22.1 Cycles, circles and trigonometry 442
22.2 Extending the definitions 448
22.3 Calculus with circular functions 455
22.4 Polar coordinates 461
Problems on Chapter 22 463

23 COMPLEX NUMBERS 466
23.1 The complex number system 466
23.2 The trigonometric form 471
23.3 Complex exponentials and polynomials 475

Problems on Chapter 23 481

24 FURTHER DYNAMICS — 483
24.1 Second-order differential equations 483
24.2 Qualitative behaviour 492
24.3 Second-order difference equations 499
Problems on Chapter 24 507
Appendix to Chapter 24 509

25 EIGENVALUES AND EIGENVECTORS — 511
25.1 Diagonalisable matrices 511
25.2 The characteristic polynomial 516
25.3 Eigenvalues of symmetric matrices 524
Problems on Chapter 25 528
Appendix to Chapter 25 531

26 DYNAMIC SYSTEMS — 533
26.1 Systems of difference equations 533
26.2 Systems of differential equations 541
26.3 Qualitative behaviour 546
26.4 Nonlinear systems 558
Problems on Chapter 26 565
Appendix to Chapter 26 568

Notes on Further Reading — 570

Answers — 572
Answers to odd-numbered exercises 572
Answers to selected problems 593

Index — 607

Preface

A glance at the Table of Contents reveals that this book is ambitious. Chapter 1 on linear equations is accessible to students with a very limited amount of school mathematics. By the time Chapter 26 on dynamic systems is reached, the reader will have covered most of the mathematics required in Master's courses in economics.

Our approach is to teach the student of economics how to *do* mathematics and how to *use* it sensibly. We emphasise the reasons why results are true and how they are related. We promote active learning with plentiful exercises and problems: rather than merely describe how mathematics is used in economics, we have included numerous problems where the student is asked to practise just this.

A distinctive feature of our approach is that we attempt to be introductory in both senses of the word: we assume little in the way of prerequisites, but also provide a sound preparation for more advanced work. Combining these two attributes means more than just writing a long book. First, it means paying attention to pace, achieving momentum without breathlessness. We have made considerable effort to achieve this, and are particularly proud of our success in the pre-calculus chapters (1–5) and in Chapters 22 and 23 on circular functions and complex numbers.

Secondly, we have been very careful in the organisation of our material. A good example of this is our treatment of the exponential function, which we introduce relatively late, after a thorough account of the rules of differentiation and maxima and minima; our concern here was to avoid piling on too much material at once. When the exponential function does appear, in Chapter 9, our exposition is based on compound interest; this leads directly to those properties of the function that are most relevant to the economist. The one major property of the exponential function omitted from Chapter 9 is its series expansion, which is used as the definition of the function in many books on calculus but has few economic applications; the series is given in Chapter 10.

A third aspect of our determination to be introductory in both senses is our attitude to proof. We have attempted wherever possible to provide some explanation of what follows from what, giving non-rigorous (but not, we hope, misleading) plausibility arguments for results whose precise proofs are well beyond our scope. We discourage rote-learning and try to avoid magic formulae. At the same time, we have deliberately adopted a discursive style, and do not burden the reader with the definition-theorem-proof format. Our terminology follows a similar 'middle way'. We define our terms, and strive to avoid serious ambiguity. On the other hand, we consider a certain laxity of language appropriate in a book of this nature; the use of "the function f", "the function $f(x)$" and "the function $y = f(x)$" in close proximity to mean the same thing should not embarrass writer or reader.

An earlier book which, in our view, strikes the right balance between rigour and accessibility is Alpha C. Chiang's classic *Fundamental Methods of Mathematical Economics*. There are many differences between our approach and Chiang's, but the most important are a result of what has happened to economics and its teaching over the last thirty years: in Paul Krugman's phrase, "the nerds won". When Chiang's book first appeared in 1969,[1] undergraduate economics was typically taught by means of verbal argument with the help of simple diagrams; the word 'model' was rarely mentioned. Chiang therefore found it necessary to explain and advocate a particular, 'mathematical' approach to economics. Three decades on, all the best textbooks on intermediate microeconomics and macroeconomics are written by authors well versed in mathematical model-building, and reflect the model-builder's attitude to the subject. There is therefore no need for us to provide lengthy discussions of the relevant economics 'done mathematically'. But for a thorough understanding of modern economics, attitude is not enough: the student also needs mathematical knowledge, technique and self-confidence. These needs become stronger when he or she progresses to more advanced material.

Our aim, then, is to teach students of economics the mathematical skills they require, leaving the economics itself to be done elsewhere. We provide applications to many branches of economics in the text, in worked examples and especially in the exercises and problems. But the emphasis throughout is on helping the reader to master the mathematics.

Special features

The following list is a mixture of topics we emphasise more strongly than other books, things we believe we do particularly well and assorted idiosyncrasies and obsessions that have found their way into our book after many years of teaching. It is not intended to be exhaustive in any respect, but should give a flavour of what is to come.

- The material on linear programming in Chapter 2 has very little direct connection with anything else that happens before Chapter 18. It is, however, a wonderfully simple illustration of how to combine algebra with diagrams, a skill that is essential for understanding calculus.

---

[1]Published by McGraw-Hill. The current (third) edition was published in 1984, also by McGraw-Hill.

- Our treatment of differentiation consistently stresses links with linear approximations.

- Starting in Chapter 8, we provide a very full discussion of how traditional calculus needs to be tailored to economic optimisation problems. In particular we emphasise the distinction between global and local optima, non-negativity constraints and the relevance of concavity and convexity.

- Our treatment of matrix algebra in Chapters 11 and 12 has two main themes: first, systems of linear equations and the use of row operations as the main tool for solving them; secondly, the interpretation of matrices as mappings. Only after this, in Chapter 13, do we come on to determinants. These we treat rather briefly; we do not think that 21st-century economics requires more. We say rather more about quadratic forms, which are important both for optimisation (see Chapter 16) and for econometrics.

- The chapters on differential calculus of several variables follow those on matrix algebra. There is a very good reason for this: use of vectors and matrices makes it much easier to explain n–variable results by single-variable analogies. The gain is substantial even when $n = 2$.

- Chapter 15 contains an unusually full treatment of comparative statics.

- Eigenvalues and eigenvectors turn up very late, in the penultimate chapter: our initial discussion of quadratic forms in Chapter 13 does not require them. The treatment of eigenvalue theory in Chapter 25 is elementary but thorough; we explain all the results needed in the final chapter on dynamic systems, and also include material much used in econometrics.

- As we have already explained, it is not our intention to duplicate material taught in economics textbooks. But with respect to interstitial topics, which tend to be omitted from mathematics courses because they are economics and vice versa, our policy has been "when in doubt, include". Examples are Section 9.3 on time in economics, the examples of phase diagrams in Chapter 26 and much of Chapter 18 on advanced topics in constrained optimisation; this chapter gives a thorough account of envelope theorems and the Kuhn–Tucker theorem.

Prerequisites and pathways

The minimal prerequisites for reading this book are some competence at algebraic manipulation, and familiarity with graphs. At the same time, there is plenty in the book for students who have already studied some calculus. As a rough guide to the amount of time required to get through the book in typical undergraduate courses, we suggest three semesters for students without calculus and two semesters for students with a good grounding in one-variable calculus.

Here are some suggestions for courses based on the book. A *first course for economics students with no previous knowledge of calculus* would consist of Chapters 1 to 9 and 19, possibly with selected material from Chapters 10 and/or 20. A *second course covering matrix algebra, functions of several variables and some simple dynamics* could start with a review of Sections 1.2 and 1.3 and then cover Chapters 11–17 and 21; some material from Chapter 18 could substitute for the harder comparative statics in Chapter 15. A course on *further calculus for economists* for students who are competent in one-variable calculus could start with a review of Chapters 8 and 9 with emphasis on the economic applications, give a brief account of partial differentiation using selected material from Chapter 14, review Chapters 19 and 20 with emphasis on economic applications, and then proceed through Chapters 21–24. A course on *optimisation and dynamics for advanced undergraduates and beginning Master's students* could be based on Chapters 16–18 and 21–26, with the amount of time devoted to the trigonometric chapters 22 and 23 depending on the students' backgrounds. There are numerous other possibilities.

Style

Chapters are of course numbered, as are sections within chapters. We do not have any lower levels of numbering. When we number propositions or worked examples, the numbering starts afresh within each section. Equation numbering, by contrast, is by chapter rather than section. The object of these conventions is to avoid intimidating the reader with a surfeit of dots.

At the risk of belabouring the obvious, we emphasise that *equations are numbered for future reference and for no other reason*. Numbered equations should *not* be regarded as more important than unnumbered ones.

Some chapters are followed by appendices, which take up particular points, largely in order to add a little more rigour to the argument. Knowledge of the material in the appendices is not necessary for doing the exercises or problems (which is why we have put the appendices after the problems). However, we hope that we have sufficiently stimulated our readers' curiosity that the appendices answer questions they wanted to ask.

This book contains several hundred exercises and 104 problems (four per chapter). Exercises are at the end of sections and are relatively undemanding. Problems are at the end of chapters: they are often related to more than one section of the chapter, and some of them are quite tough. At the end of the book we provide brief answers to odd-numbered exercises and complete solutions to selected problems (one per chapter). We have prepared answers to all the other exercises and problems with a view to producing a solution manual, but have not yet decided what form this will take.

On nice points of mathematical terminology we have followed E. J. Borowski and J. M. Borwein's *Collins Dictionary of Mathematics* (HarperCollins, 1989). This excellent reference book also served as a role-model for LaTeX typography.

Acknowledgments

This book has been much tested in teaching at UCL over the years, and we are grateful to past and present students, colleagues and teaching assistants. Georg von Graevenitz did a wonderful job with the diagrams, and in assembling assorted LaTeX documents into an integrated book.

During the many years that this book has been in preparation, we have dealt with three editors at MUP: Tony Mason, Nicola Viinikka and the late Francis Brooke. We thank them all, and are sorry that Francis did not live to see the completion of the project he encouraged. And many thanks to Zeina Khalil, Irene Pemberton and Jeannie Rau for their support.

London, April 2001

The Greek Alphabet

α	A	alpha	ν	N	nu
β	B	beta	ξ	Ξ	xi
γ	Γ	gamma	o	O	omicron
δ	Δ	delta	π	Π	pi
ε	E	epsilon	ρ	P	rho
ζ	Z	zeta	σ	Σ	sigma
η	H	eta	τ	T	tau
θ	Θ	theta	υ	Υ	upsilon
ι	I	iota	ϕ	Φ	phi
κ	K	kappa	χ	X	chi
λ	λ	lambda	ψ	Ψ	psi
μ	M	mu	ω	Ω	omega

Chapter 1

LINEAR EQUATIONS

In this chapter we introduce two of the main themes of the book. The first is the fact that a relationship between two quantities — for example price and output, or income and consumption — can often be expressed either as an equation or by means of a diagram. Building on this fact will lead us later on into curve-sketching and calculus. Here we start with the simplest case, where the relevant 'curves' are straight lines.

The second topic of Chapter 1 is the solution of systems of linear equations. This is also something we shall build on later in the book, using the powerful techniques of matrix algebra. But, as we shall see in this chapter, the basic method of solution can be explained very simply, as can its applications to the economics of market equilibrium and input-output analysis.

When you have studied this chapter you will be able to:

- sketch graphs of linear relations;

- solve systems of two linear equations in two unknowns, and of three linear equations in three unknowns;

- calculate price and quantity in market equilibrium, given linear supply and demand schedules;

- solve simple problems in input-output analysis.

1.1   Straight line graphs

Suppose we have two perpendicular lines as shown in Figure 1.1. The horizontal line is called the x–**axis**, the vertical line the y–**axis** and the plane containing the two lines the xy–**plane**. The position of a point is then specified by its perpendicular distances from the two axes. The perpendicular distance from the y–axis is known as the x–**coordinate** and the perpendicular distance from the x–axis is known as the y–**coordinate**. For example the x–coordinate of P in Figure 1.1 is 3 and the y–coordinate is 4; the point is referred to as $(3, 4)$. Distances to the left of the y–axis are negative and, similarly, distances below the x–axis are negative. For instance Q, R and S are the points $(-1, 2)$, $(4, -1.5)$ and $(-2, -3.5)$ respectively.

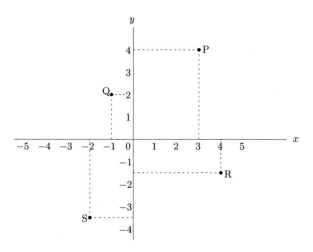

Figure 1.1: **Axes and coordinates**

Points on the x–axis have the y–coordinate zero and points on the y–axis have the x–coordinate zero. The point of intersection of the axes is known as the **origin** and has coordinates $(0, 0)$.

Now that we have explained what we mean by coordinates, we can move on to considering how to draw a picture of all the points whose x and y coordinates satisfy a relation of the form

$$y = ax + b,$$

where a and b are given numbers. This procedure is referred to as **sketching the graph** of the relation. The relation under consideration here is said to be **linear** because its graph turns out to be a straight line.

For example, the graph of the linear relation $y = 2x + 6$ is the line depicted in Figure 1.2. We could convince ourselves of this by taking a series of values of x, say $0, 1, -1, 2, -2$ and so on, and then calculating the corresponding values of y. In this way, we see that the points $(0, 6), (1, 8), (-1, 4), (2, 10), (-2, 2)$, and so on, all lie on the graph. If we then plot these on graph paper, we would see that they lie on a straight line.

To sketch the graph of a linear relation we do not need to plot lots of points. All we need to do is to find *two* points on the graph and draw the line which passes through them. It is often convenient to choose our two points to be those where the graph crosses the axes.

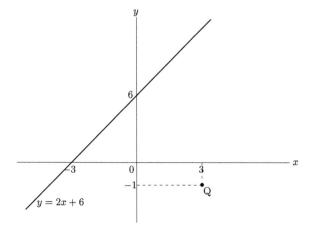

Figure 1.2: **The line** $y = 2x + 6$

For example, we sketch the straight line of Figure 1.2 as follows. Since the y–axis consists of the points whose x–coordinate is zero, our line crosses the y–axis where $x = 0$ and $y = 0 + 6$: this is the point $(0, 6)$. Similarly, the line we are interested in crosses the x-axis where $y = 0$ and $2x + 6 = 0$, giving an x–coordinate of -3. Having worked out that the line $y = 2x + 6$ crosses the axes at the points $(0, 6)$ and $(-3, 0)$, we sketch the graph by marking these two points and drawing the line that passes through both of them.

Since a straight line is the graph of a linear relation, the points which are not on the line have coordinates that do not satisfy the relation. For example, we see in Figure 1.2 that the point $(3, -1)$, denoted by Q, is not on the line $y = 2x + 6$. To verify algebraically that the coordinates of Q do not satisfy that linear relation, note that, at Q, $y = -1$ whereas $2x + 6 = +12$.

Slope and intercept

Returning to the general linear relation $y = ax + b$, we call b the **intercept** of the relation; b is the value taken by y when $x = 0$. The number a is called the **slope** or **gradient** of the relation and measures the amount by which y increases when x goes up by 1 unit.

In geometrical terms, the slope measures the steepness of the straight line graph. Figure 1.3 depicts three linear relations, all with the same intercept as the one of Figure 1.2, but with different gradients:

(A) $y = 3x + 6$;   (B) $y = 6x + 6$;   (C) $y = -x + 6$.

Each straight line can be sketched by finding the points where it cuts the axes. For instance line (A) cuts the y–axis where $x = 0$ and $y = 6$, and cuts the x–axis where $y = 0$ and $x = -2$.

According to relation (A), y increases by 3 units for every unit of increase of x; thus when x increases by 2 units from 3 to 5, y increases by 6 units from 15 to 21. In relation (B), y increases by 6 units for every unit of increase of x, which is why the line depicting this relation is steeper than the graph of (A). According to relation (C), y *decreases* by 1 unit for every unit of increase of x, so that the graph is downward-sloping: notice that this relation may be written $y = 6 - x$.

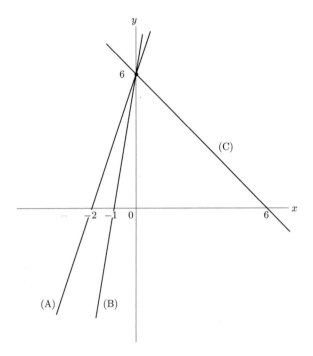

Figure 1.3: **Straight lines** — **same intercept, different slopes**

As a further illustration of negative slopes, consider the three downward-sloping straight lines of Figure 1.4: the top one depicts the relation $y = 6 - 2x$, the middle one $y = 1 - 2x$ and the bottom one $y = -3 - 2x$. These lines have different intercepts but the same slope (-2 in each case) and are therefore parallel to each other.

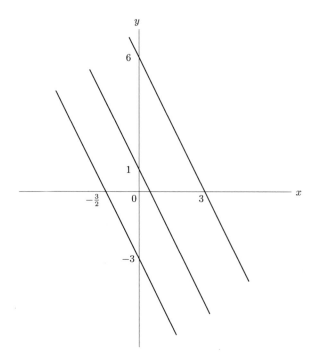

Figure 1.4: **Straight lines — same slopes, different intercepts**

To summarise, a relation of the form

$$y = ax + b$$

is represented by an upward-sloping straight line if a is a positive number, and a downward-sloping straight line if a is a negative number. Provided neither a nor b is zero, the straight line can be sketched by finding the two points where it crosses the axes. If $b = 0$, the graph passes through the origin $(0,0)$, and we may sketch the graph by choosing as our two points the origin and one other point, for example the point $(1, a)$. On the other hand, if $a = 0$ the relation reduces to $y = b$ and the graph is parallel to the x–axis, for example the horizontal line $y = 4$ of Figure 1.5.

The only straight lines whose equations *cannot* be put in the form $y = ax + b$ are those parallel to the y–axis. These lines have equations of the form

$$x = c$$

where c is a constant, for example the vertical line $x = -3$ of Figure 1.5.

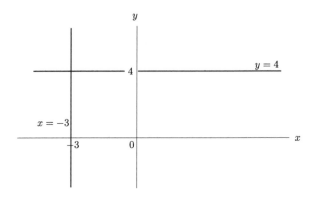

Figure 1.5: **Lines parallel to the axes**

An economic application: supply and demand

As application of straight line graphs, we consider a simple example of supply and demand in a market. Suppose the demand schedule for a good, say honey, is given by

$$q = 8 - 4p,$$

where p denotes price and q denotes quantity demanded. The graph is a straight line of slope -4 and intercept 8, hitting the p–axis when $p = 2$. The negative slope reflects the 'law of demand' whereby consumers demand less honey the higher its price.

Suppose also that the supply schedule for honey is given by

$$q = p + 3,$$

with the interpretation that bee-keepers wish to produce $p + 3$ units of honey when the price of honey is p. This is represented by a straight line of slope 1 and intercept 3, hitting the p–axis when $p = -3$. The line slopes upward because a higher price of honey induces people to devote more time and effort to keeping bees.

The supply and demand schedules are sketched in Figure 1.6. The only part of the diagram of any economic relevance is that in which neither price nor quantity is negative; the corresponding parts of the graphs have therefore been drawn solid, and the economically irrelevant parts dotted.

The equilibrium, where demand and supply are equal, is at the point E where the two lines intersect. At this point the two equations

$$q = 8 - 4p, \quad q = p + 3$$

must be satisfied simultaneously. Thus at E,

$$8 - 4p = p + 3.$$

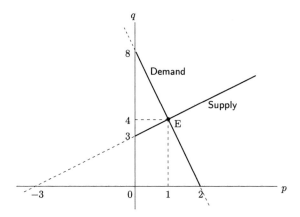

Figure 1.6: **Supply and demand**

Rearranging, we have $5 = 5p$, whence $p = 1$; and substituting this into either the supply or the demand equation gives $q = 4$. Thus in this case the equilibrium (market-clearing) price and quantity are

$$p = 1, \quad q = 4.$$

We now redraw Figure 1.6 in a way that will be more familiar to many readers. For historical reasons, economists tend to draw supply and demand curves with quantity q on the horizontal axis and price p on the vertical axis.

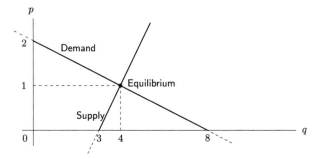

Figure 1.7: **Supply and demand, the economist's way**

To see what the diagram looks like with this labelling of axes, we first re-arrange the demand equation for honey to bring p on to the left hand side: starting with

$$q = 8 - 4p$$

we have

$$4p + q = 8$$

and hence
$$p = 2 - \frac{q}{4}.$$

This can be interpreted as saying that $2 - q/4$ is the largest price at which q units of honey would find buyers.

Similarly the supply equation can also be written with p on the left hand side, as
$$p = q - 3.$$

This can be interpreted as saying that $q - 3$ is the smallest price at which bee-keepers would be prepared to supply q units of honey.

The supply and demand schedules are redrawn in Figure 1.7; as we know from our earlier calculation, the market clears when $q = 4$ and $p = 1$.

Exercises

1.1.1 Show the point $(-2, 3)$ in the xy–plane. Show also its reflexions in the x and y axes.

The three points you have marked form three of the four vertices of a rectangle. What are the coordinates of the fourth?

1.1.2 Sketch the graphs of the following linear relations:

(a) $y = 8$,   (b) $x = -7$,   (c) $y = -2x + 5$,   (d) $y = 4x - 1$.

1.1.3 Sketch in the same diagram the graphs of the following linear relations:

(a) $y = x + 1$,   (b) $y = x - 3$,   (c) $y = x + 8$.

What do you notice?

Find the equation of the line of slope 1 which passes through the point $(-1, 5)$.

1.1.4 Sketch in the same diagram the graphs of the following linear relations:

(a) $y = 2x + 3$,   (b) $y = -x + 3$,   (c) $y = -8x + 3$.

What do you notice?

Find the equation of the line of intercept 3 which passes through the point $(1, 0)$.

1.1.5 Suppose the demand and supply schedules for milk are
$$q = 11 - 3p, \quad q = 1 + 2p$$

respectively. Sketch these schedules in the pq–plane,

1.2 Simultaneous equations

In our example of the supply and demand for honey, the algebra of finding
equilibrium price and quantity was an exercise in solving a system of two linear
equations in two unknowns. We now explain a systematic procedure for doing
this. Later in the section we generalise the method to more complicated systems
of linear equations.

Consider the pair of equations

$$3x + 2y = 8$$
$$2x + 5y = 9.$$

These equations are called linear because they can be represented by straight
lines, as we show in Figure 1.8. To sketch these lines, we can write their equations with y on the left-hand side and proceed as in Section 1.1. Alternatively
we can sketch each straight line by working out directly where it cuts the axes.
Thus the line representing the first equation crosses the x-axis where $3x + 0 = 8$,
so that $x = 8/3$, and the y-axis where $y = 4$. Similarly, the other straight line
passes through the points $(9/2, 0)$ and $(0, 9/5)$.

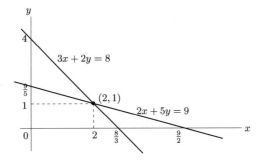

Figure 1.8:   **Two equations, two unknowns, unique solution**

Solving the system of two equations means finding values of x and y that
satisfy both equations simultaneously. What this means geometrically is finding
the intersection of the two straight lines of Figure 1.8. We can see in the figure
that the point of intersection has coordinates $(2, 1)$, so that the solution to our
system of equations is

$$x = 2, \ y = 1.$$

We now explain why this is so.

Our problem is to solve the system of equations

$$3x + 2y = 8$$
$$2x + 5y = 9.$$

To do this we start by eliminating one unknown from one equation, leaving one equation in one unknown. This is achieved by the following step:

(S)   Leave the first equation as it is and eliminate x from the second equation by subtracting a suitable multiple of the first equation.

If we subtract t times the first equation from the second we get an equation in which the coefficient of x is $2-3t$: to eliminate x we should make this expression zero by choosing t to be $2/3$.

Thus carrying out step (S) above leads to the new system

$$3x + 2y = 8$$
$$(5 - \tfrac{4}{3})y = 9 - \tfrac{16}{3}.$$

The second equation of the new system says that $\frac{11}{3}y = \frac{11}{3}$, so that $y = 1$; substituting this into the first equation, we see that

$$x = \tfrac{1}{3}(8 - 2y) = \tfrac{1}{3}(8 - 2) = 2.$$

The solution to our system is indeed

$$x = 2, \ y = 1.$$

Complications

We have just solved a system of two linear equations in two unknowns which had a unique solution: the corresponding straight lines, sketched in Figure 1.8, had a unique point of intersection. To see that this does not always happen, consider the system

$$3x + 2y = 8$$
$$6x + 4y = 9.$$

In this case, carrying out step (S) means subtracting twice the first equation from the second. This gives a new system of which the second equation is the absurd statement

$$0 = -7.$$

This is a signal that the system of equations we started with was inconsistent and therefore has no solution. The geometry of this is panel A of Figure 1.9: the two lines are parallel and therefore have no point of intersection.

The final kind of outcome of solving two linear equations in two unknowns is shown by the following:

$$3x + 2y = 8$$
$$6x + 4y = 16.$$

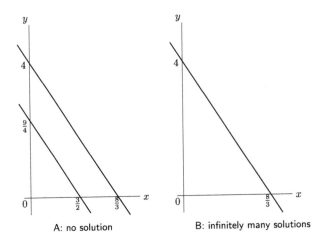

Figure 1.9:   **Two equation, two unknowns — the awkward cases**

Here, carrying out step (S) by subtracting twice the first equation from the second gives the new system

$$3x + 2y = 8$$
$$0 = 0.$$

The second equation is true in all circumstances, and therefore uninteresting. We are left with only one equation: any values of x and y which satisfy that equation solve the system. If we assign an arbitrary value p to y we can solve the first equation for x, giving $x = \frac{1}{3}(8 - 2p)$. We write the solution

$$x = \tfrac{2}{3}(4 - p), \ y = p.$$

This is the complete solution in the sense that we get all the different solutions of the system by assigning all possible numerical values to p. This means that the system has infinitely many solutions. Geometrically, the two equations of the system represent the same line — see Figure 1.9, panel B — and any one of the infinite number of points on that line represents a solution.

Two equations, two unknowns: summary

Given a system of two linear equations in two unknowns, there are three possibilities:

either there is a unique solution
or   there is no solution
or   there are infinitely many solutions.

In each case, the system may be solved by starting with step (S): 'solving' the system means finding the unique solution in the first case, tracking down an inconsistency in the second case, and describing the complete solution in the third. You do not have to know before you start which case you are in, since this is revealed by the solution procedure, as the examples above demonstrated.

The three cases can be thought of geometrically as follows. Each of the two equations represents a straight line. If the lines are different and intersect, they intersect in exactly one point: the system has a unique solution. If the equations represent parallel lines there is no solution. The remaining case is where the two equations represent the same line: here we have an infinite number of solutions.

Three equations in three unknowns

The method we used to solve a system of two linear equations in two unknowns x, y may be extended to solve systems of three linear equations in three unknowns x, y, z.

It is helpful to start with a 'triangular' system, so called because of the pattern made by the non-zero coefficients on the left-hand side:

$$
\begin{aligned}
2x + 7y + \ z &= 2 \\
3y - \ 2z &= 7 \\
4z &= 4.
\end{aligned}
$$

The third equation gives $z = 1$; substituting this into the second equation gives $y = (7+2)/3 = 3$; and substituting our values for y and z into the first equation gives

$$
x = \frac{2 - 21 - 1}{2} = -10.
$$

The solution is

$$
x = -10, \ y = 3, \ z = 1.
$$

This process of repeated substitution into the previous equation is called **back-substitution** and can be applied to any triangular system, yielding a unique solution.

For systems which are not triangular, we eliminate unknowns from equations until, if possible, we arrive at a triangular system. This is most easily achieved by a generalisation of step (S) above.

To see how the procedure works, consider the system

$$
\begin{aligned}
2x + 4y + \ z &= 5 \\
x + \ y + \ z &= 6 \\
2x + 3y + 2z &= 6.
\end{aligned}
$$

To solve this, we begin by carrying out the following generalisation of (S):

(S1)   Leave the first equation alone and eliminate x from the second and third equations by subtracting from those equations suitable multiples of the first equation.

In our example this means subtracting $1/2$ times the first equation from the second equation and (since $2/2 = 1$) subtracting the first equation from the third equation. This gives the new system

$$\begin{aligned}
2x + 4y + \;\; z &= 5 \\
- \;\; y + z/2 &= 7/2 \\
- \;\; y + \;\; z &= 1 \;.
\end{aligned}$$

The system is not yet triangular because of the presence of y in the third equation. The next stage is to perform the following step:

(S2)   Leave the first and second equations alone and eliminate y from the third equation by subtracting a suitable multiple of the second.

In this case the 'suitable multiple' is $(-1)/(-1) = 1$: we subtract the second equation from the third, obtaining the triangular system

$$\begin{aligned}
2x + 4y + \;\; z &= 5 \\
- \;\; y + z/2 &= 7/2 \\
z/2 &= -5/2.
\end{aligned}$$

We can now apply back-substitution: $z = -5$, $y = (-5 - 7)/2 = -6$, $x = (5 + 5 + 24)/2 = 17$. The solution to the system is

$$x = 17, \; y = -6, \; z = -5.$$

Gaussian elimination

In addition to the elimination steps (S1) and (S2), it is sometimes necessary to change the order of the equations. Thus, in the system

$$\begin{aligned}
- \;\; 3y + 4z &= -2 \\
x + 5y + 2z &= 9 \\
x + \;\; y + \;\; z &= 6,
\end{aligned}$$

we cannot eliminate x from the second and third equations by subtracting multiples of the first equation. We therefore begin by interchanging the first two equations and then proceeding as above.

In general, then, the elimination procedure can be carried out using a sequence of elementary operations. These are of two kinds:

(EO1)   writing the equations in a different order;
(EO2)   subtracting a multiple of one equation from another equation.

The particular procedure we use to simplify a system of equations by successive elementary operations is called **Gaussian elimination**:[1] (EO1) operations, if required, alternate with elimination steps such as (S1) and (S2) in which multiples of an equation are subtracted from each of the equations below it.

The following three properties of the procedure are extremely important.

1. *Elementary operations are reversible.* If we exchange two equations and then exchange again, we are back where we started. And if we perform the (EO2) of subtracting 7 times the second equation from the third equation, and then perform the further (EO2) of adding 7 times the second equation to the new third equation, we are again back where we started. The fact that elementary operations are reversible is important for the following reason: when we simplify a system of equations using these operations, the simplified system is logically equivalent to the one we started off with, and therefore has the same solution. This is the reason why Gaussian elimination always works.

2. Any system of three linear equations in three unknowns which has a unique solution can be reduced by Gaussian elimination to a triangular system. The solution is then found by back-substitution. And the same is true of systems of n linear equations in n unknowns, where n can be $2, 3, 4, 27$ or whatever.

3. It is possible for a system of n linear equations in n unknowns not to have a unique solution. We have already seen this for $n = 2$ (recall Figure 1.9) and the same is true for larger values of n. In such cases reduction to triangular form is not possible, but Gaussian elimination is still helpful. If the elimination procedure gives rise to an absurd equation like $0 = 3$, the system has no solution. And if the procedure leads to a vanishing equation $(0 = 0)$ and there are no absurdities, there are infinitely many solutions. In such cases the complete solution can be found, as in the two-equation case. For details, and further discussion of systems of linear equations, see Chapter 12.

Exercises

1.2.1 Solve the following equations simultaneously:

$$x + 2y = 3$$
$$2x - 3y = 13.$$

1.2.2 Show that the following system of equations has no solution unless $c = \frac{1}{2}$:

$$2x - 5y = c$$
$$4x - 10y = 1.$$

---

[1] After the great German mathematician and scientist Carl Friedrich Gauss (1777–1855).

When $c = \frac{1}{2}$, find the complete solution.

1.2.3 Suppose the demand and supply schedules for wine are

$$q = k - 4p, \quad q = 1 + 3p$$

respectively, where k is a constant parameter. Find the equilibrium price and quantity in terms of k.

In each of the following cases, sketch the demand and supply schedules and write down the equilibrium price and quantity:

$$\text{(a) } k = 3, \quad \text{(b) } k = 4, \quad \text{(c) } k = 2.$$

What happens when $k = \frac{1}{2}$?

1.2.4 Solve the system of equations

$$
\begin{aligned}
x + 2y + 2z &= 1 \\
2x - 2y + z &= 2 \\
x - y + 3z &= 3.
\end{aligned}
$$

1.3 Input-output analysis

One application in economics of systems of simultaneous linear equations is the input-output model, which has proved helpful in forecasting and planning. We illustrate it with a simple example.

Suppose an economy produces three goods X, Y and Z. There may also be non-produced goods such as labour, land, imported raw materials and so on. We assume **no joint production**: this means that we can think of 'industry X' producing positive quantities only of good X, using goods Y and Z, and possibly X itself as inputs. The other two industries produce Y and Z.

We define the **gross output** of good X to be the total amount produced, including that fed back into the system as industrial input. This is to be contrasted with the **net output** of X, which is the amount of X produced and *not* fed back into the system, being therefore available for consumption, accumulation and export. The relation between net and gross output of good X is

net output of X = gross output of X
      − quantity of X required as input in industry X
      − quantity of X required as input in industry Y
      − quantity of X required as input in industry Z.

Similar relations hold for goods Y and Z.

Input requirements per unit of *gross* output of each produced good are given in the following table, known as an **input-output table**. This says for example that each unit of gross output of good Y requires the input of 0.2 units of good X, 0.5 units of good Y and 0.3 units of good Z.

		OUTPUT		
		X	Y	Z
	X	0.2	0.2	0.2
INPUT	Y	0.4	0.5	0.1
	Z	0.4	0.3	0.3

Our final assumption is **constant returns to scale**, which in this context means that the figures given in the table for input requirements per unit of gross output are independent of the levels of gross output. Thus, if gross outputs of Y and Z are y and z, $0.1z$ units of Y are required as input in the Z industry and $0.3y$ units of Z are required as input in the Y industry, however large or small y and z happen to be.

Let the gross outputs of X, Y, Z be x, y, z and the net outputs x^*, y^*, z^*. Then the relation between net and gross output of good X may be written

$$x^* = x - 0.2x - 0.2y - 0.2z.$$

The equivalent relations for Y and Z are:

$$y^* = y - 0.4x - 0.5y - 0.1z$$
$$z^* = z - 0.4x - 0.3y - 0.3z.$$

Simplifying, we have the equations

$$x^* = 0.8x - 0.2y - 0.2z$$
$$y^* = -0.4x + 0.5y - 0.1z$$
$$z^* = -0.4x - 0.3y + 0.7z.$$

It is a matter of simple arithmetic to use these equations to obtain the net outputs, given the gross outputs. More interestingly, one can also use the equations to find out how much gross output of each good must be produced if a given list of net outputs is required.

Suppose for example that required net outputs of X, Y and Z are 10, 15 and 7 respectively. To find the gross outputs, we must solve the above system of linear equations for x, y and z, given that $x^* = 10$, $y^* = 15$ and $z^* = 7$. This is done in the usual way by Gaussian elimination. Our first step is to leave the first equation alone and eliminate x from the second and third equations by

adding 0.5 times the first equation to each of these equations. We obtain the
system

$$0.8x - 0.2y - 0.2z = 10$$
$$0.4y - 0.2z = 20$$
$$-0.4y + 0.6z = 12.$$

Leaving the first two equations alone and adding the second equation to the
third, we obtain the triangular system

$$0.8x - 0.2y - 0.2z = 10$$
$$0.4y - 0.2z = 20$$
$$0.4z = 32.$$

Solving this system by back-substitution, we have $z = 80$, $y = \frac{1}{2}(100 + z) = 90$
and $x = \frac{1}{4}(50 + y + z) = 55$. The required gross outputs are 55 units of X, 90
units of Y and 80 units of Z.

This is of course a particularly simple and stylised example of input-output
analysis, which can be made much more general and practical. As early as
the 1950s the economist Wassily Leontief and his associates were constructing
80-sector input-output tables for the United States. Since then input-output
analysis has been greatly extended to bring in time-lags in production, choice
of technique, natural resources and many other complications.

Exercises

1.3.1 For the example of the input-output model given in the text, find the gross
outputs corresponding to net outputs of 12, 10, 10 of X, Y, Z respectively.

1.3.2 Suppose an economy produces two goods X and Y under conditions of no
joint production and constant returns to scale. Input requirements per
unit of gross output are given by the following input-output table.

		OUTPUT	
		X	Y
INPUT	X	0.1	0.2
	Y	0.7	0.4

Find the gross outputs when the required net outputs of X and Y are 30
and 10 respectively.

Problems on Chapter 1

1–1. (i) Find the equation of the straight line in the xy–plane that has slope s and passes through the point $(4, 7)$.

(ii) If you know that the straight line of (i) passes through the point (x_1, y_1), where $x_1 \neq 4$, what is s?

(iii) By reasoning by analogy to your solutions to (i) and (ii), find the equation of the straight line that passes through the points (x_0, y_0) and (x_1, y_1), where $x_1 \neq x_0$.

(iv) Using the result of (iii), find the equation of the straight line that passes through the points $(-1, 3)$ and $(1, -5)$.

1–2. Show that the following system of equations has no solution when $k = -4$:

$$
\begin{aligned}
x + 3y - 2z &= 2 \\
2x - 5y + z &= 0 \\
3x - 2y - z &= k.
\end{aligned}
$$

When $k = 2$, show that the system reduces to two equations in three unknowns and hence find the complete solution.

1–3. In the following macroeconomic model, the unknowns are Y (national income), C (consumption) and T (tax collection):

$$
Y = C + I + G, \quad C = 2 + 0.8(Y - T), \quad T = 1 + 0.2Y.
$$

I (investment) and G (government expenditure) are assumed to be known. Find Y, C and T in terms of I and G. What happens to Y, C and T when G increases by x units?

1–4. Consider again the input-output table of Exercise 1.3.2. Find the gross outputs corresponding to net output levels a, b of X, Y respectively. How do you know the gross outputs are positive?

Chapter 2

LINEAR INEQUALITIES

Not all economic statements can be expressed as equations. The statements that Ireland's GDP is *greater* this year than last, and that *at most* 20% of the British labour force is employed in manufacturing, are examples of inequalities. In this chapter we show how inequalities may be treated in a similar way to equations in Chapter 1: they may be manipulated algebraically and sketched in the xy–plane. As before, we deal with straight lines rather than curves: hence the word 'linear' in the chapter's title.

Section 2.3 introduces optimisation subject to constraints, one of the main themes of this book. The exercises in that section are good training in combining algebraic and diagrammatic reasoning.

When you have studied this chapter you will be able to:

- rearrange inequalities using the three main algebraic rules;

- depict linear inequalities as regions in a plane;

- apply linear inequality diagrams in economic examples;

- solve simple problems in linear programming.

2.1 Inequalities

If u and v are numbers, then

$$u < v$$

means that u is less than v. Such a relation is called an **inequality** and the symbol $<$ is called an inequality sign.

If u and v are represented as points on the horizontal axis, the relation means that u is to the left of v. Figure 2.1 illustrates, among other things, the facts that $-2 < -1$, $-1 < \frac{1}{2}$ and $\frac{1}{2} < 3$.

$$-2 \qquad -1 \qquad 0 \ \tfrac{1}{2} \ 1 \qquad 2 \qquad 3$$

Figure 2.1: **Points on the horizontal axis**

The other inequality signs are defined as follows:

- $u > v$ means that u is greater than v (u is to the right of v);

- $u \leq v$ means that u is less than or equal to v;

- $u \geq v$ means that u is greater than or equal to v.

Thus $u > v$ means the same as $v < u$, and $u \geq v$ means the same as $v \leq u$. Statements involving $<$ and $>$ are called **strict inequalities**, while those involving $\leq$ and $\geq$ are called **weak inequalities**.

A number x is said to be **positive** if $x > 0$, **negative** if $x < 0$, non-negative if $x \geq 0$ and non-positive if $x \leq 0$.

Rules for manipulating inequalities

Let u and v be two numbers such that $u < v$. Suppose that a red button is placed on the axis at the point marked u, and a blue button at the point marked v. If we move both buttons to the right *by the same amount*, say 2 units, then the red button will still be to the left of the blue button: in other words, $u + 2 < v + 2$. If instead we had moved both buttons to the left by 3 units, the red button would again be to the left of the blue one: $u - 3 < v - 3$. In general, we have the following rule:

Rule 1 If the same number is added to both sides of an inequality, the inequality is preserved.

Again let u and v be numbers such that $u < v$; then $2u < 2v$. This is true when both u and v are positive numbers, when both u and v are negative numbers and when u is negative and v positive.[1] For suppose u is Pemberton's wealth and v is Rau's wealth. If u and v are positive numbers, then $u < v$ means that Pemberton has positive net wealth but is less wealthy than Rau, and this will remain true if the wealth of both men is doubled. If u and v are negative numbers, then $u < v$ means that Pemberton is even more seriously in debt than Rau, and this will remain true if the debts of both are doubled.

---

[1]The assumption that $u < v$ rules out the case where u is positive and v negative.

Finally, if $u < 0$ and $v > 0$, then Pemberton is in debt while Rau has positive net wealth, and this remains true when Pemberton's debts and Rau's wealth are doubled.

All of this is equally valid when doubling is replaced by multiplication by any positive number, so we have:

Rule 2 If both sides of an inequality are multiplied by the same **positive** number, the inequality is preserved.

The third and final rule for dealing with inequalities is more subtle:

Rule 3 If both sides of an inequality are multiplied by the same **negative** number, the inequality is **reversed**.

A special case of Rule 3 is where the negative multiplier is -1:

$$\text{if } u < v \text{ then } -u > -v. \tag{$*$}$$

This is easily verified using Figure 2.1: for example, if u is to the right of 0 and v still further to the right, then $-u$ is to the left of 0 and $-v$ still further to the left. Alternatively one can prove $(*)$ by adding the number $-v - u$ to both sides of the inequality $u < v$ and applying Rule 1.

Rule 3 tells us, for example, that if $u < v$ then $-5u > -5v$. Another way of demonstrating this is as follows: if $u < v$, then $-u > -v$ by $(*)$, so $5(-u) > 5(-v)$ by Rule 2, so $-5u > -5v$. The longer demonstration explains where Rule 3 comes from: since the argument works equally well when 5 is replaced by any other positive number, Rule 3 is a consequence of the special case $(*)$ and Rule 2.

Two points about the rules

First, they may be combined: if $u < v$ then $4 + 5u < 4 + 5v$ by Rules 1 and 2, and $6 - 7u > 6 - 7v$ by Rules 1 and 3. Secondly, *the rules apply to weak as well as strict inequalities*: if $a \geq b$ then $a + 2 \geq b + 2$, $3a \geq 3b$ and $-4a \leq -4b$.

Inequalities in the xy–plane

We now show how inequalities can be depicted in the xy–plane. Recall from Figure 1.5 that the equation $x = -3$ represents a line parallel to the y–axis, and the equation $y = 4$ a line parallel to the x–axis. These lines are redrawn in Figure 2.2. The shaded region consists of points above or on the line $y = 4$; these are the points whose y–coordinate is greater than or equal to 4. Thus the hatched region depicts the weak inequality $y \geq 4$. Similarly, the shaded , consisting of points on or to the left of the line $x = -3$, depicts the inequality $x \leq -3$. The region which is both hatched and shaded consists of points satisfying the two inequalities $x \leq -3$, $y \geq 4$.

Figure 2.2 is simple because it depicts regions whose boundaries are parallel to the axes. We now give some more complicated examples.

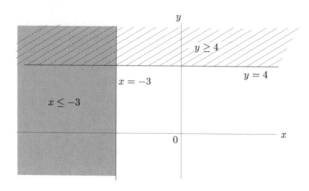

Figure 2.2: **The inequalities** $x \leq -3$ **and** $y \geq 4$

Example 1 Depict the inequality $3x + 4y \leq 6$.

We start by drawing the straight line $3x + 4y = 6$ in the usual way, as the line through the point on the x-axis where $x = 2$ and the point on the y-axis where $y = 3/2$. The inequality is satisfied by all points on or on one side of the line.

To decide which side, we choose a point not on the line and see whether its coordinates satisfy the inequality. The simplest point to test is the origin: when $x = y = 0$, $3x + 4y = 0 < 6$, and the inequality is satisfied. Thus the inequality $3x + 4y \leq 6$ corresponds to the set of points which are either on the line L through the points $(2,0)$ and $(0,3/2)$ or on the *same* side of that line as the origin. This set of points is shaded in panel A of Figure 2.3. Panel B depicts the set of points satisfying the strict inequality $3x + 4y < 6$: this set consists of all points on the same side of L as the origin, but does not include points on the line. For this reason we draw L in panel B as a broken rather than a solid line.

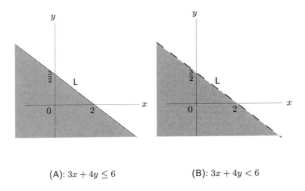

(A): $3x + 4y \leq 6$ \qquad\qquad (B): $3x + 4y < 6$

Figure 2.3: **Weak and strict inequalities**

Example 2 Determine the region in the xy–plane which satisfies simultaneously the inequalities

$$3x + 4y \leq 6, \quad x - 2y \leq 0.$$

The set of points satisfying the first inequality is shaded in panel A of
Figure 2.3, and again in Figure 2.4. Now consider the second inequality.
The line $x - 2y = 0$ is the line through the origin with slope $\frac{1}{2}$; the points
(x, y) for which $x - 2y \leq 0$ lie either on this line or on one side of it. To
decide which side, we cannot use the origin as test point since it is on the
line. Instead, we note that $x - 2y \leq 0$ if $y = 0$ and $x < 0$; the inequality is
therefore satisfied by all points on the *negative* part of the x–axis. Since
these points are to the *left* of the line $y = \frac{1}{2}x$, the region $x - 2y \leq 0$
consists of the points which are either on or to the left of that line. This
set of points is hatched in Figure 2.4.

The set of points satisfying the two inequalities $3x + 4y \leq 6$ and $x - 2y \leq 0$
is therefore the region which is both hatched and shaded in Figure 2.4.
The boundary lines of the region intersect at the point $(6/5, 3/5)$: you
should check this algebraically.

Exercises

2.1.1 Use the rules for manipulating inequalities to determine the values of x
which satisfy the following:

(a) $2x + 1 > 0$ \qquad\qquad (b) $8 - 3x \leq 0$

(c) $2x + 7 \geq x - 5$ \qquad\quad (d) $1 - 4x < 3 + x$.

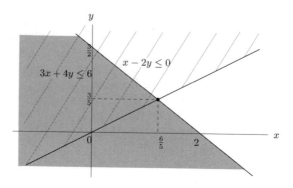

Figure 2.4: **The inequalities** $3x + 4y \leq 6$ **and** $x - 2y \leq 0$

2.1.2 Shade the region in the xy–plane which satisfies

$$x + 2y \leq 3, \quad 2x - 3y \geq 13.$$

[HINT. If you have done Exercise 1.2.1, you will already have found the point of intersection of the relevant straight lines.]

2.2   Economic applications

As we said at the beginning of this chapter, constraints in economics often take the form of inequalities. We now show how such constraints can be represented graphically, using the methods of the last section.

The budget set and the budget line

Suppose that there are only two goods labelled 1 and 2, and that Ian consumes quantities x_1 of good 1 and x_2 of good 2. If the prices of the goods are p_1 and p_2, Ian spends $p_1 x_1$ on good 1 and $p_2 x_2$ on good 2; his total expenditure is then $p_1 x_1 + p_2 x_2$. If Ian's income is m, then the statement that he cannot consume more than his income may be written

$$p_1 x_1 + p_2 x_2 \leq m.$$

This inequality is called the **budget constraint**. Since goods can be consumed only in non-negative quantities, $x_1 \geq 0$ and $x_2 \geq 0$. The set of points in the $x_1 x_2$–plane satisfying these two inequalities and the budget constraint is called the **budget set**. The **budget line** is the straight line with equation

$$p_1 x_1 + p_2 x_2 = m;$$

points on this line whose coordinates are both non-negative represent consumption choices such that Ian spends all his income.

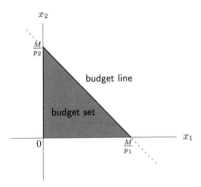

Figure 2.5: **The budget line and the budget set**

To sketch the budget set, we begin by drawing the budget line, noting that it passes through the point on the horizontal axis where $x_1 = m/p_1$ and the point on the vertical axis where $x_2 = m/p_2$. By using the origin as test point in the usual way, we see that the set of all points satisfying the budget constraint consists of the budget line and those points on the same side of it as the origin. The budget set, drawn shaded in Figure 2.5, consists of those points which satisfy the budget constraint and have both coordinates non-negative.

Sketching production possibilities

Suppose a firm manufactures two products X and Y. Let the production process involve three departments A, B and C, with time (in minutes) required in each department per unit output of each product given by the table below.

	Department		
	A	B	C
Product X	20	30	45
Product Y	40	30	30

Let x and y be the amounts of X and Y produced each day by the firm. Then the table above states that the amount of time required each day in department A is $20x$ minutes for the production of X and $40y$ minutes for the production of Y, in all $20x + 40y$ minutes. Similarly the total amount of time per day required in department B is $30x + 30y$ minutes, and the amount of time per day required in department C is $45x + 30y$ minutes.

Suppose that Departments A and B are each available for 8 hours per day, and that Department C is available for 11 hours per day. Then each department imposes a constraint on x and y of the form

$$\text{time required} \leq \text{time available.}$$

Using the above data and the fact that there are 60 minutes in each hour, we see that the time constraint for Department A is

$$20x + 40y \leq 480.$$

The corresponding constraints for B and C are

$$30x + 30y \leq 480,$$

$$45x + 30y \leq 660.$$

Dividing the first of these three inequalities by 20, the second by 30 and the third by 15, we have

$$
\begin{aligned}
x + 2y &\leq 24 &&\text{(constraint A)}\\
x + y &\leq 16 &&\text{(constraint B)}\\
3x + 2y &\leq 44 &&\text{(constraint C).}
\end{aligned}
$$

Output levels x and y must of course be non-negative, which gives us the additional inequalities

$$x \geq 0, \ y \geq 0.$$

The set of points in the xy–plane satisfying these five inequalities is called the **feasible set** for the firm's production plan.

   To sketch the feasible set, we begin by drawing three lines corresponding to the time constraints in the three departments.

$$
\begin{aligned}
x + 2y &= 24 &&\text{(line A)}\\
x + y &= 16 &&\text{(line B)}\\
3x + 2y &= 44 &&\text{(line C).}
\end{aligned}
$$

Using the origin as test point in the usual way, we see that the set of points satisfying constraint A consist of all points on or to the left of line A. Similar results hold for B and C. Since the feasible set consists of all points which satisfy the three time constraints *and have both coordinates non-negative*, it is the shaded region ODEFG in Figure 2.6.

   The coordinates of the corners of the feasible set are easily found using the methods of Chapter 1. D is the point where line A crosses the y–axis and is therefore the point $(0, 12)$. E is the point of intersection of lines A and B; its coordinates are found by solving simultaneously the equations

$$x + 2y = 24, \ x + y = 16$$

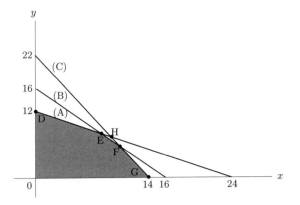

Figure 2.6: **The feasible set for a two-product firm**

and turn out to be $(8, 8)$. Similarly, since F is the point of intersection of lines B and C, its coordinates are $(12, 4)$. G is the point where line C crosses the x-axis and is therefore the point $(44/3, 0)$.

Notice finally that the point H where A crosses C is outside the feasible set. The interpretation of this is that the firm cannot use departments A *and* C to full capacity: if it did, it would be producing too much X and Y per day for department B to handle in eight hours.

Exercises

2.2.1 Judy has an income of 10 which she spends on fish and chips, the prices of which are 2 and 3 respectively. Sketch the budget set.

Also sketch the budget set if the prices of the two goods are reversed.

2.2.2 Henry has an income of 18 which he can spend on two goods labelled 1 and 2, with prices 1 and 3 respectively. Sketch the budget set.

Sketch also the budget set in each of the following cases:

(a) income 36, prices 2 and 6;

(b) income 90, prices 5 and 15;

(c) income 9, prices 0.5 and 1.5.

What do you notice? Can you formulate a general result?

2.2.3 A firm produces two products X and Y, using a production process involving two departments A and B. The time in minutes required in each department per unit output of each product is given by the following table.

| | Department | |
	A	B
Product X	16	10
Product Y	8	20

Department A is available for 4 hours per day and Department B is available for 5 hours per day. Sketch the feasible set.

2.2.4 Suppose the situation is as in Exercise 2.2.3, but with the additional information that production per unit of X and Y causes the emission of 2 and 3 units of carbon respectively. Sketch the feasible set if total carbon emissions are to be restricted to 48 units per day.

Sketch also the feasible set if total carbon emissions per day are to be restricted to (a) 60 units, (b) 24 units.

2.3   Linear programming

The two most important concepts in economic theory are equilibrium and optimisation. We introduced equilibrium, in the special sense of a single market clearing, in our supply-and-demand example in Section 1.1. Optimisation means doing as well as one can subject to given constraints.

To illustrate this, we continue with the example of the two-product firm of the last section, and assume in addition that the firm is attempting to maximise profit. Suppose that products X and Y yield profits of £30 and £40 per unit respectively. If the firm produces per day x units of X and y of Y, its profit in £ per day is $30x + 40y$. The firm's problem is to choose the output combination (x, y) which makes profit as large as possible, subject to the constraint that (x, y) be feasible. Recalling from Section 2.2 the inequalities that define our firm's feasible set of output combinations, we may write the profit-maximisation problem as follows:

$$
\begin{aligned}
\text{maximise} \quad & 30x + 40y \\
\text{subject to} \quad & x + 2y \leq 24 \\
& x + y \leq 16 \\
& 3x + 2y \leq 44 \\
& x \geq 0, \quad y \geq 0.
\end{aligned}
$$

This particular kind of optimisation problem, in which a linear expression is being maximised subject to linear inequalities, is called a **linear maximisation programme**. The expression to be maximised, in this case representing profit, is called the **objective function**.

To solve our maximisation programme we must search over the feasible set to locate the point of maximal profit. We start by considering the different output combinations which yield a given level of profit, say z. If (x, y) is such a combination,

$$30x + 40y = z;$$

the point (x, y) therefore lies on the straight line which cuts the x–axis at $(z/30, 0)$ and the y–axis at $(0, z/40)$. Such a straight line is called an **isoprofit line**: its equation may be written

$$y = -\tfrac{3}{4}x + \tfrac{1}{40}z,$$

with slope $-3/4$ and intercept $z/40$.

Taking a different value of z gives us a new isoprofit line, also with slope $-3/4$ but with a different intercept. As we allow z to vary, we obtain a collection of parallel lines, each one corresponding to a particular level of profit. This collection is known as the **family** of isoprofit lines. Four members of the family are sketched in Figure 2.7, which also reproduces the feasible set from Figure 2.6. The isoprofit line IP_2 has a larger intercept than the isoprofit line IP_1 and therefore corresponds to a higher level of profit. IP_3 and IP_4 correspond to still higher levels of profit: note that the latter does not meet the feasible set.

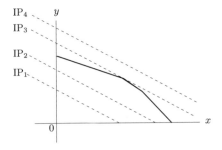

Figure 2.7: **Profit maximisation for a two-product firm**

It is now easy to solve our linear programme. Moving outward from the origin to isoprofit lines corresponding to increasingly high profits, we reach the highest one that meets the feasible set. This is the line IP_3 which meets the feasible set at just one point, namely E. This point gives the profit-maximising output combination. Recalling from Section 2.2 that the coordinates of E are $(8, 8)$, we see that profits are maximized when $x = y = 8$: maximal profit is

$$30 \times 8 + 40 \times 8 = 560.$$

One feature of the solution deserves special attention: at the optimum point E, the slope of the isoprofit lines lies between the slopes of DE and EF, the two parts of the boundary of the feasible set which meet at E. This is important because it points to a method of solving our linear programme that avoids the element of trial-and-error involved in sketching isoprofit lines.

The key to the improved method is the fact that the slope of each part of the constraint boundary DEFG is easily inferred from the construction of the feasible set. The line DE is a segment of what we called line A in Section 2.2 and therefore has slope $-\frac{1}{2}$; EF is a segment of line B and therefore has slope -1; similarly the slope of FG is $-\frac{3}{2}$. The feasible set is drawn yet again, with these slopes labelled, in Figure 2.8. We know from the data on profits that the slope of each isoprofit line is $-30/40$, or $-\frac{3}{4}$. To solve the problem, we simply note that $-\frac{3}{4}$ is between $-\frac{1}{2}$ and -1, which locates the optimum point at E.

To summarise, we have solved our profit-maximisation programme by the following method, which is the one we recommend for problems of this type:

1. Sketch the feasible set, calculating the coordinates of its corners and the slopes of its edges (the line-segments that make up the constraint boundary).

2. Calculate the common slope s of the isoprofit lines: it is *not* necessary to sketch these lines.

3. If s lies between the slopes of two adjacent edges, profits are maximised at the corner where these edges meet.

This solution method is illustrated in Figure 2.8.

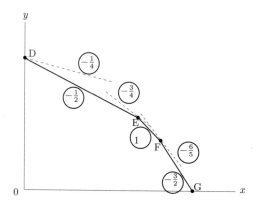

Figure 2.8: **The two-product problem: alternative assumptions**

We now use the recommended method to solve some variants of the problem we have just solved, corresponding to different assumptions about profits; these solutions are also depicted in Figure 2.8. Suppose the unit profits for X and Y are not 30 and 40 as above, but z_X and z_Y respectively. The common slope s of the isoprofit lines is then $-z_X/z_Y$. For example, if $z_X = 60$ and $z_Y = 50$, the slope of each isoprofit line is $-6/5$, which lies between the slopes of EF and FG: hence the optimum is at F. Since F has coordinates $(12, 4)$, maximal profit is 920.

A case of some interest is that where $z_X = 16$ and $z_Y = 54$; here the isoprofit lines are even flatter than DE and the optimum is at the point D on the y–axis; 0 units of X and 12 units of Y are produced, giving a maximal profit of 768. Notice that in this as in all the other cases, it is the profit *ratio* z_X/z_Y that determines the optimal level of output of each product; the absolute levels of z_X and z_Y serve only to determine the maximal amount of profit.

Another interesting case occurs where $z_X = z_Y = 25$. Here $z_X/z_Y = 1$, so the slope of each isoprofit line is equal to the slope of EF. This implies that the profit-maximisation problem has multiple solutions: any (x, y) combination on the edge EF maximises profits, with a profit of 400.

Generalities and complications

Having analysed the example of a two-product firm in some detail, we are now in a position to make some general points about linear programming. Recall that a linear maximisation programme is an optimisation problem in which a linear expression, called the objective function, is maximised subject to constraints taking the form of linear inequalities. The set of points in the xy–plane which satisfy the constraints is called the feasible set.

It is possible that there are *no* points which satisfy all the constraints, in which the programme is said to be **infeasible**; if it *is* possible to satisfy all constraints simultaneously, the programme is said to be **feasible**. Thus our profit-maximisation programme, in all its variants, was feasible. An example of an infeasible programme is

$$\text{maximise } 2x + 3y \text{ subject to } x + y \leq 2 \text{ and } x + y \geq 3.$$

In some feasible linear maximisation programmes, the objective function may be made arbitrarily large without violating the constraints. Thus in the linear programme

$$\text{maximise } x + y \text{ subject to } x \geq 0 \text{ and } y \geq x,$$

the point $(M, 2M)$ is in the feasible set for any positive number M; the objective function then takes the value $3M$, which may be made as large as we like by choosing M large enough. This programme is illustrated in Figure 2.9: the feasible region is shaded, the downward-sloping lines with slope -1 are the 'isoprofit lines', and upward movement along the line $y = 2x$ represents the method just described of increasing the objective function indefinitely. In such cases the programme is said to be **unbounded**; otherwise the programme is said to be **bounded**.

The production problem considered earlier in this section is feasible and bounded in all its variants. A linear programme which is feasible and bounded always has at least one solution. If there is a unique solution, it occurs at a corner of the feasible set. If there are multiple solutions, as in our production

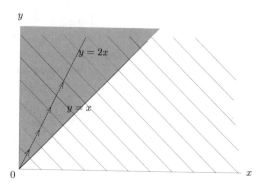

Figure 2.9: **An unbounded linear programme**

problem when $z_X = z_Y = 25$, then a solution can still be found at a corner (in our example, either E or F in Figure 2.8 will do).

The observant reader will have noticed that we have considered only weak inequality constraints in this section. In more general linear programming problems, equation constraints may occur, but strict inequality constraints are not allowed. To see the reason for this, consider the innocent-looking problem

maximise x subject to $x < 1$.

This problem has no solution: $x = 0.99$ does better than $x = 0.9$, $x = 0.999$ does better still, and so on, but $x = 1$ violates the constraint. To avoid technical difficulties of this kind, linear programming restricts attention to constraints which are equations or weak inequalities. In many problems in economics this is the realistic way to proceed; thus in our production problem it makes sense to assume that the firm can use each of its three departments to maximum availability if it so wishes.

Extensions

When there are more than two variables, the graphical approach is no longer possible. It is however possible to generalise the method. The reader should be able to visualise a 'corner' in three dimensions as a point where three planes meet. In dimensions higher than three, no pictorial representation is available but the concept of a corner can still be defined algebraically. The significance of corners is that, if a solution exists, there is a solution at a corner of the feasible set. Thus solution of a linear programme reduces to a search over corners. The most popular way of doing this is known as the simplex algorithm and explained in textbooks on linear programming.

Linear minimisation programmes are just like maximisation programmes, except that we are now minimising a linear expression subject to linear constraints. With two variables, the standard graphical method of solution is as for maximisation: we carefully draw the feasible set and then proceed by comparison of slopes. When there are more than two variables, the simplex algorithm is again needed.

Exercises

2.3.1 Suppose the situation is as in Exercise 2.2.3, and that products X and Y yield profits of £12 and £16 per unit respectively. Find the profit-maximising output levels.

How would your answer change if the profits per unit were £4 and £1?

2.3.2 Suppose the situation is as in Exercise 2.2.4, and that products X and Y yield profits of £12 and £16 per unit respectively. Find the profit-maximising output levels when total carbon emissions are restricted to 48 units per day.

How would your answer change if permitted carbon emissions were to fall to 24 units per day?

Problems on Chapter 2

2–1. The following is a general version of the macroeconomic model of Problem 1–3. As before, the unknowns are Y (national income), C (consumption) and T (tax collection); I (investment) and G (government expenditure) are assumed to be known. The equations of the model are

$$Y = C + I + G, \quad C = c_0 + c_1(Y - T), \quad T = t_0 + t_1 Y;$$

c_0, c_1, t_0, t_1 are constant parameters, with $0 < c_1 < 1$ and $0 < t_1 < 1$. Find Y, C and T in terms of I, G and the parameters. What happens to Y, C and T when G increases by x units?

2–2. Consider again our consumer Ian of Section 2.2, who has income m and consumes two goods labelled 1 and 2. Assume as before that good 2 has price p_2. Good 1 is priced at p_1 up to consumption level z, and at $p_1 + t$ per unit on all consumption in excess of z, where $t > 0$. Sketch the budget set.

Also sketch the budget set

(i) when $t < 0$;

(ii) when consumption of good 1 is rationed at z.

2–3. Consider again the economy of Exercise 1.3.2 and Problem 1–4. Suppose that, in addition to the produced goods X and Y, there are two kinds of non-produced input, labour and land. Assume that production of each unit of gross output of X requires the use of 7 units of labour and 3 units of land, and production of each unit of gross output of Y requires the use of 6 units of labour and 2 units of land.

(i) Using your answer to Problem 1–4, calculate total usage of labour and land when the *net* outputs of X and Y are a and b respectively.

(ii) Suppose the the economy's total endowments of labour and land are 800 and 300 units respectively. What conditions must be satisfied by the numbers a and b if the economy can produce net outputs of a units of X and b units of Y? Draw a diagram illustrating feasible combinations of a and b.

2–4. The diet of Oleg the Russian Blue consists of only two food items, FishBits and KittyCrackers. Prices and nutrient contents per unit are as follows.

	FB	KC
Price	2	1
Calcium	10	4
Protein	5	5
Calories	2	6

Oleg has minimum daily requirements of 20 units of calcium, 20 units of protein and 12 units of calories. Find the combination of the two food items which will satisfy his daily requirements and entail least cost. State the least cost.

How does the solution change if the prices change to

(i) 4 and 2,   (ii) 3 and 2,   (iii) 3 and 1?

Find a value of the price ratio of the two food items for which the solution is not unique. Is there more than one such value?

Chapter 3

SETS AND FUNCTIONS

In this chapter we begin to discuss relations between variables which cannot be graphed as straight lines. To do this, we need to be rather more precise than we were in Chapters 1 and 2 about basic notions such as 'number' and 'relation'. The most important concept which we introduce is that of a function, which is central to much of the remainder of the book. Along the way we give a quick summary of the rules of elementary algebra.

When you have studied this chapter you will be able to:

- describe sets in $\mathcal{R}$ and $\mathcal{R}^n$;

- rearrange algebraic expressions by simple operations, including that of completing the square;

- understand what it means to sketch the graph of a function;

- sketch the graphs of x^2, $|x|$ and functions closely related to them.

3.1 Sets and numbers

A collection of objects viewed as a single entity is called a **set**. The objects in the collection are called the **elements** or **members** of the set.

For instance, a firm's workforce can be considered as a single entity; the members of this set are the individual employees. The Roman alphabet is also a set, its members being the 26 letters. A very different example of a set is a straight line; the elements of the set are the points on the line.

Sets are sometimes described by listing their members in braces, for example

$$\{1, 3, 4, 8\}.$$

The order in which elements are listed does not matter: $\{1, 3, 4, 8\}$ is the same set as $\{4, 3, 8, 1\}$.

Sets can also be described by their defining property. For example, the set E of all positive whole numbers which are divisible by 2 can be written as

$$E = \{2, 4, 6, 8, ...\}$$

or as

$$E = \{\, x : x \text{ is a positive whole number divisible by } 2 \,\},$$

where the colon is read as 'such that'.

If the object x is a member of the set X we write $x \in X$ (read: x belongs to X). If x is not a member of X we write $x \notin X$. Thus with E as above, $12 \in E$ but $13 \notin E$.

Given two sets A and B such that every member of A is also a member of B, we say that A is a **subset** of B, and write $A \subset B$. Thus if E is as above and F is the set of all positive whole numbers divisible by 4, then $F \subset E$; other subsets of E are $\{2, 4, 6\}$, $\{4, 16, 36\}$ and E itself.

The set with no members is called the **empty set** and is always denoted by $\emptyset$. Thus if F is the set of all positive whole numbers which are divisible by 4,

$$\{\, x \in F : x \le 3 \,\} = \emptyset.$$

Numbers

The set of numbers used for counting, namely $\{1, 2, 3, \ldots\}$, is called the set of **natural numbers** and is denoted by $\mathcal{N}$. The set of **integers**, denoted by $\mathcal{Z}$, consists of the natural numbers, their negatives $-1, -2, -3, \ldots$ and the number 0: thus

$$\mathcal{Z} = \{0, 1, -1, 2, -2, \ldots\}.$$

The integers may be represented as points at equally spaced intervals on a line: think of the horizontal axis of the last two chapters. We can also represent on the line ratios of integers such as $1/2$ and $-5/3$: numbers of this type are known as **rational numbers**. Do they account for all the points on the line? The answer is no: even if we were to mark all the rational numbers, we would have failed to mark points corresponding to numbers such as $\sqrt{2}$ and $-\sqrt{7}$.[1] If we put in all the missing numbers we have the set of **real numbers**. This set, denoted by $\mathcal{R}$, can be represented by all the points on a straight line, with all the gaps filled in.

---

[1] How do we know that $\sqrt{2}$ is not a rational number? The following proof is over 2000 years old. Let k be an integer which *can* be expressed as the square of a rational number: we want to show that $k \ne 2$. By assumption, $k = (m/n)^2$, where m and n are integers. Dividing through by common factors if necessary, we may assume that m and n are not both even: hence either (i) m is odd, or (ii) m is even and n is odd. Now the square of an odd integer is odd, and the square of an even integer is divisible by 4; this, together with the fact that $m^2 = kn^2$, implies that k is odd in case (i), while k is divisible by 4 in case (ii). Since k is either odd or divisible by 4, k cannot be 2.

Intervals

At various points in this book we shall be focussing attention on a particular kind of subset of $\mathcal{R}$ known as an **interval**. Let a and b be real numbers, with $a < b$. An example of an interval is

(1) the set of all real numbers which are greater than a and less than b.

In general, an interval is a set of type (1) or of one of the following related types:

(2) the set of all real numbers which are greater than a;

(3) the set of all real numbers which are less than b;

(4) the set of all real numbers;

(5) as (1) or (2), but with 'greater than a' replaced by 'greater than or equal to a';

(6) as (1), (3) or (5), but with 'less than b' replaced by 'less than or equal to b'.

Examples of intervals are $\{\, x \in \mathcal{R} : x \geq 4 \,\}$ and $\{\, x \in \mathcal{R} : -2 < x \leq \sqrt{2} \,\}$. Two subsets of $\mathcal{R}$ which are not intervals are $\mathcal{Z}$ and $\{\, x \in \mathcal{R} : x \neq 0 \,\}$.

Some simple algebra

Because the real numbers are usually discussed in connection with algebraic operations, we often refer to $\mathcal{R}$ as the real number *system*. We assume familiarity with the rules of simple algebraic manipulation, which we state here as a reminder:

$$
\begin{aligned}
a(b + c) &= ab + ac \\
(a + b)c &= ac + bc \\
(a + b)(c + d) &= ac + bc + ad + bd.
\end{aligned}
$$

These rules can be used to multiply out expressions involving brackets. For example:

$$
\begin{aligned}
(a + b)^2 &= a^2 + 2ab + b^2 \\
(a - b)^2 &= a^2 - 2ab + b^2 \\
(a + b)(a - b) &= a^2 - b^2 \\
3x(2y - 4) &= 6xy - 12x \\
(2x + 3)(4x - 5) &= 8x^2 + 12x - 10x - 15 \\
&= 8x^2 + 2x - 15.
\end{aligned}
$$

Completing the square

A consequence of the expression just given for $(a + b)^2$ is that

$$x^2 + 2bx + c = (x + b)^2 + (c - b^2).$$

This rule is usually applied in the cases where b and c are given numbers but x is not: for example

$$x^2 - 10x + 38 = (x - 5)^2 + 13.$$

The point of this rearrangement — known as **completing the square** — is that the original expression $x^2 + 2bx + c$ is written as the sum of a squared term involving x and a given number.

As a more complicated example of completing the square, consider the expression

$$3x^2 - 10x + 38.$$

To complete the square, we can divide through by 3 and apply the formula above with $b = -5/3$ and $c = 38/3$:

$$x^2 - \tfrac{10}{3}x + \tfrac{38}{3} = \left(x - \tfrac{5}{3}\right)^2 + \tfrac{38}{3} - \left(\tfrac{5}{3}\right)^2.$$

Hence

$$3x^2 - 10x + 38 = 3(x - \tfrac{5}{3})^2 + 38 - \tfrac{25}{3}$$
$$= 3(x - \tfrac{5}{3})^2 + \tfrac{89}{3}.$$

To get this result with less use of fractions, begin by *multiplying* by 3:

$$3(3x^2 - 10x + 38) = (3x)^2 - 2 \times 5 \times 3x + 114$$
$$= (3x - 5)^2 - 25 + 114,$$

whence

$$3x^2 - 10x + 38 = \tfrac{1}{3}(3x - 5)^2 + \tfrac{89}{3}.$$

In the next chapter, we shall expain why completing the square is often a useful operation.

The plane as a set

An important set related to $\mathcal{R}$ whose members are not themselves numbers is denoted by $\mathcal{R}^2$ and consists of all **ordered pairs** of real numbers:

$$\mathcal{R}^2 = \{\, (x, y) : x \in \mathcal{R} \text{ and } y \in \mathcal{R} \,\}.$$

Each member of $\mathcal{R}^2$ is an **ordered** pair in the sense that the order now matters — thus the first number in the pair (x, y) might be the age of a woman in years, the second her income in £ per year.

Just as the members of $\mathcal{R}$ can be thought of as points on a line, the members of $\mathcal{R}^2$ can be regarded as points in a plane on which two axes have been drawn. Thus $(3, -1)$ and $(-2, 2)$ are members of $\mathcal{R}^2$, represented respectively by the points P and Q in Figure 3.1.

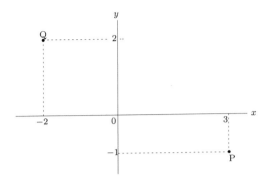

Figure 3.1:   **P and Q are members of $\mathcal{R}^2$**

Of course, the xy–plane is something we have discussed at some length in Chapters 1 and 2. All the straight lines and shaded regions that we drew in those chapters may be regarded as subsets of $\mathcal{R}^2$.

Examples

1. The straight line $y = 2x + 6$ is the set

$$\{\,(x, y) \in \mathcal{R}^2 : y = 2x + 6\,\}.$$

2. A subset of $\mathcal{R}^2$ which is particularly relevant for economic applications is the set

$$\{\,(x, y) \in \mathcal{R}^2 : x \geq 0 \text{ and } y \geq 0\,\},$$

known as the **non-negative quadrant**.

3. In Section 2.2 we sketched the the budget set of a consumer we called Ian, who has income m and consumes two goods with prices p_1 and p_2. This is the set

$$\{\,(x_1, x_2) \in \mathcal{R}^2 : x_1 \geq 0,\ x_2 \geq 0 \text{ and } p_1 x_1 + p_2 x_2 \leq m\,\},$$

which is of course a subset of the non-negative quadrant.

In this context we call an ordered pair (x_1, x_2) a **consumption bundle**, so that the budget set consists of all consumption bundles which the consumer can afford at the given income and prices. Notice the relevance of *ordered* pairs: the bundle consisting of 11 units of good 1 and 26 units of good 2 is clearly different from that consisting of 26 units of good 1 and 11 units of good 2.

4. The feasible set of a linear programme in two variables is a subset of $\mathcal{R}^2$, namely

$$\{\,(x, y) \in \mathcal{R}^2 : (x, y) \text{ satisfies the constraints of the programme}\,\}.$$

To say that this set is not empty is to say that the programme is feasible.

Lists

A generalisation of the idea of an ordered pair is that of an **ordered list**. For instance, if T_1, T_2, T_3 and T_4 denote the value in £ of the income tax paid by a taxpayer in 1991, 1992, 1993 and 1994, then (T_1, T_2, T_3, T_4) is an ordered list of 4 real numbers.

For each positive integer n, we use the symbol $\mathcal{R}^n$ for the set of all ordered lists of n real numbers:

$$\mathcal{R}^n = \{ (x_1, x_2, \ldots, x_n) : x_i \in \mathcal{R} \text{ for } i = 1, 2, \ldots, n \}.$$

If we have a sample of taxpayers and compute for each one the list (T_1, T_2, T_3, T_4) as defined above, the set of all such lists is a subset of $\mathcal{R}^4$.

Similarly, the budget set of a consumer who consumes five goods is a subset of $\mathcal{R}^5$; the feasible set of a linear programme in 9 variables is a subset of $\mathcal{R}^9$; and so on.

Exercises

3.1.1 For each of the following pairs of sets A and B, state which, if either, is a subset of the other:

    (a) A is the set of people living in Scotland; B is the set of people living in the UK.

    (b) A is the set of people living in the USA; B is the set of people living in California.

    (c) A is the set of natural numbers divisible by 6; B is the set of natural numbers divisible by 2.

    (d) A is the set of natural numbers divisible by 5; B is the set of natural numbers divisible by 7.

    (e) $A = \{ x \in \mathcal{R} : -4 < x < 4 \}$, $B = \{ x \in \mathcal{R} : -7 < x < 7 \}$.

    (f) $A = \{ x \in \mathcal{R} : -1 < x < 2 \}$, $B = \{ x \in \mathcal{R} : -2 < x < 1 \}$.

3.1.2 Multiply out the following expressions:

    (a) $(x-6)^2$,   (b) $(2x-3y)(2x+3y)$,   (c) $6a(2a+b)$,   (d) $(x-1)(x+3)$.

3.1.3 Express each of the following as a product of two factors:

    (a) $x^2 - 18x + 81$,   (b) $16a^2 - 25b^2$,   (c) $5x^2 - 15xy$,   (d) $x^2 - 3x - 10$.

3.1.4 Complete the square in each of the following expressions:

    (a) $x^2 + 12x + 3$,   (b) $4x^2 - 12x + 9$,   (c) $-x^2 + 8x - 7$.

3.1.5 Suppose you have a data set consisting of the values of imports and exports for 18 countries.

(a) If an element of the set is considered to be the values of the two variables for one particular country, how many elements does the data set contain? Which $\mathcal{R}^n$ do they belong to?

(b) If an element of the set is considered to be the values of one of the variables for all the countries, how many elements does the data set contain? Which $\mathcal{R}^n$ do they belong to?

3.2 Functions

In Chapter 1 we explained how to draw graphs of equations of the form

$$y = ax + b.$$

We can think of this equation as a rule which transforms any real number x into the real number $ax + b$.

A rule which transforms each real number into another real number is called a **function defined on $\mathcal{R}$ with values in $\mathcal{R}$**, or simply a function from $\mathcal{R}$ to $\mathcal{R}$. If the function is denoted by f, the number into which f transforms x is denoted by $f(x)$. This number $f(x)$ is referred to as the **value of the function f at x**.

For example, given two real numbers a and b, we may denote by f the rule which transforms any real number x into the real number $ax + b$:

$$f(x) = ax + b \text{ for all } x \text{ in } \mathcal{R}.$$

Such a rule is called a **linear function** from $\mathcal{R}$ to $\mathcal{R}$. We now give examples of functions from $\mathcal{R}$ to $\mathcal{R}$ which are not linear.

Example 1: Squares   Let $f(x) = x^2$. The rule f transforms the number 2 into 2^2, and we can write

$$f(2) = 2^2 = 4.$$

Similarly $f(-3) = (-3)^2 = 9$, and so on. Since the square of any real number is non-negative (remember that minus times minus equals plus), this function takes only non-negative values.

Example 2: Absolute value   The expression $|x|$ is defined as follows:

$$|x| = \begin{cases} x & if \ x \geq 0 \\ -x & if \ x < 0. \end{cases}$$

$|x|$ is called the **absolute value** or **modulus** of x; it is usually pronounced 'mod x'. If we define a function f from $\mathcal{R}$ to $\mathcal{R}$ by setting $f(x) = |x|$, then f leaves non-negative numbers unchanged transforms negative numbers into the corresponding positive ones. For example, $|8| = 8$ and $|-2| = 2$. This function, like that of Example 1, takes only non-negative values.

Graphs

The **graph** of a function f from $\mathcal{R}$ to $\mathcal{R}$ is the set

$$\{\, (x,y) \in \mathcal{R}^2 : y = f(x) \,\}.$$

Thus the graph of f can be depicted in the xy–plane by joining up the points $(x, f(x))$ for all values of x. This is exactly what we did for linear functions in Chapter 1.

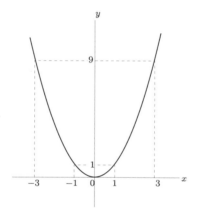

Figure 3.2: $y = x^2$

The graphs of the functions of Examples 1 and 2 are sketched in Figures 3.2 and 3.3 respectively. We now explain the diagrams, and in the process give a brief homily about what 'sketching a graph' does and does not mean. To sketch a graph is to draw a picture which illustrates the general shape of the graph and marks any points of particular interest. Thus Figure 3.2 shows that the graph of $y = x^2$ is U-shaped with the bottom of the U at the origin, while Figure 3.3 demonstrates that the graph of $y = |x|$ is V-shaped, with a right angle at the origin. The 'points of interest' in these sketches were chosen rather arbitrarily, just to remind the reader that $1^2 = (-1)^2 = 1$, $3^2 = (-3)^2 = 9$ and $|2| = |-2| = 2$.

The V-shape in Figure 3.3 arises from the definition of the absolute value function: the graph is the line through the origin of slope 1 when $x > 0$, and the line through the origin of slope -1 when $x < 0$. The reason for the U-shape in

Figure 3.2 is as follows: the graph gets steeper as x increases along the positive part of the x–axis because

$$1^2 - 0^2 < 2^2 - 1^2 < 3^2 - 2^2 < \cdots,$$

and the graph is symmetrical about the y–axis because $(-x)^2 = x^2$ for all x.

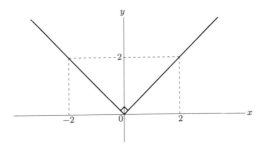

Figure 3.3: $y = |x|$

Since a considerable amount of attention will be devoted to curve-sketching in subsequent chapters, it is however worth spelling out at this stage what the object of the exercise is.

The point of sketching graphs is to *illustrate mathematical arguments*. A sketch need not be drawn on graph paper, and need not be even approximately to scale, as long as it brings over the main features, such as the U shape in Figure 3.2. A corollary of this is that

SKETCH DOES NOT MEAN PLOT.

Plotting data points on graph paper and joining them up with curves is obviously a useful activity in applied economics, statistics, history and so on. It can even be useful in mathematics, for example when finding approximate solutions to complicated equations. However, it is not the same thing as graph-sketching, and it is the latter activity which we emphasise in this book.

Example 3 Let the function f be defined by

$$f(x) = 4 - |x|.$$

This is similar to the function of Example 2, except that the graph has been turned upside down and then shifted up by 4 units. The right-angled corner is therefore at the point $(0, 4)$. The graph is sketched in Figure 3.4. As 'points of interest' we mark those points where the graph crosses the x–axis: at these points $|x| = 4$, so that $x = \pm 4$.

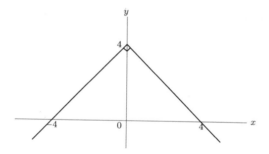

Figure 3.4: $y = 4 - |x|$

Functions in general

The general definition of a function from a set A to a set B is a rule which transforms each element of A into an element of B. If f is a function from a set A to a set B, and x is a member of A, we refer to the element $f(x)$ of B as the **image of x under** f. In the case where B is a set of numbers we often refer to images as 'values', just as we do in the case of functions from $\mathcal{R}$ to $\mathcal{R}$.

Example 4: Factorials   Given a natural number n, the natural number $n!$ (pronounced 'n–factorial') is given by

$$n! = 1 \times 2 \times \ldots \times (n-1) \times n.$$

It is conventional to define $0!$ to be 1.

Let $\mathcal{N}$ denote as usual the set of natural numbers, and let $\mathcal{Z}_+$ be the set of all non-negative integers ($\mathcal{N}$ together with 0). Then $n!$ is a natural number for all n in $\mathcal{Z}_+$. We may therefore define a function f from $\mathcal{Z}_+$ to $\mathcal{N}$ by

$$f(n) = n!.$$

If $n \in \mathcal{N}$, then $n!$ is the number of ways of arranging n objects in order, for example along a line.[2] For instance, if we have two objects a and b, these may be arranged in the order (a,b) or (b,a). If we now bring in a third object c, there are three ways of placing it on the line relative to the objects a and b: to the left of them, between them, or to the right of them. Since any of these three moves may be combined with either of the two ways of arranging a and b, we have $3 \times 2 = 3!$ arrangements for the three objects. Similarly, a fourth

---

[2]A justification sometimes given for $0!$ being 1 is that there is exactly one way of arranging 0 objects along a line, namely to do nothing. As a logical argument, this is no more convincing than the counter-argument that if there are no objects to arrange there is no way of arranging them, so $0!$ should be zero rather than one. It turns out, however, that the ways in which factorials are typically used in mathematics fit in better with the former line of reasoning than the latter. Hence, purely as a matter of convenience, $0!$ is defined to be 1.

object d can be placed in any of four ways relative to the three objects already on the line; and since each of these may be combined with any of the 3! ways of arranging a, b, c we have $4 \times 3! = 4!$ arrangements of a, b, c, d. And so on.

Example 5: Square roots   For any positive real number x, the **positive square root** of x is defined to be the unique number y such that $y^2 = x$ and $y > 0$. The positive square root of x is denoted by $\sqrt{x}$ (read: 'root x'). $\sqrt{0}$ is defined to be 0.

Let $\mathcal{R}_+$ be the set of non-negative real numbers: for each member x of $\mathcal{R}_+$, $\sqrt{x}$ is also a member of $\mathcal{R}_+$. We may therefore define a function f from $\mathcal{R}_+$ to $\mathcal{R}_+$ by

$$f(x) = \sqrt{x}.$$

The graph of this function is sketched in Figure 3.5.

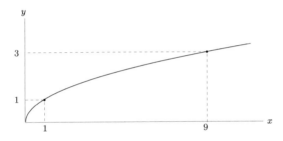

Figure 3.5: $y = \sqrt{x}$

Properties of square roots

We assume that the reader has some familiarity with square roots, but the following reminders may be helpful.

(i) It should be clear from Figure 3.2 that for any positive number b, there are *two* real numbers a for which $a^2 = b$: these are the positive square root $\sqrt{b}$ and the negative square root $-\sqrt{b}$. If c is a negative number there is *no* real number a for which $a^2 = c$.

(ii) If p and q are positive numbers then

$$\sqrt{pq} = \sqrt{p} \times \sqrt{q}, \quad \sqrt{p/q} = \sqrt{p}/\sqrt{q}.$$

(iii) The functions of Examples 1, 2 and 5 are related by the useful formula

$$|x| = \sqrt{x^2} \text{ for all } x \text{ in } \mathcal{R}.$$

More examples

In Examples 1–5 we were concerned with functions from A to B, where both A and B were subsets of $\mathcal{R}$. In our next two examples, B is a subset of $\mathcal{R}$ but A is not.

Example 6: Distance in $\mathcal{R}^2$ Let $\mathcal{R}_+$ be the set of all non-negative real numbers. We may define a function f from $\mathcal{R}^2$ to $\mathcal{R}_+$ by

$$f(x,y) = \sqrt{x^2 + y^2}.$$

The geometrical interpretation of this is that $f(x,y)$ is the distance from the origin to the point (x,y). This follows from a geometrical theorem about right-angled triangles which states the following: if x and y are the lengths of the sides which meet at the right angle, and z is the length of the third side, then $z^2 = x^2 + y^2$. This theorem is known as **Pythagoras' theorem** and is illustrated in Figure 3.6.

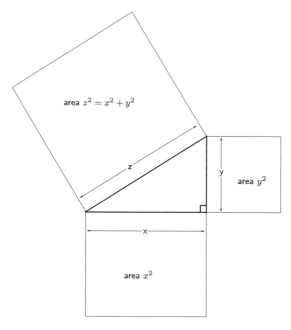

Figure 3.6: **The area of the largest square is the sum of the areas of the other two.**

More generally, Pythagoras' theorem gives us a general formula for the distance between any two points in the plane: If P is the point in the plane with coordinates (a, b) and Q is the point in the plane with coordinates (c, d), the distance from P to Q is

$$\sqrt{(a - c)^2 + (b - d)^2}.$$

The reason why this formula follows from Pythagoras' theorem should be clear from Figure 3.7 — the relevant right-angled triangle is PQR. The diagram is drawn with $0 < c < a$ and $0 < d < b$ but the formula is general: for instance the distance from the point $(-1, 5)$ to the point $(-4, 7)$ is $\sqrt{3^2 + (-2)^2} = \sqrt{13}$.

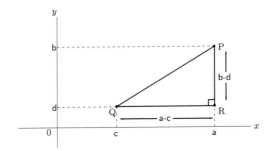

Figure 3.7:   **Distance between two points**

The next example comes from economics.

Example 7 Suppose there are 4 goods in an economy labelled $1, 2, 3, 4$; let the prices of the goods be $3, 5, 7, 9$ respectively. If a consumer buys quantities x_1, x_2, x_3, x_4 of the goods, his or her expenditure is

$$3x_1 + 5x_2 + 7x_3 + 9x_4.$$

We may therefore define a function f which transforms each possible consumption bundle into the expenditure required to purchase it. Let

$$C = \{\, (x_1, x_2, x_3, x_4) \in \mathcal{R}^4 : x_i \geq 0 \text{ for } i = 1, 2, 3, 4\,\};$$

then f is the function from C to $\mathcal{R}_+$ defined by

$$f(x_1, x_2, x_3, x_4) = 3x_1 + 5x_2 + 7x_3 + 9x_4.$$

Terminology

In our subsequent treatment of functions, we shall often be a little looser with language than we were in the examples above. It is common practice to refer to the value of a function at x when, strictly speaking, we should be referring to the function itself. Thus the function of Example 1 which transforms x to x^2 will often be referred to simply as 'the function x^2'. We shall also often refer to this function as

$$y = x^2,$$

especially when considering its graph.

When discussing a function such as $y = x^2$, we shall often call x the **independent variable** and y the **dependent variable**. Similarly, the function of Example 6 which transforms the coordinates of a point into the distance from the origin to that point may be referred to as

$$z = \sqrt{x^2 + y^2}.$$

Here the dependent variable is z and we have two independent variables x, y. And in Example 7 we have four independent variables x_1, x_2, x_3, x_4; the dependent variable is expenditure.

Exercises

3.2.1 Let

$$f(x) = 2x^2 + 5x - 3.$$

Find the values of $f(0)$, $f(-3)$, $f(\frac{1}{2})$, $f(a)$, $f(-b)$ and $f(a - b)$.

3.2.2 Sketch in the same xy–plane the graphs of $y = |x|$, $y = |2x|$ and $y = |\frac{1}{2}x|$.

3.2.3 Sketch in the same xy–plane the graphs of $y = x^2$, $y = 2x^2$ and $y = \frac{1}{2}x^2$.

3.2.4 Find the distance of each of the points $(3, 4)$ and $(4, -3)$ from the origin.

Let the point (x, y) lie on the circle with centre the origin and radius 5: find the equation satisfied by (x, y).

3.2.5 Suppose there are three goods in an economy labelled $1, 2, 3$; let the prices of the goods be $4, 2, 1$ respectively. Write down the function giving the expenditure required to purchase quantities x_1, x_2, x_3 respectively of the three goods. How does this function change when the prices change to $3, 3, 2$?

Suppose that at the original prices Bill buys quantities g_1, g_2, g_3 of the goods, and that with the new prices he buys h_1, h_2, h_3. Use the functions you have specified above to evaluate:

(a) the cost of the original bundle at the original prices;

(b) the cost of the original bundle at the new prices;

(c) the cost of the new bundle at the new prices;

(d) the cost of the new bundle at the original prices.

3.3 Mappings

As we noted above, the general definition of a function from a set A to a set B is a rule which transforms each element of A into an element of B. In the last section we considered only cases where B is a set of numbers such as $\mathcal{N}$ or $\mathcal{R}$. A common (but not universal) convention is to use the word 'function' only for this case, and **mapping** for the more general case where B is not necessarily a set of numbers.

We now give an example of a mapping from A to B where neither A nor B is a set of numbers.

Example Consider the mapping g from $\mathcal{R}^2$ to $\mathcal{R}^2$ defined by

$$g(x, y) = (-y, x).$$

This mapping has a simple geometrical interpretation. Given any point P in the xy–plane, let OP_g be the line obtained by rotating the line OP anti-clockwise through a right angle, as in Figure 3.8. If the coordinates of P are (a, b), then those of P_g are $(-b, a)$; thus P_g is the image of P under g.

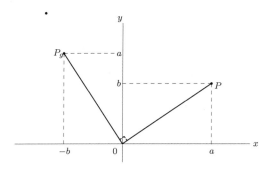

Figure 3.8:   **Rotation through a right angle**

Composite mappings

Mappings can be combined as follows. Suppose A, B, C are sets; let g be a mapping from A to B and f a mapping from B to C; then we define the **composite mapping** $f \circ g$ from A to C by

$$(f \circ g)(x) = f(g(x)).$$

Example If g is the mapping from $\mathcal{R}^2$ to $\mathcal{R}^2$ defined by

$$g(x, y) = (-y, x)$$

as in the last example, and f is the mapping from $\mathcal{R}^2$ to $\mathcal{R}$ defined by

$$f(x, y) = 2x^2 - y^2,$$

then $f \circ g$ is the mapping from $\mathcal{R}^2$ to $\mathcal{R}$ defined as follows:

$$(f \circ g)(x, y) = f(g(x, y)) = f(-y, x) = 2(-y)^2 - x^2.$$

Thus

$$(f \circ g)(x, y) = 2y^2 - x^2.$$

If f and g are mappings from a set A to the same set A, we may define the two mappings $f \circ g$ and $g \circ f$, both from A to A. *These two composite mappings are not in general the same.*

Example Let f and g be the functions from $\mathcal{R}$ to $\mathcal{R}$ defined by

$$f(x) = 1 + x, \quad g(x) = x^2.$$

Then for every real number x,

$$(f \circ g)(x) = f(x^2) = 1 + x^2$$

and

$$(g \circ f)(x) = g(1 + x) = (1 + x)^2 = 1 + x^2 + 2x.$$

It follows that $(f \circ g)(x) = (g \circ f)(x)$ only when $x = 0$: $f \circ g$ and $g \circ f$ are not the same function.

Exercises

3.3.1 Interpret geometrically the mapping h from $\mathcal{R}^2$ to $\mathcal{R}^2$ defined by

$$h(x, y) = (x, -y).$$

Identify the points which remain unchanged under this mapping.

3.3.2 Let g be the mapping from $\mathcal{R}^2$ to $\mathcal{R}^2$ defined by

$$g(x, y) = (y, -x),$$

and let the mapping h be as in Exercise 3.3.1. Find the image of (x, y) under each of the composite mappings $g \circ h$ and $h \circ g$.

Problems on Chapter 3

3–1. Two concepts encountered in elementary set theory are the **union** of two sets A and B, denoted $A \cup B$, and the **intersection** of two sets A and B, denoted $A \cap B$.[3] They are defined as follows:

$$A \cup B = \{ x : x \in A \text{ or } x \in B \}, \quad A \cap B = \{ x : x \in A \text{ and } x \in B \}.$$

Suppose $A = \{ x \in \mathcal{R} : -2 < x < 2 \}$, $B = \{ x \in \mathcal{R} : -3 < x < -1 \}$ and $C = \{ x \in \mathcal{R} : 1 < x < 3 \}$. Illustrate geometrically $A \cup B$, $B \cup C$, $A \cup C$, $A \cap B$, $B \cap C$ and $A \cap C$. Show that

$$A \cap (B \cup C) = (A \cap B) \cup (A \cap C) \text{ and } A \cup (B \cap C) = (A \cup B) \cap (A \cup C).$$

3–2. Consider the function
$$y = 2 + (x - 3)^2.$$

By writing $X = x - 3$ and $Y = y - 2$, sketch the graph of the function in the XY–plane. Find which point in the xy–plane corresponds to $(0, 0)$ in the XY–plane. Use this information to sketch the graph of the function in the xy–plane.

Use the same method to sketch the graph of the function

$$y = 5 + |x - 2|.$$

3–3. Sandra pays income tax according to the schedule

$$T(X) = \begin{cases} 0 & if \ X < E \\ t(X - E) & if \ X \geq E \end{cases}$$

where X is her pre-tax income; E and t are positive constants with $t < 1$. Sandra is also eligible for an income-related transfer

$$B(X) = \begin{cases} s(P - X) & if \ X < P \\ 0 & if \ X \geq P \end{cases}$$

where P and s are constants such that $P > 0$ and $t < s < 1$. Sandra's disposable income Y is therefore equal to $F(X)$, where

$$F(X) = X - T(X) + B(X).$$

Sketch the graph $Y = F(X)$ in each of the following cases:

(i) $E > P$;   (ii) $E < P, \ s + t < 1$;   (iii) $E < P, \ s + t > 1$.

---

[3]The symbols $\cup$ and $\cap$ are sometimes read 'cup' and 'cap' respectively.

3-4. A survey gives the values of the following variables for a sample of households in the UK:

$$v_1 = \text{number of people in household}$$
$$v_2 = \text{total household income}$$
$$v_3 = \text{total household expenditure on food}$$
$$v_4 = \text{total household expenditure on clothing}$$
$$v_5 = \text{total household expenditure on alcohol and tobacco}$$
$$v_6 = \text{total household expenditure on other goods}$$

Write down the functions which give

(i) total household expenditure;

(ii) total household saving;

(iii) income per person;

(iv) expenditure on clothing per person;

For each function state how many variables it involves. Write down also the mappings which give

(v) the ordered pair consisting of income per person and total expenditure per person;

(vi) the list consisting of income per person, saving per person and expenditure per person on alcohol and tobacco.

For each mapping state how many variables it involves.

Chapter 4

QUADRATICS, INDICES AND LOGARITHMS

We now turn from functions in general to particular functions which are constantly applied in economic analysis. Quadratic functions are especially useful for problems involving maximisation or minimisation. At the end of the chapter, we introduce a procedure for transforming some non-linear relationships into linear ones. This trick has applications both in economics and in statistics, where linear relations are much easier to estimate than nonlinear ones.

When you have studied this chapter you will be able to:

- sketch the graphs of quadratic functions

- solve quadratic equations

- maximise and minimise quadratic functions, and apply the method in simple economic examples

- rearrange and simplify algebraic expressions involving indices (including fractional indices) and logarithms (to any base).

4.1   Quadratic functions

In Section 3.2 we sketched the graph of the function $y = x^2$. We now generalise slightly and consider the function

$$y = ax^2,$$

where a is a real number such that $a \neq 0$. The graph of such a function has one of two possible shapes, depending on whether a is positive or negative. If $a > 0$ the graph is U-shaped with the bottom of the U at the origin: we say that the origin is the **vertex** or **minimum point** of the graph. This case is depicted in Panel A of Figure 4.1. If $a < 0$ the graph is $\cap$-shaped, and the origin is now the **maximum point**, as in Panel B of Figure 4.1. In each case the graph is called a **parabola**.

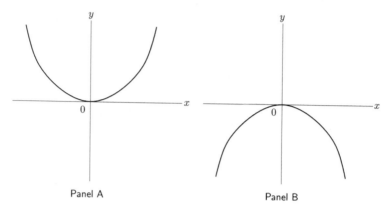

Panel A

Panel B

Figure 4.1: **Parabolas with vertex at the origin**

To generalise further, we define a **quadratic function** to be a function of the form

$$f(x) = ax^2 + bx + c,$$

where a, b, c are real numbers with $a \neq 0$. The graph of such a function has the same parabolic shape as in Figure 4.1, being U-shaped or $\cap$-shaped according as a is positive or negative the only difference is that the vertex of the parabola is not necessarily at the origin.

We now explain, via examples, how to sketch the graph of any quadratic function. *The essential trick is to complete the square.*

Example 1 Sketch the graph of the function $f(x) = 2x^2 + 8x + 9$.

$$\begin{aligned} f(x) &= 2(x^2 + 4x) + 9 \\ &= 2([x + 2]^2 - 4) + 9 \quad \text{by completing the square} \\ &= 2(x + 2)^2 + 1. \end{aligned}$$

Thus the equation $y = f(x)$ may be written

$$y - 1 = 2(x + 2)^2.$$

This has the same graph as $y = 2x^2$ except that the axes have been shifted: the vertex is not at the point where $x = y = 0$ but at the point where $x + 2 = y - 1 = 0$, which is the point $(-2, 1)$.

The U-shaped curve is sketched in Figure 4.2, which illustrates the principle that when we sketch a graph we mark points of particular interest. In this case these are the vertex $(-2, 1)$ and the point where the curve crosses the y–axis: since $f(0) = 0 + 0 + 9$, this is the point $(0, 9)$.

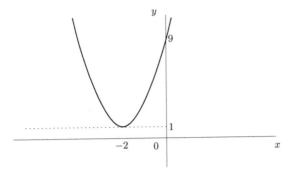

Figure 4.2: $y = 4x^2 + 8x + 9$

Example 2 Sketch the parabola $y = -3x^2 + 30x - 27$.

$$
\begin{aligned}
y &= -3(x^2 - 10x + 9) \\
&= -3((x - 5)^2 + (9 - 5^2)) \quad \text{by completing the square} \\
&= -3(x - 5)^2 + 48
\end{aligned}
$$

This has the same graph as $y = -3x^2$ except that the vertex is at $(5, 48)$ rather than the origin.

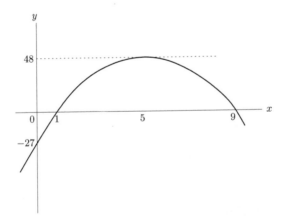

Figure 4.3: $y = -3x^2 + 30x - 27$

The $\cap$-shaped curve is sketched in Figure 4.3. To complete the sketch we mark the points where the curve cuts the axes. Since $y = -27$ when $x = 0$, the graph cuts the y–axis at the point $(0, -27)$. Also, the graph cuts the x–axis at the points $(1, 0)$ and $(9, 0)$; we now explain why.

Quadratic equations

To find where the curve crosses the x–axis in Figure 4.3, we need to find those values of x for which

$$3x^2 + 30x - 27 = 0. \qquad (4.1)$$

This is an example of a **quadratic equation**: an equation of the form

$$f(x) = 0$$

where f is a quadratic function. In this instance we have already shown, by completing the square, that

$$f(x) = -3(x - 5)^2 + 48.$$

Thus equation (4.1) says that $(x - 5)^2 = 16$. Taking square roots, $x - 5 = \pm 4$, so that x is either 1 or 9. Hence, as shown in Figure 4.3, the curve

$$y = -3x^2 + 30x - 27$$

crosses the x–axis at the points $(1,0)$ and $(9,0)$.

The general case

We wish to solve the equation

$$ax^2 + bx + c = 0, \qquad (4.2)$$

where a, b, c are real numbers such that $a \neq 0$.

Denote the left-hand side of the equation by $f(x)$. Then

$$\begin{aligned} 4af(x) &= 4a^2x^2 + 4abx + 4ac \\ &= (2ax)^2 + 2b(2ax) + 4ac \\ &= (2ax + b)^2 - b^2 + 4ac \end{aligned}$$

by completing the square. It follows that $f(x) = 0$ if and only if

$$(2ax + b)^2 = b^2 - 4ac. \qquad (4.3)$$

The left-hand side of (4.3) must be nonnegative for all x. To solve the equation for x we need the right hand side also to be non-negative. We assume for the moment that this is so, so that $b^2 \geq 4ac$. Then equation (4.2) may be solved for x by taking square roots in (4.3):

$$2ax + b = \pm\sqrt{b^2 - 4ac}.$$

Rearranging, we obtain an important formula for the solutions (or **roots**) of the quadratic equation (4.2):

$$x = \frac{-b \pm \sqrt{b^2 - 4ac}}{2a}. \qquad (4.4)$$

We now have **two** methods of solving a quadratic equation. The first is to complete the square with the given numbers, just as we did to solve (4.1). The second, known as the formula method, consists of applying (4.4) with the given values of a, b and c.

Example 3   Solve the quadratic equation $x^2 + x - 12 = 0$.

To solve this equation by completing the square, we rearrange the left-hand side so that the equation reads

$$(x + \tfrac{1}{2})^2 - \tfrac{1}{4} - 12 = 0.$$

Hence $(x + \tfrac{1}{2})^2 = \tfrac{49}{4}$. Taking square roots, $x + \tfrac{1}{2} = \pm\tfrac{7}{2}$ thus the solutions are $x = 3$ and $x = -4$.

Alternatively, we may apply the formula (4.4) with $a = 1$, $b = 1$ and $c = -12$. Here $b^2 - 4ac = 1 + 48 = 7^2$ the roots are therefore $(-1 \pm 7)/2$, in short 3 and -4.

Solution by factorisation

This is a third method of solving quadratic equations. Denote the left hand side of (4.2) by $f(x)$, and suppose for simplicity that $a = 1$. Then

$$f(x) = x^2 + bx + c.$$

Suppose we can spot numbers p and q such that

$$b = -(p + q) \quad \text{and} \quad c = pq.$$

Then $f(x) = (x - p)(x - q)$ in particular, $f(x) = 0$ if and only if x is either p or q. Hence the roots of the quadratic equation $f(x) = 0$ are p and q.

This method can be applied to the equation of Example 3, which we have just solved by the other two methods. It is not terribly hard to see that two numbers p and q such that

$$p + q = -1 \quad \text{and} \quad pq = -12$$

are given by $p = 3$, $q = -4$. Hence the equation may be written

$$(x - 3)(x + 4) = 0$$

and the roots are 3 and -4 as before.

In practice, we invite you to solve quadratic equations by whichever method you find most convenient. The choice between the first two methods is purely a matter of taste. The factorisation method requires a certain amount of guess-work, but is very quick when that is successful.

How many roots?

In explaining how to solve the equation (4.2), we assumed that $b^2 \geq 4ac$. If $b^2 < 4ac$, equation (4.3) has a non-negative left hand side and a negative right hand side, and therefore cannot be true for any real number x. But (4.3) is just another way of writing (4.2). Thus in the case where $b^2 < 4ac$, equation (4.2) has no solution.

Example 1 (continued)   Consider the equation $f(x) = 0$, where

$$f(x) = 2x^2 + 8x + 9$$

as in Example 1. In this case $b^2 - 4ac = 64 - 72 < 0$. The equation therefore has no solution. What this means in geometrical terms is that the curve $y = f(x)$ never meets the x–axis, a fact we already know from Figure 4.2.

Returning to equations where solutions do exist, notice the distinction between the cases $b^2 > 4ac$ and $b^2 = 4ac$. In the former case, equation (4.2) always has two distinct roots, thanks to the $\pm$ in (4.4). In the case where $b^2 = 4ac$, equation (4.2) has the single solution $x = -b/(2a)$. This is known as the case of **coincident roots**. Geometrically, this means that the curve

$$y = ax^2 + bx + c$$

has its vertex on the x–axis.

Example 4 The equation $2x^2 + 8x + 8 = 0$ has coincident roots at $x = -2$. To see the geometry of this, shift the curve of Figure 4.2 downwards by 1 unit, obtaining a parabola with vertex at the point $(-2, 0)$.

Properties of the roots

We now give more information on how the roots of a quadratic equation are related to the coefficients. We shall use the following proposition in Chapter 24.

Proposition If the roots of the quadratic equation $ax^2 + bx + c = 0$ are p and q, then

$$p + q = -\frac{b}{a} \text{ and } pq = \frac{c}{a}.$$

To see why this proposition is true, suppose we divide the equation by a and solve by factorisation. Then

$$x^2 + (b/a)x + (c/a) = 0 \text{ and } (x - p)(x - q) = 0$$

are the same quadratic equation. Therefore

$$x^2 + (b/a)x + (c/a) \text{ and } x^2 - (p + q)x + pq$$

are indeed the same quadratic function.

Another way of proving the proposition is to use (4.4) and direct calculation. For the details of the proof, see Exercise 4.1.4.

Maximising and minimising quadratic functions

Let $f(x) = ax^2 + bx + c$, where $a < 0$. The curve $y = f(x)$ is then $\cap$-shaped, as in Figure 4.3, and the method we used to sketch that graph enables us to locate the vertex of the curve. Let the vertex be the point (x^*, y^*). Then y^* is the greatest value that $f(x)$ can possibly take, and is attained when $x = x^*$. For this reason we say that the function f has its **maximum point** at (x^*, y^*).

We now give a typical example from economics of finding the maximum point of a quadratic function. Suppose a monopolist can produce quantity x of a product at total cost $7 + 6x$. Let the demand function for the product be given by

$$x = 15 - \tfrac{1}{2}p,$$

where p is the price charged. We wish to find the profit-maximising price and output, and the maximal profit.

We begin by expressing profit as a function of output x. From the demand function, $p = 30 - 2x$. Thus

$$\text{revenue} = px = (30 - 2x)x.$$

Letting y denote profit and using the fact that

$$\text{profit} = \text{revenue} - \text{cost},$$

we see that

$$\begin{aligned}
y &= (30x - 2x^2) - (7 + 6x) \\
&= -2x^2 + 24x - 7 \\
&= -2(x^2 - 12x) - 7 \\
&= -2[(x - 6)^2 - 36] - 7
\end{aligned}$$

by completing the square. It follows that

$$y = -2(x - 6)^2 + 65. \tag{4.5}$$

It is clear from (4.5) that the curve depicting profit y as a function of output x is $\cap$-shaped, with its vertex at the point $(6, 65)$. The maximal profit is 65, attained when $x = 6$ and $p = 30$.

Notice the logic behind this last step. Since a square cannot be negative, equation (4.5) says that

$$y = 65 - (\text{something non-negative}).$$

Thus the best we can do in the way of maximising y is to choose x such that the non-negative 'something' is zero, in which case $y = 65$. Since the 'something' is $2(x - 6)^2$, making it zero requires that $x = 6$.

Minimisation

Similarly, given the function $f(x) = ax^2 + bx + c$ where $a > 0$, the curve $y = f(x)$ is now U-shaped. If the vertex is (x^*, y^*), then y* is the *least value* that the function f can take, and we call the vertex the **minimum point** of the function.

Example 1 (further continued)   Consider yet again the function

$$f(x) = 2x^2 + 8x + 9 = 2(x+2)^2 + 1.$$

As we noted in connection with Figure 4.2, the vertex is $(-2, 1)$. The minimal value of f is 1, attained when $x = -2$.

Notice again the logic behind the result. Since

$$f(x) = 1 + (\text{something non-negative}),$$

the minimum value of $f(x)$ is 1, and is attained by choosing x such that the 'something' is zero since the 'something' is $2(x+2)^2$, we minimise $f(x)$ by letting $x = -2$.

In the last example, the optimum value of x happens to be negative. But in many examples in economics — for instance, choosing output to maximise profit — it is natural to require the variable x to be non-negative. In such cases, there is everything to be said for sketching the graph. For example, it is clear from Figure 4.2 that the minimum value of $2x^2 + 8x + 9$ subject to the constraint $x \geq 0$ is 9, attained when $x = 0$.

Exercises

4.1.1 Sketch the graphs of

$$\text{(a) } y + 3 = 2(x+2)^2, \quad \text{(b) } y = 3x^2 + 2x - 1.$$

4.1.2 Solve the following equations:

$$\text{(a) } x^2 - 6x + 8 = 0 \qquad \text{(b) } x^2 - 8x + 16 = 0$$

$$\text{(c) } 2x^2 - 5x + 1 = 0 \qquad \text{(d) } x^2 + 2x + 4 = 0$$

4.1.3 Sketch the graph of

$$y = x^2 - 4.$$

Find:

(a) the coordinates of the points where the graph meets the x–axis

(b) the values of x for which $x^2 - 4 > 0$

(c) the values of x for which $x^2 - 4 < 0$.

Repeat the question for
$$y = x^2 + 4.$$

4.1.4 Show by direct calculation that if
$$p = \frac{-b + \sqrt{b^2 - 4ac}}{2a}, \quad q = \frac{-b - \sqrt{b^2 - 4ac}}{2a},$$

then $p + q = -b/a$ and $pq = c/a$.

4.1.5 Sketch the graphs of

(a) $y = 2 - (x + 1)^2$ (b) $y = 4 - (2x - 1)^2$

(c) $y = -x^2 + 6x - 5$ (d) $y = -4x^2 - 4x + 1$

In each case state the maximum value of y.

If, in each case, the constraint $x \geq 0$ is imposed, what are the maximum values of y?

4.1.6 A monopolist can produce quantity x of a product X at total cost $3 + 2x$. The demand schedule for the product is
$$p = 11 - 2x,$$

where p is the price charged for X. Find the profit-maximising output and the maximum profit.

4.2 Indices

You are probably familiar with expressions such as x^3 and x^{12}, but here is a reminder of their meaning. Given a real number x, we define
$$x^3 = x \times x \times x, \quad x^4 = x \times x \times x \times x$$

and so on. In general, for any natural number n,
$$x^n = \overbrace{x \times x \times \ldots \times x}^{n \text{ times}}.$$

In this expression, the natural number n is called the **power**, **index** or **exponent**.

Rules for handling indices

Assume that $x \neq 0$. From the definition of powers we have, for instance,

$$x^5 \times x^2 = (x \times x \times x \times x \times x) \times (x \times x) = x^7; \quad \text{and;} \quad x^5/x^2 = \frac{x \times x \times x \times x \times x}{x \times x} = x^3.$$

These equations generalise as follows:

IR1 $x^m \times x^n = x^{m+n}$

and, if $m > n$,

IR2 $x^m/x^n = x^{m-n}$.

Further, if we define

IR3 $x^{-n} = 1/x^n$,

IR4 $x^0 = 1$,

then **IR2** continues to hold when $m \leq n$.

We have now defined x^k for any non-zero real number x and *any* integer k. With these definitions,

> the index rules **IR1–IR4** hold for any $x \neq 0$ and any integers m, n.

IR3 gives a convenient notation for very small numbers; thus 0.000000321 may be written as 3.21×10^{-7}.

We now generalise further. A **rational number** is a ratio of integers: for example all integers are rational numbers, as are $5/2$ and $-1/3$. Given a positive real number x and a rational number r, we may define x^r so as to be compatible with **IR1–IR3** above.

For example, since we require $x^{1/2}$ to be such that $x^{1/2} \times x^{1/2} = x^1 = x$,

$$x^{1/2} = \sqrt{x}.$$

More generally, if $x > 0$ and n is a positive integer, $x^{1/n}$ is defined as the positive nth root of x: thus $27^{1/3} = 3$ and $32^{1/5} = 2$. More generally still, $x^{2/3}$ can be defined as $(x^2)^{1/3}$, $x^{-5/2}$ as $(x^{-5})^{1/2}$ and so on.

Given these definitions, the rules **IR1–IR4** hold for any positive real number x and any rational numbers m and n. The following also hold:

IR5 $(x^m)^n = x^{mn}$

IR6 $(xy)^n = x^n y^n$.

IR5 tells us for example that $x^{2/3}$, which we defined above as $(x^2)^{1/3}$, is the same as $(x^{1/3})^2$, and that $x^{-5/2}$ is equal to $(x^{1/4})^{-10}$.

Examples

To illustrate how rules **IR1–IR6** may be applied, we simplify the expressions

$$a = (x^8 \times x^{-9})/x^{-4}, \qquad b = (x^{1/3} \times x^{1/6})/x^{3/2},$$

$$c = (x^2 y^2)^{-1/4} \sqrt{y}, \qquad d = (64x^6)^{-1/3} \times (9x)^{1/2}.$$

Using rules **IR1** and **IR2**,

$$a = x^{8-9}/x^{-4} = x^{-1-(-4)} = x^{4-1} = x^3.$$

To simplify b, we notice first that $x^{1/3} x^{1/6} = x^{1/2}$: this follows from **IR1** and the fact that $\frac{1}{3} + \frac{1}{6} = \frac{1}{2}$. Hence by **IR2** and **IR3**,

$$b = x^{(\frac{1}{2} - \frac{3}{2})} = x^{-1} = 1/x.$$

To simplify c, we note that by **IR6** and **IR5**,

$$(x^2 y^2)^{-1/4} = ((xy)^2)^{-1/4} = (xy)^{2 \times (-1/4)} = (xy)^{-1/2}.$$

Hence by **IR6** and **IR1**,

$$c = x^{-1/2} y^{-1/2} y^{1/2} = x^{-1/2} y^0.$$

Using **IR3** and **IR4**, $c = \left(1/x^{1/2}\right) \times 1 = 1/\sqrt{x}$.

Finally,

$$
\begin{aligned}
d &= ((2x)^6)^{-1/3} \times (9x)^{1/2} \quad && \text{by } \textbf{IR6} \\
&= (2x)^{-2} \times (9x)^{1/2} \quad && \text{by } \textbf{IR5} \\
&= 3x^{1/2}/(4x^2) \quad && \text{by } \textbf{IR6 and IR3} \\
&= 3/(4x^{3/2}) \quad && \text{by } \textbf{IR2}.
\end{aligned}
$$

Extending the rules

So far we have defined x^r only in the case where r is a rational number. Not all real numbers are rational, as we pointed out in Section 3.1. However, it is true that any real number can be approximated arbitrarily closely by rational numbers, and this fact may be used to define x^r for any positive real number x and any real number r for example, since $\sqrt{2}$ is a real number between $7/5$ and $13/9$, $3^{\sqrt{2}}$ is a real number between $3^{7/5}$ and $3^{13/9}$.

The rules **IR1–IR6** *hold for any positive real numbers* x, y *and any real numbers* m, n. In particular, $1^r = 1$ for every real number r.

Notice that as we define x^r for more and more general kinds of exponent r, we become more restrictive about x. If r is a natural number, the expression x^r makes sense for any real number x. If r is a negative integer, the expression x^r makes sense only if $x \neq 0$. And we can be sure that the expression x^r makes sense for every real number r only if $x > 0$.

Indices and inequalities

We gave the basic rules for manipulating inequalities in Section 2.1. We now explain how the properties of indices may be used to add to these rules.

Let c be a real number such that $c > 1$. Then $c^2 > c > 1$, $c^3 > c^2 > 1$, and generally $c^n > 1$ for every natural number n. Rather less obviously, $c^{1/n} > 1$ for every natural number n.[1] Using these facts, it may be shown that $c^a > 1$ for every positive real number a. Summarising, we see that

$$\text{if } c > 1 \text{ and } a > 0 \text{ then } c^a > 1.$$

Using this fact, and the rules **IR1–IR6**, it is not hard to demonstrate the following:

(A) if u, v, a are positive numbers such that $u < v$, then $u^a < v^a$ and $u^{-a} < v^{-a}$

(B) if u, v, a are positive numbers such that $u < v$, then $a^u < a^v$ if $a > 1$, and $a^u > a^v$ if $a < 1$.

Note in particular the special case of (A) when $a = 1$: if $0 < u < v$, then $\frac{1}{u} > \frac{1}{v}$.

One use for (A) and (B) is that they enable us to rank complicated numbers without using a calculator. For example, is $0.2^{0.3}$ greater or less than $0.3^{0.2}$? The answer is less: $0.2^{0.3} < 0.3^{0.3}$ by (A), and $0.3^{0.3} < 0.3^{0.2}$ by (B), so $0.2^{0.3} < 0.3^{0.2}$.

Exercises

4.2.1 Let $f(x) = x^2$ and $g(x) = x^4$.

(a) Explain why $f(-a) = f(a)$ and $g(-a) = g(a)$.

(b) Find the values of $f(\frac{1}{2})$, $f(1)$, $f(2)$, $g(\frac{1}{2})$, $g(1)$ and $g(2)$.

Use the information you have obtained in (a) and (b) to sketch in the same xy–plane the graphs of $y = x^2$ and $y = x^4$. What do you notice? What would the graph of $y = x^6$ look like?

4.2.2 Let $f(x) = x^3$ and $g(x) = x^5$.

(a) Explain why $f(-a) = -f(a)$ and $g(-a) = -g(a)$.

(b) Find the values of $f(\frac{1}{2})$, $f(1)$, $f(2)$, $g(\frac{1}{2})$, $g(1)$ and $g(2)$.

Use the information you have obtained in (a) and (b) to sketch in the same xy–plane the graphs of $y = x^3$ and $y = x^5$. What do you notice? What would the graph of $y = x^7$ look like?

---

[1]The reason is as follows. Let $b = c^{1/n}$. If we had $b \le 1$ we would have $b^2 = b \times b \le 1 \times b \le 1$, $b^3 \le b^2 \le 1$ and so on up to $b^n \le 1$ but this is absurd, because $b^n = c > 1$. Hence $b > 1$.

4.2.3 Express the following numbers in the form $a \times 10^b$ where a is a number between 0 and 10 and b is an integer:

(a) 372.8, (b) 0.003728, (c) 3.728.

4.2.4 Simplify the following:

(a) $(x^5)x(x^8)/x^4$ (b) $(x^{1/2}x^{4/3})/x^{1/6}$

(c) $(x^{1/4}y^{-2})^{-4}$ (d) $(125x^6)^{1/3}(4y)^{-2}$

4.2.5 If $z = x^{1/2}y^{1/4}$ and $y = 2x$, find x and y in terms of z.

4.2.6 A firm's output Y is related to capital input K and labour input L by the production function

$$Y = 2K^{2/3}L^{1/3}.$$

Suppose that initially $K = a$ and $L = b$. Find the percentage increase in Y resulting from 1% increases in both K and L. What happens when the changes are each 10%? Can you formulate a general result?

4.3   Logarithms

Given a real number a such that $a > 1$, we may define the function

$$y = a^x \quad (x \in \mathcal{R}).$$

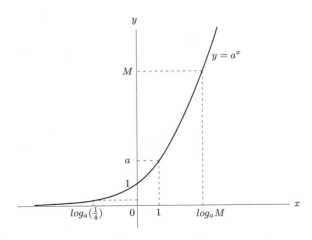

Figure 4.4: $y = a^x$

Figure 4.4 sketches the graph of this function. The graph illustrates three facts about indices which we explained in the preceding section: $a^x > 0$ for all real x, $a^0 = 1$, and $a^u < a^v$ whenever $u < v$. The third fact, which follows from our assumption that $a > 1$, is shown in the graph by the curve's upward slope from left to right. Two more features of the graph are worth noting at this stage, although the reasons for them will not become clear until later in the book: the curve is close to the x–axis for large negative x, and becomes steeper as x increases.

Figure 4.4 shows that for any given positive number y, there is exactly one real number x such that $a^x = y$. This x is called the **logarithm of y to base a** and is denoted by $\log_a y$. Thus

$$x = \log_a y \text{ if and only if } y = a^x.$$

In Figure 4.4 we illustrate the concept of logarithm by depicting $\log_a y$ for $y = 1/4$ and for $y = M$, where M is some positive number greater than a.

Example To illustrate how the definition of logarithm may be applied, we find u and v where

$$u = \log_4 8 \text{ and } v = \log_3(1/27).$$

Here $4^u = 8$, which may be written $2^{2u} = 2^3$ hence $u = 3/2$. Similarly $3^v = 1/27 = 3^{-3}$, whence $v = -3$.

Properties of logarithms

The main properties are as follows:

L1 $\log_a(yz) = \log_a y + \log_a z$.

L2 $\log_a(y/z) = \log_a y - \log_a z$.

L3 $\log_a(1/z) = -\log_a z$.

L4 $\log_a 1 = 0$.

L5 $\log_a(y^b) = b \times \log_a y$.

These properties are easily derived from the corresponding properties of indices. Another useful fact about logarithms is the **change-of-base formula**

L6 $\log_a y = \log_a b \times \log_b y$.

To see why this is true, let $x = \log_b y$. Then $y = b^x$. But then by **L5** we have $\log_a y = x \times \log_a b$, as required.

Logarithms to base 10 are called **common logarithms**. Any 'scientific' calculator, however inexpensive, has a 'log' key, which gives $\log_{10} y$ for any $y > 0$. The change-of-base formula may then be used to calculate logarithms to any base: for by **L6** with $a = 10$, $\log_b y$ can be calculated as $\log_{10} y / \log_{10} b$ for any $b > 1$ and any $y > 0$. For example,

$$\log_{1.7} 0.2 = \log_{10} 0.2 / \log_{10} 1.7 = -\frac{0.69897}{0.23045} = -3.0331.$$

More interesting uses of common logarithms in calculation will appear in the next chapter.

Logarithms in economics: an example

Suppose that a firm's output Y is related to capital input K and labour input L by the production function

$$Y = \tfrac{1}{5} K^{0.4} L^{0.6}. \tag{4.6}$$

Let $y = \log Y$, $k = \log K$ and $\ell = \log L$, where all logarithms are to the same base. Then

$$y = 0.4k + 0.6\ell - \log 5. \tag{4.7}$$

Equation (4.7) is a linear relationship between the logarithms of the economic variables. For this reason, relations such as (4.6) are said to be **log-linear**. The procedure of transforming a non-linear relationship into a linear one by taking logarithms is a very useful one, and we shall return to it in Chapter 9.

Exercises

4.3.1 Evaluate, without using a calculator, the following:

(a) $\log_5 125$, (b) $\log_5(1/125)$, (c) $\log_8 64$, (d) $\log_8 4$, (e) $\log_8 256$.

4.3.2 Use the properties of logarithms to show that $\log_a x = 1/\log_x a$.

4.3.3 A firm's output Y is related to capital input K, labour input L and natural resource input R by the production function

$$Y = 2K^{1/2} L^{1/3} R^{1/6}.$$

Write down a linear relationship between the logarithms to base 10 of Y, K, L, R.

Problems on Chapter 4

4–1. Solve simultaneously the equations $q = 5 - p^2$, $q = 2p - 3$.

Now suppose p represents price and q quantity, and that the equations represent demand and supply curves respectively. Sketch the parts of the curves which lie in the non-negative quadrant state the equilibrium price and quantity.

4–2. Suppose the situation is as in Exercise 4.1.6 but that the government now imposes a tax of t per unit of output produced. Find the new profit-maximising output.

Find also an expression for the total tax revenue and find the value of t which maximises it.

4–3. This problem is concerned with a class of functions which are not quadratic but can be minimised by completing the square.

(i) Let the function $f(x)$ be defined for $x > 0$ by

$$f(x) = ax + b + c/x,$$

where a, b, c are constants such that $a > 0$ and $b > 0$. By expressing $f(x)$ in the form

$$\left(\sqrt{ax} - \sqrt{c/x}\right)^2 + \text{constant},$$

find the value of x that minimises $f(x)$. Hence find the minimum value of $f(x)$.

(ii) The cost function of a firm is

$$C(x) = 50 + 2x + 0.08x^2,$$

where x is output. Using the result of (i), find the level of output that minimises average cost $C(x)/x$ also find the minimum average cost.

4–4. Sketch the graph of the following supply function for petrol:

$$q = \tfrac{1}{4}p^4,$$

where p represents price and q represents quantity.

Now consider the function

$$q = 8p^{-1}$$

where p is positive. Explain why q decreases as p increases. If this function is the demand function for petrol, find the equilibrium price and quantity.

Also find the equilibrium price and quantity by expressing the supply and demand functions in log-linear form and solving the resulting linear system simultaneously.

Chapter 5

SEQUENCES AND SERIES

This chapter has a practical and a theoretical purpose. The practical one is to acquaint the reader with certain formulae that appear in all parts of economics and finance which involve growth and the payment of interest; the key words here are compounding, discounting and present value. The theoretical one is to introduce the important mathematical concept of a limit, which will play an essential role in the rest of the book.

When you have studied this chapter you will be able to:

- sum arithmetic and geometric progressions;

- find limits of sequences in simple cases;

- understand the difference between flat rate of interest and annual percentage rate, and derive the latter from the former;

- calculate present values and compound values of income streams.

5.1 Sequences

Economic data often take the form of sequences of numbers. For example we may think of the sequence

$$b_1, \ b_2, \ b_3, \ \ldots$$

where b_1 denotes the Gross Domestic Product of Belgium in 1991, b_2 the Belgian GDP in 1992 and so on. An example from the foreign exchange market could be

$$c_1, \ c_2, \ c_3, \ \ldots$$

where c_1 is the US\$/Yen exchange rate at noon on 15 January 2001 and $c_2, c_3, \ldots$ denote the US\$/Yen exchange rate at noon on subsequent trading days.

Despite the fragility of human institutions, we can in principle think of both the sequences just mentioned as going on for ever. In fact, the term 'sequence' in mathematics is most commonly used to mean 'infinite sequence'.

To be precise about this, let $\mathcal{N}$ denote as usual the set of all natural numbers; we define a **sequence** of real numbers to be a function from $\mathcal{N}$ to $\mathcal{R}$. If u is such a function, we may write the values it takes as $u(1)$, $u(2)$, $u(3)$ and so on. It is conventional to denote these values by

$$u_1, u_2, u_3, \ldots$$

and to refer to the sequence as $\{u_n\}$.

Example 1 Letting $u_n = 2n$ for $n = 1, 2, \ldots$ gives the sequence

$$2, 4, 6, 8, \ldots$$

Example 2 Let $u_n = 29 - 9n$ for $n = 1, 2, \ldots$; then the sequence $\{u_n\}$ is

$$20, 11, 2, -7, \ldots$$

Example 3 Letting $u_n = -3^n/5$ for $n = 1, 2, \ldots$ gives the sequence

$$-\frac{3}{5}, -\frac{9}{5}, -\frac{27}{5}, -\frac{81}{5}, \ldots$$

Example 4 Let $u_n = 8 \times (-4)^{1-n}$ for $n = 1, 2, \ldots$; then the sequence $\{u_n\}$ is

$$8, -2, \frac{1}{2}, -\frac{1}{8}, \ldots$$

Example 5 Letting $u_n = (n+1)/(2n)$ for $n = 1, 2, \ldots$ gives the sequence

$$1, \frac{3}{4}, \frac{2}{3}, \frac{5}{8}, \ldots$$

Arithmetic and geometric progressions

An **arithmetic progression** is a sequence $\{u_n\}$ with the property that the difference between each pair of successive terms is the same: in other words, $u_{n+1} - u_n$ is the same for all n. The arithmetic progression with first term a and common difference d is

$$a, a + d, a + 2d, a + 3d, \ldots;$$

the nth term is given by
$$u_n = a + (n - 1)d.$$

A **geometric progression** is a sequence $\{u_n\}$ in which each term is obtained from the preceding one by multiplication by the same number: in other words, the ratio u_{n+1}/u_n is the same for all n. The geometric progression with first term a and common ratio x is

$$a, \ ax, \ ax^2, \ ax^3, \ \ldots ;$$

the nth term is given by

$$u_n = ax^{n-1}.$$

How do these concepts relate to the examples of sequences given above? Example 1 is the arithmetic progression with first term 2 and common difference 2. Example 2 is the arithmetic progression with $a = 20$ and $d = -9$. Example 3 is the geometric progression with first term $-3/5$ and common ratio 3. Example 4 is the geometric progression with $a = 8$ and $x = -1/4$. Example 5 is neither an arithmetic nor a geometric progression.

Limits

One question we might ask about a sequence is: what happens eventually? In some cases, the terms of the sequence $\{u_n\}$ appear to cluster round a particular number z when n becomes large: this happens in Example 5 above, with $z = \frac{1}{2}$. In other cases, for instance Example 1, nothing like this occurs. This brings us to the notion of limit.

The limit of a sequence is defined as follows. We say that the sequence $\{u_n\}$ tends to the limit z if, given any positive real number p, there is a positive integer N such that

$$|u_n - z| < p \quad \text{for all } n > N. \tag{5.1}$$

When the sequence $\{u_n\}$ tends to the limit z we write

$$\lim u_n = z.$$

What this definition means, roughly speaking, is that we can make u_n as close as we like to z for all sufficiently large n. To go into these matters in more detail, it is helpful to start with (5.1). This statement may be illustrated in a diagram by representing the sequence $\{u_n\}$ by a set of points in the xy–plane with x–coordinates $1, 2, 3, \ldots$ and y–coordinates $u_1, u_2, u_3, \ldots$. The statement (5.1) means that all the points of the sequence to the right of the vertical line $x = N$ lie between the two horizontal lines $y = z + p$ and $y = z - p$: see Figure 5.1. The statement $\lim u_n = z$ means that for any positive p, however small, one can choose a number N such that Figure 5.1 is applicable.

A story often used to explain the definition of a limit is the following. There is a small person (D De V) and a large person (AS). D De V chooses a small positive number, say 0.01. AS then looks for a natural number N_1 such that $|u_n - z| < 0.01$ for all $n > N_1$. Suppose he finds such an N_1. Then D De V chooses an even smaller number, say 10^{-7}, and AS tries to find an integer N_2 such that u_n is squeezed between $z - 10^{-7}$ and $z + 10^{-7}$ for all $n > N_2$. If this process can be repeated indefinitely, $\lim u_n = z$; if not, not.

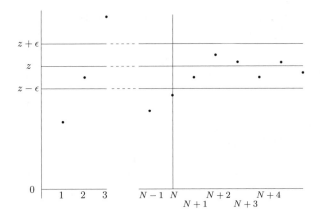

Figure 5.1: **The limit of a sequence**

Examples

To illustrate the concept of limit, we look again at the geometric progressions of Examples 3 and 4. Consider first Example 4: $u_n = 8 \times (-4)^{1-n}$ for $n = 1, 2, \ldots$. A glance at the sequence suggests that the limit is 0, and we now show that this is correct.

Since $u_1 = 8$, $|u_1| < 10$. Also $4^{-5} = 1/1024 < 10^{-3}$. Hence $|u_n| < 0.01$ for all $n > 5$, $|u_n| < 10^{-5}$ for all $n > 10$, $|u_n| < 10^{-8}$ for all $n > 15$ and so on. Thus $\lim u_n = 0$.

Now look at Example 3: $u_n = -3^n/5$ for $n = 1, 2, \ldots$. In this case, u_n becomes arbitrarily large and negative as n gets larger: the sequence does not tend to any limit.

Notation

There are other ways of writing the statement that the sequence $\{u_n\}$ tends to the limit z. As well as the familiar

$$\lim u_n = z,$$

these include

$$\lim_{n \to \infty} u_n = z$$

and 'u_n tends to z as n tends to infinity'. The last statement is often abbreviated to

$$u_n \to z \text{ as } n \to \infty.$$

Here $\to$ is the symbol for 'tends to' and ∞ is the usual symbol for infinity. We shall say something about what 'infinity' means after we have explored the algebra of limits a little further.

Working with limits

More advanced books give systematic methods for investigating whether a sequence tends to a limit. Here we merely note that one can get a lot of mileage out of the following two facts:

Fact 1 Given a real number x, $\lim_{n\to\infty} x^n = 0$ if and only if $-1 < x < 1$.

Fact 2 Given a real number b, $\lim_{n\to\infty} n^b = 0$ if and only if $b < 0$.

Fact 1 tells us, for example, that a geometric progression with common ratio $1/2$ or $-2/3$ tends to the limit 0. Conversely, a geometric progression with common ratio 2 or -3 does not tend to any limit.

Fact 2 implies in particular that for any positive integer k,

$$n^{-k} \to 0 \text{ as } n \to \infty.$$

We now show how this may be applied.

Example 5 (continued) Let

$$u_n = \frac{n+1}{2n} = \frac{1}{2}\left(1 + \frac{1}{n}\right).$$

As $n \to \infty$, $n^{-1} \to 0$, and therefore $1 + n^{-1} \to 1$. Hence $\lim u_n = \frac{1}{2}$.

Example 6 Let

$$v_n = \frac{(-1)^n (n+1)^2}{n^4}.$$

Taking absolute values, which turns the $(-1)^n$ into $+1$ for all n, and dividing above and below by n^2, we see that $|v_n| = (1 + n^{-1})^2 \times n^{-2}$. As $n \to \infty$, $n^{-1} \to 0$ and $n^{-2} \to 0$. Therefore $v_n \to (1+0)^2 \times 0 = 0$, so $v_n \to 0$.

If we were to modify this example by replacing $(n+1)^2$ by $(n+1)^4$, then v_n would be close to $+1$ for large even n and close to -1 for large odd n, and the sequence would not tend to any limit.

'Infinity'

In our discussion of limits, we have sometimes used the word 'infinity', and the reader may wonder what it means. We give a simple, if evasive, answer: the word occurs in this book only in phrases such as 'tends to infinity', which is another way of saying 'becomes arbitrarily large'. In terms of symbols, we have explained what $\to \infty$ means, and ∞ on its own is not something we need to define. Similarly, '$\to -\infty$' means 'becomes arbitrarily large and negative'.

Exercises

5.1.1 Write down the first three terms of each of the following sequences:

$$\text{(a)} \; u_n = 4 + 3n \quad \text{(b)} \; u_n = 5 - 6n \quad \text{(c)} \; u_n = 4^n$$

$$\text{(d)} \; u_n = 5 \times (-2)^n \quad \text{(e)} \; u_n = n \times 3^n$$

In each case, state whether the sequence is an arithmetic progression, a geometric progression or neither.

5.1.2 Write down the first three terms and a formula for the nth term of each of the following sequences:

(a) the arithmetic progression with first term 2 and common difference 5;

(b) the geometric progression with first term 4 and common ratio 3.

5.1.3 In each of the following cases, state whether the sequence $\{u_n\}$ tends to a limit, and find the limit if it exists:

$$\text{(a)} \; u_n = 1 + \tfrac{1}{2}n \quad \text{(b)} \; u_n = 1 - \tfrac{1}{2}n \quad \text{(c)} \; u_n = \left(\tfrac{1}{2}\right)^n \quad \text{(d)} \; u_n = \left(-\tfrac{1}{2}\right)^n$$

5.2   Series

The **series** generated by a sequence $\{u_n\}$ is defined to be the sequence $\{s_n\}$, where

$$s_1 = u_1, \quad s_2 = u_1 + u_2, \quad s_3 = u_1 + u_2 + u_3$$

and so on. A useful general notation for $\{s_n\}$ is

$$\sum_{r=1}^{n} u_r,$$

Here $\sum$ is the upper-case Greek letter *sigma* and stands for 'sum'.[1]

We now derive explicit formulae for s_n when $\{u_n\}$ is an arithmetic or geometric progression.

---

[1]In fact sigma-notation has more flexible uses than summation of the *first n* terms of a sequence: for instance

$$\sum_{r=6}^{9} u_r = u_6 + u_7 + u_8 + u_9 \quad \text{and} \quad \sum_{r=1}^{4} u_{3r} = u_3 + u_6 + u_9 + u_{12}.$$

Summing arithmetic progressions

We begin by deriving a simple formula for the sum of the first n natural numbers. Let

$$i_n = 1 + \quad 2 \quad + \ldots + (n-1) + n.$$

Then

$$i_n = n + (n-1) + \ldots + \quad 2 \quad + 1.$$

Adding the last two equations,

$$2i_n = \overbrace{(n+1) + \ldots + (n+1)}^{n \text{ times}}.$$

Hence

$$1 + 2 + \ldots + n = \tfrac{1}{2}n(n+1). \tag{5.2}$$

We can use similar reasoning to find the sum of the first n terms of a general arithmetic progression. Let $\{u_n\}$ be the arithmetic progression with first term a and common difference d, and let s_n be the sum of the first n terms. Writing s_n both ways round and adding, as we did with i_n, we have

$$2s_n = (u_1 + u_n) + (u_2 + u_{n-1}) + \ldots + (u_n + u_1).$$

Let $x = u_1 + u_n$. Since $u_2 = u_1 + d$ and $u_{n-1} = u_n - d$, $u_2 + u_{n-1} = x$. Similarly $u_3 + u_{n-2} = u_2 + d + u_{n-1} - d = x$, and so on. Thus $2s_n = nx$, and

$$s_n = \frac{n}{2}(u_1 + u_n). \tag{5.3}$$

An alternative formula for s_n is sometimes useful. Recalling the formula for the nth term of the progression, we may substitute $u_1 = a$ and $u_n = a + (n-1)d$ into (5.3), obtaining

$$s_n = n\left(a + \frac{n-1}{2}d\right). \tag{5.4}$$

Notice that the standard formula (5.2) for the sum of the first n natural numbers is a special case both of (5.3) and of (5.4); we can obtain it by setting $u_1 = 1$, $u_n = n$ in (5.3), or by setting $a = d = 1$ in (5.4).

Example Find the sum of the first 15 terms of the sequence

$$48, \ 44, \ 40, \ 36, \ldots$$

This is the arithmetic progression with first term 48 and common difference -4. The 15th term is $48 - (14 \times 4) = -8$; thus by (5.3) the sum of the first 15 terms is

$$\tfrac{1}{2} \times 15 \times (48 - 8) = 300.$$

Alternatively, we can use (5.4) rather than (5.3): since $a = 48$ and $d = -4$, the sum of the first 15 terms is

$$15(48 + 7 \times (-4)) = 300.$$

Summing geometric progressions

Our object is to find a formula for the sum s_n of the first n terms of the geometric progression with first term a and common ratio x. If $x = 1$, all terms of the progression are equal to a, and $s_n = na$. From now on we ignore this uninteresting case, and assume that $x \neq 1$.

We start by considering the case where $a = 1$, so that

$$s_n = 1 + x + \cdots + x^{n-1}.$$

Multiplying by x,

$$x s_n = x + x^2 + \ldots + x^n.$$

The right-hand sides of the last two equations have a lot of terms in common. Indeed, letting

$$t = x + x^2 + \ldots + x^{n-1},$$

we have $s_n = 1 + t$ and $x s_n = t + x^n$. Hence $s_n - x s_n = 1 - x^n$. Rearranging,[2]

$$s_n = (1 - x^n)/(1 - x).$$

In the general case where a is not necessarily equal to 1, all terms of the progression are multiplied by a: therefore s_n is multiplied by a. This gives us the following important fact:

Geometric series formula The sum to n terms of the geometric progression with first term a and common ratio $x \neq 1$ is

$$a \left[\frac{1 - x^n}{1 - x} \right].$$

An alternative version of the formula is obtained by multiplying numerator and denominator by -1: the sum is

$$a \left[\frac{x^n - 1}{x - 1} \right].$$

Example Find the sum of the first 8 terms of the geometric progression

$$10, \ 50, \ 250, \ 1250, \ \ldots$$

Here $a = 10$ and $x = 5$; the sum to 8 terms is

$$10 \left[\frac{5^8 - 1}{5 - 1} \right] = \frac{390625 - 1}{0.4} = 976560.$$

---

[2]Division by $1 - x$ is allowed because $x \neq 1$.

Convergence of series

Let $\{u_n\}$ be any sequence and let $\{s_n\}$ be the series generated by it. If s_n approaches a limit S as $n \to \infty$, we say that the series $\{s_n\}$ is **convergent**, and we write

$$S = \sum_{r=1}^{\infty} u_r.$$

S is called the **sum of the series**, or the **sum to infinity**, and is sometimes written

$$S = u_1 + u_2 + \ldots$$

A series which is not convergent is said to be **divergent**.

We now focus on geometric progressions. Let a and x be real numbers with $a \neq 0$ and $x \neq 1$. As we stated above, the sum to n terms of the geometric progression with first term a and common ratio x is

$$s_n = a(1 - x^n)/(1 - x).$$

We also stated in the last section that if $-1 < x < 1$ then $x^n \to 0$ as $n \to \infty$; therefore

$$\lim_{n \to \infty} s_n = a(1 - 0)/(1 - x) = a/(1 - x).$$

What we actually stated in the last section (Fact 1 about limits) was that $x^n \to 0$ as $n \to \infty$ if *and only if* $-1 < x < 1$: this fact may be used to show that the geometric series diverges if $|x| \geq 1$. We summarise as follows:

Geometric series formula (infinite version) Given that $a \neq 0$, the series

$$a + ax + ax^2 + \ldots$$

converges if and only if $-1 < x < 1$, in which case the sum of the series is

$$\frac{a}{1 - x}.$$

Example Find the sum of the series

$$8 - 2 + \frac{1}{2} - \frac{1}{8} + \ldots$$

Applying the formula just given with $a = 8$ and $x = -1/4$, we see that the sum of the series is

$$\frac{8}{1 + \frac{1}{4}} = \frac{32}{5} = 6.4 \,.$$

Exercises

5.2.1 Find the sum of the natural numbers from 1 to 100 inclusive.

5.2.2 Find the sum of the first 6 terms and a formula for the sum of the first n terms of each of the following sequences:

(a) the arithmetic progression with first term -3 and common difference 7;

(b) the arithmetic progression with first term 3 and common difference -7;

(c) the geometric progression with first term 3 and common ratio 7;

(d) the geometric progression with first term -3 and common ratio $-1/7$.

5.2.3 For each of the cases in Exercise 5.2.2, say whether the sum to infinity exists and, when it exists, find it.

5.3   Geometric progressions in economics

The main economic application of geometric progressions is to compound interest. Let an amount of money P be invested at the beginning of year 1. Let the rate of interest be r, measured as follows: $r = 0.1$ means a rate of interest of 10% per annum, $r = 0.025$ means a rate of interest of $2\frac{1}{2}\%$ per annum and so on. We also suppose for the moment that interest is paid once a year, at the end of the year. How much is the investment worth at the beginning of year 2? Answer: principal P plus accrued interest rP equals $P(1 + r)$. Similarly, the value of the investment at the beginning of year 3 is $P(1+r)(1+r) = P(1+r)^2$; the value at the beginning of year 4 is $P(1+r)^3$; and so on.

Example 1 If £50 is invested at 4% per annum, the value in £ at the beginning of the 7th year is $50 \times (1.04)^6 = 63.27$.

Example 2 We now allow the rate of interest to vary. Suppose as in Example 1 that £50 is invested for 6 full years, but now assume that the rate of interest is 4% per annum for the first three years, rises to 5% for the fourth year, and is 6% for subsequent years. Then the value of the investment at the beginning of the 7th year is £$50 \times (1.04)^3 \times 1.05 \times (1.06)^2$, which is £66.35.

Example 3 In this example we allow compounding of interest to take place more often than once a year. Let interest be compounded quarterly; then with a rate of interest of 4% per annum, 1% of the value of the investment accrues as interest at the end of each quarter. With £50 invested at the beginning of the first year, the value in £ of the investment after 6 full years (24 quarters) is $50 \times (1.01)^{24} = 63.49$.

Generally, if a sum P is invested at a rate of interest of r per year, compounded m times per year, the value of the investment after n years is

$$(1 + r/m)^{mn} P.$$

If $m > 1$, the amount of interest earned in a year per pound invested at the beginning of the year is not r but

$$r' = (1 + r/m)^m - 1.$$

Notice that r' is greater than r: for instance, if $r = 0.04$ and $m = 4$ as in Example 3, then $r' = 0.0406$. When r and r' are expressed as percentages, r is called the **flat rate** and r' the **annual percentage rate** (APR). Given r, r' increases as m increases: given the flat rate, the APR is greater for quarterly than for annual compounding, greater still for monthly compounding and so on.

The fundamental reason why $r' > r$ is, of course, that more interest is paid each year the more frequently it is compounded. Note that in the case of a flat rate of only 4% per annum, the difference between annual and quarterly compounding is very small: comparing Examples 1 and 3, we have a difference of only 22p in the value after 6 years of an initial investment of £50. But with higher interest rates, the difference between annual and quarterly compounding becomes substantial: see Exercise 5.3.1.

For the rest of this section we shall assume annual compounding unless otherwise stated.

Repeated investments

In our examples so far, we have assumed just one intitial investment. Now suppose that an amount of money A is placed in an account at the beginning of *each* year, starting at the beginning of year 1. Then at the beginning of year n (just after the nth investment has been made) the amount of money in the account is

$$W = A(1+r)^{n-1} + A(1+r)^{n-2} + \ldots + A(1+r) + A.$$

The reason for this is that $A(1+r)^{n-1}$ is the principal plus accrued interest for the first year's investment, $A(1+r)^{n-2}$ is principal plus interest on the second year's investment and so on down to the investment just made. Thus W is the sum to n terms of the geometric progression with first term A and common ratio $1 + r$; it follows that

$$W = A\frac{(1+r)^n - 1}{(1+r) - 1}.$$

Simplifying,

$$W = \frac{A}{r}([1+r]^n - 1). \tag{5.5}$$

Example 4 If £50 is placed in an account at the beginning of each year, and the rate of interest is 4% per annum, how much money is in the account just after the 7th investment has been made?

We apply (5.5) with $A = 50$, $r = 0.04$ and $n = 7$. The amount of money in the account is £W, where $W = 1250 \times (1.04^7 - 1) = 394.91$.

Using the formulae indirectly

The compounding formulae may be applied in various ways, as the next two examples illustrate. Notice the use of fractional indices in the solution of Example 5, and logarithms in Example 6.

Example 5 If £50 is invested at a constant rate of interest r, what value of r is required for the investment to be worth £70 at the end of six years?

The required r is given by the equation $50(1 + r)^6 = 70$. Thus $r = (1.4)^{1/6} - 1 = 0.058$, an interest rate of 5.8% per annum.

Example 6 If £50 is invested in an account once per year, and the rate of interest is 4% per annum, after how many payments will there be at least £600 in the account?

Let the answer be N. By (5.5), N is the smallest integer n such that

$$\frac{50}{0.04}([1.04]^n - 1) \geq 600.$$

Thus N is the smallest integer greater than or equal to y, where

$$1.04^y = \frac{600 \times 0.04}{50} + 1 = 1.48 .$$

Taking common logarithms,

$$y = \frac{\log_{10} 1.48}{\log_{10} 1.04} = \frac{0.17026}{0.01703} = 9.996,$$

so $N = 10$.

Present value

Suppose that a sum of money M is going to be available 3 years from now. Its **present value** P is the amount of money which, if invested now, would compound to M in three years time. Assuming a constant rate of interest r, we have $P(1 + r)^3 = M$, so that $P = M(1 + r)^{-3}$. The process of finding present values from future ones is called **discounting**; it can be regarded as the opposite to compounding. When the interest rate is r, the **discount factor** is $1/(1 + r)$.

Similarly, the present value P_n of an annual income stream of Y per year for n years, *starting one year from now*, is given by

$$P_n = \frac{Y}{(1+r)} + \frac{Y}{(1+r)^2} + \ldots + \frac{Y}{(1+r)^n}.$$

To simplify this, one may apply directly the formula for summing a geometric progression. A slightly quicker way is to notice that

$$P_n = \left[Y(1+r)^{n-1} + Y(1+r)^{n-2} + \ldots + Y\right](1+r)^{-n}.$$

The term in square brackets, with Y replaced by A, is the compounded sum which we called W above. Using (5.5), we see that the term in square brackets is equal to $(Y/r)([1+r]^n - 1)$: therefore

$$P_n = \frac{Y}{r}(1 - [1+r]^{-n}). \tag{5.6}$$

Example 7 One use of (5.6) is the calculation of the regular payments on a mortgage. Suppose that £150,000 is borrowed to be repaid over 20 years. Suppose also that the (flat) rate of interest is 9% per annum, and that repayments, and compounding of interest, take place monthly. Assuming that each month's repayment is a constant amount z, what must z be?

The answer is that z is such that the present value of repayments of £z per month for 240 months, discounted at $(9/12)\%$ per month, equals the value of the loan (£150,000). Hence by (5.6),

$$15 \times 10^4 = \frac{z}{0.0075}(1 - 1.0075^{-240}).$$

Therefore $z = 1125/(1 - 0.166413) = 1349.589$; repayments are approximately £1350 per month.

Infinite streams

Returning now to the case of annual discounting, we consider what happens to (5.6) as $n \to \infty$. Consider a security which gives its holder the right to an annual income of Y per year *forever*, starting one year from now; such a security is called a **perpetuity**. The crucial fact about such securities is the following.

Valuation formula for a perpetuity Assume a constant rate of interest r. Then the value of the perpetuity giving its holder the right to an annual income of Y per year, starting one year from now, is $\dfrac{Y}{r}$.

This may be obtained by taking the limit as $n \to \infty$ of the right-hand side of (5.6), or directly as the sum of the infinite geometric series with first term $Y/(1+r)$ and common ratio $1/(1+r)$: since $0 < 1/(1+r) < 1$, the sum is

$$\frac{Y}{1+r} \bigg/ \left(1 - \frac{1}{1+r}\right) = \frac{Y}{(1+r)-1} = \frac{Y}{r}.$$

Example 7 The value at the beginning of year 1 of an income stream of £1200 received at the end of years $1, 2, 3, \ldots$ forever, discounted at 6% per annum, is £20, 000.

An interesting point about the beautifully simple valuation formula for a perpetuity is that it gives us an easy way to remember the more complicated formula (5.6) for the present value P_n of an annual income stream of Y per year for n years, starting one year from now. We can think of the finite income stream as the difference between two infinite streams. Specifically, $P_n = a - b$, where a is the present value of an income of Y received at the end of years $1, 2, 3$ and so on forever, and b is the present value of an income of Y received at the end of years $n+1, n+2, n+3$ and so on forever. Now $a = Y/r$; similarly b is the present value of a lump sum of Y/r available in n years time, and is therefore equal to $(Y/r)(1 + r)^{-n}$. Hence

$$P_n = \frac{Y}{r} - \frac{Y}{r}(1 + r)^{-n},$$

which is (5.6).

The money multiplier

A quite different application of geometric progressions concerns the determination of the money supply. A country's **money stock** M is equal to $C + D$, where C is cash held by the public outside the banks, and D is bank deposits. The **money base** (or stock of **high-powered money**) H is equal to $C + Z$ where Z is bank reserves. Notice that Z consists of cash in the tills and vaults of banks, together with banks' deposits at the country's central bank (e.g. the Bank of England); thus H is *total* cash, inside and outside the banks, *plus* banks' deposits at the central bank.

Let c denote the public's cash-to-deposits ratio and z the banks' reserves-to-deposits ratio. Then $c = C/D$ and $z = Z/D$, so $M = (c+1)D$ and $H = (c+z)D$. It follows that

$$\frac{M}{H} = \frac{c+1}{c+z}. \tag{5.7}$$

The right-hand side of (5.7) is called the **money multiplier**, and we denote it by the Greek letter μ.

Notice that c could in principle be greater or less than 1, whereas z must be less than 1, because balance sheets balance: total bank liabilities (which are approximately equal to D) must be matched by assets (of which Z is only a part). Therefore $\mu > 1$, whence the term 'multiplier'. In modern economies, both c and z are considerably less than 1, making μ much greater than 1. For example, in the United Kingdom in March 2000 H was £30 billion and M £560 billion, making μ approximately 19.[3]

---

[3]In practice, there are several different measures of the money supply; this is a consequence

A consequence of (5.7) is that if H goes up by 1 unit and c and z remain constant, then M goes up by μ units: if an extra unit of high-powered money enters the economy, say from abroad, and μ is 19, the money stock increases by 19 units! How can this happen? This is where geometric progressions enter the picture.

Suppose then that some person or firm A1 receives 1 unit of cash from abroad; the 'A' here stands for 'agent', a term commonly used by economists to mean 'person-or-firm'. To maintain the cash-to-deposits ratio at c, A1 must keep a proportion $c/(1 + c)$ of her 1 unit in the form of cash, and deposit the remaining $1/(1 + c)$ a bank (say B1). For example, if $c = 1/4$ then A1 should keep 1/5 of her money in cash and 4/5 as bank deposits.

Now consider what bank B1 does with the new deposit. To maintain its reserves-to-deposits ratio at z, B1 should allocate the deposit of $1/(1 + c)$ as follows: retain $z/(1 + c)$ as reserves and lend the remainder, say to agent A2. Suppose the loan is made in cash, and denote the amount lent by x: then

$$x = (1 - z)/(1 + c).$$

Up to this stage, the increase in the money stock is $1 + x$, consisting of 1 unit arising from A1's windfall ($c/(1 + c)$ units cash plus $1/(1 + c)$ units deposited at bank B1) and x units arising from A2's loan (all cash).

However, matters do not stop here, because A2 is now in the position that A1 was in at the beginning of the story, except that she has only x rather than 1 units of cash to dispose of. A2 (or whoever sells her goods and services) will deposit part of the cash at a bank (say B2) which will lend some of the deposit to another agent (say A3). Indeed, just as A1's 1–unit windfall generated an additional increase in the money stock of x, A2's x–unit loan generates an additional increase in the money stock of $x \times x$.

By this stage, the overall increase in the money stock is

$$1 + x + x^2.$$

But this is not the end of the story, for part of the cash arising from A3's loan will be deposited at a bank (say B3), and so on. The eventual increase in the money stock is

$$1 + x + x^2 + x^3 + \ldots = \frac{1}{1 - x}.$$

It remains to check that this expression for the increase in the money stock engendered by a 1–unit increase in the money base is equal to the money multiplier μ. Since

$$1 - x = 1 - \frac{1 - z}{1 + c} = \frac{c + z}{1 + c} = \frac{1}{\mu},$$

$1/(1 - x)$ is indeed equal to μ.

---

of the fact that there are several different ways of defining the terms 'bank' and 'deposit'. The figures given in the text for H and M are for the Bank of England's categories 'M0' and 'retail deposits and cash in M4' respectively.

Exercises

5.3.1 In the Republic of Usuria the (flat) rate of interest 40% per annum. Suppose 100 Usurian dollars are invested. Find the value of the investment at the beginning of the third year if compounding takes place (a) annually, (b) quarterly, (c) every two years, (d) every three years.

5.3.2 An amount of money is invested at a constant rate of interest r, compounded annually. What value of r is required for the investment to be worth double at the end of 10 years?

5.3.3 In this exercise assume an interest rate of 6% per annum, with annual compounding of interest.

    (a) If £100 is deposited in an account at the beginning of each year, how much money is in the account just after the 5th investment has been made?

    (b) If £A is deposited in an account at the beginning of each year, after how many payments will there be at least £8A in the account?

5.3.4 You are promised that four payments of £100 are going to be made to you at yearly intervals starting now. If the interest rate is 8% per annum, how much is this promise worth to you now?

5.3.5 Suppose that a £100,000 mortgage is to be repaid over 25 years. Assume constant repayments and monthly compounding of interest. Find what amount must be repaid each month when the rate of interest is (a) 9% per annum, (b) 8.5% per annum.

Problems on Chapter 5

5–1. Show that the sequence

$$u_n = \frac{3n}{n+3}$$

tends to a limit z. Find z. For this sequence, make a table of values giving $p = 10^{-2}$, 10^{-3}, 10^{-4}, 10^{-5} and a corresponding integer N which satisfies (5.1).

Does the sequence

$$v_n = \frac{3n^2}{n^3+3}$$

tends to a limit?

5–2. Credit card firms usually charge interest monthly and often state the interest rate charged as a rate per month. Suppose such a firm charges an interest rate of s per month. Find in terms of s:

(i) the annual flat rate;

(ii) the annual percentage rate (APR).

Suppose the firm wishes to change the APR from 20% to 25%. Find the corresponding change in the interest charged per month.

5–3. The following is the special case of the model of Problem 2–1 where there is no tax collection:

$$Y = C + I + G, \quad C = c_0 + c_1 Y.$$

The unknowns are Y (national income) and C (consumption); I (investment) and G (government expenditure) are assumed to be known. As before, c_0 and c_1 are positive constants, with $c_1 < 1$.

(i) Suppose that G increases by one unit. According to the first equation, Y will increase by one unit; but, according to the second equation, this will cause an increase in C of c_1 units which then (by the first equation) causes a further increase of c_1 units in Y. Continue this argument to obtain an expression for the total effect in the form of an infinite series. Find its sum.

(ii) Now solve the system of equations for Y and C in terms of I, G, c_0 and c_1. Use the expression obtained for Y to determine directly the change in Y produced by an increase in G of one unit. Verify that your answers to (i) and (ii) are consistent.

(iii) What happens if, instead of G increasing by one unit, I does?

[The changes in Y resulting from unit changes in G and I are called multipliers, like the money multiplier of Section 5.3.]

5–4. (i) A timber owner plants a forest at time $t = 0$, where time is measured in years. The volume of timber in the forest at time $t \geq 0$ is given by the function $f(t)$. The price per unit volume of wood harvested is p and the interest rate is r; both p and r assumed to be constant. The forest is cut down and the timber sold at time T. Find the value of the forest at time 0.

(ii) Now suppose that every T years the timber owner cuts down the forest, sells the timber and replants it with similar trees. Find the total value of the forest at time 0.

[The price p may be interpreted as net of harvesting costs. Ignore planting costs throughout.]

Chapter 6

INTRODUCTION TO DIFFERENTIATION

This is the first of several chapters on calculus, a branch of mathematics with a vast range of applications.

The word **calculus** can be used to refer to any systematic body of rules for calculation. However, a more common usage of the term in mathematics, and the way in which it will be used in this book, is as a shorthand for **infinitesimal calculus**, a branch of mathematics invented in the 17th century by the Englishman Isaac Newton (1642–1727) and the German Georg Wilhelm Leibniz (1646–1716). Calculus consists of **differential calculus**, which we introduce in this chapter and develop in Chapters 7 to 10, and **integral calculus**, which will be introduced in Chapter 19.

Differential calculus is concerned with the way in which the value of a function changes when the independent variable changes. In particular, it is concerned with defining and measuring rates of change, using the concept of a limit. The first two sections of this chapter set up the conceptual apparatus. We then give some rules for finding rates of change, and some simple applications to economics, notably the calculation of marginal functions and elasticities. The appendix to the chapter, which can be omitted at first reading, goes into the basic mathematical concepts in rather more detail.

When you have studied this chapter you will be able to:

- understand what is meant by the slope of a curve;

- find derivatives of polynomials and functions involving negative-integer powers;

- use differentiation to approximate changes in values of functions, by applying the small increments formula;

- calculate marginal functions and elasiticities in simple cases.

6.1   The derivative

The central problem of differential calculus is as follows: given a function f, we wish to find the rate at which $f(x)$ changes as x changes.

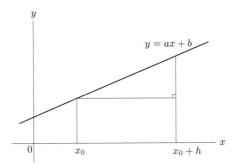

Figure 6.1: **The rate of change of a linear function**

In the case of linear functions, rates of change are easily defined and calculated. Let

$$f(x) = ax + b$$

and let x change from x_0 to $x_0 + h$, as shown in Figure 6.1. Then

$$\frac{\text{change in } f(x)}{\text{change in } x} = \frac{(a[x_0 + h] + b) - (ax_0 + b)}{(x_0 + h) - x_0} = \frac{ah}{h} = a.$$

Thus the rate of change of $f(x)$ is a constant equal to the slope of the line $y = f(x)$.

Notice the special case which occurs when $a = 0$: the function $f(x)$ is then constant and its rate of change is zero.

The slope of a parabola

The next step is to generalise the concept of rate of change, or slope, to functions whose graphs are smooth curves. The simplest case to start with is

$$f(x) = x^2,$$

whose graph is shown in Figure 6.2. As before let x change from x_0 to $x_0 + h$. Then

$$\frac{\text{change in } f(x)}{\text{change in } x} = \frac{(x_0 + h)^2 - x_0^2}{(x_0 + h) - x_0} = \frac{2x_0 h + h^2}{h} = 2x_0 + h.$$

This calculation corresponds to finding the slope of the line PQ. If we now imagine what happens geometrically as h gets smaller and smaller, we can see that the slope of PQ becomes closer and closer to the slope of the line T which touches the graph of x^2 at $x = x_0$. The line T is known as the **tangent to the curve** at the point (x_0, x_0^2); its slope measures the rate of change of the function $f(x) = x^2$ at $x = x_0$.

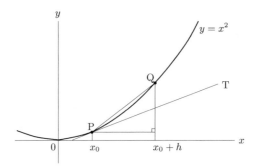

Figure 6.2: **The rate of change of** $f(x) = x^2$

The fact that the slope of PQ can be made as close as we wish to the slope of T by taking h sufficiently small can be expressed as a statement about limits, analogous to the facts about limits of sequences given in Section 5.1. We write

$$\text{slope of PQ} \to 2x_0 \text{ as } h \to 0$$

or

$$\lim_{h \to 0} (\text{slope of PQ}) = 2x_0.$$

As we noted above, the slope $2x_0$ of the tangent T measures the rate of change of the function $f(x) = x^2$ at x_0. It is called the **derivative** of $f(x)$ at x_0. Other names for the derivative include **gradient**, **differential coefficient** and, for reasons just stated, **slope** and **rate of change**.

Slopes in general

The above procedure may be carried out at a general point x (i.e. dropping the subscript 0) for a general function $f(x)$.

The slope of the line PQ is given by the expression

$$\frac{f(x+h) - f(x)}{h}. \tag{6.1}$$

Taking the limit as $h \to 0$ of (6.1) gives the derivative of $f(x)$ at x. The derivative of f at x is denoted by $f'(x)$: the symbol $'$ is known as a prime, and f' is pronounced 'eff-prime'.

The derivative $f'(x)$ is the slope of the tangent to the curve at that particular x: as with the slope of any straight line, it can be positive, negative or zero. In Figure 6.2, $f'(x)$ is positive if $x > 0$, negative for $x < 0$ and zero if $x = 0$.

In the standard notation for limits,

$$f'(x) = \lim_{h \to 0} \frac{f(x+h) - f(x)}{h}.$$

In the special case of a straight line, where $f(x) = ax + b$, $f'(x) = a$. In the case where $f(x) = x^2$, $f'(x) = 2x$. In general, the process of going from the function f to the function f' is called **differentiation**.

Alternative notation

An alternative notation for differentiation is as follows. Given a function, say $y = f(x)$, we write the change in x as Δx and the change in y as Δy; thus Δx is what we have been calling h up to now and Δy is the numerator of (6.1).[1] Notice that Δx is a single symbol, not 'Δ times x', and the same goes for Δy. The derivative is then written[2]

$$\frac{dy}{dx} = \lim_{\Delta x \to 0} \frac{\Delta y}{\Delta x}.$$

Here $\dfrac{d}{dx}$ is to be understood as specifying the operation of differentiation: dy and dx should not be regarded as the numerator and denominator of a fraction.

The alternative notation for the two special cases of differentiation at the beginning of this chapter is as follows:

$$\text{if } y = ax + b, \ \frac{dy}{dx} = a; \quad \text{if } y = x^2, \ \frac{dy}{dx} = 2x.$$

While we do not *need* two notations for differentiation, the added flexibility happens to be very useful; this will become clear as we proceed. As a very rough rule, $f'(x)$ is more convenient for theoretical argument and $\dfrac{d}{dx}$ for calculations, but this is not a rule we shall adhere to strictly.

An application: velocity

Suppose a long straight road runs from south to north past a point O. A car starts q kilometres north of O and moves along the road. We define a function f by letting $f(x)$ be the number of kilometres north of O that the car is situated after x hours have elapsed. Since the road runs south as well as north of O, and the car can move in either direction, $f(x)$ can be either positive or negative. The graph of f is shown in the upper panel of Figure 6.3.

---

[1] Δ is the upper-case (capital) form of the Greek letter 'delta'; the lower-case form is δ. Many books use δx and δy instead of Δx and Δy. We prefer Δ in this context as it has fewer alternative uses.

[2] $\frac{dy}{dx}$ is pronounced 'dee-wye-by-dee-ex'.

Suppose that, as in Figure 6.3, $0 < a < b$ and the curve $y = f(x)$ slopes upward for all x between a and b. This means that the car is moving northward between time a and time b and covers $f(b) - f(a)$ km. in that period; the average speed of the car during that time, in km. per hour, is

$$(f(b) - f(a))/(b - a).$$

All of this remains true when we bring b closer and closer to a: hence $f'(a)$ is the instantaneous speed of the car at time a.

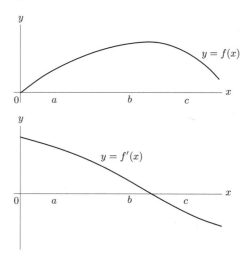

Figure 6.3: **Velocity as a derivative**

To say more about this example, it is helpful to work in terms of **velocity** rather than speed. Velocity may be defined as 'signed speed': in this example, velocity is positive if the car is moving north, negative if it is moving south. Since the car is moving north at time a, its instantaneous speed $f'(a)$ is also its instantaneous velocity: if $f'(a) = 80$, the car is moving north at time a at a speed of 80 km. per hour. By contrast, at time c the car is moving south: this is illustrated in the diagram by the fact that the curve $y = f(x)$ is downward-sloping when x is close to c, and results in the slope $f'(c)$ being negative. In this case too, slope equals velocity: for instance $f'(c) = -60$ means that the car's velocity at time c is -60 km. per hour; in other words, it is moving south at 60 km. per hour.

To summarise in the alternative notation: if x is time and y is distance (in a particular direction), dy/dx represents velocity. This application of the derivative has been known since the dawn of calculus, and has nothing to do with economics.[3] Our reason for mentioning this particular application is that

---

[3]One aspect of this example does occur frequently in economics: the independent variable represents time. We shall return to this theme in Section 9.3.

it illustrates very well an important mathematical point: *the derivative is a function in its own right.* Thus when $f(x)$ represents distance north of O at time x, $f'(x)$ represents velocity at time x. The graph of the function $f'(x)$ is sketched in the lower panel of Figure 6.3.

Exercises

6.1.1 Write down the rate of change of the function $f(x) = x^2$ at the points where $x = 1, -2, \frac{7}{2}, -\frac{1}{2}$.

What are the corresponding rates of change for the function $g(x) = 5x - 8$? Comment.

6.1.2 Find, using the method of this section, the rate of change of the function $f(x) = x^3$ at $x = x_0$.

[HINT. Use the fact that $a^3 - b^3 = (a - b)(a^2 + ab + b^2)$.]

6.1.3 Find, using the method of this section, the rate of change of the function $f(x) = x^{-1}$ at $x = x_0$.

6.1.4 Use your answer to Exercise 6.1.2 to show that the tangents at the points on the curve $y = x^3$ where $x = -k$ and $x = k$ are parallel.

6.2   Linear approximations and differentiability

We have seen that the slope of the curve $y = f(x)$ at a point P is found by finding the slope of the tangent to the curve at P. Now, instead of focusing attention solely on the point P, we consider what happens close to P. We see from Figure 6.4 that, if we stay close to P, then the tangent at P stays close to the curve $y = f(x)$. Thus the tangent at P can be viewed as a linear approximation to the curve near P.

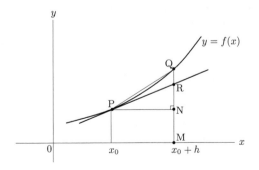

Figure 6.4: **The tangent at P is a linear approximation to the curve at P**

The form of the approximation can be found explicitly as follows. Suppose $|h|$ is small. Referring to Figure 6.4 we see that, when the independent variable takes the value $x + h$,

$$\text{value of function } f = \text{MQ} = f(x + h)$$

and

$$\text{value of linear approximation} = \text{MR} = \text{MN} + \text{NR} = f(x) + hf'(x).$$

Therefore

$$f(x + h) \approx f(x) + hf'(x) \text{ when } |h| \text{ is small.} \qquad (6.2)$$

In (6.2), x is considered fixed and the right-hand side is linear in h.

The approximation (6.2) can also be written

$$f(x + h) - f(x) \approx hf'(x) \text{ when } |h| \text{ is small} : \qquad (6.3)$$

the change in the value of the function $f(x)$ is approximately the change in x multiplied by the slope of the curve at x. This fact is sometimes called the **small increments formula**.

In the alternative notation, the small increments formula (6.3) says that when Δx is small in absolute value,

$$\Delta y \approx \frac{dy}{dx} \Delta x.$$

Here $\dfrac{dy}{dx}$ is the slope at the original point P.

Limits and continuity

Most of what we have done so far in this chapter can be summarised as follows: when we find the derivative of a function at a point, we are approximating the function by a straight line at that point. Unfortunately, not all functions are capable of being approximated by straight lines at every point, so differentiation is not always possible. We now say a few words about which functions can and cannot be differentiated. Our account will be very brief: some details are discussed at greater length in the appendix to this chapter, but even that is not at all a rigorous treatment of the subject.

We begin by going back to the idea of a limit, and saying a little more about what it means. The statement

$$f(x) \text{ tends to the limit } \ell \text{ as } x \text{ approaches } x_0 \qquad (6.4)$$

means that we may make $f(x)$ as close as we wish to ℓ for all x sufficiently close (but not equal) to x_0. A more precise definition is given in the appendix, which also discusses the analogy with the notion of a limit of a sequence introduced in Section 5.1. Briefer ways of writing (6.4) include

$$f(x) \to \ell \text{ as } x \to x_0$$

and

$$\lim_{x \to x_0} f(x) = \ell.$$

An important point about limits is that

$$\lim_{x \to x_0} f(x) \text{ **may or may not** be equal to } f(x_0).$$

To see this, consider the following three examples.

Example 1 Let $f(x) = 2x + 3$. Then $f(x)$ is close to 5 whenever x is close to 1. Hence

$$\lim_{x \to 1} f(x) = 5 = f(1).$$

Example 2 Let

$$f(x) = \begin{cases} +1, & \text{when } x \neq 4 \\ -1, & \text{when } x = 4 \end{cases}$$

Since $f(x) = 1$ whenever $x \neq 4$, however close x is to 4, $f(x) \to 1$ as $x \to 4$. But $f(4) = -1$. Therefore

$$\lim_{x \to 4} f(x) \neq f(4).$$

Example 3 Let

$$f(x) = \begin{cases} x - 1, & \text{when } x < 0 \\ x + 1, & \text{when } x \geq 0 \end{cases}$$

Then $f(x) \approx -1$ whenever x is close to *and less than* 0, while $f(x) \approx +1$ whenever x is close to *and greater than* 0. So in this case the expression $\lim_{x \to 0} f(x)$ is not even defined.

If $\lim_{x \to x_0} f(x) = f(x_0)$, we say that the function $f(x)$ is **continuous** at x_0. Thus the function of Example 1 is continuous at $x = 1$, the function of Example 2 is **discontinuous** (i.e. not continuous) at $x = 4$, and that of Example 2 is discontinuous at $x = 0$.

We say that f is a **continuous function** if it is continuous at x for *every* x. Geometrically, *a function is continuous if its graph may be drawn without lifting the pencil from the paper*. That this geometrical definition of continuity amounts to the same thing as the algebraic one given in the preceding sentence may seem mysterious. We attempt to clear up the mystery in the appendix to this chapter. Meanwhile, some insight may be obtained by looking again at the three examples above. The function of Example 1 is continuous. We have already explained that the function of Example 2 is discontinuous at $x = 4$, and its graph does indeed have a break where $x = 4$. We showed above that the function of Example 3 is discontinuous at $x = 0$, and it is easy to see that its graph jumps where $x = 0$.

The intermediate value theorem

A useful result about continuous functions is the **intermediate value theorem**: let the function $f(x)$ be continuous for all x such that $a \leq x \leq b$, and let k be a real number between $f(a)$ and $f(b)$; then there is at least one value of x such that $a \leq x \leq b$ and $f(x) = k$.

An important special case of the theorem (corresponding to the case $k = 0$) is the following: if the function $f(x)$ is continuous for all x such that $a \leq x \leq b$, and $f(a)$ and $f(b)$ have opposite signs, then the equation $f(x) = 0$ has at least one solution between a and b. This special case is illustrated in Figure 6.5.

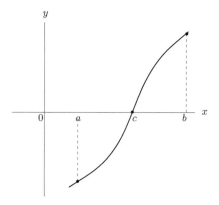

Figure 6.5: **If f is continuous and $f(a) < 0$, $f(b) > 0$ then $f(c) = 0$ for some c between a and b**

Two features of the intermediate value theorem deserve emphasis. First, the result is something one would expect given the description of continuity in terms of pencil and paper; but a rigorous proof using the definition of continuity in terms of limits is beyond the scope of this book. Secondly, the result depicted in Figure 6.5 is helpful because it gives a condition, which is often easy to verify, under which a nonlinear equation has at least one solution.

Differentiability

We now return to the topic of differentiation, and in particular the question of when that operation is possible. A function $f(x)$ has a derivative at $x = x_0$ if the expression

$$(f(x_0 + h) - f(x_0))/h$$

approaches a limit as $h \to 0$, in which case the limit is $f'(x_0)$. The derivative of $f(x)$ at $x = x_0$ can also be wriiten as a limit in a slightly different way, namely

$$f'(x_0) = \lim_{x \to x_0} \frac{f(x) - f(x_0)}{x - x_0}.$$

A function is said to be **differentiable** at a particular point if the derivative of the function can be found at that point. Recall that this means that the function can be approximated by a straight line at the point. On the other hand, a function which is discontinuous at a point clearly cannot be approximated by a straight line at that point. Hence, a function which is differentiable at a point must be continuous at that point.

Just as we went from continuity at a point to the notion of a continuous function, we can do the same with differentiability: a **differentiable function** is one that is differentiable at every point. The last paragraph implies that **every differentiable function is continuous**; in the appendix, we derive this fact from the small increments formula (6.3).

On the other hand, **not all continuous functions are differentiable**. In particular, the continuous function

$$f(x) = |x|$$

is not differentiable at $x = 0$. The geometry of this is easy to see: since x is a perfect approximation to $f(x)$ for small positive x, and $-x$ is a perfect approximation to $f(x)$ for small negative x, **no** linear function can approximate $f(x)$ both for small positive x and for small negative x. We give an algebraic demonstration at the end of the appendix to this chapter.

The moral of this is that continuous functions with kinks in them are not differentiable at kink-points. On the other hand, there are plenty of functions which are differentiable.

An important class of differentiable functions is the polynomials. A **polynomial** in x is the sum of a finite number of expressions of the form ax^n where a is a real number and n a non-negative integer: thus linear and quadratic functions are polynomials, and so is the function

$$3x^{20} - x^{12} + \tfrac{5}{3}x^8 - 6x + \sqrt{2}.$$

All polynomials are differentiable, and ratios of polynomials are differentiable wherever they are defined.

The fact that polynomials and ratios of polynomials are differentiable implies that they are continuous. This is helpful for calculating limits: for instance

$$\lim_{x \to 2} \frac{x^3 + 1}{x^2 + 7x - 6} = \frac{8 + 1}{4 + 14 - 6} = \frac{3}{4}.$$

But to say that a function is differentiable does not in itself help us to find its derivative. For that we need rules: these are the subject of the next section and most of the next chapter.

Exercises

6.2.1 Use the derivative to find the approximate change in x^2 when x changes (a) from 1 to 1.01, (b) from 1 to 0.99, (c) from 2 to 2.01, (d) from 2 to 1.99.

What happens if the function is $5x - 8$ instead of x^2?

6.2.2 Find the slope of the tangent to the curve $y = x^2$ at the point where $x = 1$. Use this and the fact that the tangent passes through the point $(1, 1)$ to find the equation of the tangent.

Verify your results for this function in Exercise 6.2.1, parts (a) and (b), by finding the corresponding changes along the tangent.

6.2.3 A function $f(x)$ is defined as follows:

$$f(x) = \begin{cases} x & \text{when } x < 1 \\ 2x - 1 & \text{when } x \geq 1 \end{cases}$$

Sketch its graph. Explain why the function is continuous at $x = 1$ but not differentiable there.

6.3   Two useful rules

The reader who has worked through the last two sections and their exercises will know how to differentiate linear functions and the power functions x^2, x^3 and x^{-1}. We now extend the set of functions we can differentiate, by means of two key rules: the power rule, which enables us to differentiate more general powers of x, and the combination rule whereby sums of multiples of powers of x can be differentiated. We consider these two rules in turn.

Power rule   If $f(x) = x^n$, where n is an integer, then $f'(x) = nx^{n-1}$.

For example, the derivative of x^{20} is $20x^{19}$ and the derivative of x^{-2} is $-2x^{-3}$.

In terms of limits, the power rule states that

$$\frac{(x + h)^n - x^n}{h} \to nx^{n-1} \text{ as } h \to 0. \tag{6.5}$$

We sketch the proof of this in the case where n is a *positive* integer. Assume that $x \neq 0$, let $t = 1 + (h/x)$ and let z be the fraction on the left-hand side of

(6.5). Then

$$z = \frac{(xt)^n - x^n}{x(t-1)} = x^{n-1} \left[\frac{t^n - 1}{t - 1} \right].$$

For reasons explained in Section 5.2, the term in square brackets is the sum of the first n terms of the geometric progression with first term 1 and common ratio t. When h is close to 0, t is close to 1; but then all terms of the progression are close to 1, and the sum to n terms is close to n. Thus, as $h \to 0$, $z \to x^{n-1} \times n$, as required.

The proof for the negative integer case is quite similar and is omitted.

Combination rule If $f(x) = af_1(x) + bf_2(x)$, where a and b are constants, then $f'(x) = af_1'(x) + bf_2'(x)$.

In the dy/dx notation, the above rules may be written as follows:

Power rule $\dfrac{d}{dx}(x^n) = nx^{n-1}$ if n is an integer.

Combination rule $\dfrac{d}{dx}(ay + bz) = a\dfrac{dy}{dx} + b\dfrac{dz}{dx}.$

We use this notation to sketch a proof of the combination rule. Let

$$w = ay + bz.$$

Suppose that when x increases by Δx, y increases by Δy, z by Δz and w by Δw. Then

$$\Delta w = a\Delta y + b\Delta z.$$

Dividing through by Δx, we see that

$$\frac{\Delta w}{\Delta x} = a\frac{\Delta y}{\Delta x} + b\frac{\Delta z}{\Delta x}.$$

If we now let $\Delta x \to 0$,

$$\frac{\Delta y}{\Delta x} \to \frac{dy}{dx}, \quad \frac{\Delta z}{\Delta x} \to \frac{dz}{dx} \quad \text{and} \quad \frac{\Delta w}{\Delta x} \to \frac{dw}{dx},$$

which gives us the combination rule.

The combination rule may be iterated — for example

$$\frac{d}{dx}(2y - 3z - 4u + 5v) = 2\frac{dy}{dx} - 3\frac{dz}{dx} - 4\frac{du}{dx} + 5\frac{dv}{dx}.$$

Combining the rules

The special cases of the power rule when n is 1 or 0 are $\dfrac{d}{dx}(x) = 1$ and $\dfrac{d}{dx}(1) = 0$. Putting these facts together with the combination rule, we retrieve the rule for differentiating linear functions given in Section 6.1, which we call the **straight line rule**. We now show how the rules can combined to differentiate more complicated functions.

Example 1 Find dy/dx when $y = 2x^3 - 3x^2$.

$$\begin{aligned} \frac{dy}{dx} &= 2\frac{d}{dx}(x^3) - 3\frac{d}{dx}(x^2) \quad \text{by the combination rule} \\ &= 2(3x^2) - 3(2x) \qquad \text{by the power rule} \\ &= 6x(x - 1). \end{aligned}$$

Example 2 Find dy/dx when $y = x^5 + x^2 - 3x + 5$.

$$\frac{dy}{dx} = \frac{d}{dx}(x^5) + \frac{d}{dx}(x^2) + \frac{d}{dx}(-3x + 5)$$
$$\text{by the combination rule}$$
$$= 5x^4 + 2x - 3$$

by the power rule and the straight line rule.

The methods used in Examples 1 and 2 can be used to differentiate any polynomial. In fact, the class of functions which can be differentiated using the rules given so far is wider than the polynomials, since the power rule allows negative-integer powers. The next example ilustrates this point and another, very important, one: *it is sometimes necessary to do some algebraic rearrangement before the rules can be applied.*

Example 3 Find $f'(x)$ when $f(x) = (3 - 4x)/x^2$.

The first step is to write $f(x)$ in a form to which the rules may be applied. We do this by noting that

$$f(x) = 3x^{-2} - 4x^{-1}.$$

Then by the combination and power rules,

$$f'(x) = 3(-2x^{-3}) - 4(-x^{-2}) = (4x - 6)/x^3.$$

Exercises

6.3.1 Write down the derivative of the function $y = x^{-1}$. What can you say about its sign? What can you say about the sign of the derivative of the function $y = x^{-2}$? Try to formulate a general result, and comment on its significance for possible equations for demand schedules.

6.3.2 Differentiate:

(a) $3x^2 - 4$ (b) $x^7 + x^{-4}$

(c) $7x^3 - 2x^2 + 5x + 1$ (d) $2x^4 - 7x^{-1}$

(e) $\frac{2}{3}x^6 + \frac{1}{6}x^{-3} - \frac{1}{2}$ (f) $0.7x^{-4} + 1.3 - 3.1x^3$

(g) $ax^3 + b$ (h) $4ax^2 - 3bx^{-2} + a^2$

In parts (g) and (h), a and b are constants.

6.3.3 Differentiate by first rewriting as sums of powers of x:

(a) $(4x - 2)x^3$ (b) $x(x + 1)(x + 2)$

(c) $\dfrac{3x^2 + 1}{2x}$ (d) $\dfrac{(2x - 1)(x + 1)}{x}$

(e) $\left(x + \dfrac{a}{x}\right)\left(x - \dfrac{a}{x}\right)$ (f) $\dfrac{x - a}{bx^3}$

In parts (e) and (f), a and b are constants.

6.4 Derivatives in economics

The most common applications of differentiation in economics concern marginal functions.

Suppose the revenue of a monopolist is some function $R(x)$ of x, where x is the quantity sold. To make things simple, at some cost in realism, we allow x to vary continuously throughout some range of non-negative real numbers and assume that $R(x)$ is differentiable.

Marginal revenue is defined to be $R'(x)$, the derivative of revenue with respect to quantity: notice that $R'(x)$ depends on x. From the small increments formula (6.3),

$$R(x + h) - R(x) \approx hR'(x) \text{ for small } h.$$

Thus 'h times marginal revenue at x' is approximately the increase in revenue when the quantity sold is increased from x to $x + h$, provided h is small.

It is important to notice that marginal revenue as just defined is **not** the same as 'increase in revenue when quantity is increased by 1 unit' and may not be even approximately equal to that change in revenue. This is because $h = 1$ may not be small enough for the small-increments approximation to be accurate.

Similarly, if $C(x)$ is the cost of producing an output level of x, marginal cost is $C'(x)$. If $H(Y)$ denotes the level of imports when national income is Y, then the marginal propensity to import is $H'(Y)$. And so on.

Two examples

(i) Suppose a monopolist faces the demand function

$$x = 27 - 3p,$$

where x is quantity sold and p is price. Then revenue, expressed as a function of x, is

$$R(x) = px = \tfrac{1}{3}(27 - x)x = 9x - \tfrac{1}{3}x^2.$$

Marginal revenue is now found by differentiation:

$$R'(x) = 9 - \tfrac{2}{3}x.$$

(ii) Suppose we have the consumption function

$$C = 10 + 0.7Y - 0.002Y^2,$$

where Y is national income and C is consumption. The marginal propensity to consume is

$$\frac{dC}{dY} = 0.7 - 0.004Y.$$

Elasticity

Marginal functions give the actual rate of response of one variable with respect to changes in the other: the value of a marginal function will therefore depend on the units in which variables are measured. It is often more useful in economics to have a unit-free measure of proportionate response.

As an example of this, consider a demand function, which gives quantity demanded as a function of price. Suppose that price changes from p to $p + \Delta p$, so that quantity demanded changes from q to $q + \Delta q$. Then

$$\frac{\text{proportional change in quantity demanded}}{\text{proportional change in price}} = \frac{\Delta q}{q} \bigg/ \frac{\Delta p}{p} = \frac{p}{q}\frac{\Delta q}{\Delta p}.$$

As $\Delta p \to 0$, this ratio approaches

$$\frac{p}{q}\frac{dq}{dp}.$$

This is called the **price elasticity of demand** at the point (p, q). For a demand curve, dq/dp will typically be negative, so the demand elasticity is negative. [Some books give simply the absolute value: we give the sign.]

For example, let the demand function be

$$q = 27 - 3p.$$

Then $\dfrac{dq}{dp} = -3$, and the demand elasticity is

$$\frac{p}{q} \times (-3) = -\frac{3p}{q}.$$

Notice that this elasticity of demand, which we denote by the Greek letter η (eta), can be written as a function of p by substituting the demand function into the denominator:

$$\eta = -\frac{3p}{27 - 3p} = \frac{p}{p - 9}.$$

From the demand function, $q = 0$ when $p = 9$, so the relevant values of p are between 0 and 9. The last expression for η tells us that the elasticity of demand is negative and depends on p; $|\eta|$ is small when p is close to zero, and becomes very large as p approaches 9.

The elasticity of demand can also be written as a function of q: since $\eta = -3p/q$ and $3p = 27 - q$, $\eta = (q - 27)/q$.

All of this generalises to an arbitrary linear demand function. Suppose that

$$q = a - bp,$$

where a and b are positive constants. Then

$$\text{elasticity of demand} = -\frac{bp}{q} = -\frac{bp}{a - bp} = \frac{q - a}{q}.$$

Elasticity of supply is defined in a similar way. Suppose the quantity q of a good supplied in a competitive market is a function of the good's price, say $q = S(p)$. Then

$$\text{elasticity of supply} = \frac{p}{q}\frac{dq}{dp} = \frac{pS'(p)}{S(p)}.$$

If, as is usually assumed, the quantity supplied increases as price increases, then $S'(p) > 0$ and the elasticity of supply is positive.

Exercises

6.4.1 A monopolist faces a demand function

$$x = 10 - 2p,$$

where x denotes sales and p denotes price. Find the firm's revenue in terms of x; also find marginal revenue.

6.4.2 Suppose the cost of producing an output level x of a good is

$$x^2 + 3x + 10.$$

Find the marginal cost.

6.4.3 Suppose the supply function for tea is

$$q = -1 + 2p,$$

where p denotes price and q denotes quantity supplied. Find the elasticity of supply at the points where $p = 1$, 1.5 and 2.

6.4.4 Suppose the supply function for coffee is

$$q = 3p^2,$$

where p denotes price and q denotes quantity supplied. Find the elasticity of supply at the points where $p = 1$, 1.5 and 2. Comment.

6.4.5 Suppose the level of a country's imports in terms of its national income Y is given by

$$7 + 0.2Y + 0.05Y^2.$$

Find the marginal propensity to import.

Problems on Chapter 6

6–1. Sketch in the same xy–plane the graphs of $y = x^3$ and its derivative.

[HINT. To solve this problem correctly, you should use simple algebra and the methods of this chapter to obtain information about where the curves cross, and signs and magnitudes of slopes. Plotting is *not* permitted.]

6–2. Find the equation of the tangent at the point on the curve $y = x^3$ where $x = 2$. Find the value of y given by the tangent when $x = 2 + h$ and use this to verify the small increments formula in this case.

Find also the value of the function when $x = 2 + h$. Hence find the error when the curve near $x = 2$ is approximated by the tangent at $x = 2$. Calculate the error as a percentage of the true value when (i) $h = 0.01$, (ii) $h = 1$.

6–3. A monopolist faces a demand function

$$x = 10 - 3p,$$

where x denotes sales and p denotes price. Find marginal revenue as a function of x.

Suppose the firm is operating at a sales level of 3. By how much does the revenue increase if sales increase by one unit? What is the value of marginal revenue when $x = 3$? Explain why these results are different.

Use marginal revenue to find the approximate change in revenue when sales increase from 3 to 3.1.

6–4 Suppose the demand function for a good is given by $q = f(p)$, where q denotes quantity demanded and p denotes price. Suppose initially that $p = p_0$ and $q = q_0$; p then increases by 1%. Use the small increments formula to find a general formula for the approximate percentage change in quantity demanded in terms of the elasticity of demand at (p_0, q_0).

What special features does the approximation have when the demand function takes the forms:

$$\text{(i) } q = a - bp \quad (a, b > 0) \qquad \text{(ii) } q = ap^{-n} \quad (a > 0, \ n \in \mathcal{N})\ ?$$

Appendix to Chapter 6

The aim of this appendix is to go a little more deeply into the reasons for some of the facts stated in Section 6.1. While the topics we discuss are those with which rigorous treatments of calculus are concerned, we make no attempt at such a treatment here. All we are trying to do is to tie up a few ends; if in the process we stimulate the reader's curiosity more than we satisfy it, so much the better.

Limits

We said in Section 6.2 that the statement

$$\lim_{x \to x_0} f(x) = \ell \qquad (6.6)$$

means that we may make $f(x)$ as close as we wish to ℓ for all x sufficiently close (but not equal) to x_0. A more precise definition of limits is as follows: $f(x) \to \ell$ as $x \to x_0$ if for any positive number ε, however small, we can choose a positive number δ such that

$$|f(x) - \ell| < \varepsilon \text{ for all } x \text{ such that } 0 < |x - x_0| < \delta.$$

The use of the Greek letters δ (delta) and ε (epsilon) in this context is traditional.

The meaning of (6.6) is often explained by a story similar to the one used to explain the limit of a sequence in Section 5.1. Instead of a small person and a large one we have two small persons, say D De V and TC. D De V chooses a small positive number, say 0.01. TC then looks for a positive number δ_1 sufficiently small that $|f(x) - \ell| < 0.01$ for all x such that $x \neq x_0$ and $x_0 - \delta_1 < x < x_0 + \delta_1$. Suppose he finds such a δ_1. Then D De V chooses an even smaller number, say 10^{-7}, and TC tries to find a positive number δ_2 so small that $f(x)$ is squeezed between $\ell - 10^{-7}$ and $\ell + 10^{-7}$ whenever $0 < |x - x_0| < \delta_2$. Suppose TC finds such a δ_2; D de V then chooses a still smaller ε, and so on. If this process can be repeated indefinitely, (6.6) holds; if not, not.

Continuous functions

In Section 6.2, we defined a function f to be continuous at x_0 if $\lim_{x \to x_0} f(x)$ exists and is equal to $f(x_0)$. We defined a continuous function to be one that is continuous at every point. We also gave a geometrical definition of a continuous function as one whose graph may be drawn without lifting the pencil from the paper.

The reason for giving two definitions of a continuous function is this. The geometrical definition is easy to understand and visualise: it also makes results such as the intermediate value theorem intuitively clear. But we also need the algebraic definition if we are to extend the concept of continuity to functions of more than one variable, as we shall later in this book. Unfortunately, it is not obvious that the two definitions of continuity are consistent with each other, and we now attempt an explanation.

Let us start with the geometrical definition of continuity and try to rephrase it in algebraic terms. As a first attempt, consider the following notion of continuity: a function f is continuous if small changes in x produce only small changes in $f(x)$. This conveys the same general idea as the geometrical definition, but is not quite equivalent to it.

To see why this is so, consider the following two functions:

$$f(x) = 10^6 x, \quad g(x) = \begin{cases} 0, & \text{if } x < 0 \\ 10^{-6}, & \text{if } x \geq 0 \end{cases}$$

Then f is continuous by the pencil-and-paper definition, while g is not; this despite the fact that a 1–unit increase in x gives rise to a one-million-unit increase in $f(x)$ and an increase of at most one-millionth of a unit in $g(x)$. Notice however that we can make the change in $f(x)$ as small as we like by making the change in x small enough; for example, if x increases by 10^{-14} units then $f(x)$ will increase by 10^{-8} units. By contrast, if x increases from 0 to the positive number h, there is no choice of h small enough to make the increase in $g(x)$ less than 10^{-6} units.

All of this suggests that we can adapt the 'small changes' notion of continuity to make it fully consistent with the pencil-and-paper definition by focusing on changes which are *arbitrarily* small: in other words, changes which are as small as we wish them to be. And that is precisely what we do when we define continuity in terms of limits.

Continuity and differentiability

Remember that

(a) every differentiable function is continuous;

(b) not all continuous functions are differentiable. In particular, the continuous function $|x|$ is not differentiable at $x = 0$.

Fact (a) comes from the small increments formula:

$$f(x + h) \approx f(x) + h f'(x) \text{ when } |h| \text{ is small.}$$

When $|h|$ is *very* small, so is $|h f'(x)|$, and $f(x + h) \approx f(x)$. This argument shows that if f is differentiable, $\lim_{h \to 0} f(x + h) = f(x)$, so that f is continuous at x; since this is true for all x, f is a continuous function.

To prove (b), we must show that the expression

$$\frac{|0+h| - |0|}{h}$$

does not tend to a limit as $h \to 0$. This is so because $|h|/h = 1$ for all positive h, however small, and $|h|/h = -1$ for all negative h, however small in absolute value.

Chapter 7

METHODS OF DIFFERENTIATION

In the last chapter we explained what a derivative is and showed how to calculate derivatives for a very narrow class of functions. In the first two sections of this chapter we introduce four rules which enable us to differentiate much more complicated functions. These are the product rule, the quotient rule, the composite function rule and a generalised version of the power rule. None of these rules is very hard to learn or to apply; the composite function rule is the trickiest and requires particularly close attention. What is important is that the rules be thoroughly understood; anything less than this will cause dreadful problems for the reader for the rest of the book.

Also in this chapter, we introduce a class of functions called monotonic functions, which have varied applications in economics and give rise to yet another rule of differentiation, the inverse function rule. The appendix to the chapter gives informal proofs of the product and quotient rules and introduces the mathematical concept of second-order small quantities, which is important for more advanced work.

When you have studied this chapter you will be able to:

- differentiate products and ratios of functions;

- differentiate composite functions;

- differentiate functions involving indices which are not whole numbers;

- test functions for monotonicity.

7.1   The product and quotient rules

The product rule is a simple recipe for differentiating a function which is expressed as the product of two other functions.

Product rule $\dfrac{d}{dx}(uv) = v\dfrac{du}{dx} + u\dfrac{dv}{dx}$

Example Find dy/dx when $y = (4x^3 + 5)(3x^2 - 8)$.

To apply the product rule, let $u = 4x^3 + 5$, $v = 3x^2 - 8$. Then

$$\frac{du}{dx} = 12x^2, \quad \frac{dv}{dx} = 6x.$$

Hence

$$v\frac{du}{dx} = 12x^2(3x^2 - 8), \quad u\frac{dv}{dx} = 6x(4x^3 + 5).$$

By the product rule,

$$\begin{aligned}
\frac{dy}{dx} &= 12x^2(3x^2 - 8) + 6x(4x^3 + 5) \\
&= 6x(6x^3 - 16x + 4x^3 + 5) \\
&= 60x^4 - 96x^2 + 30x.
\end{aligned}$$

We give an informal proof of the product rule in the appendix to this chapter. In the '$f'(x)$' notation, the rule takes the less memorable form:

if $f(x) = p(x)q(x)$ then $f'(x) = p'(x)q(x) + p(x)q'(x)$.

The quotient rule

We now turn to the second rule of this section. A proof is sketched in the appendix to this chapter, and another in Problem 7–1.

Quotient rule $\dfrac{d}{dx}\left(\dfrac{u}{v}\right) = \left(v\dfrac{du}{dx} - u\dfrac{dv}{dx}\right)\Big/ v^2$

Example Find dy/dx when $y = x^2/(x^2 - x + 1)$.

To apply the quotient rule, let $u = x^2$, $v = x^2 - x + 1$. Then

$$\frac{du}{dx} = 2x, \quad \frac{dv}{dx} = 2x - 1$$

and

$$v\frac{du}{dx} - u\frac{dv}{dx} = 2x(x^2 - x + 1) - x^2(2x - 1)$$
$$= x(2x^2 - 2x + 2 - 2x^2 + x)$$
$$= x(2 - x).$$

Hence by the quotient rule,

$$\frac{dy}{dx} = \frac{x(2 - x)}{(x^2 - x + 1)^2}.$$

As with the product rule, the '$f'(x)$' form of the quotient rule is not particularly easy to remember (so don't bother to learn it by heart), but we state it for completeness:

if $f(x) = p(x)/q(x)$ then $f'(x) = \left(p'(x)q(x) - p(x)q'(x)\right) \Big/ \left(q(x)\right)^2$.

Exercises

7.1.1 Use the product rule to differentiate:

(a) $(x^4 - 3x^2)(5x + 1)$ (b) $(6x^3 + x)(x^6 - 3x^4 - 2)$

(c) $(x^m + 8)(5x^2 + 2x^{-n})$ (d) $(4x^4 + 2x^2 - 1)(x + 5)x^n$

In parts (c) and (d), m and n are positive integers.

7.1.2 Use the quotient rule to differentiate:

(a) $(1 + 2x)/(1 - 2x)$ (b) $(x^2 + 1)/(2x^3 + 1)$

(c) $(a + bx)/(0.3x^2 + 0.6x^4)$ (d) $(3x + a)/(x^2 + b)$

In parts (c) and (d), a and b are constants.

7.1.3 Capital K and labour L in an economy are given by the linear functions

$$K = 2 + 3t, \quad L = 1 + 4t,$$

where t denotes time. Find the rate of change with respect to time of the capital-labour ratio K/L.

7.2 The composite function rule

We said something about the composition of functions in Section 3.3. For present purposes it suffices to recall that a composite function is a function of the form $p(q(x))$, where p and q are functions. For example, if $p(x) = x^9$ and $q(x) = 5x^2 - 1$, then $p(q(x)) = (5x^2 - 1)^9$.

Composite function rule   If $f(x) = p(q(x))$, $f'(x) = p'(q(x)) q'(x)$.

A simpler way of writing this is as follows. Let $u = q(x)$ and $y = p(u)$, so that $y = p(q(x)) = f(x)$. Then

$$\frac{dy}{dx} = \frac{dy}{du} \times \frac{du}{dx}. \tag{7.1}$$

To prove this rigorously would involve going into limits and differentiability much more deeply than we intend to do in this book. To give an intuitive explanation of why the composite function rule is valid, we argue as in the proof of the combination rule in Chapter 6. Suppose that when x increases by Δx, u increases by Δu and y by Δy. Then

$$\frac{\Delta y}{\Delta x} = \frac{\Delta y}{\Delta u} \times \frac{\Delta u}{\Delta x}. \tag{7.2}$$

When $\Delta x \to 0$,

$$\frac{\Delta y}{\Delta x} \to \frac{dy}{dx}, \ \frac{\Delta y}{\Delta u} \to \frac{dy}{du} \ \text{ and } \ \frac{\Delta u}{\Delta x} \to \frac{du}{dx}.$$

We may therefore obtain (7.1) by taking limits in (7.2).

Example Find dy/dx when $y = (5x^2 - 1)^9$.

To apply the composite function rule, let $u = 5x^2 - 1$; then $y = u^9$. Therefore

$$\frac{dy}{du} = 9u^8, \quad \frac{du}{dx} = 10x$$

and

$$\frac{dy}{dx} = 9u^8 \times 10x = 90xu^8 = 90x(5x^2 - 1)^8.$$

Fractional indices

Another useful rule of differentiation is an extension of one we gave earlier. It says that the power rule of the last chapter continues to be true when the integer n is replaced by *any* real number c.

Power rule (extended)   If c is any constant, $\dfrac{d}{dx}(x^c) = cx^{c-1}$.

This enables us to differentiate functions involving fractional indices: for instance

$$\frac{d}{dx}(x^{7/3}) = \frac{7}{3}x^{4/3} \quad \text{and} \quad \frac{d}{dx}(x^{2/5}) = \frac{2}{5}x^{-3/5} = \frac{2}{5x^{3/5}}.$$

Similarly, since $\sqrt{x} = x^{1/2}$,

$$\frac{d}{dx}\left(\frac{1}{\sqrt{x}}\right) = \frac{d}{dx}(x^{-1/2}) = -\frac{1}{2}x^{-3/2} = -\frac{1}{2x\sqrt{x}}.$$

The extended version of the power rule also enables us to differentiate functions such as $x^{\sqrt{2}}$, but these rarely occur in practice.

Combining the rules

The rules of differentiation can be combined in various ways. The following example is slightly complicated, but it is worth working through carefully to see which rule needs to be applied at each stage.

Example Differentiate

$$y = \frac{x}{\sqrt{a^2 + x^2}},$$

where a is a constant.

Let $w = (a^2 + x^2)^{-1/2}$. Then $y = xw$, so

$$\frac{dy}{dx} = w + x\frac{dw}{dx}$$

by the product rule. To find dw/dx, we use the composite function rule. Let $u = a^2 + x^2$. Then $w = u^{-1/2}$, and

$$\frac{dw}{dx} = \frac{dw}{du} \times \frac{du}{dx} = -\tfrac{1}{2}u^{-3/2} \times 2x$$

by the composite function rule and the power rule. Simplifying, $dw/dx = -xu^{-3/2} = -xw^3$, whence $dy/dx = w - x^2w^3 = w(1 - x^2w^2)$. But

$$1 - x^2w^2 = 1 - \frac{x^2}{a^2 + x^2} = \frac{a^2}{a^2 + x^2} = a^2w^2,$$

so

$$\frac{dy}{dx} = a^2w^3 = \frac{a^2}{(a^2 + x^2)^{3/2}}.$$

Two final points about the rules

1. There is often more than one way of differentiating a particular function: for instance, the last example could have been solved by writing $y = x/v$, where $v = (a^2 + x^2)^{+1/2}$, and using the quotient rule instead of the product rule.

2. It often saves time to **simplify before differentiating**; in particular, this avoids unnecessary use of the product and quotient rules. Thus the function $f(x) = (5x^2 + 2x)x^2$ could be differentiated using the product rule; but it is much easier to write $f(x) = 5x^4 + 2x^3$ and then differentiate, getting $f'(x) = 20x^3 + 6x^2$. Similarly, the function $(5x^2 + 2x)/x^2$ should not be differentiated by the quotient rule; instead, we write the function as $5 + 2x^{-1}$, and the derivative is easily seen to be $-2/x^2$.

Exercises

7.2.1 The functions f and g are defined as follows:

$$f(x) = x^3 + 1, \quad g(x) = x^4 - 2.$$

Find expressions for $f(g(x))$, $g(f(x))$ and their derivatives.

7.2.2 Differentiate:

    (a) $(3x - 7)^{10}$ (b) $(x^3 + 1)^5$

    (c) $(4x + 9)^{1/2}$ (d) $(x^6 - 1)^{2/3}$

    (e) $(x^{1/4} + 5)^6$ (f) $(x^4 - 3x^2 + 5x + 1)^{1/4}$

    (g) $1/(x^2 - 1)^7$ (h) $8/(\sqrt{x} + 2)^5$

7.2.3 Differentiate using the rules of this and the previous section:

    (a) $(x^2 - 1)(x^3 + 1)^5$,   (b) $(x^{1/3} - 2)/(x^5 - 2)^3$.

7.2.4 Suppose the demand function for beer is given by

$$q = 3p^{-1/4},$$

where p denotes price and q quantity supplied. Find the elasticity of demand.

[Note that the same method will give the elasticity of demand for any demand function of the form $q = ap^{-b}$, where a and b are positive real numbers. Also note that the result of part (ii) of the final part of Problem 6–4 is true in this more general case.]

7.2.5 Suppose that a firm's output Q is related to labour input L by the production function

$$Q = L^{2/5}.$$

Suppose further that L is given by the linear function

$$L = 4 + 3t.$$

Find dQ/dt.

7.3 Monotonic functions and inverse functions

Some functions have graphs that slope upward: $f(x) = x$ is an obvious example. Other functions slope downward wherever they are defined, for example demand curves in economics. In this section we explain the main properties of these two kinds of function.

We say that the function f is **strictly increasing** if $f(x_1) < f(x_2)$ whenever $x_1 < x_2$. Similarly, f is said to be **strictly decreasing** if $f(x_1) > f(x_2)$ whenever $x_1 < x_2$. In either case f is said to be a **monotonic function**. Thus in panel A of Figure 7.1, f_1 and f_2 are monotonic functions, with f_1 strictly increasing and f_2 strictly decreasing. The function F of panel B has some increasing segments and some decreasing ones and is therefore non-monotonic.

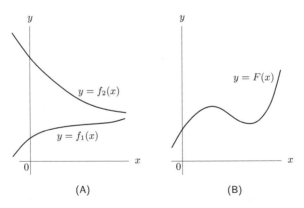

(A)   (B)

Figure 7.1: f_1 **is a strictly increasing function;** f_2 **is a strictly decreasing function,** F **is neither**

It should be clear from Figure 7.1 that if f is a monotonic function (increasing or decreasing) the equation $f(x) = y$ can be solved in principle for x, given any y. By 'in principle' we mean that the graph of f can be plotted and the solution for any given y read off to any degree of accuracy. In some cases the

solution can be written explicitly: for instance if $y = x^3 + 4$ then $x = (y-4)^{1/3}$.[1]
An example which does not admit an explicit solution is given below.

If f is monotonic and the the solution of the equation $f(x) = y$ is $x = g(y)$, then g is called the **inverse function** of f: notice that

$$f(g(y)) = y \text{ and } g(f(x)) = x.$$

Thus, if $f(x) = x^3 + 4$ the inverse function g is given by $g(y) = (y-4)^{1/3}$.
Associated with inverse functions is another rule for differentiation.

Inverse function rule Let f be a monotonic function with inverse function g; if, for given x, f is differentiable at x and $f'(x) \neq 0$, then g is differentiable at $y = f(x)$, and $g'(y) = 1/f'(x)$.

In the alternative notation, the inverse function rule can be written

$$\frac{dx}{dy} = 1 \bigg/ \frac{dy}{dx}.$$

This can be justified by noting that

$$\frac{\Delta x}{\Delta y} = 1 \bigg/ \frac{\Delta y}{\Delta x}$$

and taking limits.

Testing for monotonicity

If $f'(x) > 0$ for all x then f is strictly increasing. Notice that the converse of the statement is false: the function $f(x) = x^3$ is monotonic increasing but $f'(0) = 0$. A useful sufficient condition for monotonicity which covers this case is as follows:

> if $f'(x) \geq 0$ for all x, and if $f'(x) = 0$ for only a finite number of values of x, then f is strictly increasing.

Similarly, if $f'(x) \leq 0$ for all x, and if $f'(x) = 0$ for only a finite number of values of x, then f is strictly decreasing.

---

[1]In Section 4.2 we raised only positive numbers to fractional powers. However, it is easy and logical to define cube roots of negative numbers as follows: if $z < 0$, $z^{1/3} = -(-z)^{1/3}$. For example, $(-8)^{1/3} = -2$.

Example Consider the function

$$f(x) = x^5 - 10x^3 + 45x.$$

Here $f'(x) = 5x^4 - 30x^2 + 45 = 5(x^2 - 3)^2$. Hence $f'(x) \geq 0$ for all x, being 0 only when $x = \pm\sqrt{3}$, so f is monotonic increasing.

We may therefore define the inverse function g. In this case f can take any real value (essentially because $f(x)$ is large and positive when x is large and positive, and $f(x)$ is large and negative when x is large and negative). The function $g(y)$ is therefore defined for every real number y, even though it cannot be written explicitly in terms of y.

By the inverse function rule, $g'(y)$ is defined for all values of y except for y_1 and y_2, given by $g(y_1) = \sqrt{3}$ and $g(y_2) = -\sqrt{3}$. It is easy to check that $y_1 = f(\sqrt{3}) = 24\sqrt{3}$, and similarly $y_2 = -24\sqrt{3}$. For all values of y other than $\pm 24\sqrt{3}$, $g'(y)$ may be obtained from the inverse function rule:

$$g'(y) = \frac{1}{f'(x)} = \frac{1}{5}(x^2 - 3)^{-2} = \frac{1}{5}([g(y)]^2 - 3)^{-2}.$$

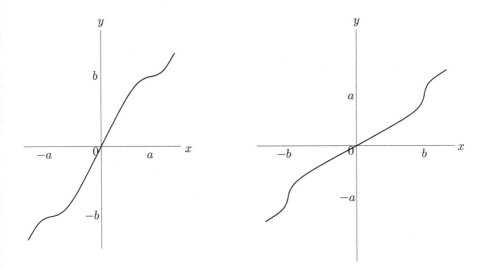

Figure 7.2: **The function** $f(x) = x^5 - 10x^3 + 45x$ **and its inverse** $(a = \sqrt{3}, b = 24\sqrt{3})$

The graphs of the function f of the last example and its inverse function g are sketched in the two panels of Figure 7.2. Do not worry if you do not understand fully why the curves bend as they do; the reasons will be made clear in the next chapter. The two points which should be appreciated at this stage are: first, the two panels depict the same equation, with a different labelling of the axes; second, the non-differentiability of $g(y)$ at $y = \pm 24\sqrt{3}$ arises because the graph in the right-hand panel 'goes vertical' at those points.

When is a function monotonic?

The test for monotonicity described above should not be applied unthinkingly, since it is often easy to verify that a function is monotonic without going to the trouble of differentiating it. There are functions which are obviously monotonic, such as the increasing functions $2x$ and x^3 and the decreasing functions $-4x$ and $2 - x^5$. There are also functions whose monotonicity can be verified by relating the function at hand to obvious cases without doing any calculus.

Consider for example the function $f(x) = x/(1 + x)$, defined for all $x \geq 0$. One could verify that this is a strictly increasing function by differentiating it using the quotient rule and showing that the derivative is always positive. However, a simpler method is to notice that

$$f(x) = 1 - \frac{1}{1 + x}$$

and argue as follows; when $x(\geq 0)$ increases, $1/(1+x)$ must *decrease* and hence $f(x)$ must *increase*.

We have just considered a function $f(x)$ defined for all *non-negative* values of x. An important general point about monotonicity which we have not emphasised so far is this: whether or not a function is monotonic depends on the set of values for which it is defined.

For example, if x is allowed to be any real number, the function

$$y = 25 - x^2$$

is clearly not monotonic: the graph slopes upward when $x < 0$ and downward when $x > 0$. But if we restrict our attention to non-negative values of x, the function is monotonic decreasing. For $x \geq 0$ and $y \leq 25$, the inverse function is given by

$$x = \sqrt{25 - y}.$$

You are strongly encouraged to draw the graph of this inverse function.

In this case, the fact that we have an explicit formula for the inverse function gives us two alternative ways of calculating dx/dy. One method is direct differentiation:

$$\frac{dx}{dy} = \frac{d}{dy}\left([25 - y]^{1/2}\right) = \frac{1}{2}(25 - y)^{-1/2} \times (-1) = \frac{-1}{2\sqrt{25 - y}},$$

using the power rule and the composite function rule. The other method is to use the inverse function rule:

$$\frac{dx}{dy} = 1 \left/ \frac{dy}{dx} \right. = \frac{1}{(-2x)} = \frac{-1}{2\sqrt{25 - y}}.$$

Weakly monotonic functions

A class of functions which includes the strictly increasing ones consists of the **non-decreasing** functions. We say that the function f is non-decreasing if $f(x_1) \leq f(x_2)$ whenever $x_1 < x_2$. Thus the non-decreasing functions include the constant functions, monotonic increasing functions, and functions whose graphs have some rising and some flat sections.

A differentiable function f is non-decreasing if and only if $f'(x) \geq 0$ for all x. Thus the usual sufficient condition for a function to be strictly increasing may be restated as follows: if f is a differentiable, non-decreasing function, and $f'(x) = 0$ for only a finite number of values of x, then f is strictly increasing.

Similarly, we say that the function f is **non-increasing** if $f(x_1) \geq f(x_2)$ whenever $x_1 < x_2$. A differentiable function f is non-increasing if and only if $f'(x) \leq 0$ for all x.

Functions which are non-increasing or non-decreasing are sometimes said to be **weakly monotonic**.

Exercises

7.3.1 Show that the function $y = x^3$ is monotonic increasing. Find dx/dy:

(a) by finding an explicit formula for the inverse function and differentiating it;

(b) by using the inverse function rule.

7.3.2 Are the following functions monotonic?

(a) $y = -x^6 + 5$,   (b) $y = -x^6 + 5 \ (x > 0)$,   (c) $y = 9x^5 + x^3 + 4x$.

For each monotonic function, find dx/dy by the inverse function rule.

7.3.3 A demand curve has equation $p = -q^2 + 3$ where p is price, q is quantity and p and q are restricted to be non-negative. Show that p is a monotonic function of q and use the inverse function rule to find dq/dp. Hence find an expression for the elasticity of demand.

Problems on Chapter 7

7–1. Derive the quotient rule from the product rule as follows: write the equation $y = u/v$ as $u = yv$, differentiate using the product rule and solve for dy/dx.

7–2. Suppose that a firm's output Q is related to capital input K and labour input L by the production function

$$Q = K^{1/2}L^{1/3}$$

Suppose further that K and L are given by the linear functions

$$K = 5 + 2t, \quad L = 2 + t.$$

Find dQ/dt.

7–3.   (i) Sometimes relations which are not given in the form $y = f(x)$ can be put in that form by means of simple algebra. Show that the relation

$$x^{1/2}y^{1/3} = c, \quad (x, y > 0) \tag{7.3}$$

where c is a positive constant, can be put in the form $y = f(x)$. Hence find the slope at any point of the curve in the xy–plane defined by (7.3).

 (ii) If a firm has the production function $Q = F(K, L)$, relating output Q to capital input K and labour input L, an **isoquant** of the production function is defined to be a curve in the KL–plane of input combinations which produce a given level of output.

Suppose the production function is as in Problem 7–2. Using your answer to (i), show that the isoquants are negatively sloped.

7–4. In each of the following cases, find the range of values of the constant a for which the function $f(x)$ is monotonic.

 (i) $f(x) = (x + a)^5 - 80x$.

 (ii) $f(x) = (x + a)^5 - 80x \quad (x > 0)$.

 (iii) $f(x) = (x + a)^{-2} + 80x \quad (x > 0)$.

Appendix to Chapter 7

Recall that the product rule states that

$$\frac{d}{dx}(uv) = v\frac{du}{dx} + u\frac{dv}{dx}.$$

We now give an informal proof.

Let $y = uv$ and suppose that when x increases by Δx, u increases by Δu, v by Δv and y by Δy. Then

$$y + \Delta y = (u + \Delta u)(v + \Delta v).$$

Subtracting $y = uv$ from this equation,

$$\Delta y = v\Delta u + u\Delta v + \Delta u\Delta v. \tag{7.4}$$

Dividing (7.4) by Δx, we have

$$\frac{\Delta y}{\Delta x} = v\frac{\Delta u}{\Delta x} + [u + \Delta u]\frac{\Delta v}{\Delta x}.$$

Now let $\Delta x \to 0$. Then all terms of the form $\Delta \cdot / \Delta x$ approach the corresponding $d \cdot / dx$; also, since $\Delta u \to 0$, the term in square brackets approaches u. Hence, taking limits in the last equation gives the product rule.

Second-order small quantities

It is helpful for future work to repeat the proof of the product rule in a slightly different way. We pick up the story at (7.4), and assume Δx is small in absolute value. Then Δu and Δv are also small, and the term $\Delta u\Delta v$ is what is known as a **second-order small quantity**: being the product of two small quantities it is not only small but *small relative to* Δx when Δx is small. In terms of limits,

$$\frac{\Delta u\Delta v}{\Delta x} \to 0 \text{ as } \Delta x \to 0.$$

Because $\Delta u\Delta v$ is a second-order small quantity, (7.4) implies that

$$\Delta y \approx v\Delta u + u\Delta v. \tag{7.5}$$

Dividing (7.5) by Δx, we have

$$\frac{\Delta y}{\Delta x} \approx v\frac{\Delta u}{\Delta x} + u\frac{\Delta v}{\Delta x}.$$

If we now let $\Delta x \to 0$, all the $\Delta \cdot / \Delta x$ terms tend to $d \cdot / dx$, and the approximation tends to equality. We therefore retrieve the product rule.

Proving the quotient rule

We now turn to the quotient rule:

$$\frac{d}{dx}\left(\frac{u}{v}\right) = \left(v\frac{du}{dx} - u\frac{dv}{dx}\right)\bigg/ v^2.$$

This may be derived from the product rule: see Problem 7–1. Here we give an alternative (informal) proof, which illustrates the technique of neglecting second-order small quantities.

Let $y = u/v$. In the usual notation,

$$y + \Delta y = \frac{u + \Delta u}{v + \Delta v}.$$

Multiplying the right-hand side above and below by $v - \Delta v$, we have

$$y + \Delta y = \frac{uv + v\Delta u - u\Delta v - \Delta u\Delta v}{v^2 - (\Delta v)^2}. \tag{7.6}$$

Now observe that $\Delta u\Delta v$ and $(\Delta v)^2$ are second-order small quantities. Therefore, just as (7.4) implied (7.5), (7.6) implies that

$$y + \Delta y \approx (uv + v\Delta u - u\Delta v)/v^2.$$

Subtracting $y = u/v$ from this equation, and then dividing by Δx,

$$\frac{\Delta y}{\Delta x} \approx \left(v\frac{\Delta u}{\Delta x} - u\frac{\Delta v}{\Delta x}\right)\bigg/ v^2.$$

Letting $\Delta x \to 0$ and arguing as in the last part of the proof of the product rule, we obtain the quotient rule.

Chapter 8

MAXIMA AND MINIMA

This chapter has two main themes. The first is **curve-sketching**, and, in particular, the significance for curve-sketching of maximum and minimum points.

The second theme of the chapter is **optimisation**, which in its simplest form means choosing the value of a variable x so as to maximise or minimise a function $f(x)$. As we shall see, this is intimately related to curve-sketching. We have already encountered optimisation — and its relevance to economics — in Sections 2.3 and 4.1, in connection with linear and quadratic functions; but now, using calculus, we can go much further.

When you have studied this chapter you will be able to:

- find the local maxima and minima of a function, with or without the use of the second derivative;

- sketch graphs of functions of the type studied in earlier chapters;

- find global maxima and minima of functions of one variable, including those cases (common in economic examples) where the independent variable is restricted to be non-negative;

- test functions for convexity and concavity.

8.1   Critical points

We stated in Section 3.2 that sketching a graph involves marking any points of particular interest. Among such points of particular interest are critical points, which we now define.

Let f be a differentiable function. The points on the curve $y = f(x)$ where $f'(x) = 0$ are called **critical points**, and the value taken by the function at such a point is called a **critical value**. At such a point the tangent to the curve is horizontal (parallel to the x-axis).[1]

---

[1] An alternative, somewhat old-fashioned term for critical point (or value) is **stationary**

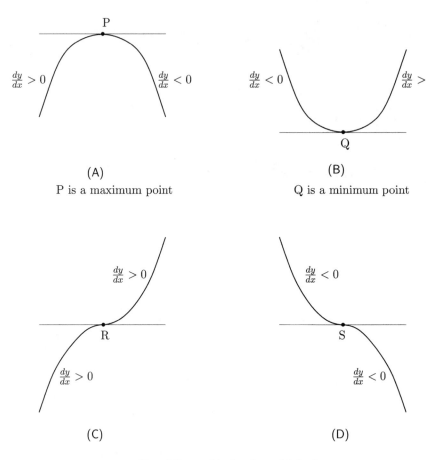

Figure 8.1: **The basic critical points**

There are three kinds of critical point, as shown in the four panels of Figure 8.1:

(a) **Maximum points** like P in panel A. At a maximum point, y has its greatest value in a neighbourhood of the point.

(b) **Minimum points** like Q in panel B. At a minimum point, y has its least value in a neighbourhood of the point.

point (or value). The origin of this term lies in the applications of the kind discussed in Section 6.1 where x represents time, $f(x)$ distance and $f'(x)$ velocity. A stationary point is then a situation of (temporarily) zero velocity.

(c) The third kind of critical point is a **critical point of inflexion**,[2] such as R and S in panels C and D. At such a point $dy/dx = 0$, but dy/dx does not change sign in passing through the point.

Maximum and minimum points of a curve are called **turning points**; critical points of inflexion are not turning points.

Finding and classifying critical points

The critical points of a function $y = f(x)$ may be found and classified in four steps. Steps 1–3 find the critical points, while step 4 classifies them.

STEP 1   Find $f'(x)$.

STEP 2   Find the values of x for which $f'(x) = 0$.

STEP 3   For each such x, find the corresponding value of y.

STEP 4   For each critical point (x^*, y^*), find the sign of $f'(x)$ when x is slightly less than x^* (which is written $x = x^*-$) and when is slightly greater than x^* (which is written $x = x^*+$). If $f'(x)$ changes from positive to negative when x changes from x^*- to x^*+, then (x^*, y^*) is a maximum; if $f'(x)$ changes from negative to positive then (x^*, y^*) is a minimum; if $f'(x)$ does not change sign then (x^*, y^*) is a critical point of inflexion.

Knowledge of the critical points of a curve is vital when sketching a curve. Conversely, if the critical points themselves are the main focus of interest, then it is usually a good idea to sketch the curve to check that the results make sense.

When sketching a curve, in addition to knowing the critical points, we will need to know how the curve behaves for large values of $|x|$ and, at least roughly, where the curve cuts the axes. We now give some examples.

Example 1 Find and classify the critical points of the curve

$$y = x^3 - 9x^2 + 24x + 2.$$

Sketch the curve.

STEP 1. $\dfrac{dy}{dx} = 3x^2 - 18x + 24 = 3(x - 2)(x - 4)$.

STEP 2. $\dfrac{dy}{dx} = 0$ when $x = 2$ or 4.

---

[2]A point of inflexion is a point where the curve crosses its tangent. If at such a point the tangent happens to be horizontal, we have a critical point of inflexion; if not, a non-critical point of inflexion. We shall say a little more on this in the next section.

STEP 3. When $x = 2$, $y = 22$; when $x = 4$, $y = 18$.

We have now found the critical points, and we use Step 4 to classify them. Consider first the critical point $(2, 22)$. When $x = 2-$, $x - 2 < 0$ and $x - 4 < 0$, so dy/dx is the product of two negative numbers and is therefore positive. When $x = 2+$, $x - 2 > 0$ and $x - 4 < 0$, so $dy/dx = (+)(-) = -$. Thus, as x goes from $2-$ to $2+$, dy/dx goes from $+$ to $-$; $(2, 22)$ is therefore a maximum point.

Now look at the other critical point $(4, 18)$. When $x = 4-$, $dy/dx = (+)(-) = -$. When $x = 4+$, $dy/dx = (+)(+) = +$. Thus $(4, 18)$ is a minimum point.

Having gone through all the steps, we must now use whatever extra information we have to sketch the curve. When $|x|$ is large, x^3 is much greater in absolute value than the other terms; thus the behaviour of y is dominated by the term in x^3. By taking x sufficiently large and positive, y can be made greater than any given positive number. This is written

$$y \to \infty \text{ as } x \to \infty.$$

Similarly, by taking $|x|$ sufficiently large with x negative, y can be made less than any given negative number. This is written

$$y \to -\infty \text{ as } x \to -\infty.$$

Finally, where does the curve cut the axes? When $x = 0$, $y = 2$: the curve cuts the y–axis at $(0, 2)$. It is clear from all the information we have obtained about the curve that it cuts the x–axis only once, at a point to the left of the y–axis.

A sketch is given in Figure 8.2.

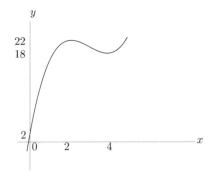

Figure 8.2: $y = x^3 - 9x^2 + 24x + 2$

Example 2 Find and classify the critical points of the curve

$$y = x^4 - 4x^3 + 5.$$

Sketch the curve.

$$\frac{dy}{dx} = 4x^3 - 12x^2 = 4x^2(x - 3),$$

which is zero when $x = 0$ and when $x = 3$. When $x = 0$, $y = 5$. When $x = 3$, $y = (3 - 4)3^3 + 5 = -22$. Thus the critical points are $(0, 5)$ and $(3, -22)$.

When x is close to but not equal to zero, $x^2 > 0$ and $x < 3$. Thus $dy/dx < 0$ both when $x = 0-$ and when $x = 0+$, so $(0, 5)$ is a critical point of inflexion. When x goes from $3-$ to $3+$, x^2 remains positive and $x - 3$ goes from negative to positive, so dy/dx goes from negative to positive: $(3, -22)$ is a therefore a minimum point.

The final piece of information we need to sketch the curve is what happens to y when $|x|$ becomes very large. Here we apply the highest-power rule for polynomials introduced in Example 1: the curve behaves like $y = x^4$ when x is very large, so $y \to \infty$ when $x \to \infty$ and when $x \to -\infty$. The graph is sketched in Figure 8.3.

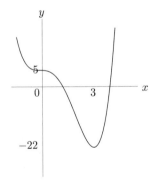

Figure 8.3: $y = x^4 - 4x^3 + 5$

Exercises

8.1.1 The graph of $y = x^2$ was sketched in Section 3.2, and you were asked to sketch the graphs of further simple powers of x in Exercises 4.2.1 and 4.2.2. We can now use the techniques of this section to confirm the shape.

Show that the graph of $y = x^2$ has a minimum point at $(0,0)$ and that that of the graph of $y = x^3$ has a critical point of inflexion at $(0,0)$. What about the graphs of $y = x^4$, $y = x^5$ and so on?

8.1.2 Find the critical points of

$$y = x^3 - 12x^2 + 21x + 1$$

and determine their nature. Sketch the curve.

8.1.3 Find the critical values of

$$y = x - 2x^4$$

and determine their nature. Sketch the curve.

8.2 The second derivative

If f is a differentiable function, then f' is a function, which may itself be differentiable. If it is, we denote the derivative of $f'(x)$ with respect to x by $f''(x)$ and call it the **second derivative** of $f(x)$. The function f is then said to be **twice differentiable**.

For example, if $f(x) = 2x^4 + 3x$ then $f'(x) = 8x^3 + 3$; differentiating again, $f''(x) = 24x^2$.

In the alternative notation, the second derivative is

$$\frac{d}{dx}\left(\frac{dy}{dx}\right),$$

and this is usually denoted by

$$\frac{d^2y}{dx^2}.$$

For example:

$$\text{if } y = 2x^4 + 3x \text{ then } \frac{dy}{dx} = 8x^3 + 3 \text{ and } \frac{d^2y}{dx^2} = 24x^2.$$

The first derivative measures the slope of a curve at a point: what is the geometrical significance of the second derivative? If $f''(x_0) > 0$, the gradient $f'(x)$ of $f(x)$ is increasing at x_0. This can happen in three ways:

(a) $f'(x_0)$ is positive and $f'(x)$ becomes more positive as x passes from x_0- to x_0+. In this case the point $(x_0, f(x_0))$ is like point A in Figure 8.4.

(b) $f'(x_0)$ is negative and $f'(x)$ becomes less negative as x passes from x_0- to x_0+, as at point B in Figure 8.4.

(c) $f'(x_0) = 0$ and $f'(x)$ goes from negative to positive as x passes from x_0- to x_0+: see point C in Figure 8.4.

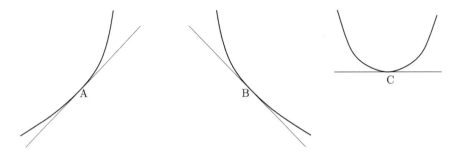

Figure 8.4: **Positive second derivative**

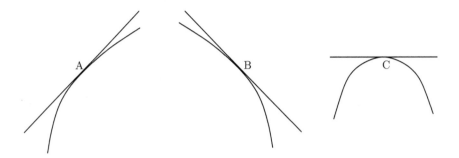

Figure 8.5: **Negative second derivative**

Notice that in all three cases the curve $y = f(x)$ lies above its tangent at x_0.

If $f''(x) < 0$ at a point then the curve lies below its tangent at that point and we have one of the situations A, B, C of Figure 8.5.

Bearing in mind the significance of the sign of the second derivative in determining whether a curve lies above or below its tangent, we can formalise the definition of a point of inflexion originally given in footnote 1 of this chapter. The curve $y = f(x)$ has a **point of inflexion** at $x = x_0$ if $f''(x_0) = 0$ **and** $f''(x)$ changes sign as x passes through x_0. In Exercise 8.2.1 you are asked to sketch the possible shapes the curve may take near a point of inflexion.

Finding and classifying critical points (continued)

Figure 8.5 tells us that if $f''(x) < 0$ **and** $f'(x) = 0$, we must be in the situation depicted by point C. Thus

$$\text{if } f(x_0) = y_0, \ f'(x_0) = 0 \text{ and } f''(x_0) < 0 \text{ then}$$
$$(x_0, y_0) \text{ is a maximum point of the curve } y = f(x).$$

Similarly, Figure 8.4 shows that if $f(x_0) = y_0$, $f'(x_0) = 0$ and $f''(x_0) > 0$ then (x_0, y_0) is a minimum point of the curve $y = f(x)$.

These facts give us an alternative method to that of the last section for classifying critical points. This is known as the **second derivative test**, and its steps are as follows:

STEP I   Find $f'(x)$ and $f''(x)$.

STEP II   Find the critical points in the usual way.

STEP III   For each critical point (x^*, y^*), calculate $f''(x^*)$. If $f''(x^*) < 0$ then (x^*, y^*) is a maximum. If $f''(x^*) > 0$ then (x^*, y^*) is a minimum. If $f''(x^*) = 0$ then (x^*, y^*) may be a maximum, minimum or point of inflexion: in this case we have to fall back on the method of the last section to classify the critical point.

Example Find and classify the critical points of the function

$$y = 2x^3 - 3x^2 - 12x + 9,$$

and sketch the curve.

Differentiating twice,

$$\frac{dy}{dx} = 6x^2 - 6x - 12, \quad \frac{d^2y}{dx^2} = 6(2x - 1).$$

To find the critical points, we solve the quadratic equation $dy/dx = 0$ by factorisation: since

$$\frac{dy}{dx} = 6(x^2 - x - 2) = 6(x + 1)(x - 2),$$

the critical points occur where $x = -1$ and where $x = 2$. When $x = -1$, $y = 16$. When $x = 2$, $y = -11$. Thus the critical points are $(-1, 16)$ and $(2, -11)$.

Now we classify the critical points using step III. When $x = -1$, $d^2y/dx^2 = -18 < 0$; we have a maximum. When $x = 2$, $d^2y/dx^2 = 6 > 0$, and we have a minimum. The critical points consist of a maximum point at $(-1, 16)$ and a minimum point at $(2, -11)$.

To sketch the curve, we use the information just obtained about critical points and the following three facts, which come straight from the equation of the curve: $y = 9$ when $x = 0$, $y \to \infty$ as $x \to \infty$ and $y \to -\infty$ as $x \to -\infty$.

The curve is sketched in Figure 8.6.

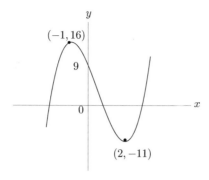

Figure 8.6: $y = 2x^3 - 3x^2 - 12x + 9$

The ambiguous case

We now focus on the last part of step III: the fall-back procedure that comes into operation when the second derivative is zero at a critical point.

To see why this is necessary, consider the following three cases:

$$\text{(i)} \quad y = x^4 \qquad \text{(ii)} \quad y = -x^4 \qquad \text{(iii)} \quad y = x^3.$$

In each case there is a critical point at the origin and $d^2y/dx^2 = 0$ when $x = 0$. The critical point is a minimum in case (i), a maximum in case (ii) and a point of inflexion in case (iii). *You are strongly encouraged to verify these facts before proceeding further.*

Exercises

8.2.1 Show in a diagram the shape of the curve $y = f(x)$ near a point of inflexion $(x_0, f(x_0))$ where:

    (a) $f'(x_0) > 0$, $f''(x_0) = 0$ and $f''(x)$ changes from negative to positive;

    (b) $f'(x_0) > 0$, $f''(x_0) = 0$ and $f''(x)$ changes from positive to negative;

    (c) $f'(x_0) < 0$, $f''(x_0) = 0$ and $f''(x)$ changes from negative to positive;

    (d) $f'(x_0) < 0$, $f''(x_0) = 0$ and $f''(x)$ changes from positive to negative.

8.2.2 Repeat Exercise 8.1.2 using the second derivative test. Find also any points of inflexion on the curve.

8.2.3 Repeat Exercise 8.1.3 using the second derivative test. Find also any points of inflexion on the curve.

8.3 Optimisation

Optimisation is concerned with finding the maximum or minimum value of a function usually, but not always, subject to some constraint(s) on the independent variable(s). Whether the maximum or minimum is required depends on whether the function represents a desirable quantity such as profit or an undesirable quantity such as cost. We have already encountered simple optimisation problems in Chapter 2 where we introduced linear programming and in Chapter 4 where we explained how to maximise or minimise a quadratic function, including the case where the constraint $x \geq 0$ was imposed.

In more general optimisation problems for functions of a single variable, the application of differential calculus to finding maximum and minimum points provides the foundation but does not by any means give the whole story. For this reason, the section we now embark on is fairly long and involved: we therefore start with an outline of what we shall do.

We begin by summarising the main results on maximum and minimum points given in the last section, emphasising the fact that a function may have many such points. In addition, the behaviour of the function for large values of $|x|$ may be such that the highest maximum and/or the lowest minimum are beaten.

We then discuss difficulties arising from the fact that most economic variables are necessarily non-negative: hence the independent variable x will often be required to satisfy the constraint $x \geq 0$. This leads to the possibility that the optimum will be on the $x = 0$ boundary.

Finally, we give an economic application which illustrates the complications and difficulties discussed earlier in the section.

Maxima and minima: local and global

To emphasise the fact that, at a maximum point, y has its greatest value *in a neighbourhood of the point*, such a point is often called a **local maximum**. Similarly a minimum point, in the sense of the last two sections, is sometimes called a **local minimum**.

Conditions for local optima

In the case of twice-differentiable functions, much of what we said in Section 8.2 about maximum and minimum points may be summarised as follows. Starting with local maxima, we have:

(1) If the function f has a local maximum where $x = x^*$ then $f'(x^*) = 0$ and $f''(x^*) \leq 0$.

(2) If $f'(x^*) = 0$ and $f''(x^*) < 0$, the function f has a local maximum where $x = x^*$.

Statement (1) gives necessary conditions for a local maximum, whereas (2) gives sufficient conditions.[3] The reason why $f''(x^*) \leq 0$ is a necessary condition for a local maximum can easily be seen by looking at what happens when $f'(x^*) = 0$ and $f''(x^*) > 0$ — there would then be a local *minimum* at $(x^*, f(x^*))$.

The condition $f'(x^*) = 0$ is called the **first-order condition** for a local maximum, as it involves the first derivative of f. Similarly the conditions $f''(x^*) \leq 0$ in (1) and $f''(x^*) < 0$ in (2) are called **second-order conditions**. The reason why they differ is of course that points where $f'(x^*)$ and $f''(x^*)$ are both zero may or may not be local maxima: this is the "ambiguous case" discussed at the end of the last section.

Similarly, the necessary and sufficient conditions for a local minimum may be summarised as follows:

(1) If the function f has a local minimum where $x = x^*$ then $f'(x^*) = 0$ and $f''(x^*) \geq 0$.

(2) If $f'(x^*) = 0$ and $f''(x^*) > 0$, the function f has a local minimum where $x = x^*$.

Local versus global

A local maximum point (x^*, y^*) of the curve $y = f(x)$, which has the additional property that

$$y^* \geq f(x) \text{ for all } x \text{ in } \mathcal{R},$$

is called a **global maximum point**. In that case, y^* is the greatest value $f(x)$ can take for any real x, and is of course unique. There may however be more than one global maximum *point*: in other words, there may be some x other than x^* for which $f(x) = y^*$.

Global maxima may be found as follows. Start by finding the local maximum points in the way described in the last two sections. *Provided a global maximum exists*, it (or they) may be found by comparing the values of y at the local maxima. The proviso is terribly important: in general, the only way to tell whether a global maximum exists is to sketch the curve, and in particular to consider how y behaves as $x \to \pm\infty$.

The following examples illustrate the distinction between global and local maxima:

- For the curve sketched in Figure 8.6, there is exactly one local maximum, which is **not** a global maximum.

---

[3]We say that A is a sufficient condition for B if A implies B; we say that A is a necessary condition for B if B implies A. Thus living in London is a sufficient but not a necessary condition for living in England; and living in London is a necessary but not a sufficient condition for living in Buckingham Palace.

- The function $f(x) = 3 + 2x - x^2$ has exactly one local maximum at $(1, 4)$, which is also the global maximum. This is easily seen using the methods of Section 4.1: calculus is not required.

- For the curve sketched in Figure 8.7, there are three local maxima, two of which are global maxima.

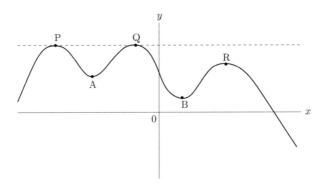

Figure 8.7: **Three local maxima, two of which are global maxima**

Global minima are defined in a similar way to global maxima: a **global minimum point** of the curve $y = f(x)$ is a local minimum point (x^*, y^*) with the additional property that

$$y^* \le f(x) \text{ for all } x \text{ in } \mathcal{R}.$$

Here are some examples of local and global minima:

- For the curve sketched in Figure 8.6, there is exactly one local minimum, which is **not** a global minimum.

- For the curve sketched in Figure 8.3, there is exactly one local minimum at $(3, -22)$, which is also the global minimum.

- For the curve sketched in Figure 8.7, there are two local minima, neither of which are global minima.

Four important points

The following two facts are very helpful; by appealing to them one can save a lot of calculation.

(a) The function f has a local minimum when $x = x^*$ if and only if the function $-f$ has a local maximum when $x = x^*$, and the same is true for global minima and maxima.

For example, we showed in the last section that the function

$$y = 2x^3 - 3x^2 - 12x + 9$$

has a local maximum at $(-1, 16)$, a local minimum at $(2, -11)$ and no global maximum or minimum. This tells us immediately that the function

$$y = -2x^3 + 3x^2 + 12x - 9$$

has a local minimum at $(-1, -16)$, a local maximum at $(2, 11)$ and no global maximum or minimum.

(b) Suppose $g(x) = H(f(x))$, where H is a *strictly increasing* function. If the function f has a global maximum point at (x^*, y^*), then the function g has a global maximum point at $(x^*, H(y^*))$.

The reason for this is simple: since

$$f(x^*) \geq f(x) \quad \text{for all } x$$

and H is a strictly increasing function,

$$H(f(x^*)) \geq H(f(x)) \quad \text{for all } x.$$

Similarly, if the function f has a global minimum point at (x^0, y^0), then the function g has a global minimum point at $(x^0, H(y^0))$.

For example, suppose we are looking for the global minimum of the function

$$g(x) = \tfrac{1}{8}(x^4 - 4x^3 + 5)^3.$$

We found in Section 8.1 that the function inside the brackets has its global minimum at the point $(3, -22)$. Also $H(u) = u^3/8$ is a monotonic increasing function. Hence the global minimum point of g is $(3, -1331)$.

And now two remarks about the advantages of using one's brain rather than applying routines mechanically.

(c) Calculus methods can be applied to finding maxima and minima only if the relevant function is differentiable. Thus common sense rather than calculus is the right tool for showing that $y = |x|$ attains its global minimum at $x = 0$.

(d) Even when calculus methods can be used, they are not always necessary or desirable. Points (a) and (b) above illustrate the fact that one can sometimes build on previous information, rather than starting afresh with differentiation: more on this in the exercises and problems. Also, as we showed in Section 4.1 and recalled earlier in this section, quadratic functions can be maximised or minimised by completing the square; this is usually the simplest and most efficient method.

Boundary maxima and minima

So far, we have been concerned with the maximum and minimum values of functions when the x variable is allowed to vary over the set $\mathcal{R}$ of all real numbers. However, as we have noted earlier, most economic variables are necessarily non-negative; we shall therefore often want to maximise or minimise a function $f(x)$ subject to the constraint $x \geq 0$.

We begin with the slightly simpler problem of finding a *local* maximum of $f(x)$ subject to the constraint $x \geq 0$. The two ways in which a local maximum can occur are illustrated in the two panels of Figure 8.8. In panel A, $f'(x) = 0$ when x takes the positive value x^* and $f'(x)$ changes from positive to negative when x goes from x^*- to x^*+. Here the maximum point A is called an **interior local maximum**. In panel B, $f'(0) \leq 0$ and $f'(0+) < 0$. Here we have a **boundary local maximum** at B.

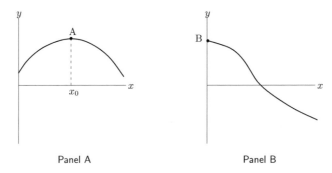

Panel A   Panel B

Figure 8.8: **Local maxima subject to** $x \geq 0$

When finding the local maxima subject to $x \geq 0$, we first find the interior local maxima (with $x > 0$) in the usual way. We then check to see if the value $x = 0$ gives the situation of Figure 8.8, panel B: notice that this happens if $dy/dx < 0$ when $x = 0$. The global maximum may then be found, as in the unconstrained case, by comparison of the local maxima and by considering the behaviour of y as $x \to \infty$.

We leave it to the reader to sketch the diagram corresponding to Figure 8.8 for local minima subject to $x \geq 0$. Once the local minima have been located, the global minimum may be found in a similar way to finding the global maximum.

An economic example

The methods explained above can be applied to the problem of the profit-maximising monopolist:

$$\text{maximise} \quad F(x) = R(x) - C(x) \quad \text{subject to } x \geq 0,$$

where x denotes output, R revenue, C cost and F profit.

Consider first the case where $x = x^*$ gives an interior local maximum. Then $R'(x^*) = C'(x^*)$:

$$\text{marginal revenue} = \text{marginal cost.}$$

Further, $F''(x^*) \leq 0$, which means that $R''(x^*) \leq C''(x^*)$. Notice that this inequality must hold if the marginal revenue curve is downward-sloping and the marginal cost curve is upward-sloping or horizontal. On the other hand, if the marginal revenue and marginal cost curves are both downward-sloping, the inequality $R''(x^*) \leq C''(x^*)$ says that the marginal revenue curve is at least as steep as the marginal cost curve at the optimum. Similarly, the *sufficient* condition for the critical point to be a local maximum, $F''(x^*) < 0$, says that the marginal revenue curve cuts the marginal cost curve from above.

The other possibility is where we have a boundary local maximum at $x = 0$. A necessary condition for such a boundary local maximum is $F'(0) \leq 0$. Similarly, a sufficient condition for a local maximum of this kind is $F'(0) < 0$: marginal cost is greater than marginal revenue at zero output.

The profit-maximisation problem is one of finding the **global** maximum, so the analyst's job does not end when the local maxima have been located. We now work through a particular example, which illustrates this point.

A numerical example

Suppose the monopolist faces the demand function

$$x = 100 - p,$$

where x is output and p is price, and let the monopolist's total cost be

$$C(x) = \tfrac{1}{3}x^3 - 7x^2 + 111x + 50.$$

We wish to find the output and price that maximise profit, and the maximal profit.

We begin by solving the demand equation for price in terms of output, and multiplying by output to obtain the revenue:

$$R(x) = px = (100 - x)x = 100x - x^2.$$

Profit $F(x)$ is given by

$$F(x) = R(x) - C(x) = -\tfrac{1}{3}x^3 + 6x^2 - 11x - 50.$$

Our object is to maximise $F(x)$ subject to $x \geq 0$.

By differentiation,

$$F'(x) = -x^2 + 12x - 11 = -(x-1)(x-11), \quad F''(x) = -2x + 12 = -2(x-6).$$

Hence $F'(x) = 0$ when $x = 1$ and when $x = 11$. Since

$$F''(1) = (-2) \times (-5) > 0 \quad \text{and} \quad F''(11) = (-2) \times (+5) < 0,$$

F has a local minimum when $x = 1$ and a local maximum when $x = 11$.

Having found that the only *interior* local maximum occurs where $x = 11$, we now calculate $F'(0)$ to find whether there is a boundary local maximum at $x = 0$: the answer is yes, because $F'(0) = -11 < 0$.

The next step is to check which of the local maxima give the higher profit. In fact $F(0) = -50$ and

$$F(11) = 121\left(-\frac{11}{3} + 6 - 1\right) - 50 = \frac{334}{3},$$

so that the more profitable of the two local maxima is $(11, 334/3)$. This suggests that the profit-maximising output is 11, but to verify this we should sketch the graph.

This is an easy task. We have already located the located the local maxima at $(0, -50)$ and $(11, 334/3)$. We also know that the remaining critical point is a local minimum occurring where $x = 1$; at that point, $F(x) = -166/3$. Finally, since $x^3/3$ is much bigger than $6x^2$ when x is very large, $F(x) \to -\infty$ as $x \to \infty$. The curve is sketched in Figure 8.9, from which it is clear that the maximal profit is $334/3$, attained when $x = 11$; the price which the monopolist should charge to maximise profit is $100 - 11 = 89$.

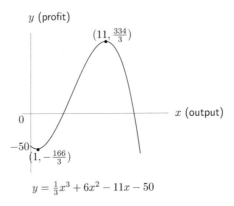

$$y = \tfrac{1}{3}x^3 + 6x^2 - 11x - 50$$

Figure 8.9: **Example of a monopolist; profit as a function of output**

Solving this example has taken several steps, and you should check that you have understood all of them. Notice in particular that serious work has to be done in getting from the classification of critical points to the global maximum.

Many of the main features of this example are depicted in Figure 8.10, which may seem more familiar than Figure 8.9. In Figure 8.10 we see the marginal revenue schedule MR ($R'(x) = 100 - 2x$) crossing the marginal cost schedule MC ($C'(x) = x^2 - 14x + 111$) from above at the local maximum of profit where $x = 11$, and from below at the local minimum of profit where $x = 1$. The same diagram also shows that MR < MC when $x = 0$, so there is another local maximum at zero output. What is not clear from Figure 8.10 — though crystal clear from Figure 8.9 — is that profit is actually greater at $x = 11$ than at $x = 0$. There is a way of inferring this from Figure 8.10, but it will not be explained until Chapter 19.

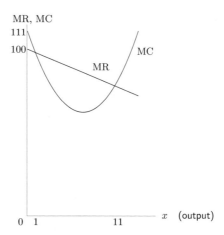

Figure 8.10: **Example of a monopolist; marginal revenue and marginal cost**

Exercises

8.3.1 Recall the function
$$y = x^3 - 12x^2 + 21x + 1$$
from Exercise 8.1.2. Use the graph you have drawn there to write down the coordinates of any local maxima, local minima, global maxima and global minima. Also write down the coordinates of any local maxima, local minima, global maxima and global minima when the constraint $x \geq 0$ is imposed.

8.3.2 (a) Use the results of Exercise 8.3.1 to write down the coordinates of any local maxima, local minima, global maxima and global minima of the function
$$y = -x^3 + 12x^2 - 21x - 1.$$

(b) Repeat part (a) when the constraint $x \geq 0$ is imposed.

(c) Repeat parts (a) and (b) for the function
$$y = (x^3 - 12x^2 + 21x + 1)^5.$$

8.3.3 A firm can produce quantity x of a product at cost

$$\tfrac{1}{3}x^3 - 6x^2 + 160x + 15.$$

The firm faces the demand function

$$x = 144 - p,$$

where p is the price of the product.

(a) Show that the marginal cost is positive at all levels of production.

(b) Find the profit-maximising level of output.

8.3.4 A differentiable function f has a local maximum at $(a, f(a))$ and no other local maximum. What do you deduce?

8.4 Convexity and concavity

The concepts of convex and concave functions are important for two reasons. First, they give us a class of cases for which it is relatively easy to find global optima. Second, they occur frequently in economics. These two reasons are related; indeed it is often said that the central role assigned by economists to convexity comes from a preference for easy problems over hard ones. Rather than entertain our readers with old jokes about economists' use of assumptions,[4] we proceed to the mathematics.

Let U be a set of points in the plane. We say that U is a **convex set** if the line segment[5] joining any two points of U is entirely contained in U. Thus in Figure 8.11 the sets U and V are convex, but W is not convex: the line segment joining the points A and B of W contains points such as C which are not in W.

Figure 8.11: U **and** V **are convex sets,** W **is not**

---

[4]A selection may be found at ⟨http://netec.mcc.ac.uk/JokEc.html⟩.

[5]From the beginning of this book, we have been using the term 'straight line' to mean something that extends infinitely far in both directions. It is therefore useful to have a separate term for that part of a straight line that lies between two given points: 'line segment' is the usual one.

A **convex function** is a function with the property that the set of all points which are on or above its graph is a convex set. In Figure 8.12, the functions f and g are convex but h is not. Given the definition of a convex set, we may describe convex functions as follows: a convex function has the property that, for any two points on its graph, the chord[6] joining the points lies on or above the graph.

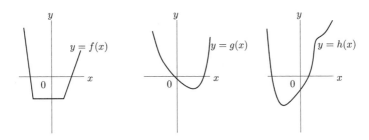

Figure 8.12: f **and** g **are convex functions,** h **is not**

This enables us to describe convex functions algebraically: the function f is convex if and only if

$$f(\alpha x_1 + (1 - \alpha)x_2) \le \alpha f(x_1) + (1 - \alpha)f(x_2) \qquad (8.1)$$

for any real numbers x_1, x_2, α such that $0 \le \alpha \le 1$.

To see why (8.1) is equivalent to the property that any chord lies on or above the graph, observe that when $0 < \alpha < 1$, $\alpha x_1 + (1 - \alpha)x_2$ is a number u lying between x_1 and x_2. In Figure 8.13, the left-hand side of (8.1) is the height PN of the *graph* at u while the right-hand side can be shown, with the help of some geometry, to be the height MN of the *chord* at u.

One point worth noticing in connection with the algebra of convex functions is that the inequality in (8.1) is weak ($\le$ rather than $<$). This allows for the fact that a convex function may contain straight line segments. This does not happen in Figure 8.13, but it is true of the convex function f of Figure 8.12; in that case, it is easy to choose values of x_1 and x_2 such that the chord coincides with the graph.

A convex function need not be differentiable; for example, the convex function f of Figure 8.12 has two kinks. However, in this book, we shall mainly be concerned with functions that are sufficiently smooth to be twice-differentiable. An important proposition relating convexity to the derivative is the following:

a differentiable function f is convex if and only if
f' is a non-decreasing function.

---

[6]A chord is a line-segment joining two points of a curve.

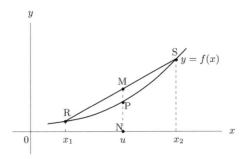

Figure 8.13: f **is a convex function; the chord RS lies above the curve**

Another way of stating this proposition is to say that f is convex if and only if $f'(a) \leq f'(b)$ whenever $a \leq b$. For twice-differentiable functions, the proposition may be restated in terms of the second dervative:

a twice-differentiable function f is convex if and only if $f''(x) \geq 0$ for all x.

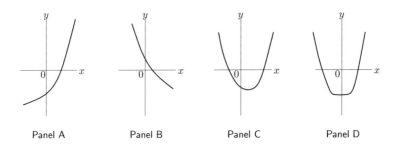

Figure 8.14: **Twice-differentiable convex functions**

Four examples of convex functions, each assumed to be twice-differentiable, are depicted in the four panels of Figure 8.14. Notice that in each case the following hold:

(i) There is either no global minimum (panels A and B) or one global minimum point (panel C) or an interval of such points (panel D).

(ii) There is no local minimum point other than the global minimum points.

(iii) There is no local maximum.

Properties (i), (ii) and (iii) hold for all convex functions. In fact, we have the following general proposition.

> given a differentiable convex function f, the point $(x^*, f(x^*))$
> is a global minimum point if and only if $f'(x^*) = 0$.

This result is of considerable importance; it says that if we can find a critical point of a convex function, we know it is a global minimum without having to go through the process of classification described in the last two sections. This fact is not the tremendous effort-saver that it might seem, for we often have to calculate the second derivative to verify that the function is convex in the first place. However, there are instances where we have extraneous information that the function in question is convex and in such situations the result is very useful indeed.

Strictly convex functions

A convex function with *no* straight line segments is said to be strictly convex. More precisely, a function is said to be **strictly convex** if, for any two points on its graph, all óther points of the chord joining them lie *above* the graph. Algebraically: the function f is convex if and only if

$$f(\alpha x_1 + (1 - \alpha)x_2) < \alpha f(x_1) + (1 - \alpha)f(x_2) \tag{8.2}$$

for any real numbers x_1, x_2, α such that $x_1 \neq x_2$ and $0 < \alpha < 1$.

A differentiable function f is convex if and only if its derivative f' is a strictly increasing function. It follows from the test for monotonicity in Section 7.3 that a convex function f is strictly convex if $f''(x) > 0$ for all except a finite number of values of x. For example, if $f(x) = x^4$ then $f''(x) = 12x^2$, which is non-negative for all x and zero only at $x = 0$; f is therefore strictly convex.

Convex functions defined on intervals

Convex functions can be defined not on all of $\mathcal{R}$ but on some interval[7] of $\mathcal{R}$. The rules just stated above continue to apply, with appropriate modifications. In particular, fact (iii) must be modified to allow for boundary maxima: see Exercise 8.4.2.

As an illustration of a convex function defined on an interval, we sketch the graph of the function $y = 1/x$, defined for $x > 0$. For all positive x,

$$\frac{dy}{dx} = -\frac{1}{x^2} < 0 \quad \text{and} \quad \frac{d^2y}{dx^2} = \frac{2}{x^3} > 0.$$

Thus the curve is downward-sloping and strictly convex.

For this function, y is small and positive when x is large and positive; indeed we can make y as close to zero as we wish by taking x sufficiently large and positive. This may be written

$$y \downarrow 0 \text{ as } x \to \infty.$$

---

[7]Intervals were defined in Section 3.1.

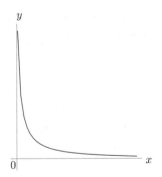

Figure 8.15: $y = x^{-1}$ **for** $x > 0$

A slightly different way of putting this is to say that the graph of $y = 1/x$ approaches the line $y = 0$ as $x \to \infty$. The line $y = 0$ is then said to be an **asymptote** of the curve $y = 1/x$, and the curve $y = 1/x$ is said to be asymptotic to the x–axis as $x \to \infty$.

Now consider the case where the independent variable x (still restricted to be positive) is very small. Then y is large and positive. More precisely, we can make y as large as we wish by choosing x suitably small and positive; this statement is written

$$y \to \infty \text{ as } x \downarrow 0$$

and implies that the y–axis also an asymptote. The graph of the function $y = 1/x$ for $x > 0$ is shown in Figure 8.15.

Concave functions

We say that a function is **concave** if the set of all points which are *on or below* its graph is a convex set. It follows that

the function f is concave if and only if $-f$ is convex.

Thanks to this fact, we can infer the properties of concave functions from the corresponding properties of convex functions. In particular:

(a) The function f is concave if and only if

$$f(\alpha x_1 + (1 - \alpha)x_2) \geq \alpha f(x_1) + (1 - \alpha)f(x_2)$$

for any real numbers x_1, x_2, α such that $0 \leq \alpha \leq 1$.

(b) A differentiable function f is convex if and only if f' is a non-increasing function.

(c) A twice-differentiable function f is concave if and only if $f''(x) \leq 0$ for all x.

(d) Given a differentiable concave function f, the point $(x^*, f(x^*))$ is a global maximum point if and only if $f'(x^*) = 0$.

We say that f is a **strictly concave** function if $-f$ is a strictly convex function. It follows that a function f is strictly concave if $f''(x) \leq 0$ for all x, with equality for at most a finite number of values of x. For example, the function $y = 3 - 2x^6$ is strictly concave: this is because $d^2y/dx^2 = -60x^4$, which is non-positve for all x and zero only for $x = 0$.

As an example of a function which is strictly concave on an interval of $\mathcal{R}$, consider $y = 1/x$ for $x < 0$. Then

$$\frac{dy}{dx} = -\frac{1}{x^2} < 0 \quad \text{and} \quad \frac{d^2y}{dx^2} = \frac{2}{x^3} < 0 \quad \text{whenever } x < 0.$$

Thus the function is negatively sloped and strictly concave. The remaining information one needs to sketch the graph comes from investigating its behaviour for x large and negative and for x small and negative. You are invited to do this in Exercise 8.4.3.

Non-negativity constraints again

Suppose we are maximising the concave function $f(x)$ subject to $x \geq 0$. If there exists a number x^* such that $x^* > 0$ and $f'(x^*) = 0$ then an interior global maximum is attained at $x = x^*$. If $f'(0) \leq 0$ then a boundary-maximum is attained at $x = 0$, and this will be the global maximum, given the non-negativity constraint.

Similar considerations apply to minimising a convex function $f(x)$ subject to the constraint $x \geq 0$.

Minimising a convex function: an economic example

Here we consider a firm's cost function $C(x)$, which expresses the dependence of total cost on output x. Average cost is defined to be $C(x)/x$. We find, in a particular case, the level of output which minimises average cost.

Suppose the cost function is

$$C(x) = x^2 + 10x + 36.$$

Denoting average cost by $G(x)$, we have

$$G(x) = x + 10 + 36/x$$

for all $x > 0$. Differentiating, we see that

$$G'(x) = 1 - 36x^{-2} \quad \text{and} \quad G''(x) = 72x^{-3}.$$

Since $G''(x) > 0$ for all positive x, the function G is convex, so the global minimum is given by equating $G'(x)$ to zero. Thus average cost is minimised when $x = \sqrt{36} = 6$, and minimal average cost is $6 + 10 + 6 = 22$.

Three points should be noted about this example.

1. Observe how easy minimisation becomes once we have established that the function is convex.

2. In this example, marginal cost $C'(x)$ is $2x + 10$; thus, when average cost is minimised by setting $x = 6$,

$$\text{marginal cost} = 22 = \text{average cost.}$$

This is no accident. If we have an arbitrary cost function $C(x)$ and denote average cost $C(x)/x$ by $G(x)$, then by the quotient rule

$$G'(x) = [xC'(x) - C(x)]/x^2 = [C'(x) - G(x)]/x.$$

If $G(x)$ is minimised when $x = x^* > 0$, then $G'(x^*) = 0$, so $C'(x^*) = G(x^*)$: *marginal cost equals average cost at the level of output which minimises the latter.*

3. Our cost-minimisation problem is easily generalised in the following way. Suppose we have the function

$$G(x) = ax + b + c/x,$$

defined for all $x > 0$; here a, b, c are constants with a and c positive.[8] Then

$$G'(x) = a - cx^{-2} \quad \text{and} \quad G''(x) = 2cx^{-3}.$$

The function G is therefore convex, and is minimised where $a = c/x^2$: the global minimum point is $\left(\sqrt{c/a}, \, b + 2\sqrt{ac} \right)$.

Exercises

8.4.1 Show that function

$$y = -x^4 + 4x^3 - 6x^2 + 8x + 3,$$

is concave everywhere, and that its slope is zero when $x = 2$. Deduce the coordinates of the global maximum point.

---

[8]In fact this function can be minimised without the use of calculus: recall Problem 4–3. This does not alter the fact that it provides a neat illustration of minimising a convex function via calculus.

8.4.2 Suppose the function of Exercise 8.4.1 is defined only for $x \geq 0$. Write down the coordinates of the local minimum point and the global maximum point

What happens if the function is defined only for (a) $x \geq 1$, (b) $x \geq 2$, (c) $x \geq 3$?

8.4.3 Complete the discussion of the function $y = x^{-1}$ given earlier in this section by investigating the behaviour of y when x is

(a) large and negative;   (b) small and negative.

Sketch the graph of $y = x^{-1}$.

Problems on Chapter 8

8-1. Find the critical points of

$$y = x^5(2 - x)^4$$

and determine their nature. Find also any points of inflexion and determine the ranges of x for which the function is (i) convex, (ii) concave.

Sketch the curve.

8-2. The volume of timber available for harvest in a forest at time t is given by the differentiable function $f(t)$ which satisfies the following conditions:

(i) $f(0) = 0$;
(ii) $f(t)$ is convex and increasing for $0 \leq t \leq a$;
(iii) $f(t)$ is concave and increasing for $a \leq t \leq b$;
(iv) $f(t)$ is decreasing for $t \geq b$.

Show in a diagram the shape of $y = f(t)$.

Suppose the forest is to be harvested when $f(t)/t$ is at its global maximum. Describe the optimum geometrically, and show that it is obtained at the unique value of t for which $f(t)/t = f'(t)$.

[This condition is known as the forester's rule because it has been traditionally favoured by that profession.]

8-3. Show that for the production function

$$Q = K^{1/2}L^{1/3}$$

the equation of a typical isoquant[9] can be put in the form $L = f(K)$. Hence show that the isoquants are convex.

Show that each isoquant has two asymptotes and state their equations. Sketch the pattern of isoquants.

---

[9]Isoquants were defined in problem 7–3.

8–4. A monopolist sells quantity x of a product; denote the price by p. Since $p = \dfrac{px}{x}$, we may refer to p as **average revenue**. Thus the average revenue schedule (or curve, or function), expressing the dependence of average revenue on x, is the demand function for the product written with p as dependent variable.

Suppose average revenue is given by

$$p = 36,000 - 1800x + 50x^2 - \tfrac{1}{2}x^3 \quad (0 \le x \le 60).$$

(i) Verify that this function is monotonic.

(ii) Find marginal revenue; show that it is **not** a monotonic function of x.

(iii) Sketch the average revenue curve and the marginal revenue curve in the same diagram.

[This example demonstrates that a downward-sloping demand curve does not necessarily imply a downward-sloping marginal revenue curve.]

Chapter 9

EXPONENTIAL AND LOGARITHMIC FUNCTIONS

This chapter brings together differential calculus and the functions introduced in the second half of Chapter 4. Up to now we have differentiated x^c but not c^x, and have not found the derivative of anything involving logarithms; these gaps will be filled. Along the way we introduce a real number called e which has many interesting properties.

When you have studied this chapter you will be able to:

- differentiate functions involving exponential and logarithmic terms;

- understand continuous compounding and discounting;

- use 'the economist's favourite approximation';

- calculate growth rates of economic varaibles, using discrete or continuous time.

The material of this chapter has widespread applications in the natural sciences and the social sciences. In particular, it plays an essential role in any serious economic analysis involving compound interest or growth of income or wealth. We begin our story with compound interest.

9.1 The exponential function

Suppose you invest £1 for one year at an interest rate of x per year. How much is your pound worth at the end of the year? As we know from Section 5.3, the answer to this question (call it £y) depends on how often interest is compounded: $y = 1 + x$ with annual compounding, $y = (1 + \frac{x}{4})^4$ with quarterly compounding and so on. In general, if interest is compounded n times a year at equal intervals of length $1/n$ years, we will have

$$y = \left(1 + \frac{x}{n}\right)^n.$$

In the terminology of Section 5.3, $y - 1$ (expressed as a percentage) is the annual percentage rate corresponding to the flat rate x; and as we noted in that section, y is greater, the greater is n. It can be seen by examples that making n enormously large, for given x, will not make y grow indefinitely. Thus for each x there is some upper limit which y approaches as n tends to infinity. We may therefore define the **exponential function**

$$\exp x = \lim_{n \to \infty} \left(1 + \frac{x}{n}\right)^n. \tag{9.1}$$

As we increase n, the interval between compounding 'dates' becomes shorter, approaching zero as $n \to \infty$. For this reason the limiting case where $n \to \infty$ is known as **continuous compounding**. The function $\exp x$ of (9.1) is the value at the end of 1 year of £1 invested at a rate of interest $100x\%$ per annum, compounded continuously.

To give some numerical content to this, Table 9.1 tabulates $(1 + (x/n))^n$ for various values of x and n. The row marked ∞ corresponds to the exponential function, values of which are available on any scientific calculator.

$$\text{Table 9.1: } \left(1 + \frac{x}{n}\right)^n.$$

$n \backslash x$	0.03	0.10	0.30	5	-2
1	1.0300	1.1000	1.3000	6.0000	-1.0000
4	1.0303	1.1038	1.3355	25.6289	0.0625
12	1.0304	1.1047	1.3449	65.3450	0.1122
100	1.0304	1.1051	1.3492	131.5013	0.1326
∞	1.0305	1.1052	1.3499	148.4132	0.1353

The first three columns of Table 9.1 correspond to the sort of values of x which we normally associate with interest rates. But the limit on the right-hand side of (9.1) exists for **all** real values of x, including negative ones — the exponential function $y = \exp x$ may therefore be defined by (9.1) for all x in $\mathcal{R}$. This is illustrated by the last two columns of Table 9.1: notice that the '$n = 100$' entry in these columns is not such a good approximation to $\exp x$ as it is in the first three.

The graph of $y = \exp x$ is sketched in Figure 9.1. According to the graph, $\exp x$ is positive for all real x, being close to zero when x is large and negative. The exponential function is monotonic increasing and convex, and $\exp 0 = 1$.

Later in this section, we shall give reasons why the exponential function behaves in this way.

The number $\exp 1$ is denoted by e, and turns out to be 2.7182818 to 7 decimal places.

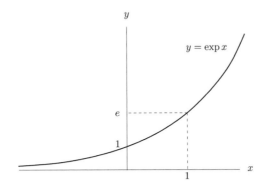

Figure 9.1: **The exponential function**

Properties of the exponential function

The exponential function is one of the most important fuctions in mathematics. It has wide applications in physics, chemistry and biology as well as in economics.

We now introduce the six main properties of the exponential function. *Please do not learn them by heart*, except possibly for the last one (**E6** below). The reason why memorising **E1**–**E5** is a complete waste of time will become clear before the end of this section

The first two properties are as follows:

E1 $\exp 0 = 1$;

E2 $\exp(a + b) = (\exp a) \times (\exp b)$.

E1 is obvious from (9.1). **E2** is very important and not at all obvious.

To see what **E2** means, think again of compound interest. Consider two securities, I and II: I bears a rate of interest of a per year for the first year, and b per year for the second year; II yields no interest for the first year and bears a rate of interest of $a + b$ per year for the second year. **E2** tells us that *if compounding is continuous*, each pound invested in security II is worth exactly the same after two years as a pound invested in security I. As we have just said, this is not obvious, and it is not even true if continuous compounding is replaced by compounding at discrete intervals: for example, with $a = 0.05$, $b = 0.10$ and annual compounding, £1000 invested in security II is worth £1150 after two years, while £1000 invested in security I is worth £1155 after two years. In the appendix to this chapter we give a (not fully rigorous) account of why **E2** follows from (9.1).

We now make some simple deductions from **E1** and **E2**. Setting $b = -a$ in **E2** and using **E1** gives

E3 $\exp(-a) = 1/(\exp a)$,

while **E2** and **E3** imply that

E4 $\exp(a - b) = (\exp a)/(\exp b)$.

The next property is more subtle: for any real numbers a and c,

E5 $\exp(ac) = (\exp a)^c$.

Notice that **E5** reduces to **E1** when $c = 0$, to **E2** (with $a = b$) when $c = 2$ and to **E3** when $c = -1$. It takes a little effort to go from these special cases to the case where c can be any integer, and a lot more work (beyond the scope of this book) to show that **E5** still holds when c is any real number.

Properties **E1**–**E5** tell us that the x in $\exp x$ behaves like an index. We will make this explicit presently; before doing that, we bring in some calculus.

Differentiating the exponential function

The last of the main properties of the function $\exp x$ is that *it is its own derivative*:

E6 $\dfrac{d}{dx}(\exp x) = \exp x$.

We shall give an informal explanation of this remarkable result in the appendix to this chapter.

Given the properties **E1**–**E6**, we can now explain why Figure 9.1 looks as it does. It follows immediately from the definition of the exponential function (9.1) that $\exp x$ is positive for all positive x. Applying **E1** and **E3**, we see that that $\exp 0 = 1$ and $\exp x$ is positive for all real x. That $\exp x$ is monotonic increasing follows from **E6**; also, two applications of **E6** show that

$$\frac{d^2y}{dx^2} = \exp x > 0,$$

so $\exp x$ is a convex function. All of this implies that $\exp x$ becomes very large and positive when x is large and positive, and this, together with **E3**, shows that $\exp x$ is close to zero when x is large and negative.

The number e and the function e^x

We now take a closer look at property **E5** of the exponential function, which states that $\exp(ac) = (\exp a)^c$ for any real numbers a and c. Letting $a = 1$ and recalling that $\exp 1 = e$, we see that $\exp c = e^c$ for all c. Replacing c by x, we have

$$\exp x = e^x \quad \text{for all } x \in \mathcal{R}. \tag{9.2}$$

The importance of (9.2) is this: *once one thinks of the exponential function as e^x, the properties* **E1–E5** *reduce to simple algebra*. This is the reason why we implored you not to learn these properties by heart.

Summary of properties

There is a real number e, approximately equal to 2.7183, such that the function e^x has the following two properties:

$$(A) \quad \frac{d}{dx}(e^x) = e^x.$$

$$(B) \quad e^x = \lim_{n \to \infty} \left(1 + \frac{x}{n}\right)^n \quad \text{for all } x \in \mathcal{R}.$$

The function e^x is known as the exponential function and is sometimes denoted by $\exp x$.

Points to notice

1. A useful generalisation of (A) is this: for any constant a,

$$\frac{d}{dx}(e^{ax}) = ae^{ax}. \tag{9.3}$$

   This is easily derived from (A) and the composite function rule. Let $y = e^{ax}$. Then $y = e^u$, where $u = ax$. Hence

$$\frac{dy}{dx} = \frac{dy}{du} \times \frac{du}{dx} = e^u a = ae^{ax}.$$

2. From now on we shall usually denote the exponential function by e^x, but we retain the 'exp' notation for occasional use. This is especially helpful when one is dealing with expressions of the form $e^{f(x)}$. For instance,

$$\exp(\sqrt{1 + x^2})$$

   has exactly the same meaning as

$$e^{\sqrt{1+x^2}},$$

   but the former expression is much easier to read without a magnifying glass.

3. The key giving the exponential function on most scientific calculators is the one labelled e^x and not the one marked EXP.

Formulae for continuous compounding and discounting

We now consider fact (B) about the exponential function. This is of course equation (9.1) in a slightly different notation, and is the basis of what we said at the beginning of the section about compound interest.

We recall the basic fact about continuous compounding, using the 'e' notation and following the common practice of denoting the interest rate by r rather than x: £1 compounded continuously at a rate of r per year becomes £e^r after one year. The rate r is sometimes called the **instantaneous** rate of interest: the APR (annual percentage rate) is $e^r - 1$, expressed as a percentage.

During a second year, every £1 becomes £e^r, and therefore £e^r becomes £$(e^r)^2$. Thus, after two years, £1 becomes £e^{2r}. Similarly, after T years, £1 becomes £e^{rT}, and £P becomes £Pe^{rT}.

Summarising, the value F of an amount P after continuous compounding for T years at a rate of interest of r per year is given by

$$V = Pe^{rT}. \tag{9.4}$$

Notice that, because compounding is continuous, the number T in (9.4) does not have to be an integer: see Exercise 9.1.2.

Similarly, the present value P of a given amount V which is to be available T years from now is given by solving (9.4) for P, given V: the present value is

$$P = Ve^{-rT}. \tag{9.5}$$

The formulae (9.4) and (9.5) assume a constant interest rate r. Also, we have not yet considered the continuous-discounting analogue of finding the present value of an income stream, which we did for annual discounting in Section 5.3. So there is a lot more to be said on this topic, but that will have to wait until Chapter 19.

Exercises

9.1.1 Use a calculator to verify

(a) $e^2 e^3 = e^5$, (b) $e^8/e^2 = e^6$, (c) $e^{-4} = 1/e^4$, (d) $(e^{1.5})^4 = e^6$.

9.1.2 Find the value after 10 years of £500 compounded (a) annually, (b) monthly, (c) continuously, at an interest rate of 4% per annum. Comment.

How do your answers change when the time period involved is $2\frac{1}{2}$ years?

9.1.3 Find the present value of £400 to be paid in 5 years time if it is discounted (a) annually, (b) monthly, (c) continuously, at a rate of 7% per annum. Comment.

9.1.4 Differentiate

(a) $e^{2x} + 3e^{-4x}$, (b) xe^{2x}.

9.2 Natural logarithms

Let x be a positive number. The **natural logarithm** of x is the logarithm to base e of x, where e is as in the last section. Using the definition of logarithms given in Section 4.3, we see that

$$y = \log_e x \text{ if and only if } x = e^y.$$

It is common[1] to denote $\log_e x$ by $\ln x$: thus

$$\exp(\ln x) = x \text{ for every positive number } x;$$
$$\ln(\exp y) = y \text{ for every real number } y.$$

In short, the natural logarithm function is the inverse function of the exponential function.

The graph of the natural logarithm function is sketched in Figure 9.2. Since 'ln' is the inverse function of 'exp', Figure 9.2 is just Figure 9.1 with the axes interchanged. For this reason the natural logarithm function is monotonic increasing and concave, with $\ln 1 = 0$, and with $\ln x$ becoming very large and negative as x tends to zero.

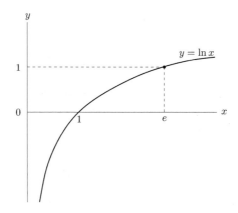

Figure 9.2: **The natural logarithm function**

Properties

The main properties of natural logarithms are as follows:

L1 $\ln 1 = 0$;

L2 $\ln(a \times b) = \ln a + \ln b$;

---

[1]But not universal. Some authors use '$\log_e$' or just 'log' instead of 'ln'; but see footnote 2.

L3　　$\ln(1/a) = -\ln a$;

L4　　$\ln(a/b) = \ln a - \ln b$;

L5　　$\ln(a^c) = c \ln a$;

L6　　$\dfrac{d}{dx}(\ln x) = \dfrac{1}{x}$.

Rules **L1**–**L5** are true for logarithms to any base. That **L6** holds for natural logarithms can be shown as follows. Let $y = \ln x$: then $x = e^y$. Using the inverse function rule of Section 7.3 and the fact that the exponential function is its own derivative,

$$\frac{1}{dy/dx} = \frac{dx}{dy} = e^y = x.$$

Thus $\dfrac{dy}{dx} = \dfrac{1}{x}$, proving **L6**.

'The economist's favourite approximation'

The phrase is, we believe, due to the late Professor Sherwin Rosen of the University of Chicago. The approximation in question is a property of natural logarithms which has many applications in economics:

L7　　$\ln(1 + h) \approx h$　when $|h|$ is small.

One way of justifying this is in terms of compound interest. It is not hard to see that $\ln(1+h)$ is the flat rate which, with continuous compounding, yields an APR of h. Thus **L7** is just another way of saying that if the rate of interest is small, the difference between annual and continuous compounding is very small.

A more direct way of deriving **L7** is to apply the small increments approximation of Section 6.2: if f is a differentiable function and $|h|$ is small,

$$f(x + h) \approx f(x) + hf'(x).$$

We apply this formula with $f(x) = \ln x$ and $x = 1$; then $f(1) = 0$ by **L1** and $f'(1) = 1/1 = 1$ by **L6**. Therefore $\ln(1 + h) \approx 0 + h$, which is **L7**.

The approximation **L7** is particularly accurate when h is small and *positive*. For example, **L7** states that $\ln 1.05 \approx 0.05$, and in fact $\ln 1.05 = 0.0488$ to 4 decimal places. Even for h as large as 0.15, h is not a bad approximation to $\ln(1 + h)$; the calculator tells us that $\ln 1.15 = 0.140$ to 3 decimal places. For small negative h, the accuracy of the approximation **L7** is slightly less impressive: $\ln 0.95 = -0.0513$ to 4 decimal places, and $\ln 0.85 = -0.163$ to 3 decimal places. We shall have more to say about this approximation in Section 10.3.

More examples of differentiation

The rules for differentiating 'exp' and 'ln' may be combined with the other rules of differentiation given in Chapters 6 and 7, especially the composite function rule. We have already given an example of this in equation (9.3), and we now give some more.

Example 1 Differentiate c^x, where c is a positive constant.

Let $y = c^x$, $a = \ln c$. Then $c = e^a$, so $y = e^{ax}$. Hence by (9.3),

$$\frac{dy}{dx} = ae^{ax} = (\ln c)y.$$

Summarising,

$$\frac{d}{dx}(c^x) = c^x \ln c.$$

Example 2 **L6** is a property of *natural* logarithms and does not hold for logarithms to other bases such as 10.[2] The correct formula for the derivative of the logarithm to an arbitrary base b is

$$\frac{d}{dx}(\log_b x) = \frac{1}{x \ln b}.$$

This is easily derived from the change-of-base formula of Section 4.3. Since

$$\log_e x = \log_e b \times \log_b x,$$

$\log_b x = (\ln x)/(\ln b)$. Differentiating this expression using **L6**, we obtain the required formula.

Example 3 It follows immediately from the composite function rule that

$$\frac{d}{dx}(\ln f(x)) = \frac{f'(x)}{f(x)}$$

for any (positive-valued) function f. In particular

$$\frac{d}{dx}\ln(x + c) = \frac{1}{x + c}$$

for any constant c.

Example 4 A function that occurs frequently in mathematical statistics is

$$y = \exp(-\tfrac{1}{2}x^2).$$

To differentiate this, we use the composite function rule: since $y = e^{-u}$, where $u = x^2/2$,

$$dy/dx = -e^{-u} \times x = -xf(x).$$

---

[2]It is easy to forget this important point if you denote the natural logarithm of x by 'log x'. This is one reason why we prefer 'ln'.

The rules for differentiating 'exp' and 'ln' may also be combined with the methods of optimisation and curve-sketching explained in Chapter 8. This is explored in Excercise 9.2.4 and the Problems.

More on elasticity

Recall from Section 6.4 that the elasticity of a supply or demand function $q = f(p)$ is $\dfrac{p}{q}\dfrac{dq}{dp}$. Now $\dfrac{d}{dp}\ln q = \dfrac{1}{q}\dfrac{dq}{dp}$ by the composite function rule, so the elasticity is equal to

$$p\frac{d}{dp}\ln q.$$

When calculating elasticities it is often useful to take natural logarithms before differentiating.

The case of constant elasticity

Suppose that the demand function for a good is $q = ap^{-b}$ where a and b are positive constants. Then

$$\ln q = \ln a - b\ln p.$$

Differentiating, remembering that $\ln a$ is a constant, we have

$$\frac{d}{dp}\ln q = 0 - \frac{b}{p}.$$

Multiplying through by p, we see that the elasticity of demand is the constant $-b$.

In fact, demand functions of the form $q = ap^{-b}$ are the only ones for which elasticity of demand is constant. Similarly, the only constant-elasticity supply functions are those of the form $q = ap^{b}$, where a and b are positive constants.

Elasticity of supply: an example

As a slightly more complicated example, suppose that the supply function of a competitive industry is

$$q = 5(p - 4)^3.$$

Then $\ln q = \ln 5 + 3\ln(p - 4)$; the elasticity of supply is

$$p\frac{d}{dp}\ln q = p\left[0 + 3\frac{d}{dp}\ln(p - 4)\right] = \frac{3p}{p - 4}.$$

This supply function is defined only for $p > 4$: the assumption is that price must exceed 4 for firms to be tempted into the industry. Elasticity of supply is very large for p only just greater than 4 and falls as p increases, being close to 3 when p is very large.

Exercises

9.2.1 We showed in Section 9.1 that an instantaneous rate of interest of r yields an APR (annual percentage rate) of $100r'\%$ per annum, where $r' = e^r - 1$. If compounding is continuous and you know that the APR is $100s\%$ per annum, what is the instantaneous rate of interest?

9.2.2 Differentiate

$$\text{(a)} \ \ln(ax), \quad \text{(b)} \ \ln(x^4 + 1), \quad \text{(c)} \ \exp(x^3 + x), \quad \text{(d)} \ x\ln x,$$
$$\text{(e)} \ e^x/(e^x + 1) \quad \text{(f)} \ \ln\left(x^2/(x^4 + 1)\right).$$

9.2.3 (a) In Example 1 of this section we found the derivative of c^x. Now do this another way by taking natural logarithms of both sides of the equation $y = c^x$ and then differentiating with respect to x.

(b) In Example 4 of this section we found the derivative of $\exp(-\frac{1}{2}x^2)$. Now do this another way, using the same method as in part (a) of this exercise.

9.2.4 Find the critical point of

$$y = xe^{-x}$$

and determine its nature. Find also the point of inflexion and the ranges of values for which the function is (a) convex, (b) concave.

[Note that we are not quite in a position to sketch the graph of this function: although its behaviour for x large and negative is obvious, that for x large and positive is not. This gap will be filled in Exercise 10.4.3.]

9.2.5 Suppose that the supply function of a competitive industry is

$$q = Ap^a + Bp^b,$$

where A, B, a, b are positive constants, with $a > b$. Find the elasticity of supply. Explain what happens to the elasticity of supply when $p \to 0$, and when $p \to \infty$.

9.3 Time in economics

Many problems in economics are concerned with variables which change over time. There are two standard ways of formalising such problems, known as discrete-time and continuous-time analysis.

Consider an economic variable, say income, which varies over time. In discrete-time analysis, the time variable t takes the values $1, 2, 3, \ldots$ and the values of the economic variable y form a sequence $\{y_t\}$. In continuous-time analysis, by contrast, we write

$$y = f(t)$$

where t varies continuously through some interval of real numbers.[3] It is common to assume that f is a differentiable function, so that calculus may be applied.

The choice between continuous and discrete time depends on the task in hand. With regard to realism, each method of analysis corresponds to an aspect of reality: discrete time to the fact that economic statistics appear at regular intervals (for example the monthly 'claimant count' of unemployed people in Britain), continuous time to the fact that different people are making economic decisions all the time. Also, in many financial markets, available data are generated so frequently as to be virtually a continuous flow.

Although discrete-time analysis is the natural tool when use is being made of data produced at discrete intervals, this does not mean that any economic model which must eventually be tested on such data has to be formulated in discrete time from the beginning. It is in fact very common for economists to analyse mathematical models using continuous time, and then use a discrete-time approximation to confront the theory with the data. The reason for this is that continuous-time analysis is often easier, precisely because one has the tools of calculus at one's disposal.

Rate of change and rate of growth

Suppose for the moment we are treating time continuously. Let the economic variable y be given by $y = f(t)$, where t represents time and f is a differentiable function. We define the **rate of change** of y to be

$$\frac{dy}{dt} = f'(t).$$

The (proportional) **rate of growth** of y is

$$\frac{1}{y}\frac{dy}{dt} = \frac{f'(t)}{f(t)}.$$

For example, if $y = a + bt^2$, where a and b are constants, then the rate of change of y is $2bt$ and the rate of growth is $2bt/(a + bt^2)$.

If, as is often the case for economic variables, y takes only positive values, then $\ln y$ may be defined. In this case it follows from the composite function rule that

$$\frac{1}{y}\frac{dy}{dt} = \frac{d}{dt}\ln y. \qquad (9.6)$$

The rate of growth can then be calculated as the right-hand side of (9.6). For example, if $y = Ae^{ct}$, where A and c are constants with $A > 0$, then $\ln y =$

---

[3]In theoretical modelling it is often convenient to 'kick the system off' at a time designated $t = 0$; the relevant interval then consists of non-negative real numbers. We shall adopt this procedure in Chapter 21, but it is not essential: t could in principle take negative values, as in the conventional dating system for historical events, where 'BC' corresponds to $t < 0$.

$\ln A + ct$. Differentiating with respect to t, we see that the rate of growth of y is the constant c.

The corresponding definitions in discrete time are $y_{t+1} - y_t$ for rate of change, and $(y_{t+1} - y_t)/y_t$ for rate of growth. In fact, growth rates provide a good illustration of a point we made earlier about continuous time being easier than discrete time.

In continuous-time analysis, the rate of growth of consumption per head is equal to the rate of growth of consumption minus the rate of growth of heads: for if C is aggregate consumption and L the size of the population,

$$\frac{d}{dt} \ln \frac{C}{L} = \frac{d}{dt} (\ln C - \ln L) = \frac{d}{dt} (\ln C) - \frac{d}{dt} (\ln L).$$

In discrete-time analysis, by contrast, the rate of growth of consumption per head is not in general the same as the rate of growth of consumption minus the rate of growth of heads, though there will be approximate equality when growth rates are small.

One way in which this problem may be eased is to redefine the discrete-time growth rate as

$$\ln y_{t+1} - \ln y_t,$$

by analogy with the right-hand side of (9.6). With this definition, the rate of growth of consumption per head is equal to the rate of growth of consumption minus the rate of growth of heads. Also, the two definitions of the growth rate give very similar numbers for slowly-growing variables — this follows from properties **L4** and **L7** of natural logarithms, given in the last section. But discrete-time analysis with liberal use of logarithms presents its own problems, and in general continuous time lends itself to easier mathematics.

Exercises

9.3.1 Suppose
$$y = a + bt + ct^2,$$

where a, b, c are constants. Find (a) the continuous-time rate of growth, (b) the discrete-time rate of growth.

9.3.2 Suppose that aggregate wealth W and population size L are given by
$$W = a + bt, \quad L = Ae^{mt},$$

where a, b, A and m are constants. Find the continuous-time growth rates of wealth, population and wealth per head.

9.3.3 (a) Verify that the discrete-time rate of growth, as usually defined, is approximately equal to
$$\ln y_{t+1} - \ln y_t$$

if the variable y grows slowly.

(b) Verify that if the discrete-time rate of growth of a variable y is redefined as

$$\ln y_{t+1} - \ln y_t,$$

then the rate of growth of consumption per head is equal to the rate of growth of consumption minus the rate of growth of heads. Can you formulate a general result?

9.3.4 Suppose $y = Ae^{rt}$, where A and r are constants. Find

(a) the continuous-time rate of growth;

(b) the discrete-time rate of growth;

(c) $\ln y_{t+1} - \ln y_t$.

Under what circumstances are (b) and (c) close to each other?

9.3.5 By using the results of Exercise 9.3.4, or otherwise, repeat Exercise 9.3.4 for $y = Ac^t$, where A and c are constants.

Problems on Chapter 9

9–1. As a generalisation of Example 4 of Section 9.2, consider the function

$$y = \exp(-ax^2),$$

where a is a positive constant.

(i) Find dy/dx. Without calculating the second derivative, show that the unique global maximum is at $x = 0$.

(ii) Find d^2y/dx^2. Hence find the points of inflexion and the ranges of values for which the function is convex and concave.

(iii) Sketch the graph.

9–2. (i) A sum of money is invested at a constant (instantaneous) rate of interest r per year, compounded continuously. Let $R = 100r$, so that the instantaneous rate of interest, treated as a percentage, is $R\%$ per annum. Suppose the investment is worth double at the end of T years;[4] show that

$$T \approx \frac{69}{R}.$$

---

[4]Since time is measured continuously, T does not have to be an integer.

(ii) The approximation in (i) is known in finance as the **rule of 69**. It is often convenient to use an alternative approximation for the doubling time in which the denominator is the APR rather than the instantaneous flat rate; the numerator should then be somewhat greater than 69, and increase with the APR. Show that the 'rule of 70' provides a reasonable approximation when the APR is below 5% per annum, and the 'rule of 72' when it is 5–10%. [Hint: use part (i), and your answer to Exercise 9.2.1.]

9–3. (i) By expressing the limit as the value of a derivative at $x = 0$, show that

$$\lim_{x \to 0} \frac{e^{ax} - 1}{x} = a.$$

Hence show that

$$\lim_{a \to 0} \frac{e^{ax} - 1}{a} = x.$$

(ii) For each real number $a \neq 0$, the function f_a is defined as follows:

$$f_a(x) = \frac{e^{ax} - 1}{a}.$$

Also let $f_0(x) = x$: by the second result of (i),

$$\lim_{a \to 0} f_a(x) = f_0(x) \quad \text{for all } x.$$

Find $f_a'(x)$, $f_a''(x)$, $f_a(0)$ and $f_a'(0)$. Use these results to sketch the curves $y = f_a(x)$ in the same xy–plane for $a = 0$, ± 1 and ± 5.

(iii) For each real number $b \neq 0$, the function g_b is defined as follows:

$$g_b(x) = \frac{x^b - 1}{b} \quad (x > 0).$$

Also let $g_0(x) = \ln x$. Use the second result of (i) to show that

$$\lim_{b \to 0} g_b(x) = g_0(x) \quad \text{for all } x > 0.$$

Find $g_b'(x)$, $g_b''(x)$, $g_b(1)$ and $g_b'(1)$. Use these results to sketch the curves $y = g_b(x)$ in the same xy–plane for $b = 0$, $\frac{1}{2}$, ± 1 and ± 2.

[The functions of part (ii) of this problem are known in financial economics as 'constant absolute risk aversion' (CARA) utility functions: the coefficient of absolute risk aversion is $-a$. The functions of part (iii) are known in statistics as 'Box–Cox transformations' and in financial economics as 'constant relative risk aversion' (CRRA) utility functions: the coefficient of relative risk aversion is $1 - b$.]

9–4.   (i) As in part (i) of Problem 5–3, a timber owner plants a forest at time 0. The volume of timber in the forest at time $t \geq 0$ is given by the function $f(t)$. The price per unit volume of wood harvested is p and the interest rate is r; both p and r assumed to be constant, p is net of harvesting costs, and planting costs are ignored.

Suppose now that time is measured continuously and discounting is continuous, with r being the instantaneous rate of interest. If the forest is cut down and the timber sold at time T, what is the value of the forest at time 0? Show that this value, considered as a function of T, has a critical point where T satisfies

$$f'(T)/f(T) = r. \tag{9.7}$$

[Equation (9.7) is called the **Fisher rule**, after the famous American economist Irving Fisher (1867–1947).]

(ii) Assume everything is as in (i), except that at time T, $2T$, $3T$, ... the timber owner cuts down the forest, sells the timber and replants it with similar trees.[5] Express the value of the forest at time 0 as a function of T, and show that it has a critical point where

$$f'(T)/f(T) = re^{rT}/(e^{rT} - 1). \tag{9.7$'$}$$

[Equation (9.7$'$) is called the **Faustmann rule**, after the nineteenth-century German landowner and forester Martin Faustmann.]

(iii) Show that the right-hand side of (9.7$'$) approaches $1/T$ as $r \to 0$.

[This means that, when the interest rate is very low, the Faustmann rule approximates the 'forester's rule' of Problem 8–2.]

(iv) Assuming $f(t)$ has the shape specified in Problem 8–2, discuss the circumstances in which the critical points of parts (i) and (ii) are global maxima.

---

[5]T is called the **rotation period**, and does not have to be an integer.

Appendix to Chapter 9

In this appendix we sketch non-rigorous proofs of two important properties of the exponential function:

E2 $\exp(a + b) = (\exp a) \times (\exp b)$.

E6 $\dfrac{d}{dx}(\exp x) = \exp x$.

What we mean by a 'proof' is a derivation from the original definition (9.1) of the exponential function. **E2** is obvious if you think of $\exp x$ as e^x, but that is not the point at issue here; we needed **E2** as part of the build-up to the number e and the function e^x, and our aim in this appendix is to fill in gaps in that argument. Our 'proofs' are non-rigorous in that we do not fully justify our operations with limits, but they are a serious attempt to explain why **E2** and **E6** hold. We think this is worth doing, because the exponential function is so central that it is not healthy to think of it as a deep mystery, or of e as a magic number.

We start with **E2**. For each $n \in \mathcal{N}$, let

$$u_n = \left(1 + \frac{a}{n}\right)^n, \quad v_n = \left(1 + \frac{b}{n}\right)^n, \quad w_n = \left(1 + \frac{a+b}{n}\right)^n.$$

By (9.1), $\exp a$, $\exp b$ and $\exp(a + b)$ are the limits of the sequences $\{u_n\}$, $\{v_n\}$ and $\{w_n\}$ respectively as $n \to \infty$. **E2** follows from the fact that $w_n \approx u_n v_n$ when n is large. To justify this approximation, we note that, for all n,

$$u_n v_n = \left(1 + \frac{1}{n}\left[a + b + \frac{ab}{n}\right]\right)^n.$$

When n is large, the term in square brackets is close to $a + b$, so $u_n v_n$ is indeed close to w_n.

Differentiating the exponential function, again

We now give an explanation for **E6**, which states that

$$\lim_{h \to 0} \frac{\exp(x + h) - \exp x}{h} = \exp x. \tag{9.8}$$

For any real number h, let $h' = \exp h - 1$. A few minutes with a calculator should satisfy you that when h is small and positive, the difference between h' and h is small even relative to h;[6] hence $(h' - h)/h$ is small, and h'/h is close to 1. For example, if $h = 0.01$, $h'/h = 1.00502$;[7] if $h = 0.002$, $h'/h = 0.00100$.

---

[6]In the language of compound interest: if the flat rate is small, the difference between the APR and the flat rate is *very* small, regardless of how often interest is compounded.

[7]This and subsequent numerical results are correct to 5 decimal places.

Similarly, h'/h is close to 1 if h is small and negative: for example, if $h = -0.004$, $h'/h = 0.99800$.[8] All of this may be summarised in terms of limits: as $h \to 0$, $h'/h \to 1$.

(9.8) is now easy to prove. By **E2**, $\exp(x + h) = \exp x \exp h$, whence

$$\frac{\exp(x + h) - \exp x}{h} = \frac{h'}{h} \exp x.$$

As $h \to 0$, $h'/h \to 1$, and (9.8) holds as required.

Chapter 10

APPROXIMATIONS

In Chapter 6 we introduced the idea that the derivative at a point on a curve provides a linear approximation to the curve at that point. In this chapter we apply and extend that idea.

Our first application is Newton's method for finding approximate solutions to nonlinear equations. This algorithm and its extensions are of great importance in numerical work. In Section 10.2 we look at linear approximations from a slightly different viewpoint and introduce the mean value theorem, which is at the heart of more rigorous treatments of differential calculus. In the remainder of the chapter, we explain how use of the second derivative leads to a quadratic approximation, and then generalise further to consider approximations by polynomials of higher degree.

We included this chapter because the material in it is used quite extensively by economists. It is, however, somewhat demanding. Therefore, instead of our usual list of things you should know when you have studied the whole chapter, we give some advice on what can and cannot be skipped. *A minimal reading of the chapter should include:*

- the discussion of the small increments formula (first half of Section 10.1), which gives a fuller account of the geometry of that all-important formula than we provided in Section 6.2;

- Newton's method (Section 10.1, second half);

- the formulae for higher derivatives at the beginning of Section 10.3 (just the first two paragraphs and the Example);

- the series for e^x and $\ln(1+x)$ in Section 10.4.

If you desire rather more understanding of the theory but do not want to read the entire chapter, you should read the first part of Section 10.2, up to but not including the material on l'Hôpital's rule. This will give you a good idea of the reasons for the oft-invoked propositions labelled (10.4) and (10.5).

10.1   Linear approximations

We begin by recalling the small increments formula of Section 6.2:

$$f(x + h) - f(x) \approx h f'(x) \quad \text{when } |h| \text{ is small.}$$

The approximation is illustrated in the two panels of Figure 10.1. In each panel, the vertical distance PR is equal to $f(a + h) - f(a)$ and the distance PQ is the approximation to PR obtained by setting $x = a$ in the small increments formula.

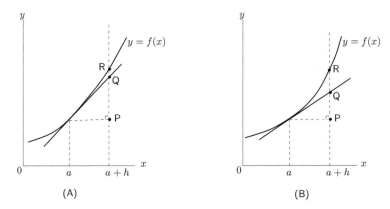

Figure 10.1: **The small-increments formula**

In Figure 10.1, PQ is quite a good approximation to PR in panel A and a terrible one in panel B. Why? One obvious way in which the function f of panel A differs from that of panel B is that the former function is not far from being linear, while the latter has a sharply increasing slope.

Now the rate of increase of the slope at a particular point is the second derivative. This suggests that in cases where the small increments formula provides a poor approximation, we can get a better one by using information on second derivatives. We shall obtain such an approximation at the end of the next section. Before turning to that, we see what we can do with first derivatives alone.

It is helpful for what follows to connect the algebra and the geometry of the small increments formula more explicitly than we have done up to now. In each panel of Figure 10.1, the linear approximation to the curve $y = f(x)$ at the point P is the tangent T, whose equation we denote by $y = L(x)$. Since T is a straight line of slope $f'(a)$,

$$L(x) = x f'(a) + c$$

for some constant c. Since T passes through the point P with coordinates $(a, f(a))$, $L(a) = f(a)$; therefore $c = f(a) - a f'(a)$, and

$$L(x) = f(a) + (x - a) f'(a).$$

To approximate the curve $y = f(x)$ by its tangent at P ($y = L(x)$) is the same as approximating $f(a + h)$ by $L(a + h) = f(a) + hf'(a)$; this brings us back to the familiar small increments formula. Notice that all of this is true whether the approximation is good, as in panel A of Figure 10.1, or bad as in panel B.

Newton's method

This is one of the classic methods of finding approximate solutions to nonlinear equations.[1] Suppose we are trying to solve the equation $f(x) = 0$. By analogy with the quadratic case, we call a value of x which satisfies the equation a **root** of the equation. Suppose we start with some value of x, say $x = a$, which we take as our first approximation to a root. Let $L(x)$ be the linear approximation to $f(x)$ at the point P with coordinates $(a, f(a))$. Then, as our second approximation to a root of $f(x) = 0$, we choose the value x such that $L(x) = 0$: call that value b.

We now describe this approximate solution b both geometrically and algebraically. Since the line $y = L(x)$ is the tangent to the curve $y = f(x)$ at the point P, the coordinates of the point where this tangent meets the x–axis are $(b, 0)$. This is illustrated in Figure 10.2. To find b in terms of algebra, recall that $L(x) = f(a) + (x - a)f'(a)$. Equating this to zero, we see that

$$b = a - \frac{f(a)}{f'(a)}. \tag{10.1}$$

We thus have **Newton's method**: starting with a first approximation a to a root of the equation $f(x) = 0$, we choose as our second approximation b, given by (10.1). This is illustrated in Figure 10.2, where b is indeed a better approximation than a.

Once the method has been applied to improve the approximation from a to b, it can be applied again starting at b to give an even closer approximation c, as in Figure 10.2. The algebra of this is as follows: define a function U (standing for 'update') by

$$U(x) = x - \frac{f(x)}{f'(x)}. \tag{10.2}$$

Then by (10.1), $b = U(a)$. Similarly, $c = U(b)$. A further approximation is $U(c)$, and so on.

When does one stop? Typically, one will have found a good approximation to a root if two conditions are met: the value taken by f is small *and* differences between successive approximations are small. The first condition will guarantee the second provided the value taken by f' is *not* particularly small.

Newton's method will not always be as successful as it is in the case above. It is clear in Figure 10.3 that, rather than getting closer to the root, the method

---

[1]Why *approximate* solutions? Because exact solutions can be found only in special cases, such as the quadratic equations of Section 4.1.

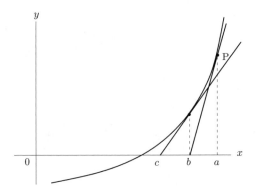

Figure 10.2: **Newton's method**

actually takes you further away. The reason for this failure is simply that the tangent at P is not a good approximation of the curve near the root. The way around this problem is to try several alternative starting points. In relatively simple examples, sketching the curve using the methods of Chapter 8 provides a good safeguard against being led astray.

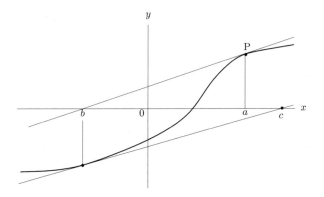

Figure 10.3: **A case where Newton's method fails**

Example Find an approximate solution of the equation

$$x^5 - 5x + 2 = 0.$$

Denote the left-hand side of the equation by $f(x)$. Then $f(x) = 2$ when $x = 0$ and $f(x) = -2$ when $x = 1$; therefore, by the intermediate value theorem of Section 6.2 (illustrated in Figure 6.5), the equation has a root between 0 and 1. Since x^5 is fairly small for all x in this range, it makes sense to choose our initial approximation a such that $-5a + 2 = 0$: thus $a = 0.4$.

To improve on this, we use the update function U of (10.2). In this case $U(x) = x - V(x)$, where

$$V(x) = \frac{x^5 - 5x + 2}{5(x^4 - 1)}.$$

In particular,

$$V(a) = \frac{(0.4)^5 \times 0.2}{(0.4)^4 - 1} = -0.0021$$

to four decimal places, and our second approximation b is 0.4021. Notice that $f(b) = 1.8 \times 10^{-6}$ and $|b - a|$ is only just over 0.002, so we are already doing pretty well. Just to try one more turn, observe that

$$V(b) = \frac{0.36 \times 10^{-6}}{b^4 - 1} = -3.7 \times 10^{-7}.$$

Since both $|f(b)|$ and $|V(b)|$ are extremely small numbers we can be confident that we have located a root correct to 3 decimal places, namely 0.402.

The solution we have approximated is only one of the roots of the equation $x^5 - 5x + 2 = 0$. In Problem 10–1 you are asked to find approximate values of the others.

Exercises

10.1.1 Find the equations of the tangents to the curve $y = x^3$ at the points where (a) $x = 2$, (b) $x = 3$.

Show in a table the approximate values given by each tangent and the true values when $x = 2.1, 2.2, \ldots, 2.9$. Comment.

10.1.2 Find an approximation to $\sqrt{2}$, correct to 3 decimal places, by applying Newton's method to the equation $x^2 - 2 = 0$. Take $x = 1.5$ as the initial approximation.

Without doing any further calculation, say what you think would happen if you applied Newton's method to the same equation, taking $x = -1.5$ as the initial approximation.

10.1.3 Show that the equation

$$x^7 - 6x + 4 = 0$$

has a root between 0 and 1. Find an initial approximation by ignoring the term x^7. Use Newton's method to find the root correct to 3 decimal places.

10.2 The mean value theorem

Th mean value theorem gives a relation between derivatives of functions and slopes of lines other than the usual one involving tangents. Being an exact result, the theorem has implications which do not concern limits or approximations. We shall discuss two of these here, and then an application to finding limits. After that we return to the main theme of this chapter.

The key result is as follows.

Mean value theorem   If f is a differentiable function and a and b are real numbers such that $a < b$, there exists a real number c such that $a < c < b$ and

$$f'(c) = \frac{f(b) - f(a)}{b - a}. \tag{10.3}$$

The theorem is illustrated in Figure 10.4. Given the chord AB, there is a point C on the curve such that the tangent at C is parallel to the line-segment AB. Denote the x–coordinate of C by c: then the slope of the tangent is $f'(c)$ and the slope of the chord is

$$(f(b) - f(a))/(b - a).$$

Equating the slopes, we see that c satisfies (10.3). In Figure 10.4, there happens to be just one real number c with the required property, but in other cases there is more than one. we encourage you to draw a diagram which illustrates this point.

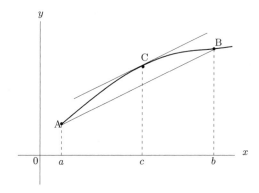

Figure 10.4: **The mean value theorem: The tangent at C is parallel to the chord** AB

In the special case where $f(a) = f(b) = 0$, the theorem says that *between any two roots of the equation $f(x) = 0$, there is at least one root of $f'(x) = 0$.* This result is known as **Rolle's theorem** and is very useful in both theoretical and practical aspects of solving equations. We say more about Rolle's theorem in the appendix to this chapter.

Application to constant functions

The derivative of a constant is zero. More interestingly, the converse is also true:

$$\text{if } f'(x) = 0 \text{ for all } x, \quad f(x) = \text{constant.} \tag{10.4}$$

This fact, which will be used to great effect in Chapter 19, is in fact a consequence of the mean value theorem.

To prove (10.4), suppose $f'(x) = 0$ for all x, and let a and b be real numbers such that $a < b$: we wish to show that $f(a) = f(b)$. By the mean value theorem there is a number c satisfying (10.3); but $f'(c) = 0$ by assumption; hence $f(a) = f(b)$.

Application to monotonic functions

We stated the following proposition in Section 7.3:

$$\text{if } f'(x) > 0 \text{ for all } x, \text{ then } f \text{ is monotonic increasing.} \tag{10.5}$$

This makes sense geometrically, though the reason why it holds is not entirely obvious: saying that $f'(x_0) > 0$ merely means that the graph $y = f(x)$ is upward-sloping when x is close to x_0, and it is not immediately clear that one can always chain upward-sloping segments together to get an upward-sloping curve.

In fact there is no need to discuss these mysteries, since (10.5) follows easily from the mean value theorem. The proof is very similar to that of (10.4). Suppose $f'(x) > 0$ for all x, and let a and b be real numbers such that $a < b$: we wish to show that $f(a) < f(b)$. By the mean value theorem there is a number c satisfying (10.3); but $f'(c) > 0$ by assumption; hence $f(a) < f(b)$.

L'Hôpital's rule

An important application of the mean value theorem is to 'indeterminate forms'. Let f and g be differentiable functions, with continuous derivatives. Suppose we want to calculate

$$\lim_{x \to a} \frac{f(x)}{g(x)}.$$

If $g(a) \neq 0$ the limit is simply $f(a)/g(a)$. If $g(a) = 0$ and $f(a) \neq 0$, no limit exists. The tricky case, or **indeterminate form**, is when $f(a) = g(a) = 0$.

The rule for dealing with this case is known as **l'Hôpital's rule**[2] and states that

$$\text{if } f(a) = g(a) = 0, \quad \lim_{x \to a} \frac{f(x)}{g(x)} = \lim_{x \to a} \frac{f'(x)}{g'(x)}. \tag{10.6}$$

---

[2]After the French aristocrat, mathematician and suspected plagiarist Guillaume de l'Hôpital (1661–1704). The rule is much used in literature of microeconomic theory, often to derive results which could have been obtained directly from the definition of a derivative. But there are occasions when l'Hôpital's rule is genuinely helpful.

We derive the rule from the mean value theorem in the case where $f(a) = g(a) = 0$ and $g'(a) \neq 0$. In this case the rule reduces to

$$\lim_{x \to a} f(x)/g(x) = f'(a)/g'(a). \tag{10.7}$$

To obtain this, we apply the mean value theorem to f and g separately: given any $x \neq a$,

$$f(x) = f(a) + (x - a)f'(p) \quad \text{and} \quad g(x) = g(a) + (x - a)g'(q)$$

for some numbers p and q between a and x. Since $f(a) = g(a) = 0$,

$$f(x)/g(x) = f'(p)/g'(q).$$

As x approaches a, so do p and q, and we obtain (10.7).

In the case just considered where $g'(a) \neq 0$, l'Hôpital's rule is applied in the form (10.7). Notice however that the general form of the rule, namely (10.6), is not restricted to this case. If $g'(a) = 0$, we need to do some work to evaluate the right-hand side of (10.6); we may even need to apply l'Hôpital's rule again, though this is not always necessary.

Example Evaluate the limit $\ell = \lim_{x \to 0} \dfrac{x - \ln(1 + x)}{x^2}$.

Writing $f(x) = x - \ln(1 + x)$, $g(x) = x^2$ and using the fact that $\ln 1 = 0$, we have $f(0) = g(0) = 0$. We may therefore apply l'Hôpital's rule:

$$\ell = \lim_{x \to 0} \frac{1 - (1 + x)^{-1}}{2x}.$$

The right-hand side still looks like an indeterminate form, but its evaluation does not require calculus: as long as x is neither 0 nor -1,

$$\frac{1 - (1 + x)^{-1}}{2x} = \frac{1 + x - 1}{2x(1 + x)} = \frac{1}{2(1 + x)}.$$

Letting $x \to 0$, we have $\ell = \frac{1}{2}$.

Back to approximations

We now take up the theme, presaged in Section 10.1, of using quadratic approximations when linear ones are inadequate. The key to the analysis is the following extension of the mean value theorem.

Second mean value theorem   If f is a twice-differentiable function and a and b are real numbers such that $a < b$, there exists a real number d such that $a < d < b$ and

$$f(b) = f(a) + (b - a)f'(a) + \tfrac{1}{2}(b - a)^2 f''(d). \tag{10.8}$$

The proof of this is outlined in the appendix to this chapter. Here we concentrate on explaining its relevance to approximations.

We begin by restating the original mean value theorem in a slightly different way. Let a, b, c be as in (10.3) and let $h = b - a$. Since c lies between a and b we can write $c = a + sh$ where $0 < s < 1$. Thus

$$f(a + h) = f(a) + hf'(a + sh), \quad \text{where } 0 < s < 1. \tag{10.9}$$

This was derived under the assumption that $h > 0$ but it also holds when $h < 0$.

We can rephrase (10.8) in the same way that we rephrased (10.3): the second mean value theorem states that, given a and h, there is a number t such that

$$f(a + h) = f(a) + hf'(a) + \tfrac{1}{2}h^2 f''(a + th), \quad \text{where } 0 < t < 1. \tag{10.10}$$

Now let us see how (10.9) and (10.10) lead to approximations. If $|h|$ is small, we may approximate the term $hf'(a + sh)$ in (10.9) by $hf'(a)$. Thus

$$f(a + h) \approx f(a) + hf'(a) \quad \text{when } |h| \text{ is small.}$$

This is the familiar small increments formula, which approximates $f(a + h)$ by a linear function of h. But now suppose that instead of (10.9) we use (10.10), approximating the term $\tfrac{1}{2}h^2 f''(a + th)$ by $\tfrac{1}{2}h^2 f''(a)$; then

$$f(a + h) \approx f(a) + hf'(a) + \tfrac{1}{2}h^2 f''(a) \quad \text{when } |h| \text{ is small,} \tag{10.11}$$

which approximates $f(a + h)$ by a *quadratic* function of h.

Setting $x = a + h$, we see that the linear approximation to the function $f(x)$ when x is close to a is

$$L(x) = f(a) + (x - a)f'(a).$$

As we stated earlier, the straight line $y = L(x)$ is the tangent to the curve $y = f(x)$ at the point $(a, f(a))$. By (10.11), the quadratic approximation to the same curve at the same point is the parabola $y = Q(x)$, where

$$Q(x) = f(a) + (x - a)f'(a) + \tfrac{1}{2}(x - a)^2 f''(a).$$

Because the quadratic approximation allows curvature, it is typically more accurate than the linear one, though not quite so simple to apply.

Example We approximate the function $f(x) = x^2 \ln x$ by linear and quadratic functions of x when x is close to 1.

Using the product rule and the fact that the derivative of $\ln x$ is $1/x$,

$$f'(x) = 2x \ln x + x \quad \text{and} \quad f''(x) = 2 \ln x + 3.$$

Since $\ln 1 = 0$ we have $f(1) = 0$, $f'(1) = 1$ and $f''(1) = 3$. Let the linear and quadratic approximations to $f(x)$ when x is close to 1 be $L(x)$ and $Q(x)$: then

$$L(x) = x - 1, \quad Q(x) = (x - 1) + \tfrac{3}{2}(x - 1)^2 = \tfrac{1}{2}(x - 1)(3x - 1).$$

The table below gives values of $L(x)$, $Q(x)$ and $f(x)$ for various values of x close to 1. Notice that Q provides a rather better approximation to f than L.

x	0.80	0.95	1.02	1.10	1.25
$L(x)$	−0.20	−0.05	0.02	0.10	0.25
$Q(x)$	−0.1400	−0.0462	0.0206	0.1150	0.3437
$f(x)$	−0.1428	−0.0463	0.0206	0.1153	0.3487

Exercises

10.2.1 If $f(x) = 5 + 6x - x^2$, $a = 1$ and $b = 3$, find the number c satisfying the conclusion of the mean value theorem.

10.2.2 If $f(x) = x^3$, $a = -1$ and $b = 1$, find the two numbers c satisfying the conclusion of the mean value theorem.

10.2.3 Use l'Hôpital's rule to evaluate

$$\lim_{x \to 0} \frac{a^x - b^x}{e^{ax} - e^{bx}}.$$

10.2.4 In the Example above, we found the linear and quadratic approximations to the function $f(x) = x^2 \ln x$ when x is close to 1. Now find the corresponding approximations when x is close to 2. Give also a numerical table similar to that in the Example for $x = 1.80$, 1.95, 2.02, 2.10 and 2.25.

10.3   Higher derivatives and Taylor's theorem

We can generalise the ideas of the last section by introducing 'higher derivatives'. Let f be a function; assuming all relevant functions are differentiable we may define the **third derivative**

$$f^{(3)}(x) = \frac{d}{dx} f''(x),$$

the **fourth derivative**

$$f^{(4)}(x) = \frac{d}{dx} f^{(3)}(x),$$

and so on. $f^{(3)}(x)$ is sometimes written as $f'''(x)$.

The notation may be adapted to still higher derivatives. A function f which can be differentiated any number of times is called a **smooth function**, and its nth derivative, for each $n \in \mathcal{N}$, is denoted by $f^{(n)}(x)$. If $f(x) = y$, then we sometimes refer to the nth derivative as

$$\frac{d^n y}{dx^n}.$$

Example Recall from the last section that if $f(x) = x^2 \ln x$ then $f'(x) = 2x \ln x + x$ and $f''(x) = 2 \ln x + 3$. This $f(x)$ is a smooth function, defined for all positive x. In particular $f^{(3)}(x) = 2/x$, $f^{(4)}(x) = -2/x^2$ and so on.

An important property of smooth functions is the following proposition.

Taylor's theorem If f is a smooth function and n is a positive integer,

$$f(a+h) = f(a) + hf'(a) + \frac{h^2}{2}f''(a) + \ldots + \frac{h^{(n-1)}}{(n-1)!}f^{n-1}(a) + \frac{h^n}{n!}f^n(a+th),$$

where t is some number such that $0 < t < 1$.

Here, as in Section 3.2, $n!$ means n–factorial, defined as $1 \times 2 \times \ldots \times n$. The special case of Taylor's theorem where $a = 0$ is called **Maclaurin's theorem**[3].

Taylor's theorem may look pretty complicated, but it is a natural generalisation of the second mean value theorem. Indeed, an argument very similar to the proof of the second mean value theorem given in the appendix to this chapter may be used to prove Taylor's theorem for any n.

Taylor approximations

We showed in the last section that the first and second mean value theorems enable us to approximate $f(a + h)$, when $|h|$ is small, by linear or quadratic functions of h. Similarly, Taylor's theorem allows us to approximate $f(a + h)$ by higher-degree polynomials.

To see how this works, notice that Taylor's theorem may be written

$$f(a + h) = S_{n-1} + R_n.$$

Here S_{n-1} is a polynomial in h of degree $n - 1$ (in other words, the highest power of h in the polynomial is $n - 1$) and R_n is the remainder term

$$\frac{h^n}{n!}f^n(a + th).$$

---

[3]Brook Taylor and Colin Maclaurin were British mathematicians of the early eighteenth century.

The $(n-1)$th order **Taylor approximation** is obtained by approximating R_n by zero (since h^n is very small for small h and sizeable n), giving

$$f(a+h) \approx S_{n-1}.$$

The nth order approximation is obtained by approximating R_n by $\dfrac{h^n}{n!} f^n(a)$, giving

$$f(a+h) \approx S_n = f(a) + hf'(a) + \frac{h^2}{2} f''(a) + \ldots + \frac{h^n}{n!} f^n(a).$$

More on the coefficients

Although we have not proved Taylor's theorem, we can give some insight into why the coefficients in the polynomial S_n are as they are, and why the polynomial gives a good approximation to $f(a+h)$ for small h.

Consider the fourth-order approximation, which we may write as

$$S_4(h) = c_0 + c_1 h + c_2 h^2 + c_3 h^3 + c_4 h^4,$$

where

$$c_0 = f(a), \quad c_1 = f'(a), \quad c_2 = f''(a)/2, \quad c_3 = f^{(3)}(a)/6 \text{ and } c_4 = f^{(4)}(a)/24.$$

Differentiating, we have

$$\begin{aligned}
S_4'(h) &= c_1 + 2c_2 h + 3c_3 h^2 + 4c_4 h^3, \\
S_4''(h) &= 2c_2 + 6c_3 h + 12c_4 h^2, \\
S_4^{(3)}(h) &= 6c_3 + 24c_4 h, \\
S_4^{(4)}(h) &= 24c_4.
\end{aligned}$$

Setting $h = 0$, we see that

$$S_4(0) = c_0 = f(a), \qquad S_4'(0) = c_1 = f'(a), \qquad S_4''(0) = 2c_2 = f''(a),$$

$$S_4^{(3)}(0) = 6c_3 = f^{(3)}(a) \qquad \text{and} \qquad S_4^{(4)}(0) = 24c_4 = f^{(4)}(a).$$

What all this means in words is that if we consider $f(a+h)$ and $S_4(h)$ as functions of h, the values of the two functions, and those of their first four derivatives, coincide when $h = 0$.

Obviously, this generalises. For any positive integer n, $S_n(h)$ is the nth-degree polynomial whose value and first n derivatives coincide at $h = 0$ with those of $f(a+h)$. It is therefore not surprising that for sizeable n and small h, $S_n(h)$ is close to $f(a+h)$.

Exercises

10.3.1 Suppose
$$f(x) = x^4 - 3x^3 + 8x^2 + 5x - 2.$$
Find the first four derivatives. What can you say about all the derivatives higher than the fourth?

Evaluate the first four derivatives at $x = 0$. What do you notice? Try to formulate a general result.

10.3.2 In the Example at the end of Section 10.2, we found the linear and quadratic approximations to the function $f(x) = x^2 \ln x$ when x is close to 1. Now find the corresponding third-order approximation and the corresponding row of the numerical table.

10.4   Taylor series

So far, we have considered Taylor's theorem as an approximation device in the sense that the remainder term R_n becomes very small when $|h|$ is small. A different kind of approximation using Taylor's theorem focuses on the case where n is large. It is true in many cases that $R_n \to 0$ as $n \to \infty$, even when h is not particularly small in absolute value. In such cases we have the **Taylor series expansion** of $f(a + h)$:

$$f(a + h) = f(a) + hf'(a) + \frac{h^2}{2!}f''(a) + \frac{h^3}{3!}f^{(3)}(a) + \cdots,$$

where the right hand side is to be interpreted as a convergent series in the sense of Section 5.2.

The special case of the Taylor series expansion when $a = 0$ is called the **Maclaurin expansion** of f. We now derive some examples of this, without any attempt at verifying that $R_n \to 0$ as $n \to \infty$.

The exponential function

If $f(x) = e^x$ then $f(x) = f'(x) = \cdots = f^{(n)}(x) = e^x$, whence
$$f(0) = f'(0) = \cdots = f^{(n)}(0) = 1.$$
The Maclaurin expansion is therefore
$$e^x = 1 + x + \frac{x^2}{2!} + \cdots + \frac{x^n}{n!} + \cdots$$
This may be shown to be valid for every real number x. Replacing x by $-x$ in the above, we obtain
$$e^{-x} = 1 - x + \frac{x^2}{2!} - \cdots + (-1)^n \frac{x^n}{n!} + \cdots$$
for all $x \in \mathcal{R}$.

Natural logarithms

The first point to notice is that there is no Maclaurin series expansion for $\ln x$, since $\ln x$ is defined only when $x > 0$. The standard Maclaurin expansion relating to natural logarithms is therefore the one for the function

$$f(x) = \ln(1 + x).$$

We have $f'(x) = (1 + x)^{-1}$, $f''(x) = -(1 + x)^{-2}$, $f^{(3)}(x) = 2(1 + x)^{-3}$, $f^{(4)}(x) = -(3!)(1 + x)^{-4}$ and so on. Hence

$$f'(0) = 1, \quad \frac{f''(0)}{2} = -\frac{1}{2}, \quad \frac{f^{(3)}(0)}{3!} = \frac{1}{3}, \quad \frac{f^{(4)}(0)}{4!} = -\frac{1}{4}$$

and so on; notice also that $f(0) = \ln 1 = 0$. The Maclaurin expansion is therefore

$$\ln(1 + x) = x - \frac{x^2}{2} + \frac{x^3}{3} - \ldots + (-1)^{n+1}\frac{x^n}{n} + \ldots$$

It may be shown that the expansion is valid when $-1 < x \leq 1$.

Replacing x by $-x$, we have

$$\ln(1 - x) = -x - \frac{x^2}{2} - \frac{x^3}{3} - \ldots - \frac{x^n}{n} - \ldots$$

The expansion is valid when $-1 \leq x < 1$.

These expansions are intimately related to the 'economist's favourite approximation' of Section 9.2:

$$\ln(1 + h) \approx h \quad \text{if } |h| \text{ is small.}$$

This can be obtained from the Maclaurin expansion above, using the fact that h^2, h^3 and so on are very small in absolute value when $|h|$ is small.

More generally, if $0 < x < \frac{1}{2}$ just a few terms of the Maclaurin expansion will give a good approximation to $\ln(1 + x)$, and similarly for $\ln(1 - x)$. The former approximation is particularly good, since the terms of the expansion alternate in sign; thus omitted terms partly compensate for each other.

Binomial series

Consider the function

$$f(x) = (1 + x)^c,$$

where c is a constant. Here $f'(x) = c(1 + x)^{c-1}$,

$$f''(x) = c(c - 1)(1 + x)^{c-2}, \quad f^{(3)}(x) = c(c - 1)(c - 2)(1 + x)^{c-3}$$

and so on. Setting

$$a_1 = c, \quad a_2 = \frac{c - 1}{2}, \quad a_3 = \frac{c - 2}{3}, \quad \ldots \tag{10.12}$$

we see that

$$f'(0) = a_1, \quad \frac{f''(0)}{2} = a_1 a_2, \quad \frac{f^{(3)}(0)}{3!} = a_1 a_2 a_3$$

and so on. Also, $f(0) = 1$; the Maclaurin expansion is therefore

$$(1+x)^c = 1 + a_1 x + a_1 a_2 x^2 + a_1 a_2 a_3 x^3 + \ldots \tag{10.13}$$

The expansion is valid when $-1 < x < 1$. The series expansion given by (10.12) and (10.13) is called a **binomial series**.

Two special cases are worth noting. The first is where $c = -1$. In that case $a_n = -1$ for every positive integer n. Hence by (10.13),

$$\frac{1}{1+x} = 1 - x + x^2 - \ldots + (-1)^n x^n + \ldots \quad \text{whenever } |x| < 1.$$

Replacing x by $-x$, we have

$$\frac{1}{1-x} = 1 + x + x^2 + \ldots + x^n + \ldots \quad \text{whenever } |x| < 1.$$

This is the geometric series formula which we first encountered in Section 5.2 and applied to economics in Section 5.3.

The second important special case of (10.12) and (10.13) is where c is equal to a positive integer m. Then $a_{m+1} = 0$, which implies that the coefficient of x^n on the right hand side of (10.12) is zero for all $n > m$. The Maclaurin expansion therefore consists of only a finite number of terms:

$$(1+x)^m = 1 + mx + \frac{m(m-1)}{2!}x^2 + \frac{m(m-1)(m-2)}{3!}x^3 + \ldots + x^m.$$

This result, which is valid for every positive integer m **and every real number** x, is called the **binomial theorem**.

The theorem may be written in the form

$$(1+x)^m = 1 + \binom{m}{1}x + \binom{m}{2}x^2 + \ldots + \binom{m}{r}x^r + \ldots + x^m,$$

where

$$\binom{m}{r} = \frac{m(m-1)\ldots(m+1-r)}{r!} = \frac{m!}{r!(m-r)!}.$$

Some readers may know, for example from statistics courses, that $\binom{m}{r}$ is the number of ways of choosing r objects from m, without replacement and without regard to order. This fact may be used to prove the binomial theorem without the use of calculus. It is however worth knowing that the binomial theorem is — among other things — a special case of a Maclaurin expansion.

Exercises

10.4.1 (a) Obtain the value of e correct to 3 decimal places by taking a sufficiently large number of terms of the power series for e^x.

(b) The series for $\ln(1 + x)$ is to be used to evaluate $\ln 1.1$. Find the values obtained by taking one, two, and three terms of the series. Compare these with the true value and comment on your results.

10.4.2 Use the series for e^x to show that

$$\frac{e^x - 1}{x} \approx 1 + \tfrac{1}{2}x \quad \text{when } |x| \text{ is small.}$$

10.4.3 (a) Use the series for e^x to show that $xe^{-x} \to 0$ as $x \to \infty$. Hence sketch the graph of $y = xe^{-x}$. [You were asked to provide the rest of the information required to sketch the curve in Exercise 9.2.4.]

(b) Show also that $x^2 e^{-x} \to 0$ as $x \to \infty$. Try to formulate a general result.

10.4.4 Use the series for $\ln(1 + x)$ and $\ln(1 - x)$ to obtain a series expansion for $\ln \dfrac{1 + x}{1 - x}$. For what values of x is the expansion valid? By putting $x = \tfrac{1}{2}$ and taking a sufficiently large number of terms of the series, find $\ln 3$ correct to 3 decimal places.

10.4.5 Use the series given in the text to obtain the series for

(a) e^{2x}, (b) $\ln(1 + 3x)$, (c) $(1 + x)^{\frac{1}{2}}$, (d) $(1 - 5x)^{-1}$.

In each case, give the first three terms, the general term and the range of values of x for which the expansion is valid.

10.4.6 Use the binomial theorem to write down the expansions of

(a) $(1 + x)^3$, (b) $(1 + x)^4$, (c) $(1 - 2x)^3$, (d) $(x + y)^4$.

Problems on Chapter 10

10–1. Explain how Rolle's theorem can be used to obtain a restriction on the number of roots of the polynomial equation $f(x) = 0$ when

(i) $f'(x) = 0$ has no roots;

(ii) $f'(x) = 0$ has one root;

(iii) $f'(x) = 0$ has two distinct roots.

Try to formulate a general result.

10–2. As in the Example of Section 10.1, consider the equation

$$x^5 - 5x + 2 = 0.$$

(i) By sketching the graph of the left-hand side, show that this equation has exactly three real roots x_1, x_2, x_3, where $x_1 < -1$ and $0 < x_2 < 1 < x_3$.

(ii) We showed in Section 10.1 that $x_2 = 0.402$ to 3 decimal places. Using your sketch and a *small* amount of arithmetic (hint: $1.5^4 \approx 5$), show that x_1 is between -2 and -1.5, while x_3 is between 1 and 1.5. Then use Newton's method to approximate x_1 and x_3, each to 3 decimal places.

(iii) The fact that the equation has exactly three roots can be obtained without any curve-sketching, by using the result of Problem 10–1 and the intermediate value theorem of Section 6.2. Fill in the details.

10–3. The CES production function is

$$Y = A[\delta K^\gamma + (1 - \delta)L^\gamma]^{1/\gamma},$$

where A, γ, δ are constants such that $A > 0$, $\gamma < 1$ and $0 < \delta < 1$. Show that $\ln(Y/A)$ can be expressed in the form $m(\gamma)/n(\gamma)$ where $m(0) = n(0) = 0$. Using l'Hôpital's rule, or otherwise, show that

$$\lim_{\gamma \to 0} \ln \frac{Y}{A} = \delta \ln K + (1 - \delta) \ln L.$$

Hence find $\lim_{\gamma \to 0} Y$.

[The reason for the name CES, which stands for constant elasticity of substitution, will be explained in Problem 17–2.]

10–4. This problem is about wage 'differentials', in the sense of labour economics and industrial relations. These differentials have nothing to do with differential calculus.

Suppose workers of grade 1 receive the wage w_1 and workers of grade 2 receive the wage w_2, where $w_1 < w_2$. The differential between the two wages may be defined in three non-equivalent ways: as the difference between the wages as a proportion of the lower wage ($D_a = (w_2 - w_1)/w_1$), the difference between the wages as a proportion of the higher wage ($D_b = (w_2 - w_1)/w_2$) or the difference between the natural logarithms of the wages ($D_c = \ln w_2 - \ln w_1$). Show that if $D_b = x$ then

$$D_a = x + x^2 + x^3 + \dots \quad \text{and} \quad D_c = x + \frac{x^2}{2} + \frac{x^3}{3} + \dots.$$

Hence show that $D_b < D_c < D_a$.

Appendix to Chapter 10

As in the appendices to earlier chapters, our object is to give more theoretical backbone to the mathematics of the chapter. As usual, our argument will not be completely rigorous, as it will rely in part on appeals to geometric intuition. We do however provide a much fuller account of the reasons underlying the first and second mean value theorems than we did in Section 10.2.

We begin by recalling Rolle's theorem, the special case of the mean value theorem where $f(a) = f(b) = 0$:

Rolle's theorem   If f is a differentiable function, and a and b are real numbers such that $a < b$ and $f(a) = f(b) = 0$, there exists a real number c such that $a < c < b$ and $f'(c) = 0$.

Rolle's theorem may be illustrated by a diagram similar to the one we drew to illustrate the mean value theorem (Figure 10.4), but simpler. *You are strongly encouraged to draw such a diagram.* Having done so, you will find it easy to appreciate the logic behind Rolle's theorem: since the function $f(x)$ takes the same value at $x = a$ and $x = b$, it must have a critical point for some x between a and b.

Although Rolle's theorem looks like (and is) a very special case of the mean value theorem, the latter can in fact be derived from the former. We shall now go through this proof of the mean value theorem. We do this for two reasons. First, Rolle's theorem is such a simple and intuitive result that it is interesting to see how much can be extracted from it. Second, the argument used here is one that can be adapted to prove many results, including the second mean value theorem (see below) and Taylor's theorem (though we do not go that far).

Let f, a and b be as in the statement of the mean value theorem: f is a differentiable function, and a, b are real numbers such that $a < b$. We wish to find a real number c such that $a < c < b$ and

$$f'(c) = \frac{f(b) - f(a)}{b - a}. \tag{10.3}$$

To do this, we define the function

$$R(x) = f(x) - f(a) - K(x - a),$$

where K is a constant. Obviously $R(a) = 0$; also, the constant K can be chosen to make $R(b) = 0$, by letting

$$K = (b - a)^{-1}(f(b) - f(a)).$$

Since $R(a) = R(b) = 0$ we may apply Rolle's theorem, obtaining a real number c such that $a < c < b$ and $R'(c) = 0$. Hence

$$K = f'(c).$$

Equating our two expressions for K, we see that c satisfies (10.3), and the mean value theorem is proved.

Proof of the second mean value theorem

A slightly more complicated version of the argument just used to prove the mean value theorem may also be used to prove the second mean value theorem, which we now recall.

Let f be a twice-differentiable function, and let a and b be real numbers such that $a < b$. The theorem says that there is a real number d such that $a < d < b$ and

$$f(b) = f(a) + (b-a)f'(a) + \tfrac{1}{2}(b-a)^2 f''(d). \tag{10.8}$$

To prove this, we define the function

$$R(x) = f(x) - f(a) - (x-a)f'(a) - K(x-a)^2,$$

where K is a constant. Obviously $R(a) = 0$ and $R'(a) = 0$; also, the constant K can be chosen to make $R(b) = 0$, by letting

$$K = (b-a)^{-2}\left(f(b) - f(a) - (b-a)f'(a)\right). \tag{10.14}$$

Since $R(a) = R(b) = 0$ we may apply Rolle's theorem, obtaining a real number c such that $a < c < b$ and $R'(c) = 0$. And since $R'(a) = R'(c) = 0$ we may apply Rolle's theorem *again*, with R' and c replacing R and b.

This gives us a real number d such that $a < d < c < b$ and $R''(d) = 0$. Hence $f''(d) = 2K$. Writing the left-hand side of (10.14) as $\tfrac{1}{2}f''(d)$, we see that d satisfies (10.8): the second mean value theorem is proved.

Chapter 11

MATRIX ALGEBRA

In this chapter and the two that follow it we explain the rudiments of a branch of mathematics called **linear algebra**.

The starting problem of linear algebra is to solve a system of m simultaneous linear equations in n unknowns, but the theory and applications range far beyond this. In particular, linear algebra is an essential tool in the differential calculus of several variables, in the theory of differential equations and in statistics and econometrics. We shall give a thorough account of how to solve systems of linear equations in Chapter 12; differential calculus of several variables will be covered in Chapters 14–18, and differential equations introduced in Chapters 21 and 24. For this chapter, we are concerned with preliminary matters of definition and rules of operation.

Our initial objective is to introduce a notation which is useful for dealing with several variables at the same time. This leads us to work with arrays of numbers known as vectors and matrices, and to explain the laws of arithmetic for these arrays. We start with vectors in Section 11.1, and devote the remaining three sections to matrices. Matrices are somewhat more complicated than vectors, since they may be viewed from two different perspectives: as arrays in their own right, and as mappings transforming vectors into other vectors.

When you have studied this chapter you will be able to:

- perform on vectors the basic operations of addition and multiplication by scalars, and interpret these operations geometrically;

- add and multiply matrices;

- test sets of vectors for linear dependence, in simple cases;

- formulate systems of linear equations in matrix notation.

11.1 Vectors

A **vector** is a list of numbers. For reasons that will become clear in the next section, it is convenient to write vectors as columns. Thus

$$\begin{bmatrix} 3 \\ 2 \end{bmatrix}, \quad \begin{bmatrix} -4 \\ 5 \\ -7 \\ 8 \end{bmatrix}, \quad \begin{bmatrix} 0 \\ -6 \\ 9 \end{bmatrix}$$

are all vectors.

The number in the ith position of the vector $\mathbf{a}$ is denoted by a_i and is referred to as the ith **component** of $\mathbf{a}$. Thus if $\mathbf{a}$ is the middle one of the three vectors above, then $\mathbf{a}$ has four components, and $a_3 = -7$. Here, and for the rest of this book, we employ the widely-used convention of denoting vectors by lower case letters in bold Roman type ($\mathbf{a}, \mathbf{b}, \mathbf{x}$ and so on), and their components by the correspondng letters in italic type.

In the examples just given, components of vectors were integers. This is too restrictive for the operations which we want to perform, and in what follows we shall allow all real numbers to be components of vectors. More generally, books on linear algebra use the term **scalar** to denote a member of the number system from which components of vectors are drawn. For our purposes a scalar is the same as a real number.

A vector with n components is called an n–vector. In this chapter we shall use the symbol $\mathcal{R}^n$ to mean the set of all n–vectors, with real numbers as components. This differs from the notation of Chapter 3 only in that we are now writing members of $\mathcal{R}^n$ as columns rather than rows.

The order of the components of a vector matters: thus

$$\begin{bmatrix} 2 \\ 0 \\ -1 \end{bmatrix} \quad \text{and} \quad \begin{bmatrix} -1 \\ 2 \\ 0 \end{bmatrix}$$

are different vectors. Two vectors are equal if and only if they have the same number of components and corresponding components are equal. Thus, if $\mathbf{x}$ and $\mathbf{y}$ are both n–vectors, the single vector equation

$$\mathbf{x} = \mathbf{y}$$

is equivalent to the n scalar equations

$$x_i = y_i \ \text{ for } i = 1, 2, \ldots, n.$$

Vector arithmetic

The simplest operations of vector arithmetic are addition and multiplication by a scalar.

Addition of two vectors **a** and **b** can be performed when and only when **a** and **b** have the same number of components and is performed component by component: for example

$$\begin{bmatrix} 4 \\ 5 \\ 6 \end{bmatrix} + \begin{bmatrix} 3 \\ -1 \\ 2 \end{bmatrix} = \begin{bmatrix} 7 \\ 4 \\ 8 \end{bmatrix}.$$

Multiplication by a scalar is also performed component by component:

$$2 \begin{bmatrix} 4 \\ 5 \\ 6 \end{bmatrix} = \begin{bmatrix} 8 \\ 10 \\ 12 \end{bmatrix}, \quad (-3) \begin{bmatrix} 3 \\ -1 \\ 2 \end{bmatrix} = \begin{bmatrix} -9 \\ 3 \\ -6 \end{bmatrix}.$$

The vector $(-1)\mathbf{a}$ is often denoted by $-\mathbf{a}$.

As in Chapter 1 we can represent members of $\mathcal{R}^2$ by points in the plane. The operations of addition and multiplication by scalars are interpreted geometrically as follows. To obtain $\mathbf{a} + \mathbf{b}$ from **a** and **b**, complete the parallelogram. To obtain $2\mathbf{a}$ from **a**, stretch the line from the origin to **a** by a factor of 2. To obtain $-\mathbf{b}$ from **b**, reflect **b** in the origin. All of this is depicted in Figure 11.1.

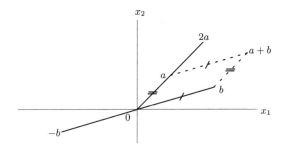

Figure 11.1: **Vector arithmetic**

Combined operations

The operations of addition and multiplication by a scalar are put together in the obvious way:

$$4 \begin{bmatrix} 1 \\ 3 \end{bmatrix} + 5 \begin{bmatrix} 2 \\ 1 \end{bmatrix} = \begin{bmatrix} 4 \\ 12 \end{bmatrix} + \begin{bmatrix} 10 \\ 5 \end{bmatrix} = \begin{bmatrix} 14 \\ 17 \end{bmatrix}.$$

In particular, subtraction is defined by letting

$$\mathbf{a} - \mathbf{b} = \mathbf{a} + (-\mathbf{b}).$$

The zero n–vector, whose components are all zero, is denoted by $\mathbf{0}_n$, or simply **0** if there is no ambiguity about n. $\mathbf{0}_2$ is represented by the origin in Figure 11.1.

The following laws of vector arithmetic always hold:

(a) $\mathbf{a} + \mathbf{b} = \mathbf{b} + \mathbf{a}.$

(b) $(\mathbf{a} + \mathbf{b}) + \mathbf{c} = \mathbf{a} + (\mathbf{b} + \mathbf{c}).$

(c) $\lambda(\mathbf{a} + \mathbf{b}) = \lambda\mathbf{a} + \lambda\mathbf{b}.$

(d) $(\lambda + \mu)\mathbf{a} = \lambda\mathbf{a} + \mu\mathbf{a}.$

(e) $\lambda(\mu\mathbf{a}) = \mu(\lambda\mathbf{a}) = (\lambda\mu)\mathbf{a}.$

These laws are not worth learning by heart: the important thing to notice is the strong analogy with ordinary arithmetic.

Laws (a) and (b) have names: (a) is called the **commutative law** of vector addition, and (b) the **associative law** of vector addition. The associative law is useful because it makes unambiguous expressions like

$$\mathbf{a} + \mathbf{b} + \mathbf{c} + \mathbf{d} + \mathbf{e}.$$

Finally, note in connection with the last three laws the liberal use of Greek letters[1] for scalars, which is common in vector algebra.

Given the laws, it is easy to calculate expressions like $\alpha\mathbf{a} - \beta\mathbf{b} + \gamma\mathbf{c}$; for example

$$4\begin{bmatrix} 2 \\ 1 \\ 3 \end{bmatrix} - 5\begin{bmatrix} -1 \\ 2 \\ 1 \end{bmatrix} + 3\begin{bmatrix} 3 \\ 1 \\ -1 \end{bmatrix} = \begin{bmatrix} 8 + 5 + 9 \\ 4 - 10 + 3 \\ 12 - 5 - 3 \end{bmatrix} = \begin{bmatrix} 22 \\ -3 \\ 4 \end{bmatrix}.$$

Linear dependence

Expressions such as $\mathbf{a} + \mathbf{b}$ and $2\mathbf{a} - 3\mathbf{b}$ are examples of **linear combinations** of the vectors $\mathbf{a}$ and $\mathbf{b}$. Generally, a linear combination of two vectors $\mathbf{a}$ and $\mathbf{b}$ is a vector of the form $\alpha\mathbf{a} + \beta\mathbf{b}$, where α and β are scalars; a linear combination of four vectors $\mathbf{a}, \mathbf{b}, \mathbf{c}, \mathbf{d}$ is a vector of the form

$$\alpha\mathbf{a} + \beta\mathbf{b} + \gamma\mathbf{c} + \delta\mathbf{d}$$

where $\alpha, \beta, \gamma, \delta$ are scalars; and so on. Notice that, in this definition, the scalars α, β and so on are allowed to be zero; for example the vectors $3\mathbf{a} + \mathbf{b}$, $\mathbf{b} - \mathbf{c}$ and $-\mathbf{d}$ are all linear combinations of the four vectors $\mathbf{a}, \mathbf{b}, \mathbf{c}, \mathbf{d}$.

Suppose we have a set of k n–vectors, say $\mathbf{b}^1, \mathbf{b}^2, \ldots, \mathbf{b}^k$.[2] We say that the vectors $\mathbf{b}^1, \mathbf{b}^2, \ldots, \mathbf{b}^k$ are **linearly dependent** if it is possible to express one of them as a linear combination of the others. We say that the vectors $\mathbf{b}^1, \mathbf{b}^2, \ldots, \mathbf{b}^k$ are **linearly independent** if they are not linearly dependent;

---

[1] In this instance, λ (lambda) and μ (mu).

[2] The superscripts $1, 2, \ldots, k$ are not powers but simply labels to denote different vectors. The use of superscripts when listing vectors helps to avoid confusion with labelling the components of a single vector, for which subscripts are usually employed.

thus $\mathbf{b}^1, \mathbf{b}^2, \ldots, \mathbf{b}^k$ are linearly independent if none of the vectors can be expressed as a linear combination of the others.

A simple criterion for linear dependence is the following: $\mathbf{b}^1, \mathbf{b}^2, \ldots, \mathbf{b}^k$ are linearly dependent if and only if there exist scalars $\alpha_1, \alpha_2, \ldots, \alpha_k$, *not all zero*, such that

$$\alpha_1 \mathbf{b}^1 + \alpha_2 \mathbf{b}^2 + \ldots + \alpha_k \mathbf{b}^k = \mathbf{0}. \tag{11.1}$$

To establish this criterion in the case of three vectors $\mathbf{a}, \mathbf{b}, \mathbf{c}$, suppose first that the vectors are linearly dependent. Then one of them can be written as a linear combination of the others. Supposing for definiteness that $\mathbf{a}$ is a linear combination of $\mathbf{b}$ and $\mathbf{c}$, we have $\mathbf{a} = \lambda \mathbf{b} + \mu \mathbf{c}$ for some scalars λ and μ. Then

$$(-1)\mathbf{a} + \lambda \mathbf{b} + \mu \mathbf{c} = \mathbf{0},$$

and (11.1) holds with scalars $-1, \lambda, \mu$, which are not all zero since one of them is -1. Conversely, suppose there are scalars α, β, γ, not all zero, such that

$$\alpha \mathbf{a} + \beta \mathbf{b} + \gamma \mathbf{c} = \mathbf{0}.$$

Suppose for definiteness that $\alpha \neq 0$: then

$$\mathbf{a} = \lambda \mathbf{b} + \mu \mathbf{c},$$

where $\lambda = -\beta/\alpha$ and $\mu = -\gamma/\alpha$; therefore $\mathbf{a}, \mathbf{b}, \mathbf{c}$ are linearly dependent.

This criterion provides a simple way of testing whether a given set of vectors are linearly dependent or independent. Start with a relation of the form (11.1). If you can show that the only scalars $\alpha_1, \alpha_2, \ldots, \alpha_k$ which satisfy this are all zero, then the vectors are linearly independent; if you can find $\alpha_1, \alpha_2, \ldots, \alpha_k$ which satisfy (11.1) and are *not* all zero, then the vectors are linearly dependent.

To see the test in action, consider the vectors

$$\mathbf{a} = \begin{bmatrix} 2 \\ 1 \end{bmatrix} \quad \mathbf{b} = \begin{bmatrix} 1 \\ 2 \end{bmatrix}, \quad \mathbf{c} = \begin{bmatrix} 1 \\ 1 \end{bmatrix}.$$

Here $\mathbf{a}$ and $\mathbf{b}$ are linearly independent, since the only scalars α and β for which $2\alpha + \beta$ and $\alpha + 2\beta$ are both zero are given by $\alpha = \beta = 0$. The three vectors $\mathbf{a}, \mathbf{b}, \mathbf{c}$ are linearly dependent, since $\mathbf{a} + \mathbf{b} - 3\mathbf{c} = \mathbf{0}$.

Exercises

11.1.1 The components of the 3–vector $\mathbf{a}$ are Anne's weekly expenditures on food, clothing and housing. The components of the 3–vector $\mathbf{b}$ are Bill's weekly expenditures on food, clothing and housing. Interpret the vectors $\mathbf{a} + \mathbf{b}$ and $52\mathbf{a}$.

11.1.2 If

$$\mathbf{a} = \begin{bmatrix} 2 \\ 2 \end{bmatrix} \quad \text{and} \quad \mathbf{b} = \begin{bmatrix} 1 \\ 3 \end{bmatrix},$$

find $\mathbf{a} + \mathbf{b}$, $3\mathbf{a}$, $-4\mathbf{b}$ and $3\mathbf{a} - 4\mathbf{b}$. Show the points representing $\mathbf{a}$, $\mathbf{b}$, $\mathbf{a} + \mathbf{b}$, $3\mathbf{a}$, $-4\mathbf{b}$ and $3\mathbf{a} - 4\mathbf{b}$ in a plane with axes labelled x_1, x_2.

11.1.3 Suppose

$$\mathbf{x} = \begin{bmatrix} 3 \\ 2q \\ 6 \end{bmatrix}, \quad \mathbf{y} = \begin{bmatrix} p+2 \\ -5 \\ 3r \end{bmatrix}.$$

If $\mathbf{x} = 2\mathbf{y}$, find p, q and r.

11.1.4 Which of the following sets of vectors are linearly dependent?

(a) $\begin{bmatrix} 1 \\ 0 \end{bmatrix}, \begin{bmatrix} 0 \\ 1 \end{bmatrix}, \begin{bmatrix} 1 \\ 1 \end{bmatrix}.$ (b) $\begin{bmatrix} 0 \\ 1 \\ 1 \end{bmatrix}, \begin{bmatrix} 1 \\ 0 \\ 1 \end{bmatrix}, \begin{bmatrix} 1 \\ 1 \\ 0 \end{bmatrix}.$

(c) $\begin{bmatrix} 1 \\ 2 \\ 3 \end{bmatrix}, \begin{bmatrix} 4 \\ 5 \\ 6 \end{bmatrix}, \begin{bmatrix} 7 \\ 8 \\ 9 \end{bmatrix}.$ (d) $\begin{bmatrix} 13 \\ 7 \\ 9 \\ 2 \end{bmatrix}, \begin{bmatrix} 0 \\ 0 \\ 0 \\ 0 \end{bmatrix}, \begin{bmatrix} 3 \\ -2 \\ 5 \\ 8 \end{bmatrix}.$

11.2 Matrices

A **matrix**[3] is a rectangular array of numbers. For example,

$$\begin{bmatrix} 1 & 2 & 0 \\ 5 & 1 & 9 \end{bmatrix}$$

is a matrix with 2 rows and 3 columns. In general, a matrix with m rows and n columns is called an $m \times n$ matrix.[4] Matrices, like vectors, will be denoted by letters in bold Roman type; we shall normally use upper-case letters for matrices and lower-case ones for vectors.

The numbers that form the matrix are called its **entries** or **elements**. The entry in the ith row and jth column of a matrix $\mathbf{A}$ is called the (i, j) entry of $\mathbf{A}$: the standard notation for this entry is a_{ij}. Thus if

$$\mathbf{A} = \begin{bmatrix} 1 & 2 & 6 & 7 \\ 9 & 1 & 8 & 0 \\ 4 & 2 & 5 & 3 \end{bmatrix}$$

then $a_{12} = 2$, $a_{24} = 0$, the $(3, 3)$ entry of $\mathbf{A}$ is 5, and so on.

The order in which the entries enter a matrix does matter: two matrices $\mathbf{A}$ and $\mathbf{B}$ are said to be equal ($\mathbf{A} = \mathbf{B}$) only if they are exactly the same, with the same number of rows, the same number of columns and the same entries in the same order.

$$\begin{bmatrix} 1 & 2 & 0 \\ 5 & 1 & 9 \end{bmatrix}$$

is *not* the same 2×3 matrix as

$$\begin{bmatrix} 2 & 1 & 9 \\ 1 & 5 & 0 \end{bmatrix}$$

---

[3]The plural of matrix is matrices, with the c pronounced as in 'peace'.
[4]The $\times$ in '$m \times n$ matrix' is usually pronounced 'by'.

since the entries have been placed in different positions.

As with vectors, the entries of a matrix can be any real numbers and, again as with vectors, the term scalar is used to denote a member of the number system from which entries of matrices are drawn.

The operations of matrix addition, and multiplication of a matrix by a scalar, are defined in a fashion analogous to that for vectors. Addition of two matrices $\mathbf{A}$ and $\mathbf{B}$ can be performed when and only when $\mathbf{A}$ and $\mathbf{B}$ have the same number of rows and the same number of columns, and is performed entry by entry; multiplication by a scalar is also performed entry by entry. The two kinds of operation are put together in the obvious way:

$$2 \begin{bmatrix} 1 & 6 \\ 3 & -5 \end{bmatrix} + 3 \begin{bmatrix} 2 & -4 \\ 1 & 6 \end{bmatrix} = \begin{bmatrix} 8 & 0 \\ 9 & 8 \end{bmatrix}.$$

In particular, subtraction is defined by letting

$$-\mathbf{A} = (-1)\mathbf{A}, \quad \mathbf{A} - \mathbf{B} = \mathbf{A} + (-\mathbf{B}).$$

The $m \times n$ matrix whose entries are all zero is called the $m \times n$ **zero matrix** and is denoted by $\mathbf{O}_{mn}$, or simply $\mathbf{O}$ if there is no ambiguity about m and n. If $\mathbf{A}$ is any $m \times n$ matrix, then $\mathbf{A} - \mathbf{A} = \mathbf{O}$. Notice that we also obtain $\mathbf{O}_{mn}$ when we multiply any $m \times n$ matrix by the scalar 0. In short, the matrix $\mathbf{O}$ plays the same role for matrices that the number 0 does in ordinary arithmetic.

Again as with vectors, the operations of addition and multiplication by scalars satisfy laws similar to those of ordinary arithmetic. In particular we have the commutative law of matrix addition

$$\mathbf{A} + \mathbf{B} = \mathbf{B} + \mathbf{A}$$

and the associative law of matrix addition

$$(\mathbf{A} + \mathbf{B}) + \mathbf{C} = \mathbf{A} + (\mathbf{B} + \mathbf{C});$$

the latter makes expressions like $\mathbf{A} + \mathbf{B} + \mathbf{C} + \mathbf{D} + \mathbf{E}$ unambiguous.

Given the laws, it is easy to calculate expressions of the form

$$\alpha \mathbf{A} + \beta \mathbf{B} + \gamma \mathbf{C}.$$

Thus, our previous example of matrix arithmetic may be extended as follows:

$$2 \begin{bmatrix} 1 & 6 \\ 3 & -5 \end{bmatrix} + 3 \begin{bmatrix} 2 & -4 \\ 1 & 6 \end{bmatrix} - 4 \begin{bmatrix} 1 & -3 \\ -1 & 2 \end{bmatrix}$$

$$= \begin{bmatrix} 8 & 0 \\ 9 & 8 \end{bmatrix} + \begin{bmatrix} -4 & 12 \\ 4 & -8 \end{bmatrix} = \begin{bmatrix} 4 & 12 \\ 13 & 0 \end{bmatrix}.$$

Up to now, the only difference between matrices and vectors has been the arrangement of the numbers that go into them. We now introduce another operation that leads us to view the relation between vectors and matrices in a very different way.

Matrix-vector multiplication

We start with an example. Given the 2×3 matrix

$$\mathbf{A} = \begin{bmatrix} 6 & 8 & 7 \\ 5 & 1 & 9 \end{bmatrix},$$

and any 3–vector $\mathbf{x}$, we define the 2–vector $\mathbf{Ax}$ as follows:

$$\begin{bmatrix} 6 & 8 & 7 \\ 5 & 1 & 9 \end{bmatrix} \begin{bmatrix} x_1 \\ x_2 \\ x_3 \end{bmatrix} = \begin{bmatrix} 6x_1 + 8x_2 + 7x_3 \\ 5x_1 + x_2 + 9x_3 \end{bmatrix}. \tag{11.2}$$

This definition is helpful in two ways. First, consider the system of two linear equations in three unknowns

$$6x_1 + 8x_2 + 7x_3 = -3$$
$$5x_1 + x_2 + 9x_3 = 4.$$

In view of (11.2), this system of equations may be written as the single vector equation

$$\mathbf{Ax} = \mathbf{b},$$

where $\mathbf{b}$ is the 2–vector with components -3 and 4.

The second important point about (11.2) is that it gives a new perspective on what a matrix is. Notice that $\mathbf{x}$ is a 3–vector and $\mathbf{Ax}$ is a 2–vector. Thus we can think of the 2×3 matrix $\mathbf{A}$ as a machine for transforming 3–vectors into 2–vectors. In the language of Section 3.3, $\mathbf{A}$ *is a mapping from* $\mathcal{R}^3$ *to* $\mathcal{R}^2$. This is related to systems of linear equations in the following way: we can think of the problem of solving the system $\mathbf{Ax} = \mathbf{b}$ as that of finding all the 3–vectors that are transformed by the mapping $\mathbf{A}$ into the 2–vector $\mathbf{b}$.

All of this generalises. Given an $m \times n$ matrix $\mathbf{A}$ and an n–vector $\mathbf{x}$, we can form the m–vector $\mathbf{Ax}$ by the following process, known as **matrix-vector multiplication**.

If $\mathbf{A}$ consists of a single row $\mathbf{w} = [w_1 \; w_2 \; \ldots \; w_n]$, then $\mathbf{Ax}$ is the scalar

$$\mathbf{wx} = w_1 x_1 + w_2 x_2 + \ldots + w_n x_n.$$

This is called a **row-column product**: for example,

$$[\,3 \; 1\,] \begin{bmatrix} 2 \\ 7 \end{bmatrix} = 3 \times 2 + 1 \times 7 = 13.$$

If $\mathbf{A}$ has m rows, where $m > 1$, then $\mathbf{Ax}$ is the m–vector whose components are the row-column products of the rows of $\mathbf{A}$ with $\mathbf{x}$. For example,

$$\begin{bmatrix} 3 & 1 \\ 4 & -1 \\ -2 & 0 \end{bmatrix} \begin{bmatrix} 2 \\ 7 \end{bmatrix} = \begin{bmatrix} 6+7 \\ 8-7 \\ -4+0 \end{bmatrix} = \begin{bmatrix} 13 \\ 1 \\ -4 \end{bmatrix}.$$

Any system of m linear equations in n unknowns $x_1, x_2, \ldots, x_n$ may be written in the form $\mathbf{Ax} = \mathbf{b}$, where $\mathbf{A}$ is an $m \times n$ matrix. For example the system of 3 linear equations in 4 unknowns

$$
\begin{aligned}
e_1 x_1 + e_2 x_2 + e_3 x_3 + e_4 x_4 &= b_1 \\
f_1 x_1 + f_2 x_2 + f_3 x_3 + f_4 x_4 &= b_2 \\
g_1 x_1 + g_2 x_2 + g_3 x_3 + g_4 x_4 &= b_3
\end{aligned}
$$

may be written $\mathbf{Ax} = \mathbf{b}$ where

$$
\mathbf{A} = \begin{bmatrix} e_1 & e_2 & e_3 & e_4 \\ f_1 & f_2 & f_3 & f_4 \\ g_1 & g_2 & g_3 & g_4 \end{bmatrix}, \quad \mathbf{b} = \begin{bmatrix} b_1 \\ b_2 \\ b_3 \end{bmatrix}.
$$

An $m \times n$ matrix $\mathbf{A}$ can be regarded as a mapping from $\mathcal{R}^n$ to $\mathcal{R}^m$, transforming the n–vector $\mathbf{x}$ into the m–vector $\mathbf{Ax}$. To solve the system of linear equations $\mathbf{Ax} = \mathbf{b}$ is to find all those n–vectors $\mathbf{x}$ which the mapping $\mathbf{A}$ transforms into the m–vector $\mathbf{b}$.

Facts about Ax

Two important properties of matrix-vector multiplication are the following:

(I) $\mathbf{A}(\lambda \mathbf{x} + \mu \mathbf{y}) = \lambda \mathbf{Ax} + \mu \mathbf{Ay}$.

(II)   If the columns of the matrix $\mathbf{A}$ are the vectors $\mathbf{a}^1, \mathbf{a}^2, \ldots, \mathbf{a}^n$, so that $\mathbf{A}$ can be written as $[\mathbf{a}^1 \ \mathbf{a}^2 \ \ldots \ \mathbf{a}^n]$, then $\mathbf{Ax} = x_1 \mathbf{a}^1 + x_2 \mathbf{a}^2 + \ldots + x_n \mathbf{a}^n$.

Property (I) is another rule of vector arithmetic: it shows how matrix-vector multiplication interacts with addition and multiplication by scalars. Property (II) is helpful because it shows how $\mathbf{Ax}$ relates to the *columns* of $\mathbf{A}$: recall that our original definition was in terms of the rows. For example, the 2–vector on the right-hand side of (11.2) may be written

$$
x_1 \begin{bmatrix} 6 \\ 5 \end{bmatrix} + x_2 \begin{bmatrix} 8 \\ 1 \end{bmatrix} + x_3 \begin{bmatrix} 7 \\ 9 \end{bmatrix}.
$$

A consequence of (II) is the following criterion for matrix equality:

$$\text{if } \mathbf{Ax} = \mathbf{Bx} \text{ for all } \mathbf{x}, \text{ then } \mathbf{A} = \mathbf{B}.$$

For suppose $\mathbf{Ax} = \mathbf{Bx}$ for all $\mathbf{x}$. Then $\mathbf{Ax} = \mathbf{Bx}$ when $\mathbf{x}$ is the vector whose first component is 1 and whose other components are all zero; by (II), this implies that $\mathbf{A}$ and $\mathbf{B}$ have the same first column. Similar arguments apply to all the other columns, so $\mathbf{A} = \mathbf{B}$.

Exercises

11.2.1 Let

$$\mathbf{A} = \begin{bmatrix} 2 & -1 & 0 \\ 1 & 3 & 5 \end{bmatrix}, \quad \mathbf{B} = \begin{bmatrix} 4 & 1 & 7 \\ -2 & 4 & -1 \end{bmatrix}.$$

Find $\mathbf{A} + \mathbf{B}$, $5\mathbf{A}$, $-2\mathbf{B}$ and $5\mathbf{A} - 2\mathbf{B}$.

11.2.2 Let the vectors $\mathbf{a}$ and $\mathbf{b}$ be as in Exercise 11.1.1, and let $\mathbf{w} = [1 \ 1 \ 1]$. Interpret the row-column products $\mathbf{wa}$ and $\mathbf{w}(\mathbf{a} - \mathbf{b})$.

11.2.3 Let $\mathbf{x} = \begin{bmatrix} x_1 \\ x_2 \end{bmatrix}$ be any 2–vector. Find $\mathbf{Ax}$ when $\mathbf{A}$ takes each of the following forms:

$$\text{(a)} \begin{bmatrix} -1 & 0 \\ 0 & -1 \end{bmatrix}, \quad \text{(b)} \begin{bmatrix} 3 & 0 \\ 0 & 3 \end{bmatrix}, \quad \text{(c)} \begin{bmatrix} -2 & 0 \\ 0 & -2 \end{bmatrix}.$$

Interpret your results geometrically.

11.2.4 Express the following system of equations in matrix form:

$$\begin{aligned} x_1 - 3x_2 + x_3 &= 0 \\ 2x_1 - 4x_2 + 4x_3 &= 0. \end{aligned}$$

Given that $\mathbf{c} = \begin{bmatrix} -4 \\ -1 \\ 1 \end{bmatrix}$, verify that $\mathbf{x} = \mathbf{0}$ and $\mathbf{x} = \mathbf{c}$ are solutions to the system. For which values of λ is $\lambda\mathbf{c}$ a solution?

11.2.5 (a) Verify property (I) of matrix-vector multiplication when

$$\mathbf{A} = \begin{bmatrix} a & b \\ c & d \end{bmatrix}, \quad \mathbf{x} = \begin{bmatrix} x_1 \\ x_2 \end{bmatrix}, \quad \mathbf{y} = \begin{bmatrix} y_1 \\ y_2 \end{bmatrix}, \quad \lambda = 2 \text{ and } \mu = -3.$$

(b) Verify property (II) of matrix-vector multiplication when

$$\mathbf{A} = \begin{bmatrix} a_1 & b_1 & c_1 & d_1 \\ a_2 & b_2 & c_2 & d_2 \\ a_3 & b_3 & c_3 & d_3 \end{bmatrix}, \quad \mathbf{x} = \begin{bmatrix} -4 \\ 3 \\ 2 \\ -1 \end{bmatrix}.$$

11.3   Matrix multiplication

Multiplication of matrices is defined as follows. Suppose $\mathbf{A}$ is an $m \times n$ matrix and $\mathbf{B}$ an $n \times s$ matrix, so that $\mathbf{A}$ has the same number of columns as $\mathbf{B}$ has rows. Denote the rows of $\mathbf{A}$ by $\mathbf{a}_1, \mathbf{a}_2, \ldots, \mathbf{a}_m$ and the columns of $\mathbf{B}$ by $\mathbf{b}^1, \mathbf{b}^2, \ldots, \mathbf{b}^s$. Then $\mathbf{AB}$ is the $m \times s$ matrix whose (i, k) entry is the row-column product $\mathbf{a}_i \mathbf{b}^k$ for all relevant i and k.

For example, if

$$\mathbf{A} = \begin{bmatrix} 1 & 5 \\ 2 & -3 \\ 4 & -8 \end{bmatrix}, \quad \mathbf{B} = \begin{bmatrix} 2 & -7 & 3 & 0 \\ 1 & 0 & 4 & -5 \end{bmatrix}$$

then $\mathbf{A}$ is a 3×2 matrix and $\mathbf{B}$ is a 2×4 matrix. Therefore $\mathbf{AB}$ is the 3×4 matrix

$$\begin{bmatrix} 1 \times 2 + 5 \times 1 & -1 \times 7 + 5 \times 0 & 1 \times 3 + 5 \times 4 & 1 \times 0 - 5 \times 5 \\ 2 \times 2 - 3 \times 1 & -2 \times 7 - 3 \times 0 & 2 \times 3 - 3 \times 4 & 2 \times 0 + 3 \times 5 \\ 4 \times 2 - 8 \times 1 & -4 \times 7 - 8 \times 0 & 4 \times 3 - 8 \times 4 & 4 \times 0 + 8 \times 5 \end{bmatrix}.$$

Performing the arithmetic, we see that

$$\mathbf{AB} = \begin{bmatrix} 7 & -7 & 23 & -25 \\ 1 & -14 & -6 & 15 \\ 0 & -28 & -20 & 40 \end{bmatrix}.$$

This definition raises three questions.

Question 1 *When can we multiply two matrices?*

The product $\mathbf{AB}$ is defined if, and only if, the number of columns of $\mathbf{A}$ is equal to the number of rows of $\mathbf{B}$. When the product $\mathbf{AB}$ is defined, it has the same number of rows as $\mathbf{A}$ and the same number of columns as $\mathbf{B}$:

$$\underset{m \times n}{\mathbf{A}} \ \underset{n \times s}{\mathbf{B}} \ = \ \underset{m \times s}{\mathbf{C}}$$

Question 2 *How is matrix multiplication related to matrix-vector multiplication?*

Very closely, since we can think of matrix multiplication taking place column by column. If the columns of $\mathbf{B}$ are $\mathbf{b}^1, \mathbf{b}^2, \ldots, \mathbf{b}^s$ then the columns of $\mathbf{AB}$ are $\mathbf{Ab}^1, \mathbf{Ab}^2, \ldots, \mathbf{Ab}^s$.

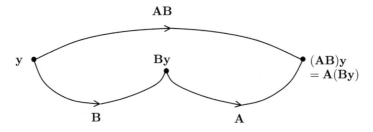

Figure 11.2: **Matrix multiplication**

Question 3 *Why is matrix multiplication defined like this anyway?*

The answer is that *multiplication of matrices is composition of mappings.* This is illustrated in Figure 11.2. Suppose as before that $\mathbf{A}$ is $m \times n$ and $\mathbf{B}$ is $n \times s$. Then $\mathbf{A}$ is the mapping from $\mathcal{R}^n$ to $\mathcal{R}^m$ which transforms any n–vector $\mathbf{x}$ into the m–vector $\mathbf{Ax}$. Similarly, $\mathbf{B}$ is the mapping from $\mathcal{R}^s$ to $\mathcal{R}^n$ which transforms any s–vector $\mathbf{y}$ into the n–vector $\mathbf{By}$. Now consider the composite mapping from $\mathcal{R}^s$ to $\mathcal{R}^m$ which transforms the s–vector $\mathbf{y}$ into the m–vector $\mathbf{A(By)}$. *This mapping turns out to be the matrix* $\mathbf{AB}$: for any s–vector $\mathbf{y}$,

$$(\mathbf{AB})\mathbf{y} = \mathbf{A}(\mathbf{By}).\tag{11.3}$$

We now explain why (11.3) is true. To do this, we use the properties (I) and (II) of matrix-vector multiplication given at the end of Section 11.2. To keep things simple, we give the argument only in the case where $s = 2$.

Let the two columns of $\mathbf{B}$ be $\mathbf{b}^1$ and $\mathbf{b}^2$. Then for any 2-vector $\mathbf{y}$,

$$\mathbf{By} = y_1\mathbf{b}^1 + y_2\mathbf{b}^2$$

by property (II). Hence

$$
\begin{aligned}
\mathbf{A}(\mathbf{By}) &= y_1\mathbf{Ab}^1 + y_2\mathbf{Ab}^2 && \text{by (I)}\\
&= [\mathbf{Ab}^1 \ \ \mathbf{Ab}^2]\mathbf{y} && \text{by (II)}\\
&= (\mathbf{AB})\mathbf{y}
\end{aligned}
$$

by the answer to Question 2 above, and (11.3) is satisfied.

Rules of matrix multiplication

The **associative law of matrix multiplication** states that

$$(\mathbf{AB})\mathbf{C} = \mathbf{A}(\mathbf{BC}).\tag{11.4}$$

Notice that this makes expressions like $\mathbf{ABCDE}$ unambiguous — we assume, of course, that the relevant products are defined.

The associative law (11.4) is a consequence of (11.3). Applying (11.3), with $\mathbf{y}$ chosen to be the first column of $\mathbf{C}$, we see that both sides of (11.4) have the same first column; a similar argument applies to all columns, so (11.4) holds. Notice that one can interpret the associative law in terms of composite mappings: if $\mathbf{A}$ has m rows and $\mathbf{C}$ has t columns, then both sides of (11.4) represent the mapping from $\mathcal{R}^t$ to $\mathcal{R}^m$ which transforms the t–vector $\mathbf{z}$ into the m–vector

$$\mathbf{A}(\mathbf{B}(\mathbf{C}(\mathbf{z}))).$$

The other rules of matrix multiplication show how it interacts with the other operations of matrix arithmetic. The rules

$$(\mathbf{A} + \mathbf{B})\mathbf{C} = \mathbf{AC} + \mathbf{BC}, \quad \mathbf{A}(\mathbf{B} + \mathbf{C}) = \mathbf{AB} + \mathbf{AC},$$

known as the **distributive laws**, tell us that matrix multiplication interacts in the obvious way with addition. Equally obvious rules combine matrix multiplication with multiplication by scalars:

$$(\lambda\mathbf{A})\mathbf{B} = \lambda(\mathbf{AB}) = \mathbf{A}(\lambda\mathbf{B}).$$

These rules are very natural analogues of the rules of ordinary arithmetic, and there is no point in learning them by heart. We now encounter something quite unlike ordinary arithmetic.

Matrix multiplication is not commutative

In general,

$$\mathbf{AB} \neq \mathbf{BA}.$$

Though this has no analogue in numerical arithmetic, it is not surprising at all when we recall that multiplication of matrices is composition of mappings. For we saw in Section 3.3 that when we compose two mappings, the order does matter.

To see what this means for matrices, suppose that $\mathbf{A}$ is an $m \times n$ matrix. For the matrix $\mathbf{AB}$ to be defined, $\mathbf{B}$ needs to have n rows; for the matrix $\mathbf{BA}$ to be defined, $\mathbf{B}$ needs to have m columns; thus both products are defined only when $\mathbf{B}$ is an $n \times m$ matrix. Given this, $\mathbf{AB}$ is an $m \times m$ matrix and $\mathbf{BA}$ is $n \times n$. If $m \neq n$, $\mathbf{AB}$ and $\mathbf{BA}$ are obviously different matrices. Therefore the only case where $\mathbf{AB}$ has a chance of being equal to $\mathbf{BA}$ is where $\mathbf{A}$ and $\mathbf{B}$ are both $n \times n$ matrices, for some n; and in this case $\mathbf{AB}$ *may or may not* be equal to $\mathbf{BA}$.

To see this, suppose $n = 2$. Notice first that

$$\text{if } \mathbf{A} = \begin{bmatrix} 3 & 0 \\ 0 & 1 \end{bmatrix} \text{ and } \mathbf{B} = \begin{bmatrix} 1 & 0 \\ 0 & 2 \end{bmatrix} \text{ then } \mathbf{AB} = \begin{bmatrix} 3 & 0 \\ 0 & 2 \end{bmatrix} = \mathbf{BA}.$$

On the other hand,

$$\text{if } \mathbf{A} = \begin{bmatrix} 0 & 1 \\ 1 & 0 \end{bmatrix} \text{ and } \mathbf{B} = \begin{bmatrix} 0 & 1 \\ 2 & 0 \end{bmatrix}$$

$$\text{then } \mathbf{AB} = \begin{bmatrix} 2 & 0 \\ 0 & 1 \end{bmatrix} \text{ and } \mathbf{BA} = \begin{bmatrix} 1 & 0 \\ 0 & 2 \end{bmatrix}.$$

In this case, $\mathbf{AB} \neq \mathbf{BA}$.

Because matrix multiplication is not commutative, the instruction "multiply $\mathbf{A}$ by $\mathbf{B}$" is ambiguous and should not be used. Instead we use the terms **premultiply** or **postmultiply** as appropriate: premultiplication of $\mathbf{A}$ by $\mathbf{B}$ means forming the product $\mathbf{BA}$, postmultiplication of $\mathbf{A}$ by $\mathbf{B}$ means forming the product $\mathbf{AB}$.

Partitioned matrices

This useful notational device is most easily explained by an example. Given the 3×5 matrix

$$\mathbf{A} = \begin{bmatrix} 2 & 4 & 6 & 8 & 0 \\ 1 & 3 & 5 & 7 & 9 \\ 4 & 0 & 4 & 0 & 4 \end{bmatrix},$$

we may partition $\mathbf{A}$ into four 'blocks' $\mathbf{A}_1, \mathbf{A}_2, \mathbf{A}_3, \mathbf{A}_4$ by writing

$$\mathbf{A} = \begin{bmatrix} \mathbf{A}_1 & \mathbf{A}_2 \\ \mathbf{A}_3 & \mathbf{A}_4 \end{bmatrix},$$

where

$$\mathbf{A}_1 = \begin{bmatrix} 2 & 4 & 6 \\ 1 & 3 & 5 \end{bmatrix} \quad \mathbf{A}_2 = \begin{bmatrix} 8 & 0 \\ 7 & 9 \end{bmatrix}$$

$$\mathbf{A}_3 = \begin{bmatrix} 4 & 0 & 4 \end{bmatrix} \quad \mathbf{A}_4 = \begin{bmatrix} 0 & 4 \end{bmatrix}.$$

Obviously there are other ways of partitioning $\mathbf{A}$, for example $\mathbf{A} = [\mathbf{B}\ \mathbf{C}\ \mathbf{D}]$ where

$$\mathbf{B} = \begin{bmatrix} 2 & 4 \\ 1 & 3 \\ 4 & 0 \end{bmatrix}, \quad \mathbf{C} = \begin{bmatrix} 6 \\ 5 \\ 4 \end{bmatrix}, \quad \mathbf{D} = \begin{bmatrix} 8 & 0 \\ 7 & 9 \\ 0 & 4 \end{bmatrix}.$$

Provided all block products are defined, we can multiply two partitioned matrices block by block using the same rule as for ordinary matrix multiplication:

$$\begin{bmatrix} \mathbf{A} & \mathbf{B} \\ \mathbf{C} & \mathbf{D} \end{bmatrix} \begin{bmatrix} \mathbf{P} & \mathbf{Q} \\ \mathbf{R} & \mathbf{S} \end{bmatrix} = \begin{bmatrix} \mathbf{AP} + \mathbf{BR} & \mathbf{AQ} + \mathbf{BS} \\ \mathbf{CP} + \mathbf{DR} & \mathbf{CQ} + \mathbf{DS} \end{bmatrix}.$$

Exercises

11.3.1 Let

$$\mathbf{A} = \begin{bmatrix} 1 & 2 \\ 2 & 0 \\ 1 & -2 \\ 5 & -2 \end{bmatrix}, \quad \mathbf{B} = \begin{bmatrix} 1 & 0 & -1 \\ 2 & 1 & 4 \end{bmatrix}, \quad \mathbf{C} = \begin{bmatrix} 4 & -4 & 3 & 1 \\ 1 & 0 & -1 & 0 \end{bmatrix}.$$

Find $\mathbf{AB}$, $\mathbf{AC}$ and $\mathbf{CA}$.

11.3.2 Verify equation (11.3) in the case where

$$\mathbf{A} = \begin{bmatrix} 1 & -1 \\ 2 & 0 \\ -1 & 3 \end{bmatrix}, \quad \mathbf{B} = \begin{bmatrix} 0 & 2 & -3 \\ -2 & 1 & 4 \end{bmatrix}, \quad \mathbf{y} = \begin{bmatrix} y_1 \\ y_2 \\ y_3 \end{bmatrix}.$$

11.3.3 Let $\mathbf{A}$ and $\mathbf{B}$ be 4×4 matrices partitioned as follows:

$$\mathbf{A} = \begin{bmatrix} \mathbf{A}_1 & \mathbf{O} \\ \mathbf{O} & \mathbf{A}_2 \end{bmatrix}, \quad \mathbf{B} = \begin{bmatrix} \mathbf{B}_1 & \mathbf{O} \\ \mathbf{O} & \mathbf{B}_2 \end{bmatrix},$$

where $\mathbf{A}_1, \mathbf{A}_2, \mathbf{B}_1, \mathbf{B}_2$ are 2×2 matrices. Find $\mathbf{AB}$.

11.4   Square matrices

An $n \times n$ matrix is called a **square matrix** of **order** n. In this section we explain some special properties of such matrices. Our final summary of matrix arithmetic applies to all matrices, square or otherwise.

Powers

If **A** is a square matrix we may define the matrices

$$\mathbf{A}^2 = \mathbf{AA}, \quad \mathbf{A}^3 = \mathbf{A}^2\mathbf{A}, \quad \mathbf{A}^4 = \mathbf{A}^3\mathbf{A}$$

and so on.

Two points about this are worth noting. First, to calculate $\mathbf{A}^2$ from **A** one actually has to premultiply the matrix **A** by the matrix **A**; simply squaring each entry of **A** will not in general give the right answer!

Secondly, results such as $\mathbf{A}^4 = (\mathbf{A}^2)^2$ and

$$\mathbf{A}^3\mathbf{A}^5 = \mathbf{A}^8 = \mathbf{A}^5\mathbf{A}^3$$

are just as true for square matrices as for numbers: they follow, in fact, from the associative law of matrix multiplication. Hence the case where **B** and **C** are both powers of the same matrix **A** is one of those rare cases where **BC** = **CB**.

Triangular and diagonal matrices

Given a 3×3 matrix

$$\mathbf{A} = \begin{bmatrix} a_{11} & a_{12} & a_{13} \\ a_{21} & a_{22} & a_{23} \\ a_{31} & a_{32} & a_{33} \end{bmatrix}$$

we call a_{11}, a_{22} and a_{33} the **diagonal entries** of **A**; the other 6 entries are said to be **off-diagonal**. These definitions extend in an obvious way to square matrices of any order.

A square matrix is said to be **upper triangular** if all entries below the diagonal are zero, **lower triangular** if all entries above the diagonal are zero. A **triangular matrix** is a matrix which is either upper or lower triangular, and a **diagonal matrix** is one that is both upper and lower triangular, so that all off-diagonal entries are zero. For example, if

$$\mathbf{A} = \begin{bmatrix} 5 & 1 & 4 \\ 0 & 2 & 1 \\ 0 & 0 & 3 \end{bmatrix}, \quad \mathbf{B} = \begin{bmatrix} 2 & 0 & 0 \\ 5 & 3 & 0 \\ 7 & 0 & 4 \end{bmatrix}, \quad \mathbf{C} = \begin{bmatrix} 6 & 0 & 0 \\ 0 & 9 & 0 \\ 0 & 0 & 2 \end{bmatrix},$$

then **A** is upper triangular, **B** is lower triangular and **C** is a diagonal matrix.

The general definition of a triangular matrix allows zeros on the diagonal. An upper triangular matrix with *no* zeros on the diagonal is called a **regular**

upper triangular matrix (RUT, for short). Systems of linear equations with RUTs as coefficient matrix are the 'triangular systems' of Section 1.2, which can be solved uniquely by back-substitution.

Example Let

$$A = \begin{bmatrix} 2 & 7 & 1 \\ 0 & 3 & -2 \\ 0 & 0 & 4 \end{bmatrix}, \quad b = \begin{bmatrix} 2 \\ 7 \\ 4 \end{bmatrix}.$$

Then the system of linear equations $Ax = b$ may be written

$$
\begin{aligned}
2x_1 + 7x_2 + x_3 &= 2 \\
3x_2 - 2x_3 &= 7 \\
4x_3 &= 4.
\end{aligned}
$$

We solved this system by back-substitution in Section 1.2, with a slightly different notation for the unknowns; the unique solution is $x_1 = -10$, $x_2 = 3$, $x_3 = 1$.

The identity matrix

An $n \times n$ diagonal matrix of particular importance is the one whose diagonal entries are all 1's. This is called the $n \times n$ **identity matrix**: it is denoted by I_n, or simply I if there is no ambiguity about n. Thus

$$I_3 = \begin{bmatrix} 1 & 0 & 0 \\ 0 & 1 & 0 \\ 0 & 0 & 1 \end{bmatrix}.$$

For any vector x, $Ix = x$. Thus the identity matrix is the mapping which transforms vectors into themselves (or, to put it more simply, leaves them unchanged).

We said in Section 11.2 that the zero matrix plays the same role for matrices that the number 0 does in ordinary arithmetic. Similarly, the identity matrix plays the same role in matrix multiplication that the number 1 plays in ordinary arithmetic: for any $m \times n$ matrix A,

$$I_m A = A = A I_n.$$

Summary of matrix arithmetic

We said in the last section that there is no point in learning the rules of matrix arithmetic by heart. This is because it is much easier to remember what is forbidden than what is allowed. Matrix arithmetic is just like ordinary arithmetic, except for the following:

1. Addition and multiplication are subject to dimension restrictions: $\mathbf{A} + \mathbf{B}$ and $\alpha\mathbf{A} + \beta\mathbf{B}$ are defined only when $\mathbf{A}$ and $\mathbf{B}$ have the same number of rows and the same number of columns; $\mathbf{AB}$ is defined only when the number of columns of $\mathbf{A}$ is equal to the number of rows of $\mathbf{B}$.

2. Matrix multiplication is not commutative.

3. There is no such thing as matrix division.

Exercises

11.4.1 Show that, if $\mathbf{A}$ and $\mathbf{B}$ are square matrices of the same order, then $\mathbf{A}^2 - \mathbf{B}^2$ is *not* in general equal to $(\mathbf{A} + \mathbf{B})(\mathbf{A} - \mathbf{B})$.

11.4.2 (a) Find a nonzero 2×2 matrix $\mathbf{A}$ such that $\mathbf{A}^2 = \mathbf{O}$.

(b) Find a 2×2 matrix $\mathbf{A}$, with real entries, such that $\mathbf{A}^2 = -\mathbf{I}$.

11.4.3 Find all 2×2 matrices $\mathbf{A}$ such that $\mathbf{A}^2$ is the matrix obtained from $\mathbf{A}$ by squaring each entry.

11.4.4 Calculate $\mathbf{AB}$ when

$$\mathbf{A} = \begin{bmatrix} a & b & c \\ 0 & d & e \\ 0 & 0 & f \end{bmatrix}, \quad \mathbf{B} = \begin{bmatrix} 3 & -1 & 6 \\ 0 & 2 & 1 \\ 0 & 0 & -5 \end{bmatrix}.$$

What general result about upper triangular matrices does your answer suggest? What is the corresponding result for lower triangular matrices?

Problems on Chapter 11

11–1. (i) Let

$$\mathbf{a}^1 = \begin{bmatrix} 1 \\ 0 \\ 0 \end{bmatrix}, \quad \mathbf{a}^2 = \begin{bmatrix} 0 \\ 1 \\ 0 \end{bmatrix}, \quad \mathbf{a}^3 = \begin{bmatrix} 0 \\ 0 \\ 1 \end{bmatrix}.$$

Show that

(a) $\mathbf{a}^1, \mathbf{a}^2, \mathbf{a}^3$ are linearly independent;

(b) any 3–vector $\mathbf{x}$ can be expressed as a linear combination of $\mathbf{a}^1, \mathbf{a}^2, \mathbf{a}^3$.

(ii) As (i), but with

$$\mathbf{a}^1 = \begin{bmatrix} 1 \\ 0 \\ 0 \end{bmatrix}, \quad \mathbf{a}^2 = \begin{bmatrix} 1 \\ 1 \\ 0 \end{bmatrix}, \quad \mathbf{a}^3 = \begin{bmatrix} 1 \\ 1 \\ 1 \end{bmatrix}.$$

[A set of 3–vectors with properties (a) and (b) is called a **basis** of $\mathcal{R}^3$.]

11–2. [This problem reformulates in matrix notation the exercises of Section 3.3.]

Find matrices $\mathbf{A}$ and $\mathbf{B}$ such that

$$\mathbf{Ax} = \begin{bmatrix} -x_2 \\ x_1 \end{bmatrix}, \quad \mathbf{Bx} = \begin{bmatrix} x_1 \\ -x_2 \end{bmatrix} \quad \text{for every 2-vector } \mathbf{x} = \begin{bmatrix} x_1 \\ x_2 \end{bmatrix}.$$

Interpret these mappings geometrically. Verify that $\mathbf{AB} \neq \mathbf{BA}$ and interpret this result geometrically.

11–3. Let

$$\mathbf{A} = \begin{bmatrix} 2 & -1 & 3 \\ 0 & -1 & 1 \\ 0 & 0 & 2 \end{bmatrix}, \quad \mathbf{B} = \begin{bmatrix} 4 & 0 & 0 \\ 3 & -2 & 0 \\ 1 & 1 & -1 \end{bmatrix}, \quad \mathbf{C} = \begin{bmatrix} -3 & 0 & 0 \\ 0 & 2 & 0 \\ 0 & 0 & 1 \end{bmatrix}$$

and let $\mathbf{y}$ be a given 3-vector with components y_1, y_2, y_3.

Solve each of the following systems of equations:

$$\text{(i) } \mathbf{Ax} = \mathbf{y}, \quad \text{(ii) } \mathbf{Bx} = \mathbf{y}, \quad \text{(iii) } \mathbf{Cx} = \mathbf{y}.$$

What feature of the solution procedure distinguishes (iii) from (i) and (ii)?

11–4. In this problem we ask you to formulate in general terms the input-output model of Section 1.3.

Suppose an economy produces n goods labelled $1, \ldots, n$. We assume there is **no joint production**, so that we can think of 'industry j' producing positive quantities only of good j, using the other produced goods, and possibly j itself as inputs. There may also be non-produced goods such as labour and raw materials that are used as inputs, but these do not matter for this problem. For each good j, we define the gross output x_j of j be the total amount produced, including that fed back into the system as industrial input; the net output y_j of j is the amount of j produced and not fed back into the system, being therefore available for final use.

For any pair of goods i, j, let a_{ij} be the input of good i required in industry j, per unit of gross output of good j. We assume **fixed coefficients** and **constant returns to scale**: the n^2 numbers $\{a_{ij}\}$ are constants, and in particular do not depend on the values of $x_1, \ldots, x_n$.

(i) Write down a system of linear equations expressing the net outputs $y_1, \ldots, y_n$ in terms of the gross outputs $x_1, \ldots, x_n$ and the input-output coefficients $\{a_{ij}\}$.

(ii) Let $\mathbf{x}$ be the **gross output vector** with components $x_1, \ldots, x_n$; let $\mathbf{y}$ be the **net output vector** with components $y_1, \ldots, y_n$. Also let $\mathbf{A}$ be the **input-output matrix**, defined as the $n \times n$ matrix with

(i, j) entry a_{ij} for all i and j. Write the system of equations of (i) as a single vector equation. Find a matrix $\mathbf{B}$, related to $\mathbf{A}$, such that this vector equation takes the form $\mathbf{Bx} = \mathbf{y}$.

Chapter 12

SYSTEMS OF LINEAR EQUATIONS

Systems of simultaneous linear equations were discussed at some length in Chapter 1, and mentioned in Chapter 11 as one of the reasons for matrix notation. In the first two sections of this chapter we give a general method of solving a system of m simultaneous linear equations in n unknowns. The method is essentially that used for simple cases in Section 1.2: Gaussian elimination and back-substitution. With regard to Gaussian elimination, we have little to add to what was said in Chapter 1, apart from a few suggestions about how to set out the calculations. Back-substitution, by contrast, is more complicated in the general case, and requires some care: this is the subject of Section 12.1. Section 12.2 completes the story, and introduces an alternative to Gaussian elimination known as Gauss–Jordan elimination.

As we said at the beginning of the last chapter, solving systems of linear equations is merely the starting problem of the branch of mathematics known as linear algebra. We devote the last two sections of this chapter to showing how the techniques of Gaussian and Gauss–Jordan elimination may be applied to two problems other than that of solving a single system of linear equations. The first is that of inverting a matrix, which brings us back to the concept of matrices as mappings. The second is that of calculating an important number associated with any matrix, known as the rank.

When you have studied this chapter you will be able to:

- solve general systems of linear equations;

- invert matrices using the Gauss–Jordan method;

- manipulate algebraic expressions involving inverse matrices;

- determine the rank of a matrix.

12.1   Echelon matrices

In this section we show how back-substitution can be applied to systems rather more general than the triangular ones of Section 1.2. To do this we introduce a class of matrices known as echelon matrices.

An **echelon matrix** is a matrix, not necessarily square, with the following two properties:

(i) There is at least one non-zero entry; rows consisting entirely of zeros, if any, lie below rows with at least one non-zero entry.

(ii) In each non-zero row after the first, the left-most non-zero entry lies to the right of the left-most non-zero entry in the preceding row.

These properties give us the following 'staircase' pattern, where each $\star$ denotes a number which must be non-zero, and the entries marked $\cdot$ may be zero or non-zero:

$$\begin{bmatrix} \star & \cdot & \cdot & \cdot & \cdot & \cdot \\ 0 & \star & \cdot & \cdot & \cdot & \cdot \\ 0 & 0 & 0 & 0 & \star & \cdot \\ 0 & 0 & 0 & 0 & 0 & 0 \end{bmatrix}$$

In each of the non-zero rows of an echelon matrix, the left-most non-zero entry is called the **pivot**; and the columns containing the pivots are said to be **basic columns**. In the illustration the pivots are the entries marked $\star$; the first, second and fifth columns are basic. *For any echelon matrix,*

number of pivots = number of non-zero rows = number of basic columns.

The four types of echelon matrix

Recall from Section 11.4 that a regular upper triangular matrix, or RUT, is a square matrix with all entries below the diagonal equal to zero and all entries on the diagonal non-zero. In an echelon matrix which has no row consisting entirely of zeros, the basic columns form a RUT whose diagonal entries are the pivots.

We therefore define a **Type 1 echelon matrix** to be the same thing as a RUT; a **Type 2 echelon matrix** is an echelon matrix consisting of a RUT and one or more additional columns. Every echelon matrix which has no row consisting entirely of zeros must be of Type 1 or Type 2. Notice that a Type 1 echelon matrix is a square matrix, while a Type 2 echelon matrix has more columns than rows.

Now consider an echelon matrix which has one or more rows consisting entirely of zeros. If we delete those rows, we obtain an echelon matrix of Type

1 or Type 2. There are therefore just two types of echelon matrix in addition
to Types 1 and 2. A **Type 3 echelon matrix** consists of a Type 1 echelon
matrix, followed by one or more rows of zeros; a **Type 4 echelon matrix**
consists of a Type 2 echelon matrix, followed by one or more rows of zeros. A
Type 3 echelon matrix has more rows than columns; the number of rows of a
Type 4 echelon matrix may be greater than, equal to or less than the number
of columns.

Echelon systems

We now explain how to solve a system of equations of the form $\mathbf{Ax} = \mathbf{b}$, where
$\mathbf{A}$ is an echelon matrix. We consider each type in turn.

Type 1

In this case the coefficient matrix is a RUT. The system is solved by back-
substitution, giving a unique solution.

Type 2

Recall that in a Type 2 echelon matrix the basic columns form a RUT, and there
are also one or more non-basic columns. Since each component of $\mathbf{x}$ corresponds
to a column of $\mathbf{A}$, we may speak of 'basic' and 'non-basic' unknowns. To solve
the system, we assign arbitrary values to non-basic unknowns, and then solve
for the basic unknowns by back-substitution.

Example 1 Solve the system $\mathbf{Ax} = \mathbf{b}$, where

$$\mathbf{A} = \begin{bmatrix} 2 & -4 & 1 & -8 \\ 0 & 0 & 5 & 10 \end{bmatrix}, \quad \mathbf{b} = \begin{bmatrix} -4 \\ 20 \end{bmatrix}.$$

Here $\mathbf{A}$ is a Type 2 echelon matrix, with first and third columns basic. We
therefore assign arbitrary values λ and μ to x_2 and x_4, giving the system

$$2x_1 + x_3 = 4\lambda + 8\mu - 4$$
$$5x_3 = -10\mu + 20.$$

We now find x_1 and x_3 by back-substitution: $x_3 = 4 - 2\mu$ and

$$x_1 = \tfrac{1}{2}(4\lambda + 8\mu - 4 + 2\mu - 4) = 2\lambda + 5\mu - 4.$$

Summarising, the complete solution is

$$x_1 = 2\lambda + 5\mu - 4, \quad x_2 = \lambda, \quad x_3 = 4 - 2\mu, \quad x_4 = \mu$$

where λ and μ are arbitrary; or in vector form,

$$
\mathbf{x} = \begin{bmatrix} -4 \\ 0 \\ 4 \\ 0 \end{bmatrix} + \lambda \begin{bmatrix} 2 \\ 1 \\ 0 \\ 0 \end{bmatrix} + \mu \begin{bmatrix} 5 \\ 0 \\ -2 \\ 1 \end{bmatrix}.
$$

Type 3

If $\mathbf{A}$ is a Type 3 echelon matrix we may write

$$
\mathbf{A} = \begin{bmatrix} \mathbf{H} \\ \mathbf{O} \end{bmatrix}, \tag{12.1}
$$

where $\mathbf{H}$ is a Type 1 echelon matrix. A system of linear equations with $\mathbf{A}$ as coefficient matrix may therefore be written in two blocks, an upper block with coefficient matrix $\mathbf{H}$ and a lower one with coefficient matrix $\mathbf{O}$. If there are any non-zero numbers on the right hand side of the lower block, the system contains absurdities and therefore has no solution. If on the other hand all the numbers on the right in the lower block are zeros, the lower block says only that $0 = 0$ and may therefore be ignored. We are then left with the upper block, which may be solved by back-substitution to give a unique solution.

Type 4

If $\mathbf{A}$ is a Type 4 echelon matrix we may again write (12.1), but $\mathbf{H}$ is now a Type 2 echelon matrix. As with Type 3, a system of linear equations with $\mathbf{A}$ as coefficient matrix may be written in two blocks, say

$$
\mathbf{Hx} = \mathbf{p} \qquad \text{(upper block)}
$$
$$
\mathbf{Ox} = \mathbf{q} \qquad \text{(lower block)}
$$

Again, if $\mathbf{q} \neq \mathbf{0}$ we have no solution, while if $\mathbf{q} = \mathbf{0}$ we only have to solve the upper block. Since $\mathbf{H}$ is now Type 2 rather than Type 1 the solution is not unique, and we find the complete solution as above.

Example 2 Solve the system $\mathbf{Ax} = \mathbf{b}$ where

$$
\mathbf{A} = \begin{bmatrix} 2 & -4 & 1 & -8 \\ 0 & 0 & 5 & 10 \\ 0 & 0 & 0 & 0 \end{bmatrix}, \quad \mathbf{b} = \begin{bmatrix} -4 \\ 20 \\ 0 \end{bmatrix}.
$$

Here $\mathbf{A}$ is the matrix of Example 1 with a final row of zeros added. It is therefore of Type 4. The lower block of the system of equations says that $0 = 0$, so we only have to solve the upper block. This is exactly the system solved in Example 1, and the solution is as stated there.

Note that if the third component of $\mathbf{b}$ had been a nonzero number, then there would be no solution.

Exercises

12.1.1 Write down

(a) a 3×4 echelon matrix $\mathbf{A}$ in which the third column consists entirely of zeros;

(a) a 4×3 echelon matrix $\mathbf{A}$ in which the first column consists entirely of zeros.

In each case, what special feature does the system of equations $\mathbf{Ax} = \mathbf{b}$ have?

12.1.2 Solve the system $\mathbf{Ax} = \mathbf{b}$ in each of the following cases:

(a) $\quad \mathbf{A} = \begin{bmatrix} 3 & -5 & 0 & 1 \\ 0 & 2 & -1 & 0 \end{bmatrix}, \quad \mathbf{b} = \begin{bmatrix} -4 \\ 1 \end{bmatrix}.$

(b) $\quad \mathbf{A} = \begin{bmatrix} 7 & 3 & -2 & 1 \\ 0 & 8 & 4 & -3 \\ 0 & 0 & -1 & 2 \\ 0 & 0 & 0 & 1 \\ 0 & 0 & 0 & 0 \end{bmatrix}, \quad \mathbf{b} = \begin{bmatrix} 0 \\ 2 \\ 1 \\ -2 \\ 0 \end{bmatrix}.$

(c) $\quad \mathbf{A} = \begin{bmatrix} 6 & 3 & 9 & 5 \\ 0 & 0 & 0 & 2 \\ 0 & 0 & 0 & 0 \end{bmatrix}, \quad \mathbf{b} = \begin{bmatrix} 1 \\ -8 \\ 2 \end{bmatrix}.$

(d) As (b), except that the final component of $\mathbf{b}$ is -1 rather than 0.

(e) As (c), except that the final component of $\mathbf{b}$ is 0 rather than 2.

12.2 More on Gaussian elimination

Having said all that needs to be said about systems of linear equations whose coefficient matrix is an echelon matrix, we turn to the general system

$$\mathbf{Ax} = \mathbf{b},$$

where $\mathbf{A}$ is an $m \times n$ matrix. If $\mathbf{A} = \mathbf{O}$ and $\mathbf{b} \neq \mathbf{0}$, there is no solution; if $\mathbf{A} = \mathbf{O}$ and $\mathbf{b} = \mathbf{0}$ then *every* n-vector is a solution. For the rest of this section we ignore these uninteresting cases and assume that $\mathbf{A}$ has at least one non-zero entry.

To solve the system, we apply Gaussian elimination as in Section 1.2. It is convenient not to write out equations in full but instead to operate on the rows of the **augmented matrix** $[\mathbf{A} \quad \mathbf{b}]$. The 'elementary operations' of Section 1.2 now become the following **elementary row operations**:

(EO1)   exchanging two rows;
(EO2)   subtracting a multiple of one row from another row.

In Gaussian elimination, (EO2) operations are packaged together in **elimination steps** in which multiples of one row (the **pivot row**) are subtracted from each of the rows below it. The procedure is continued until we obtain a matrix $[\mathbf{E} \quad \mathbf{c}]$ *in which* $\mathbf{E}$ *is an echelon matrix*. The solution to $\mathbf{Ax} = \mathbf{b}$ is then found by solving $\mathbf{Ex} = \mathbf{c}$.

To summarise, the procedure is as in Section 1.2, with two differences. First, we do not bother to write the equations out in full; we are therefore operating on rows rather than equations. Second and much more important, we aim for echelon form rather than triangular form: in particular, we do not need to assume that $m = n$. We illustrate with three examples.

Example 1 Solve the system $\mathbf{Ax} = \mathbf{b}$ where

$$\mathbf{A} = \begin{bmatrix} 2 & -4 & 1 & -8 \\ 4 & -8 & 7 & -6 \\ -1 & 2 & 1 & 7 \end{bmatrix}, \quad \mathbf{b} = \begin{bmatrix} -4 \\ 12 \\ 8 \end{bmatrix}.$$

Starting with the augmented matrix $[\mathbf{A} \quad \mathbf{b}]$, we notice that the entry in the first row and first column is non-zero; it may therefore serve as pivot for our first elimination step. We subtract multiples of the first row from the other rows so as to produce zero entries below the pivot. In this case we must subtract *twice* the first row from the second and *add* $\frac{1}{2}$ times the first row to the third, giving the matrix

$$\begin{bmatrix} 2 & -4 & 1 & -8 & | & -4 \\ 0 & 0 & 5 & 10 & | & 20 \\ 0 & 0 & 3/2 & 3 & | & 6 \end{bmatrix}.$$

Keeping the first row unchanged, we focus on the other rows. The first column has been constructed to have all entries zero below the first row, and in this case the second column happens to have the same property. We therefore move on to the third column. The entry in that column and the second row is non-zero, so we use it as pivot for the second elimination step, which is to subtract $3/10$ times the second row from the third. This gives the matrix

$$\begin{bmatrix} 2 & -4 & 1 & -8 & | & -4 \\ 0 & 0 & 5 & 10 & | & 20 \\ 0 & 0 & 0 & 0 & | & 0 \end{bmatrix}.$$

We have reduced our system of equations to one in which the coefficient matrix is a Type 4 echelon matrix. The bottom row consisting only of zeros tells us only that $0=0$ and may therefore be ignored. Now look at the first two rows. The 'upper block' equation system given by these rows is in fact the equation system of Example 1 of the last section. The complete solution is therefore as before:

$$\mathbf{x} = \begin{bmatrix} -4 \\ 0 \\ 4 \\ 0 \end{bmatrix} + \lambda \begin{bmatrix} 2 \\ 1 \\ 0 \\ 0 \end{bmatrix} + \mu \begin{bmatrix} 5 \\ 0 \\ -2 \\ 1 \end{bmatrix},$$

where λ and μ are arbitrary.

Example 2 Let the system $\mathbf{Ax} = \mathbf{b}$ be as in Example 1, but with the third component of $\mathbf{b}$ equal to 10 rather than 8. Proceeding as above, we reach an echelon form with the first two rows as before, but with third row

$$[\,0 \quad 0 \quad 0 \quad 0 \mid 2\,].$$

This row corresponds to the absurd equation $0 = 2$ and indicates that our system has no solution.

Example 3 Solve the system $\mathbf{Ax} = \mathbf{b}$ where

$$\mathbf{A} = \begin{bmatrix} 2 & 1 & 4 \\ 2 & 1 & 1 \\ 4 & 8 & 7 \\ 4 & 3 & 9 \end{bmatrix}, \quad \mathbf{b} = \begin{bmatrix} 5 \\ 8 \\ 5 \\ 8 \end{bmatrix}.$$

Starting with $[\mathbf{A} \quad \mathbf{b}]$, we use as our first pivot the top left entry; the first elimination step is to subtract the first row from the second row, and twice the first row from each of the other rows, giving

$$\begin{bmatrix} 2 & 1 & 4 & \mid & 5 \\ 0 & 0 & -3 & \mid & 3 \\ 0 & 6 & -1 & \mid & -5 \\ 0 & 1 & 1 & \mid & -2 \end{bmatrix}.$$

Keeping the first row unchanged and focussing on the other rows, we see that the second column has non-zero entries below the first row, but the entry in the second row is not one one of them. So we need a row exchange before our next elimination step. To avoid messy arithmetic we exchange the second and fourth rows, getting

$$\begin{bmatrix} 2 & 1 & 4 & \mid & 5 \\ 0 & 1 & 1 & \mid & -2 \\ 0 & 6 & -1 & \mid & -5 \\ 0 & 0 & -3 & \mid & 3 \end{bmatrix}.$$

Two more elimination steps yield

$$\begin{bmatrix} 2 & 1 & 4 & \mid & 5 \\ 0 & 1 & 1 & \mid & -2 \\ 0 & 0 & -7 & \mid & 7 \\ 0 & 0 & -3 & \mid & 3 \end{bmatrix}.$$

and

$$\begin{bmatrix} 2 & 1 & 4 & 5 \\ 0 & 1 & 1 & -2 \\ 0 & 0 & -7 & 7 \\ 0 & 0 & 0 & 0 \end{bmatrix}$$

which is our (Type 3) echelon form. Ignoring the bottom row (0=0) we have a triangular system: back-substitution gives the unique solution

$$x_1 = 5, \quad x_2 = -1, \quad x_3 = -1.$$

We encourage you to check that if the fourth component of **b** were 7 rather than 8 there would be no solution.

Number of equations, number of unknowns

The method described above works for any system of linear equations, regardless of whether the number of equations is greater than, equal to, or less than the number of unknowns. But in any practical example we know which one of the three possibilities obtains. What does this information tell us about the complete solution?

We begin by looking again at the four types of echelon matrix. Recall from Section 12.1 that a Type 1 echelon matrix is square, a Type 2 echelon matrix has more columns than rows, a Type 3 echelon matrix has more rows than columns and a Type 4 echelon matrix may have any ranking of number of rows and number of columns. Putting this another way, a square echelon matrix must be of Type 1 or Type 4, an echelon matrix with more columns than rows must be of Type 2 or Type 4 and an echelon matrix with more rows than columns must be of Type 3 or Type 4.

Now consider a general system of linear equations $\mathbf{Ax} = \mathbf{b}$, where $\mathbf{A}$ is an $m \times n$ matrix. Suppose that $[\mathbf{A} \quad \mathbf{b}]$ is reduced by Gaussian elimination to $[\mathbf{E} \quad \mathbf{c}]$ where $\mathbf{E}$ is an $m \times n$ echelon matrix. If $m \geq n$, $\mathbf{E}$ may be of Type 1, 3 or 4; thus in this case there may be a unique solution, no solution or infinitely many solutions. If $m < n$, $\mathbf{E}$ is either of Type 2 (in which case there are infinitely many solutions) or of Type 4 (in which case there are either no solutions or infinitely many); thus if $m < n$ we can be sure that there is *not* a unique solution. We summarise as follows:

Proposition 1 Given a system of m linear equations in n unknowns, there are three possibilities:

either	there is a unique solution
or	there is no solution
or	there are infinitely many solutions.

If there are at least as many equations as unknowns, any one of of these cases can occur. If there are more unknowns than equations, only the last two cases can occur.

The next question to consider is whether there is anything special about the case where the number of equations is the same as the number of unknowns. Suppose as before that $[\mathbf{A} \quad \mathbf{b}]$ is reduced to $[\mathbf{E} \quad \mathbf{c}]$, where $\mathbf{E}$ is an echelon matrix. Also suppose that $\mathbf{A}$ is square, so that $\mathbf{E}$ is also square. Then $\mathbf{E}$ is either Type 1 or Type 4, with a unique solution only in the former case. And since all the pivots in Gaussian elimination are chosen to the left of the vertical line, the type of $\mathbf{E}$ depends only on the coefficient matrix $\mathbf{A}$ and not on the vector $\mathbf{b}$. The conclusion is as follows:

Proposition 2 If $\mathbf{A}$ is a *square* matrix, then whether or not the system $\mathbf{Ax} = \mathbf{b}$ has a unique solution depends only on $\mathbf{A}$, not on $\mathbf{b}$.

The consequences of this will be explored in the next section.

Gauss–Jordan elimination

To complete our discussion of Gaussian elimination, we mention a variant. Like Gaussian elimination, Gauss–Jordan elimination alternates row exchanges (if necessary) with elimination steps in which multiples of the pivot row are subtracted from other rows. But in a Gauss–Jordan elimination step we subtract multiples of the pivot row from *all* the other rows, not just the lower ones. The purpose of this is to end with an echelon matrix in which there are zeros above as well as below the pivots. This involves more work in elimination — the advantage is that the back-substitution stage reduces to simple division by the pivots.

To illustrate this we repeat Example 1 above, using the Gauss–Jordan method. Starting with the augmented matrix $[\mathbf{A} \quad \mathbf{b}]$ we perform the first elimination step as before, obtaining

$$\begin{bmatrix} 2 & -4 & 1 & -8 & -4 \\ 0 & 0 & 5 & 10 & 20 \\ 0 & 0 & 3/2 & 3 & 6 \end{bmatrix}.$$

We now subtract $3/10$ times the second row from the third as before, *and* subtract $1/5$ times the second row from the first. This gives the matrix

$$\begin{bmatrix} 2 & -4 & 0 & -10 & -8 \\ 0 & 0 & 5 & 10 & 20 \\ 0 & 0 & 0 & 0 & 0 \end{bmatrix}.$$

This is echelon form. Ignoring the bottom row $(0 = 0)$ and setting $x_2 = \lambda$, $x_4 = \mu$, we have

$$2x_1 = 4\lambda + 10\mu - 8, \quad 5x_3 = -10\mu + 20.$$

The solution is therefore

$$x_1 = 2\lambda + 5\mu - 4, \quad x_2 = \lambda, \quad x_3 = 4 - 2\mu, \quad x_4 = \mu$$

as in Example 1.

Applying Gauss–Jordan

For practical computation one may use either Gaussian or Gauss–Jordan elimination; computer software typically uses the former. You should however make yourself familiar with both methods, since both will be used later in this book.

An advantage of the Gauss–Jordan method is that it is sometimes possible to avoid row exchanges by choosing the pivot *columns* in an order other than the natural one. Consider Example 2 above, in which the first elimination step yielded

$$\left[\begin{array}{ccc|c} 2 & 1 & 4 & 5 \\ 0 & 0 & -3 & 3 \\ 0 & 6 & -1 & -5 \\ 0 & 1 & 1 & -2 \end{array}\right]$$

Rather than performing a row exchange as we did earlier, we can move on to the third column and perform a Gauss–Jordan elimination step with the $(3,3)$ entry as pivot. This gives

$$\left[\begin{array}{ccc|c} 2 & 25 & 0 & -15 \\ 0 & -18 & 0 & 18 \\ 0 & 6 & -1 & -5 \\ 0 & 7 & 0 & -7 \end{array}\right]$$

We may now return to the second column and perform a Gauss–Jordan elimination step with the $(2,2)$ entry as pivot, getting

$$\left[\begin{array}{ccc|c} 2 & 0 & 0 & 10 \\ 0 & -18 & 0 & 18 \\ 0 & 0 & -1 & 1 \\ 0 & 0 & 0 & 0 \end{array}\right]$$

As before, the unique solution is $x_1 = 5$, $x_2 = -1$, $x_3 = -1$.

Solving several systems with the same coefficient matrix

One use for Gauss–Jordan is in solving two or more systems with the same coefficient matrix. If we want to solve the systems $\mathbf{Ax} = \mathbf{b}^1$ and $\mathbf{Ax} = \mathbf{b}^2$, there is no point in going through the elimination procedure twice. Instead we start with the doubly augmented matrix $[\mathbf{A} \quad \mathbf{b}^1 \quad \mathbf{b}^2]$ and eliminate down to $[\mathbf{E} \quad \mathbf{c}^1 \quad \mathbf{c}^2]$ where $\mathbf{E}$ is an echelon matrix. We can then solve our original systems by solving $\mathbf{Ex} = \mathbf{c}^1$ and $\mathbf{Ex} = \mathbf{c}^2$. This procedure works equally well whether elimination is Gaussian or Gauss–Jordan, but the latter option makes the final back-substitution less tedious.

Exercises

12.2.1 Solve the system $\mathbf{Ax} = \mathbf{b}$ in each of the following cases:

(a) $\quad \mathbf{A} = \begin{bmatrix} 2 & -1 & 4 & 1 \\ 4 & 3 & 3 & 7 \end{bmatrix}, \quad \mathbf{b} = \begin{bmatrix} 0 \\ -1 \end{bmatrix}.$

(b) $\quad \mathbf{A} = \begin{bmatrix} 2 & 3 & 4 \\ 5 & 6 & 7 \\ 8 & 9 & 10 \end{bmatrix}, \quad \mathbf{b} = \begin{bmatrix} 1 \\ 2 \\ 4 \end{bmatrix}.$

(c) As (b), except that the final component of $\mathbf{b}$ is 3 rather than 4.

12.2.2 Solve the system $\mathbf{Ax} = \mathbf{b}$ when

$$\mathbf{A} = \begin{bmatrix} 1 & 3 & 1 \\ 3 & 9 & 11 \\ 4 & 12 & 6 \end{bmatrix}, \quad \mathbf{b} = \begin{bmatrix} 0 \\ 0 \\ 0 \end{bmatrix}.$$

What do you notice?

12.2.3 State what the following two systems of linear equations have in common, and use this information to solve both of them.

(a) $\quad 2x_1 + 4x_2 + x_3 = 5, \quad x_1 + x_2 + x_3 = 6, \quad 2x_1 + 3x_2 + x_3 = 6.$

(b) $\quad 2x_1 + 4x_2 + x_3 = 3, \quad x_1 + x_2 + x_3 = -2, \quad 2x_1 + 3x_2 + x_3 = 8.$

12.3 Inverting a matrix

Suppose $\mathbf{A}$ is a square matrix. Does the system $\mathbf{Ax} = \mathbf{0}$ have a solution? Obviously yes: $\mathbf{x} = \mathbf{0}$ will do. Are there other solutions? Answer: maybe. For example,

$$\begin{bmatrix} 1 & 2 \\ 2 & 4 \end{bmatrix} \begin{bmatrix} 2 \\ -1 \end{bmatrix} = \begin{bmatrix} 0 \\ 0 \end{bmatrix}.$$

On the other hand, if

$$\begin{bmatrix} 1 & 2 \\ 2 & 3 \end{bmatrix} \begin{bmatrix} x_1 \\ x_2 \end{bmatrix} = \begin{bmatrix} 0 \\ 0 \end{bmatrix}$$

then $x_1 = x_2 = 0$.

The point we are making here is that there are two kinds of square matrix. Given a square matrix $\mathbf{A}$, we say that $\mathbf{A}$ is **singular** if the system $\mathbf{Ax} = \mathbf{0}$ has some non-zero solution; we say that $\mathbf{A}$ is **nonsingular** if the unique solution of $\mathbf{Ax} = \mathbf{0}$ is $\mathbf{x} = \mathbf{0}$.

Section 12.2 gives us the standard method for testing whether a square matrix $\mathbf{A}$ is singular or nonsingular. This consists of solving the system of equations $\mathbf{Ax} = \mathbf{0}$ in the usual way. As you may have realised when doing

Exercise 12.2.2, it is a waste of time to write explicitly the column of zeros that should appear on the right of each augmented matrix. All that needs to be done is is to reduce $\mathbf{A}$ to an echelon matrix $\mathbf{E}$ by elementary row operations: if $\mathbf{E}$ is Type 4, $\mathbf{A}$ is singular; if $\mathbf{E}$ is Type 1, $\mathbf{A}$ is nonsingular.

Proposition 2 of the last section says that if $\mathbf{A}$ is a square matrix, then whether or not the system $\mathbf{Ax} = \mathbf{b}$ has a unique solution depends only on $\mathbf{A}$, not on $\mathbf{b}$. From this we may infer an important fact about nonsingular matrices: *if $\mathbf{A}$ is a nonsingular $n \times n$ matrix and $\mathbf{y}$ is any n–vector, there is exactly one n–vector $\mathbf{x}$ such that $\mathbf{Ax} = \mathbf{y}$.* Returning to the idea of matrices as mappings, which we introduced in Section 11.2, we may rephrase this fact as follows: if $\mathbf{A}$ is nonsingular and $\mathbf{y}$ is a given vector, exactly one vector $\mathbf{x}$ is transformed by $\mathbf{A}$ into $\mathbf{y}$.

Associated with every nonsingular matrix is another matrix known as its inverse, and we now work towards defining it. Let $\mathbf{A}$ be a nonsingular $n \times n$ matrix, and let $\mathbf{u}^1, \mathbf{u}^2, \ldots, \mathbf{u}^n$ be the columns of the $n \times n$ identity matrix $\mathbf{I}_n$. Since $\mathbf{A}$ is nonsingular the system $\mathbf{Ax} = \mathbf{u}^1$ has a unique solution, say $\mathbf{x} = \mathbf{v}^1$. Similarly there is exactly one n–vector $\mathbf{v}^2$ such that $\mathbf{Av}^2 = \mathbf{u}^2$. And so on up to $\mathbf{v}^n$. Letting $\mathbf{A}^{-1}$ be the $n \times n$ matrix with columns $\mathbf{v}^1, \mathbf{v}^2, \ldots, \mathbf{v}^n$, we see that $\mathbf{AA}^{-1} = \mathbf{I}$.

This brings us to the following definition and proposition:

Definition A square matrix $\mathbf{A}$ is said to be **invertible** if there is a square matrix $\mathbf{A}^{-1}$ with the property that

$$\mathbf{Ax} = \mathbf{y} \ \text{ if and only if } \ \mathbf{x} = \mathbf{A}^{-1}\mathbf{y}.$$

The matrix $\mathbf{A}^{-1}$ is called the **inverse matrix** of $\mathbf{A}$.

Proposition A square matrix is invertible if and only if it is nonsingular.

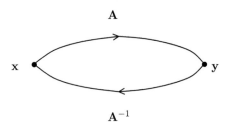

Figure 12.1: **Inverse of a matrix**

The definition of the inverse matrix is illustrated in Figure 12.1, which uses the idea of matrices as mappings. If we start from any n–vector $\mathbf{x}$ and let $\mathbf{y} = \mathbf{Ax}$, then multiplication by $\mathbf{A}^{-1}$ transforms $\mathbf{y}$ back into $\mathbf{x}$. Conversely, if we start from any n–vector $\mathbf{y}$ and let $\mathbf{x} = \mathbf{A}^{-1}\mathbf{y}$, then multiplication by $\mathbf{A}$ transforms $\mathbf{x}$ back into $\mathbf{y}$.

To prove the proposition, notice first that if $\mathbf{A}$ is invertible and $\mathbf{Ax} = \mathbf{0}$, then $\mathbf{x} = \mathbf{A}^{-1}\mathbf{0} = \mathbf{0}$; thus $\mathbf{A}$ is nonsingular. Conversely, suppose $\mathbf{A}$ is a nonsingular $n \times n$ matrix, and let $\mathbf{A}^{-1}$ be the matrix constructed above so as to make $\mathbf{AA}^{-1} = \mathbf{I}$. We want to show that this matrix is indeed the inverse of $\mathbf{A}$.

If $\mathbf{x} = \mathbf{A}^{-1}\mathbf{y}$, then $\mathbf{Ax} = \mathbf{AA}^{-1}\mathbf{y} = \mathbf{Iy} = \mathbf{y}$. Going the other way, let $\mathbf{x}$ and $\mathbf{y}$ be vectors such that $\mathbf{Ax} = \mathbf{y}$. Since $\mathbf{A}$ is nonsingular, $\mathbf{x}$ is the *only* vector transformed by $\mathbf{A}$ into $\mathbf{y}$; but since $\mathbf{AA}^{-1} = \mathbf{I}$, $\mathbf{A}(\mathbf{A}^{-1}\mathbf{y}) = \mathbf{y}$; therefore $\mathbf{A}^{-1}\mathbf{y} = \mathbf{x}$. We have now demonstrated that $\mathbf{A}^{-1}$ has all the properties shown in Figure 12.1; the proposition is proved.

Application and calculation

What is the point of inverting a matrix? The definition of the inverse gives us a clue: if $\mathbf{A}$ is an invertible $n \times n$ matrix and $\mathbf{b}$ is an n–vector, then $\mathbf{A}^{-1}\mathbf{b}$ is the only vector $\mathbf{x}$ such that $\mathbf{Ax} = \mathbf{b}$. We can therefore find the unique solution of the system $\mathbf{Ax} = \mathbf{b}$ by computing $\mathbf{A}^{-1}$ and post-multiplying it by $\mathbf{b}$.

Now this in itself is not very interesting: if we want to solve a single system we should use the methods of the last section and not waste our time computing $\mathbf{A}^{-1}$. Notice however that knowing $\mathbf{A}^{-1}$ enables us to solve $\mathbf{Ax} = \mathbf{b}$ for *any* vector $\mathbf{b}$; and this can be very useful.

To invert a matrix, one follows the steps we went through in building up to the definition of the inverse. Let $\mathbf{u}^1, \mathbf{u}^2, \ldots, \mathbf{u}^n$ be the columns of the identity matrix: then we know that the first column of $\mathbf{A}^{-1}$ is the unique solution to the system $\mathbf{Ax} = \mathbf{u}^1$, the second column of $\mathbf{A}^{-1}$ is the unique solution to the system $\mathbf{Ax} = \mathbf{u}^2$, and so on. We therefore solve all these systems simultaneously by the method suggested at the end of Section 12.2. Starting with the matrix $[\mathbf{A}\ \ \mathbf{I}]$, we reduce it by Gauss–Jordan elimination to the form $[\mathbf{D}\ \ \mathbf{B}]$, where $\mathbf{D}$ is a diagonal matrix with no diagonal entry equal to zero.[1] $\mathbf{A}^{-1}$ is then found by dividing each row of $\mathbf{B}$ by the corresponding diagonal entry of $\mathbf{D}$.

Example Invert the matrix

$$\mathbf{A} = \begin{bmatrix} 2 & 1 & 2 \\ 3 & 1 & 1 \\ 3 & 1 & 2 \end{bmatrix}.$$

Starting with the augmented matrix $[\mathbf{A}\ \ \mathbf{I}]$, we subtract $3/2$ times the first row from each of the other rows to get

$$\left[\begin{array}{ccc|ccc} 2 & 1 & 2 & 1 & 0 & 0 \\ 0 & -1/2 & -2 & -3/2 & 1 & 0 \\ 0 & -1/2 & -1 & -3/2 & 0 & 1 \end{array} \right]$$

Our next Gauss–Jordan elimination step is to add twice the second row to the first row, and to subtract the second row from the third row. We

---

[1]This cannot be done if $\mathbf{A}$ is singular: thus the method provides a built-in test for whether the matrix we start with can be inverted.

obtain

$$\left[\begin{array}{ccc|ccc} 2 & 0 & -2 & -2 & 2 & 0 \\ 0 & -1/2 & -2 & -3/2 & 1 & 0 \\ 0 & 0 & 1 & 0 & -1 & 1 \end{array}\right]$$

One more elimination step gives

$$[\mathbf{D} \ \ \mathbf{B}] = \left[\begin{array}{ccc|ccc} 2 & 0 & 0 & -2 & 0 & 2 \\ 0 & -1/2 & 0 & -3/2 & -1 & 2 \\ 0 & 0 & 1 & 0 & -1 & 1 \end{array}\right]$$

To obtain $\mathbf{A}^{-1}$ we divide the first row of $\mathbf{B}$ by 2, the second row by $-\frac{1}{2}$ and the third by 1:

$$\mathbf{A}^{-1} = \left[\begin{array}{ccc} -1 & 0 & 1 \\ 3 & 2 & -4 \\ 0 & -1 & 1 \end{array}\right].$$

General facts about inverses

Some important facts about inverses follow almost immediately from Figure 12.1.

Fact 1 $\mathbf{A}\mathbf{A}^{-1} = \mathbf{A}^{-1}\mathbf{A} = \mathbf{I}$.

To see why this is so, look again at Figure 12.1. The diagram shows that $\mathbf{A}^{-1}\mathbf{A}\mathbf{x} = \mathbf{x}$ for every $\mathbf{x}$. Recalling the criterion for matrix equality introduced at the end of Section 11.2, we infer that $\mathbf{A}^{-1}\mathbf{A} = \mathbf{I}$. The fact that $\mathbf{A}\mathbf{A}^{-1} = \mathbf{I}$ has already been demonstrated and used; but it also follows from Figure 12.1, which shows that $\mathbf{A}\mathbf{A}^{-1}\mathbf{y} = \mathbf{y}$ for all $\mathbf{y}$.

Figure 12.1 also shows that $\mathbf{A}$ bears the same relation to $\mathbf{A}^{-1}$ that $\mathbf{A}^{-1}$ does to $\mathbf{A}$. We therefore have:

Fact 2 If $\mathbf{A}$ is invertible, so is $\mathbf{A}^{-1}$, and $(\mathbf{A}^{-1})^{-1} = \mathbf{A}$.

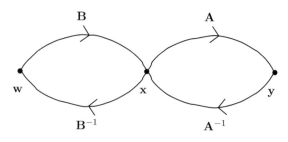

Figure 12.2: **Inverse of a product**

Our next fact shows how inversion interacts with matrix multiplication. Let $\mathbf{A}$ and $\mathbf{B}$ be invertible $n \times n$ matrices. Figure 12.2, which is an extension of Figure 12.1, shows that $\mathbf{ABw} = \mathbf{y}$ is if and only if $\mathbf{w} = \mathbf{B}^{-1}\mathbf{A}^{-1}\mathbf{y}$. This implies:

Fact 3 If $\mathbf{A}$ and $\mathbf{B}$ are invertible so is $\mathbf{AB}$, and

$$(\mathbf{AB})^{-1} = \mathbf{B}^{-1}\mathbf{A}^{-1}.$$

Note that since matrix multiplication is not commutative, $(\mathbf{AB})^{-1}$ is not in general equal to $\mathbf{A}^{-1}\mathbf{B}^{-1}$.

The formula of Fact 3 may be iterated: for example

$$(\mathbf{ABCD})^{-1} = \mathbf{D}^{-1}\mathbf{C}^{-1}\mathbf{B}^{-1}\mathbf{A}^{-1}.$$

Again, notice the order of multiplication!

Our last general fact gives a criterion for invertiblility that is often useful in theoretical work.

Fact 4 If $\mathbf{A}, \mathbf{B}$ are square matrices such that $\mathbf{AB} = \mathbf{I}$, then both $\mathbf{A}$ and $\mathbf{B}$ are invertible, $\mathbf{A}^{-1} = \mathbf{B}$ and $\mathbf{B}^{-1} = \mathbf{A}$.

We now explain why Fact 4 is true. Suppose $\mathbf{AB} = \mathbf{I}$. If $\mathbf{x}$ is any vector such that $\mathbf{Bx} = \mathbf{0}$, then

$$\mathbf{x} = \mathbf{Ix} = \mathbf{ABx} = \mathbf{A0} = \mathbf{0}.$$

Hence $\mathbf{B}$ is nonsingular and therefore invertible. But then

$$\begin{aligned}\mathbf{B}^{-1} &= \mathbf{ABB}^{-1} \quad \text{since } \mathbf{AB} = \mathbf{I}\\ &= \mathbf{A} \quad\quad\quad\ \text{since } \mathbf{BB}^{-1} = \mathbf{I}.\end{aligned}$$

We have shown that $\mathbf{B}$ is invertible, with inverse $\mathbf{A}$. Applying Fact 2 with $\mathbf{A}$ replaced by $\mathbf{B}$, we see that $\mathbf{A}$ is invertible, with inverse $\mathbf{B}$.

The inversion formula for 2×2 matrices

One consequence of Fact 4 is the following helpful formula:

$$\text{if } \mathbf{A} = \begin{bmatrix} a & b \\ c & d \end{bmatrix} \text{ and } ad \neq bc,$$

$$\text{then } \mathbf{A} \text{ is invertible and } \mathbf{A}^{-1} = \frac{1}{ad - bc}\begin{bmatrix} d & -b \\ -c & a \end{bmatrix}.$$

For example,

$$\text{if } \mathbf{A} = \begin{bmatrix} 9 & 7 \\ 2 & 1 \end{bmatrix} \text{ then } \mathbf{A}^{-1} = \frac{1}{(-5)}\begin{bmatrix} 1 & -7 \\ -2 & 9 \end{bmatrix} = \begin{bmatrix} -0.2 & 1.4 \\ 0.4 & -1.8 \end{bmatrix}.$$

To see why the inversion formula is true, let $\mathbf{C} = \begin{bmatrix} d & -b \\ -c & a \end{bmatrix}$, $\lambda = ad - bc$. A simple calculation shows that $\mathbf{AC}$ has both diagonal entries equal to λ and both off-diagonal entries equal to 0: hence $\mathbf{AC} = \lambda\mathbf{I}$. If $\lambda \neq 0$, we may define the matrix $\mathbf{B} = \lambda^{-1}\mathbf{C}$; then $\mathbf{AB} = \mathbf{I}$, so $\mathbf{A}^{-1} = \mathbf{B}$ by Fact 4.

Three points about notation

Returning to the general $n \times n$ case, we make the following important points:

1. The adjectives singular, nonsingular and invertible apply only to square matrices.

2. $\mathbf{AB}^{-1}$ always means $\mathbf{A}(\mathbf{B}^{-1})$, not $(\mathbf{AB})^{-1}$.

3. Fact 1 shows that inverse matrices bear some resemblance to reciprocals. This similarity is responsible for the superscript -1 in the usual notation for the inverse, but it should not be taken too literally. In particular, if $\mathbf{A} \neq \mathbf{B}$ then $\mathbf{AB}^{-1}$ and $\mathbf{B}^{-1}\mathbf{A}$ are in general different matrices; it is therefore *not* a good idea to denote either of these matrices by $\dfrac{\mathbf{A}}{\mathbf{B}}$. As we said at the end of the last chapter, there is no such thing as matrix division.

Exercises

12.3.1 "A square matrix with a row or column consisting entirely of zeros must be singular." Why?

12.3.2 Determine whether the following matrices are singular or nonsingular:

$$\begin{bmatrix} 1 & 2 \\ 3 & 4 \end{bmatrix}, \quad \begin{bmatrix} -2 & -3 \\ 4 & 6 \end{bmatrix}, \quad \begin{bmatrix} 1 & 0 & -2 \\ -1 & 2 & 3 \\ 0 & 2 & 1 \end{bmatrix}, \quad \begin{bmatrix} 2 & -1 & 1 \\ 1 & 0 & 2 \\ -1 & 1 & 3 \end{bmatrix}.$$

12.3.3 Invert the matrices

$$\begin{bmatrix} 3 & -1 \\ 2 & 1 \end{bmatrix}, \quad \begin{bmatrix} 1 & 3 & 5 \\ 1 & 7 & 5 \\ 5 & 10 & 15 \end{bmatrix}, \quad \begin{bmatrix} 0 & 3 & 4 \\ 2 & 0 & 3 \\ -1 & 1 & 0 \end{bmatrix}.$$

Hence solve the systems of equations:

(a) $3x_1 - x_2 = 5$, $2x_1 + x_2 = 15$.

(b) $3x_2 + 4x_3 = 5$, $2x_1 + 3x_3 = -1$, $-x_1 + x_2 = 2$.

12.3.4 Let $\mathbf{A}, \mathbf{B}, \mathbf{C}$ be invertible matrices of the same order. Simplify the expressions

$$(\mathbf{I} + \mathbf{A})\mathbf{A}^{-1}(\mathbf{I} - \mathbf{A}), \quad \mathbf{A}(3\mathbf{A}^{-1} + 4\mathbf{B}^{-1})\mathbf{B}, \quad (\mathbf{AB}^{-1}\mathbf{C})^{-1}.$$

12.3.5 (a) Show that if $\mathbf{A}$ and $\mathbf{B}$ are square matrices such that $\mathbf{A} \neq \mathbf{O}$, $\mathbf{B} \neq \mathbf{O}$ and $\mathbf{AB} = \mathbf{O}$, then both $\mathbf{A}$ and $\mathbf{B}$ must be singular.

(b) Let $\mathbf{A}$ be a square matrix such that $\mathbf{A}^2 = \mathbf{O}$. [Recall from Exercise 11.4.2 that this does not necessarily imply that $\mathbf{A} = \mathbf{O}$.] What can be said about the matrices $\mathbf{I} + \mathbf{A}$ and $\mathbf{I} - \mathbf{A}$?

12.3.6 Let $\mathbf{A} = \begin{bmatrix} t & 1 \\ 1 & t \end{bmatrix}$. Use the inversion formula for 2×2 matrices to find $\mathbf{A}^{-1}$ if t is neither 1 nor -1. What happens if $t = \pm 1$, and why?

12.4 Linear dependence and rank

We introduced linear dependence and independence in Section 11.1, and described a test for finding whether vectors were linearly dependent or independent. However, we said very little about how to apply the test. We now return to this topic.

Let $\mathbf{a}, \mathbf{b}, \mathbf{c}$ be n–vectors and let α, β, γ be scalars. Then we know from Section 11.2 (specifically, property (II) of matrix-vector multiplication) that

$$\alpha\mathbf{a} + \beta\mathbf{b} + \gamma\mathbf{c} = [\mathbf{a} \ \mathbf{b} \ \mathbf{c}] \begin{bmatrix} \alpha \\ \beta \\ \gamma \end{bmatrix}.$$

Now let $\mathbf{A}$ denote the matrix $[\mathbf{a} \ \mathbf{b} \ \mathbf{c}]$ and recall the criterion for linear dependence given at the end of Section 11.1: we see that $\mathbf{a}, \mathbf{b}, \mathbf{c}$ are linearly dependent if and only if the system $\mathbf{A}\mathbf{x} = \mathbf{0}$ has a non-zero solution.

This generalises as follows: *the columns of a matrix $\mathbf{A}$ are linearly dependent if and only if the system $\mathbf{A}\mathbf{x} = \mathbf{0}$ has some non-zero solution.* In particular, the columns of a *square* matrix are linearly dependent if and only the matrix is singular.

Now we showed in the last section how to find whether a square matrix is singular or invertible. The standard test of whether the columns of a general matrix $\mathbf{A}$ are linearly dependent or independent is similar. We reduce $\mathbf{A}$ by elementary row operations to an echelon matrix $\mathbf{E}$. If $\mathbf{E}$ is of Type 1 or Type 3, so that the system $\mathbf{A}\mathbf{x} = \mathbf{0}$ has the unique solution $\mathbf{x} = \mathbf{0}$, the columns of $\mathbf{A}$ are linearly independent. Conversely, if $\mathbf{E}$ is of Type 2 or Type 4 the columns of $\mathbf{A}$ are linearly dependent.

If $\mathbf{A}$ has more columns than rows then $\mathbf{E}$ must be of Type 2 or Type 4, and the columns of $\mathbf{A}$ must be linearly dependent. We have therefore arrived at a general result about dependence of vectors: *if we have a set of **more than** n vectors in $\mathcal{R}^n$, these vectors must be linearly dependent.*

Rank of a matrix

The rank of a matrix is a number, associated with that matrix, which helps to describe the solutions of the corresponding equation systems. The concept of rank has numerous applications in econometrics.

The **rank** of a matrix $\mathbf{A}$ is defined to be the maximal number of linearly independent columns of $\mathbf{A}$. The meaning of 'maximal' is this: if the rank of $\mathbf{A}$ is 5, one can choose a set of 5 linearly independent columns of $\mathbf{A}$, but one cannot choose a set of 6 or more linearly independent columns of $\mathbf{A}$.

Example 1 The purpose of this example is to illustrate the concept of rank; a systematic method of finding the rank is given later in the section. Let

$$\mathbf{A} = \begin{bmatrix} 1 & 0 & 1 \\ 0 & 1 & 1 \\ 1 & 1 & 2 \end{bmatrix}.$$

It is easy to see that any two columns of $\mathbf{A}$ are linearly independent; but the three columns of $\mathbf{A}$ are linearly dependent, since the third columns is the sum of the first two. Thus the rank of $\mathbf{A}$ is 2.

Finding the rank

We begin with echelon matrices. We said at the beginning of this chapter that for any echelon matrix,

number of pivots = number of non-zero rows = number of basic columns.

This number is the rank of the matrix.

To see why this is so, consider first echelon matrices of types 1 and 2. Let $\mathbf{E}$ be an echelon matrix with r rows, none of which consists entirely of zeros. The r basic columns of $\mathbf{E}$ form an invertible triangular matrix and are therefore linearly independent; but since the columns of $\mathbf{E}$ are r–vectors, it is not possible to choose a set of more than r linearly independent columns. Thus the rank of $\mathbf{E}$ is r.

Now notice that three n–vectors $\mathbf{a}, \mathbf{b}, \mathbf{c}$ are linearly dependent if and only if the three $(n+1)$–vectors

$$\begin{bmatrix} \mathbf{a} \\ 0 \end{bmatrix}, \quad \begin{bmatrix} \mathbf{b} \\ 0 \end{bmatrix}, \quad \begin{bmatrix} \mathbf{c} \\ 0 \end{bmatrix}$$

are linearly dependent. This generalises as follows: the rank of a matrix is unaffected if we append or delete rows consisting entirely of zeros. But this implies that the proposition that the rank of an echelon matrix is its number of non-zero rows is just as true for echelon matrices of types 3 and 4 as it is for types 1 and 2.

Having explained how to calculate the rank of an echelon matrix, we now give a method for finding the rank of a general matrix. The principle underlying the method is this: *the rank of a matrix is unaffected by elementary row operations.* To see why this is true, recall from Section 1.2 that the elementary operations transform a system of linear equations into an equivalent one. For this reason, elementary row operations transform a set of linearly independent columns into another set of linearly independent columns, and similarly for linearly dependent columns, leaving the rank of the matrix unchanged.

Thus one way of finding the rank of a matrix is to transform it, by Gaussian elimination, into a matrix whose rank is easy to find; and echelon matrices fall into that category. The method of finding the rank of a matrix $\mathbf{A}$ is therefore as follows: *reduce* $\mathbf{A}$ *to an echelon matrix* $\mathbf{E}$ *by Gaussian elimination; the rank of* $\mathbf{A}$ *is then the number of non-zero rows of* $\mathbf{E}$.

Example 2 Find the rank of the matrix

$$\mathbf{A} = \begin{bmatrix} 2 & -4 & 1 & -8 \\ 4 & -8 & 7 & -6 \\ -1 & 2 & 1 & 7 \end{bmatrix}.$$

In Example 1 of Section 12.2, we reduced this $\mathbf{A}$ by Gaussian elimination to the echelon matrix

$$\mathbf{E} = \begin{bmatrix} 2 & -4 & 1 & -8 \\ 0 & 0 & 5 & 10 \\ 0 & 0 & 0 & 0 \end{bmatrix}.$$

Since $\mathbf{E}$ has exactly two rows which do not consist entirely of zeros, the rank of $\mathbf{A}$ is 2.

Exercises

12.4.1 (a) Let

$$\mathbf{A} = \begin{bmatrix} 1 & 5 & -2 \\ 1 & 3 & 1 \\ 2 & 2 & 0 \end{bmatrix}.$$

Find the complete solution of the system $\mathbf{A}\mathbf{x} = \mathbf{0}$, and say whether the columns of $\mathbf{A}$ are linearly independent. If they are dependent, find scalars $\alpha_1, \alpha_2, \alpha_3$, not all zero, such that

$$\alpha_1 \mathbf{a}^1 + \alpha_2 \mathbf{a}^2 + \alpha_3 \mathbf{a}^3 = \mathbf{0},$$

where $\mathbf{a}^1, \mathbf{a}^2, \mathbf{a}^3$ are the columns of $\mathbf{A}$.

(b) As (a), but with

$$\mathbf{A} = \begin{bmatrix} -1 & 0 & 4 \\ 1 & 2 & 4 \\ 1 & -1 & -8 \end{bmatrix}.$$

12.4.2 Find the ranks of the following matrices directly from the definition:

(a) $\begin{bmatrix} 3 & 0 \\ 5 & 1 \\ 9 & 1 \end{bmatrix}$ (b) $\begin{bmatrix} 1 & 2 & 3 & 4 \\ 3 & 6 & 9 & 12 \end{bmatrix}$ (c) $\begin{bmatrix} 1 & 2 & 3 & 4 \\ 3 & 6 & 9 & 11 \end{bmatrix}.$

12.4.3 Use the results of exercise 11.1.4 to find the ranks of the following matrices:

(a) $\begin{bmatrix} 1 & 0 & 1 \\ 0 & 1 & 1 \end{bmatrix}$ (b) $\begin{bmatrix} 0 & 1 & 1 \\ 1 & 0 & 1 \\ 1 & 1 & 0 \end{bmatrix}$

(c) $\begin{bmatrix} 1 & 4 & 7 \\ 2 & 5 & 8 \\ 3 & 6 & 9 \end{bmatrix}$ (d) $\begin{bmatrix} 13 & 0 & 3 \\ 7 & 0 & -2 \\ 9 & 0 & 5 \\ 2 & 0 & 8 \end{bmatrix}$

In cases (b) and (c), check your results by reduction to echelon form.

12.4.4 Let $\mathbf{A}$ and $\mathbf{B}$ be matrices such that the product $\mathbf{AB}$ is defined.

(a) Show that, if the columns of $\mathbf{B}$ are linearly dependent, so are the columns of $\mathbf{AB}$.

(b) If the second, fourth and fifth columns of $\mathbf{B}$ form a linearly dependent set of vectors, can we be sure that the same is true of the second, fourth and fifth columns of $\mathbf{AB}$?

(c) If we have a set of four linearly independent columns of $\mathbf{AB}$, how can we find a set of four linearly independent columns of $\mathbf{B}$?

(d) How is the rank of $\mathbf{AB}$ related to that of $\mathbf{B}$?

Problems on Chapter 12

12–1. (i) Let

$$\mathbf{A} = \begin{bmatrix} 2 & 1 & 5 & 2 \\ 1 & 0 & 4 & 3 \\ 4 & 3 & 7 & 0 \end{bmatrix}, \quad \mathbf{b} = \begin{bmatrix} t \\ t \\ t \end{bmatrix}.$$

For which values of t does the system $\mathbf{Ax} = \mathbf{b}$ have a solution? Find the rank of $\mathbf{A}$; also find the rank of the augmented matrix $[\mathbf{A} \quad \mathbf{b}]$ for all values of t. Comment on your results.

(ii) As (i), but with

$$\mathbf{A} = \begin{bmatrix} 1 & 6 & -7 & 3 & 5 \\ 1 & 9 & -6 & 4 & 9 \\ 1 & 3 & -8 & 4 & 2 \\ 2 & 15 & -13 & 11 & 16 \end{bmatrix}, \quad \mathbf{b} = \begin{bmatrix} 1 \\ 2 \\ 2 \\ t \end{bmatrix}.$$

12–2. Consider the partitioned matrix

$$\mathbf{A} = \begin{bmatrix} \mathbf{A}_1 & \mathbf{O} \\ \mathbf{O} & \mathbf{A}_2 \end{bmatrix},$$

where $\mathbf{A}_1$ and $\mathbf{A}_2$ are invertible square matrices. Show that $\mathbf{A}$ is invertible, with

$$\mathbf{A}^{-1} = \begin{bmatrix} \mathbf{A}_1^{-1} & \mathbf{O} \\ \mathbf{O} & \mathbf{A}_2^{-1} \end{bmatrix}.$$

Hence find the inverses of

$$\begin{bmatrix} 5 & -2 & 0 & 0 \\ 2 & 3 & 0 & 0 \\ 0 & 0 & 1 & 4 \\ 0 & 0 & -1 & 2 \end{bmatrix} \quad \text{and} \quad \begin{bmatrix} 1 & 4 & -3 & 0 \\ 2 & 0 & 1 & 0 \\ 4 & -1 & 3 & 0 \\ 0 & 0 & 0 & 2 \end{bmatrix}.$$

12–3. Let

$$\mathbf{A} = \begin{bmatrix} a_1 & a_2 & a_3 \\ b_1 & b_2 & b_3 \\ c_1 & c_2 & c_3 \end{bmatrix}, \quad \mathbf{B} = \begin{bmatrix} a_1 & a_2 \\ b_1 & b_2 \end{bmatrix}.$$

Suppose $\mathbf{B}$ is nonsingular.

(i) Explain *briefly* why there is a unique 2–vector $\mathbf{z}$ such that

$$\mathbf{Bz} = \begin{bmatrix} a_3 \\ b_3 \end{bmatrix}.$$

(ii) Let $\mathbf{x}$ be a 3–vector. Show that

$$\begin{bmatrix} a_1 & a_2 & a_3 \\ b_1 & b_2 & b_3 \end{bmatrix} \mathbf{x} = \begin{bmatrix} 0 \\ 0 \end{bmatrix}$$

if and only if there is a scalar λ such that

$$\mathbf{x} = \lambda \begin{bmatrix} z_1 \\ z_2 \\ -1 \end{bmatrix}.$$

(iii) Show that $\mathbf{A}$ is singular if and only if

$$c_1 z_1 + c_2 z_2 = c_3.$$

(iv) Show that, if $\mathbf{A}$ is singular, it can be transformed into an invertible matrix by replacing its $(3,3)$ entry by any number other than c_3.

[This problem will be followed up in Problem 13–1, and its relevance for applications explained.]

12–4. In this problem we consider the n–good input-output model of Problem 11–4. Notation is as in that problem.

Suppose we wish to find a gross output vector $\mathbf{x}$ which yields a given vector $\mathbf{y}$ of net outputs. What properties must the input-output matrix $\mathbf{A}$ have if this problem is to have a unique solution for every vector $\mathbf{y}$ with non-negative components? Bear in mind that gross outputs are also required to be non-negative.

Chapter 13

DETERMINANTS AND QUADRATIC FORMS

This chapter is mainly concerned with square matrices, and in particular with real-valued functions of square matrices.

The first function we consider is the determinant. The determinant of a square matrix $\mathbf{A}$, denoted by $\det \mathbf{A}$, is a scalar associated with $\mathbf{A}$, defined by rules which we state at the beginning of Section 13.1. In nineteenth-century mathematics, and in some textbooks written for students of economics as recently as the 1970s, more importance was attached to determinants than to matrices. While it is now generally recognised that determinants play a rather small part in the theory of linear algebra and have a strictly limited usefulness in applications, some facility at handling them is an essential part of an economist's mathematical education. Our approach to determinants is in the spirit of last chapter's emphasis on row operations, and we restrict ourselves to the most basic properties.

The other main topic of this chapter, quadratic forms, has many applications in statistics and econometrics, mainly in connection with calculation of standard errors of estimates. Quadratic forms are also used widely in the calculus of functions of several variables, as we shall see in Chapter 16.

While this is not a rigorous book, we have attempted in most chapters to give some explanation, albeit informal, of why the main results are true. This chapter is something of an exception, in that most of the important facts about determinants are stated without any attempt at proof. This is because the proofs tend to be intricate and, in our view, not much help to understanding. The price the reader has to pay is to take a lot of results on trust; anyone who feels short-changed should consult the books by Cohn and Strang cited in 'Notes on Further Reading' at the end of this book.

A notational device which we sometimes use in this and subsequent chapters is that of **row vectors**: we apply the concepts of vector addition, multiplication by scalars and linear dependence to lists of numbers *written as rows*. In particular, we treat rows of matrices in this way: notice that when we do this we are merely making explicit something that was implicit in the use of row operations in the last chapter. Because we shall be using row vectors, we shall often use the term **column vector** to mean what we called simply a vector in Chapters 11 and 12.

When you have studied this chapter you will be able to:

- calculate determinants using Gaussian elimination and via row and column expansions;

- use transposition in conjunction with the other operations of matrix algebra;

- invert matrices by the adj-over-det method, and solve systems of linear equations using Cramer's rule;

- test symmetric matrices for definiteness and semidefiniteness.

13.1 Determinants

We begin by defining the determinant of a triangular matrix:

D1 The determinant of a triangular matrix is the product of its diagonal entries.

We showed in Section 12.1 that any square matrix can be reduced to a triangular matrix by elementary row operations. We can therefore complete our definition of the determinant of a matrix by specifying the effects of row operations. The rules are:

D2 The determinant changes sign when two rows are exchanged.

D3 If a multiple of one row is subtracted from another row, the determinant remains unchanged.

The determinant of a matrix $\mathbf{A}$ is denoted by $\det \mathbf{A}$.

Some determinants can be evaluated using just **D1** and **D2**: for example

$$\det \begin{bmatrix} 0 & 0 & 6 \\ 0 & 4 & 5 \\ 1 & 2 & 3 \end{bmatrix} = -\det \begin{bmatrix} 1 & 2 & 3 \\ 0 & 4 & 5 \\ 0 & 0 & 6 \end{bmatrix} = -24.$$

Two very special cases are worthy of mention. First, consider the case of a 1×1 matrix $[a]$, where a is a scalar: here

$$\det [a] = a,$$

by **D1**. Second, *a matrix with two identical rows has determinant* 0. For if two rows of $\mathbf{A}$ are identical, then $\det \mathbf{A} = -\det \mathbf{A}$ by **D2**, so $\det \mathbf{A} = 0$.

In general, however, we need all three defining properties **D1–D3** to find the determinant of a given $n \times n$ matrix. The basic procedure is to reduce the matrix to triangular form by Gaussian elimination, keeping track of the effects of the row operations on the determinant by means of **D2** and **D3**. Once a triangular matrix is reached, the determinant can be calculated using **D1**.

We now discuss this procedure in more detail.

Applying the rules

Consider first the case $n = 2$. Let

$$\mathbf{A} = \begin{bmatrix} a & b \\ c & d \end{bmatrix}.$$

If $a = 0$, exchanging the rows of $\mathbf{A}$ gives a triangular matrix with diagonal entries c and b; thus $\det \mathbf{A} = -bc$ by **D1** and **D2**. If $a \neq 0$ we may subtract c/a times the first row of $\mathbf{A}$ from the second row and apply **D2** and **D3**: we then have

$$\det \mathbf{A} = a \left(d - \frac{bc}{a} \right).$$

Putting all this together we see that, whether or not a is zero,

$$\det \mathbf{A} = ad - bc.$$

It is conventional to write

$$\det \begin{bmatrix} a & b \\ c & d \end{bmatrix} = \begin{vmatrix} a & b \\ c & d \end{vmatrix},$$

with a similar notation for matrices of higher order. The formula for a 2×2 determinant that we have just derived may be written

$$\begin{vmatrix} a & b \\ c & d \end{vmatrix} = ad - bc. \tag{13.1}$$

Formulae for determinants of higher order may be derived similarly, but are too complicated to be of much use. Instead, we apply Gaussian elimination[1] directly, reducing the given matrix $\mathbf{A}$ to an upper triangular matrix $\mathbf{U}$. By **D1**, $\det \mathbf{U}$ is the product of the diagonal entries of $\mathbf{U}$. And by **D2** and **D3**,

$$\det \mathbf{A} = (-1)^k \det \mathbf{U},$$

where k is the number of times two rows have been exchanged in the reduction process.

---

[1] Here, as throughout this book, we are using 'Gaussian elimination' to mean repeated application of just two kinds of elementary row operation: row exchanges, and subtraction of multiples *of* the pivot row *from* other rows.

Example 1 Compute det $\mathbf{A}$ when

$$\mathbf{A} = \begin{bmatrix} 2 & 3 & 4 \\ 2 & 3 & 7 \\ 5 & 8 & 6 \end{bmatrix}.$$

The obvious elimination step yields the matrix

$$\begin{bmatrix} 2 & 3 & 4 \\ 0 & 0 & 3 \\ 0 & \frac{1}{2} & -4 \end{bmatrix}.$$

Exchanging the second and third rows gives us the triangular matrix

$$\begin{bmatrix} 2 & 3 & 4 \\ 0 & \frac{1}{2} & -4 \\ 0 & 0 & 3 \end{bmatrix},$$

which we denote by $\mathbf{U}$. Since there has been *one* row exchange,

$$\det \mathbf{A} = (-1)^1 \det \mathbf{U} = -(2 \times \tfrac{1}{2} \times 3) = -3.$$

More properties

A consequence of the standard method of calculating determinants is:

D4 A square matrix is singular if and only if its determinant is zero.

To see why this is so, consider the evaluation of det $\mathbf{A}$ by reducing $\mathbf{A}$ to an upper triangular matrix $\mathbf{U}$. If $\mathbf{A}$ is invertible then $\mathbf{U}$ is a Type 1 echelon matrix, with all diagonal entries non-zero: in this case det $\mathbf{A} \neq 0$. If $\mathbf{A}$ is singular then $\mathbf{U}$ is a Type 4 echelon matrix, with at least one zero on the diagonal; in this case det $\mathbf{A} = 0$.

It is clear from **D1** that det $\mathbf{I}_n = 1$ for all n, and det $2\mathbf{I}_n$ depends on n: det $2\mathbf{I}_2 = 2 \times 2 = 4$, det $2\mathbf{I}_3 = 2^3 = 8$ and so on. These examples demonstrate two important facts: $\det(\mathbf{A} + \mathbf{B})$ is not in general equal to det $\mathbf{A}$ + det $\mathbf{B}$, and $\det(\lambda\mathbf{A})$ is not in general equal to $\lambda(\det \mathbf{A})$.

The fundamental reason for this is that determinants are directly related to the operations of addition and multiplication by scalars, but *applied to individual rows rather than the whole matrix*. The relevant rules are as follows:

D5 If the matrices $\mathbf{A}, \mathbf{B}, \mathbf{C}$ are identical in all rows except one (say the rth), and

$$r\text{th row of } \mathbf{A} + r\text{th row of } \mathbf{B} = r\text{th row of } \mathbf{C},$$

then det $\mathbf{A}$ + det $\mathbf{B}$ = det $\mathbf{C}$.

D6 If *one* row of a matrix is multiplied by the scalar λ, *and the others are left unchanged*, the determinant is multiplied by λ.

D5 implies, for example, that

$$\begin{vmatrix} a & b \\ c & d \end{vmatrix} + \begin{vmatrix} a' & b' \\ c & d \end{vmatrix} = \begin{vmatrix} a + a' & b + b' \\ c & d \end{vmatrix}.$$

D6 can be iterated: for instance, multiplying the first row of a matrix by 2 and the second by -5, leaving all other rows unchanged, multiplies the determinant by -10. Notice that if we multiply the whole matrix by a scalar λ we are multiplying *every* row by λ. Hence:

D7 If $\mathbf{A}$ is $n \times n$, $\det(\lambda \mathbf{A}) = \lambda^n \det \mathbf{A}$.

Row expansions and cofactors

Consider the 3×3 matrix

$$\mathbf{A} = \begin{bmatrix} a_{11} & a_{12} & a_{13} \\ a_{21} & a_{22} & a_{23} \\ a_{31} & a_{32} & a_{33} \end{bmatrix}. \tag{13.2}$$

It can be shown that

$$\det \mathbf{A} = a_{11} \begin{vmatrix} a_{22} & a_{23} \\ a_{32} & a_{33} \end{vmatrix} - a_{12} \begin{vmatrix} a_{21} & a_{23} \\ a_{31} & a_{33} \end{vmatrix} + a_{13} \begin{vmatrix} a_{21} & a_{22} \\ a_{31} & a_{32} \end{vmatrix}. \tag{13.3}$$

This equation is called **expansion of** $\det \mathbf{A}$ **by the first row**. Used in conjunction with (13.1), it provides another method of computing a 3×3 determinant. For instance, if

$$\mathbf{A} = \begin{bmatrix} 2 & 3 & 4 \\ 2 & 3 & 7 \\ 5 & 8 & 6 \end{bmatrix},$$

as in Example 1, then

$$\begin{aligned} \det \mathbf{A} &= 2 \begin{vmatrix} 3 & 7 \\ 8 & 6 \end{vmatrix} - 3 \begin{vmatrix} 2 & 7 \\ 5 & 6 \end{vmatrix} + 4 \begin{vmatrix} 2 & 3 \\ 5 & 8 \end{vmatrix} \\ &= 2(18 - 56) - 3(12 - 35) + 4(16 - 15) \\ &= -76 + 69 + 4. \end{aligned}$$

Hence $\det \mathbf{A} = -3$, as before.

For the purpose of generalisation, it is helpful to write (13.3) in a slightly different way. Let $\mathbf{A}$ be as in (13.2). For each $i = 1, 2, 3$ and $j = 1, 2, 3$ we define the (i, j) **cofactor** of $\mathbf{A}$ to be the scalar

$$\tilde{a}_{ij} = (-1)^{i+j} \det \mathbf{A}_{ij},$$

where $\mathbf{A}_{ij}$ is the 2×2 matrix obtained from $\mathbf{A}$ by deleting its ith row and jth column. Then

$$\tilde{a}_{11} = + \begin{vmatrix} a_{22} & a_{23} \\ a_{32} & a_{33} \end{vmatrix}, \quad \tilde{a}_{12} = - \begin{vmatrix} a_{21} & a_{23} \\ a_{31} & a_{33} \end{vmatrix}$$

and so on. The formula (13.3) for expansion of $\det \mathbf{A}$ by its first row may then be written

$$\det \mathbf{A} = a_{11}\tilde{a}_{11} + a_{12}\tilde{a}_{12} + a_{13}\tilde{a}_{13}.$$

We now state some generalisations of this formula. First, we can let $\mathbf{A}$ be a square matrix of any order $n > 1$. For such a matrix, we define cofactors as above, except that each $\mathbf{A}_{ij}$ is now an $(n - 1) \times (n - 1)$ matrix; to calculate $\tilde{a}_{ij}$, one therefore needs to compute a determinant of order $n - 1$. Expansion of $\det \mathbf{A}$ by the first row is given by

$$\det \mathbf{A} = a_{11}\tilde{a}_{11} + a_{12}\tilde{a}_{12} + \ldots + a_{1n}\tilde{a}_{1n}. \tag{13.4}$$

Notice that this reduces to (13.3) in the case $n = 3$ (and to (13.1) in the case $n = 2$, if we think of scalars as 1×1 determinants).

Second, expansion by the first row can be generalised to expansion by any row. We could expand by the rth row by performing $r - 1$ row exchanges to bring the rth row on top, with the other rows in their original order, and then applying (13.4). But, by **D2** and the definition of cofactors, we do not actually have to perform the exchanges since their effect may be summarised as follows:

$$\det \mathbf{A} = a_{r1}\tilde{a}_{r1} + a_{r2}\tilde{a}_{r2} + \ldots + a_{rn}\tilde{a}_{rn}. \tag{13.5}$$

This is known as **expansion by the rth row** and is true for $r = 1, \ldots, n$.

The formula (13.5) gives us n different ways of expanding $\det \mathbf{A}$ in terms of determinants of order $n - 1$. If $n > 3$, these in turn can be expressed in terms of determinants of order $n - 2$, and so on until we get down to order 2 and apply (13.1).

For determinants of order 3 or more whose entries are fully specified as numbers, Gaussian elimination is usually a quicker method of computation than row expansion. The latter method can however be useful when entries are given as symbols rather than numbers. Generally, it saves effort to expand by a row with some zero entries.

Example 2 Compute $\det \mathbf{A}$ when

$$\mathbf{A} = \begin{bmatrix} p & 1 & q \\ 2 & 0 & 3 \\ r & 4 & s \end{bmatrix}.$$

Expanding by the second row,

$$\begin{aligned} \det \mathbf{A} &= 2 \times (-1)^{2+1} \times \begin{vmatrix} 1 & q \\ 4 & s \end{vmatrix} + 3 \times (-1)^{2+3} \times \begin{vmatrix} p & 1 \\ r & 4 \end{vmatrix} \\ &= -2(s - 4q) - 3(4p - r) \\ &= -12p + 8q + 3r - 2s. \end{aligned}$$

Determinants and matrix multiplication

A very important property of determinants is

D8 $\det(\mathbf{AB}) = \det \mathbf{A} \times \det \mathbf{B}.$

A consequence of this is a formula for the determinant of an inverse matrix. Let $\mathbf{A}$ be an invertible matrix. Then $\mathbf{AA}^{-1} = \mathbf{I}$; hence by **D8** and **D1**,

$$\det \mathbf{A} \times \det \mathbf{A}^{-1} = 1.$$

Therefore

D9 $\det \mathbf{A}^{-1} = \dfrac{1}{\det \mathbf{A}}.$

Exercises

13.1.1 Evaluate the determinants

$$\begin{vmatrix} 1 & 3 & 2 \\ 8 & 4 & 0 \\ 2 & 1 & 2 \end{vmatrix}, \quad \begin{vmatrix} 0 & a & 1 \\ 1 & 0 & b \\ c & 1 & 0 \end{vmatrix}, \quad \begin{vmatrix} 1 & 1 & 1 & -1 \\ 1 & 1 & -1 & 1 \\ 1 & -1 & 1 & 1 \\ -1 & 1 & 1 & 1 \end{vmatrix}.$$

13.1.2 Determine the values of t for which the matrix

$$\begin{bmatrix} t & 1 & 0 \\ 0 & t & 0 \\ 0 & 0 & t+3 \end{bmatrix}$$

is invertible.

13.1.3 Verify **D5** and **D6** for general 3×3 matrices using row expansions.

13.2   Transposition

The **transpose** of a (not necessarily square) matrix $\mathbf{A}$ is the matrix $\mathbf{A}^{\mathrm{T}}$ whose rows are the columns of $\mathbf{A}$: thus

$$\text{if } \mathbf{A} = \begin{bmatrix} 3 & 1 & 4 \\ 8 & 9 & 6 \end{bmatrix} \text{ then } \mathbf{A}^{\mathrm{T}} = \begin{bmatrix} 3 & 8 \\ 1 & 9 \\ 4 & 6 \end{bmatrix}.$$

Some books denote the transpose of $\mathbf{A}$ by $\mathbf{A}'$ rather than $\mathbf{A}^{\mathrm{T}}$.

    Transposition interacts in the obvious way with addition and multiplication by scalars:

$$(\alpha \mathbf{A} + \beta \mathbf{B})^{\mathrm{T}} = \alpha \mathbf{A}^{\mathrm{T}} + \beta \mathbf{B}^{\mathrm{T}}.$$

The interaction with matrix multiplication is more subtle:

$$(\mathbf{AB})^{\mathrm{T}} = \mathbf{B}^{\mathrm{T}}\mathbf{A}^{\mathrm{T}}. \tag{13.6}$$

Notice the order of multiplication! In particular, notice that $(\mathbf{AB})^{\mathrm{T}}$ is not in general equal to $\mathbf{A}^{\mathrm{T}}\mathbf{B}^{\mathrm{T}}$.

To illustrate these points, suppose $\mathbf{A}$ is a 2×3 matrix and $\mathbf{B}$ is a 3×4 matrix. Then $\mathbf{A}^{\mathrm{T}}$ has 2 columns and $\mathbf{B}^{\mathrm{T}}$ has 4 rows, so $\mathbf{A}^{\mathrm{T}}\mathbf{B}^{\mathrm{T}}$ is not even defined. On the other hand, $(\mathbf{AB})^{\mathrm{T}}$ and $\mathbf{B}^{\mathrm{T}}\mathbf{A}^{\mathrm{T}}$ are well-defined 4×2 matrices: that they are the same matrix is not so obvious, but it does follow from the definition of matrix multiplication.

One way of remembering the order of multiplication in transposing a product is to note that it is similar to that when inverting a product. There are two other points of similarity here. First, (13.6) can be iterated: for example

$$(\mathbf{ABCD})^{\mathrm{T}} = \mathbf{D}^{\mathrm{T}}\mathbf{C}^{\mathrm{T}}\mathbf{B}^{\mathrm{T}}\mathbf{A}^{\mathrm{T}}.$$

Secondly, $\mathbf{AB}^{\mathrm{T}}$ always means $\mathbf{A}(\mathbf{B}^{\mathrm{T}})$, not $(\mathbf{AB})^{\mathrm{T}}$.

For any matrix $\mathbf{A}$, two transpositions get you back where you started:

$$(\mathbf{A}^{\mathrm{T}})^{\mathrm{T}} = \mathbf{A}.$$

Note that this is so whether or not $\mathbf{A}$ is square.

If $\mathbf{A}$ is an invertible square matrix, then

$$\mathbf{A}^{\mathrm{T}}(\mathbf{A}^{-1})^{\mathrm{T}} = (\mathbf{A}^{-1}\mathbf{A})^{\mathrm{T}} = \mathbf{I}^{\mathrm{T}} = \mathbf{I}.$$

Hence $\mathbf{A}^{\mathrm{T}}$ is also invertible and

$$(\mathbf{A}^{\mathrm{T}})^{-1} = (\mathbf{A}^{-1})^{\mathrm{T}}.$$

More on rank

In Section 12.4 we defined the rank of a (not necessarily square) matrix as its maximal number of linearly independent columns. We also gave a method for computing the rank via Gaussian elimination.

By considering how the method works, one can show that *the rank of a matrix is equal to the maximal order of its invertible square submatrices.*[2] This means the following: if $\mathbf{A}$ is a matrix of rank r one can obtain an invertible $r \times r$ matrix by deleting rows and/or columns of $\mathbf{A}$, but one cannot obtain an invertible matrix of order $r + 1$ in that way.

This description of rank in terms of invertible submatrices, together with the fact that the transpose of an invertible matrix is invertible, implies that

$$\text{rank of } \mathbf{A}^{\mathrm{T}} = \text{rank of } \mathbf{A}$$

---

[2] A submatrix of a matrix $\mathbf{A}$ is a matrix obtained from $\mathbf{A}$ by deleting some (or none) of its rows and some (or none) of its columns. If a matrix is partitioned into blocks, as in the last part of Section 11.3, these blocks are submatrices of the original matrix.

for any matrix $\mathbf{A}$. This in turn implies that the rank of a matrix is equal to its maximal number of linearly independent *rows*.

For example, consider the matrix

$$\begin{bmatrix} 1 & 0 & -3 & 2 & -4 & 7 \\ 3 & -4 & 5 & 0 & 0 & -3 \\ 2 & -2 & 1 & 1 & -2 & 2 \end{bmatrix}.$$

There are various ways of showing that the rank of this matrix is 2, but the easiest is by inspection of the rows: the first and second are linearly independent, while the third is half the sum of the first two.

Transposition and determinants

The crucial rule here is that

$$\det \mathbf{A}^{\mathrm{T}} = \det \mathbf{A}.$$

For example, when $n = 2$ we have

$$\begin{vmatrix} a & c \\ b & d \end{vmatrix} = ad - cb = ad - bc = \begin{vmatrix} a & b \\ c & d \end{vmatrix}.$$

For $n > 2$ the rule is much less obvious; it is one of the many properties of determinants that we ask the reader to take on trust.

Because transposition leaves the determinant unchanged, all the general properties of determinants in the last section remain true when we replace the word 'rows' by 'columns'. For example, the determinant changes sign when two columns are exchanged; and if a multiple of one column is subtracted from another column, the determinant remains unchanged.

Similarly, one can express determinants in terms of their cofactors using expansions based on columns rather than rows: the rule for expansion by the kth column is

$$\det \mathbf{A} = a_{1k}\tilde{a}_{1k} + a_{2k}\tilde{a}_{2k} + \ldots + a_{nk}\tilde{a}_{nk}. \tag{13.5'}$$

This holds for $k = 1, \ldots, n$. Notice that (13.5) and (13.5'), taken together, give $2n$ possible expansions of an $n \times n$ determinant.

Associated with the expansion formulae are the so-called **alien cofactors formulae**

$$a_{r1}\tilde{a}_{s1} + a_{r2}\tilde{a}_{s2} + \ldots + a_{rn}\tilde{a}_{sn} = 0 \quad \text{if } r \neq s \tag{13.7}$$

and

$$a_{1k}\tilde{a}_{1\ell} + a_{2k}\tilde{a}_{2\ell} + \ldots + a_{nk}\tilde{a}_{n\ell} = 0 \quad \text{if } k \neq \ell. \tag{13.7'}$$

To see why (13.7) holds, let $\mathbf{B}$ be the matrix whose sth row is the rth row of $\mathbf{A}$ and whose other rows, including the rth, are as in $\mathbf{A}$. Then the left hand side of (13.7) is the expansion of $\det \mathbf{B}$ by its sth row. But since the rth and sth rows of $\mathbf{B}$ are identical, $\det \mathbf{B} = 0$. Hence (13.7) is true; similar reasoning using expansion by columns establishes (13.7').

The adjoint matrix

The **cofactor matrix** of an $n \times n$ matrix $\mathbf{A}$ is, not surprisingly, the matrix of its cofactors: it is the matrix $\tilde{\mathbf{A}}$ whose (i, j) entry $\tilde{a}_{ij}$ is the (i, j) cofactor of $\mathbf{A}$. The transpose of $\tilde{\mathbf{A}}$ is called the **adjoint matrix** of $\mathbf{A}$ and is denoted by $\mathbf{A}^*$: thus

$$\mathbf{A}^* = \tilde{\mathbf{A}}^{\mathrm{T}}.$$

Now consider the matrix $\mathbf{A}\mathbf{A}^*$. The row expansion formula (13.5) tell us that each diagonal entry of $\mathbf{A}\mathbf{A}^*$ is equal to $\det \mathbf{A}$, while the alien cofactors formula (13.7) tells us that each off-diagonal entry of $\mathbf{A}\mathbf{A}^*$ is 0. Hence $\mathbf{A}\mathbf{A}^* = (\det \mathbf{A})\mathbf{I}$. Similarly, it follows from (13.5') and (13.7') that $\mathbf{A}^*\mathbf{A} = (\det \mathbf{A})\mathbf{I}$. Summarising,

$$\mathbf{A}\mathbf{A}^* = \mathbf{A}^*\mathbf{A} = (\det \mathbf{A})\mathbf{I}. \tag{13.8}$$

Adj-over-det and Cramer's rule

From (13.8) follows a famous formula for the inverse of a matrix, often called the 'adj-over-det' formula: if $\mathbf{A}$ is invertible,

$$\mathbf{A}^{-1} = \frac{1}{\det \mathbf{A}} \mathbf{A}^*. \tag{13.9}$$

The special case of (13.9) for 2×2 matrices is the inversion formula given near the end of Section 12.3.

From (13.9) can be derived a formula for the solution to a system of linear equations:

Cramer's rule If $\mathbf{A}$ is invertible, the solution to the system $\mathbf{A}\mathbf{x} = \mathbf{b}$ is

$$x_j = \frac{\det \mathbf{B}_j}{\det \mathbf{A}} \quad \text{for } j = 1, \dots, n$$

where, for each j, $\mathbf{B}_j$ is the matrix obtained from $\mathbf{A}$ by replacing its jth column by $\mathbf{b}$.

How useful are adj-over-det and Cramer's rule? In our opinion, not very. For matrices of order 4 or more, Gauss–Jordan is the preferred method of matrix inversion: formula (13.9) is too complicated to apply. Similarly, Cramer's rule is a terrible way of solving a numerical system of linear equations: Gaussian elimination or Gauss-Jordan is far better. Cramer's rule can sometimes be useful when coefficients are expressed in symbolic form rather than taking specific numerical values. This is the context in which the rule is sometimes used in the literature of economic theory, though such techniques are much less popular now than they were thirty years ago.

Exercises

13.2.1 In Section 12.3, we showed that

$$\text{if } \mathbf{A} = \begin{bmatrix} 2 & 1 & 2 \\ 3 & 1 & 1 \\ 3 & 1 & 2 \end{bmatrix} \quad \text{then } \mathbf{A}^{-1} = \begin{bmatrix} -1 & 0 & 1 \\ 3 & 2 & -4 \\ 0 & -1 & 1 \end{bmatrix}.$$

Use this result to write down the inverse of the matrix

$$\begin{bmatrix} 2 & 3 & 3 \\ 1 & 1 & 1 \\ 2 & 1 & 2 \end{bmatrix}.$$

13.2.2 An **orthogonal matrix** is an invertible square matrix whose inverse is its transpose. By Facts 1 and 4 of Section 12.3, a square matrix $\mathbf{A}$ is orthogonal if and only if $\mathbf{A}\mathbf{A}^{\mathrm{T}} = \mathbf{I}$.

(a) Show that

$$\begin{bmatrix} 1 & 0 \\ 0 & 1 \end{bmatrix} \quad \text{and} \quad \frac{1}{\sqrt{2}}\begin{bmatrix} 1 & 1 \\ 1 & -1 \end{bmatrix}$$

are orthogonal matrices.

(b) Prove that the determinant of an orthogonal matrix is either 1 or -1. Show that both cases can occur.

13.2.3 Find the inverse of the third matrix of Exercise 12.3.3 using the adj-over-det rule.

13.2.4 Let a, b, c be constants such that $abc \neq -1$. Use Cramer's rule to solve the system of equations

$$ay + z = 1, \quad x + bz = 1, \quad cx + y = 1.$$

[You were asked to calculate the determinant of the coefficient matrix in Exercise 13.1.1.]

13.2.5 Recall the macroeconomic model of Problem 2–1. The unknowns are Y (national income), C (consumption) and T (tax collection); I (investment) and G (government expenditure) are assumed to be known. The equations of the model are

$$Y = C + I + G, \quad C = c_0 + c_1(Y - T), \quad T = t_0 + t_1 Y;$$

c_0, c_1, t_0, t_1 are constant parameters, with $0 < c_1 < 1$ and $0 < t_1 < 1$. Use Cramer's rule to find Y, C and T in terms of I, G and the parameters.

13.3   Inner products and quadratic forms

Having discussed transposition of matrices, we turn to transposition of vectors. Given a column-vector $\mathbf{x}$ in $\mathcal{R}^n$, $\mathbf{x}^T$ is the row vector $(x_1, x_2, \ldots, x_n)$. Thus if $\mathbf{x}$ and $\mathbf{y}$ belong to $\mathcal{R}^n$, $\mathbf{x}^T\mathbf{y}$ is the scalar

$$x_1 y_1 + x_2 y_2 + \ldots + x_n y_n.$$

This expression is known as the **inner product** of $\mathbf{x}$ and $\mathbf{y}$. Notice that

$$\mathbf{x}^T\mathbf{y} = \mathbf{y}^T\mathbf{x}.$$

Inner products occur in economics in contexts such as the following. There are n goods labelled $1, 2, \ldots, n$ with prices $p_1, p_2, \ldots, p_n$. A consumer buys quantities $x_1, x_2, \ldots, x_n$ of the goods: then the consumer's total expenditure is

$$p_1 x_1 + p_2 x_2 + \ldots + p_n x_n.$$

If we list the prices as an n–vector $\mathbf{p}$ and the quantities as an n–vector $\mathbf{x}$, then expenditure is the inner product $\mathbf{p}^T\mathbf{x}$.

If $\mathbf{x}$ is any n–vector,

$$\mathbf{x}^T\mathbf{x} = x_1^2 + x_2^2 + \ldots + x_n^2.$$

This is a very simple example of a 'quadratic form', a concept we explain below. Since $\mathbf{x}^T\mathbf{x}$ is a sum of squares,

$$\mathbf{x}^T\mathbf{x} > 0 \quad \text{if } \mathbf{x} \neq \mathbf{0}.$$

When we write inner products in full, it is often convenient to use the sigma-notation for sums that we introduced in Section 5.2. If $\mathbf{x}$ and $\mathbf{y}$ are n–vectors,

$$\mathbf{x}^T\mathbf{y} = \sum_{i=1}^{n} x_i y_i, \quad \mathbf{x}^T\mathbf{x} = \sum_{i=1}^{n} x_i^2.$$

Quadratic forms and symmetric matrices

In Chapter 4 we defined a quadratic function to be a function of the form

$$f(x) = ax^2 + bx + c$$

where a, b, c are constants. A slight generalisation of this is the expression

$$g(x, y) = ax^2 + bxy + cy^2,$$

which is known as a quadratic form in the two variables x, y. Notice that $g(x, y)$ reduces to $f(x)$ when we set $y = 1$.

By the rules of matrix multiplication, we may write

$$g(x, y) = [x \ \ y] \begin{bmatrix} a & p \\ q & c \end{bmatrix} \begin{bmatrix} x \\ y \end{bmatrix},$$

where p and q are any two numbers such that $p + q = b$. Consider in particular what happens when $p = q = b/2$: then

$$g(x, y) = \mathbf{z}^\mathrm{T} \mathbf{A} \mathbf{z}, \quad \text{where} \quad \mathbf{z} = \begin{bmatrix} x \\ y \end{bmatrix} \quad \text{and} \quad \mathbf{A} = \begin{bmatrix} a & b/2 \\ b/2 & c \end{bmatrix}.$$

The point to notice here is that $\mathbf{A}$ has the property that $\mathbf{A}^\mathrm{T} = \mathbf{A}$: this property is known as symmetry.

To put these ideas in a more general context, we define a **symmetric matrix** to be a square matrix whose transpose is itself. Associated with each symmetric $n \times n$ matrix $\mathbf{A}$ is the **quadratic form $\mathbf{x}^\mathrm{T} \mathbf{A} \mathbf{x}$**, where $\mathbf{x}$ is an arbitrary n–vector. The typical 2×2 symmetric matrix is

$$\mathbf{A} = \begin{bmatrix} a & p \\ p & c \end{bmatrix},$$

in which case

$$\mathbf{x}^\mathrm{T} \mathbf{A} \mathbf{x} = a x_1^2 + c x_2^2 + 2 p x_1 x_2.$$

Similarly, the typical 3×3 symmetric matrix is

$$\mathbf{A} = \begin{bmatrix} a & p & q \\ p & b & r \\ q & r & c \end{bmatrix},$$

in which case

$$\mathbf{x}^\mathrm{T} \mathbf{A} \mathbf{x} = a x_1^2 + b x_2^2 + c x_3^2 + 2 p x_1 x_2 + 2 q x_1 x_3 + 2 r x_2 x_3.$$

The relation between quadratic forms and symmetric matrices is discussed in more detail in the appendix to this chapter.

Definite and semidefinite quadratic forms

When we discussed quadratic functions in Chapter 4, we devoted some attention to the question whether a function $f(x)$ was positive for all values of x. There is no direct analogue of this property for quadratic forms, since $\mathbf{x}^\mathrm{T} \mathbf{A} \mathbf{x}$ is always zero when $\mathbf{x} = \mathbf{0}$. However, given a symmetric matrix $\mathbf{A}$, we can however ask whether $\mathbf{x}^\mathrm{T} \mathbf{A} \mathbf{x} > 0$ for every *non-zero* vector $\mathbf{x}$; if so, we say that $\mathbf{A}$ is a **positive definite** symmetric matrix. Similarly, the symmetric matrix $\mathbf{A}$ is said to be **positive semidefinite** if $\mathbf{x}^\mathrm{T} \mathbf{A} \mathbf{x} \geq 0$ for every vector $\mathbf{x}$.

Example 1 Let **A** be the symmetric matrix

$$\begin{bmatrix} 1 & 0 & 0 \\ 0 & 1 & -1 \\ 0 & -1 & 1 \end{bmatrix}.$$

Then $\mathbf{x}^{\mathrm{T}}\mathbf{A}\mathbf{x} = x_1^2 + (x_2 - x_3)^2$, which, being a sum of squares, is non-negative.

Thus **A** is positive semidefinite. Notice that **A** is not positive definite since $\mathbf{x}^{\mathrm{T}}\mathbf{A}\mathbf{x} = \mathbf{0}$ for any vector **x** of the form $(0 \ c \ c)^{\mathrm{T}}$. If all the diagonal entries were 2 rather than 1, then **A** would be positive definite, as you are asked to show in Exercise 13.3.4.

We say that a symmetric matrix **A** is **negative semidefinite** if $-\mathbf{A}$ is positive semidefinite; this happens if and only if $\mathbf{x}^{\mathrm{T}}\mathbf{A}\mathbf{x} \leq 0$ for every vector **x**. Similarly, **A** is said to be **negative definite** if $-\mathbf{A}$ is positive definite.

Many symmetric matrices are neither positive semidefinite nor negative semi-definite: an example is

$$\begin{bmatrix} -1 & 0 \\ 0 & 1 \end{bmatrix},$$

since the associated quadratic form takes the value -1 when $\mathbf{x} = \begin{bmatrix} 1 \\ 0 \end{bmatrix}$ and the value $+1$ when $\mathbf{x} = \begin{bmatrix} 0 \\ 1 \end{bmatrix}$.

The terms 'positive definite', 'negative semidefinite' and so on are often applied to the quadratic forms themselves as well as the symmetric matrices which define them.

Testing symmetric matrices

Given a symmetric matrix, how do we test whether it is positive definite, negative semidefinite or whatever? We begin with the 2×2 case:

(a) A 2×2 symmetric matrix is positive definite if and only if its diagonal entries are both positive and its determinant is positive.

(b) A 2×2 symmetric matrix is positive semidefinite if and only if its diagonal entries are both non-negative and its determinant is non-negative.

(c) A 2×2 symmetric matrix is negative definite if and only if its diagonal entries are both negative and its determinant is positive.

(d) A 2×2 symmetric matrix is negative semidefinite if and only if its diagonal entries are both non-positive and its determinant is non-negative.

Example 2 Let

$$\mathbf{A} = \begin{bmatrix} 2+t & 1 \\ 1 & 2-t \end{bmatrix}.$$

Then $\mathbf{A}$ is symmetric and $\det \mathbf{A} = 3 - t^2$. If $-\sqrt{3} < t < \sqrt{3}$, the determinant and both diagonal entries are positive: thus $\mathbf{A}$ is positive definite. If $t = \pm\sqrt{3}$, $\mathbf{A}$ is positive semidefinite but not positive definite. If $|t| > \sqrt{3}$, $\det \mathbf{A} < 0$: in this case $\mathbf{A}$ is neither positive semidefinite nor negative semidefinite.

We now discuss briefly why these tests for 2×2 symmetric matrices are valid. We focus on (a). Consider the symmetric matrix

$$\mathbf{A} = \begin{bmatrix} a & p \\ p & c \end{bmatrix},$$

and the associated quadratic form

$$g(x,y) = ax^2 + 2pxy + cy^2.$$

Then $a = g(1,0)$ and $c = g(0,1)$: for our matrix to be positive definite, we need these diagonal entries to be positive.

To see the relevance of the determinant, consider the case where $a = c = 1$. Then $\det \mathbf{A} = 1 - p^2$. To verify (a) in this case, we need to show that $g(x,y) > 0$ for all (x,y) other than $(0,0)$ if and only if $p^2 < 1$. In fact,

$$g(x,y) = x^2 + 2pxy + y^2 = (x + py)^2 + (1 - p^2)y^2$$

by completing the square. This is clearly positive if $p^2 < 1$ and at least one of x and y is not zero; while if $p^2 \geq 1$ we can make $g(x,y)$ non-positive by setting $x = p$, $y = -1$. Thus (a) holds for this matrix. The proofs of (a)–(d) in the general case consist of more elaborate versions of the same argument.

Higher dimensions

We now say a few words about generalising tests (a)–(d) to symmetric matrices of order n. For this we need a few definitions.

A **submatrix** of a matrix $\mathbf{A}$ is a matrix obtained from $\mathbf{A}$ by deleting some (or none) of its rows and some (or none) of its columns. A **principal submatrix** of a square matrix $\mathbf{A}$ is a submatrix obtained using the rule that the kth row of $\mathbf{A}$ is deleted if and only if the kth column of $\mathbf{A}$ is deleted. A **leading principal submatrix** of a square matrix $\mathbf{A}$ is a submatrix obtained by deleting the *last* m rows and columns, for some m.

For example, if

$$\mathbf{A} = \begin{bmatrix} a & b & c \\ p & q & r \\ u & v & w \end{bmatrix},$$

then the principal submatrices of $\mathbf{A}$ are its three diagonal entries a, q, w (considered as 1×1 matrices), the three 2×2 matrices

$$\begin{bmatrix} a & b \\ p & q \end{bmatrix}, \quad \begin{bmatrix} a & c \\ u & w \end{bmatrix}, \quad \begin{bmatrix} q & r \\ v & w \end{bmatrix}$$

and $\mathbf{A}$ itself. The first, fourth and seventh of these matrices are the leading principal submatrices of $\mathbf{A}$.

A **minor** of a square matrix $\mathbf{A}$ is the determinant of a square submatrix of $\mathbf{A}$; a **principal minor** is the determinant of a principal submatrix and a **leading principal minor** is the determinant of a leading principal submatrix. In the 3×3 example just given, the leading principal minors of $\mathbf{A}$ are a, $aq - bp$ and $\det \mathbf{A}$; the other principal minors are b, c, $aw - cu$ and $qw - rv$.

Tests (a) and (b) for 2×2 symmetric matrices generalise as follows:

(a) An $n \times n$ symmetric matrix is positive definite if and only if its principal minors are all positive.

(b) An $n \times n$ symmetric matrix is positive semidefinite if and only if its principal minors are all non-negative.

These tests are usually cumbersome to apply. A somewhat more user-friendly version of (a) is the following:

(a′) An $n \times n$ symmetric matrix is positive definite if and only if its *leading* principal minors are all positive.

For example, the 3×3 symmetric matrix

$$\begin{bmatrix} f & 1 & 4 \\ 1 & g & 5 \\ 4 & 5 & h \end{bmatrix}$$

is positive definite if and only if the following three conditions are met: $f > 0$, $fg > 1$ and the determinant of the matrix is positive. The test (a′) is often implemented in the following form:

(a″) An $n \times n$ symmetric matrix is positive definite if and only if it can be reduced by Gaussian elimination, *without row exchanges*, to an upper triangular matrix whose diagonal entries are all positive.

By contrast, non-negativity of the leading principal minors is *not* a sufficient condition for a symmetric matrix to be positive semidefinite; for example, the 3×3 diagonal matrix with diagonal entries $1, 0, -1$ has leading principal minors $1, 0, 0$ but is not positive semidefinite.

It is possible to generalise rules (c) and (d) to $n \times n$ symmetric matrices. However, it is usually easier to test for negative definiteness or semidefiniteness by applying (a′) or (b) to the matrix $-\mathbf{A}$.

Three propositions

We end this section with three general propositions about positive definite and semidefinite symmetric matrices. We give the proofs because they are good illustrations of the use of simple logical reasoning employing the algebra of inner products, but the reader may omit them without loss of continuity.

Proposition 1 If $\mathbf{A}$ is a positive semidefinite symmetric matrix, and $\mathbf{x}$ is a vector such that $\mathbf{Ax} \neq \mathbf{0}$, then $\mathbf{x}^T\mathbf{Ax} > 0$.

PROOF Let $\mathbf{y} = \mathbf{Ax}$, and suppose $\mathbf{y} \neq \mathbf{0}$; we wish to show that $\mathbf{x}^T\mathbf{y} > 0$. Since $\mathbf{A}$ is symmetric, $\mathbf{y}^T = \mathbf{x}^T\mathbf{A}$; hence the expressions $\mathbf{y}^T\mathbf{Ax}$ and $\mathbf{x}^T\mathbf{Ay}$ are both equal to $\mathbf{y}^T\mathbf{y}$. Therefore, for every scalar λ,

$$(\mathbf{x} - \lambda\mathbf{y})^T\mathbf{A}(\mathbf{x} - \lambda\mathbf{y}) = \mathbf{x}^T\mathbf{y} - 2\lambda\mathbf{y}^T\mathbf{y} + \lambda^2\mathbf{y}^T\mathbf{Ay}.$$

Since $\mathbf{A}$ is positive semidefinite, the left-hand side of this equation is non-negative. Thus

$$\mathbf{x}^T\mathbf{y} \geq \lambda(2\mathbf{y}^T\mathbf{y} - \lambda\mathbf{y}^T\mathbf{Ay})$$

for every real number λ. But since $\mathbf{y} \neq \mathbf{0}$, $\mathbf{y}^T\mathbf{y} > 0$. We may therefore choose the scalar λ to be positive but sufficiently small that $\lambda\mathbf{y}^T\mathbf{Ay} < 2\mathbf{y}^T\mathbf{y}$. Hence $\mathbf{x}^T\mathbf{y} > 0$.

Proposition 2 A symmetric matrix is positive definite if and only if it is positive semidefinite and invertible.

PROOF We showed in Section 12.3 that a square matrix is invertible if and only if it is nonsingular. We may therefore prove the proposition by showing that a positive semidefinite symmetric matrix $\mathbf{A}$ is positive definite if and only if it is nonsingular. If $\mathbf{A}$ is positive definite then, for any non-zero n–vector $\mathbf{x}$, $\mathbf{x}^T\mathbf{Ax} > 0$; thus $\mathbf{Ax} \neq \mathbf{0}$, so $\mathbf{A}$ is nonsingular. Conversely, if $\mathbf{A}$ is nonsingular then, for any non-zero n–vector $\mathbf{x}$, $\mathbf{Ax} \neq \mathbf{0}$; but then $\mathbf{x}^T\mathbf{Ax} > 0$ by Proposition 1, so $\mathbf{A}$ is positive definite.

Proposition 3 If $\mathbf{A}$ is a positive definite symmetric matrix, so is $\mathbf{A}^{-1}$.

PROOF Let $\mathbf{A}$ be a positive definite, symmetric $n \times n$ matrix. By Proposition 2, $\mathbf{A}$ is invertible. Recall that for any invertible matrix $\mathbf{B}$, $\mathbf{B}^{-1}$ is an invertible matrix whose inverse is $\mathbf{B}$ and whose transpose is $(\mathbf{B}^T)^{-1}$. Hence $\mathbf{A}^{-1}$ is invertible and symmetric; by Proposition 2, it remains to prove that $\mathbf{A}^{-1}$ is positive semidefinite. Let $\mathbf{x}$ be any n–vector and let $\mathbf{y} = \mathbf{A}^{-1}\mathbf{x}$; we want to show that $\mathbf{x}^T\mathbf{y} \geq 0$. But $\mathbf{x}^T\mathbf{y} = \mathbf{y}^T\mathbf{x}$ and $\mathbf{x} = \mathbf{Ay}$; therefore $\mathbf{x}^T\mathbf{y} = \mathbf{y}^T\mathbf{Ay}$, which is non-negative because $\mathbf{A}$ is positive definite.

Exercises

13.3.1 (a) Find 3–vectors $\mathbf{p}$ and $\mathbf{q}$, neither of which has a component equal to zero, such that $\mathbf{p}^{\mathrm{T}}\mathbf{q} = 0$.

(b) Show that if $\mathbf{p}$ and $\mathbf{q}$ are n–vectors such that $\mathbf{p}^{\mathrm{T}}\mathbf{q} = 0$, then

$$(\mathbf{p} + \mathbf{q})^{\mathrm{T}}(\mathbf{p} + \mathbf{q}) = \mathbf{p}^{\mathrm{T}}\mathbf{p} + \mathbf{q}^{\mathrm{T}}\mathbf{q}.$$

13.3.2 Suppose you have a data set consisting of n observations on two variables x_1 and x_2; the ith observation is denoted (x_{1i}, x_{2i}). Let $\mathbf{X}$ be the $n \times 2$ matrix whose ith row is $(x_{1i}\ x_{2i})$.[3] Calculate the matrix $\mathbf{X}^{\mathrm{T}}\mathbf{X}$, expressing its entries in $\sum$–notation.

13.3.3 Prove that if $\mathbf{A}$ is a symmetric matrix, so is $\mathbf{B}^{\mathrm{T}}\mathbf{A}\mathbf{B}$.

13.3.4 Show directly from the definitions that the symmetric matrix

$$\begin{bmatrix} 2 & 0 & 0 \\ 0 & 2 & -1 \\ 0 & -1 & 2 \end{bmatrix}$$

is positive definite.

13.3.5 Determine the symmetric matrix $\mathbf{A}$ such that

$$\mathbf{x}^{\mathrm{T}}\mathbf{A}\mathbf{x} = 2x_1^2 + 3x_2^2 + 4x_1x_2$$

for every 2–vector $\mathbf{x}$. Use the test given in the text to show that the matrix $\mathbf{A}$ is positive definite.

13.3.6 Determine the values of t for which the symmetric matrix $\begin{bmatrix} 2t & 2 \\ 2 & t \end{bmatrix}$ is

(a) positive definite;

(b) positive semidefinite but not positive definite;

(c) negative definite;

(d) negative semidefinite but not negative definite;

(e) none of the above.

13.3.7 Determine the definiteness of the symmetric matrices

$$\begin{bmatrix} 3 & -1 & 1 \\ -1 & 1 & 2 \\ 1 & 2 & 9 \end{bmatrix}, \quad \begin{bmatrix} 3 & -1 & 1 \\ -1 & 1 & 2 \\ 1 & 2 & 6 \end{bmatrix}, \quad \begin{bmatrix} -1 & 1 & 0 \\ 1 & -2 & 1 \\ 0 & 1 & -1 \end{bmatrix}.$$

---

[3]This notation, which is standard in the statistical literature, departs from the usual one for matrices, in that the second subscript indicates the row and the first the column.

Problems on Chapter 13

13–1. (i) Let

$$\mathbf{A} = \begin{bmatrix} a_1 & a_2 & a_3 \\ b_1 & b_2 & b_3 \\ c_1 & c_2 & c_3 \end{bmatrix}, \quad \mathbf{B} = \begin{bmatrix} a_1 & a_2 \\ b_1 & b_2 \end{bmatrix}.$$

Suppose $\mathbf{B}$ is nonsingular and $\mathbf{A}$ is singular. In Problem 12–3 you were asked to prove that $\mathbf{A}$ can be transformed into an invertible matrix by replacing its $(3,3)$ entry by any number other than c_3. Give another proof of the same result, by expanding det $\mathbf{A}$ by its third row.

(ii) Sketch a proof of the following proposition: any singular square matrix can be transformed into an invertible matrix by arbitrarily small changes to its diagonal entries.

[HINT First prove the proposition for 2×2 matrices. Then use the argument of (i) to extend the proposition to 3×3 matrices. Finally, explain how the same logic may be used to prove the proposition for square matrices of higher order.]

(iii) Explain why the proposition of (ii) ceases to be true when the words 'singular' and 'invertible' are interchanged.

[This problem shows that when we are dealing with square matrices, invertible matrices can be considered as the normal case and singular ones as peculiar. For this reason, it is common in applications to assume that square matrices are invertible unless one has a good reason to suppose otherwise.]

13–2. This problem develops further the n–good input-output model of Problems 11–4 and 12–4. Notation is as in those problems.

Suppose each industry j uses as inputs not only the produced goods $1, \ldots, n$ but also non-produced goods such as labour and raw materials; let the cost of such inputs, per unit of gross output of j, be c_j. Let p_j be the price of good j. Write down an expression for the cost of producing each unit of gross output of good j. Derive a system of linear equations which must hold if all industries exactly break even (price equals average cost).

Let $\mathbf{c}$ be the vector with components $c_1, \ldots, c_n$ and let $\mathbf{p}$ be the **price vector**, with components $p_1, \ldots, p_n$. What properties must the input-output matrix $\mathbf{A}$ have if, for every vector $\mathbf{c}$ with non-negative components, there is a corresponding vector $\mathbf{p}$ of non-negative prices such that all industries break even? How are these properties related to the answer to Problem 12–4?

13–3. Suppose $\mathbf{C}$ is an $n \times k$ matrix. Show that $\mathbf{C}^{\mathrm{T}}\mathbf{C}$ is a positive semidefinite symmetric matrix. Show also that $\mathbf{C}^{\mathrm{T}}\mathbf{C}$ is positive definite if the columns of $\mathbf{C}$ are linearly independent. What restriction on n and k does this condition impose?

13–4. This problem is concerned with the most popular of all econometric techniques, **least-squares estimation**.

Suppose you have a data set consisting of n observations on three variables y, x_1, x_2; the ith observation is denoted (y_i, x_{1i}, x_{2i}). You wish to find a linear function of the form

$$y = b_1 x_1 + b_2 x_2$$

which fits the data as well as possible in the following sense: b_1 and b_2 are chosen so as to minimise the expression

$$Q(b_1, b_2) = \sum_{i=1}^{n} (y_i - b_1 x_{1i} - b_2 x_{2i})^2.$$

Let $\mathbf{y}$ be the n–vector whose ith component is y_i, $\mathbf{X}$ the $n \times 2$ matrix whose ith row is $(x_{1i} \ \ x_{2i})$.[4] Assume that the columns of $\mathbf{X}$ are linearly independent. Let $\mathbf{b}$ be the 2–vector $(b_1 \ \ b_2)^{\mathrm{T}}$.

(i) Show that $Q(\mathbf{b}) = (\mathbf{y} - \mathbf{Xb})^{\mathrm{T}}(\mathbf{y} - \mathbf{Xb})$.

(ii) Suppose that $\mathbf{b}^*$ is a 2–vector such that

$$\mathbf{X}^{\mathrm{T}}(\mathbf{y} - \mathbf{Xb}^*) = \mathbf{0}. \tag{$*$}$$

Using the result of Exercise 13.3.1(b), show that

$$Q(\mathbf{b}) = (\mathbf{y} - \mathbf{Xb}^*)^{\mathrm{T}}(\mathbf{y} - \mathbf{Xb}^*) + (\mathbf{b}^* - \mathbf{b})^{\mathrm{T}}\mathbf{X}^{\mathrm{T}}\mathbf{X}(\mathbf{b}^* - \mathbf{b}).$$

(iii) Since the columns of $\mathbf{X}$ are linearly independent, the symmetric 2×2 matrix $\mathbf{X}^{\mathrm{T}}\mathbf{X}$ is positive definite (recall Problem 13–3) and therefore invertible (Proposition 2 of Section 13.3). Deduce that there is only one vector $\mathbf{b}^*$ satisfying $(*)$, and find an explicit expression for $\mathbf{b}^*$.

(iv) Show that $Q(\mathbf{b})$ is minimised when $\mathbf{b} = \mathbf{b}^*$.

[All of this generalises easily to the case where the data set consists of n observations on $1 + k$ variables $y, x_1, \ldots, x_k$. In particular, the case of three variables y, x_1, x_2, where the function to be fitted is of the form

$$y = b_1 x_1 + b_2 x_2 + b_3,$$

may be treated in this framework by letting $k = 3$, $x_{3i} = 1$ for all i.]

---

[4]We commented on this notation in an earlier footnote, in connection with Exercise 13.3.2.

Appendix to Chapter 13

This appendix explains how quadratic forms are related to symmetric matrices. The points we make are not difficult or complicated; indeed they are often omitted from textbooks, presumably on grounds of triviality. However, we have found that students are often confused by these issues, and we therefore take this opportunity to spell out the details.

Let $\mathbf{A}$ be a symmetric matrix of order n, and let $\mathbf{B}$ be an $n \times n$ matrix such that

$$\mathbf{B} + \mathbf{B}^{\mathrm{T}} = 2\mathbf{A}.$$

Then $\mathbf{x}^{\mathrm{T}}\mathbf{A}\mathbf{x} = \mathbf{x}^{\mathrm{T}}\mathbf{B}\mathbf{x}$ for every n–vector $\mathbf{x}$. For example, if

$$\mathbf{A} = \begin{bmatrix} 1 & 3 \\ 3 & 2 \end{bmatrix}$$

and $\mathbf{B}$ is any of the matrices

$$\begin{bmatrix} 1 & 4 \\ 2 & 2 \end{bmatrix}, \quad \begin{bmatrix} 1 & 6 \\ 0 & 2 \end{bmatrix}, \quad \begin{bmatrix} 1 & 8 \\ -2 & 2 \end{bmatrix}$$

then the quadratic form $\mathbf{x}^{\mathrm{T}}\mathbf{A}\mathbf{x}$ may be written $\mathbf{x}^{\mathrm{T}}\mathbf{B}\mathbf{x}$.

Because of this, it is not wrong to define a quadratic form to be an expression of the form $\mathbf{x}^{\mathrm{T}}\mathbf{B}\mathbf{x}$, where $\mathbf{B}$ is any square matrix, not necessarily symmetric. In practice, however, quadratic forms are always considered in connection with symmetric matrices. There are two reasons for this.

The first concerns uniqueness. Given a quadratic form $g(x_1, \ldots, x_n)$, where $n > 1$, there are lots of $n \times n$ matrices $\mathbf{B}$ such that

$$g(\mathbf{x}) = \mathbf{x}^{\mathrm{T}}\mathbf{B}\mathbf{x} \quad \text{for all } \mathbf{x},$$

but only one of these matrices is symmetric.

Secondly, *the tests for positive definiteness and so on given in Section 13.3 are valid only for symmetric matrices.* To illustrate this, we consider the matrix

$$\mathbf{B} = \begin{bmatrix} 1 & 8 \\ -2 & 2 \end{bmatrix}.$$

Then $\det \mathbf{B} = 18$, so the determinant and both diagonal entries of $\mathbf{B}$ are positive. Nevertheless, the expression

$$g(\mathbf{x}) = \mathbf{x}^{\mathrm{T}}\mathbf{B}\mathbf{x} = x_1^2 + 2x_2^2 + 6x_1x_2$$

is *not* a positive definite quadratic form. This may be seen in either of two ways. First, it is clear by inspection that $g(1, -1) = -3$. Alternatively, we may write $g(\mathbf{x})$ in the form $\mathbf{x}^{\mathrm{T}}\mathbf{A}\mathbf{x}$, where $\mathbf{A}$ is the symmetric matrix given above, and apply the usual test; it is easy to see that $\det \mathbf{A}$ is the negative number -7.

Chapter 14

FUNCTIONS OF SEVERAL VARIABLES

Our study of calculus up to now has been limited to situations where one variable depends on one other variable. We now consider cases where the dependent variable depends on several independent variables. Examples in economics abound: the quantity demanded of a good depends on its price, the prices of some other goods and on income; aggregate consumption depends on aggregate income and aggregate wealth; total cost incurred by a firm depends on its level of output and on the prices of inputs; and so on.

In terms of technique, much of this chapter and the next consists of fairly straightforward generalisations of the rules and methods of Chapters 6 and 7: the small increments formula, the composite function rule and so forth. Matrix algebra is also useful here, both in providing a convenient notation and in highlighting analogies between the one-variable and several-variable cases. Vector and matrix notation is particularly helpful when we deal with functions of n variables, where n can be any natural number. But to fix ideas it is simplest to begin with the case where $n = 2$.

When you have studied this chapter you will be able to:

- find partial derivatives, with applications to marginal products of production functions and price and income elasticities of demand functions;

- obtain gradient vectors and Hessian matrices;

- apply the small increments formula and the chain rule;

- calculate the degree of homogeneity of a homogeneous function.

14.1 Partial derivatives

One reason for beginning with functions of two variables is that one can draw diagrams. We can depict a function $f(x, y)$ graphically in three-dimensional space by taking three mutually perpendicular axes Ox, Oy, Oz. It is conventional to choose the orientation of the axes so that a right-handed corkscrew, when screwed in the direction from Ox to Oy, moves along Oz. Such a system of axes is said to be **right-handed**.

Provided the function f is well behaved, the equation

$$z = f(x, y)$$

is represented by a smooth surface, as in Figure 14.1. The conditions under which this is true are described in the appendix to this chapter.

The figure shows a typical point (x_0, y_0, z_0) such that $z_0 = f(x_0, y_0)$. As (x_0, y_0) varies over the xy–plane, a surface is traced out in three-dimensional space.

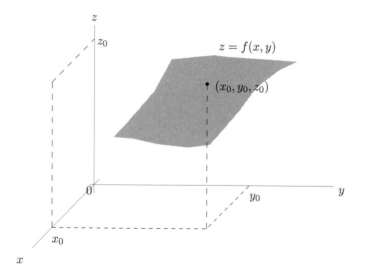

Figure 14.1: **The surface** $z = f(x, y)$

Our aim is to analyse how $f(x, y)$ changes when x and y change. We embark on this by considering first what happens to $f(x, y)$ when x changes and y remains fixed. Notice that this approach fits in with that taken in economic theory, much of which consists of tracing the effects on a dependent variable of changes in *one* of the dependent variables, *all other things being equal.*[1]

Keeping y fixed essentially reduces $f(x, y)$ to a function of the one variable x, and we may then use the ideas developed in Chapters 6–10. In particular, we can differentiate $f(x, y)$ with respect to x, treating y as a constant. The

---

[1]Many economists like to enunciate the phrase 'other things being equal' in Latin as *ceteris paribus*, sometimes abbreviated to *cet. par.*

resulting derivative is called the **partial derivative** of f with respect to x, and is written

$$\frac{\partial f}{\partial x},$$

pronounced 'partial dee-eff-by-dee-ex'.[2] In a completely analogous way, the derivative of f with respect to y, treating x as constant, is called the partial derivative of f with respect to y, and is written $\dfrac{\partial f}{\partial y}$.

Example 1 Let

$$f(x, y) = x^2 y + y^5.$$

Partially differentiating with respect to x,

$$\frac{\partial f}{\partial x} = \frac{\partial}{\partial x}(x^2 y) + \frac{\partial}{\partial x}(y^5).$$

The first term on the right hand side is $2xy$ *and the second is zero*; for since y is being treated as a constant, so also is y^5. Thus

$$\frac{\partial f}{\partial x} = 2xy.$$

Similarly

$$\frac{\partial f}{\partial y} = \frac{\partial}{\partial y}(x^2 y) + \frac{\partial}{\partial y}(y^5) = x^2 + 5y^4.$$

Methods and rules

As we noted at the beginning of this chapter, the methods of partial differentiation are those of ordinary differentiation: the product and quotient rules, the composite function rule and so on. For instance, the composite function rule tells us that

$$\frac{\partial}{\partial x}\left([f(x, y)]^2\right) = 2f(x, y)\frac{\partial f}{\partial x} \quad \text{and} \quad \frac{\partial}{\partial y}\left(e^{f(x,y)}\right) = e^{f(x,y)}\frac{\partial f}{\partial y}.$$

Second derivatives

Having differentiated, we may differentiate again. Under suitable conditions, discussed below, one may define the expressions

$$\frac{\partial^2 f}{\partial x^2} = \frac{\partial}{\partial x}\left(\frac{\partial f}{\partial x}\right), \quad \frac{\partial^2 f}{\partial y^2} = \frac{\partial}{\partial y}\left(\frac{\partial f}{\partial y}\right).$$

---

[2]The symbol ∂ is different from d and δ and is not a letter in any alphabet we know of. Perhaps because of its unfamiliarity, some students tend to avoid the symbol ∂ and use d or δ instead. *We do not encourage this practice*: partial differentiation is a distinct mathematical operation and the correct symbol should be used for it.

These are known as the **second partial derivatives** of the function $f(x, y)$. Similarly we may define the expressions $\dfrac{\partial}{\partial x}\left(\dfrac{\partial f}{\partial y}\right)$ and $\dfrac{\partial}{\partial y}\left(\dfrac{\partial f}{\partial x}\right)$, known as the **mixed partial derivatives** of $f(x, y)$.

Example 2 As in Example 1, let $f(x, y) = x^2 y + y^5$. We showed above that

$$\frac{\partial f}{\partial x} = 2xy \quad \text{and} \quad \frac{\partial f}{\partial y} = x^2 + 5y^4.$$

Hence

$$\frac{\partial^2 f}{\partial x^2} = \frac{\partial}{\partial x}(2xy) = 2y \quad \text{and} \quad \frac{\partial^2 f}{\partial y^2} = \frac{\partial}{\partial y}(x^2 + 5y^4) = 20y^4.$$

Similarly

$$\frac{\partial}{\partial x}\left(\frac{\partial f}{\partial y}\right) = \frac{\partial}{\partial x}(x^2 + 5y^4) = 2x \quad \text{and} \quad \frac{\partial}{\partial y}\left(\frac{\partial f}{\partial x}\right) = \frac{\partial}{\partial y}(2xy) = 2x.$$

The mixed derivative theorem

For the function f of Examples 1 and 2,

$$\frac{\partial}{\partial x}\left(\frac{\partial f}{\partial y}\right) = \frac{\partial}{\partial y}\left(\frac{\partial f}{\partial x}\right). \qquad (14.1)$$

This is in fact a property of a very wide class of functions, including all those encountered in examples in this and the next three chapters.

To give some idea of the class of functions for which (14.1) holds, we need to say a little about continuity of functions of two variables: a taste of how this can be made rigorous is given in the appendix to this chapter. Roughly speaking, continuity of the function $f(x, y)$ means that the surface $z = f(x, y)$ is unbroken. This is necessary but not sufficient for existence of partial derivatives: for that one also needs the surface to have no kinks or sharp ridges. We say that the continuous function $f(x, y)$ is a **smooth function**[3] if its first, second and mixed partial derivatives exist and are continuous functions of x and y. *Equation (4.1) holds whenever $f(x, y)$ is a smooth function*; this result is known as the **mixed derivative theorem**, and it is conventional to write

$$\frac{\partial^2 f}{\partial x\, \partial y} = \frac{\partial}{\partial x}\left(\frac{\partial f}{\partial y}\right) = \frac{\partial}{\partial y}\left(\frac{\partial f}{\partial x}\right).$$

---

[3]We are using the term 'smooth function' here in a slightly different sense from that of Section 10.3.

An economic application

We have already mentioned that partial derivatives are tailor-made for the ceteris paribus methodology so widely used in economics. We now give an example
of this.

Recall from Section 6.4 that, if a firm's revenue is given by the function
$R(x)$ where x denotes the sales of its product, then the marginal revenue is
defined to be $R'(x)$. Now suppose the firm produces two products X and Y,
and its revenue is a smooth function $R(x, y)$ of the sales of the two products.
The marginal revenue of X is defined to be $\dfrac{\partial R}{\partial x}$. Similarly, the marginal revenue
of Y is defined to be $\dfrac{\partial R}{\partial y}$. Then the inequality

$$\frac{\partial^2 R}{\partial x^2} < 0$$

means that marginal revenue of X is a decreasing function of sales of that
product, *given the sales of the other one*. Similarly,

$$\frac{\partial^2 R}{\partial x \, \partial y} > 0$$

means that increasing the sales of X, at constant sales of Y, increases the
marginal revenue of Y. By the mixed derivative theorem, this happens if and
only if increasing the sales of Y, at constant sales of X, increases the marginal
revenue of X.

Gradient and Hessian

Given the smooth function $f(x, y)$, it is sometimes useful to denote $\partial f / \partial x$ by
$f_1(x, y)$, where the subscript 1 indicates that partial differentiation is being
performed with respect to the *first* component of the vector (x, y). Similarly
we write

$$f_2(x, y) = \frac{\partial f}{\partial y}, \quad f_{11}(x, y) = \frac{\partial^2 f}{\partial x^2}, \quad f_{22}(x, y) = \frac{\partial^2 f}{\partial y^2},$$

$$f_{12}(x, y) = \frac{\partial}{\partial x}\left(\frac{\partial f}{\partial y}\right), \quad f_{21}(x, y) = \frac{\partial}{\partial y}\left(\frac{\partial f}{\partial x}\right).$$

Since f is a smooth function the mixed derivative theorem applies:

$$f_{12}(x, y) = \frac{\partial^2 f}{\partial x \, \partial y} = f_{21}(x, y).$$

At each point (x, y) in the plane we may define the **gradient vector**

$$Df(x, y) = \begin{bmatrix} f_1(x, y) \\ f_2(x, y) \end{bmatrix}.$$

We may also define the **Hessian matrix**[4]

$$D^2 f(x,y) = \begin{bmatrix} f_{11}(x,y) & f_{12}(x,y) \\ f_{21}(x,y) & f_{22}(x,y) \end{bmatrix}.$$

By the mixed derivative theorem, the Hessian matrix is a symmetric matrix in the sense of Section 13.3.

Example 3 Let

$$f(x,y) = xy^4 + x^3 y^2.$$

Calculating the partial derivatives in the usual way,

$$\frac{\partial f}{\partial x} = y^4 + 3x^2 y^2, \quad \frac{\partial f}{\partial y} = 4xy^3 + 2x^3 y.$$

Hence

$$\frac{\partial^2 f}{\partial x^2} = 6xy^2, \quad \frac{\partial^2 f}{\partial y^2} = 12xy^2 + 2x^3, \quad \frac{\partial^2 f}{\partial x\, \partial y} = 4y^3 + 6x^2 y.$$

The gradient is

$$Df(x,y) = \begin{bmatrix} (3x^2 + y^2)y^2 \\ (2x^2 + 4y^2)xy \end{bmatrix}$$

and the Hessian is

$$D^2 f(x,y) = \begin{bmatrix} 6xy^2 & 2y(3x^2 + 2y^2) \\ 2y(3x^2 + 2y^2) & 2x(x^2 + 6y^2) \end{bmatrix}.$$

In particular, setting $x = 1$ and $y = -1$ gives

$$Df(1,-1) = \begin{bmatrix} 4 \\ -6 \end{bmatrix}, \quad D^2 f(1,-1) = \begin{bmatrix} 6 & -10 \\ -10 & 14 \end{bmatrix}.$$

More on notation

The subscript notation, and the use of the gradient vector and Hessian matrix, are particularly useful for theoretical work. By contrast, yet another notational style is often adopted in applications. Given $z = f(x,y)$, it is quite common in applied work to denote the partial derivatives $\dfrac{\partial f}{\partial x}$ and $\dfrac{\partial f}{\partial y}$ by $\dfrac{\partial z}{\partial x}$ and $\dfrac{\partial z}{\partial y}$ respectively, with a similar convention for second derivatives. This notation can lead to confusion and we shall be sparing with it, but we shall use it from time to time.

---

[4]Named after the German mathematician L.O. Hesse (1811–74).

As an economic example of this notation, we consider elasticities of demand. Recall from Section 6.4 that if x, the quantity demanded of a good, depends on its price p, then the price elasticity of demand is defined to be

$$\frac{p}{x}\frac{dx}{dp}.$$

Now suppose there are two goods labelled $1, 2$ and the quantity demanded of each good depends on both prices. We denote quantiies by x_1, x_2 and prices by p_1, p_2. We may then define the **own-price elasticities of demand**

$$\frac{p_1}{x_1}\frac{\partial x_1}{\partial p_1} \text{ for good 1,} \qquad \frac{p_2}{x_2}\frac{\partial x_2}{\partial p_2} \text{ for good 2.}$$

The **cross-price elasticities of demand** are

$$\frac{p_2}{x_1}\frac{\partial x_1}{\partial p_2} \quad \text{and} \quad \frac{p_1}{x_2}\frac{\partial x_2}{\partial p_1}.$$

Exercises

14.1.1 In each of the following cases, find the gradient vector and the Hessian matrix of the function $f(x, y)$.

(a) $f(x, y) = 3x + 4y^3$ (b) $f(x, y) = x^3 \ln y + 6x^2y^3 + e^{2x}y$

(c) $f(x, y) = (x^2 + 4y^2)^{-1/2}$ (d) $f(x, y) = (x + 4y)(e^{-2x} + e^{-3y})$.

14.1.2 In each of the following cases, find the gradient vector and the Hessian matrix of the function $f(x, y)$, and evaluate them at $(1, -2)$.

(a) $f(x, y) = 3x^2 + 2y^5$ (b) $f(x, y) = 3x^2y^3 + 2x^3y^2$

(c) $f(x, y) = (3x - 2y)/(x^2 + y^2)$ (d) $f(x, y) = x \ln(1 + y^2)$.

14.1.3 A monopolist sells quantities x and y respectively of products X and Y. The prices p_x and p_y charged for X and Y are given by the following functions:

$$p_x = 25 - 2x + y, \qquad p_y = 20 + x - y.$$

Find the total revenue and the marginal revenues of X and Y.

The expressions for p_x and p_y in terms of quantities sold are called **inverse demand functions**. Why would this question have been harder if you had been given the demand functions in direct rather than inverse form?

14.1.4 Two goods 1 and 2 have demand functions

$$x_1 = 8p_1^{-2}p_2^{1/2}, \qquad x_2 = 4p_1^{1/2}p_2^{-1/2},$$

where x_i and p_i denote respectively the quantity demanded and the price of good i. Find the own-price elasticity of demand for each good and the two cross-price elasticities of demand.

[HINT. You may find it helpful to start by taking natural logarithms.]

14.2 Approximations and the chain rule

In Section 6.2 we introduced the small increments formula for differentiable functions of one variable:

$$f(x+h) - f(x) \approx hf'(x) \text{ when } |h| \text{ is small.}$$

We now generalise this approximation to functions of two variables.

Let (a, b) be a point in the plane and let h and k be real numbers. Let $f(x, y)$ be a smooth function of two variables; we use the subscript notation for partial derivatives. The small increments formula for functions of two variables says that

$$f(a+h, y+k) - f(a, b) \approx hf_1(a, b) + kf_2(a, b) \tag{14.2}$$

when $|h|$ and $|k|$ are small. The sense of the approximation is that when h and k are both small in absolute value, the difference between the two sides of (14.2) is small even relative to $|h|$ and $|k|$. This property of f is known as **differentiability** at the point (a, b). All 'smooth' functions, in the sense of the last section, are differentiable; differentiable functions do not have to be smooth (though they do have to be continuous), but we consider only smooth functions in what follows. A non-rigorous explanation why (14.2) holds when f is smooth is given in the appendix to this chapter.

There are two helpful ways of interpreting (14.2) and relating it to the small increments formula for functions of one variable. First, notice that the special cases of (14.2) when $k = 0$ and when $h = 0$ follow immediately from the one-variable formula and the definition of a partial derivative. Thus (14.2) tells us that the approximate change in the value of f in the general two-variable case is the *sum* of the approximate changes in the two special cases.

The second interpretation of (14.2) is geometrical, and is the counterpart of the description of the one-variable formula given in Section 10.1 in terms of the tangent to a curve. Given the real numbers a and b, and the differentiable function $f(x, y)$, we may define the function

$$L(x, y) = f(a, b) + (x - a)f_1(a, b) + (y - b)f_2(a, b).$$

Then $z = L(x, y)$ is the equation of a plane in 3–dimensional space; denoting this plane by T and the surface $z = f(x, y)$ by S, and letting $c = f(a, b)$, we see that the point (a, b, c) belongs both to S and to T. In a diagram similar to Figure 14.1, the plane T touches the surface S at the point (a, b, c), and is therefore called the **tangent plane** to the surface at that point. The approximation (14.2) says that for points in the xy–plane which are close to (a, b), the height above the xy–plane of the surface S is close to the height of the tangent plane T.

A more concise way of phrasing (14.2) is to say that if $z = f(x, y)$ then, for small changes Δx and Δy in x and y, the change in z is

$$\Delta z \approx \frac{\partial f}{\partial x}\Delta x + \frac{\partial f}{\partial y}\Delta y. \tag{14.3}$$

This is the form of the small increments formula which we shall use most frequently in what follows.

The chain rule

We now present an important generalisation of the composite function rule to functions of two variables.

Let $z = f(x, y)$, where f is a smooth function. Suppose that x and y themselves depend on a variable t: let $x = g(t)$ and $y = h(t)$, where g and h are differentiable functions. Then z may be written as a function of t, say

$$z = F(t) = f(g(t), h(t)).$$

The **chain rule** states that, under these assumptions,

$$F'(t) = f_1(g(t), h(t)) \, g'(t) + f_2(g(t), h(t)) \, h'(t).$$

In a more user-friendly notation,

$$\frac{dz}{dt} = \frac{\partial f}{\partial x}\frac{dx}{dt} + \frac{\partial f}{\partial y}\frac{dy}{dt}. \tag{14.4}$$

A non-rigorous proof of the chain rule is as follows. Suppose that t changes by an amount Δt and let the consequent changes in x, y, z be $\Delta x, \Delta y, \Delta z$. Assume that Δt is small: then by continuity Δx and Δy are also small. Applying the small increments formula (14.3) and dividing through by Δt,

$$\frac{\Delta z}{\Delta t} \approx \frac{\partial f}{\partial x}\frac{\Delta x}{\Delta t} + \frac{\partial f}{\partial y}\frac{\Delta y}{\Delta t}.$$

Taking limits as $\Delta t \to 0$, we get (14.4).

Example To see how the chain rule may be applied, suppose that

$$f(x, y) = xy^4 + x^3 y^2,$$

as in Example 3 of Section 14.1. Suppose also that

$$x = 2 - 3t, \quad y = 4 + 5t.$$

Let $z = f(x, y)$. Then z can be expressed as a function of the single variable t. One way of finding dz/dt would be to write down this function explicitly and differentiate it. This, however, would be rather tedious, and it is simpler to use the chain rule.

We know from the earlier example that

$$\frac{\partial f}{\partial x} = y^4 + 3x^2 y^2, \quad \frac{\partial f}{\partial y} = 4xy^3 + 2x^3 y.$$

Also, it is obvious that $dx/dt = -3$ and $dy/dt = 5$. So by the chain rule,

$$\frac{dz}{dt} = -3(y^4 + 3x^2 y^2) + 5(4xy^3 + 2x^3 y)$$
$$= 10x^3 y - 9x^2 y^2 + 20xy^3 - 3y^4.$$

An important special case

We sometimes need to apply the chain rule in the case where $t = x$. Suppose that $z = f(x, y)$ and y depends on x, say $y = h(x)$. Then z may be written as a function of x alone, say $z = F(x)$, where $F(x) = f(x, h(x))$. The expression $F'(x)$ is denoted by dz/dx and called the **total derivative** of z with respect to x, to distinguish it from the partial derivative $\partial f / \partial x$ which treats y as a constant. Since $dx/dx = 1$, the chain rule gives the following relation between total and partial derivatives:

$$\frac{dz}{dx} = \frac{\partial f}{\partial x} + \frac{\partial f}{\partial y}\frac{dy}{dx}.$$

This equation has a simple interpretation. Recall that the left-hand side is the same as $F'(x)$, the derivative of z with respect to x taking into account both the direct effect of x on z via the first argument of f and the indirect effect via y. The equation expresses $F'(x)$ as the sum of these two effects.

Differentials

The small increments formula (14.3) and the chain rule (14.4) are perhaps the most useful results in differential calculus. Some textbooks associate with these results a process known as "taking differentials". Suppose we are given the function of two variables $z = f(x, y)$; then taking differentials yields the equation

$$dz = \frac{\partial f}{\partial x}dx + \frac{\partial f}{\partial y}dy. \tag{14.4'}$$

What sense are we to make of this equation? In particular, what is the meaning of the terms dx, dy, dz?

Some books interpret (14.4') as another way of writing the small increments formula (14.3). This does not appeal to us, as we think it is important to distinguish between approximations (for example (14.3)) and equations (which is what (14.4') purports to be). A much more sensible interpretation of (14.4') is as a shorthand way of writing the chain rule (14.4), with the variable t left unspecified. If and when the reader comes across differentials in books and articles on economics, we strongly recommend this interpretation. Our usual practice in this book will be to write the chain rule in full when we need it, and to avoid the use of differentials.[5]

Several independent variables

Everything we have done so far in this chapter is easily generalised to functions of more than two variables.

---

[5]A third interpretation of (14.4'), used in many books on calculus, is as the equation of the tangent plane at a particular point. Using differential notation in this way is very helpful if one wants to go more deeply into the geometry of surfaces than we do in this book.

Let $f(x_1, x_2, \ldots, x_n)$ be a real-valued function of n variables. Partial derivatives of f with respect to $x_1, x_2, \ldots, x_n$ are defined in the obvious way: for example, if $n = 4$ then $\partial f/\partial x_2$ is the derivative of f with respect to x_2, treating x_1, x_3 and x_4 as constants. As in the 2–variable case, we assume that f is sufficiently well behaved for these and second order partial derivatives to exist and be well behaved themselves. We again refer to this by saying that the function f is smooth.

The use of vector and matrix notation is particularly helpful when we deal with functions of more than two variables. The gradient vector of a function $f(\mathbf{x})$ on $\mathcal{R}^n$ is the n–vector $Df(\mathbf{x})$ whose components are the partial derivatives of x with respect to $x_1, \ldots, x_n$. The Hessian matrix of $f(\mathbf{x})$ is now an $n \times n$ matrix $D^2 f(\mathbf{x})$. The mixed derivative theorem applies to smooth functions of n variables, so the Hessian matrix is symmetric.

Example Consider the function of three variables

$$f(x, y, z) = xe^y + ye^z + ze^x.$$

Here

$$\frac{\partial f}{\partial x} = e^y + 0 + z\frac{\partial}{\partial x}(e^x) = e^y + ze^x,$$

and similarly $\dfrac{\partial f}{\partial y} = e^z + xe^y$, $\dfrac{\partial f}{\partial z} = e^x + ye^z$. Second derivatives are easily calculated; for example,

$$\frac{\partial^2 f}{\partial x^2} = ze^x, \qquad \frac{\partial^2 f}{\partial y \partial z} = e^z.$$

Therefore, the gradient vector and Hessian matrix are

$$Df(x, y, z) = \begin{bmatrix} e^y + ze^x \\ e^z + xe^y \\ e^x + ye^z \end{bmatrix}, \qquad D^2 f(x, y, z) = \begin{bmatrix} ze^x & e^y & e^x \\ e^y & xe^y & e^z \\ e^x & e^z & ye^z \end{bmatrix}.$$

Back to the chain rule

The small increments formula and the chain rule generalise in obvious ways to functions of n variables. The small increments formula says that if $\Delta x_1, \ldots, \Delta x_n$ are small in absolute value then

$$\Delta f(x_1, \ldots, x_n) \approx \frac{\partial f}{\partial x_1}\Delta x_1 + \ldots + \frac{\partial f}{\partial x_n}\Delta x_n,$$

or, in the inner-product notation of Section 13.3,

$$\Delta f(\mathbf{x}) \approx [Df(\mathbf{x})]^{\mathrm{T}}\Delta\mathbf{x}.$$

Similarly, the chain rule may be written

$$\frac{d}{dt} f(x_1, \ldots, x_n) = \frac{\partial f}{\partial x_1} \frac{dx_1}{dt} + \ldots + \frac{\partial f}{\partial x_n} \frac{dx_n}{dt}$$

or simply as

$$\frac{d}{dt} f(\mathbf{x}) = [Df(\mathbf{x})]^{\mathrm{T}} \frac{d\mathbf{x}}{dt}.$$

One further generalisation is often useful. Suppose $y = f(x_1, \ldots, x_n)$, where $x_1, \ldots, x_n$ depend on several variables, say the m variables $t_1, \ldots, t_m$. Then we may apply the chain rule as above, with differentiation with respect to t replaced by partial differentiation with respect to t_i for each $i = 1, \ldots, m$.

For example, let $z = f(x, y)$ where the (scalar) variables x and y themselves depend on two variables t and u. Then z may be written as a function of t and u, say $z = F(t, u)$. The chain rule tells us that

$$\frac{\partial F}{\partial t} = \frac{\partial f}{\partial x} \frac{\partial x}{\partial t} + \frac{\partial f}{\partial y} \frac{\partial y}{\partial t} \quad \text{and} \quad \frac{\partial F}{\partial u} = \frac{\partial f}{\partial x} \frac{\partial x}{\partial u} + \frac{\partial f}{\partial y} \frac{\partial y}{\partial u}.$$

Exercises

14.2.1 Suppose the monopolist of Exercise 14.1.3 is operating at a sales level of $x = 5$, $y = 6$. Use the small increments formula to find the approximate change in revenue when

(a) x increases by 0.01 and y stays constant;

(b) x stays constant and y increases by 0.02;

(c) x increases by 0.01 and y increases by 0.02;

(d) x increases by 0.03 and y decreases by 0.01.

14.2.2 If
$$z = x^3 y^4 + x e^y, \quad x = 1 + 6t, \quad y = -2 - 3t,$$
use the chain rule to find dz/dt.

14.2.3 Find the gradient vector and the Hessian matrix of the function

$$f(x, y, z) = xy^2 + yz^2.$$

Then write down the gradient vector and the Hessian matrix of the function

$$f(x_1, x_2, x_3, x_4, x_5) = x_1 x_2^2 + x_2 x_3^2 + x_3 x_4^2 + x_4 x_5^2.$$

14.2.4 Let the demand functions for two goods 1 and 2 be as in Exercise 14.1.4.

(a) Suppose prices are given as the following functions of time t:

$$p_1 = 2t^{1/2}, \quad p_2 = 3t^{3/2}.$$

Use the chain rule to find dx_1/dt and dx_2/dt.

(b) Suppose now that prices are given as the following functions of time t and the exchange rate u:

$$p_1 = 2ut^{1/2}, \quad p_2 = 3t^{3/2}.$$

Use the chain rule to find $\partial x_1/\partial t$, $\partial x_2/\partial t$, $\partial x_1/\partial u$ and $\partial x_2/\partial u$. Explain in words what the expression $\partial x_1/\partial t$ means in this context.

14.2.5 Suppose consumption C in an economy is specified as $C = f(Y, T)$, where Y denotes national income and T the tax collection. Suppose also that the tax collection is specified as $T = g(Y)$. Find an expression for dC/dY in terms of the partial derivatives of f and the derivative of g.

14.3 Production functions

The classic example in economics of a function of two variables is the production function. Suppose the output Q of a firm depends on capital input K and labour input L, according to the relation

$$Q = F(K, L).$$

The inputs are sometimes called **factors of production**, and F is the firm's **production function**.

The **average product of capital** is defined as the expression

$$\frac{Q}{K} = \frac{F(K, L)}{K}.$$

Similarly, the average product of labour is the ratio

$$\frac{Q}{L} = \frac{F(K, L)}{L}.$$

The **marginal product**[6] **of capital** is defined as the derivative of output with respect to capital *with the other input (labour) held constant*; in short, the marginal product of capital is $\partial F/\partial K$. Using the notation introduced at the end of Section 14.1, we shall sometimes denote the marginal product of capital by $\partial Q/\partial K$. Similarly, the marginal product of labour is $\partial F/\partial L$, otherwise known as $\partial Q/\partial L$.

---

[6] Also known as the 'marginal productivity' or 'marginal physical product'.

Just as with functions of one variable, it is often helpful to work with elasticities rather than derivatives. Given the production function $F(K, L)$, the elasticities of output with respect to capital and labour are

$$\eta_K = \frac{K}{Q}\frac{\partial Q}{\partial K} \quad \text{and} \quad \eta_L = \frac{L}{Q}\frac{\partial Q}{\partial L}.$$

By the results of Section 9.2,

$$\eta_K = K\frac{\partial}{\partial K}\ln F(K, L), \quad \eta_L = L\frac{\partial}{\partial L}\ln F(K, L). \tag{14.5}$$

The Cobb–Douglas case

The **Cobb–Douglas production function** is

$$Q = AK^\alpha L^\beta,$$

where A, α, β are positive constants[7]. Here the average product of capital is $K^{\alpha-1}L^\beta$ and the average product of labour is $K^\alpha L^{\beta-1}$.

In this case the marginal product of capital is

$$\frac{\partial Q}{\partial K} = A\left(\alpha K^{\alpha-1}\right)L^\beta = \alpha\frac{Q}{K}.$$

It follows immediately that the elasticity of output with respect to capital, denoted above by η_K, is the constant α.

An alternative way of finding $\partial Q/\partial K$ and η_K is to take logarithms from the start:

$$\ln Q = \ln A + \alpha \ln K + \beta \ln L.$$

Differentiating with respect to K and using (14.5),

$$\eta_K/K = 0 + \alpha/K + 0.$$

Hence $\eta_K = \alpha$. Using the original definition of η_K, we see that

$$\frac{\partial Q}{\partial K} = \eta_K\frac{Q}{K} = \alpha\frac{Q}{K},$$

as before. Similarly

$$\eta_L = \beta, \quad \frac{\partial Q}{\partial L} = \beta\frac{Q}{L}.$$

---

[7]Some authors call this function the **generalised Cobb–Douglas production function**, reserving Cobb–Douglas (unqualified) for the special case where $\alpha + \beta = 1$. The function has been popular in empirical economics ever since the researches in the 1920s of the mathematician Charles W. Cobb and the economist (formerly lumberjack, later US senator) Paul H. Douglas.

Diminishing returns to factors

We say that the production function $F(K, L)$ displays **diminishing returns to capital** if $\partial F/\partial K$ is a decreasing function of K, for any given L. A sufficient condition for this is that

$$\frac{\partial^2 F}{\partial K^2} < 0$$

for all (K, L). Similarly, we have **diminishing returns to labour** if $\partial F/\partial L$ is a decreasing function of L, for any given K.

For example, the production function $Q = 6(KL)^{2/3}$ exhibits diminishing returns to each factor. Here,

$$\frac{\partial Q}{\partial K} = 4K^{-1/3}L^{2/3},$$

which is decreasing in K for given L because K is raised to a negative power. Diminishing returns to labour are demonstrated in a similar way.

The chain rule and growth rates

We now give an economic application of the chain rule. The application concerns production functions; but now we consider the output of an entire economy rather than an individual firm.

Let $Q = F(K, L)$, where Q is some measure of aggregate output and K and L denote respectively the economy's capital stock and employed labour force. Obviously there is more than one measure of aggregate output (Gross Domestic Product is a popular one) and it is sensible to adjust K for utilisation and L for hours worked, but these issues need not concern us here. This F is known as the **aggregate production function**.

Let time be measured as a continuous variable (recall Section 9.3) and denote it by t. Then Q, K, L all depend on t; applying the chain rule to the aggregate production function, we have

$$\frac{dQ}{dt} = \frac{\partial F}{\partial K}\frac{dK}{dt} + \frac{\partial F}{\partial L}\frac{dL}{dt}. \tag{14.6}$$

It is instructive to rewrite this equation in terms of growth rates. Recall from Section 9.3 that the (continuous–time) growth rate of a variable x is $\dfrac{1}{x}\dfrac{dx}{dt}$. Denoting the growth rates of output, capital and labour by g_Q, g_K and g_L, we may write (14.6) in the form

$$Qg_Q = \frac{\partial F}{\partial K}Kg_K + \frac{\partial F}{\partial L}Lg_L. \tag{14.6'}$$

Now let η_K and η_L denote, as above, the elasticities of output with respect to capital and labour. Then

$$K\frac{\partial F}{\partial K} = Q\eta_K, \quad L\frac{\partial F}{\partial L} = Q\eta_L.$$

Dividing (14.6′) by Q, we have

$$g_Q = \eta_K g_K + \eta_L g_L \tag{14.7}$$

This equation says that the growth rate of output is a weighted sum of the growth rates of the inputs, the weights being the elasticities of output with respect to the inputs. We shall say something about the empirical relevance of (14.7) in the next section.

Exercises

14.3.1 For the production function

$$Q = \frac{KL}{K+L},$$

find the average and marginal products of labour.

14.3.2 This exercise is concerned with the CES production function, first introduced in Problem 10–3. The production function is

$$Q = A[\delta K^\gamma + (1-\delta)L^\gamma]^{1/\gamma},$$

where A, γ, δ are constants such that $A > 0$, $\gamma < 1$ and $0 < \delta < 1$.

  (a) Show that the marginal product of capital is $\delta A^\gamma (Q/K)^{1-\gamma}$. Write down a similar expression for the marginal product of labour.

  (b) Show that that this production function exhibits diminishing returns to each factor.

  (c) Show that when $A = \frac{1}{2}$, $\delta = \frac{1}{2}$ and $\gamma = -1$, the CES production function reduces to the function of Exercise 14.3.1.

14.3.3 For the Cobb–Douglas production function

$$Q = AK^\alpha L^\beta \qquad (A, \alpha, \beta > 0)$$

find the ranges of values of α and β for which it exhibits diminishing returns to each factor.

14.3.4 Suppose the production function of an economy is as in Exercise 14.3.3, where Q, K and L denote aggregate output, capital and labour respectively. Suppose further that K and L have constant rates of growth m and n respectively. Find the rate of growth of output by each of the following methods:

  (a) using the chain rule;

  (b) taking natural logs in the production function, and differentiating the resulting log-linear equation with respect to time.

14.4   Homogeneous functions

One question we may ask about a function of n variables, say $f(x_1, \ldots, x_n)$, is: what happens to the value of the function when $x_1, \ldots, x_n$ are all increased in the same proportion? In general the only sensible answer is: it all depends on which values of the independent variables we start with. There is however a class of functions for which more definite statements may be made.

Let $f(x_1, \ldots, x_n)$ be defined for all positive $x_1, \ldots, x_n$ and let r be a real number. We say that the function f is **homogeneous of degree** r if

$$f(\lambda x_1, \ldots, \lambda x_n) = \lambda^r f(x_1, \ldots, x_n)$$

for all positive values of $x_1, \ldots, x_n$ and any positive number λ. We have defined such functions only for the case where the independent variables are restricted to be positive so as to avoid problems concerning fractional indices. The restriction is adequate for all economic applications of homogeneous functions, of which there are many.

As an example of a homogeneous function, suppose that $f(x, y)$ is a quadratic form in two variables, in the sense of Section 13.3:

$$f(x, y) = ax^2 + bxy + cy^2$$

where a, b, c are constants. Then for any positive constant λ,

$$f(\lambda x, \lambda y) = a(\lambda x)^2 + b(\lambda x)(\lambda y) + c(\lambda y)^2 = \lambda^2(ax^2 + bxy + cy^2) = \lambda^2 f(x, y).$$

The function f is therefore homogeneous of degree 2. It is not hard to show that a quadratic form in n variables is homogeneous of degree 2, for any n.

A more complicated example of a homogeneous function is

$$f(x, y, z) = \frac{2\sqrt{x} + 3\sqrt{y}}{8y + 9z}.$$

In this case multiplication of x, y and z by λ multiplies the numerator on the right hand side by $\sqrt{\lambda}$ and the denominator by λ, so the value of the function is multiplied by $1/\sqrt{\lambda}$: f is therefore homogeneous of degree $-\frac{1}{2}$.

An example of a function which is not homogeneous is

$$f(x, y) = 4x^2 + 3y + 1.$$

In this case, the ratio $f(2x, 2y)/f(x, y)$ depends on x and y.

Euler's theorem

An important proposition about the partial derivatives of homogeneous functions is **Euler's theorem on homogeneous functions**:[8]

---

[8]Leonhard Euler (1707–1783), a Swiss who spent much of his working life in Russia, was one of the greatest and most prolific mathematicians of the 18th century. His name is pronounced 'oiler'.

The function $f(x_1, \ldots, x_n)$ is homogeneous of degree r if and only if

$$x_1 \frac{\partial f}{\partial x_1} + \ldots + x_n \frac{\partial f}{\partial x_n} = r\, f(x_1, \ldots, x_n)$$

for all positive $x_1, \ldots, x_n$.

A proof of this theorem in the case where $n = 2$ is given in the appendix to this chapter. We now explain how the theorem turns up in economics in connection with production functions.

Returns to scale

Suppose as usual that the output Q of a firm (or an economy) depends on capital input K and labour input L, according to the production function $Q = F(K, L)$. We say that the production function F displays **increasing returns to scale** if multiplying both K and L by the same number $\lambda\,(>1)$ multiplies output by more than λ. In general, this could happen for some values of K, L and λ but not for others. However, things are made very simple if we assume that F is a homogeneous function.

Suppose the production function is homogeneous of degree r. Then for any K, L, λ we have

$$\frac{F(\lambda K, \lambda L)}{F(K, L)} = \lambda^r.$$

Given that $\lambda > 1$, we have $\lambda^r > \lambda$ if and only if $r > 1$. Thus a production function which is homogeneous of degree r will display increasing returns to scale if and only if $r > 1$.

Similarly, we say that a production function displays **decreasing returns to scale** if multiplying both K and L by the same number $\lambda\,(>1)$ multiplies output by less than λ. In particular, a production function which is homogeneous of degree r displays decreasing returns to scale if and only if $r < 1$. Homogeneity of degree $r < 1$ implies, for instance, that doubling both capital and labour inputs will raise output by a factor of 2^r, which is less than 2.

Finally, a production function displays **constant returns to scale** if multiplying both inputs by the same positive number λ multiplies output by exactly λ. This happens for all λ and all levels of inputs if and only if the production function is homogeneous of degree 1.

Example Consider the production function

$$F(K, L) = [a\sqrt{K} + b\sqrt{L}]^c$$

where a, b, c are positive constants. In this case, multiplying both inputs by λ multiplies the term in square brackets by $\sqrt{\lambda}$, and therefore multiplies output by $\lambda^{c/2}$. Hence F is homogeneous of degree $c/2$: this production function displays decreasing returns to scale if $c < 2$, constant returns to scale if $c = 2$, and increasing returns to scale if $c > 2$.

Returning to the general case of a homogeneous production function, we consider how returns to scale relate to the elasticities η_K and η_L of output with respect to capital and labour. Let $Q = F(K, L)$. By Euler's theorem, F is homogeneous of degree r if and only if

$$K\frac{\partial F}{\partial K} + L\frac{\partial F}{\partial L} = r\, F(K, L).$$

Dividing through by Q, we see that F is homogeneous of degree r if and only if

$$\eta_K + \eta_L = r. \tag{14.8}$$

Hence there are increasing, constant or decreasing returns to scale, depending on whether the sum of the elasticities is greater, equal to or less than 1.

Notice that diminishing returns to each factor is compatible with increasing, constant or decreasing returns to scale. For example, we showed in the last section that the production function $Q = 6(KL)^{2/3}$ displays diminishing returns to each factor. This production function is homogeneous of degree $\frac{4}{3}$, as may be verified either directly or by noting that $\eta_K + \eta_L = \frac{2}{3} + \frac{2}{3} = \frac{4}{3}$ and applying Euler's theorem. We therefore have increasing returns to scale. Similarly, the production functions $6(KL)^{1/2}$ and $6(KL)^{1/3}$ also display diminishing returns to each factor; the former exhibits constant returns to scale, the latter decreasing returns to scale.

Economic growth and technical progress

Let us now see how equation (14.8) relates to our discussion of economic growth in the last section. In many industrial countries over the last 30 years, output and capital stock have each grown on average at about 3% per year, whereas labour input has grown much more slowly, say at 0.5% per year. If we assume that each country has an aggregate production function $F(K, L)$, we may substitute $g_Q = g_K = 0.03$ and $g_L = 0.005$ into (14.7). Doing this and dividing through by 0.03 gives

$$\eta_K + \tfrac{1}{6}\eta_L = 1. \tag{14.9}$$

Now this is clearly incompatible with constant returns to scale, except in the absurd case where $\eta_L = 0$. The reason why this case is absurd is that it implies that additional labour, applied to given capital, produces no more output! In fact, empirical studies suggest a value of η_L between $\frac{1}{2}$ and 1. So to make sense of (14.9) we have to assume increasing returns to scale. But even then the numbers look rather unrealistic. For example, suppose we assume a homogeneous production function. Then by (14.8), the sum of the elasticities is equal to r, the degree of homogeneity, which is a measure of the strength of increasing returns. If $\eta_L = 0.6$, then (14.9) implies that $\eta_K = 0.9$ and $r = 1.5$: both of these numbers look rather large relative to the econometric evidence. If on the other hand we let $\eta_L = 0.9$, then η_K falls to 0.85 but r rises to 1.75.

How can we explain (14.9) without invoking increasing returns to scale of this order of magnitude? A common approach is to take issue with the notion of an aggregate production function of the form $F(K, L)$, and argue that output depends not only on capital and labour but also on the state of technology. The simplest way to formalise this is to represent technical progress by the passage of time, replacing $Q = F(K, L)$ by $Q = F(K, L, t)$ where t denotes time.

This formulation provides an illustration of the distinction between total and partial derivatives introduced in Section 14.2. The total derivative dQ/dt is the actual rate of change of output, whereas the partial derivative $\partial F/\partial t$ is what the rate of change of output *would* be if K and L did not change. The relation between total and partial derivatives is given by the chain rule as

$$\frac{dQ}{dt} = \frac{\partial F}{\partial K}\frac{dK}{dt} + \frac{\partial F}{\partial L}\frac{dL}{dt} + \frac{\partial F}{\partial t}. \qquad (14.10)$$

The consequences of (14.10) are explored in Problem 14–3.

Consumer demand

Homogeneous functions also occur in economics in the theory of household demand for consumer goods. Consider a consumer with income m, who consumes quantities of n goods labelled $1, \ldots, n$. Let the prices of the goods be $p_1, \ldots, p_n$, and let the quantities of the n goods that the consumer purchases be $x_1, \ldots, x_n$. As we noted in Section 2.2 for the case $n = 2$, the consumer's purchases must satisfy the budget constraint

$$p_1 x_1 + \ldots + p_n x_n \leq m.$$

The quantities of the goods which the consumer decides to purchase therefore depend on the prices $p_1, \ldots, p_n$ and on income m. We express this dependence by the demand functions

$$x_1 = f_1(p_1, \ldots, p_n, m), \quad \ldots, \quad x_n = f_n(p_1, \ldots, p_n, m).$$

Notice that in this case the subscripts on f do not represent partial derivatives: $f_1, \ldots, f_n$ are just n different functions. This is one of the notational difficulties one has to learn to live with; we shall always be careful to dispel ambiguities as and when they arise.

If we double all prices and income, the set of consumption bundles that satisfy the budget constraint remains the same; so if preferences do not change we would expect the quantities purchased to remain unchanged also. And the same is true if we replace the word 'double' by 'multiply by λ', where λ is any positive number. Thus

$$f_i(\lambda p_1, \ldots, \lambda p_n, \lambda m) = f_i(p_1, \ldots, p_n, m) \quad \text{for } i = 1, \ldots, n.$$

This, together with the fact that $1 = \lambda^0$, implies that *consumer demand functions are homogeneous of degree zero.*

Differentiating homogeneous functions

We return to the mathematics of homogeneous functions. Let the function $f(x, y)$ be homogeneous of degree r. Differentiating the equation

$$f(\lambda x, \lambda y) = \lambda^r f(x, y)$$

with respect to x, and using the subscript notation for partial derivatives,

$$\lambda f_1(\lambda x, \lambda y) = \lambda^r f_1(x, y).$$

Dividing by λ, we see that

$$f_1(\lambda x, \lambda y) = \lambda^{r-1} f_1(x, y).$$

Since this is true for all positive x, y, λ, the function f_1 is homogeneous of degree $r - 1$.

Obviously the same is true for the function f_2, and a similar argument is valid when we have n independent variables rather than 2. We therefore have the following important result: *if a function is homogeneous of degree r, each of its partial derivatives is homogeneous of degree $r - 1$.*

As an application of this result in economics, consider a three-factor production function $F(K, L, N)$, where K and L have their usual meanings and N denotes natural resources. Suppose we have constant returns to scale, in the sense that multiplying all three inputs by a common multiple λ multiplies output by λ; then F is homogeneous of degree 1. It follows that $\partial F/\partial K$ is homogeneous of degree 0: doubling K, L and N leaves the marginal product of capital unchanged. Similarly, $\partial F/\partial L$ and $\partial F/\partial N$ are homogeneous of degree 0.

The result also has applications in consumer demand theory. Suppose there are n goods and let $f_1(p_1, \ldots, p_n, m)$ be a consumer's demand function for good 1. The partial derivative $\partial f_1/\partial m$ is sometimes called the marginal propensity to consume good 1. Since the function f_1 is homogeneous of degree 0, the marginal propensity to consume good 1 is homogeneous of degree -1 in the variables $p_1, \ldots, p_n, m$: doubling all prices and income halves the marginal propensity to consume good 1, with similar consequences for the other goods.

Exercises

14.4.1 For the Cobb–Douglas production function

$$Q = AK^\alpha L^\beta \qquad (A, \alpha, \beta > 0)$$

determine how the returns to scale depend on α and β. What special form does the function take in the case of constant returns to scale?

14.4.2 For the CES production function

$$Q = A[\delta K^\gamma + (1 - \delta)L^\gamma]^{1/\gamma},$$

where A, γ, δ are constants such that $A > 0$, $\gamma < 1$ and $0 < \delta < 1$, determine the returns to scale. How are your answers modified for the production function

$$Q = A[\delta K^\gamma + (1 - \delta)L^\gamma]^{\nu/\gamma},$$

where $\nu > 0$?

14.4.3 It is given that the demand $f_1(p_1, p_2, m)$ for good 1 stays the same when the prices and income all change in the same proportion. Use Euler's theorem to show that the sum of the own-price elasticity, the cross-price elasticity and the income elasticity is zero.

Problems on Chapter 14

14–1. (i) Find the equation of the tangent plane to the surface $z = xy$ at the point where $x = 4$ and $y = 3$. Find the value of z given by the tangent plane when $x = 4 + h$ and $y = 3 + k$. Verify that this is the value of z predicted by the small increments formula.

(ii) Now find the value of the function $f(x, y) = xy$ when $x = 4 + h$ and $y = 3 + k$. Hence find the error when the surface $z = xy$ near the point $(4, 3, 12)$ is approximated by the tangent plane at that point. Calculate the error as a percentage of the true value when

(a) $h = 0.01$, $k = 0.01$;   (b) $h = 1$, $k = 1$.

14–2. In a model of a small open economy, the demand for money is given by

(A) $M = f(Y, i)$,

where Y is national income and i is the rate of interest. Suppose that national income is determined by the aggregate demand relation

(B) $Y = g(i, u)$,

where u is the exchange rate. Substituting (B) into (A), we have

(C) $M = f(g(i, u), i)$.

Let the right-hand side of (C) be denoted by $H(i, u)$.

Show how the expressions $\partial H/\partial i$ and $\partial H/\partial u$ are related to the partial derivatives of the functions f and g. Verify your answers in the case where

$$f(Y, i) = AY e^{-ai}, \quad g(i, u) = B e^{-bi} u^c$$

for some positive constants A, B, a, b, c.

14-3. Suppose the production function of an economy has the form

$$Q = F(K, L, t)$$

where Q, K, L and t denote output, capital, labour and time respectively. Recall that, under this assumption, equation (14.10) expresses dQ/dt in terms of the partial derivatives of the production function and the time-derivatives of K and L.

(i) Suppose that K and L have constant rates of growth m and n respectively, and

$$F(K, L, t) = AK^\alpha L^\beta e^{\mu t},$$

where A, α, β, μ are positive constants. Find the rate of growth of output.

(ii) Now suppose that K and L have the *same* constant rate of growth n, and

$$F(K, L, t) = H(K, L) e^{\mu t},$$

where μ is a positive constant and $H(K, L)$ is homogeneous of degree $r > 0$. Find the rate of growth of output.

14-4. Suppose the production function $F(K, L)$ of a firm is homogeneous of degree 1.

(i) Show that the average products of capital and labour can be expressed as functions only of the capital-labour ratio K/L.

(ii) Show that the marginal products of capital and labour can be expressed as functions only of K/L.

(iii) Deduce that the average and marginal products are homogeneous of degree zero in K and L.

Appendix to Chapter 14

Our aim here is to do for functions of two variables what we did for functions of one variable in the appendix to chapter 6: to give a rather more precise account of what is meant by limits and continuity, and to relate these concepts to differentiation. The material of this appendix extends in a fairly obvious way to functions of more than two variables.

We end with a proof of Euler's theorem on homogeneous functions: again, we consider only the case of two independent variables, but the extension to n merely involves messier notation. The proof does not involve precise notions of limits and continuity, but it does use the chain rule in a rather subtle way, and readers with a strong aversion to proofs should omit it.

Limits and continuity

Let $f(x, y)$ be a function of two variables and let (x_0, y_0) be a point in the xy–plane. We say that $f(x, y)$ tends to the limit ℓ as (x, y) approaches (x_0, y_0) if we can make $f(x, y)$ as close as we like to $f(x_0, y_0)$ for all points (x, y) sufficiently close to, but not identical with, (x_0, y_0). More rigorously,

$$f(x, y) \to \ell \text{ as } (x, y) \to (x_0, y_0)$$

if, for any positive number ε, we can choose a positive number δ with the property that

$$|f(x, y) - \ell| < \varepsilon$$

for all points (x, y) other than (x_0, y_0) such that $|x - x_0| < \delta$ and $|y - y_0| < \delta$.

This is pretty similar to the definition of a limit for functions of one variable given in Section 6.5. The only new idea to grasp is the way in which closeness of two real numbers generalises to closeness of points in the plane: both the x–coordinates and the y–coordinates of the two points need to be close together.

Continuity generalises in the obvious way. We say that the function $f(x, y)$ is continuous at the point (x_0, y_0) if $f(x, y)$ tends to a limit ℓ as (x, y) approaches (x_0, y_0), and $\ell = f(x_0, y_0)$. We say that f is a continuous function if it is continuous at each point where it is defined.

Partial derivatives again

Partial differentiation is defined in terms of limits in the same way as ordinary differentiation. Using the subscript notation for partial derivatives, we have

$$f_1(x, y) = \lim_{h \to 0} \frac{f(x + h, y) - f(x, y)}{h},$$

assuming that the limit exists. The other partial derivative $f_2(x, y)$ is defined similarly. Suppose the function f is continuous and can be partially differentiated with respect both to x and to y for at each point where $f(x, y)$ is

defined, and the partial derivatives $f_1(x,y)$ and $f_2(x,y)$ are themselves continuous functions; then the equation $z = f(x,y)$ may be represented by a surface
in (x,y,z)–space as in Figure 14.1 with no breaks, kinks or sharp ridges. If f_1
and f_2 also have the properties just ascribed to f, then f is a smooth function
in the sense of Section 14.1.

Using these definitions, we say more about two key results of Chapter 14:
the small increments formula (which underlies the chain rule) and the mixed
derivative theorem. We give a proof of the first result, albeit a somewhat
informal one. For the mixed derivative theorem we give a plausibility argument
that falls some way short of a proof.

The small increments formula

Let $f(x,y)$ be a smooth function, and let (a,b) and $(a+h,b+k)$ be points in
the xy–plane. Suppose that $|h|$ and $|k|$ are small; we wish to show that

$$f(a+h,b+k) - f(a,b) \approx hf_1(a,b) + kf_2(a,b). \qquad (14.2)$$

The meaning of the approximation is that the difference between the two sides
of (14.2) is small even relative to $|h|$ and $|k|$.

We begin the proof by noting that

$$f(a+h,b+k) - f(a,b) = [f(a+h,b+k) - f(a,b+k)] + [f(a,b+k) - f(a,b)].$$

By the small increments formula for functions of one variable, the first term
in square brackets is approximately equal to $hf_1(a,b+k)$ and the second to
$kf_2(a,b)$. Hence

$$f(a+h,b+k) - f(a,b) \approx hf_1(a,b+k) + kf_2(a,b). \qquad (14.2')$$

We obtain (14.2) from (14.2') by showing that the difference between their
right-hand sides is a second-order small quantity, in the sense of the appendix
to Chapter 7. Since f is smooth and $|k|$ is small, $|f_1(a,b+k) - f_1(a,b)|$ is small.
Since $|h|$ is also small, $h(f_1(a,b+k) - f_1(a,b))$ is indeed a second-order small
quantity, and the proof is complete.

The mixed derivative theorem

Let $f(x,y)$ be a smooth function ,and let

$$\ell = \frac{\partial}{\partial x}\left(\frac{\partial f}{\partial y}\right), \quad \ell' = \frac{\partial}{\partial y}\left(\frac{\partial f}{\partial x}\right),$$

both evaluated at the point (a,b). The theorem states that $\ell = \ell'$.

To get some insight into why this is so, let h be a number whose absolute
value is small. Then

$$\ell \approx \frac{1}{h}[f_2(a+h,b) - f_2(a,b)].$$

But if k is a number whose absolute value is small, then

$$f_2(a+h,b) \approx \frac{1}{k}[f(a+h,b+k) - f(a+h,b)],$$

with a similar approximation for $f_2(a,b)$. Putting all of this together,

$$\ell \approx \frac{1}{hk}[f(a+h,b+k) - f(a+h,b) - f(a,b+k) + f(a,b)] \qquad (14.11)$$

when $|h|$ and $|k|$ are small.

What follows from this is that if the right hand side of (14.11) approaches a limit m as $(h,k) \to (0,0)$, then $\ell = m$. Similar reasoning, introducing k first and then h, shows that $\ell' = m$. Hence $\ell' = \ell$, as the theorem states. To turn this argument into a serious proof we would have to show that smoothness of f is sufficient for the limit m to exist, but we prefer to stop here.

Proof of Euler's theorem

The two-variable case of Euler's theorem on homogeneous functions runs as follows: the function $f(x,y)$ is homogeneous of degree r if and only if

$$x f_1(x,y) + y f_2(x,y) = r f(x,y) \qquad (14.12)$$

for all x, y. As in our treatment of homogeneous functions in Section 14.4, all variables are assumed to be positive (though the constant r is not).

To set up the proof, we introduce the function of three variables

$$F(s,x,y) = s^{-r} f(sx, sy).$$

If f is homogeneous of degree r then $F(s,x,y)$ is equal to $f(x,y)$ for all (x,y) and therefore depends only on (x,y), not on s. Conversely, if $F(s,x,y)$ depends only on x and y then $F(s,x,y) = F(1,x,y)$ for all (s,x,y), so f is homogenoeous of degree r. Summarising, we see that $f(x,y)$ *is homogeneous of degree* r *if and only if* $F(s,x,y)$ *does not depend on* s. For future reference, we differentiate $F(s,x,y)$ with respect to s, making careful use of the chain rule:

$$F_1(s,x,y) = s^{-r} G(s,x,y),$$

where

$$G(s,x,y) = x f_1(sx,sy) + y f_2(sx,sy) - \frac{r}{s} f(sx,sy).$$

Suppose $f(x,y)$ is homogeneous of degree r. Then $F(s,x,y)$ does not depend on s, so $\partial F/\partial s = 0$. But then $G(s,x,y) = 0$ for all s,x,y; in particular $G(1,x,y) = 0$ for all x,y, so (14.12) also holds.

Conversely, if (14.12) holds for all x and y, it also holds when x is replaced by sx and y by sy. Dividing through by s, we see that $G(s,x,y) = 0$, and hence $F_1(s,x,y) = 0$ for all (s,x,y). Now recall from Section 10.2 that a function of one variable whose derivative is always zero must be a constant; thus the statement that $F_1(s,x,y) = 0$ for all (s,x,y) implies that $F(s,x,y)$ does not depend on s, but only on x and y. Hence $f(x,y)$ is homogeneous of degree r, as required.

Chapter 15

IMPLICIT RELATIONS

In Section 7.4 we saw how a monotonic function $y = f(x)$ gives rise to another function $x = g(y)$, called the inverse function of f. We also saw how to obtain the derivative of the inverse function g from the derivative of f. We now ask a more general question. Given a function of two variables $F(x, y)$, we consider the equation

$$F(x, y) = 0. \tag{15.1}$$

We ask whether this equation defines y as a function of x: if we fix x, does (15.1) have a unique solution for y? Once we have determined the conditions under which the answer is yes, we show how to find the derivative of y with respect to x.

Applications of this in economics are as diverse as the occurrence of nonlinear functions. Here we restrict our attention to finding the slopes of isoquants and indifference curves, and to simple comparative static analysis.

When you have studied this chapter you will be able to:

- calculate derivatives by the rule of implicit differentiation;

- test production functions and utility functions for diminishing marginal rate of substitution;

- sketch the isoquant diagram of a production function, and the indifference-curve diagram of a utility function;

- perform simple exercises in comparative statics.

15.1 Implicit differentiation

An equation of the form (15.1) is called an **implicit relation** between the variables x and y, in contrast with the more familiar explicit form $y = f(x)$. Sometimes implicit relation can be reduced to explicit form by simple algebraic manipulation. Thus, for $x \neq 0$, the equation $xy - 3 = 0$ is obviously equivalent to $y = 3/x$: in this case the given implicit relation does indeed define y as a function of x.

In many cases, however, the situation is not so straightforward. Thus, if

$$F(x, y) = x^2 + y^2,$$

the only point in the xy–plane satisfying (15.1) is the origin. And if

$$F(x, y) = x^2 + y^2 + 1,$$

there are *no* points in the xy–plane satisfying (15.1): in other words, it is not possible to find real numbers x and y such that $x^2 + y^2 = -1$.

A rather more subtle example is that where

$$F(x, y) = x^2 + y^2 - 4.$$

In this case, the relation $F(x, y) = 0$ may be written

$$x^2 + y^2 = 4. \tag{15.2}$$

Since a point (x, y) satisfies this relation if and only if its distance from the origin is exactly 2, the relation (15.2) describes the circle in the xy–plane with centre at the origin and radius 2. If $|x| > 2$ there is no y satisfying (15.2). On the other hand, if $-2 \le x \le 2$ we may 'solve' (15.2) for y in terms of x, getting

$$y = \pm\sqrt{4 - x^2}.$$

The $\pm$ presents a problem, in that we have more than one solution y for any given x whose absolute value is less than 2. However, if we specify that the solution curve goes through a particular point, we can determine whether we have $+$ or $-$. For example, given the point $(-1, \sqrt{3})$, the only solution for y in terms of x *which passes through that point* is $y = +\sqrt{4 - x^2}$, defined whenever $-2 \le x \le 2$. This is illustrated in Figure 15.1. The relation (15.2) is described by the entire circle; the unique solution for y which goes through the point $(-1, \sqrt{3})$ consists of all points on the upper semicircle.

Local solutions

The idea of a unique local solution can be described in general terms as follows. Let (x_0, y_0) be a point in the xy–plane satisfying the implicit relation (15.1). We say that $y = f(x)$ is the **unique local solution** of the relation in the neighbourhood of (x_0, y_0) if, for all points in the xy–plane sufficiently close to (x_0, y_0), we have

$$F(x, y) = 0 \text{ if and only if } y = f(x).$$

Existence and nonexistence of a local solution are illustrated in the two panels of Figure 15.2. In panel (A) we may draw a box around the point

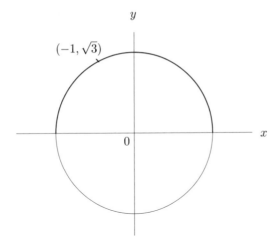

Figure 15.1: **The relation** $x^2 + y^2 = 4$

(x_0, y_0) such that the set of points within the box for which $F(x, y) = 0$ takes the form of a curve $y = f(x)$. In panel (B), by contrast, the following are true in any box we draw around the point (x_0, y_0): if $x > x_0$ there is no value of y for which $F(x, y) = 0$, while if $x < x_0$ there are two values of y for which $F(x, y) = 0$.

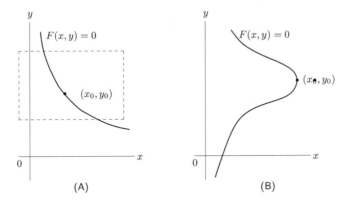

Figure 15.2: **Existence and nonexistence of a unique solution to the relation** $F(x, y) = 0$ **near** (x_0, y_0)

The fundamental result on unique local solutions is as follows.

Proposition Let F be a smooth function, in the sense of Chapter 14. Suppose that If $F(x_0, y_0) = 0$ and

$$F_2(x_0, y_0) \neq 0. \tag{15.3}$$

Then the equation $F(x, y) = 0$ has a unique local solution $y = f(x)$ in the neighbourhood of the point (x_0, y_0).

In (15.3) we use the subscript notation for partial derivatives introduced in Section 14.1. The inequality states that the partial derivative $\partial F / \partial y$ does not vanish at the point (x_0, y_0).

The reason why a unique local solution exists under the conditions stated is explained in the appendix to this chapter. We now show that under these conditions the function f is differentiable at x_0, and we derive an expression for $f'(x_0)$.

We do this by a simple geometrical argument. Recall that the equation $z = F(x, y)$ is represented by a surface S in three-dimensional space. The points (x, y) in the xy–plane such that $F(x, y) = 0$ correspond to those points in xyz–space which belong both to the surface S and to the plane $z = 0$. This set of points — call it A — contains the point $(x_0, y_0, 0)$, which we denote by P. Since (15.3) guarantees a unique local solution, the points of A *which are sufficiently close to* P form a curve C, described by the equation $y = f(x)$.

Let T be the tangent plane to the surface S at the point P. Recalling our discussion of tangent planes in Section 14.2, we can write down the equation of T: it is

$$z = u(x - x_0) + v(y - y_0),$$

where $u = F_1(x_0, y_0)$ and $v = F_2(x_0, y_0)$. Since T is the tangent plane to the surface S at the point P, the line of intersection of T and the plane $z = 0$[1] is the tangent to the curve C at (x_0, y_0). Hence the tangent to the curve $y = f(x)$ at the point (x_0, y_0) is the straight line

$$u(x - x_0) + v(y - y_0) = 0.$$

Since $v \neq 0$ by (15.3), the slope of the line, and hence of the curve at (x_0, y_0), is $-u/v$. Therefore

$$f'(x_0) = -\frac{F_1(x_0, y_0)}{F_2(x_0, y_0)}. \tag{15.4}$$

The formula (15.4) for the derivative of the local solution is called the **rule of implicit differentiation**.

Assuming that (15.3) holds and F is a smooth function, we have $F_2(x, y) \neq 0$ for all points (x, y) sufficiently close to (x_0, y_0). Hence, if (x_1, y_1) is suitably close to (x_0, y_0) and $F(x_1, y_1) = 0$, we can repeat the argument above with (x_1, y_1) replacing (x_0, y_0); we obtain the same local solution f. In particular, (15.4) continues to hold when (x_0, y_0) is replaced by (x_1, y_1).

---

[1]How do we know that the planes T and $z = 0$ intersect in a line? Because any pair of planes in 3–dimensional space are either parallel or coincident or intersect in a straight line. In the case in hand, the planes cannot be parallel since they share the point P, and they cannot be coincident, because $v \neq 0$ by (15.3).

Because of this, the rule of implicit differentiation may be written in a simpler notation as follows:

$$\frac{dy}{dx} = -\frac{\partial F}{\partial x} \bigg/ \frac{\partial F}{\partial y}. \tag{15.5}$$

This holds for all points (x, y) which satisfy (15.1) and are suitably close to a point (x_0, y_0) satisfying (15.1) and (15.3).

An alternative derivation of (15.5) runs as follows. For all points (x, y) which satisfy $F(x, y) = 0$ and are sufficiently close to (x_0, y_0), we have $F_2(x, y) \neq 0$ and $y = f(x)$. Hence $F(x, f(x)) = 0$. We now differentiate this equation (totally) with respect to x, using the chain rule:

$$\frac{\partial F}{\partial x} + \frac{\partial F}{\partial y} f'(x) = 0.$$

Rearranging, using the fact that $\partial F/\partial y \neq 0$, we obtain (15.5).

This derivation of the rule of implicit differentiation using the chain rule is quick and simple; it is also much less informative than the geometrical derivation given earlier in the section, and completed in the appendix to this chapter. The chain-rule argument shows that if (a) $\partial F/\partial y \neq 0$ at, and hence near, (x_0, y_0), *and* (b) there exists a unique local solution, *and* (c) the local solution can be differentiated, *then* (15.5) holds. The geometrical argument also shows that (a) guarantees (b) and (c), a useful and surprising fact.

An economic application: isoquants

In Section 14.3, we considered the production function of a firm using two inputs, capital and labour. Let $F(K, L)$ be such a production function; as in Section 14.3, the marginal products of capital and labour are $\partial F/\partial K$ and $\partial F/\partial L$. We assume that $F(K, L)$, $\partial F/\partial K$ and $\partial F/\partial L$ are positive for all positive values of K and L: an additional dose of capital or labour increases output.

An **isoquant** is an implicit relation between K and L giving those (K, L) combinations which give rise to a given level of output. A typical isoquant has the equation

$$F(K, L) = \overline{Q},$$

where $\overline{Q}$ is a positive constant representing a particular output level. Given that marginal products are positive, this isoquant will be a downward-sloping curve in the KL–plane: if capital input is increased while output remains unchanged at $\overline{Q}$, labour input must be lowered to compensate.

The equation of the isoquant can be written $G(K, L) = 0$ where $G(K, L)$ is defined to be $F(K, L) - \overline{Q}$. By implicit differentiation, the slope of the isoquant curve is

$$\frac{dL}{dK} = -\frac{\partial G}{\partial K} \bigg/ \frac{\partial G}{\partial L}.$$

Since $\overline{Q}$ is constant, the functions $F(K, L)$ and $G(K, L)$ have the same partial derivatives; therefore

$$\frac{dL}{dK} = -\frac{\partial F}{\partial K} \bigg/ \frac{\partial F}{\partial L}.$$

The expression $-dL/dK$ measures the rate at which labour must be substituted for capital to retain the same total output and is known as the **marginal rate of substitution of labour for capital**, often abbreviated to MRS. The equation just derived states that the MRS is the ratio of the marginal product of capital to the marginal product of labour.

The production function F is said to have the property of **diminishing marginal rate of substitution** if the MRS decreases as we increase capital and decrease labour along an isoquant. Thus, diminishing MRS means that the slope of a typical isoquant becomes more gentle as we move rightward along it. This in turn is the same as saying that isoquants are convex, in the sense of Section 8.4, and have no linear segments. Figure 15.3 shows three isoquants of a production function with diminishing MRS.

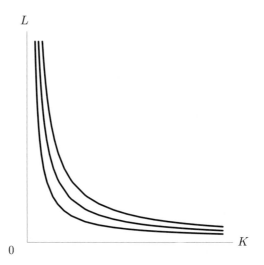

Figure 15.3: **Isoquants of a production function**

Example 1 In Section 14.3 we considered the Cobb–Douglas production function

$$F(K, L) = AK^{\alpha}L^{\beta},$$

where A, α, β are positive constants. Recall that for this production function, the marginal products are

$$\frac{\partial F}{\partial K} = A\left(\alpha K^{\alpha-1}\right)L^{\beta} = \frac{\alpha}{K}F(K, L),$$

and similarly

$$\frac{\partial F}{\partial L} = \frac{\beta}{L} F(K, L).$$

Hence the slope of the isoquant through the point (K, L) is

$$\frac{dL}{dK} = -\frac{\alpha}{K} \Big/ \frac{\beta}{L} = -\frac{\alpha L}{\beta K}.$$

We now show that this production function displays diminishing marginal rate of substitution. We could in principle do this by calculating d^2L/dK^2 and showing that it is positive, but it is easier to use a straightforward algebraic argument. The MRS is

$$\left|\frac{dL}{dK}\right| = \frac{\alpha L}{\beta K}.$$

As we move rightwards along an isoquant, K increases and L decreases: therefore the numerator in the expression for the MRS decreases and the denominator increases. Hence the marginal rate of substitution becomes smaller as we move rightwards along an isoquant, as required.

Example 2 Consider the production function

$$F(K, L) = 8\,K^{0.5}L^{0.7} + 9\,K^{0.3}L^{0.4}.$$

In this case

$$\frac{\partial F}{\partial K} = 4\,K^{-0.5}L^{0.7} + 2.7\,K^{-0.7}L^{0.4}$$

and

$$\frac{\partial F}{\partial L} = 5.6\,K^{0.5}L^{-0.3} + 3.6\,K^{0.3}L^{-0.6}.$$

Hence the slope of the isoquant through the point (K, L) is

$$\frac{dL}{dK} = -\frac{4\,K^{-0.5}L^{0.7} + 2.7\,K^{-0.7}L^{0.4}}{5.6\,K^{0.5}L^{-0.3} + 3.6\,K^{0.3}L^{-0.6}}.$$

We now show that this production function displays diminishing marginal rate of substitution. Here it would be possible but totally insane to calculate d^2L/dK^2 and show that it is positive. Instead, as in the Cobb–Douglas case, we use an algebraic argument.

We look first at the expression for $\partial F/\partial K$, and in particular at the term $K^{-0.5}L^{0.7}$. Since this term is the product of K raised to a negative power and L raised to a positive power, $K^{-0.5}L^{0.7}$ is a decreasing function of K and an increasing function of L. Similarly, $K^{-0.7}L^{0.4}$ is a decreasing function of K and an increasing function of L. Therefore, as we move rightwards along an isoquant, increasing K and decreasing L, the terms

$K^{-0.5}L^{0.7}$ and $K^{-0.7}L^{0.4}$ become smaller, and therefore so does $\partial F/\partial K$. By similar reasoning, the terms $K^{0.5}L^{-0.3}$ and $K^{0.3}L^{-0.6}$ become larger as we move rightwards along an isoquant, and therefore $\partial F/\partial L$ increases.

We have shown that the MRS is the ratio of two terms, of which the numerator becomes smaller and the denominator becomes larger as we move rightwards along an isoquant. Therefore the MRS becomes smaller as we move rightwards along an isoquant, as required.

Isoquant diagrams

All we did in the two examples above was to verify diminishing MRS. To sketch an isoquant, one also needs to find its asymptotes, or the points where it meets the axes.[2] An **isoquant diagram** depicts a few (usually three or four) typical isoquants.

Another application: indifference curves

Another economic application of implicit relations is to consumer theory. Suppose a household consumes quantities x, y of two goods X and Y. Suppose that the household's preferences may be represented by a utility function $U(x, y)$: in other words, U is a function with property that the household prefers (x_0, y_0) to (x_1, y_1) if and only if $U(x_0, y_0) > U(x_1, y_1)$. The expressions $\partial U/\partial x$ and $\partial U/\partial y$ are called the **marginal utilities** of the two goods X, Y. A typical indifference curve has equation

$$U(x, y) = \overline{U},$$

where $\overline{U}$ is a constant representing a particular level of utility.

Assuming that marginal utilities are positive (so that the household prefers more of either good), indifference curves will be downward sloping. The marginal rate of substitution (MRS) is defined as the ratio of the marginal utilities: diminishing MRS means that indifference curves are convex. Thus the indifference curves of a household displaying diminishing MRS look like the isoquants of Figure 15.3, except that the axes are now labelled x and y instead of K and L.

As with isoquants, one may draw an **indifference curve diagram**, depicting three or four typical indifference curves. Again, drawing such a diagram usually requires information in the form of the asymptotes of each indifference curve, or the points where it cuts the axes.

---

[2]At this point you may find it helpful to review the material on curve-sketching in Chapter 8.

Exercises

15.1.1 Consider the function corresponding to the upper semicircle of the set of points in the xy–plane satisfying

$$x^2 + y^2 = 4.$$

Find dy/dx

(a) by finding and differentiating an explicit formula for y as a function of x;

(b) by using the rule for implicit differentiation.

15.1.2 By analogy with the production function discussed in the text, a utility function of the form

$$U(x, y) = x^\alpha y^\beta,$$

where α and β are positive constants, is called a Cobb–Douglas utility function. For such a function, show that each indifference curve is negatively sloped, convex and has the axes as asymptotes. Hence sketch an indifference curve diagram.

15.1.3 For the production function

$$Q = (aK^{-2} + bL^{-2})^{-1/2} \qquad (a, b > 0)$$

show that the isoquants are negatively sloped and convex.

Find the equations of the asymptotes of the isoquant $Q = \overline{Q}$. Hence sketch an isoquant diagram.

15.2 Comparative statics

Much of economics is concerned with equilibrium analysis, and one of the most important aspects of this is comparative statics; it is 'comparative' because the object of the exercise is to compare equilibria, 'static' because we are not concerned with how the system moves from one equilibrium to another.

To illustrate the method, we consider supply and demand for a good in a single market. We start with the case of linear supply and demand schedules, as in Section 1.1; our analysis here is slightly more general, in that we do not specify numerically the parameters of the supply and demand schedules, and we explicitly assume that quantity demanded depends on income (measured, for example, as the aggregate income of buyers in the market).

We denote the price of the good by p and income by y; the quantities demanded and supplied of the good are denoted by q^D and q^S. Then q^D depends on p and y, while q^S depends only on p. We have the demand and supply functions

$$q^D = \alpha - \beta p + \gamma y, \quad q^S = \delta + \epsilon p.$$

For the usual reasons (recall Section 1.1) we assume that β and ϵ are positive. We also assume that γ is positive, in other words that the quantity demanded increases when income rises and price remains the same. Equilibrium, which in this instance means that the market clears, requires that

$$q^D = q^S.$$

Thus, in equilibrium, price p and quantity q are determined as the solution to the pair of simultaneous equations

$$q = \alpha - \beta p + \gamma y, \quad q = \delta + \epsilon p.$$

In solving these equations, we take income y as given; the equilibrium values of p and q then depend on y. *A typical exercise in comparative statics is to see how the equilibrium changes as y changes.*

Before going into the algebra of the comparative statics, it is helpful to draw a diagram to illustrate the qualitative effect of a change in income. Figure 15.4 depicts the supply schedule and two demand schedules, corresponding to two income levels y_0 and y_1, with $y_0 < y_1$. The diagram is drawn with price p on the vertical axis and quantity q on the horizontal, following economists' convention — recall Figure 1.7 and the discussion leading up to it. Because $\gamma > 0$, an increase in income from y_0 to y_1 shifts the demand schedule to the right; hence, as shown in Figure 15.4, equilibrium price rises from p_0 to p_1 and equilibrium quantity rises from q_0 to q_1.

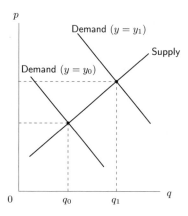

Figure 15.4: **Supply and demand - comparative statics**

Now for the algebra. Recalling the pair of simultaneous equations giving equilibrium price and quantity, and equating the expressions for q given by the two equations, we have

$$\alpha - \beta p + \gamma y = \delta + \epsilon p.$$

Solving for p, we see that equilibrium price is given by

$$p = \frac{\alpha - \delta + \gamma y}{\beta + \epsilon}.$$

We assume throughout that y is large enough for the numerator in this expression to be positive, so that equilibrium price is positive. Equilibrium q is then given by feeding equilibrium p into the supply equation:

$$q = \delta + \epsilon p = \frac{\beta \delta + \epsilon(\alpha + \gamma y)}{\beta + \epsilon}.$$

It is clear from the expressions for p and q that we have just derived, and the assumptions that β, γ and ϵ are positive, that an increase in income increases equilibrium price and quantity. But we knew that from Figure 15.4. What then is to be gained from doing the algebra? Mainly that we now have explicit expressions for the changes in p and q induced by a change in y. Focusing on the equation for equilibrium price, we see that if income rises from y_0 to y_1 the increase in equilibrium price is

$$p_1 - p_0 = \frac{\gamma}{\beta + \epsilon}(y_1 - y_0). \tag{15.6}$$

This implies, for example, that if γ is large, the change in price will be large; that if β is large, the change in price will be small; and that the parameters β and ϵ affect the response of price to changes in income only via their sum $\beta + \epsilon$. All of these consequences of the linear supply-and-demand model could have been derived geometrically, with sufficient effort and ingenuity — but the algebra gets you there more quickly.

The nonlinear case

We now drop the assumption that all relevant functions are linear. Suppose that, with market variables defined as above, the demand and supply functions are

$$q^D = f(p, y), \quad q^S = g(p).$$

We assume as usual that an increase in price, other things equal, reduces quantity demanded and increases quantity supplied: thus for all positive p and y, $\frac{\partial f}{\partial p} < 0$ and $g'(p) > 0$. We also assume as above that the good in question is what economists call a **normal good**: when income rises, other things equal, quantity demanded increases. This means that $\frac{\partial f}{\partial y} > 0$.

Equilibrium requires that $q^D = q^S$, so that equilibrium price is related to income by the equation

$$f(p, y) = g(p).$$

Comparative statics is then a matter of solving this equation for p as a function of y, and investigating how p changes as y changes.

To bring this into line with the mathematics of the first part of this chapter, it is helpful to introduce the function of two variables

$$E(p, y) = f(p, y) - g(p).$$

Observe that $E(p, y)$ is equal to $q^D - q^S$, the excess of quantity demanded over quantity supplied at the given levels of price and income. For this reason, $E(p, y)$ is known as the **excess demand function**. The equilibrium condition then reduces to the following relation between income and price:

$$E(p, y) = 0.$$

We shall analyse this relation using the techniques of Section 15.1. Before we do that, two points of clarification need to be made.

First, nothing in the assumptions made so far about the functions f and g ensures that a positive equilibrium price exists for all relevant income levels. In what follows we simply assume that it does, just as we did in the linear case. Secondly, there is a slight difference in notation from Section 15.1. There, we were concerned with reducing an implicit relation $F(x, y) = 0$ to an equation of the form $y = f(x)$; in other words, the second argument of F was being expressed as a function of the first. Here, we start with the implicit relation $E(p, y) = 0$ and see how the *first argument* of E, namely p, behaves *as a function of the second*, namely y. The variation in the formulae for implicit differentiation that this switch of variables calls for should be obvious, but perhaps a little extra care is required.

We can now proceed with the comparative statics. Given income y, equilibrium price p is given by the implicit relation $E(p, y) = 0$. From the definition of the function E,

$$\frac{\partial E}{\partial p} = \frac{\partial f}{\partial p} - g'(p) < 0, \qquad \frac{\partial E}{\partial y} = \frac{\partial f}{\partial y} > 0.$$

Notice that E is a monotonically decreasing function of p for given y. Thus, given y, there is at most one value of p such that $E(p, y) = 0$; as noted above, we are assuming that such a p does exist for relevant values of y. The equilibrium price p is therefore determined as a function of income y. In particular, this function is the local solution obeying the rules of Section 15.1; thus

$$\frac{dp}{dy} = -\frac{\partial E}{\partial y} \Big/ \frac{\partial E}{\partial p}.$$

Using our information about the partial derivatives of E, we may write the last equation in terms of the original supply and demand functions:

$$\frac{dp}{dy} = \frac{\partial f / \partial y}{(-\partial f / \partial p) + g'(p)}. \qquad (15.7)$$

This is the analogue to (15.6) for the nonlinear case.

(15.7) is more general than (15.6) in the sense that $\dfrac{\partial f}{\partial y}$, $-\dfrac{\partial f}{\partial p}$ and $g'(p)$ reduce to γ, β and ϵ in the special case where demand and supply functions are linear. On the other hand, (15.7) is less general than (15.6) in the sense that (15.6) applies to changes in y of any size, whereas (15.7) tells us only about the effect of small changes in y. This is the price we have to pay for allowing nonlinearity.

As well as illustrating comparative statics, this model of supply and demand also provides an example of an important distinction between two kinds of economic variable. The price and quantity of the good are called **endogenous variables**, since they are determined within the model ('endo' is Greek for 'within'); income is an **exogenous variable**, since it is determined outside the model[3] ('ex' is Greek for 'out of'). The purpose of comparative statics is to analyse the effects on endogenous variables of changes in exogenous ones.

Comparative statics of optima

The methods of comparative statics can also be applied to first-order conditions resulting from optimising behaviour. A typical example is as follows.

Suppose a monopolist's revenue is $R(x)$, where x is quantity produced and sold. Suppose that the only input is labour, which the monopolist can hire at a given wage w per unit, and that $N(x)$ units of labour are required to produce x units of output. The monopolist's total cost is therefore $wN(x)$, and her profit is $R(x) - wN(x)$. It is reasonable to assume that required labour input is an increasing function of output; in fact we make the slightly stronger assumption that $N'(x) > 0$ for all x.

Assuming that profit-maximising output x^* is positive, it satisfies the necessary conditions for an interior maximum, familiar from Chapter 8. These are the first-order condition

$$R'(x^*) - wN'(x^*) = 0$$

and the second-order condition

$$R''(x^*) - wN''(x^*) \leq 0.$$

We now use these conditions to find how the endogenous variable x^* responds to a change in the exogenous variable w.

To apply the rule of implicit differentiation to the first-order condition, we need to assume that

$$R''(x^*) - wN''(x^*) \neq 0. \tag{15.8}$$

---

[3]Whether a variable is endogenous or exogenous depends on the model being considered. Income is exogenous in the supply-and-demand model considered here, but there are plenty of macroeconomic models in which income is an endogenous variable.

Notice that this is *not* guaranteed by the second-order necessary condition for profit maximisation, which is a weak inequality. However, if we assume for simplicity that (15.8) is true, then this, together with the second-order condition, ensures that

$$R''(x^*) - wN''(x^*) < 0.$$

Implicit differentiation then tells us that

$$\frac{dx^*}{dw} = \frac{N'(x^*)}{R''(x^*) - wN''(x^*)}.$$

Since $N'(x^*) > 0$ and $R''(x^*) < wN''(x^*)$, $dx^*/dw < 0$.

Exercises

15.2.1 Consider the following macroeconomic model:

$$Y = C + I, \quad C = a + bY \quad (a > 0, \ 0 < b < 1).$$

The endogenous variables Y and C are national income and consumption respectively, and the exogenous variable I is investment.

Find the equilibrium values of Y and C in terms of I and the parameters a, b. Find also an expression for the change in Y when I increases from I_0 to I_1, determine its sign and comment on its magnitude.

15.2.2 Now consider the following nonlinear version of the model in Exercise 15.2.1:

$$Y = C + I, \quad C = f(Y) \quad (0 < f'(Y) < 1).$$

Find dY/dI, determine its sign and comment on its magnitude.

15.2.3 Suppose the demand function facing a monopolist is $x = sf(p)$, where x is output, p is price, f is a decreasing function and s is a parameter denoting market size. Let the monopolist's total cost be

$$C(x) = c_0 + c_1 x,$$

where c_0 and c_1 are positive constants.

(a) Show that the monopolist's revenue may be written $xg(x/s)$, where g is a decreasing function. Hence find how the profit-maximising output and price change when s increases.

(b) How are the results of (a) affected when

$$C(x) = c_0 + c_1 x + c_2 x^2,$$

where c_0, c_1 and c_2 are positive constants?

15.3 Generalising to higher dimensions

Returning to mathematical principles, we now explain briefly how implicit differentiation can be generalised to functions of many variables.

The simplest case is where we have a single implicit relation involving $m+1$ variables, say

$$F(x_1, \ldots, x_m, y) = 0. \tag{15.9}$$

Suppose that at some particular values $\bar{x}_1, \ldots, \bar{x}_m, \bar{y}$ of $x_1, \ldots, x_m, y$, (15.9) holds and $\partial F / \partial y \neq 0$. Then there is a unique local solution f for y in the sense that, for all $x_1, \ldots, x_m, y$ sufficiently close to $\bar{x}_1, \ldots, \bar{x}_m, \bar{y}$,

$$F(x_1, \ldots, x_m, y) = 0 \quad \text{if and only if} \quad y = f(x_1, \ldots, x_m).$$

The implicit differentiation rule giving the partial derivatives of f is

$$\frac{\partial f}{\partial x_i} = - \frac{\partial F}{\partial x_i} \Big/ \frac{\partial F}{\partial y} \quad \text{for } i = 1, \ldots, m.$$

Jacobian matrices

Now suppose we have more than one implicit relation. To begin with a simple case, suppose we have two implicit relations in three variables x, y, z, say

$$F(x, y, z) = 0, \quad G(x, y, z) = 0.$$

Suppose also that these two equations admit a unique solution for y and z in terms of x in the neighbourhood of a point $(\bar{x}, \bar{y}, \bar{z})$. We denote this local solution by

$$y = f(x), \quad z = g(x).$$

In fact, this pair of equations represents a curve in three-dimensional xyz–space. On this curve,

$$F(x, f(x), g(x)) = 0 \quad \text{and} \quad G(x, f(x), g(x)) = 0.$$

Totally differentiating these equations, we have

$$\frac{\partial F}{\partial x} + \frac{\partial F}{\partial y} f'(x) + \frac{\partial F}{\partial z} g'(x) = 0$$

$$\frac{\partial G}{\partial x} + \frac{\partial G}{\partial y} f'(x) + \frac{\partial G}{\partial z} g'(x) = 0.$$

This pair of equations may be written in matrix form as

$$\mathbf{J} \begin{bmatrix} f'(x) \\ g'(x) \end{bmatrix} = - \begin{bmatrix} \partial F / \partial x \\ \partial G / \partial x \end{bmatrix} \tag{15.10}$$

where

$$\mathbf{J} = \left[\begin{array}{cc} \partial F/\partial y & \partial F/\partial z \\ \partial G/\partial y & \partial G/\partial z \end{array} \right]$$

The 2×2 matrix $\mathbf{J}$ is called the **Jacobian matrix**[4] of the pair of functions (F, G) with respect to the pair of variables (y, z). Recalling that

$$\frac{dy}{dx} = f'(x) \quad \text{and} \quad \frac{dz}{dx} = g'(x)$$

along the solution curve, and assuming that the matrix $\mathbf{J}$ is invertible, we may solve the equations (15.10) as follows:

$$\left[\begin{array}{c} dy/dx \\ dz/dx \end{array} \right] = -\mathbf{J}^{-1} \left[\begin{array}{c} \partial F/\partial x \\ \partial G/\partial x \end{array} \right] \tag{15.11}$$

Equation (15.11) extends the implicit-differentiation rule (15.5) to the case where the single variable y is replaced by the two variables y, z. It is shown in advanced textbooks that invertibility of the matrix $\mathbf{J}$ at the point $(\bar{x}, \bar{y}, \bar{z})$ is sufficient for a unique local solution $y = f(x)$, $z = g(x)$ to exist and to be differentiable. In other words, invertibility of the Jacobian matrix is the relevant generalisation of the condition $\partial F/\partial y \neq 0$ used in Section 15.1.

Full generality

For the sake of completeness, and to illustrate the convenience of matrix notation in these matters, we note that all of the above may be generalised to the case of n implicit relations involving $m + n$ variables.

Consider the n relations

$$F_j(\mathbf{x}, \mathbf{y}) = 0 \quad (j = 1, \dots, n),$$

where $\mathbf{x}$ is an m–vector of variables, $\mathbf{y}$ is an n–vector of variables and subscripts on functions *do not* represent partial differentiation. Let $\mathbf{J}$ denote the Jacobian matrix of the Fs with respect to the components of $\mathbf{y}$: thus $\mathbf{J}$ is the $n \times n$ matrix whose (j, k) entry is $\partial F_j/\partial y_k$ for all j and k.

Suppose that, at some particular pair of vectors $(\bar{\mathbf{x}}, \bar{\mathbf{y}})$, the relations all hold and the matrix $\mathbf{J}$ is invertible. Then there is a unique local solution

$$y_j = f_j(\mathbf{x}) \quad (j = 1, \dots, n).$$

Further, this local solution may be differentiated with respect to the components of $\mathbf{x}$:

$$\frac{d\mathbf{f}}{d\mathbf{x}} = -\mathbf{J}^{-1} \frac{\partial \mathbf{F}}{\partial \mathbf{x}},$$

---

[4]Jacobian matrices are named after the nineteenth-century German mathematician Carl Jacobi. See Exercise 15.3.1 for further discussion of such matrices.

where $\dfrac{d\mathbf{f}}{d\mathbf{x}}$ is the $n \times m$ matrix whose (j, i) entry is $\partial f_j / \partial x_i$ and $\dfrac{\partial \mathbf{F}}{\partial \mathbf{x}}$ is the $n \times m$ matrix whose (j, i) entry is $\partial F_j / \partial x_i$.

This result is called the **implicit function theorem**.

Comparative statics again

The method of comparative statics may be extended to quite complicated economic models. When we analyse models with many variables, the method requires application of the implicit function theorem, and in particular the use of Jacobian matrices. We now consider a supply-and-demand model which is only a slight generalisation of that discussed in the last Section but is just complicated enough to require the use of Jacobian matrices.

We consider the supply of and demand for two goods A and B, the markets for which are interrelated in the following way: the supply of each good depends only on its own price, but the demand for each good depends on both prices and on income. We assume that both goods are normal.

Let the demand function for good A be $f(p, P, y)$, where p is the price of A, P is the price of B and y is income as before; let the supply function for A be $g(p)$. Similarly, let $F(p, P, y)$ and $G(P)$ be the demand and supply functions for good B. We assume that

$$\frac{\partial f}{\partial p} < 0 < g'(p), \quad \frac{\partial f}{\partial y} > 0, \quad \frac{\partial F}{\partial P} < 0 < G'(P), \quad \frac{\partial F}{\partial y} > 0.$$

For the moment, we make no assumptions about the cross-price effects $\partial f / \partial P$ and $\partial F / \partial p$: the two goods may be substitutes or complements.

Defining the excess demand functions

$$x(p, P, y) = f(p, P, y) - g(p), \quad X(p, P, y) = F(p, P, y) - G(P),$$

we see that the equilibrium conditions may be written

$$x(p, P, y) = 0, \quad X(p, P, y) = 0. \tag{15.12}$$

Let us assume that, for a given value of y, there is a unique pair of equilibrium prices (p, P) which satisfy the relations (15.12). Our object is to analyse what happens to the equilibrium when income changes. To apply the mathematics discussed above, we must consider the Jacobian matrix

$$\mathbf{J} = \begin{bmatrix} \partial x / \partial p & \partial x / \partial P \\ \partial X / \partial p & \partial X / \partial P \end{bmatrix}$$

The implicit function theorem tells us that if $\mathbf{J}$ is invertible at the given equilibrium, there is a unique local solution for p and P in terms of y, which may be differentiated as follows;

$$\begin{bmatrix} dp / dy \\ dP / dy \end{bmatrix} = -\mathbf{J}^{-1} \begin{bmatrix} \partial x / \partial y \\ \partial X / \partial y \end{bmatrix}$$

Before going into the details, let us see what invertibility of **J** means. Recall from Section 13.1 that a matrix is invertible if and only if its determinant is not zero. Letting $\Delta = \det \mathbf{J}$, we have

$$\Delta = S - T,$$

where

$$S = \frac{\partial x}{\partial p}\frac{\partial X}{\partial P} = \left(\frac{\partial f}{\partial p} - g'(p)\right)\left(\frac{\partial F}{\partial P} - G'(P)\right)$$

and

$$T = \frac{\partial x}{\partial P}\frac{\partial X}{\partial p} = \frac{\partial f}{\partial P}\frac{\partial F}{\partial p}.$$

Now S is the product of two negative terms and is therefore positive. Hence Δ will be positive if $\partial f/\partial P$ and $\partial F/\partial p$ have opposite signs, or if they have the same sign and are suitably small in absolute value. What this means in economic terms is that $\Delta > 0$ if cross-price effects on demand are not so big as to swamp the own-price effects on supply and demand. From now on we assume this is so.

Given that $\Delta > 0$, the matrix **J** is invertible. From the formula for the inverse of a 2×2 matrix[5] we have

$$\mathbf{J}^{-1} = \frac{1}{\Delta}\begin{bmatrix} \partial X/\partial P & -\partial x/\partial P \\ -\partial X/\partial p & \partial x/\partial p \end{bmatrix}$$

It follows that

$$\frac{dp}{dy} = -\frac{1}{\Delta}\left(\frac{\partial X}{\partial P}\frac{\partial x}{\partial y} - \frac{\partial x}{\partial P}\frac{\partial X}{\partial y}\right) = \frac{1}{\Delta}\left(\left[G'(P) - \frac{\partial F}{\partial P}\right]\frac{\partial f}{\partial y} + \frac{\partial f}{\partial P}\frac{\partial F}{\partial y}\right).$$

Now Δ and the term in square brackets are both positive; also, since both goods are assumed to be normal, $\partial f/\partial y$ and $\partial F/\partial y$ are positive. We therefore have the following information about the sign of dp/dy: if $\partial f/\partial P > 0$ then $dp/dy > 0$; if $\partial f/\partial P < 0$ then dp/dy could be negative if $\partial F/\partial y$ were large enough relative to $\partial f/\partial y$. A similar analysis applies to dP/dy.

Exercises

15.3.1 In the text, the Jacobian matrix was defined in the context of two implicit relations

$$F(x, y, z) = 0, \quad G(x, y, z) = 0$$

in three variables x, y, z. Suppose these relations can be solved to yield solutions $x = f(y, z)$ and $x = g(y, z)$ respectively. The Jacobian matrix of the pair of functions (f, g) with respect to the pair of variables (y, z) is now defined as in the text but with F, G replaced by f, g respectively.

---

[5]This was given near the end of Section 13.2, as a special case of the 'adj-over-det' formula.

Find the Jacobian matrix in the case where

$$f(y, z) = y^2 - z^2, \quad g(y, z) = 2yz.$$

15.3.2 In the two-market example above, let

$$f(p, P, y) = p^{-1}P^\alpha y^{1/2}, \quad g(p) = p^2, \quad F(p, P, y) = p^\beta P^{-2}y^2, \quad G(P) = P.$$

(a) Find explicit expressions for p and P in terms of y. [Hint: take logarithms.]

(b) Show how the signs of dp/dy and dP/dy depend on α and β.

(c) Comment on the relation between your answer to (b) and the results of the text.

Problems on Chapter 15

15–1. Exercise 15.1.2 was about the Cobb–Douglas utility function

$$U(x, y) = x^\alpha y^\beta,$$

where α and β are positive constants. Now consider the utility function

$$V(x, y) = \alpha \ln x + \beta \ln y.$$

Show that V gives rise to the same indifference curve diagram as U, but with different utility levels for corresponding indifference curves.

Hence sketch an indifference curve diagram for the utility function

$$W(x, y) = \alpha \ln(x - a) + \beta \ln(y - b) \qquad (x > a, \ y > b)$$

where α, β, a, b are positive constants.

15–2. For the CES production function

$$Q = A[\delta K^\gamma + (1 - \delta)L^\gamma]^{1/\gamma} \quad (A > 0, \ \gamma < 1, \ 0 < \delta < 1).$$

(i) Show that the isoquants are negatively sloped and convex.

(ii) Suppose $\gamma < 0$. Find the equations of the asymptotes of the isoquant $Q = \overline{Q}$. Hence sketch an isoquant diagram.

(iii) Now suppose that $0 < \gamma < 1$. Find the coordinates of the points where the isoquant $Q = \overline{Q}$ meets the K and L axes. Also find the slope of the isoquant at each of these points. Hence sketch an isoquant diagram.

How are your answers to (i)–(iii) modified for the production function

$$Q = A[\delta K^\gamma + (1-\delta)L^\gamma]^{r/\gamma} \quad (A > 0,\ r > 0,\ \gamma < 1,\ 0 < \delta < 1)?$$

15–3. Recall the timber owner of Problem 9–4; notation and assumptions are as in that problem.

(i) Suppose that the forest is cut down at time T and not replanted, and that T is chosen to maximise the value of the forest at time 0. By the Fisher rule,

$$f'(T)/f(T) = r.$$

Using the inverse function rule of Chapter 7, find dT/dr. What can you say about the sign of dT/dr?

(ii) Now suppose that the timber owner cuts down the forest, sells the timber and replants it with similar trees at time T, $2T$, $3T$, ... Again suppose that T is chosen to maximise the value of the forest at time 0. By the Faustmann rule,

$$f'(T)/f(T) = re^{rT}/(e^{rT} - 1)$$

Use the rule for implicit differentiation to find dT/dr. What can you say about the sign of dT/dr?

15–4. Here is a version of the popular IS–LM macroeconomic model:

$$Y = C + I + G, \quad C = f(Y), \quad I = \phi(r), \quad L(Y,r) = M,$$

where $0 < f'(Y) < 1$, $\phi'(r) < 0$, $\partial L/\partial Y > 0$ and $\partial L/\partial r < 0$.

The endogenous variables Y, C, I, r are respectively national income, consumption investment and the rate of interest. The exogenous variables are government expenditure G and the money supply M. The first two equations of the model are as in the simple model of Exercise 15.2.2, except for the presence of G. The third equation says that investment is a decreasing function of the rate of interest. The final equation describes equilibrium in the money market, equating the supply of money M to the demand $L(Y,r)$.

(i) Using the first three equations of the model and eliminating the variables C and I, obtain a relation of the form

$$F(Y,r) = G.$$

This is known as the 'IS relation'.

(ii) Now observe that the money-market equilibrium equation $L(Y, r) = M$ gives a relation between the variables Y, r, M known as the 'LM relation'. To analyse the IS and LM relations using the methods of this chapter, we define the functions

$$\Phi(Y, r, G, M) = F(Y, r) - G, \quad \Psi(Y, r, G, M) = L(Y, r) - M.$$

Find the Jacobian matrix of (Φ, Ψ) with respect to (Y, r).

(iii) By definition of the functions Φ and Ψ, the IS and LM relations may be written respectively as

$$\Phi(Y, r, G, M) = 0, \quad \Psi(Y, r, G, M) = 0.$$

Assume that for any given positive values of G and M, these equations have a unique solution in the (Y, r) plane, with both components positive. Comment on this assumption with the aid of a diagram. Using your answer to (ii), find $\partial Y/\partial G$, $\partial Y/\partial M$, $\partial r/\partial G$ and $\partial r/\partial M$. What can you say about their signs?

(iv) Compare the expression for $\partial Y/\partial G$ in your answer to (iii) with the the expression for dY/dI in your answer to Exercise 15.2.2. Comment.

Appendix to Chapter 15

In this appendix we fill in a missing step in the argument of Section 15.1, by providing an informal proof of the main result on the existence of a unique local solution.

As before, let (x_0, y_0) be a point in the xy–plane satisfying the implicit relation $F(x, y) = 0$, where F is a smooth function. We say that the equation $F(x, y) = 0$ has a unique local solution $y = f(x)$ in the neighbourhood of the point (x_0, y_0) if, for all points in the xy–plane sufficiently close to (x_0, y_0), we have

$$F(x, y) = 0 \text{ if and only if } y = f(x).$$

The result we want to demonstrate is that a unique local solution exists if $F_2(x_0, y_0) \neq 0$.

Our proof uses Figure 15.5, which reproduces Figure 15.2. Panel (A) represents the 'good' case where there is a unique local solution: we may draw a box around the point (x_0, y_0) such that the set of points within the box for which $F(x, y) = 0$ is the curve $y = f(x)$. Panel (B) is the 'bad' case: if $x > x_0$ there is no value of y for which $F(x, y) = 0$, while if $x < x_0$ there are two values of y for which $F(x, y) = 0$.

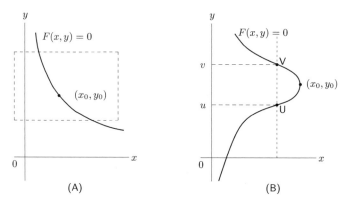

(A)   (B)

Figure 15.5: **Existence and nonexistence of a unique solution to the relation $F(x, y) = 0$ near (x_0, y_0)**

Now look more closely at panel (B). Suppose that $x_1 < x_0$ and that, as in the diagram, the curve $F(x, y) = 0$ crosses the vertical line $x = x_1$ at the two points U and V, with y-coordinates u and v. It follows that if we fix x at x_1 and regard $F(x_1, y)$ as a function of y, say $g(y)$, then $g(u) = g(v) = 0$. By the mean value theorem,[6] $g'(y_1) = 0$ for some y_1 between u and v. Hence $F_2(x_1, y_1) = 0$.

---

[6]Or, to be more precise, the special case of the mean value theorem known as Rolle's theorem. Both theorems were explained in Chapter 10.

We have just shown that the only way a case like that of panel (B) can occur is for $F_2(x_1, y_1)$ to be zero for some point (x_1, y_1) close to (x_0, y_0). We may put this the other way round: as long as $F_2(x, y) \neq 0$ for all points (x, y) sufficiently close to (x_0, y_0), a unique local solution exists as in panel (A). And given our assumptions about continuity, a sufficient condition for this to happen is that $F_2(x_0, y_0) \neq 0$.

Chapter 16

OPTIMISATION WITH SEVERAL VARIABLES

In this chapter we show how the concepts of optimisation, convexity and concavity, which we introduced in Chapter 8, extend to functions of more than one variable. The main focus in examples, exercises and problems will be on the case $n = 2$, but we shall explain all the major results in the general case. The theory of symmetric matrices and quadratic forms will play a major part in our story, and we strongly advise you to re-read the first four pages of Section 13.3 before proceeding further.

When you have studied this chapter you will be able to:

- find and classify critical points of functions of two variables;

- test functions of two variables for concavity and convexity;

- find global maxima of concave functions of two variables, and of monotonic transformations of such functions;

- understand how the methods you have applied to functions of two variables extend to functions of more than two variables.

16.1 Critical points and their classification

We begin by extending to functions of two variables the discussion of critical points of Sections 8.1–8.3.

Let $f(x, y)$ be a smooth function of two variables. The equation

$$z = f(x, y)$$

is then represented by a smooth surface, as in the three panels of Figure 16.1. The points on the surface where the gradient $Df(x, y)$ is the zero-vector **0** are called **critical points**, or **stationary points**. The value of the function at a critical point is called a **critical value**, or **stationary value**. At these points, the tangent plane to the surface is parallel to the xy–plane.

Important examples of critical points are local maximum and local minimum points.

A **local maximum point** for the function f is a point on the surface such that z has its greatest value in a neighbourhood of the point. In panel A of Figure 16.1, the point P with coordinates (x^*, y^*, z^*) is a local maximum point. If we hold y fixed at y^*, it is clear that z has a maximum with respect to x at P; thus $\partial f/\partial x = 0$ at P. Similarly, keeping x fixed at x^* and seeing what happens to $f(x, y)$ for values of y close to y^*, we infer that $\partial f/\partial y = 0$ at P. This shows that local maxima are critical points.

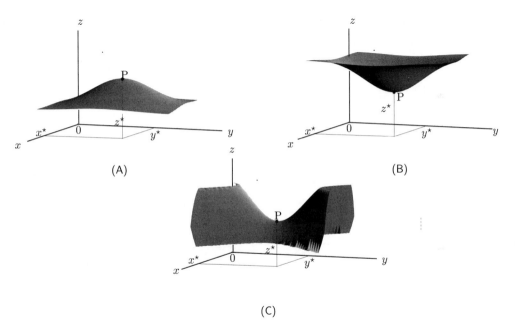

Figure 16.1: **The basic critical points**

A **local minimum point** for the function f is a point on the surface such that z has its least value in a neighbourhood of the point. Such a point is shown in panel B of Figure 16.1. By an argument similar to that for a local maximum, both partial derivatives of f are zero at such a point: local minima are critical points.

In applications, a local maximum or minimum is often called a **local optimum**, depending one whether the object of the exercise is to maximise or minimise the function in question.

It is important to note that local maxima and minima are not the only kinds of critical point. An interesting type of critical point which is *not* a local maximum or minimum is a **saddle point**. This is defined to be a point which is a maximum for movements in one direction but a minimum for movements in another. Panel C of Figure 16.1 shows a saddle point which is a maximum in the x direction and a minimum in the y direction.

One can draw pictures of critical points of functions of two variables using only the xy–plane, by means of a **contour diagram**. A **contour** of the function $f(x, y)$ is a curve depicting a relation of the form $f(x, y) = k$, where k is a constant: thus the isoquants and indifference curves which we discussed at the end of Section 15.1 are contours of production and utility functions respectively. Panel A of Figure 16.2 shows a point (x^*, y^*) corresponding to a local minimum of a function f, and some surrounding contours of that function. Panel B does the same for a local minimum, and panel C for a saddle point. Arrows show directions in which the value of the function increases.

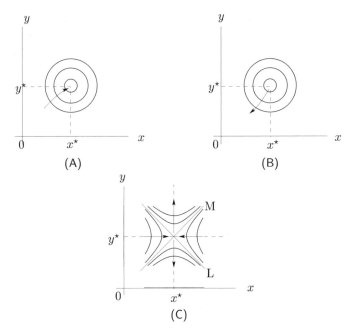

Figure 16.2: **Contours — the arrows show directions of increasing** z.

Notice that panels A and B, the contour diagrams for a maximum and a minimum, are similar: the only difference is the direction of the arrow. Panel C, the contour diagram for a saddle point, looks quite different. Here the straight lines L and M separate the directions along which $f(x, y)$ is maximised at the critical point, from those in which it is minimised there.

We shall use contour diagrams in next two chapters. For the rest of this chapter, we are concerned with the algebra of critical points. We begin by investigating how to determine the nature of a critical point. In the single-variable case, our initial approach in Section 8.1 was to look at tests for maxima and minima which involved only the first derivative. The analogue for a function of two variables would be to consider changes of sign of $\partial f/\partial x$ and $\partial f/\partial y$ as we pass through the critical point. In fact, this does not get us very far; the reason is that it is perfectly possible for $f(x, y)$ to have a maximum in both the x and y directions but a minimum in some other direction (see Exercise 16.1.1).

Thus, to generalise the method of Section 8.1 to the two-variable case, we would need to consider the changes of sign of 'derivatives' in all directions, not just the x and y directions. As this is complicated in general, we proceed no further with this line of reasoning, and instead see how we can generalise the methods of Sections 8.2 and 8.3 which use the second derivative. One helpful fact does come out of the remarks we have just made: if we can find a direction through a critical point in which the function is *not* a maximum, this is enough to show that the point is *not* a maximum point.

Conditions for local maxima and minima

The necessary and sufficient conditions for a local maximum of a function of one variable were summarised in Section 8.3.

(1) If the function $f(x)$ has a local maximum where $x = x^*$ then $f'(x^*) = 0$ and $f''(x^*) \leq 0$.

(2) If $f'(x^*) = 0$ and $f''(x^*) < 0$, the function $f(x)$ has a local maximum where $x = x^*$.

Result (2) is the second derivative test for a maximum: if we have a point where the first derivative is zero and the second derivative is negative, then the point must be a maximum. The significance of result (1) is that it provides a restriction on what can happen at a maximum: the second derivative cannot be positive at such a point.

How would you expect results (1) and (2) to extend to functions of two variables? Vector notation is very useful here. The two-variable analogue of the first derivative is the gradient vector, and it is easy to guess that statements about first derivatives being zero translate into statements about gradients being zero-vectors. The two-variable analogue of the second derivative is the Hessian, which is a symmetric matrix; and it is reasonable to guess that *statements about second derivatives being negative translate into statements about Hessians being negative definite, and statements about second derivatives being non-positive translate into statements about Hessians being negative semidefinite.* These guesses turn out to be correct, and that is all there is to extending results (1) and (2) to functions of two variables!

The extended results are therefore as follows:

(1') If the function $f(x, y)$ has a local maximum at (x^*, y^*) then $Df(x^*, y^*) = \mathbf{0}$ and $D^2 f(x^*, y^*)$ is a negative semidefinite symmetric matrix.

(2') If $Df(x^*, y^*) = \mathbf{0}$ and $D^2 f(x^*, y^*)$ is a negative definite symmetric matrix, then the function $f(x, y)$ has a local maximum at (x^*, y^*).

Result (2') is the analogue of the second derivative test, while result (1') provides the analogue of the restriction contained in (1). For the benefit of readers who distrust arguments by guesswork and analogy, a sketch of the proof of (1') is given in the appendix to this chapter.

By analogy with the one-variable case, statements about gradients are called **first-order conditions** and statements about Hessians are called **second-order conditions**. Notice that the second-order condition in (2') is stronger than that in (1'), requiring the Hessian be negative definite rather than negative semidefinite. This is exactly analogous to the distinction between the $f''(x^*) < 0$ in (2) and the $f''(x^*) \leq 0$ in (1), which we discussed at length in Chapter 8 in connection with the "ambiguous case".

The conditions just given for local maxima translate easily into conditions for local minima.

(1'') If the function $f(x, y)$ has a local minimum at (x^*, y^*) then $Df(x^*, y^*) = \mathbf{0}$ and $D^2 f(x^*, y^*)$ is a positive semidefinite symmetric matrix.

(2'') If $Df(x^*, y^*) = \mathbf{0}$ and $D^2 f(x^*, y^*)$ is a positive definite symmetric matrix, then the function $f(x, y)$ has a local minimum at (x^*, y^*).

These statements follow immediately from (1'), (2') and the fact that local minima of f correspond to local maxima of $-f$.

Example 1 Consider the function

$$f(x, y) = x^3 + y^2 - 4xy - 3x.$$

To find and classify the critical points, we begin by computing the gradient and Hessian in the usual way:

$$Df(x, y) = \begin{bmatrix} 3x^2 - 4y - 3 \\ 2y - 4x \end{bmatrix}, \quad D^2 f(x, y) = \begin{bmatrix} 6x & -4 \\ -4 & 2 \end{bmatrix}.$$

When $Df(x, y) = \mathbf{0}$, we have

$$3x^2 - 4y - 3 = 0, \quad 2y - 4x = 0.$$

We now have two equations to solve simultaneously. From the second, we see that $y = 2x$. Substituting this into the first equation, we get

$$3x^2 - 8x - 3 = 0.$$

Solving this quadratic equation by factorising the left hand side, we have $x = 3$ or $x = -\frac{1}{3}$. Substituting back into $y = 2x$ and then into $f(x, y)$ gives the following:

(a) when $x = 3$, $y = 6$ and $f(x, y) = -18$;

(b) when $x = -\frac{1}{3}$, $y = -\frac{2}{3}$ and $f(x, y) = \frac{14}{27}$.

Thus the critical points are $(3, 6, -18)$ and $(-\frac{1}{3}, -\frac{2}{3}, \frac{14}{27})$. We now determine their nature by evaluating $D^2 f$ at each point. The matrix

$$D^2 f(3, 6) = \begin{bmatrix} 18 & -4 \\ -4 & 2 \end{bmatrix}$$

has positive diagonal entries, and its determinant is $18 \times 2 - (-4)^2 = +20$. Therefore $D^2 f(3, 6)$ is positive definite, and $(3, 6, -18)$ is a local minimum point.

Now consider the other critical point.

$$D^2 f(-\tfrac{1}{3}, -\tfrac{2}{3}) = \begin{bmatrix} -2 & -4 \\ -4 & 2 \end{bmatrix},$$

which has diagonal entries of opposite signs, and therefore cannot be positive semidefinite or negative semidefinite. Hence the point $(-\frac{1}{3}, -\frac{2}{3}, \frac{14}{27})$ is neither a local maximum nor a local minimum. We shall say a little more about this below.

More on saddle points and ambiguous cases

If $Df(x^*, y^*) = \mathbf{0}$ and $D^2 f(x^*, y^*)$ is neither negative definite nor positive definite, then f may have a maximum, a minimum or neither at (x^*, y^*). One thing we do know from Section 13.3 is that if $\det D^2 f(x^*, y^*) < 0$, then $D^2 f(x^*, y^*)$ is neither negative semidefinite nor positive semidefinite; hence, by (1′) and (1″), f cannot have a local maximum or a local minimum at (x^*, y^*). In fact, f must have a saddle point at (x^*, y^*) in this case; the reasons for this are explained in the appendix to this chapter.

For instance, in Example 1 we have

$$\det D^2 f(-\tfrac{1}{3}, -\tfrac{2}{3}) = -4 - 16 < 0,$$

so the critical point $(-\frac{1}{3}, -\frac{2}{3}, \frac{14}{27})$ is a saddle point.

If $\det D^2 f(x^*, y^*) = 0$, then ad hoc investigation will be needed. An illustration is provided by the next example.

Example 2 Let $f(x, y) = 2x^2 + 2y^2 - 4xy - x^4 - y^4$. Then

$$Df(x, y) = \begin{bmatrix} 4x - 4y - 4x^3 \\ 4y - 4x - 4y^3 \end{bmatrix}, \quad D^2 f(x, y) = \begin{bmatrix} 4 - 12x^2 & -4 \\ -4 & 4 - 12y^2 \end{bmatrix}.$$

At a critical point, $Df(x, y) = \mathbf{0}$, and hence

$$x - y = x^3 = -y^3.$$

Since $x^3 + y^3 = 0$, $y = -x$. Substituting this into the condition $x - y = x^3$ gives $x(2 - x^2) = 0$. Thus at a critical point, x is either 0 or $\pm\sqrt{2}$, $y = -x$ and $z = f(x, y) = 8x^2 - 2x^4$. There are therefore three critical points: $\mathbf{a} = (0, 0, 0)$, $\mathbf{b} = (\sqrt{2}, -\sqrt{2}, 8)$ and $\mathbf{c} = (-\sqrt{2}, \sqrt{2}, 8)$.

Temporarily postponing classification of $\mathbf{a}$, we consider $\mathbf{b}$ and $\mathbf{c}$. The matrix

$$D^2 f(\sqrt{2}, -\sqrt{2}) = \begin{bmatrix} -20 & -4 \\ -4 & -20 \end{bmatrix}$$

has negative diagonal entries and determinant 384; it is therefore negative definite. Hence $\mathbf{b}$ is a local maximum; so is $\mathbf{c}$, by similar reasoning.

We now turn to $\mathbf{a}$. The matrix $D^2 f(0, 0)$ has diagonal entries $4, 4$ and determinant 0; it is therefore positive semidefinite but not positive definite. Thus $\mathbf{a}$ may or may not be a local minimum; we now show that it is not. When $y = 0$, $f(x, y) = 2x^2 - x^4$, which has a local minimum at $x = 0$; but when $y = x$, $f(x, y) = -2x^4$, which has a local maximum at $x = 0$. Thus when (x, y) passes through the origin along the x–axis, $f(x, y)$ has a local minimum; but when (x, y) passes through the origin along the line $y = x$, $f(x, y)$ has a local maximum. We conclude that $\mathbf{a}$ is a saddle point.

Higher dimensions

We now consider briefly the case where we have a function of n variables, say $f(x_1, x_2, \ldots, x_n)$. Taking advantage of vector notation, we may write our function as $f(\mathbf{x})$, where $\mathbf{x} \in \mathcal{R}^n$. Then, for any given $\mathbf{x}$, $Df(\mathbf{x})$ is also a vector in $\mathcal{R}^n$, and $D^2 f(\mathbf{x})$ is a symmetric $n \times n$ matrix.

Let $\mathbf{x}^*$ be an n–vector. We say that the function f has a local maximum at $\mathbf{x}^*$ if $f(\mathbf{x}^*) \geq f(\mathbf{x})$ for all n–vectors $\mathbf{x}$ whose components are sufficiently close to those of $\mathbf{x}^*$. Similarly, we say that f has a local minimum at $\mathbf{x}^*$ if $-f$ has a local maximum at $\mathbf{x}^*$. In applied problems when we are trying to maximise (or minimise) something, local maxima (minima) are sometimes referred to as local optima.

The conditions for local maxima and minima given earlier for functions of two variables extend in an entirely obvious fashion to functions of n variables:

(1′) If the function $f(\mathbf{x})$ has a local maximum at $\mathbf{x}^*$ then $Df(\mathbf{x}^*) = \mathbf{0}$ and $D^2 f(\mathbf{x}^*)$ is a negative semidefinite symmetric matrix.

(2′) If $Df(\mathbf{x}^*) = \mathbf{0}$ and $D^2 f(\mathbf{x}^*)$ is a negative definite symmetric matrix, then the function $f(\mathbf{x})$ has a local maximum at $\mathbf{x}^*$.

(1″) If the function $f(\mathbf{x})$ has a local minimum at $\mathbf{x}^*$ then $Df(\mathbf{x}^*) = \mathbf{0}$ and $D^2 f(\mathbf{x}^*)$ is a positive semidefinite symmetric matrix.

(2″) If $Df(\mathbf{x}^*) = \mathbf{0}$ and $D^2 f(\mathbf{x}^*)$ is a positive definite symmetric matrix, then the function $f(\mathbf{x})$ has a local minimum at $(\mathbf{x}^*)$.

That is really all there is to it, except for two awkward points. First, as we explained in Section 13.3, testing for definiteness and semidefiniteness of an $n \times n$ matrix becomes much more tedious when $n > 2$.

Secondly, one may wonder whether the information just given is of any use. In Chapter 8, we originally motivated critical points in terms of curve-sketching, which clearly becomes infeasible when we increase the number of independent variables. The second half of Chapter 8 was concerned with optimisation problems and their economic applications, a topic which it is useful to extend to functions of many variables. But in that context local optima are helpful only insofar as they give information about global optima. It turns out to be very difficult to make general statements about global optima with more than one independent variable. Instead, we often confine our attention to a class of functions for which a critical point, if there is one, must definitely be a global maximum, and to a similar class for which a critical point, if there is one, must be a global minimum. The next section is devoted to these issues.

Exercises

16.1.1 Show that the function

$$f(x, y) = 5xy - 2x^2 - 2y^2$$

has a critical point at $(0, 0, 0)$. Show also that:

(a) $f(x, 0)$ has a maximum when $x = 0$;

(b) $f(0, y)$ has a maximum when $y = 0$;

(c) $f(t, t)$ has a minimum when $t = 0$.

Illustrate these results in a contour diagram.

16.1.2 For each of the following functions, use the methods of this section to show that $(0, 0, 0)$ is a critical point and to determine whether it is a local maximum, a local minimum, a saddle point or none of these:

(a) $x^2 + y^2$,   (b) $-x^2 - y^2$,   (c) $x^2 - y^2$,   (d) $-x^2 + y^2$.

How could you have answered this question without using the methods of this section?

16.1.3 Try to repeat Exercise 16.1.2 for the following functions:

$$\text{(a) } x^4 + y^4, \quad \text{(b) } -x^4 - y^4, \quad \text{(c) } x^4 - y^4, \quad \text{(d) } -x^4 + y^4.$$

What happens?

16.1.4 Show that the function $z = x^2 + y^3$ has a critical point at $(0,0,0)$ and show that this point is neither a local maximum, nor a local minimum, nor a saddle point.

16.1.5 Find the critical points of the following functions and classify each as a local maximum, a local minimum, a saddle point or none of these.

(a)　$z = 3x^2 - y^3 + 12xy - 36y$.

(b)　$z = 3x^2 - 6xy + y^2 + y^4$.

(c)　$z = x^4 + y^4 - (x + y)^2$.

16.2　Global optima, concavity and convexity

As in the last section, we begin with functions of two variables. Our immediate task is to extend to this case the notion of global maximum introduced in Section 8.3. For this purpose it is convenient to refer to the xy–plane as $\mathcal{R}^2$ and to 3–dimensional xyz–space as $\mathcal{R}^3$, while continuing to describe points as rows — (x,y) and (x,y,z) — rather than columns: recall our remarks about 'row vectors' at the beginning of Chapter 13.

We say that the function $f(x,y)$ attains a **global maximum** at the point (x^*, y^*) if

$$f(x^*, y^*) \geq f(x,y) \quad \text{for all } (x,y) \text{ in } \mathcal{R}^2.$$

In that case, the point (x^*, y^*, z^*) in $\mathcal{R}^3$, where $z^* = f(x^*, y^*)$, is highest (in the z–direction) on the surface $z = f(x,y)$.[1]

Obviously, global maxima are local maxima; and if a global maximum exists, it may in principle be found by comparing the values of z at the local maxima and choosing the highest. However, this information on its own is even less helpful than in the case of functions of one variable, because it gives no guidance as to whether a global maximum does in fact exist. It is therefore sensible to start with a particular class of functions, analogous to the concave functions of one variable which we considered in Section 8.4.

Before introducing the algebra, we set the scene with a qualitative, geometrical example. One kind of surface which clearly has a global maximum is a dome. Let S be the surface of a dome and let V be the set of points which are *on or beneath* the surface S. Then the line segment joining any two points

---

[1]There may of course be more than one global maximum point, as in the case where the surface $z = f(x,y)$ is a flat-topped hill.

of V is entirely contained in V: following the lead of Section 8.4, we say that V is a convex set in three-dimensional space. Now, how do we generalise this example, or recognise 'dome-like' surfaces when we see them? For instance, is it true that any surface S, with the property that the set of points on or beneath it is convex, has a global maximum point? The answer is no: any non-horizontal plane has the property just mentioned, and no global maximum point. But such a plane has no local maximum point either; indeed it does not have a critical point of any kind. This suggests a more sensible question: given a surface S, with the properties that (a) the set of points on or beneath S is convex, and (b) S has a critical point P, is P a global maximum? The answer is yes, and our next task is to express all this in algebra.

Convex sets and concave functions

We say that a set V of points in $\mathcal{R}^3$ is a **convex set** if the line segment joining any two points of V is entirely contained in V. The term **convex body** is sometimes used to describe such sets, presumably so as to emphasise their solid character. The set of points *on or inside* a sphere is a convex set, but the surface of the sphere is not. Similarly, the set of points on or beneath a dome is convex; the surface of the dome is not.

We say that the function $f(x, y)$ is a **concave function** if the set of points (x, y, z) such that $z \leq f(x, y)$ is convex. Notice the weak inequality: the definition requires that the set of points *on or beneath* the surface $z = f(x, y)$ be convex, which is precisely what we had in the case of the dome.

As in the case of functions of one variable, which we discussed in Section 8.4, the definition of a concave function of two variables may be put in algebraic form. The function $f(x, y)$ is concave if and only if

$$f(\alpha x_1 + (1 - \alpha)x_2, \, \alpha y_1 + (1 - \alpha)y_2) \geq \alpha f(x_1, y_1) + (1 - \alpha)f(x_2, y_2)$$

whenever (x_1, y_1) and (x_2, y_2) are points in $\mathcal{R}^2$ and $0 \leq \alpha \leq 1$.

Two important facts about concave functions of one variable, which we emphasised in Section 8.4, were as follows.

(I) A twice-differentiable function $f(x)$ is concave if and only if $f''(x) \leq 0$ for all x.

(II) A differentiable concave function $f(x)$ attains a global maximum where $x = x^*$ **if and only if** $f'(x^*) = 0$.

(I) is the standard test of concavity for functions of one variable. Fact (II) gives the standard method of finding a global maximum point of a function which is known to be concave.

To obtain similar results for functions of two variables, we use the translation procedure of Section 16.1: statements about first derivatives being zero translate into statements about gradients being zero-vectors, and statements about second derivatives being non-positive translate into statements about Hessians being negative semidefinite.[2] Restricting ourselves as usual to smooth functions, we have:

(I') The function $f(x, y)$ is concave if and only if the matrix $D^2 f(x, y)$ is negative semidefinite for all (x, y).

(II') The concave function $f(x, y)$ attains a global maximum at (x^*, y^*) if and only if $Df(x^*, y^*) = \mathbf{0}$.

These facts have the same significance for functions of two variables that (I) and (II) have for functions of one variable. (II') is a precise statement of a point made earlier in our informal discussion of 'dome-like' surfaces: **a critical point of a concave function is a global maximum.**

(I') gives the standard test for concavity. Unfortunately, the test is difficult to apply in many cases. To verify that the function f is concave using (I'), one needs to show that $D^2 f(x, y)$ is negative semidefinite for *all* (x, y); this is in general a much harder task than applying the test of Section 13.3 to a particular, numerically specified matrix. In examples and exercises below, we confine ourselves to cases where this does not present great difficulties.

Example 1 Show that the function

$$f(x, y) = -5x^2 - y^2 + 2xy + 6x + 2y + 7$$

is concave and find its global maximum.

To apply (I') and (II'), we calculate the gradient and Hessian:

$$Df(x, y) = \begin{bmatrix} -10x + 2y + 6 \\ -2y + 2x + 2 \end{bmatrix}, \quad D^2 f(x, y) = \begin{bmatrix} -10 & 2 \\ 2 & -2 \end{bmatrix}.$$

For all (x, y) the Hessian has diagonal entries $-10, -2$ and determinant $+16$, and is therefore negative definite. Hence the function f is concave, and to find a global maximum we need only look for a critical point. When $Df(x, y) = \mathbf{0}$,

$$10x - 2y = 6 \quad \text{and} \quad 2x - 2y = -2.$$

Solving these two equations simultaneously, we get $x = 1$, $y = 2$. Further, $f(1, 2) = -9 + 4 + 17 = 12$, so the global maximum point is $(1, 2, 12)$.

Example 2 We now give an economic example. Consider a monpolist producing two goods X and Y. Let the quantities produced of the two goods be x and y, and let the prices charged be p_X and p_Y. The demand functions for the two goods are

$$x = -4p_X + p_Y + 12, \quad y = 2p_X - 3p_Y + 18,$$

[2]For comments on how such analogies may be justified, see the appendix to this chapter.

and the firm's total cost is

$$C(x, y) = 8 + 1.5\,x + 1.8\,y.$$

We wish to find the values of x, y, p_X and p_Y which maximise profit, and the maximal profit.

The method of solution is to express profit as a function of the two variables x, y. We begin by solving the demand functions for p_X and p_Y in terms of x and y. This gives the **inverse demand functions**

$$p_X = \tfrac{1}{10}(54 - 3x - y), \quad p_Y = \tfrac{1}{5}(48 - x - 2y).$$

Hence revenue is

$$R(x, y) = p_X x + p_Y y = \tfrac{1}{10}(54x + 96y - 3x^2 - 3xy - 4y^2)$$

and profit is

$$\Pi(x, y) = R(x, y) - C(x, y) = \tfrac{1}{10}(-80 + 39x + 78y - 3x^2 - 3xy - 4y^2).$$

We now maximise $\Pi(x, y)$ using the same method as in Example 1. We have

$$\frac{\partial \Pi}{\partial x} = \frac{1}{10}(39 - 6x - 3y), \quad \frac{\partial \Pi}{\partial y} = \frac{1}{10}(78 - 3x - 8y).$$

The Hessian matrix $D^2\Pi(x, y)$ has diagonal entries -0.6, -0.8 and determinant 0.39, and is therefore negative definite for all (x, y). Hence the function Π is concave, and the global maximum is found by solving the first-order conditions $\partial \Pi / \partial x = 0$, $\partial \Pi / \partial y = 0$ for x and y.

Solving the pair of linear equations $6x + 3y = 39$, $3x + 8y = 78$ gives

$$x = 2, \quad y = 9.$$

From the inverse demand functions, $p_X = 5.4 - 1.5 = 3.9$ and $p_Y = 9.6 - 4 = 5.6$. At the optimum, revenue is $7.8 + 50.4 = 58.2$, cost is $8 + 3 + 16.2 = 27.2$ and profit is 31.

Two points are worth noting about Example 2. First, the first-order conditions $\partial \Pi / \partial x = 0$ and $\partial \Pi / \partial y = 0$ have a simple interpretation in terms of marginal revenue and marginal cost. If we define the marginal revenue of X as $\partial R / \partial x$ and the marginal cost of X as $\partial C / \partial x$, and similarly for good Y, then the first-order conditions state that marginal revenue equals marginal cost for each good. It is important to note that $\partial R / \partial x$ is *not* the same as $\partial(p_X x)/\partial x$: the difference between them is $y(\partial p_Y / \partial x)$. A similar remark applies to the marginal revenue of Y.

Secondly, the problem makes sense only if x and y are constrained to be nonnegative. In the example as stated we did not need to mention this constraint since the maximum obtained when it was ignored happened to satisfy it. This will not in general remain true if the numbers in the example are changed. We shall return to this point in the next section.

Global minima and convex functions

Everything we have done in this section about concavity and maximisation translates into statements about convexity and minimisation. Recall that convex functions of one variable are concave functions turned upside down, and the same applies when we have two independent variables.

We say that the function $f(x, y)$ attains a **global minimum** at the point (x^*, y^*) if

$$f(x^*, y^*) \leq f(x, y) \quad \text{for all } (x, y) \text{ in } \mathcal{R}^2.$$

Notice that this happens if and only if the function $-f(x, y)$ attains a global minimum at (x^*, y^*).

We say that the function $f(x, y)$ is a **convex function** if the set of points (x, y, z) such that $z \geq f(x, y)$ is a convex set in $\mathcal{R}^3$. This happens if and only if $-f$ is a concave function.

The following facts about convex functions are analogous to (I') and (II'):

(I') The function $f(x, y)$ is convex if and only if the matrix $D^2 f(x, y)$ is positive semidefinite for all (x, y).

(II') The convex function $f(x, y)$ attains a global minimum at (x^*, y^*) if and only if $Df(x^*, y^*) = \mathbf{0}$.

Two extensions

(a) Logarithms and all that

All the results of this section can be extended to cases where the relevant functions are defined only for positive values of x and/or y. For example, $\ln x$ is defined only for positive x, and $1/y$ is defined only when we keep away from the x–axis, which in the current context is usually achieved by considering only positive values of y. These restrictions imposed by mathematical necessity are quite different from constraints on variables imposed for other reasons, which we shall consider in the next section and the next chapter.

Example 3 The function

$$f(x, y) = (x + y)^2 - \ln x - y,$$

is defined for $x > 0$ and all real y. We show that it is convex and find its global minimum.

As usual, we begin by calculating the gradient and Hessian:

$$Df(x, y) = \begin{bmatrix} 2(x + y) - x^{-1} \\ 2(x + y) - 1 \end{bmatrix}, \quad D^2 f(x, y) = \begin{bmatrix} 2 + x^{-2} & 2 \\ 2 & 2 \end{bmatrix}.$$

For all (x, y) the Hessian has positive diagonal entries, and the determinant is $2/x^2 > 0$. Thus $D^2 f(x, y)$ is positive definite, and f is convex. The global minimum is therefore attained at a point (x, y) such that

$$2(x + y) = x^{-1} = 1.$$

This happens if and only if $x = 1$ and $y = -\frac{1}{2}$, in which case $f(x, y) = \frac{1}{4} - 0 + \frac{1}{2} = \frac{3}{4}$. The global minimum point is $(1, -\frac{1}{2}, \frac{3}{4})$.

(b) Monotonic transformations

One useful result about global maxima in Section 8.3 was the following:[3]

> Suppose $g(x) = H(f(x))$, where H is a strictly increasing function. If the function $f(x)$ has a global maximum point where $x = x^*$, so does the function $g(x)$. Similarly, if the function $f(x)$ has a global minimum point where $x = x_0$, so does the function $g(x)$.

This result extends in an obvious way to functions of two variables $f(x, y)$ and $g(x, y)$: notice that H remains a monotonic increasing function of *one* variable.

The following example involves only trivial calculations but illustrates an important point.

Example 4 Let $g(x, y) = (4 - x^2 - y^2)^3$. Then $g(x, y) = [f(x, y)]^3$, where $f(x, y) = 4 - x^2 - y^2$. Without using any calculus, we can see that f attains its global maximum at $(0, 0)$, in which case $f(x, y) = 4$. Since $H(w) = w^3$ is a strictly increasing function, g attains its global maximum at $(0, 0)$, and the global maximum value is 64.

The key feature of Example 4 is that f is a concave function but g is not: indeed it is easy to see that when $x = 1$ and $y = 0$, $\partial^2 g/\partial x^2 = +18$. This suggests a useful method of maximising a function $g(x, y)$ which is not known to be concave and may not even be concave: find a concave function $f(x, y)$ and a strictly increasing function H such that $g(x, y) = H(f(x, y))$; then the point (x^*, y^*) which maximises f also maximises g.

The good thing about this procedure is that it will help to locate the global maxima of many functions which are not concave: for example, functions which may be represented in xyz–space by a bell-shaped surface. The bad news is that finding an appropriate monotonic function H requires guesswork. An example is provided in Exercise 16.2.4, and Problem 16–1 explains how the procedure is related to contour diagrams.

---

[3] See point (b) on page 133.

Higher dimensions

The definitions and results of this section extend to functions of n variables in the obvious way. Thus a function $f(\mathbf{x})$, where $\mathbf{x} \in \mathcal{R}^n$, attains a global maximum where $\mathbf{x} = \mathbf{x}^*$ if $f(\mathbf{x}^*) \geq f(\mathbf{x})$ for all $\mathbf{x}$ in $\mathcal{R}^n$. The function $f(\mathbf{x})$ is concave if

$$f(\alpha\mathbf{x}^1 + (1 - \alpha)\mathbf{x}^2) \geq \alpha f(\mathbf{x}^1) + (1 - \alpha)f(\mathbf{x}^2)$$

whenever $\mathbf{x}^1$ and $\mathbf{x}^2$ are points in $\mathcal{R}^n$ and $0 < \alpha < 1$.

The n-variable version of (I′) states that

(I′) The function $f(\mathbf{x})$ is concave if and only if the matrix $D^2 f(\mathbf{x})$ is negative semidefinite for all $\mathbf{x}$.

(II′) The concave function $f(\mathbf{x})$ attains a global maximum at $\mathbf{x}^*$ if and only if $Df(\mathbf{x}^*) = \mathbf{0}$.

Since the test for concavity (I′) is often difficult to apply, it is worth looking for shortcut methods of recognising concave functions when we see them. Two simple but useful facts are as follows:

(i) If $f(x_1, x_2, \ldots, x_n) = g(x_1)$, where g is a concave function of one variable, then f is a concave function.

(ii) A sum of concave functions is concave.

These facts enable us to build up concave functions of n variables from concave functions of one variable.

For example, it is easy to check that if a is a positive constant, the function $g(x) = a \ln x$, defined for all $x > 0$, is concave. Now let a_1, a_2, a_3, a_4 be positive constants, and define the function

$$f(x, y, z, w) = a_1 \ln x + a_2 \ln y + a_3 \ln z + a_4 \ln w$$

for all 4–vectors (x, y, z, w) whose components are all positive. Then by (i) and (ii), f is a concave function.

All these remarks are easily translated into statements about global minima and convex functions. We shall extend these ideas a little further in the next chapter when we introduce the class of quasi-concave functions.

Exercises

16.2.1 In which of the cases in Exercises 16.1.2 and 16.1.3 is $(0, 0, 0)$ the global optimum?

16.2.2 For the function

$$z = -2x^2 + 4xy - 3y^2 + 10x - 14y - 3,$$

find the gradient vector and the Hessian matrix. Show that the function is concave, and find the global maximum value of z.

16.2.3 A monopolist can produce quantities x and y of two products X and Y at cost $4x^2 + xy + 2y^2$. The inverse demand functions are

$$p_X = 150 - 5x + y, \quad p_Y = 30 + 2x - 2y,$$

where p_X and p_Y are the prices charged for X and Y. What outputs maximise profits?

16.2.4 Write down the global maximum value of the function

$$f(x, y) = -(3x^2 + 4y^2).$$

Hence find the global maximum value of the function

$$g(x, y) = \exp(-3x^2 - 4y^2).$$

Verify that:

(a) f is concave;

(b) $g(x, y)$ is of the form $H(f(x, y))$ where H is a strictly increasing function.

[The function g is *not* concave: if you have done Problem 9–1, you should be able to give a geometrical proof. It is possible to demonstrate non-concavity of g by computing the Hessian, but we do not advise this.]

16.2.5 Show that the function $f(x, y, z) = e^x + e^y + e^z$ is convex.

16.2.6 (a) Let A, α, β be positive constants. Show that the Cobb–Douglas production function

$$Q = AK^\alpha L^\beta$$

is concave if and only if $\alpha + \beta \le 1$.

(b) Let a, b, α, β be positive constants. Show that the utility function

$$U(x, y) = \alpha \ln(x - a) + \beta \ln(y - b) \quad (x > a, \ y > b)$$

is concave. What about the utility function

$$V(x, y) = (x - a)^\alpha (y - b)^\beta \quad (x > a, \ y > b)?$$

16.3   Non-negativity constraints

We noted in Section 8.3 that optimisation problems encountered in economics usually require the independent variables to be non-negative. We showed in that section that if a function $f(x)$ is maximised, subject to the constraint $x \ge 0$, at $x = x^*$ then

$$f'(x^*) \le 0, \quad \text{with equality if } x^* > 0.$$

This was demonstrated graphically — recall Figure 8.8 —- but a verbal argument will also suffice. Clearly $f'(x^*)$ cannot be positive: for if it were we could increase the value of $f(x)$ above $f(x^*)$, while keeping x non-negative, by choosing x slightly greater than x^*. And if $x^* > 0$ then $f'(x^*)$ cannot be negative: for if it were we could increase the value of $f(x)$ above $f(x^*)$, while keeping x non-negative, by choosing x slightly less than x^*.

Now consider the analogous problem for two variables:

$$\text{maximise } f(x,y) \text{ subject to } x \geq 0, \ y \geq 0. \tag{16.1}$$

Suppose that (x^*, y^*) is a solution to the problem (16.1). Then the following conditions must hold there:

$$\frac{\partial f}{\partial x} \leq 0, \text{ with equality if } x > 0; \quad \frac{\partial f}{\partial y} \leq 0, \text{ with equality if } y > 0. \tag{16.2}$$

This can be demonstrated exactly as in the one-dimensional case. At (x^*, y^*), $\partial f / \partial x$ cannot be positive: for if it were we could make $f(x,y)$ greater than $f(x^*, y^*)$ while satisfying the constraints by raising x slightly above x^* and keeping y at y^*. If in addition $x^* > 0$ then we are allowed small movements in the opposite direction, so $\partial f / \partial x$ cannot be negative either. Similar remarks apply to $\partial f / \partial y$.

Local and global maxima

The distinction between local and global maxima also applies when there are non-negativity constraints. Let (x^*, y^*) be a point in the plane such that $x^* \geq 0$ and $y^* \geq 0$. We say that $f(x,y)$ attains a global maximum subject to the constraints $x \geq 0$, $y \geq 0$ at the point (x^*, y^*) if $f(x^*, y^*) \geq f(x,y)$ for all points (x,y) which satisfy the constraints. Similarly, we say that $f(x,y)$ attains a local maximum subject to the constraints $x \geq 0$, $y \geq 0$ at the point (x^*, y^*) if $f(x^*, y^*) \geq f(x,y)$ for all points (x,y) which satisfy the constraints and are sufficiently close to (x^*, y^*).

The first-order conditions (16.2) are a property of *local* maxima. This is easily seen by looking again at the argument which justified those conditions: recall in particular the phrases "slightly above x^*" and "small movements in the opposite direction".

Again as in the unconstrained case, the first-order conditions are sufficient for a global maximum when the function to be maximised is concave. More precisely, if f is a concave function, and (x^*, y^*) is a point with non-negative coordinates at which (16.2) holds, then $f(x,y)$ attains a global maximum subject to the constraints $x \geq 0$, $y \geq 0$ at (x^*, y^*). This is the generalisation to functions of two variables of a result of Section 8.4.

Example 1 Maximise

$$f(x,y) = 1 - 8x + 10y - 2x^2 - 3y^2 + 4xy$$

subject to $x \geq 0$ and $y \geq 0$.

As usual, we begin by calculating the gradient and Hessian:

$$Df(x,y) = \begin{bmatrix} -8 - 4x + 4y \\ 10 - 6y + 4x \end{bmatrix}, \quad D^2 f(x,y) = \begin{bmatrix} -4 & 4 \\ 4 & -6 \end{bmatrix}.$$

For all (x, y), the Hessian matrix has diagonal entries $-4, -6$ and determinant $+8$, and is therefore negative definite. Hence f is a concave function, and any (x, y) which satisfies (16.2) is a global constrained maximum. It remains to locate such a point.

Our first pass at the problem is to look for a solution with $x > 0$, $y > 0$ so that $Df(x,y) = \mathbf{0}$. Equating the gradient to the zero-vector gives

$$x - y = -2, \quad 2x - 3y = -5.$$

These equations are satisfied only when $x = -1$ and $y = 1$, which obviously violates the constraint $x \geq 0$.

Thus our problem is not yet solved. However, the calculation just made was not a wasted effort, for we have in fact found the unconstrained maximum; and since this has $x < 0$, it is likely that $x = 0$ at the constrained maximum. We therefore look for a solution with $x = 0$ and $y > 0$, so that $\partial f / \partial y = 0$. Equating x and $\partial f / \partial y$ to zero we see that $10 - 6y + 0 = 0$, so $y = \frac{5}{3}$. Thus the point $(0, \frac{5}{3})$ satisfies the conditions

$$x = 0, \quad y > 0, \quad \partial f / \partial y = 0,$$

and it remains to show that this point satisfies the remaining condition for a constrained maximum, namely $\partial f / \partial x \leq 0$. At $(0, \frac{5}{3})$,

$$\partial f / \partial x = -4(2 + 0 - \tfrac{5}{3}) = -\tfrac{4}{3} < 0,$$

so the condition is satisfied.

Thus the constrained maximum is attained when $x = 0$ and $y = \frac{5}{3}$; the constrained maximum value of f is therefore $\frac{28}{3}$. This is of course less than the value taken by f at the unconstrained maximum $(-1, 1)$, which is in fact 10.

Example 2 We amend the monopolist's problem of Example 2 of the last section by making total cost $8 + 3x + 1.8\,y$. Profit is now

$$\Pi(x, y) = \tfrac{1}{10}(-80 + 24x + 78y - 3x^2 - 3xy - 4y^2),$$

where x and y are the quantities of the two goods. We wish to choose x and y so as to maximise $\Pi(x, y)$ subject to the constraints $x \geq 0$ and $y \geq 0$.

In this case, $\partial\Pi/\partial x = \frac{1}{10}(24 - 6x - 3y)$ and $\partial\Pi/\partial y = \frac{1}{10}(78 - 3x - 8y)$. The Hessian matrix is as in the earlier example and is therefore negative definite for all x, y. Hence the function Π is concave, and the first-order conditions give a global constrained maximum. It is not hard to see that the only values of x and y for which $\partial\Pi/\partial x = \partial\Pi/\partial y = 0$ are $x = -\frac{14}{13}$ and $y = \frac{132}{13}$, which clearly violates the constraints. We therefore look for a solution (x, y) such that $x = 0$, $y > 0$, $\partial\Pi/\partial x \le 0$ and $\partial\Pi/\partial y = 0$.

The first, second and fourth of these conditions are satisfied when $x = 0$ and $y = 9.75$. Since $9.75 > 8$, the third condition is also satisfied. Hence the solution is $x = 0$, $y = 9.75$ and the maximal profit is $-8 + 7.8 \times 9.75 - 0.4 \times (9.75)^2 = 30.025$.

Extensions

The results just stated about maximisation subject to non-negativity constraints can be generalised in the obvious way to functions of n variables, and translated into statements about minimisation.

For example, suppose we wish to *minimise* the function $g(x, y, z, w)$ subject to the constraint that x, y, z, w are all non-negative. Necessary conditions for a local minimum are:

$$\frac{\partial g}{\partial x} \ge 0, \text{ with equality if } x > 0; \quad \frac{\partial g}{\partial y} \ge 0, \text{ with equality if } y > 0.$$

$$\frac{\partial g}{\partial z} \ge 0, \text{ with equality if } z > 0; \quad \frac{\partial g}{\partial w} \ge 0, \text{ with equality if } w > 0.$$

If g is a *convex* function, these conditions are sufficient for a global minimum.

Exercises

16.3.1 For the function

$$z = -2x^2 + 4xy - 3y^2 + 10x - 14y - 3$$

of Exercise 16.2.2, find the global maximum value subject to the constraints $x \ge 0$ and $y \ge 0$.

16.3.2 Repeat Exercise 16.2.3 when the expression for the cost is $4x^2 + 8xy + 2y^2$.

16.3.3 The market demand for a commodity with only two sellers is $x = 20 - 2p$. For seller 1, the cost of producing output x_1 is $5 + 4x_1$, where $x_1 \ge 0$; for seller 2, the cost of producing output x_2 is $7 + x_2$, where $x_2 \ge 0$. Use the methods of this section to determine the output combination which maximises total profit, and the maximum profit.

In this simple case, but not in more general examples of this situation, there is an easier method. Can you spot it?

Problems on Chapter 16

16–1. Sketch the contour diagram for the function $f(x,y) = x^2 + y^2$, showing in the diagram the contours $f(x,y) = k$ where $k = 0, 1, 2, 3, 4, 5$.

Explain why the contour diagram for the function $g(x,y) = x^2 + y^2 - 2$ is identical to that for $f(x,y)$ except that the values taken by $g(x,y)$ are different.

Sketch contour diagrams for

$$\text{(i) } (x^2 + y^2 - 2)^2, \quad \text{(ii) } (x^2 + y^2 - 2)^3$$

and in each case state the global minimum value of the function. Comment.

Sketch also the contour diagram for $(x^2 + y^2 - 2)^{-1}$. Comment.

16–2. A firm has a Cobb–Douglas production function

$$F(K, L) = AK^\alpha L^\beta$$

where A, α, β are positive constants. Let the prices of capital, labour and the firm's output be r, w and p respectively.

Write down an expression for the firm's profit in terms of K and L. Show that it is a concave function of K and L if and only if $\alpha + \beta \leq 1$.

Write down the firm's profit maximisation problem. Assuming $\alpha + \beta < 1$, find the profit-maximising levels of K and L and the maximum profit in terms of p, r and w. [Hint: you may find it useful to express the first-order conditions as a pair of linear equations in $\ln K$ and $\ln L$.] What happens in the case $\alpha + \beta = 1$?

16–3. In Problem 13–4 you were asked to find the values of b_1 and b_2 that minimise the expression

$$\sum_{i=1}^{n} (y_i - b_1 x_{1i} - b_2 x_{2i})^2,$$

where $\{(y_i, x_{1i}, x_{2i}) : i = 1, \ldots, n\}$ are $3n$ given numbers. Let $\mathbf{X}$ be the $n \times 2$ matrix whose ith row is $(x_{1i} \ x_{2i})$ for $i = 1, \ldots, n$; it is assumed that the columns of $\mathbf{X}$ are linearly independent.

Solve this minimisation problem using the methods of this chapter, and verify that your answer is the same as in Problem 13–4.

16–4. Jane lives for two periods. In the first period, she works: her income is y, her consumption is c and her saving is therefore $y - c$. In the second period, she is retired: her consumption is $(1 + r)(y - c)$, where r is the rate of interest.

Suppose that Jane chooses c and y so as to maximise the utility function

$$U(c,y) + V((1+r)(y-c)),$$

where $\partial U/\partial c > 0$, $\partial U/\partial y < 0$ and $V' > 0$. The reason why y is an object of choice is that Jane can earn more income in the first period by working harder; the reason why $\partial U/\partial y < 0$ is that she finds work unpleasant.

Using the results of Section 15.3, state conditions under which the optimal values of c and y are differentiable functions of r. Assuming these conditions are met, find dc/dr and dy/dr. Using the second-order conditions for a maximum, and making any additional assumptions you think reasonable about the functions U and V, discuss the signs of dc/dr and dy/dr.

Appendix to Chapter 16

The four main results of this chapter may be summarised as follows.

(1′) If the function $f(x, y)$ has a local maximum at (x^*, y^*) then $Df(x^*, y^*) = \mathbf{0}$ and $D^2 f(x^*, y^*)$ is a negative semidefinite symmetric matrix.

(2′) If $Df(x^*, y^*) = \mathbf{0}$ and $D^2 f(x^*, y^*)$ is a negative definite symmetric matrix, then the function $f(x, y)$ has a local maximum at (x^*, y^*).

(I′) The function $f(x, y)$ is concave if and only if the matrix $D^2 f(x, y)$ is negative semidefinite for all (x, y).

(II′) The concave function $f(x, y)$ attains a global maximum at (x^*, y^*) if and only if $Df(x^*, y^*) = \mathbf{0}$.

We now sketch a proof of (1′).

Let the function $f(x, y)$ have a local maximum at (x^*, y^*). Choose any pair of real numbers a, b and define a function g of one variable by setting

$$g(t) = f(x^* + ta, \ y^* + tb).$$

Then $g(0) = f(x^*, y^*)$; and since f has a local maximum at (x^*, y^*), $g(0) \geq g(t)$ whenever $|t|$ is sufficiently small. Therefore $g(t)$ has a local maximum at $t = 0$. We now use the crucial tool of the proof, namely the one-variable counterpart of the result we are trying to prove. By the necessary conditions for a local maximum of a function of one variable,

$$g'(0) = 0 \quad \text{and} \quad g''(0) \leq 0.$$

To turn these conditions into statements about the function f, we must find expressions for $g'(t)$ and $g''(t)$. Differentiating $g(t)$ by the chain rule and using the subscript notation for partial derivatives,

$$g'(t) = af_1(x^* + ta, \ y^* + tb) + bf_2(x^* + ta, \ y^* + tb).$$

Differentiating again,

$$g''(t) = a^2 f_{11}(x^* + ta, \ y^* + tb) + 2ab f_{12}(x^* + ta, \ y^* + tb) + b^2 f_{22}(x^* + ta, \ y^* + tb).$$

Hence the first-order condition $g'(0) = 0$ may be written

$$af_1(x^*, y^*) + bf_2(x^*, y^*) = 0, \tag{16.3}$$

and the second-order condition $g''(0) \leq 0$ becomes

$$a^2 f_{11}(x^*, y^*) + 2ab f_{12}(x^*, y^*) + b^2 f_{22}(x^*, y^*) \leq 0. \tag{16.4}$$

Since (16.3) holds for all a and b, $f_1(x^*, y^*) = f_2(x^*, y^*) = 0$: $Df(x^*, y^*) = \mathbf{0}$, as required. Also, the left-hand side of (16.4) is the quadratic form corresponding to the symmetric matrix $D^2 f(x^*, y^*)$; since (16.4) holds for all a and b, the matrix is negative semidefinite. This proves (1').

We now make some brief remarks about the proofs of (2'), (I') and (II'). The proof of (I') is similar to that of (1'): we define a function g as above and use the chain rule to derive the two-dimensional result from the one-dimensional one. (2') and (II') are harder to prove, but the general approach is the same.

Similar remarks apply to the n–variable counterparts of the four main results. The method, as before, is to treat $f(\mathbf{x} + t\mathbf{a})$, where $\mathbf{x}$ and $\mathbf{a}$ are given n–vectors, as a function of the scalar variable t, and to apply differential calculus of one variable. The same trick may be used to prove the variant of (II') applicable to maxima under non-negativity constraints which we stated in Section 16.3. The remainder of this appendix is devoted to two other applications of this technique.

More on saddle points

Let (x^*, y^*, z^*) be a point on the surface $z = f(x, y)$ such that $Df(x^*, y^*) = \mathbf{0}$ and $\det D^2 f(x^*, y^*) < 0$. We stated in Section 16–1 that under these conditions (x^*, y^*, z^*) is a saddle point. We now explain why this is so.

Let $\mathbf{Q} = D^2 f(x^*, y^*)$. Since $\det \mathbf{Q} < 0$, the symmetric matrix $\mathbf{Q}$ is neither positive semidefinite nor negative semidefinite. Hence there exist 2–vectors

$$\mathbf{a} = \begin{bmatrix} a_1 \\ a_2 \end{bmatrix}, \quad \mathbf{b} = \begin{bmatrix} b_1 \\ b_2 \end{bmatrix}$$

such that $\mathbf{a}^T\mathbf{Q}\mathbf{a} < 0 < \mathbf{b}^T\mathbf{Q}\mathbf{b}$. Now consider the functions of one variable

$$g(t) = f(x^* + ta_1, y^* + ta_2), \quad h(t) = f(x^* + tb_1, y^* + tb_2).$$

Since $Df(x^*, y^*) = \mathbf{0}$, $g'(0) = h'(0) = 0$ by the chain rule. Also by the chain rule, $g''(0) = \mathbf{a}^T\mathbf{Q}\mathbf{a} < 0$ and $h''(0) = \mathbf{b}^T\mathbf{Q}\mathbf{b} > 0$. Hence $g(t)$ has a local maximum where $t = 0$ and $h(t)$ has a local minimum where $t = 0$. It follows that $f(x, y)$ has a saddle point at (x^*, y^*).

Taylor approximations

We begin by recalling some results from Chapter 10. Let $f(x)$ be a smooth function of one variable, and let a and h be real numbers, with $|h|$ small. The first-order Taylor approximation to $f(a + h)$ is

$$f(a + h) \approx f(a) + hf'(a).$$

This is of course the small increments formula for functions of one variable, which we introduced in Chapter 6 and discussed further in Section 10.1. The second-order Taylor approximation to $f(a+h)$ is

$$f(a+h) \approx f(a) + hf'(a) + \tfrac{1}{2}h^2 f''(a).$$

This was derived in Section 10.2 as a consequence of the second mean value theorem. Higher-order Taylor approximations were derived in Section 10.3, but these are not our present concern. What we are interested in is the extesion of the linear and quadratic approximations to functions of two or more variables.

Let $f(x, y)$ be a smooth function of two variables, and let (a_1, a_2) and (h_1, h_2) be points in the xy–plane. We take a_1 and a_2 as given and assume that $|h_1|$ and $|h_2|$ are small. The first-order Taylor approximation to $f(a_1 + h_1, a_2 + h_2)$ is

$$f(a_1 + h_1, a_2 + h_2) \approx f(a_1, a_2) + h_1 f_1(a_1, a_2) + h_2 f_2(a_1, a_2),$$

where the subscript notation is used for partial differentiation. This is the small increments formula of Section 14.2. The second-order Taylor approximation to $f(a_1 + h_1, a_2 + h_2)$, which is typically more accurate, is as follows:

$$f(a_1 + h_1, a_2 + h_2) \approx f(a_1, a_2) + h_1 f_1(a_1, a_2) + h_2 f_2(a_1, a_2)$$
$$+ \tfrac{1}{2}h_1^2 f_{11}(a_1, a_2) + h_1 h_2 f_{12}(a_1, a_2) + \tfrac{1}{2}h_2^2 f_{22}(a_1, a_2).$$

This may be written more concisely in the form

$$f(\mathbf{a} + \mathbf{h}) \approx f(\mathbf{a}) + \mathbf{h}^{\mathsf T}\mathbf{p} + \tfrac{1}{2}\mathbf{h}^{\mathsf T}\mathbf{Q}\mathbf{h}, \tag{16.5}$$

where $\mathbf{p}$ is the gradient $Df(a_1, a_2)$ and $\mathbf{Q}$ is the Hessian matrix $D^2 f(a_1, a_2)$. The approximation (16.5) generalises in an obvious fashion to functions of n variables.

We now derive (16.4) from the second-order Taylor approximation for functions of one variable. For any real number t, we let $g(t) = f(a_1 + th_1, a_2 + th_2)$. Then

$$g(t) \approx g(0) + tg'(0) + \tfrac{1}{2}t^2 g''(0) \tag{16.6}$$

when $|t|$ is small. But by the chain rule

$$g'(t) = h_1 f_1 + h_2 f_2, \quad g''(t) = h_1^2 f_{11} + 2h_1 h_2 f_{12} + h_2^2 f_{22},$$

where all derivatives are evaluated at $(a_1 + th_1, a_2 + th_2)$. Setting $t = 0$ and using the same notation as in (16.5), we have

$$g(0) = f(\mathbf{a}), \quad g'(0) = \mathbf{h}^{\mathsf T}\mathbf{p}, \quad g''(0) = \mathbf{h}^{\mathsf T}\mathbf{Q}\mathbf{h}.$$

This, together with (16.6), implies that (16.5) holds when $\mathbf{h}$ is replaced by $t\mathbf{h}$ and $|t|$ is small. When the components of $\mathbf{h}$ are themselves small, $t = 1$ is small enough for the approximation to be applicable, and (16.5) holds as stated.

Chapter 17

PRINCIPLES OF CONSTRAINED OPTIMISATION

In Chapter 16 we were concerned with maxima and minima of functions of several variables. We now continue this theme and look at cases where optimisation takes place subject to constraints on the variables. Problems of this sort occur frequently in economics and management science: maximisation of profit subject to capacity constraints, minimisation of cost of a diet satisfying nutritional requirements and so on. In this chapter we develop the basic method and give some important applications in economics, leaving the more advanced topics to Chapter 18.

When you have studied this chapter you will be able to:

- use Lagrange's method to maximise and minimise functions subject to equation constraints;

- derive demand functions from utility functions, and conditional input demands from production functions;

- recognise quasi-concave functions;

- distinguish between constrained maxima and minima using diagrams and considerations of convexity.

17.1 Lagrange multipliers

Constrained optimisation has appeared at various places in earlier chapters, notably in connection with linear programming in section 2.3 and non-negativity constraints in Secton 16.3. What is new in this chapter is that we deal systematically with constraints in the form of equations. We begin with the simple case of two variables and one constraint.

Let $f(x, y)$ and $g(x, y)$ be functions of two variables. We wish to

maximise $f(x, y)$ subject to the constraint $g(x, y) = 0$. $\qquad$ (17.1)

Suppose that $\partial g/\partial y \neq 0$. Then we know from our discussion of implicit relations in Section 15.1 that the constraint may be solved, at any rate locally, for y in terms of x. So one way to solve the problem might be to substitute the solution to $g(x, y) = 0$, say $y = h(x)$, into the maximand. This gives us a function of one variable,

$$F(x) = f(x, h(x)),$$

which can be maximised with respect to x. A constrained maximum of the original problem is an unconstrained maximum of the function F. At such a point, $F'(x) = 0$.

Unfortunately, the explicit expression for $h(x)$ may be messy, or even impossible to find. For this reason, we need to express the condition $F'(x) = 0$ in terms of the data of the problem, namely the functions f and g. By the chain rule,

$$F'(x) = \frac{\partial f}{\partial x} + \frac{\partial f}{\partial y} h'(x).$$

But $h(x)$ was defined to be the solution for y of the implicit relation $g(x, y) = 0$: so by implicit differentiation,

$$h'(x) = -\frac{\partial g}{\partial x} \Big/ \frac{\partial g}{\partial y}. \qquad (17.2)$$

Hence the condition for a maximum, $F'(x) = 0$, may be written as follows:

$$\frac{\partial f}{\partial x} - \frac{\partial f}{\partial y} \left(\frac{\partial g}{\partial y}\right)^{-1} \frac{\partial g}{\partial x} = 0. \qquad (17.3)$$

The next step is to make (17.3) look less intimidating. Let

$$\lambda = \frac{\partial f}{\partial y} \Big/ \frac{\partial g}{\partial y}.$$

Then (17.3) states that

$$\frac{\partial f}{\partial x} - \lambda \frac{\partial g}{\partial x} = 0.$$

Putting the last two equations together, we have

$$\frac{\partial f}{\partial x} - \lambda \frac{\partial g}{\partial x} = 0, \quad \frac{\partial f}{\partial y} - \lambda \frac{\partial g}{\partial y} = 0. \qquad (17.4)$$

We summarise as follows. At a solution of the constrained maximisation problem (17.1), the two equations (17.4) hold for some real number λ. These equations are the counterpart for constrained problems of the zero-gradient condition of optimisation without constraints, and are therefore known as **first-order conditions** for a constrained maximum.

Geometry of the first-order conditions

To emphasise the crucial importance of the first-order conditions, we give an alternative derivation of (17.4), which uses a diagram instead of the chain rule. Figure 17.1 depicts the curve $g(x, y) = 0$, labelled C (for constraint). The other curves in the diagram are contours of the function f, with each curve representing the relation $f(x, y) = k$ for a different constant k. The arrow indicates the direction of increase of f. The contour labelled M (for maximum) touches the curve C at the point P. The constraint is satisfied at P, and all other points on C lie on contours giving a lower value of f. Hence P is the solution to problem (17.1).

The curves C and M have the same slope at P. But by the rule of implicit differentiation, the slope of C at P is the value at P of the right-hand side of (17.2). Similarly, the slope of M at P is the value at P of the expression

$$-\frac{\partial f}{\partial x} \bigg/ \frac{\partial f}{\partial y}.$$

Equating the slopes and rearranging, we see that (17.3) holds at P, and (17.4) follows as before.

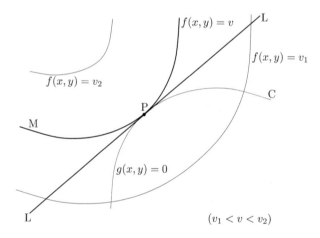

Figure 17.1: v **is the maximum value of** $f(x, y)$ **subject to** $g(x, y) = 0$

The Lagrangian

We now write the first-order conditions in yet another way. We define a function L of three variables by setting

$$L(x, y, \lambda) = f(x, y) - \lambda g(x, y). \tag{17.5}$$

L is called the **Lagrangian function** for the problem (17.1), and its third argument λ is called the **Lagrange multiplier**.[1] The relationship between the function L and the constrained maximisation problem (17.1) is as follows:

If (x^*, y^*) is a solution of the constrained maximisation problem

$$\text{maximise } f(x, y) \text{ subject to } g(x, y) = 0,$$

then there is a real number λ^* such that the Lagrangian L has a critical point at (x^*, y^*, λ^*).

To see why this is so, recall that the conditions for a critical point of L are

$$\frac{\partial L}{\partial x} = 0, \quad \frac{\partial L}{\partial y} = 0, \quad \frac{\partial L}{\partial \lambda} = 0. \tag{17.6}$$

The first two conditions are the two equations of (17.4), and we have just shown that these hold at a constrained maximum. The third condition is simply the constraint $g(x, y) = 0$.

This way of looking at (17.4) gives us a method of solving the problem (17.1). We introduce a new unknown quantity λ (the Lagrange multiplier) and form the Lagrangian function L as in (17.5). The critical points of this function are then investigated: the first two coordinates of one of these points will be a constrained maximum of the original problem. If there is more than one critical point of L, some of these points may not correspond to constrained maxima of (17.1), and ad hoc methods are typically employed to find the ones which do; we shall have more to say about this at various points in this chapter.

The whole procedure is known as **Lagrange's method of undetermined multipliers**, or the **Lagrange multiplier rule**. The usual way to find critical points of L is to solve the first two equations of (17.6) for x and y in terms of λ and then use the third equation, which is the constraint $g(x, y) = 0$, to solve for λ.[2]

Example 1 Use Lagrange's method to

$$\text{maximise } 4xy - 2x^2 + y^2 \text{ subject to } 3x + y = 5.$$

We may put this problem in the form (17.1) by setting

$$f(x, y) = 4xy - 2x^2 + y^2, \quad g(x, y) = 3x + y - 5.$$

We therefore form the Lagrangian

$$L(x, y, \lambda) = f(x, y) - \lambda g(x, y) = -2x^2 + y^2 + 4xy - 3\lambda x - \lambda y + 5\lambda.$$

---

[1] After Joseph-Louis Lagrange (1736–1813), one of the leading mathematicians of his time, and one of the first professors at the Ecole Polytechnique in Paris.

[2] The fact that λ is usually solved for last is the reason for the term '*undetermined* multipliers'.

At a critical point of the Lagrangian we must have $\partial L/\partial x = \partial L/\partial y = 0$; thus

$$-4x + 4y = 3\lambda, \quad 4x + 2y = \lambda.$$

We now solve this pair of simultaneous equations for x and y in terms of λ. Adding the two equations gives $6y = 4\lambda$: hence

$$y = \tfrac{2}{3}\lambda, \quad x = y - \tfrac{3}{4}\lambda = -\tfrac{1}{12}\lambda.$$

We are not finished yet, as we still have to determine λ. We do this by substituting the solutions for x and y into the constraint:

$$(-\tfrac{1}{4} + \tfrac{2}{3})\lambda = 5.$$

Thus $\lambda = 12$, whence $x = -1$ and $y = 8$: the corresponding value of $f(x,y)$ is $-32 - 2 + 64 = 30$.

We have now found the values of x and y that satisfy the first-order conditions for a constrained maximum. To show that this actually *is* the constrained maximum, various arguments may be employed. A simple one is to note that if we were to try to solve the problem by solving the constraint for y in terms of x and substitute into the function we are trying to maximise, we would obtain a quadratic function of x in which the coefficient of x^2 is -6. Such a function has a maximum but no minimum, as we showed in Chapter 4: hence the point we have found is the constrained maximum.

Example 2 Maximise $3x + 2y$ subject to $x^2 + 4y^2 = 10$.

In this case $f(x,y) = 3x + 2y$, $g(x,y) = x^2 + 4y^2 - 10$, so the Lagrangian is

$$L(x,y,\lambda) = (3x - \lambda x^2) + (2y - 4\lambda y^2) + 10\lambda.$$

At a critical point of the Lagrangian, $\partial L/\partial x = \partial L/\partial y = 0$; thus $3 = 2\lambda x$ and $2 = 8\lambda y$. Solving for x and y in terms of λ, we see that

$$x = \frac{3}{2\lambda}, \quad y = \frac{1}{4\lambda}.$$

Substituting back into the constraint, we have

$$\left(\frac{3}{2\lambda}\right)^2 + \left(\frac{1}{2\lambda}\right)^2 = 10,$$

whence $\lambda = \pm\tfrac{1}{2}$. When the $+$ sign is taken, $2\lambda = 1$, so $x = 3$ and $y = \tfrac{1}{2}$. Similarly, when the $-$ sign is taken, $x = -3$ and $y = -\tfrac{1}{2}$.

We have shown the points (x,y) corresponding to critical points of the Lagrangian are $(3, \tfrac{1}{2})$ and $(-3, -\tfrac{1}{2})$. It is obvious that the former point gives the higher value of f and is therefore the constrained maximum. The constrained maximum value of $f(x,y)$ is $9 + 1 = 10$.

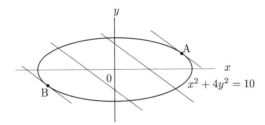

Figure 17.2: **Point A gives the constrained maximum**

Example 2 illustrates some important points. The problem and its solution are depicted in Figure 17.2.[3] Lagrange's method has located the point of tangency A with coordinates $(3, \frac{1}{2})$ as the constrained maximum. The other point of tangency B, with coordinates $(-3, -\frac{1}{2})$, was also located by Lagrange's method and dismissed as not being a constrained maximum; it is in fact the point which *minimises* $3x + 2y$ subject to $x^2 + 4y^2 = 10$. Thus Lagrange's method locates constrained minima as well as maxima. We say more about this at the end of this section.

Local and global maxima

As in Section 16.3, we may distinguish between local and global constrained maxima. Let (x^*, y^*) be a point in the plane such that $g(x^*, y^*) = 0$. We say that $f(x, y)$ attains a global maximum subject to the constraint $g(x, y) = 0$ at the point (x^*, y^*) if $f(x^*, y^*) \geq f(x, y)$ for all points (x, y) which satisfy the constraint. Similarly, we say that $f(x, y)$ attains a local maximum subject to the constraint $g(x, y) = 0$ at the point (x^*, y^*) if $f(x^*, y^*) \geq f(x, y)$ for all points (x, y) which satisfy the constraint and are sufficiently close to (x^*, y^*).

The first-order conditions given in (17.4), and restated in terms of the Lagrangian in (17.6), are a property of local constrained maxima. However, since the focus of this chapter is on problems such as (17.1), we shall mainly be concerned with global constrained optima. Therefore, *in this chapter and the next, the term 'constrained maximum' will mean 'global constrained maximum' unless otherwise stated.* Notice that this terminology differs from that of Sections 8.1 and 8.2; the change reflects the fact that our emphasis is now on optimisation rather than the geometry of critical points.

---

[3]Here is a brief explanation why the constraint curve in Figure 17.2 looks as it does. Let a, b, c be positive numbers and let E be the set of points in the xy–plane such that $ax^2 + by^2 = c$. In the special case where $a = b$, E is the circle with centre at the origin and radius $\sqrt{c/a}$. In the general case the curve crosses the axes at the points $(\pm\sqrt{c/a}, 0)$ and $(0, \pm\sqrt{c/b})$. Thus E looks like a circle with centre at the origin that has been stretched vertically or horizontally, according to whether a is greater or less that b: in Figure 17.2, $a = 1$ and $b = 4$, so the stretch is horizontal. The correct name for a stretched circle is an **ellipse**.

Constrained minimisation

As we noted in connection with Example 2, Lagrange's method locates constrained minima as well as maxima. Indeed, it is just as applicable when the object of the exercise is minimisation as when it is maximisation. Since the method is concerned only with first-order conditions, exactly the same algebra applies: to

$$\text{minimise } f(x, y) \text{ subject to } g(x, y) = 0,$$

we may define the Lagrangian L as in (17.5) and find its critical points as before.

We may distinguish between local and global constrained minima in the same way that we do for maxima. The first-order conditions are a property of local minima, but our interest centres on global ones. For this reason, we use the term 'constrained minimum' to mean 'global constrained minimum' unless otherwise stated. A similar convention applies to the word 'optimum' (maximum or minimum).

Second-order conditions exist which can in principle be used to test for maxima or minima, but these are rather complicated, and are usually applicable only to local optima. In general, it is better to distinguish between max and min by ad hoc methods (including graphical ones) and considerations of convexity. We say more about this in Sections 17.3 and 17.4.

Exercises

17.1.1 Find the maximum value of xy subject to $3x + 4y = 12$. Draw a diagram to show how you know the value you have found is the maximum.

17.1.2 Find the minimum value of $3x + 4y$ subject to $xy = 2$; it is assumed that x and y are positive numbers. Draw a diagram to show how you know the value you have found is the minimum. What happens if instead the constraint is $xy = a$ where a is the maximum value found in Exercise 17.1.1?

17.1.3 Find the maximum value of $6xy + 2x^2 - 3y^2$ subject to $x + 2y = 5$.

17.1.4 Find the maximum and minimum values of $2x + y$ subject to $x^2 + y^2 = 4$. Draw a diagram to show how you know the values you have found are the maximum and minimum.

17.1.5 Consider the following two problems where, in each case, a is a positive constant:

(a) maximise $x^2 + y^2$ subject to $2x + y = a$;

(b) minimise $x^2 + y^2$ subject to $2x + y = a$.

Explain by means of a diagram which, if either, has a solution.

17.2 Extensions and warnings

Section 17.1 introduced Lagrange's method of undetermined multipliers in its most basic form. This section is an assortment of generalisations and qualifications of the method. We begin with straightforward extensions, first increasing the number of variables beyond two, and the number of constraints beyond one. We then give two warnings, one concerning the interpretation of the method and the other its applicability.

Higher dimensions

(a) More variables

Lagrange's method can be applied to problems with any number of variables. The following example illustrates the procedure.

Example 1 We solve the three-variable problem:

$$\text{minimise} \quad e^x + e^y + e^z \quad \text{subject to} \quad 2x + 3y + 5z = 10.$$

The Lagrangian for this problem is

$$\begin{aligned} L(x, y, z, \lambda) &= e^x + e^y + e^z - \lambda(2x + 3y + 5z - 10) \\ &= (e^x - 2\lambda x) + (e^y - 3\lambda y) + (e^z - 5\lambda z) + 10\lambda. \end{aligned}$$

At a critical point of the Lagrangian,

$$e^x = 2\lambda, \quad e^y = 3\lambda, \quad e^z = 5\lambda. \tag{17.7}$$

Setting $\mu = \ln \lambda$ we have

$$x = \mu + \ln 2, \quad y = \mu + \ln 3, \quad z = \mu + \ln 5. \tag{17.8}$$

Substituting into the constraint, we see that

$$10\mu + 2\ln 2 + 3\ln 3 + 5\ln 5 = 10.$$

A little work with the calculator now shows that $\mu = -0.2729$: this and all subsequent numerical answers are given to 4 decimal places. Using (17.8) we have, at the constrained minimum,

$$x = 0.4202, \quad y = 0.8257, \quad z = 1.3365.$$

The constrained minimum value of the function we are minimising is

$$\begin{aligned} e^x + e^y + e^z &= 10e^\mu \quad \text{by (17.7)} \\ &= 7.6114. \end{aligned}$$

How do we know that this is a minimum rather than a maximum? The function

$$f(x, y, z) = e^x + e^y + e^z$$

is convex (recall Exercise 16.2.5) and it can be shown that when we are minimising a convex function subject to a linear constraint, any critical point of the Lagrangian is a constrained minimum. We discuss this and similar facts in Section 17.4.

Example 1 illustrates a useful point of technique. After writing the first-order conditions, and before doing anything with them, we defined $\mu = \ln \lambda$ and from then on worked with μ instead of λ. This simplification of the calculations by transforming the Lagrange multiplier into something more manageable is often helpful. Of course, the fact that the helpful transformation in Example 1 consisted of taking the natural logarithm was a feature of this particular problem, and other problems call for other transformations.

(b) More constraints

When we have more than one constraints we formulate the Lagrangian with a different multiplier for each constraint. Thus, to maximise $f(x, y, z, w)$ subject to the two constraints

$$g(x, y, z, w) = 0, \quad h(x, y, z, w) = 0$$

we work with the Lagrangian

$$L(x, y, z, w, \lambda, \mu) = f(x, y, z, w) - \lambda g(x, y, z, w) - \mu h(x, y, z, w).$$

In this case L is a function of six variables whose last two arguments are the Lagrange multipliers λ and μ, one for each constraint. As before, we attempt to find the constrained maximum by looking at the critical points of L.

Similarly, with three constraints we have three Lagrange multipliers, and so on. Use of the method with more than one constraint is subject to some restrictions, the most important being that the number of constraints should not exceed the number of variables. We say a little more about this at the end of this section, when we discuss constraint qualifications.

Two warnings

We now alert you to an error concerning the interpretation of Lagrange's method which is often made by students and sometimes, alas, by their teachers. We then go on to warn you against unthinking application of the method: there are occasions when it fails to locate the optimum.

(a) Behaviour of the Lagrangian

The essence of Lagrange's method is that a constrained maximum is a critical point of the Lagrangian; it is not necessarily a local maximum of the Lagrangian. To go into this in more detail, we focus on the two-variables, one-constraint case considered in the last section. We make two points. First, the constrained maximum hardly ever gives a maximum for the Lagrangian with respect to all three variables x, y, λ. Secondly, and contrary to what many economists seem to believe, the constrained maximum need not even be a maximum for L with respect to x and y, given λ.

Example 2 Consider the problem

$$\text{maximise } xy \text{ subject to } x + y = 2.$$

One does not have to use calculus to see that the constrained maximum is attained when $x = y = 1$. For if we let $w = x - 1$, then the constraint requires that $y = 1 - w$, and

$$xy = (1 + w)(1 - w) = 1 - w^2,$$

which is clearly maximised when $w = 0$.

Now consider what happens when we solve this problem by Lagrange's method. The Lagrangian is

$$L(x, y, \lambda) = xy - \lambda(x + y) + 2\lambda.$$

For $\partial L/\partial x$ and $\partial L/\partial y$ to be zero when $x = y = 1$, we need $\lambda = 1$. Now we come to the point: if we set

$$H(x, y) = L(x, y, 1) = xy - x - y + 2,$$

then the function $H(x, y)$ has a critical point at $x = y = 1$ which is not a local maximum but a saddle point. This is easily verified using the methods of Section 16.1: when $x = y = 1$, both partial derivatives of H are zero, and the Hessian matrix $D^2 H(1, 1)$ has determinant -1.

(b) Constraint qualifications

As we remarked earlier, there are awkward cases when Lagrange's method fails to detect the constrained optimum.

To see how this can arise, consider the problem

$$\text{maximise } (1 + x)(1 - y) \text{ subject to } x^3 - y^3 = 0.$$

Here the constraint is equivalent to $x = y$ and the problem may easily be solved by substitution: the constrained maximum occurs where $x = y = 0$. Now suppose we try to solve the problem by Lagrange's method, with the constraint written in its original form. The Lagrangian is

$$L(x, y, \lambda) = (1 + x)(1 - y) - \lambda(x^3 - y^3).$$

It is easy to see that $(0, 0, \lambda)$ is not a critical point of the Lagrangian, for any λ. For when $x = y = 0$, $\partial L/\partial x = 1$ and $\partial L/\partial y = -1$, whatever the value of λ. In this case, therefore, the constrained maximum is not a critical point of the Lagrangian: it cannot be detected by Lagrange's method.

What has gone wrong? The constraint function $g(x, y)$ is $x^3 - y^3$; thus at the constrained maximum $(x = y = 0)$ we have $\partial g/\partial x = \partial g/\partial y = 0$. But this means that the implicit-differentiation argument of Section 17.1 cannot be applied, so it is not very surprising that Lagrange's method fails.

Since Lagrange's method does not work in all conceivable cases, we have to look for conditions under which we can be sure that it does work. The easiest conditions to apply consist of restrictions on the constraint functions and are known as **constraint qualifications**.

When there is only one constraint, the appropriate constraint qualification is immediate from the implicit-differentiation argument of the preceding section. The proposition justifying Lagrange's method may be stated as follows:

Proposition If there is only one constraint, *and the gradient of the constraint function at the constrained maximum is not the zero-vector*, the constrained maximum is a critical point of the Lagrangian.

When there is more than one constraint the corresponding constraint qualification is that the *gradients of the constraint functions at the optimum are linearly independent*.[4] This imposes certain general restrictions on the constraints. First, since a set of linearly independent vectors cannot contain the zero-vector, the gradients of the constraint functions at the constrained maximum must all be non-zero vectors. Secondly, recall from Section 12.4 that $n + 1$ n–vectors must be linearly dependent; thus the constraint qualification requires that there be at least as many variables as constraints.

From now on we shall assume that the constraint qualification discussed above is satisfied.

Exercises

17.2.1 Find the maximum and minimum values of $2x + 3y + z$ subject to

$$x^2 + y^2 + z^2 = 9.$$

---

[4]Linear dependence and independence of vectors were introduced at the end of Section 11.1 and discussed further in Section 12.4.

17.2.2 Find the maximum value of xyz subject to $3x + 2y + z = 12$.

17.2.3 Find the maximum value of $yz + xz$ subject to the two constraints

$$y + 2z = 1, \quad x + z = 3.$$

17.2.4 Verify that the relevant constraint qualification is satisfied at the optimal points in Exercises 17.2.1 and 17.2.3.

17.3 Economic applications

We now give some simple illustrations of Lagrange multipliers may be used in microeconomics. We begin with an example from the theory of consumer demand and then turn to the theory of the firm; we end the section with some remarks about extensions to higher dimensions.

The utility-maximising consumer

You may recall our consumer Ian of Section 2.2, who consumes two goods labelled 1 and 2 in quantities x_1 and x_2. Suppose that Ian's preferences are represented by a utility function $U(x_1, x_2)$: in other words, given two alternative bundles of commodities (a_1, a_2) and (b_1, b_2), we have $U(a_1, a_2) > U(b_1, b_2)$ if and only if Ian prefers (a_1, a_2) to (b_1, b_2).

Suppose Ian's total income, to be spent on the two goods, is m; let the prices of the goods be p_1 and p_2. Ian's budget constraint is then

$$p_1 x_1 + p_2 x_2 = m. \tag{17.9}$$

To reach the point of maximum satisfaction, given his budget, Ian must choose x_1 and x_2 so as to maximise $U(x_1, x_2)$ subject to (17.9).

Before applying Lagrange's method, we need to make two points about this formulation of the problem.

Non-negative consumption

First, we normally think of goods being consumed in non-negative quantities. Therefore, to ensure that the problem makes sense, we should supplement the budget constraint with the non-negativity constraints $x_1 \geq 0, x_2 \geq 0$. In some cases, however, especially when dealing with specific functions, it will be clear from the start that the optimum will have both components strictly positive. We will restrict our attention to this case for the moment, deferring a proper treatment of non-negativity constraints to the next chapter.

Non-satiation

The second point to be made about the above formulation of the consumer's problem is that (17.9) is not quite the same as the budget constraint as we defined it in Section 2.2, namely the weak inequality

$$p_1 x_1 + p_2 x_2 \leq m.$$

However, as far as utility maximisation is concerned, the difference between this inequality and (17.9) is not great. For if we make the reasonable assumption that Ian always prefers more of at least one of the two goods, then it is never in his interest to spend less than his income.

The assumption just mentioned is known as the **non-satiation property** of the consumer's preferences. The corresponding restriction on the utility function is that, for every bundle (x_1, x_2), at least one of the partial derivatives $\partial U/\partial x_1$, $\partial U/\partial x_2$ is positive. All our examples and exercises satisfy this restriction.

One small point about non-satiation is worth mentioning before we move on. In practice, households devote some of their income to saving, donations to charity and other outlets in addition to consumer goods and services. These facts can be incorporated into the standard model of consumer behaviour by allowing the list of goods in the utility function to include saving and so on, or by restricting m to be that part of income allocated to consumer goods, or in various other ways. All of these issues are matters of *interpretation*;[5] they are conceptually quite separate from the question of whether the budget constraint should be written as an equation or an inequality.

Given the non-satiation assumption, there is no loss of generality in formulating the maximisation problem with the budget constraint written as an equation. We shall consider inequality constraints in the next chapter.

First-order conditions

We return to Ian's problem, formulated as follows:

maximise $U(x_1, x_2)$ subject to $p_1 x_1 + p_2 x_2 = m$.

It is instructive to start by considering contour diagrams like Figure 17.1, bearing in mind that the contours of the function U are indifference curves. As usual, we assume that indifference curves are convex.

In the case shown in Figure 17.3, where the solution has both components strictly positive, it occurs at a point of tangency between the budget constraint B and the indifference curve I. This is completely analogous to the case in Figure 17.1. We can therefore introduce the Lagrangian

$$L(x_1, x_2, \lambda) = U(x_1, x_2) - \lambda(p_1 x_1 + p_2 x_2 - m)$$

---

[5]And of extending the number of goods beyond two, something we shall consider at the end of this section.

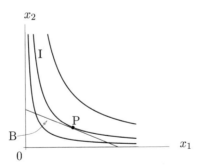

Figure 17.3: **Solution to the consumer's problem with both goods consumed in positive amounts**

and write down the first-order conditions in the usual way. At the point of maximum satisfaction we have $\partial L/\partial x_1 = \partial L/\partial x_2 = 0$: hence

$$\frac{\partial U}{\partial x_1} = \lambda p_1, \quad \frac{\partial U}{\partial x_2} = \lambda p_2. \tag{17.10}$$

These equations, together with the budget constraint (17.9), can be solved for x_1, x_2 and the Lagrange multiplier λ.

The resulting optimal levels of x_1, x_2 obviously depend on p_1, p_2 and m. We therefore write

$$x_1 = f_1(p_1, p_2, m), \quad x_2 = f_1(p_1, p_2, m). \tag{17.11}$$

These functions f_1, f_2 are called the consumer's **demand functions**: they express the dependence of utility-maximising choices of goods on prices and income. In this case subscripts on functions do not represent partial differentiation.

It turns out that the value of λ which emerges from the solution to the constrained maximisation problem has a natural economic interpretation. Once we have found the demand functions, we can express the maximum utility in terms of p_1, p_2 and m by substituting (17.11) into the utility function. The resulting function $V(p_1, p_2, m)$ is known as the **indirect utility function**. We shall show in the next chapter that the value of the multiplier λ at the optimum is related to this function by the simple equation

$$\lambda = \frac{\partial V}{\partial m}.$$

We now consider briefly when the first-order conditions (17.10) become sufficient for an optimum. In Figure 17.3, it is clear that points of higher utility than P must lie above the budget line and hence P is indeed the optimum. Thus, provided the indifference curves are negatively sloped and convex, the first-order conditions are sufficient for an optimum.

Without the assumption of convexity of the indifference curves, situations like the one shown in Figure 17.4 can occur. Here conditions (17.10) are satisfied at the points X and Y, but Y is the unique optimum.

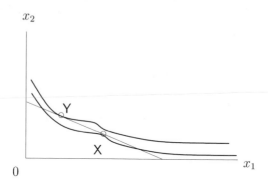

Figure 17.4: **What goes wrong with non-convex indifference curves**

An example: Stone–Geary utility

We illustrate the standard method of deriving demand functions from a utility function, using the function

$$U(x_1, x_2) = b_1 \ln(x_1 - c_1) + b_2 \ln(x_2 - c_2),$$

where b_1, b_2, c_1, c_2 are positive constants. This is the two-dimensional case of the **Stone–Geary utility function**, much used in applied work.[6] Since $\ln x$ is defined only for positive x, the utility function is defined only for $x_1 > c_1$ and $x_2 > c_2$. These inequalities may be interpreted as minimal conditions for a tolerable standard of life. Because of these survival conditions, the standard consumer problem makes sense only when the consumer has enough income to buy quantities c_1 of good 1 and c_2 of good 2 and have some money left over. We therefore assume:

$$p_1 c_1 + p_2 c_2 < m. \tag{17.12}$$

The indifference curves corresponding to this utility function are sketched in Figure 17.5. The strict inequality (17.12) is depicted in the diagram by the fact that the point (c_1, c_2) lies below and to the left of the budget line B. This, together with the fact that each indifference curve is asymptotic to the lines $x_1 = c_1$ and $x_2 = c_2$, implies that the line B is tangent to an indifference curve at a point where the survival conditions are satisfied (and, in particular, x_1 and x_2 are strictly positive). Such a point will be located by Lagrange's method; and

---

[6]Notably by Sir Richard Stone (1913–1991), a British economist who won the Nobel prize in 1984, and Robert Geary (1896–1983), the leading Irish economist of his generation.

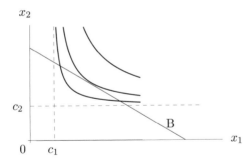

Figure 17.5: **Indifference curves for the Stone-Geary utility function** $(c_1 > 0, c_2 > 0)$

since the indifference curves are negatively sloped and convex, the first-order conditions are sufficient for a maximum.

Applying the first-order conditions in the form (17.10), we see that, at the constrained optimum,

$$b_1/(x_1 - c_1) = \lambda p_1, \quad b_2/(x_2 - c_2) = \lambda p_2.$$

Solving these equations for x_1 and x_2, we have

$$x_1 = c_1 + \frac{b_1}{\lambda p_1}, \quad x_2 = c_2 + \frac{b_2}{\lambda p_2}. \tag{17.13}$$

Equations (17.13) are not yet the demand functions, since they involve the Lagrange multiplier λ. To obtain demand functions as in (17.11), we must substitute (17.13) into the budget constraint and solve for λ in terms of p_1, p_2 and m. Before doing this, it is helpful to write the budget constraint (17.9) in the form

$$p_1(x_1 - c_1) + p_2(x_2 - c_2) = m', \tag{17.9'}$$

where $m' = m - p_1c_1 - p_2c_2$: note that $m' > 0$ by (17.12). Substituting (17.13) into (17.9'), $b_1/\lambda + b_2/\lambda = m'$. Hence $\lambda = (b_1 + b_2)/m'$. Substituting back into (17.13), we obtain the demand functions:

$$x_1 = c_1 + \frac{\beta m'}{p_1}, \quad x_2 = c_2 + \frac{(1 - \beta)m'}{p_2}, \tag{17.14}$$

$$\text{where} \quad \beta = \frac{b_1}{b_1 + b_2}, \quad m' = m - p_1c_1 - p_2c_2.$$

The demand functions in this case have a simple interpretation. Recall that quantities c_1 of good 1 and c_2 of good 2 may be regarded as the bare necessities of life. We can think of the consumer as dividing his expenditure into necessary expenditure $p_1c_1 + p_2c_2$ and discretionary expenditure m', and then dividing discretionary expenditure into that on good 1, namely $p_1(x_1 - c_1)$, and that on good 2, namely $p_2(x_2 - c_2)$. What the demand functions (17.14) tell us is that discretionary expenditures on goods 1 and 2 are fixed proportions of total discretionary expenditure: β for good 1, $1 - \beta$ for good 2.

Cost functions

Our next application of Lagrange multipliers is to the theory of the firm, and concerns the derivation of cost functions.

Suppose a firm produces a single kind of output using two inputs labelled 1 and 2. Let the prices of the inputs be w_1 and w_2; we assume that the firm takes these as given. Denote the firm's output by q and take it also as given; in practice q will be determined by the firm's decisions made in pursuit of profit or whatever, but that is not our concern here.

Suppose production of q units of output requires a quantity $a_i(q)$ of input i, for $i = 1, 2$. If $a_1(q)$ and $a_2(q)$ are completely determined by q, then the firm's cost function is

$$C(w_1, w_2, q) = w_1 a_1(q) + w_2 a_2(q),$$

and Lagrange multipliers have nothing to do with it. This, however, is a rather extreme case. It is more usual to think of the firm as having some choice of what technique to use when producing a given output level — for example, a choice between a capital-intensive technique and a labour-intensive one. The firm's cost function $C(w_1, w_2, q)$ is then defined as the *minimal* cost of producing q units of output when input prices are w_1 and w_2, and constrained optimisation is relevant after all.

To be specific, let the firm have the production function $F(x_1, x_2)$: thus quantities x_1 and x_2 of inputs 1 and 2 produce $F(x_1, x_2)$ units of output. The firm wants to choose an input combination (x_1, x_2) so as to produce a given output q at minimal cost. Its problem is therefore to

$$\text{minimise } w_1 x_1 + w_2 x_2 \text{ subject to } F(x_1, x_2) = q. \qquad (17.15)$$

As in the consumer case, the particular formulation of the problem that we have adopted requires two comments. First, economic sense requires that input quantities be non-negative; thus we should really add to the problem the constraints $x_1 \geq 0, x_2 \geq 0$. However, there are some cases — for example, if the production function is such that positive output requires positive quantities of both inputs — where it is clear from the start that the optimum will have $x_1 > 0$ and $x_2 > 0$. We shall restrict our attention to this case in what follows, giving explicit consideration to non-negativity constraints in the next chapter.

Secondly, by stating the constraint as an equation rather than as the inequality $F(x_1, x_2) \geq q$, we are ignoring the possibility that the firm manufactures more output than it needs to do. Given that both inputs have positive prices, this is a sensible assumption.

Having formulated the firm's problem as in (17.15), we may write the Lagrangian as

$$w_1 x_1 + w_2 x_2 - \mu(F(x_1, x_2) - q),$$

where μ is the Lagrange multiplier. The first-order conditions are

$$w_i = \mu \frac{\partial F}{\partial x_i} \quad \text{for } i = 1, 2. \tag{17.16}$$

These conditions are sufficient for an optimum provided the isoquants of the production function are convex: recall our discussion of isoquants and diminishing marginal rate of substitution in Section 15.1.

The levels of x_1 and x_2 which solve the problem (17.15) clearly depend on w_1, w_2 and q. The resulting functions of w_1, w_2 and q are sometimes called **conditional demand functions**: 'conditional' here means conditional on output. As noted above, the minimal cost of producing q units of output when input prices are w_1 and w_2 is the firm's cost function $C(w_1, w_2, q)$.

An example

We give an illustration of finding a cost function, and the associated conditional demand functions using a specific production function and a notation more familiar from earlier chapters.

As in Exercise 15.1.3, let the production function be

$$F(K, L) = \left(aK^{-2} + bL^{-2}\right)^{-1/2},$$

where K and L denote capital and labour respectively, and a and b are positive constants. Two important features of the isoquants for this function are that (a) they do not meet the axes, so we do not have to mention non-negativity constraints explicitly; (b) they are negatively sloped and convex, so the first-order conditions are sufficient for an optimum.

Let the prices of capital and labour be r and w respectively. The firm's problem is then to

$$\text{minimise } rK + wL \text{ subject to } F(K, L) = q,$$

with r, w and the output level q taken as given. The first-order conditions corresponding to (17.16) are then

$$r = \mu \, \partial F / \partial K, \quad w = \mu \, \partial F / \partial L,$$

where μ is the Lagrange multiplier.

To apply these conditions to the production function considered here, notice that

$$\frac{\partial F}{\partial K} = (-2aK^{-3}) \times (-\tfrac{1}{2})(aK^{-2} + bL^{-2})^{-3/2} = aK^{-3}[F(K, L)]^3 = a\left(\frac{q}{K}\right)^3,$$

and similarly

$$\frac{\partial F}{\partial L} = b\left(\frac{q}{L}\right)^3.$$

The first-order conditions for a constrained minimum are therefore

$$r = \mu a(q/K)^3, \quad w = \mu b(q/L)^3.$$

It follows that

$$K = (\mu a/r)^{1/3}q, \quad L = (\mu b/w)^{1/3}q. \tag{17.17}$$

The next step is to substitute (17.17) into the output constraint and solve for μ. Since

$$[F(K, L)]^{-2} = aK^{-2} + bL^{-2},$$

the constraint may be written $a(q/K)^2 + b(q/L)^2 = 1$. Hence by (17.17),

$$a^{1/3}(r/\mu)^{2/3} + b^{1/3}(w/\mu)^{2/3} = 1.$$

Solving for μ, we have

$$\mu = [a^{1/3}r^{2/3} + b^{1/3}w^{2/3}]^{3/2}. \tag{17.18}$$

We must now substitute the expression for μ given by (17.18) into (17.17). Letting

$$\theta = \frac{a^{1/3}r^{2/3}}{a^{1/3}r^{2/3} + b^{1/3}w^{2/3}},$$

we have $\mu = a^{1/2} r \theta^{-3/2}$ by (17.18); hence by (17.17),

$$K/q = (a^{3/2}\theta^{-3/2})^{1/3} = a^{1/2}\theta^{-1/2}.$$

Similarly, $\mu = b^{1/2} w (1 - \theta)^{-3/2}$ by (17.18), whence $L/q = b^{1/2}(1 - \theta)^{-1/2}$ by (17.17). Hence the conditional demand functions may be written as follows:

$$K = q\sqrt{\frac{a}{\theta}}, \quad L = q\sqrt{\frac{b}{1 - \theta}}.$$

To obtain the cost function, we note from (17.17) that $rK = \mu^{1/3}a^{1/3}r^{2/3}q$ and $wL = \mu^{1/3}b^{1/3}w^{2/3}q$. Adding, and using (17.18), we see that total cost $rK + wL$ is equal to $\mu^{1/3}\mu^{2/3}q$. The cost function is therefore

$$C(r, w, q) = \mu q, \tag{17.19}$$

where μ is given by (17.18). Notice two important implications of (17.19):

(i) Marginal cost $\partial C/\partial q$ is equal to μ, which was originally defined as the Lagrange multiplier in the firm's cost-minimisation problem.

(ii) Marginal cost $\partial C/\partial q$ is equal to average cost C/q, and depends only on input prices, not on q.

The question now arises: do these results generalise to production functions other than that considered in this example? Result (i) is in fact a general property of cost minimisation: it plays the same role in the theory of the firm as the equation $\partial V/\partial m = \lambda$ in the theory of the consumer, and will be discussed in more detail in the first two sections of the next chapter. Result (ii) is not nearly so general, though it is certainly not restricted to the example just considered. In fact, (ii) holds whenever the production function is homogeneous of degree 1: recall from Section 14.4 that this is the same as constant returns to scale.

Higher dimensions

It is in principle straightforward to extend the theory of the utility-maximising consumer to the case of many goods, and the theory of the cost-minimising firm to the case of many inputs. Suppose, for instance, that Ian can spend his income m on n goods whose prices are $p_1, p_2, \ldots, p_n$ and that his utility function is $U(x_1, x_2, \ldots, x_n)$. The analogous problem to that considered above is:

maximise $U(x_1, x_2, \ldots, x_n)$ subject to $p_1 x_1 + p_2 x_2 + \ldots + p_n x_n = m$.

Setting up the Lagrangian as before, we obtain the first-order conditions that generalise (17.10):

$$\frac{\partial U}{\partial x_i} = \lambda p_i \quad \text{for } i = 1, \ldots, n.$$

Similarly, the first-order conditions that generalise (17.16) to the case of the n–input firm are

$$w_i = \mu \frac{\partial F}{\partial x_i} \quad \text{for } i = 1, \ldots, n.$$

The only essential way in which such problems are more difficult when 2 is replaced by n is that the question of when the first-order conditions are sufficient for an optimum is harder to resolve; clearly, it can no longer be settled by drawing pictures of isoquants or indifference curves. The intelligent way to proceed is to investigate whether the production or utility function satisfies certain properties, which are the subject of the next section.

Exercises

17.3.1 A consumer has a Cobb–Douglas utility function

$$U(x_1, x_2) = x_1^\alpha x_2^\beta,$$

where x_1, x_2 denote the consumption of the two goods and α, β are positive constants. The prices of the goods are p_1, p_2 and the consumer's income is m.

(a) Express the consumer's problem as a constrained maximisation problem.

(b) Write down the first-order conditions and explain why, in this case, they are sufficient for a constrained maximum. Hence find the demand functions.

(c) Give an economic interpretation of the parameters α and β.

17.3.2 A firm has a Cobb–Douglas production function

$$F(K, L) = AK^\alpha L^\beta,$$

where A, α, β are positive constants. The prices of capital and labour are r and w respectively. The firm's output is q.

(a) Express the firm's cost-minimisation problem as a constrained minimisation problem.

(b) Write down the first-order conditions and explain why, in this case, they are sufficient for a constrained minimum. Hence find the conditional input demand functions and the cost function.

17.4   Quasi-concave functions

The class of quasi-concave functions is related to that of concave functions and is important in its own right in applications to optimisation and economics. It is as convenient to define such functions for n variables as for two. Before doing so, we need to say something about convex sets in $\mathcal{R}^n$.

In Section 8.4, we defined a set of points in the plane to be convex if the line segment joining any two of its points is entirely contained in the set. A similar definition of a convex set in three-dimensional space was given in Section 16.2. To generalise this notion to n–dimensional space, we must start by formulating an algebraic description of line segments.

We begin with the case $n = 2$. If (a, b) and (c, d) are points in the plane, then the mid-point of the line segment joining these points has coordinates $(\frac{1}{2}a + \frac{1}{2}c, \frac{1}{2}b + \frac{1}{2}d)$; the point two-thirds of the way along the line segment from (a, b) to (c, d) has coordinates $(\frac{1}{3}a + \frac{2}{3}c, \frac{1}{3}b + \frac{2}{3}d)$; and so on. Generally, the line segment joining the points (a, b) and (c, d) consists of all points of the form $(\alpha a + (1 - \alpha)c, \alpha b + (1 - \alpha)d)$, where $0 \le \alpha \le 1$.

The extension of this to $\mathcal{R}^n$ is straightforward. We *define* the line segment joining the n–vectors $\mathbf{x}$ and $\mathbf{y}$ to be the set of all n–vectors of the form $\alpha\mathbf{x} + (1 - \alpha)\mathbf{y}$, where $0 \le \alpha \le 1$. And we define a subset V of $\mathcal{R}^n$ to be convex if the line segment joining any two points of V is entirely contained in V.

We can now define quasi-concave functions. A function f defined on $\mathcal{R}^n$ is said to be **quasi-concave** if, for any real number c, the set of n–vectors $\mathbf{x}$ for which $f(\mathbf{x}) \ge c$ is convex.

To illustrate what this means in the case $n = 2$, consider the indifference-map diagram Figure 17.3. In this case, each of the indifference curves represents a contour $U(x_1, x_2) = c$ of a utility function U. Further, since the utility function is increasing in both of its arguments, the set of points (x_1, x_2) for which $U(x_1, x_2) \geq c$ consists of all points *on or above* the indifference curve $U(x_1, x_2) = c$. In Figure 17.3, all these sets are convex, so the utility function U is quasi-concave. This happens because, and only because, the indifference curves are convex. Thus, for utility functions which are increasing in both their arguments, quasi-concavity of the utility function is equivalent to convexity of all the indifference curves. Notice by contrast the situation depicted in Figure 17.4, where the indifference curves ar not convex and the utility function is not quasi-concave.

Concavity and quasi-concavity

All concave functions are quasi-concave. To prove this, let f be a concave function on $\mathcal{R}^n$, let c be a real number, and let $\mathbf{x}$ and $\mathbf{y}$ be n–vectors such that $f(\mathbf{x}) \geq c$ and $f(\mathbf{y}) \geq c$. Let $\mathbf{z}$ be a vector on the line segment joining $\mathbf{x}$ and $\mathbf{y}$; we want to show that $f(\mathbf{z}) \geq c$. By definition of a line segment, $\mathbf{z} = \alpha \mathbf{x} + (1 - \alpha)\mathbf{y}$, where α is a number such that $0 \leq \alpha \leq 1$. But then

$$f(\mathbf{z}) \geq \alpha f(\mathbf{x}) + (1 - \alpha)f(\mathbf{y}) \quad \text{since } f \text{ is concave}$$
$$\geq \alpha c + (1 - \alpha)c \qquad \text{since } f(\mathbf{x}) \geq c \text{ and } f(\mathbf{y}) \geq c.$$

Thus $f(\mathbf{z}) \geq c$, as required.

On the other hand, *not all quasi-concave functions are concave.* We give both an algebraic and a geometrical demonstration of this. First, consider the case where $n = 1$ and let f be a monotonic increasing function. Suppose that $f(x_0) = c$, and consider the set of all numbers x for which $f(x) \geq c$: since f is monotonic increasing, this set is the interval of all real numbers which are greater than or equal to x_0, and is therefore convex. This shows that all increasing functions of one variable are quasi-concave; but not all such functions are concave. For example, the function $f(x) = x^3$ is monotonic increasing and therefore quasi-concave, but it is obviously not concave.

As a geometrical illustration of a quasi-concave function which is not concave, let $n = 2$, and suppose the surface $z = f(x, y)$ has the shape of the upward-sloping part of a bell. Then f is not concave. This is illustrated in panel B of Figure 17.6; panel A of the figure shows, by contrast, a surface with the shape of the upward-sloping part of a dome. The function corresponding to panel A is of course concave. But in both cases, the contours have the familiar convex shape which we typically require of indifference curves and isoquants. Thus the non-concave function of panel B, like the concave one of panel A, is quasi-concave.

Monotonic transformations

You may recall that bell-shaped surfaces were mentioned in Section 16.2 in connection with functions that were not necessarily concave but were monotonic

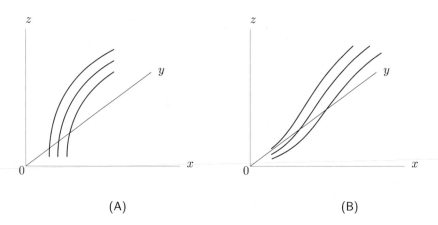

Figure 17.6: **Concave and quasi-concave functions**

(increasing) transformations of concave functions. All functions generated in this way are quasi-concave. This is a special case of the following.

Proposition Suppose $g(\mathbf{x}) = H(f(\mathbf{x}))$, where H is a strictly increasing function. If the function f is quasi-concave, so is g.

The reason why this proposition holds is straightforward. Let c be any constant: since the function H is monotonic increasing, $f(\mathbf{x}) \geq c$ if and only if $g(\mathbf{x}) \geq H(c)$. Hence a set of vectors of the form $\{\mathbf{x} : g(\mathbf{x}) \geq \text{constant}\}$ is a set of the form $\{\mathbf{x} : f(\mathbf{x}) \geq \text{constant}\}$, though not necessarily for the same constant. If f is quasi-concave, all such sets are convex; therefore g is quasi-concave.

The proposition we have just proved is often useful when checking for quasi-concavity. We now give some illustrations of this. As in the last chapter, we shall freely use functions which are defined not on the whole of $\mathcal{R}^n$ but on some subset of it. For quasi-concavity of the function to make sense, the subset in question should be convex: a typical instance is the set of n–vectors whose components are all positive.

Example 1 Let α, β, γ be positive constants and let the function f be defined by

$$f(x, y, z) = \alpha \ln x + \beta \ln y + \gamma \ln z$$

for all positive values of x, y and z. Using the method that we applied to a similar function in Section 16.2, it is easy to show that f is a concave function. In particular, f is quasi-concave. Now let A be another positive constant and consider the function

$$g(x, y, z) = A x^\alpha y^\beta z^\gamma.$$

Since $g(x, y, z) = A e^{f(x,y,z)}$, and $A e^w$ is an increasing function of w, the function g is quasi-concave.

Example 2 As a somewhat similar example, also using the fact that e^w is an increasing function, consider again the Stone–Geary utility function

$$U(x_1, x_2) = b_1 \ln(x_1 - c_1) + b_2 \ln(x_2 - c_2).$$

Also let

$$\tilde{U}(x_1, x_2) = \exp[U(x_1, x_2)] = (x_1 - c_1)^{b_1}(x_2 - c_2)^{b_2}.$$

Since U is quasi-concave (the indifference curves of Figure 17.5 are convex), so is $\tilde{U}$.

The function $\tilde{U}$ represents the same preferences as the function U: this may be seen either by simple logical reasoning[7] or by noting that the contour diagrams for the two functions are identical and the ordering of the contours is preserved. Indeed $\tilde{U}$ rather than U is often referred to as the Stone–Geary utility function.

Concavity and homogeneous functions

Homogeneous functions and their economic applications were discusssed at some length in Section 14.4. There is a useful proposition, which we do not prove here, connecting concavity, quasi-concavity and homogeneity:

Proposition A quasi-concave function which takes only positive values, and is homogeneous of degree r, is concave if and only if $r \leq 1$.

This fact provides another helpful method for testing concavity.

Example 3 As in Example 1, let

$$g(x, y, z) = Ax^\alpha y^\beta z^\gamma,$$

where A, α, β, γ are positive constants. We have already shown that this function is quasi-concave, and it is easy to see that it is homogeneous of degree $\alpha + \beta + \gamma$. It follows that g is a concave function if and only if $\alpha + \beta + \gamma \leq 1$.

Example 4 Consider the following generalisation of a production function used in the last section:

$$F(K, L) = (aK^{-2} + bL^{-2})^{-c},$$

where a, b, c are positive constants. This function can be shown to be quasi-concave, by showing that the isoquants are convex: recall Exercise

---

[7]Since $e^u > e^v$ if and only if $u > v$, $\tilde{U}(x_1, x_2) > \tilde{U}(x_1', x_2')$ if and only if $U(x_1, x_2) > U(x_1', x_2')$.

15.1.3.[8] Another way of demonstrating that F is quasi-concave is to note that $F(K, L) = H(f(K, L))$, where $f(K, L) = -a/K^2 - b/L^2$ and $H(w)$ is defined for all *negative* w as $(-w)^{-c}$; f is easily shown to be concave using the methods of Section 16.2, and H is monotonic increasing, so F is quasi-concave. Since F is also homogeneous of degree $2c$, F is a concave function if and only if $c \leq \frac{1}{2}$.

Quasi-concavity in economics

In economic theory, it is common to assume that production functions and utility functions are quasi-concave. In the case of production functions with two factors, or utility functions with two goods, quasi-concavity means diminishing marginal rate of substitution.[9]

Our comments in Example 2 on the relation between the utility functions U and $\tilde{U}$ generalise far beyond the Stone–Geary case. If $U(x_1, x_2)$ is any quasi-concave utility function and H is an increasing function of one variable, then

$$\tilde{U}(x_1, x_2) = H(U(x_1, x_2))$$

is a quasi-concave utility function which represents the same preferences as U. This observation generalises to any number of goods, and is the starting point for ordinal utility theory, which is discussed in microeconomics textbooks.

Diminishing returns and all that

We turn now from utility functions to production functions, and make an important point about definitions. The theory of production employs several related but distinct concepts concerned with the general idea of 'diminishing returns', and it is an essential if boring part of one's economic education to learn the difference between them.

To illustrate this point, consider the Cobb–Douglas production function

$$F(K, L) = AK^{\alpha}L^{\beta}$$

where A, α, β are positive constants. This function displays diminishing marginal rate of substitution (in other words, it is quasi-concave) for *all* positive α and β, however large; it displays diminishing marginal returns to each factor (in other words, $\partial^2 F/\partial K^2 < 0$ and $\partial^2 F/\partial L^2 < 0$) if and only if $\alpha < 1$ and $\beta < 1$; the production function is concave if and only if $\alpha + \beta \leq 1$; and it displays decreasing returns to scale if and only if $\alpha + \beta < 1$. Notice that each of these conditions is more stringent than the preceding one.

---

[8]In that exercise we assumed that $c = \frac{1}{2}$, but the same solution method works for any positive constant c.

[9]This is not quite correct; quasi-concavity allows isoquants or indifference curves to have flat segments, whereas (strictly) diminishing marginal rate of substitution does not.

Back to constrained optimisation

The main theorem relating quasi-concave functions to sufficient conditions for constrained optimisation is as follows.

Theorem Suppose we attempt to maximise $f(x, y)$ subject to the constraint

$$ax + by + c = 0,$$

where a, b, c are constants. Suppose the Lagrangian has a critical point when $x = x^*$ and $y = y^*$. Suppose also that f is a quasi-concave function, and that *at least one* of the following conditions are satisfied:

(i) $f(x, y) = H(F(x, y))$ for some increasing function H and some *concave* function F;

(ii) The function $f(x, y)$ does *not* have a critical point at (x^*, y^*).

Then $f(x, y)$ attains a constrained maximum at (x^*, y^*).

This theorem may be extended in two directions. First, it generalises is an obvious way to the case of more than two variables and more than one linear constraint. Secondly, the theorem is applicable to minimisation problems, with obvious modifications: minimisation of f means maximisation of $-f$, so the theorem then requires that $-f$ be quasi-concave,[10] and (i) is altered accordingly.

The seriously restrictive conditions of the theorem are that the function f be quasi-concave and the constraint(s) linear. On the first point, notice that, once we assume quasi-concavity of f, the additional conditions (i) and (ii) hold in a wide variety of cases. Thus, though not all quasi-concave functions satisfy (i), most of those encountered in economics do.[11] Also, (ii) must be satisfied if at least one of the partial derivatives of f is always positive; for then f has **no** critical points. It is for this reason that the theorem is applicable to consumer theory: *if indifference curves are downward-sloping and convex (diminishing marginal rate of substitution) then the first-order conditions for a constrained maximum are sufficient*. And, to repeat, only one of (i) and (ii) needs to be satisfied for the theorem to work.

Now consider the restriction to linear constraints. For that reason, the theorem does not cover cases such as the cost-minimisation example of Section 17.3, though it is not hard to check by geometrical means that we *did* find the optimum in that example.[12]

The moral here is that when we have nonlinear equation constraints, there are no readily applicable sufficient conditions for an optimum. In two-variable cases, sketching contours is extremely useful. Alternatively, with any number of variables, one can often make headway by transforming the problem into one with nonlinear *inequality* constraints. We shall return to this topic in the last part of the next chapter.

---

[10]This is true in particular when f is a convex function, as in Example 1 of Section 17.2.

[11]In particular, (i) must hold if f is concave: to see this, let $H(w) = w$.

[12]Recall Exercise 17.3.2.

Exercises

17.4.1 Explain why the generalised CES production function

$$F(K, L) = A[\delta K^\gamma + (1 - \delta)L^\gamma]^{\nu/\gamma} \quad (A > 0, \ \nu > 0, \ \gamma < 1, \ 0 < \delta < 1)$$

is quasi-concave. Find the range of values of ν for which it is concave.

17.4.2 Consider the 3–good Stone–Geary utility function

$$U(x_1, x_2, x_3) = b_1 \ln(x_1 - c_1) + b_2 \ln(x_2 - c_2) + b_3 \ln(x_3 - c_3),$$

where $b_1, b_2, b_3, c_1, c_2, c_3$ are positive constants. Show that this function is quasi-concave. What about the utility function

$$\tilde{U}(x_1, x_2, x_3) = \exp U(x_1, x_2, x_3) = (x_1 - c_1)^{b_1}(x_2 - c_2)^{b_2}(x_3 - c_3)^{b_3}?$$

Problems on Chapter 17

17–1. Consider a firm producing one kind of output using two inputs, labour and capital. Let r, w denote the prices of capital and labour respectively; given those prices and the required level of output q, let (K, L) be the least-cost combination of capital and labour.

   (i) Explain in words why the capital-labour ratio K/L depends only on the output level q and the input price ratio $s = r/w$.

   (ii) Let $K/L = g(s, q)$, and let

$$\sigma = -\frac{s}{(K/L)} \frac{\partial g}{\partial s}.$$

   σ is called the **elasticity of substitution** between capital and labour. Explain why you would expect σ to be positive.

   (iii) Find the function $g(s, q)$ when the firm has the CES (constant elasticity of substitution) production function

$$F(K, L) = A[\delta K^\gamma + (1 - \delta)L^\gamma]^{1/\gamma} \quad (A > 0, \ \gamma < 1, \ 0 < \delta < 1).$$

   Show that in this case the elasticity of substitution σ is indeed a constant, and find it.

   (iv) Repeat part (iii) for the generalised CES production function of Exercise 17.4.1.

   (v) What do you notice about $\partial g/\partial q$ in parts (iii) and (iv)? How do you think this result generalises?

17-2. Consider a firm producing one kind of output. The firm's output depends on hours per worker h and number of workers N according to the production function

$$F(h, N) = \frac{hN}{ah + bN}$$

where a and b are positive constants. The firm's total cost is $whN + tN$, where w and t are positive constants.

(i) How do you interpret the parameters w and t?

(ii) Find the values of h and N which minimise the cost of producing a given quantity q of output.

(iii) Use a diagram to show that your answer to (ii) does indeed give the minimum.

[Hint for part (ii): by dividing one first-order condition by the other, find a linear relation between h/N and $1/h$; use this relation and the output constraint to obtain a quadratic equation in h, and take the positive root.]

17-3.   (i) In the general model of a consumer's demand for two goods discussed in Section 17.3, write down the restriction on the demand functions imposed by the budget constraint. [This is known as the **adding-up restriction**.] Hence derive the **Engel aggregation condition**

$$p_1 \frac{\partial x_1}{\partial m} + p_2 \frac{\partial x_2}{\partial m} = 1$$

and the **Cournot aggregation conditions**

$$p_1 \frac{\partial x_1}{\partial p_1} + p_2 \frac{\partial x_2}{\partial p_1} = -x_1, \quad p_1 \frac{\partial x_1}{\partial p_2} + p_2 \frac{\partial x_2}{\partial p_2} = -x_2.$$

(ii) How do the Engel and Cournot aggregation conditions generalise to the case of n goods?

17-4. Sandra has T hours per week at her disposal, to divide between work and pleasurable activities. Her weekly income is the sum of non-labour income N and labour income wh, where h is the number of hours per week worked by Sandra and w is her hourly wage rate. T, N and w are taken as exogenous.[13]

---

[13]Think of T as 168, or 168 *less* minimal number of hours required for sleep and personal maintenance, or any other interpretation you find convenient. N may be positive, zero or negative (Sandra may be in debt). To make the problem feasible, assume that $N > -wT$. Also assume that N, if positive, is sufficiently small that Sandra chooses to work; thus the inequality $h \geq 0$ need not be considered as a constraint.

(i) Suppose Sandra divides her time between work and leisure; thus $T = h + \ell$, where ℓ is hours of leisure per week. She spends all her income on a composite consumption good whose price is p; suppose Sandra consumes x units per week of the good. Sandra chooses x, ℓ and h so as to maximise the utility function $x^\alpha \ell^\beta$, where α and β are positive constants.

By formulating Sandra's problem as one of maximisation of a function of two variables subject to one equation constraint, find the optimal values of x and ℓ. Hence find the optimal value of h. What can you say about the response of the optimal value of h to changes in w and N?

(ii) Now consider an alternative model of consumption and labour supply. Suppose Sandra spends her income on two consumption goods 1 and 2. For each good $i = 1, 2$ the price of the good is p_i, the amount of time taken to consume each unit is t_i hours and Sandra's weekly consumption is x_i units. Sandra divides her time between work and consumption of the two goods: no two of these three activities can be performed simultaneously. Sandra chooses x_1, x_2 and h so as to maximise the utility function $x_1^\alpha x_2^\beta$, where α and β are positive constants.

By formulating Sandra's problem as one of maximisation of a function of two variables subject to one equation constraint, find the optimal values of x_1 and x_2. Hence find the optimal value of h. What can you say about the response of the optimal value of h to changes in w and N?

(iii) Explain why the model of part (i) can be considered as a special case of the model of part (ii).

Chapter 18

FURTHER TOPICS IN CONSTRAINED OPTIMISATION

We now go further into the theory and economic applications of constrained optimisation. Two main topics are considered: the comparative statics of small changes in the parameters of optimisation problems, and problems with inequality constraints. Section 18.1 sets the scene for both topics, and is important in its own right. The remaining two sections are independent of each other; either or both may be omitted at a first reading.

When you have studied Section 18.2 you will be able to:

- use the envelope theorem as a tool of comparative statics;

- derive conditional input demand functions from cost functions using Shephard's lemma, and consumer demand functions from indirect utility functions using Roy's identity.

When you have studied Section 18.3 you will be able to:

- write down the Kuhn–Tucker conditions for optimality for a general constrained optimisation problem;

- solve optimisation problems with inequality constraints in simple cases.

18.1 The meaning of the multipliers

As in the preceding chapter, we begin by considering the problem:

$$\text{maximise } f(x,y) \text{ subject to the constraint } g(x,y) = 0. \qquad (18.1)$$

Let the constrained maximum for this problem be obtained when $x = x^*$ and $y = y^*$.

The function to be maximised or minimised in an optimisation problem is called the **objective function** of that problem. In what follows, we shall find sometimes find it convenient to consider a variant of problem (18.1) with the same objective function: this is the problem

$$\text{maximise } f(x,y) \text{ subject to the constraint } g(x,y) = b, \qquad (18.2)$$

where b is a constant. The constrained maximum value of the objective function $f(x,y)$ in (18.2) will in general depend on the constant b, and we denote it by $v(b)$. Observe that (18.1) is the special case of (18.2) where $b = 0$, so that $v(0) = f(x^*, y^*)$.

Our first aim in this section is to give another derivation of the Lagrange multiplier rule for (18.1). We begin by defining the function

$$H(x,y) = f(x,y) - v(g(x,y)).$$

We claim that the function H attains its (unconstrained) maximum at (x^*, y^*). To see this, choose any point (x,y) and let $b = g(x,y)$. Then $f(x,y) \le v(b)$ by definition of the function v, so $H(x,y) \le 0$. But $g(x^*, y^*) = 0$ and $f(x^*, y^*) = v(0)$, so $H(x^*, y^*) = v(0) - v(0) = 0$. Thus $H(x,y) \le 0$ for all (x,y), with equality at (x^*, y^*): this proves the claim.

We can now proceed to the Lagrange multiplier rule. Using the claim we have just proved, and the first-order conditions for an unconstrained maximum, we see that $\partial H / \partial x$ and $\partial H / \partial y$ are both zero at the point (x^*, y^*). But, by the composite function rule,

$$\frac{\partial H}{\partial x} = \frac{\partial f}{\partial x} - v'(g(x,y))\frac{\partial g}{\partial x}$$

for all (x,y), and we know that $g(x^*, y^*) = 0$. Hence, at the point (x^*, y^*) we have

$$\frac{\partial f}{\partial x} - v'(0)\frac{\partial g}{\partial x} = 0$$

and similarly

$$\frac{\partial f}{\partial y} - v'(0)\frac{\partial g}{\partial y} = 0.$$

Setting

$$\lambda = v'(0), \qquad (18.3)$$

we obtain the Lagrange multiplier rule for the problem (18.1):

$$\frac{\partial f}{\partial x} - \lambda\frac{\partial g}{\partial x} = 0, \quad \frac{\partial f}{\partial y} - \lambda\frac{\partial g}{\partial y} = 0.$$

What we have just done is useful in two ways. First, we have given a derivation of the Lagrange multiplier rule which is considerably easier to generalise to cases of many variables and many constraints than the implicit-differentiation argument of Section 17.1.[1] Secondly, equation (18.3) is important in its own right: it says that the Lagrange multiplier can be interpreted as the rate of response of the maximal value of f to variations in the right-hand side of the constraint.

The result we have just established in connection with problem (18.1) generalises in an obvious way to (18.2). This gives us the following proposition, which is the main result of this section.

Proposition For problem (18.2), let $v(b)$ be the constrained-maximal value of f, and let λ be the Lagrange multiplier at the optimum. Then $\lambda = v'(b)$.

In what follows, we refer to this proposition as the **marginal interpretation of the multiplier**.

Economic applications

Recall the utility-maximisation problem of Section 17.3:

$$\text{maximise } U(x_1, x_2) \text{ subject to } p_1 x_1 + p_2 x_2 = m.$$

As we stated in the last chapter, the maximum level of utility subject to this budget constraint is denoted by $V(p_1, p_2, m)$: this expression, considered as a function of the prices p_1, p_2 and income m, is known as the **indirect utility function**. The consumer's problem may be regarded as an illustration of (18.2), with m taking the role of b. The marginal interpretation of the Lagrange multiplier of the consumer's problem is that

$$\lambda = \frac{\partial V}{\partial m}, \tag{18.4}$$

a result stated but not proved in the last chapter.

All of this generalises to the case where the consumer chooses quantities $x_1, x_2, \ldots, x_n$ of n goods so as to maximise the utility function $U(x_1, x_2, \ldots, x_n)$ subject to the budget constraint

$$p_1 x_1 + p_2 x_2 + \ldots + p_n x_n = m.$$

The indirect utility function is now $V(p_1, p_2, \ldots, p_n, m)$, a function of $n + 1$ variables, and (18.4) holds as before.

Similar considerations apply to the firm producing one kind of output with the aid of n kinds of input. The firm chooses input quantities $x_1, x_2, \ldots, x_n$ so

---

[1]See Exercise 18.1.3. We should in honesty draw the reader's attention to one implicit assumption made in the derivation just given of Lagrange's method, namely that the function $v(b)$ is differentiable at $b = 0$. This assumption is violated in "awkward cases" such as that discussed at the end of Section 17.2 where the constrained maximum is not a critical point of the Lagrangian. There are also cases in which the differentiability assumption is violated but Lagrange's method works all the same.

as to minimise the cost of producing a given level of output q; it is assumed that the firm takes input prices $w_1, w_2, \ldots, w_n$ as given. The firm's problem is then to

minimise $w_1 x_1 + w_2 x_2 + \ldots + w_n x_n$ subject to $F(x_1, x_2, \ldots, x_n) = q$,

where F is the production function. As we stated in the last chapter, the first-order conditions for a minimum are

$$w_i = \mu \frac{\partial F}{\partial x_i} \quad \text{for } i = 1, \ldots, n,$$

where μ is the Lagrange multiplier.

The firm's cost function $C(w_1, w_2, \ldots, w_n, q)$ is defined to be the minimum level of cost subject to the output constraint. By formulating the firm's problem as a maximisation problem ('maximise $-w_1 x_1 - \ldots - w_n x_n$ subject to $\ldots$') and using the marginal interpretation of the multiplier, we may identify the Lagrange multiplier μ with marginal cost $\partial C / \partial q$.

Exercises

18.1.1 Find the maximum value of xy subject to $3x + 4y = k$, where k is a positive constant. Find also the value of the Lagrange multiplier at the optimum. Use your results to determine

(a) the maximum value when $k = 7$,

(b) the maximum value when $k = 8$,

(c) the maximum value when $k = 7.2$,

(d) the value of the Lagrange multiplier when $k = 7$.

In view of the main result of this section, how would you expect your answers to (a), (b), (c) and (d) to be related? Are your expectations fulfilled?

18.1.2 In the case of the Stone–Geary utility function discussed in Section 17.3, find the indirect utility function $V(p_1, p_2, m)$ and verify that $\partial V / \partial m$ is equal to the value of the Lagrange multiplier at the consumer's optimum.

18.1.3 Use the method of this section to derive the Lagrange multiplier rule for the problem: maximise $f(x, y, z, w)$ subject to the two constraints $g(x, y, z, w) = 0$ and $h(x, y, z, w) = 0$.

[HINT Recall from Section 17.2 that in this case there are two Lagrange multipliers, λ and μ. Let $v(b, c)$ denote the maximum value of $f(x, y, z, w)$ subject to the constraints $g(x, y, z, w) = b$, $h(x, y, z, w) = c$. Using an argument similar to that used to derive (18.3), obtain the Lagrange multiplier rule with $\lambda = v_1(0, 0)$ and $\mu = v_2(0, 0)$: here subscripts denote partial derivatives.]

18.2   Envelope theorems

Before continuing our study of comparative statics of optimisation problems, we make a brief detour to unconstrained maximisation.

Let $f(x, t)$ be a function of two variables. Suppose we maximise $f(x, t)$ with respect to x, treating t as given. Clearly the solution will depend on t: let the maximal value be $v(t)$, attained at $x = q(t)$. Then

$$v(t) = f(q(t), t) = \max_x f(x, t).$$

Now consider what happens to $v(t)$ as t varies. By the chain rule

$$v'(t) = \frac{\partial f}{\partial x} q'(t) + \frac{\partial f}{\partial t},$$

where $\partial f / \partial x$ is evaluated at $(q(t), t)$. But, precisely because $q(t)$ is the maximising choice of x, we have $\partial f / \partial x = 0$ when $x = q(t)$. It follows that

$$v'(t) = \frac{\partial f}{\partial t}.$$

Thus the derivative of v with respect to t is equal to the *partial* derivative of f with respect to t when x is evaluated at its optimal value $q(t)$; in other words, a small change in t, say from t_0 to $t_0 + \delta$, will have approximately the same effect on the value of the objective function when x adjusts optimally as when x remains fixed at $q(t_0)$. This result is the simplest example of what is known as an **envelope theorem**.

Similar results hold for functions of many variables. Let $f(\mathbf{x}, \mathbf{t})$ be a function of $n + r$ variables: instead of a scalar variable x we have an n–vector $\mathbf{x} = (x_1, \ldots, x_n)$ and instead of a scalar t we have an r–vector $\mathbf{t} = (t_1, \ldots, t_r)$. Let $v(\mathbf{t})$ be the maximal value of $f(\mathbf{x}, \mathbf{t})$ with respect to $\mathbf{x}$, with $\mathbf{t}$ taken as given. The envelope theorem states that

$$\frac{\partial v}{\partial t_k} = \frac{\partial f}{\partial t_k} \quad \text{for } k = 1, \ldots, r.$$

Here, the right-hand side denotes the partial derivative of $f(\mathbf{x}, \mathbf{t})$ with respect to t_k, with all other components of $\mathbf{t}$ held constant and with all components of $\mathbf{x}$ held constant at their optimal values, given $\mathbf{t}$.

An example: short-run and long-run cost curves

The envelope theorem is applicable to problems of minimisation as well as maximisation. For a simple example of this, consider a firm whose total cost of producing output Q depends on the quantity at hand of a fixed factor, which we identify with capital K. We may therefore write $C = G(K, Q)$. As in the last section, cost will also depend on the prices of variable inputs, but these prices are not the focus of concern here, so we do not mention them explicitly. Plotting $G(K, Q)$ against Q for any given level of K gives us the **short-run cost curve** corresponding to that level of K.

The **long-run cost curve** is the relation between C and Q obtained by choosing at each level of Q the cost-minimising level of K. Thus the equation of the long-run cost curve is $C = H(Q)$, where

$$H(Q) = \min_K G(K, Q). \tag{18.5}$$

By (18.5) and the envelope theorem, $H'(Q) = \partial G/\partial Q$. What this means in geometrical terms is that each short-run cost curve meets the long-run cost curve at a point where they have the same slope: the curves are tangential to each other. The relationship between the long-run cost curve and the family of short-run cost curves is sketched in panel A of Figure 18.1. The geometrical term for this tangential relationship between a single curve and a family of curves is that the former is the **envelope** of the latter; hence the term "envelope theorem".

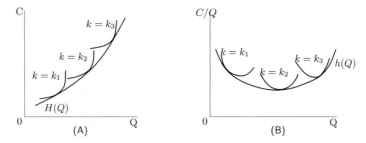

Figure 18.1: **The long-run cost curve is the envelope of the family of short run cost curves**

The relation between short-run and long-run cost curves may be discussed in terms of average rather than total cost. Let $g(K, Q)$ and $h(Q)$ denote respectively short-run and long-run average cost: thus

$$g(K, Q) = G(K, Q)/Q, \quad h(Q) = H(Q)/Q.$$

For any given value of Q, the value of K which minimises $G(K, Q)$ also minimises $G(K, Q)/Q$. Hence (18.5) implies that

$$h(Q) = \min_K g(K, Q),$$

and $h'(Q) = \partial g/\partial Q$ by the envelope theorem. This gives us the tangential relationship between the long-run average cost curve and the family of short-run average cost curves which is sketched in panel B of Figure 18.1.

Panel B of Figure 18.1 is probably more familiar to most readers than panel A; a similar diagram appears in almost every textbook on microeconomics.

A question which students sometimes ask about this diagram is: why does the long-run average cost curve not pass through the minimum points of the short-run average cost curves? The answer is as follows. As we have just demonstrated, the tangential relationship between long-run and short-run average cost curves depicts the solution to the problem of minimising $g(K, Q)$ as a function of K, for given Q. By contrast, the minimum point of each short-run average cost curve depicts the solution to the problem of minimising $g(K, Q)$ as a function of Q, for given K. Since these are quite different problems, it is not surprising that they have different solutions.

Constraints reintroduced

The next step is to extend the envelope theorem to constrained maxima. Again, it is helpful to start with a low-dimensional case. Let $f(x, y, t)$ and $g(x, y, t)$ be functions of three variables. Suppose we take t as given and choose x and y so as to maximise $f(x, y, t)$ subject to the constraint $g(x, y, t) = 0$. The maximal value of $f(x, y, t)$ subject to the constraint depends on t: call it $v(t)$. The envelope theorem states that

$$v'(t) = \frac{\partial L}{\partial t}.$$

Here the right-hand side denotes the partial derivative with respect to t of the Lagrangian

$$L(x, y, \lambda, t) = f(x, y, t) - \lambda g(x, y, t),$$

with x, y and the multiplier λ held at their optimal values.

We now explain why this is true. Let the maximal value $v(t)$ be attained when $x = p(t)$ and $y = q(t)$. Then

$$f(p(t), q(t), t) = v(t), \quad g(p(t), q(t), t) = 0.$$

By total differentiation,

$$\frac{\partial f}{\partial x} p'(t) + \frac{\partial f}{\partial y} q'(t) + \frac{\partial f}{\partial t} = v'(t),$$

$$\frac{\partial g}{\partial x} p'(t) + \frac{\partial g}{\partial y} q'(t) + \frac{\partial g}{\partial t} = 0.$$

(18.6)

Let L and λ denote as usual the Lagrangian and the Lagrange multiplier. Subtracting λ times the second equation of (18.6) from the first, we have

$$\frac{\partial L}{\partial x} p'(t) + \frac{\partial L}{\partial y} q'(t) + \frac{\partial L}{\partial t} = v'(t).$$

But by the first-order conditions for a constrained maximum, $\partial L/\partial x = \partial L/\partial y = 0$. Thus $\partial L/\partial t = v'(t)$, which is the envelope theorem.

The marginal interpretation of the Lagrange multiplier, explained in the preceding section, is a special case of the envelope theorem. The Lagrangian for the problem (18.2), regarded as a function of the four variables x, y, λ, b, is

$$L(x, y, \lambda, b) = f(x, y) - \lambda(g(x, y) - b).$$

Let $v(b)$ denote as before the constrained maximum value of f. Applying the envelope theorem with b replacing t, we see that

$$v'(b) = \frac{\partial L}{\partial b} = \frac{\partial}{\partial b}[f(x, y) - \lambda g(x, y) + \lambda b].$$

But then $v'(b) = \lambda$, which is the marginal interpretation of the multiplier.

Extensions and applications

All of the above can be extended to the case of many variables and many constraints. Let $f(\mathbf{x}, \mathbf{t})$ be a function of $n + r$ variables $x_1, \ldots, x_n, t_1, \ldots, t_r$. Suppose, to keep the notation within bounds, that there are two constraints: we take $\mathbf{t}$ as given and choose $\mathbf{x}$ so as to maximise $f(\mathbf{x}, \mathbf{t})$ subject to the constraints $g(\mathbf{x}, \mathbf{t}) = 0$ and $h(\mathbf{x}, \mathbf{t}) = 0$. The maximal value of the objective function subject to the constraints depends on the vector $\mathbf{t}$: call it $v(\mathbf{t})$. The envelope theorem states that

$$\frac{\partial v}{\partial t_k} = \frac{\partial L}{\partial t_k} \quad \text{for } k = 1, \ldots, r,$$

where L is the Lagrangian, defined as follows:

$$L(\mathbf{x}, \lambda, \mu, \mathbf{t}) = f(\mathbf{x}, \mathbf{t}) - \lambda g(\mathbf{x}, \mathbf{t}) - \mu h(\mathbf{x}, \mathbf{t}).$$

In this case there are two constraints, so there are two Lagrange multipliers λ, μ. A similar result with one multiplier holds when there is only one constraint; with three multipliers when there are three constraints; and so on for any number of constraints that does not exceed the number of components of $\mathbf{x}$.

More on the cost-minimising firm

As in the unconstrained case, the envelope theorem is applicable to minimisation as well as maximisation. As an illustration of this, we reconsider the cost-minimising firm, in the n–input setting introduced at the end of the preceding section.

Recall that the firm produces a given level of output q and faces given input prices $w_1, \ldots, w_n$. The firm's production function is F, and the firm's problem is to minimise $w_1 x_1 + \ldots + w_n x_n$ subject to the constraint $F(x_1, \ldots, x_n) = q$. The Lagrangian for the problem is

$$L(x_1, \ldots, x_n, \mu, w_1, \ldots, w_n, q) = w_1 x_1 + \ldots + w_n x_n - \mu F(x_1, \ldots, x_n) + \mu q, \quad (18.7)$$

where μ is the Lagrange multiplier.

The firm's **cost function** is defined to be the minimum level of cost subject to the output constraint, and is denoted by $C(w_1, w_2, \ldots, w_n, q)$. Recall that marginal cost is $\partial C / \partial q$. By the envelope theorem

$$\frac{\partial C}{\partial q} = \frac{\partial L}{\partial q} = \mu,$$

which illustrates yet again the marginal interpretation of the multiplier.

What can we say about the other partial derivatives of the cost function? The answer is that

$$\frac{\partial C}{\partial w_i} = x_i \quad \text{for } i = 1, \ldots, n, \tag{18.8}$$

where x_i is the optimal amount of input i employed. This result is known as **Shephard's lemma**; it shows how the conditional demand functions[2] are related to the cost function.

Shephard's lemma is a consequence of the envelope theorem. Recall that the Lagrangian L for the firm's problem was given in (18.7), and that $\partial L / \partial w_i$ is defined as the partial derivative of the Lagrangian with respect to w_i, taking all other input prices and q as constants, and treating $x_1, \ldots, x_n$ and μ as if they were constants. Writing (18.7) in the form

$$L = w_i x_i + (\text{terms not involving } w_i),$$

we see that $\partial L / \partial w_i = x_i$. By the envelope theorem, $\partial C / \partial w_i$ is equal to the value taken by $\partial L / \partial w_i$ when $x_1, \ldots, x_n$ and μ take their optimal values. Hence (18.8) holds.

As we stated earlier, Shephard's lemma holds because of the envelope theorem; it does *not* follow directly from the basic rules of partial differentiation. Since this point is often misunderstood, we spell it out in detail. Recall that the optimal choices of input quantities depend on input prices and on the level of output — this dependence is expressed formally in the conditional input demand functions. Therefore, if we differentiate the equation

$$C = w_1 x_1 + \ldots + w_n x_n$$

with respect to w_i, what follows directly from the basic rules of partial differentiation is not (18.8) but

$$\frac{\partial C}{\partial w_i} = x_i + \left[w_1 \frac{\partial x_1}{\partial w_i} + \ldots + w_n \frac{\partial x_n}{\partial w_i} \right].$$

In fact, the sum inside the square brackets is equal to zero; but that is a *consequence* of Shephard's Lemma, not a justification for it.

---

[2]Conditional demand functions for inputs were defined in Section 17.3: recall that 'conditional' here means 'given output'. Shephard's lemma is named after the American economist and engineer Ronald Shephard. It is called a lemma rather than a theorem because it is usually regarded as a step towards the properties of conditional demand functions rather than as an important result in its own right: see the 'Notes on Further Reading' for references.

More on indirect utility functions

The envelope theorem can be applied in the theory of consumer behaviour to find the partial derivatives of the consumer's indirect utility function, which we denote as in the last section by $V(p_1, \ldots, p_n, m)$. We showed in Section 18.1 that $\partial V / \partial m$ is equal to the Lagrange multiplier λ. The formula for the other partial derivatives of the function V is almost, but not quite, as simple as Shephard's lemma. The correct formula, which you are asked to prove in Exercise 18.2.3, is

$$\frac{\partial V}{\partial p_i} = -\lambda x_i,$$

where x_i is the optimal amount of good i consumed. Putting this together with the marginal interpretation of the multiplier, we obtain the following relation between the demand functions and the partial derivatives of the indirect utility function:

$$x_i = -\frac{\partial V}{\partial p_i} \bigg/ \frac{\partial V}{\partial m} \quad \text{for } i = 1, \ldots, n.$$

This result is known as **Roy's identity**, after the French econometrician René Roy.

Exercises

18.2.1 Suppose a firm's short-run cost curve for any given level of capital K is

$$C(K, Q) = bK^2(1 + (Q/K)^4).$$

   (a) Sketch the short-run cost curves corresponding to $K = \frac{1}{2}$, $K = 1$ and $K = 2$.

   (b) Find the equation of the long run cost curve.

   (c) Verify the envelope theorem in this case.

18.2.2 A firm's short-run cost curve for any given level of capital K is

$$C(K, Q) = \alpha K + \beta K^{-1/2} Q^2,$$

   where α and β are positive constants. Average cost C/Q is denoted by A. Find, and sketch in the QA–plane:

   (a) the long-run average cost curve;

   (b) the curve traced out by the minimum points of the short-run average cost curves.

18.2.3 Prove Roy's identity by applying the envelope theorem to the Lagrangian

$$U(x_1, \ldots, x_n) - \lambda(p_1 x_1 + \ldots + p_n x_n) + \lambda m.$$

18.2.4 Using Roy's identity, obtain the demand functions for the Stone–Geary utility function from the expression for the indirect utility function found in Exercise 18.1.2.

18.3   Inequality constraints

In our economic examples in the preceding chapter, we were careful to point out that various difficulties involving inequality constraints were being brushed under the carpet. First, economic variables such as inputs and outputs are typically non-negative. As the reader will now be well aware, there are cases where optimisation ignoring these constraints will nevertheless give a non-negative solution, and therefore answer the question of interest. However, this will not always be so. Similarly, a consumer's budget constraint can be formulated equally well as an equation or a weak inequality under the assumption of non-satiation; but this is not a general feature of inequality constraints, as a look back to Section 2.4 will demonstrate.

In this section we confront these problems, looking first at non-negativity constraints and then at general inequality constraints.

Non-negativity constraints

To keep things simple, we concentrate on the case of two variables and one equation constraint. To

maximise $f(x, y)$ subject to the constraints $g(x, y) = 0$, $x \geq 0$, $y \geq 0$,

we use a method which is a mixture of those of Sections 17.1 and 16.3. Specifically, we form the Lagrangian in the familiar way, but replace the usual necessary conditions for a constrained maximum by conditions similar to (16.2), with L replacing f:

$$\frac{\partial L}{\partial x} \leq 0, \text{ with equality if } x > 0; \quad \frac{\partial L}{\partial y} \leq 0, \text{ with equality if } y > 0. \quad (18.9)$$

To illustrate these conditions, we consider the following variant of Example 1 of Section 17.1: we maximise

$$f(x, y) = 4xy - 2x^2 + y^2$$

subject to the equation constraint

$$3x + y = 5$$

and the additional constraints

$$x \geq 0, \quad y \geq 0.$$

This problem can be solved by elementary means, given what we have already found in the earlier example. We showed then that the maximum ignoring the non-negativity constraints was attained when $x = -1$ and $y = 8$, in which case $f(x, y) = 30$. We also argued that if we solve the equation constraint for

y in terms of x and substitute into the function f, we obtain a quadratic function of x which is maximised when $x = -1$. It follows that the maximum of this quadratic function subject to the additional constraint $x \geq 0$ occurs when $x = 0$. But then $y = 5$ by the equation constraint, and $f(x, y) = 25$.

This solves the problem, but just to check that nothing has gone wrong with our reasoning we verify that the conditions (18.9) are satisfied when $x = 0$, $y = 5$ and λ is chosen appropriately. For the problem in hand,

$$L(x, y, \lambda) = 4xy - 2x^2 + y^2 - \lambda(3x + y - 5).$$

If the second condition of (18.9) is to be satisfied when $x = 0$ and $y = 5$, we need

$$4 \times 0 + 2 \times 5 - \lambda = 0,$$

so $\lambda = 10$. But then

$$\partial L / \partial x = 4 \times 5 - 3 \times 10 = -10 < 0,$$

and the first condition is also satisfied.

Application to consumer demand

We consider the two-good consumer's problem of Section 17.3:

maximise $U(x_1, x_2)$ subject to $p_1 x_1 + p_2 x_2 = m$, $x_1 \geq 0$, $x_2 \geq 0$.

We assume as usual that p_1, p_2, m are all positive. As before, the Lagrangian is

$$L(x_1, x_2, \lambda) = U(x_1, x_2) - \lambda(p_1 x_1 + p_2 x_2) + \lambda m.$$

By (18.9) there are three possibilities for the solution:[3]

(A) $x_1 > 0$, $x_2 > 0$, $\dfrac{\partial L}{\partial x_1} = 0$, $\dfrac{\partial L}{\partial x_2} = 0$.

(B) $x_1 > 0$, $x_2 = 0$, $\dfrac{\partial L}{\partial x_1} = 0$, $\dfrac{\partial L}{\partial x_2} \leq 0$.

(C) $x_1 = 0$, $x_2 > 0$, $\dfrac{\partial L}{\partial x_1} \leq 0$, $\dfrac{\partial L}{\partial x_2} = 0$.

Case (A) was analysed at length in Section 17.3, and is depicted in panel A of Figure 18.2: P is the optimum point. The other two possibilities, (B) and (C), are called **boundary solutions**.

---

[3]In general, (18.9) allows a fourth possibility, namely a solution at the origin. In this particular application, that case is ruled out because the origin is not on the budget line.

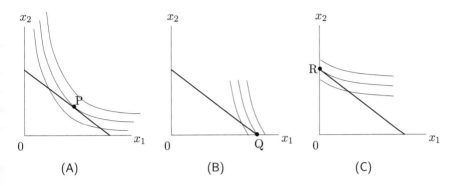

Figure 18.2: **Boundary solutions to the consumer's problem**

Cases (B) and (C) are depicted in panels B and C of Figure 18.2. Recall that in case (B), $\partial L/\partial x_1 = 0$ and $\partial L/\partial x_2 \leq 0$. Hence $\partial U/\partial x_1 = \lambda p_1$ and $\partial U/\partial x_2 \leq \lambda p_2$; eliminating λ, we see that

$$\frac{\partial U}{\partial x_1} \geq \frac{p_1}{p_2}\frac{\partial U}{\partial x_2}.$$

This inequality appears in panel B of Figure 18.2 as the fact that the indifference curve is at least as steep as the budget line at the optimum point Q.

Similarly, in case (C), $x_1 = 0$ and

$$\frac{\partial U}{\partial x_1} \leq \frac{p_1}{p_2}\frac{\partial U}{\partial x_2}.$$

This appears in panel C of Figure 18.2 as the fact that the indifference curve is *less* steep than, or tangential to, the budget line at the optimum point R.

As an illustration of how boundary optima can arise, we consider again the Stone–Geary utility function of Section 17.3:

$$U(x_1, x_2) = b_1 \ln(x_1 - c_1) + b_2 \ln(x_2 - c_2),$$

where b_1, b_2, c_1, c_2 are constants, with $b_1 > 0$ and $b_2 > 0$. However, we no longer insist that c_1 and c_2 are positive: this loses the neat interpretation of these parameters in terms of the bare necessities of life, but still gives us a perfectly respectable utility function with convex, negatively sloped indifference curves.

It is not hard to show that allowing at least one of c_1 and c_2 to be negative admits the possibility of boundary solutions to the standard consumer problem. For example, if $c_2 < 0$ the solution will be as in panel B of Figure 18.2 when p_2 is sufficiently large, given m and p_1. For a more precise account of these matters, see Exercise 18.3.3.

Extension to minimisation

Up to now, this section has discussed only maximisation. If we are minimising a function $f(x, y)$ subject to the constraints $g(x, y) = 0$, $x \geq 0$ and $y \geq 0$, similar considerations apply. In this case, the weak inequality signs in the analogue to (18.9) go the other way. At a constrained minimum,

$$\frac{\partial L}{\partial x} \geq 0, \text{ with equality if } x > 0; \quad \frac{\partial L}{\partial y} \geq 0, \text{ with equality if } y > 0.$$

General inequality constraints

We turn now to an important variant of the basic problem of Sections 17.1 and 18.1. Let $f(x, y)$ and $g(x, y)$ be functions of two variables. We wish to

$$\text{maximise } f(x, y) \text{ subject to the constraint } g(x, y) \leq 0. \tag{18.10}$$

Notice that '$g(x, y) \leq 0$' may be regarded as the general form for a weak inequality involving the variables x, y. For example, the inequality

$$F(x, y) + G(x) \geq H(y) + 7$$

can be put into that form by setting

$$g(x, y) = 7 - G(x) + H(y) - F(x, y).$$

Suppose that the constrained maximum for problem (18.10) is obtained when $x = x^*$ and $y = y^*$. Then there are two cases to consider.

Case I $g(x^*, y^*) < 0$.

In this case the constraint is said to be **slack**, or **inactive**, at (x^*, y^*). Assuming as usual that the function g is continuous, $g(x, y) < 0$ for all points (x, y) sufficiently close to (x^*, y^*): but then $f(x, y) \leq f(x^*, y^*)$ for all such (x, y). Hence the function f has a local unconstrained maximum and therefore a critical point at (x^*, y^*).

Case II $g(x^*, y^*) = 0$.

In this case the constraint is said to be **tight**, or **active**, at (x^*, y^*). In particular, (x^*, y^*) is the point which maximises $f(x, y)$ subject to $g(x, y) = 0$: hence there exists a multiplier λ such that the Lagrangian $f - \lambda g$ has a critical point at (x^*, y^*).

Now recall that (x^*, y^*) maximises $f(x, y)$ subject to the inequality constraint $g(x, y) \leq 0$, so that the feasible set is much larger than it would be if we had imposed the constraint $g(x, y) = 0$ at the outset. This provides us with an additional piece of information: if we let $v(b)$ denote the maximal value of $f(x, y)$ subject to $g(x, y) = b$, then $f(x^*, y^*) \geq v(b)$ whenever

$b < 0$. But $f(x^*, y^*) = v(0)$, so $v(0) \geq v(b)$ whenever $b < 0$; it follows that $v'(0) \geq 0$. Now we know from Section 18.1 that $v'(0)$ is the Lagrange multiplier λ, so $\lambda \geq 0$.

To summarise: in case II the Lagrange multiplier rule holds, with the additional information that the multiplier is non-negative.

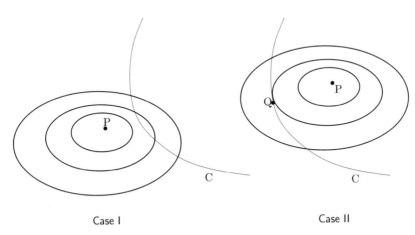

Case I   Case II

Figure 18.3: **Maximization subject to an inequality constraint (slack in case I, tight in case II**

The two cases are depicted in the two panels of Figure 18.3. In both panels, the solid curves are curves of the form $f(x, y) = k$, with inner contours corresponding to higher values of k. The broken curve C is $g(x, y) = 0$, with points to the right of the curve corresponding to $g(x, y) > 0$ and points to the left to $g(x, y) < 0$. Thus the region consisting of points on or to the left of the curve C is the feasible region for the problem (18.10). The left panel corresponds to case I; here the point P which gives the unconstrained maximum for f lies to the left of C and is therefore also the constrained maximum. In the right panel (case II), the point P which gives the unconstrained maximum for f lies to the right of C and is therefore not feasible for the constrained problem. The constrained maximum occurs at the point Q at which the curve C is tangential to an f–contour; this tangency illustrates the Lagrange multiplier rule.

We may summarise what happens at the constrained maximum (x^*, y^*) as follows. In case II, $g(x^*, y^*) = 0$, and there exists a Lagrange multiplier λ such that

$$\frac{\partial f}{\partial x} - \lambda \frac{\partial g}{\partial x} = 0, \quad \frac{\partial f}{\partial y} - \lambda \frac{\partial g}{\partial y} = 0 \text{ and } \lambda \geq 0.$$

In case I, $g(x^*, y^*) < 0$, and the function f has an unconstrained local maximum at (x^*, y^*). Therefore, at that point,

$$\frac{\partial f}{\partial x} - \lambda \frac{\partial g}{\partial x} = 0, \quad \frac{\partial f}{\partial y} - \lambda \frac{\partial g}{\partial y} = 0 \text{ where } \lambda = 0.$$

The reason for writing the first-order conditions for case I in this rather perverse way is to emphasise the resemblance to those for case II. The results for the two cases may be combined as follows.

Proposition Let the Lagrangian for problem (18.10) be defined as

$$L(x, y, \lambda) = f(x, y) - \lambda g(x, y),$$

and let $x = x^*$, $y = y^*$ be a solution of the problem. Then there exists a number λ^* with the following properties:

(a) $\partial L/\partial x = \partial L/\partial y = 0$ at (x^*, y^*, λ^*);

(b) $\lambda^* \geq 0$, $g(x^*, y^*) \leq 0$ and at least one of these two numbers is zero.

Points about the proposition

(i) Condition (b) states, among other things, that at least one of the two numbers λ^* and $g(x^*, y^*)$ is zero: in short,

$$\lambda^* g(x^*, y^*) = 0.$$

This property is known as **complementary slackness**.

(ii) Strictly speaking, we need a constraint qualification[4] for the proposition to hold. The most convenient one is this: if the constraint is tight at (x^*, y^*), the partial derivatives of g at that point are not both zero.

The Kuhn–Tucker theorem

The necessary conditions (a) and (b) for a constrained maximum may be generalised to the case of many variables and constraints.

Suppose that $f, g_1, \ldots, g_m$ are functions of n variables: our problem is to

$$\text{maximise } f(\mathbf{x}) \text{ subject to } g_i(\mathbf{x}) \leq 0 \quad (i = 1, \ldots, m).$$

We define the Lagrangian for this problem to be

$$L(x_1, \ldots, x_n, \lambda_1, \ldots, \lambda_m) = f(\mathbf{x}) - \lambda_1 g_1(\mathbf{x}) - \ldots - \lambda_m g_m(\mathbf{x}).$$

Suppose the maximum value of $f(\mathbf{x})$ subject to the constraints is obtained when $\mathbf{x} = \mathbf{x}^*$. We assume, as a constraint qualification, that the gradients of the constraints which are active at $\mathbf{x}^*$ are linearly independent.

Under these conditions there exist multipliers $\lambda_1^*, \ldots, \lambda_m^*$ with the following properties:

---

[4]Constraint qualifications for problems with equation constraints were discussed at the end of Section 17.2.

(a) At $(x_1^*, \ldots, x_n^*, \lambda_1^*, \ldots, \lambda_m^*)$, $\partial L / \partial x_j = 0$ for $j = 1, \ldots, n$.

(b) For $i = 1, \ldots, m$, $\lambda_i^* \geq 0$, $g_i(\mathbf{x}^*) \leq 0$ and $\lambda_i^* g_i(\mathbf{x}^*) = 0$.

These results are known as the **Kuhn–Tucker theorem**.[5] Conditions (a) and (b) are called the **Kuhn–Tucker conditions** for the constrained maximisation problem.

Points about the Kuhn–Tucker theorem

(i) If the function f is concave (quasi-concavity is *not* enough!) and the functions $g_1, \ldots, g_m$ are convex, then (a) may be strengthened to say that

$$L(\mathbf{x}^*, \lambda_1^*, \ldots, \lambda_m^*) \geq L(\mathbf{x}, \lambda_1^*, \ldots, \lambda_m^*).$$

Notice also that by (b),

$$L(\mathbf{x}^*, \lambda_1^*, \ldots, \lambda_m^*) \leq L(\mathbf{x}^*, \lambda_1, \ldots, \lambda_m).$$

for any non-negative values of $\lambda_1, \ldots, \lambda_m$. Thus the values of $x_1, \ldots, x_n$ and $\lambda_1, \ldots, \lambda_m$ which are optimal for the constrained maximisation problem maximise the Lagrangian with respect to $x_1, \ldots, x_n$ and minimise it with respect to $\lambda_1, \ldots, \lambda_m$. This result is sometimes useful in welfare economics and in game theory.

(ii) *Mixed constraints.* The theorem can be extended to the case where equations as well as inequalities appear among the constraints. The necessary conditions for a constrained maximum then emerge as a mixture of those we have already discussed. Suppose, for example, that we wish to maximise $f(\mathbf{x})$ subject to the constraints $g(\mathbf{x}) = 0$ and $h(\mathbf{x}) \leq 0$. Then there exist multipliers λ and μ such that at the optimal $\mathbf{x}$:

(a') $\dfrac{\partial}{\partial x_j} \big[f(\mathbf{x}) - \lambda g(\mathbf{x}) - \mu h(\mathbf{x}) \big] = 0$ for $j = 1, \ldots, n$;

(b') $\mu \geq 0$, $h(\mathbf{x}) \leq 0$ and at least one of them is zero.

Notice that the condition (b') refers only to μ, the multiplier associated with the inequality constraint; the other multiplier λ may be positive, negative or zero.

(iii) *Non-negativity constraints.* The Kuhn–Tucker theorem can also be extended to the case where some or all of the components of $\mathbf{x}$ are required to be non-negative. As one might expect, the extension consists of a modification of (a), similar to (16.2) or (18.9). If, for example, x_1 is required to be non-negative, then the condition '$\partial L / \partial x_1 = 0$' is replaced by '$\partial L / \partial x_1 \leq 0$, with equality if $x_1 > 0$'.

---

[5]The theorem is now generally attributed to the American mathematician M. Karush, who formulated and proved it in the late 1930s. The theorem was discovered independently and published in 1951 by two other American mathematicians, H. W. Kuhn and A. W. Tucker.

(iv) *More on non-negativity constraints.* The reader may recall that we did not actually derive (18.9), the first-order conditions for constrained optimisation with non-negative variables and one equation constraint. Instead, the conditions were motivated by analogy with the treatment of the unconstrained case in Section 16.3. The analogy is rather dubious, given what we said in Section 17.2 about the behaviour of the Lagrangian. A more convincing derivation of (18.9) — and of the more general case in (iii) above — relies on the Kuhn–Tucker theorem, and uses the fact that non-negativity constraints are a special case of inequality constraints: for instance, the inequality $x_1 \geq 0$ may be written $G(\mathbf{x}) \leq 0$, where $G(\mathbf{x}) = -x_1$. For more detail on how to derive results about non-negativity constraints from the Kuhn–Tucker theorem, see Exercise 18.3.4.

(v) *Minimisation.* Now consider the problem of *minimising* $f(\mathbf{x})$ subject to the constraints $g_i(\mathbf{x}) \leq 0$ $(i = 1, \ldots, m)$. Since minimising $f(\mathbf{x})$ is equivalent to maximising $-f(\mathbf{x})$, we can write the Lagrangian as above, with f replacing $-f$. it is more conventional, however, to define the Lagrangian for the minimisation problem as the negative of the expression thus described. We therefore work with the Lagrangian

$$L(x_1, \ldots, x_n, \lambda_1, \ldots, \lambda_m) = f(\mathbf{x}) + \lambda_1 g_1(\mathbf{x}) + \ldots + \lambda_m g_m(\mathbf{x}).$$

The Kuhn–Tucker necessary conditions for an optimum are then (a) and (b) as above. If we introduce non-negativity constraints on the variables, the necessary conditions for a constrained minimum have to be adjusted: if for example, x_1 is required to be non-negative, then the condition '$\partial L/\partial x_1 = 0$' is replaced by '$\partial L/\partial x_1 \geq 0$', with equality if $x_1 > 0$'. Notice that this adjustment is different from that for the constrained maximum given in (iii) above.

(vi) *So what?* The theorem is not in itself a great help in actually finding constrained maxima. However, under appropriate assumptions about convexity, the Kuhn–Tucker conditions are sufficient as well as necessary for a maximum; and if these assumptions are satisfied, the conditions may be used to find the maximum. We end the chapter with a brief discussion of this point.

Sufficient conditions

The main theorem on sufficient conditions for a maximum with inequality constraints is as follows.

Theorem Suppose we wish to maximise the function $f(\mathbf{x})$ subject to the constraints $g_i(\mathbf{x}) \leq 0$ for $i = 1, \ldots, m$. Suppose the Kuhn–Tucker conditions are satisfied at the point $\mathbf{x}^*$. Then the constrained maximum is attained at $\mathbf{x}^*$ *if* the following conditions are also satisfied:

(i) f is a quasi-concave function, and **either** f is a monotonic transformation of a concave function **or** $Df(\mathbf{x}^*) \neq \mathbf{0}$, or both;[6]

(ii) the functions $-g_1, \ldots, -g_m$ are all quasi-concave.[7]

Many things could be said about this theorem, but we restrict ourselves to two. First, we at last have sufficient conditions which are applicable to the usual problem of the cost-minimising firm, provided we state the constraint in the form

$$F(x_1, \ldots, x_n) \geq q,$$

where F is the production function. Of course, the constraint will typically be active at the optimum, since inputs are costly. The reason why we write the constraint as a weak inequality is to use the theorem above: *the point located by Lagrange's method will be the optimum if the production function is quasi-concave.* In the two-input case, this amounts to requiring that isoquants be convex.

Secondly, linear functions are quasi-concave, and concave functions satisfy condition (i). Thus *the Kuhn–Tucker conditions are sufficient for an optimum when a concave fuction is maximised subject to linear constraints.* We end with two examples in which this fact is applied.

Example 1 Maximise $2\sqrt{x} + 2\sqrt{y}$ subject to

$$2x + y \leq 3, \quad x + 2y \leq 3.$$

The Kuhn-Tucker conditions are:

(a1) $1/\sqrt{x} = 2\lambda + \mu$;   (a2) $1/\sqrt{y} = \lambda + 2\mu$;

(b1) $\lambda \geq 0$ and $2x + y \leq 3$, with complementary slackness;

(b2) $\mu \geq 0$ and $x + 2y \leq 3$, with complementary slackness.

The way we apply these conditions may be referred to as 'chasing the active constraints'. First, we try for a solution in which both constraints are active: $2x + y = x + 2y = 3$, so $x = y = 1$. (a1) and (a2) will then be satisfied provided $2\lambda + \mu = \lambda + 2\mu = 1$, which happens if and only if $\lambda = \mu = \frac{1}{3}$. But then λ and μ are positive numbers, so all conditions are met. The solution is therefore $x = y = 1$, in which case the objective function takes the value 4.

---

[6]This is the same condition on the objective function that we imposed in the theorem on sufficient conditions for a constrained optimum at the end of Section 17.4.

[7]A function g is said to be **quasi-convex** if $-g$ is quasi-concave; thus (ii) states that each of the functions g_i is quasi-convex.

Example 2 Maximise $2\sqrt{x} + 8\sqrt{y}$ subject to

$$2x + y \leq 3, \quad x + 2y \leq 3.$$

This is just like Example 1, except that the coefficient of $\sqrt{y}$ in the objective function is 8 rather than 2. The Kuhn-Tucker conditions are

(a') $1/\sqrt{x} = 2\lambda + \mu, \quad 4/\sqrt{y} = \lambda + 2\mu$,

together with (b1) and (b2) of Example 1.

As before, we begin by seeing what happen when both constraints are satisfied with equality. Then $x = y = 1$ as before; feeding this into (a') we see that $\lambda = -\frac{2}{3}$ and $\mu = \frac{7}{3}$. The negative value for λ violates (b1), so we must look further. We therefore try for a solution in which $\lambda = 0$.

Substituting $\lambda = 0$ into (a') we have $x = \mu^{-2}$ and $y = 4\mu^{-2}$. These conditions are compatible with (b2) if and only if $\mu > 0$ and $9\mu^{-2} = 3$, which happens if and only if $\mu = \sqrt{3}$. Summarising, we see that (a') and (b2) are satisfied when $\lambda = 0$, $\mu = \sqrt{3}$, $x = \frac{1}{3}$ and $y = \frac{4}{3}$. Since $\frac{2}{3} + \frac{4}{3} < 3$, these values of λ, μ, x, y also satisfy (b1) and are therefore optimal.

The solution is therefore $x = \frac{1}{3}$, $y = \frac{4}{3}$, in which case the objective function takes the value $6\sqrt{3}$.

Exercises

18.3.1 Solve the problem

    minimise $(x + 1)^2 + (y + 1)^2$ subject to $3x + y = a$, $x \geq 0$, $y \geq 0$,

(a) when $a = 16$, (b) when $a = 3$.

18.3.2 Solve the problem

    minimise $(x - 1)^2 + (y - 1)^2$ subject to $3x + 4y \leq a$,

(a) when $a = 8$, (b) when $a = 5$. In each case, verify that the Kuhn–Tucker conditions hold at the optimum. [Use any method you like to *find* the optimum.]

18.3.3 A consumer has the utility function

$$U(x_1, x_2) = b_1 \ln(x_1 - 3) + b_2 \ln(x_2 + 5) \quad (x_1 > 3, \ x_2 \geq 0)$$

where b_1 and b_2 are positive constants. The consumer chooses x_1 and x_2 so as to maximise $U(x_1, x_2)$ subject to the budget constraint

$$p_1 x_1 + p_2 x_2 = m.$$

The prices p_1 and p_2 are assumed to be positive.

Use the results on the Stone–Geary utility function given in Section 17.3 to find the optimal x_1 and x_2 in the case where $m > 3p_1 + 5(b_1/b_2)p_2$. Using this and the results of this section, find demand functions which are applicable whenever $m > 3p_1$.

Also find the demand functions corresponding to the utility function

$$\tilde{U}(x_1, x_2) = b_1 \ln(x_1 + 3) + b_2 \ln(x_2 + 5) \quad (x_1 \geq 0, \ x_2 \geq 0).$$

18.3.4 (a) For the problem considered in Section 16.3,

$$\text{maximise } f(x, y) \text{ subject to } x \geq 0, \ y \geq 0,$$

derive the first-order conditions (16.2) using the Kuhn–Tucker theorem.

(b) For the problem

$$\text{maximise } f(x, y) \text{ subject to } g(x, y) = 0, \ x \geq 0, \ y \geq 0,$$

derive the first-order conditions (18.9) using the Kuhn–Tucker theorem.

(c) Now consider the problem

$$\text{maximise } f(x, y) \text{ subject to } g(x, y) \leq 0, \ x \geq 0, \ y \geq 0.$$

Derive the first-order conditions for an optimum using the Kuhn–Tucker theorem, and simplify them to a form similar to your answer to (b).

Problems on Chapter 18

18–1. A monopolist faces the demand function $x = f(p, z)$, where x is quantity demanded, p is price, and z is a macroeconomic variable affecting demand for the product. The monopolist's total cost is $k + cx$, where k and c are positive constants. Her profit is therefore

$$\Pi(p, z) = (p - c)f(p, z) - k.$$

Let $\Phi(z) = \max_p \Pi(p, z)$, the monopolist's maximal profit given z.

In year 0, $z = z_0$, and the monopolist sets her price p_0 so as to maximise profit: thus $\Phi(z_0) = \Pi(p_0, z_0)$. In year 1, z changes to z_1. Let

$$D = \Phi(z_1) - \Pi(p_0, z_1):$$

thus D is the difference between the maximal profit the monopolist could obtain in year 1 and the profit she would obtain if she did not change the price. Let $h = z_1 - z_0$.

(i) Use the envelope theorem to show that, if $|h|$ is small, then D is small even relative to $|h|$.

(ii) In the special case where $f(p, z) = z - bp$ for some positive constant b, find an explicit expression for D. Verify that your answer has the property stated in (i).

18–2. A small open economy produces two goods labelled 1 and 2; their prices p_1 and p_2 are determined in world markets. The economy has fixed supplies K and L of capital and labour. For $i = 1, 2$ let the economy's output of good i be $F_i(K_i, L_i)$, where K_i and L_i denote the quantities of capital and labour allocated to sector i, F_i is the production function for good i and subscripts do *not* indicate partial differentiation. Under perfect competition, the economy will choose K_1, K_2, L_1, L_2 so as to maximise

$$p_1 F_1(K_1, L_1) + p_2 F_2(K_2, L_2)$$

subject to the constraints $K_1 + K_2 = K$, $L_1 + L_2 = L$. The maximal value of the objective function is denoted by $V(p_1, p_2, K, L)$.

Using the envelope theorem, show that

(i) $\dfrac{\partial V}{\partial p_i} = F_i(K_i, L_i)$ for $i = 1, 2$.

(ii) $\dfrac{\partial V}{\partial K} = p_1 \dfrac{\partial F_1}{\partial K_1} = p_2 \dfrac{\partial F_2}{\partial K_2}$.

(iii) $\dfrac{\partial V}{\partial L} = p_1 \dfrac{\partial F_1}{\partial L_1} = p_2 \dfrac{\partial F_2}{\partial L_2}$.

18–3. Ian consumes two goods, 1 and 2; notation for income, prices, and quantities is as usual. Ian's indirect utility function is

$$V(p_1, p_2, m) = a \left(\frac{m}{p_1} \right)^\alpha + b \left(\frac{m}{p_2} \right)^\beta,$$

where a, b, α, β are positive constants.

(i) Using Roy's identity, express x_1/x_2 as a function of p_1, p_2 and m.

(ii) Let s_1 and s_2 denote respectively the **expenditure shares** $p_1 x_1/m$ and $p_2 x_2/m$. Use the result of (i) and the budget constraint to express s_1 and s_2 as functions of p_1, p_2 and m.

(iii) Using the result of (i), compute $\dfrac{\partial}{\partial m}(\ln x_1 - \ln x_2)$. Use this expression and Engel aggregation to show how the income elasticities of demand

$$\frac{m}{x_1} \frac{\partial x_1}{\partial m} \quad \text{and} \quad \frac{m}{x_2} \frac{\partial x_2}{\partial m}$$

are related to s_1 and s_2.

(iv) Using a similar method to (iii), but with Cournot rather than Engel aggregation, show how the own-price elasticities of demand

$$\frac{p_1}{x_1}\frac{\partial x_1}{\partial p_1} \quad \text{and} \quad \frac{p_2}{x_2}\frac{\partial x_2}{\partial p_2},$$

and the cross-price elasticities of demand

$$\frac{p_2}{x_1}\frac{\partial x_1}{\partial p_2} \quad \text{and} \quad \frac{p_1}{x_2}\frac{\partial x_2}{\partial p_1},$$

are related to s_1 and s_2. Are the own-price elasticities of demand negative? What can be said about their absolute values? Are the cross-price elasticities of demand positive?

[Engel and Cournot aggregation were defined in Problem 17–3.]

18–4. A firm produces one kind of output using two inputs. Its production function is $F(x_1, x_2)$ where x_1 and x_2 are the input quantities. For $i = 1, 2$ the price of input i is w_i and the firm's use of each unit of i causes the emission of ϕ_i units of a pollutant.

The firm chooses x_1 and x_2 so as to minimise total cost subject to the constraints that (a) *at least* q units of output are produced; (b) *at most* E units of the pollutant are emitted. Assume that F is a quasi-concave function, that there is more than one point in the $x_1 x_2$–plane at which the constraints (a) and (b) are satisfied, and that at any such point $x_1 > 0$ and $x_2 > 0$.

(i) Draw diagrams showing the different possibilities that may occur at the optimum.

(ii) Use the Kuhn–Tucker theorem to obtain first-order conditions for an optimum.

(iii) Comment on how your answers to (i) and (ii) are related.

(iv) How does your answer to (ii) generalise to the case of n inputs?

Chapter 19

INTEGRATION

In this chapter we return to the calculus of functions of one variable. Up to this point, we have used the word 'calculus' to mean differential calculus; we now introduce the other branch of calculus, known as integral calculus.

Integral calculus, and the corresponding operation on functions known as integration, are concerned with finding the area under a curve. Just as differential calculus turned out to involve limiting operations, we shall see that the same is true of integral calculus. We shall also see that, in a sense which will be made precise later, the operation of integration is the reverse of differentiation. We can therefore think of integration in two ways: as a method for calculating areas in the plane, and as the reverse of differentiation. Most of the tools of integral calculus come from the second interpretation, while the applications draw on both.

When you have studied this chapter you will be able to:

- calculate definite and indefinite integrals of polynomial and related functions;

- obtain total cost from marginal cost, and similarly for revenue;

- calculate the present discounted value of an income stream in continuous time;

- approximate integrals numerically by the trapezium rule and Simpson's rule.

19.1   Areas and integrals

Let a and b be real numbers such that $a < b$, and let f be a continuous function. The central problem of integral calculus is to find the area bounded by the curve $y = f(x)$, the vertical lines $x = a$ and $x = b$, and the x–axis. This area is shown in Figure 19.1. Since everybody knows how to find the area of a rectangle, we start by showing how the required area can be approximated by a set of rectangles.

We define the **closed interval** $[a, b]$ to be the set $\{x \in \mathcal{R} : a \le x \le b\}$; we can think of this interval as the part of the x–axis lying between a and b, including the endpoints.[1] In Figure 19.1, the closed interval $[a, b]$ is partitioned into 7 sub-intervals of equal length. Each of these is the base of a rectangle whose top right-hand corner is on the curve $y = f(x)$. It is clear from the diagram that the sum of the areas of the 7 rectangles is a reasonably good approximation to the area under the curve.

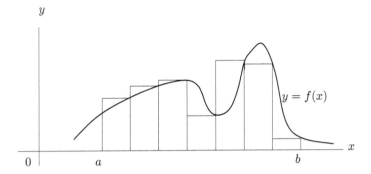

Figure 19.1: **Approximating an integral by a sum**

To give an algebraic expression for this approximation, let the end-points of the 7 sub-intervals be $x_0, x_1, \ldots, x_7$, with $x_0 = a$ and $x_7 = b$. The sum of the rectangular areas is

$$(x_1 - x_0)f(x_1) + \ldots + (x_7 - x_6)f(x_7) = \sum_{i=1}^{7} f(x_i)Dx_i,$$

where $Dx_i = x_i - x_{i-1}$ for $i = 1, \ldots, 7$. Figure 19.1 shows that this sum is approximately equal to the required area.[2]

Figure 19.1, and the subsequent discussion, suggest that we could get a better approximation to the integral by using a very large number of sub-intervals, rather than just 7: the area would then be approximated by the sum of the areas of a very large number of very narrow rectangles. In fact, if the sum of the areas of the rectangles tends to a limit as the length of the sub-intervals tends to zero, this limit gives the area. The limit is written as

$$\int_a^b f(x) \, dx,$$

---

[1]Intervals were introduced in Section 3.1. The **open interval** (a, b) is the set $\{x \in \mathcal{R} : a < x < b\}$.

[2]In Figure 19.1 and subsequent diagrams we depict a and b as positive numbers. Our only reason for doing this is to prevent the y–axis from getting in the way of the interesting part of the picture; none of the properties of integrals depend on a or b being positive.

and is called the **integral** of $f(x)$ with respect to x from $x = a$ to $x = b$. Thus $\int$ can be thought of as a continuous extension of $\sum$: indeed Leibniz introduced the symbol $\int$ for integration precisely because it looks like an elongated S (for summation).

In Figure 19.1, f takes only positive values between $x = a$ and $x = b$, so that the curve lies above the x–axis. Now consider what happens when the curve lies below the x–axis, as is the case in Figure 19.2. The area bounded by the curve, the vertical lines $x = a$ and $x = b$, and the x–axis can be approximated by rectangles as before. The function values in the approximating sum are now negative: thus

$$\int_a^b f(x)\, dx < 0.$$

The result is that the integral still gives the area but with the convention that areas below the x–axis are negative.

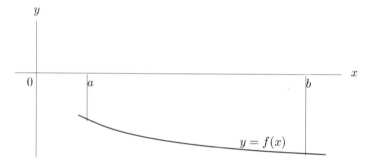

Figure 19.2: $\int_a^b f(x)dx$ **is negative**

When the function takes both positive and negative values, the integral is similarly defined, taking into account the signs of the function values. See Exercise 19.1.1 for an example of this.

Up to now, we have defined $\int_a^b f(x)\, dx$ only in the case where $a < b$. If $a > b$ we define

$$\int_a^b f(x)\, dx = -\int_b^a f(x)\, dx \tag{19.1}$$

We also define $\int_a^a f(x)\, dx$ to be zero, which is consistent with earlier remarks about sums and areas, and is the special case of (19.1) when $a = b$.

Properties of integrals

The following properties follow directly from the definition of the integral as an area.

I1   If c is a constant, $\displaystyle\int_a^b c\, dx = c(b - a)$.

I2 $\displaystyle\int_a^b x\,dx = \tfrac{1}{2}(b^2 - a^2).$

I3 $\displaystyle\int_a^b f(x)\,dx = \int_a^c f(x)\,dx + \int_c^b f(x)\,dx.$

The first two of these properties are illustrated in the two panels of Figure 19.3. **I1** follows from the formula for the area of a rectangle: see panel A. To see why **I2** holds, consider panel B: $\int_a^b x\,dx$ is the sum of the rectangular area R and the triangular area T. Now R $= a(b-a)$, while T $= \tfrac{1}{2}(b-a)^2$ by the half-base-times-height formula for the area of a triangle. Thus

$$\int_a^b x\,dx = \tfrac{1}{2}(b-a)(2a+b-a) = \tfrac{1}{2}(b-a)(b+a) = \tfrac{1}{2}(b^2 - a^2).$$

I3 is obvious when $a < c < b$ (draw the diagram); the fact that **I3** holds for any ordering of a, b, c follows from (19.1).

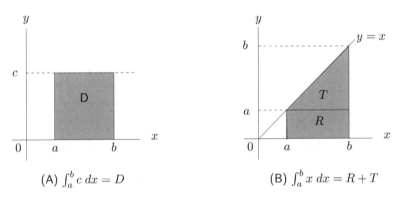

(A) $\int_a^b c\,dx = D$ (B) $\int_a^b x\,dx = R + T$

Figure 19.3: **Properties I1 and I2**

Applying the properties

The process of obtaining $\int_a^b f(x)\,dx$ from the constants a and b and the function f is known as **integration**. We now show by examples how integration may be performed using properties **I1–I3** above.

Example 1 Calculate $\displaystyle\int_0^3 f(x)\,dx$, where

$$f(x) = \begin{cases} 1 & \text{if } x \le 1 \\ x & \text{if } x > 1. \end{cases}$$

The desired integral, which we denote by J, is the shaded area in panel A of Figure 19.4. By **I3**,

$$J = \int_0^1 1\, dx + \int_1^3 x\, dx.$$

Hence by **I1** and **I2**,

$$J = 1 \times 1 + \tfrac{1}{2}(3^2 - 1^2) = 5.$$

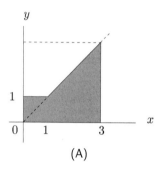
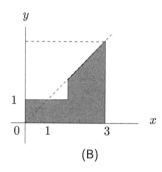

Figure 19.4: **Integrals of kinked functions**

Example 2 Calculate $\displaystyle\int_0^3 g(x)\, dx$, where

$$g(x) = \begin{cases} \tfrac{1}{2} & \text{if } x \le 1 \\ x & \text{if } x > 1. \end{cases}$$

Since the function g is discontinuous at $x = 1$, we are attempting to calculate something which has not yet been defined in this book. The integral here is in fact defined in the obvious way, as the shaded area in panel B of Figure 19.4, and the calculation follows the steps of the preceding example:

$$\int_0^3 g(x)\, dx = \int_0^1 \tfrac{1}{2}\, dx + \int_1^3 x\, dx = \tfrac{1}{2} \times 1 + \tfrac{1}{2}(3^2 - 1^2) = \tfrac{9}{2}.$$

The last example shows that one can sometimes integrate discontinuous functions. On the other hand it is possible to define functions which behave so erratically that 'area under the graph' ceases to be a well-defined concept. Generally one is on safer ground in integral calculus when the function one is trying to integrate is continuous, and we shall restrict ourselves to that case for the remainder of the chapter.

Integration and differentiation

Given a real number a and a continuous function f, we can define another function F by letting

$$F(t) = \int_a^t f(x)\, dx \quad \text{for all } t.$$

It turns out that the function F is differentiable and

$$F'(t) = f(t) \quad \text{for all } t.$$

This result is so important that it is known as the **fundamental theorem of calculus**. What it says, roughly speaking, is that if you integrate a function and then differentiate the result, you retrieve the function you started with. This justifies the statement at the beginning of this chapter that integration is the reverse of differentiation.

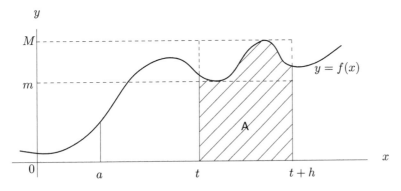

Figure 19.5: **The fundamental theorem of calculus**

To understand why the theorem holds, consider Figure 19.5 and let

$$A = \int_t^{t+h} f(x)\, dx.$$

Then A is the shaded area in Figure 19.5; it is clear from the diagram that

$$A = \int_a^{t+h} f(x)\, dx - \int_a^t f(x)\, dx = F(t+h) - F(t).$$

On the other hand, we can also see from Figure 19.5 that A lies between mh and Mh, where m and M are the least and greatest values taken by $f(x)$ when $t \leq x \leq t+h$. Putting all of this together, we obtain

$$mh \leq F(t+h) - F(t) \leq Mh. \tag{19.2}$$

If h is small then, since f is a continuous function, all the values taken by $f(x)$ when $t \le x \le t + h$ are close to $f(t)$; in particular m and M are close to $f(t)$. Therefore, (19.2) tells us that

$$\frac{1}{h}(F(t + h) - F(t))$$

is squeezed between two numbers, each of which is close to $f(t)$ when h is small. Putting this more precisely,

$$\lim_{h \to 0} \frac{F(t + h) - F(t)}{h} = f(t),$$

which is the fundamental theorem of calculus.

Integrating derivatives

We now show how the fundamental theorem leads to the most common method of integration. As a first step along the road, we establish the following proposition: if the function g has a continuous derivative,

$$\int_a^b g'(x)\, dx = g(b) - g(a). \tag{19.3}$$

To prove this proposition, let I denote the left-hand side of (19.3) and let

$$F(t) = \int_a^t g'(x)\, dx \quad \text{for all } t.$$

Then $F(a) = 0$, $F(b) = I$ and $F'(t) = g'(t)$ for all t by the fundamental theorem of calculus. We showed in Section 10.2 that a function whose derivative is always zero is a constant. Applying this result to the function $F - g$, we see that $F(t) - g(t)$ is the same for all t; in particular,

$$F(b) - g(b) = F(a) - g(a).$$

Rearranging,
$$g(b) - g(a) = F(b) - F(a) = I - 0.$$
Hence $I = g(b) - g(a)$, proving (19.3).

Primitives

Given a continuous function f, we define a **primitive** (or **anti-derivative**) of f to be a function g such that

$$g'(x) = f(x) \quad \text{for all } x.$$

The proposition we have just proved tells us that, to find $\int_a^b f(x)\, dx$, we 'only' have to find a primitive g of f; the desired integral is then equal to $g(b) - g(a)$, by (19.3). This is the most common method of integration; the serious work in the method consists of finding a primitive.

In some cases this is straightforward. For instance, since $\dfrac{d}{dx}(kx^2) = 2kx$ for any constant k, kx^2 is a primitive of $2kx$. In particular, $\frac{1}{2}x^2$ is a primitive of x. It follows that

$$\int_a^b x\, dx = \tfrac{1}{2}(b^2 - a^2).$$

This is the property of integration that we called **I2** above; it should be obvious that **I1** can be retrieved in a similar manner.

As an example of an integral which we have not already obtained by other methods, consider $\displaystyle\int_1^2 8x^3\, dx$. Since $\dfrac{d}{dx}(x^4) = 4x^3$, a primitive for $8x^3$ is $2x^4$. Hence

$$\int_1^2 8x^3\, dx = 2\times 2^4 - 2\times 1^4 = 30.$$

To apply this method of integration to more complicated functions, we need systematic ways of finding primitives. That is the subject of the next section.

Exercises

19.1.1 Use property **I2** to find $\displaystyle\int_{-2}^3 x\, dx$. Explain your answer in terms of areas.

19.1.2 By considering the relevant area, find $\displaystyle\int_a^b cx\, dx$, where c is a constant.

19.1.3 Sketch the graph of the function

$$f(x) = \begin{cases} 5 - x & \text{if } x \le 2 \\ 3 & \text{if } x > 2 \end{cases}$$

Hence find $\displaystyle\int_0^5 f(x)\, dx$.

19.1.4 Write down a primitive for $12x^5$. Hence evaluate $\displaystyle\int_2^3 12x^5\, dx$.

19.2   Rules of integration

In Section 19.1 we defined a primitive of a function f to be a function g such that $g'(x) = f(x)$ for all x. For example, since $\dfrac{d}{dx}(2x^3) = 6x^2$, $2x^3$ is a primitive of $6x^2$. Notice that $2x^3$ is not the only primitive of $6x^2$: others include $2x^3 - 2$ and $2x^3 + 47$.

Now recall the fact, proved in Section 10.2 and used in the last section, that the only functions with derivatives that are zero everywhere are the constant functions. This implies that **all** the primitives of $6x^2$ are of the form $2x^3 + C$, where C is a constant. We may generalise as follows:

Proposition If $g(x)$ is a primitive of $f(x)$, then the set of all primitives of $f(x)$ consists of the functions of the form $g(x) + C$, where C is a constant.

Given a function $f(x)$, the set of all its primitives is called the **indefinite integral** of $f(x)$ and denoted by

$$\int f(x)\, dx.$$

The proposition we have just stated gives uss the usual notation for indefinite integrals:

$$\int f(x)\, dx = g(x) + C,$$

where $g(x)$ is a particular primitive and C is an arbitrary constant, known as a **constant of integration**. For example,

$$\int 6x^2\, dx = 2x^3 + C.$$

Calculating indefinite integrals

The following general results on indefinite integrals follow from the rules of differentiation given in Chapters 6–9.

Rule 1 $\int x^\alpha\, dx = \frac{1}{\alpha+1} x^{\alpha+1} + C$ if $\alpha \neq -1$.

Rule 2 $\int \frac{1}{x}\, dx = \ln x + C$,   provided $x > 0$.

Rule 3 $\int e^x\, dx = e^x + C$.

All these results are obtained in the same way: differentiating the right-hand side yields the function integrated on the left.

Similarly, the combination rule of differentiation given in Section 6.3 yields the following properties of indefinite integrals:

Rule 4 $\int (f(x) + g(x))\, dx = \int f(x)\, dx + \int g(x)\, dx.$

Rule 5   If k is a constant, $\int k f(x)\, dx = k \int f(x)\, dx.$

In particular, Rule 1 with $\alpha = 0$, together with Rule 5, implies that

$$\int k\,dx = kx + C;$$

and rule 1 with $\alpha = 1$ states that

$$\int x\,dx = \tfrac{1}{2}x^2 + C.$$

We now demonstrate how Rules 1–5 may be used to calculate indefinite integrals.

Example 1

$$
\begin{aligned}
\int (9x^2 + 8)\,dx &= 9\int x^2\,dx + \int 8\,dx \qquad \text{by Rules 4 and 5} \\
&= 9(\tfrac{1}{3}x^3 + C_1) + (8x + C_2) \quad \text{by Rule 1}
\end{aligned}
$$

where C_1 and C_2 are arbitrary constants. Setting $C = 9C_1 + C_2$, we see that

$$\int (9x^2 + 8)\,dx = 3x^3 + 8x + C,$$

where C is a constant of integration.

Example 1 illustrates one quite important technique, that of bundling together the constants of integration arising from two indefinite integrals so that we end up with a single arbitrary constant k. From now on, we do not spell out the steps of this standard procedure.

Example 2

$$
\begin{aligned}
\int \left(6x + \frac{4}{x^3} - 9e^x\right) dx & \\
&= 6\int x\,dx + \int 4x^{-3}\,dx - 9\int e^x\,dx \ \text{by Rules 4 and 5} \\
&= 6[x^2/2] + 4[x^{-2}/(-2)] - 9e^x + k \quad \text{by Rules 1 and 3} \\
&= 3x^2 - 2x^{-2} - 9e^x + k.
\end{aligned}
$$

The next example illustrates two points. First, expressions involving brackets can sometimes be integrated by multiplying out the brackets. Second, Rule 1 works perfectly well with fractional indices.

Example 3

$$
\begin{aligned}
\int (x^{0.8} - 2)(x^{-0.6} - 3)\,dx &= \int (x^{0.2} - 3x^{0.8} - 2x^{-0.6} + 6)\,dx \\
&= x^{1.2}/1.2 - 3x^{1.8}/1.8 - 2x^{0.4}/0.4 + 6x + C \\
&= -\tfrac{5}{3}x^{1.8} - \tfrac{5}{6}x^{1.2} + 6x - 5x^{0.4} + C.
\end{aligned}
$$

Definite integrals

In contrast with the indefinite integrals dicussed above, integrals of the form $\int_a^b f(x)\,dx$, with which we were concerned in Section 19.1, are known as **definite integrals**. As we explained earlier, the most common way of calculating such integrals is to find a primitive and apply equation (19.3). Given what we have said about indefinite integrals, the method may be spelled out as follows:

(i) calculate the indefinite integral $\int f(x)\,dx$;

(ii) give the arbitrary constant C a particular value (usually 0) to get a particular primitive $g(x)$;

(iii) calculate the definite integral as $g(b) - g(a)$. This is often written as

$$\Big[\, g(x) \,\Big]_a^b.$$

Notice that if $g(x) + C$ is used as the primitive instead of $g(x)$, the definite integral becomes

$$(g(b) + C) - (g(a) + C)$$

and the Cs cancel out. For this reason, constants of integration may be omitted from the outset when we evaluate definite integrals.

Example 4   Find $I = \displaystyle\int_1^3 (9x^2 + 8)\,dx$.

Using the indefinite integral found in Example 1, we see that

$$I = \Big[\, 3x^3 + 8x \,\Big]_1^3 = (81 + 24) - (3 + 8) = 94.$$

Example 5   Find $J = \displaystyle\int_{10}^{11} 2/x\,dx$.

By Rules 2 and 5 of indefinite integration, $\displaystyle\int 2/x\,dx = 2\ln x + C$. Hence

$$J = \Big[\, 2\ln x \,\Big]_{10}^{11} = 2(\ln 11 - \ln 10) = 2\ln \tfrac{11}{10} = \ln([1.1]^2)$$

by basic properties of logarithms. Hence $J = \ln 1.21 = 0.1906$ to 4 decimal places.

Remarks on terminology

(a) In definite or indefinite integration, the function that is being integrated is called the **integrand**: thus the integrand is $9x^2 + 8$ in Example 4 and $2/x$ in Example 5.

(b) In the case of a definite integral $\int_a^b f(x)\,dx$, the numbers a and b are known as the **limits of integration**. The interval $[a, b]$ is called the **range of integration**.

(c) The indefinite integral $\int f(x)\,dx$ is an expression depending on x. On the other hand, the definite integral $\int_a^b f(x)\,dx$ depends on the limits of integration a and b but not on the variable x, which we could equally well denote by some other name. Thus

$$\int_a^b f(x)\,dx = \int_a^b f(t)\,dt = \int_a^b f(u)\,du$$

and so on. The situation is similar to that in summation, where for example

$$\sum_{i=1}^{3} i^2 = 1^2 + 2^2 + 3^2 = \sum_{r=1}^{3} r^2.$$

Extending the rules

Rules 1–3 of integration may be generalised as follows:

Rule 1' $\displaystyle\int (x-a)^\alpha\,dx = \frac{1}{\alpha+1}(x-a)^{\alpha+1} + C$ if $\alpha \neq -1$.

Rule 2' $\displaystyle\int \frac{1}{x-a}\,dx = \ln(x-a) + C$,   provided $x > a$.

Rule 3' $\displaystyle\int e^{ax}\,dx = e^{ax}/a + C$ if $a \neq 0$.

The next two examples illustrate the use of the extended rules.

Example 6

$$\int (6(x-1)^3 + 8e^{-4x})\,dx = 6[(x-1)^4/4] + 8[e^{-4x}/(-4)] + C$$

$$\text{by Rules 1' and 3'}$$

$$= \tfrac{3}{2}(x-1)^4 - 2e^{-4x} + C.$$

Example 7 Evaluate $I = \displaystyle\int_{-1}^{1} \frac{2x+3}{x+2}\, dx$.

This is a case where we need to rearrange the integrand in order to apply the rules. What we must do is to 'get rid of' the x in the numerator by expressing the numerator in terms of the denominator and constants. Specifically, since

$$2x + 3 = 2(x+2) - 1,$$

the integrand may be written

$$2 - (x+2)^{-1}.$$

Applying Rule 2′ we have

$$I = \Big[\, 2x - \ln(x+2)\, \Big]_{-1}^{1} = (2 - \ln 3) - (-2 - \ln 1).$$

Remembering that $\ln 1 = 0$, we have $I = 4 - \ln 3$.

More on Rule 2

We stated above that $\int 1/x\, dx = \ln x + C$, provided $x > 0$. The rule holds because $\ln x$ is defined only when $x > 0$, in which case

$$\frac{d}{dx}\ln x = \frac{1}{x}.$$

When $x < 0$, $\ln(-x)$ is defined and

$$\frac{d}{dx}\ln(-x) = \frac{1}{(-x)} \times (-1) \quad \text{by the composite function rule}$$

$$= \frac{1}{x}.$$

Putting the positive and negative cases together, we see that, whenever $x \neq 0$,

$$\frac{d}{dx}\ln|x| = \frac{1}{x},$$

and therefore $\displaystyle\int 1/x\, dx = \ln|x| + C$. More generally, for any constant a,

$$\int \frac{1}{x-a}\, dx = \ln|x-a| + C.$$

These generalisations of Rules 2 and 2′ should be used with caution. Notice in particular that, because of the peculiar behaviour of $1/x$ when x is close to 0, the definite integral $\int_a^b x^{-1}\, dx$ is defined only when a and b are both positive or both negative. Similarly, $\int_a^b (x-c)^{-1}\, dx$ is defined only when a and b are on the same side of c. For further information on the difficulties this may cause, see Problem 19–1 and the discussion of 'improper integrals' in the next chapter.

And finally, the bad news

We have come a long way in this section, but the class of functions which can be integrated explicitly by the rules we have described remains quite small. One reason for this is that we have not yet given the integral counterparts of the product and composite function rules of differentiation; this will be done in Chapter 20. And we shall show in Chapter 22 that functions such as $(1+x^2)^{-1}$ and $(1-x^2)^{-1/2}$ can be integrated using trigonometric functions.

However, the unfortunate fact remains that the class of functions whose primitives admit a straightforward expression in terms of known functions is not large. In other cases, definite integrals have to be calculated approximately by numerical methods. We shall explain some of the most common methods in Section 19.4.

Exercises

19.2.1 Find the following indefinite integrals:

$$\text{(a)} \int x^7 \, dx, \quad \text{(b)} \int x^{-1/2} \, dx, \quad \text{(c)} \int e^{-4t} \, dt.$$

19.2.2 Find the following definite integrals:

$$\text{(a)} \int_1^2 x^4 \, dx, \quad \text{(b)} \int_{-3}^{-2} t \, dt, \quad \text{(c)} \int_0^3 e^{w/4} \, dw.$$

19.2.3 Find the following indefinite integrals:

$$\text{(a)} \int (2x^3 + 3x - 1) \, dx, \quad \text{(b)} \int \left(3x^{1/2} - \frac{4}{x} - 1 \right) dx,$$

$$\text{(c)} \int (2e^{5t} + 5e^{-5t} - 5t) \, dt.$$

19.2.4 For each of the indefinite integrals in Exercise 19.2.3, find the definite integral over the range $[1, 2]$.

19.2.5 Find the following integrals by first simplifying the integrand:

$$\text{(a)} \int (x+1)(x-3) \, dx, \quad \text{(b)} \int (x^{3/4} - 6)/x \, dx,$$

$$\text{(c)} \int (e^{2x} + e^{-2x})(e^{3x} + e^{-3x}) \, dx.$$

19.2.6 Find $\int \dfrac{2}{x+3} \, dx$. What happens if the range of integration is $[-5, -4]$? What happens if it is $[-4, -2]$?

19.2.7 By first rearranging the integrand, find

$$\int \frac{4x+1}{x-3} \, dx.$$

19.3   Integration in economics

The simplest application is finding a 'total' quantity from a 'marginal' quantity. Suppose a firm has marginal cost

$$C'(x) = 1 + 2e^{x/3},$$

where x denotes output. Then total cost is

$$C(x) = \int (1 + 2e^{x/3})\, dx = x + 6e^{x/3} + B,$$

where B is a constant of integration.

If we also know that fixed cost is 2, then $C(0) = 2$. We can use this fact to determine completely how cost depends on output. Since $0 + 6e^0 + B = 2$ and $e^0 = 1$, $B = -4$; therefore

$$C(x) = 6e^{x/3} + x - 4.$$

Total revenue $R(x)$ can be obtained from marginal revenue $R'(x)$ by a similar method. To determine the constant of integration, it usually makes sense to assume that $R(0) = 0$.

We can now complete a piece of unfinished business left over from Chapter 8. In Section 8.3 we worked through an example concerning a profit-maximising monopolist, whose revenue and cost were given by

$$R(x) = 100x - x^2, \quad C(x) = \tfrac{1}{3}x^3 - 7x^2 + 111x + 50.$$

By writing profit as $R(x) - C(x)$, we showed that profit was maximised at $x = 11$; there was another local maximum at $x = 0$ which was not a global maximum.

We drew the MR–MC diagram for this example in Figure 8.10, which is reproduced here as Figure 19.6. We stated in Chapter 8 that it was possible to infer *from the diagram* that profit is greater at $x = 11$ than at $x = 0$, but could not explain how. Now we can.

Let E denote the excess of profit when $x = 11$ over profit when $x = 0$. Then

$$E = [R(11) - R(0)] - [C(11) - C(0)].$$

Now consider the areas marked I, J, K in Figure 19.6:

$$I + J = \int_0^{11} R'(x)\, dx = R(11) - R(0), \quad J + K = \int_0^{11} C'(x)\, dx = C(11) - C(0).$$

Hence $E = I - K$. It is clear from the diagram that I is much larger than K; hence profit at $x = 11$ exceeds profit at $x = 0$.

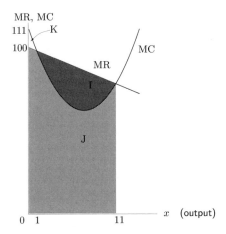

Figure 19.6: **Example of a monopolist; marginal revenue and marginal cost**

Integrating with respect to time

Another use of integration in economics arises from the treatment of time as a continuous variable. As we explained in Section 9.3, this often simplifies analysis.

Let $K(t)$ denote the capital stock of an economy at time t. Net investment at time t is defined as the rate of change of the capital stock; following the usual definition of rate of change in continuous-time analysis given in Section 9.3, net investment $I(t)$ is given by

$$I(t) = K'(t).$$

K is an example of a **stock variable**, defined as a quantity measured at a point in time; other examples of stock variables are the money supply and the labour force. I, by contrast, is a **flow variable**, defined as a quantity per unit of time; other flow variables are national income, measured in £ per year, and the inflow into unempoyment, measured in persons per month.

The relevance of integration here is as follows: if we know $I(t)$ for all t between time a and time b, the change in the capital stock between a and b is given by

$$K(b) - K(a) = \int_a^b K'(t)\,dt = \int_a^b I(t)\,dt.$$

For example, if $I(t) = 2e^{t/5}$ and $K(0) = 6$ then

$$K(5) = 6 + \int_0^5 2e^{t/5}\,dt = 6 + 10(e^1 - e^0) = 10e - 4.$$

Continuous compounding and discounting

In Section 19.1 we introduced the idea of integration as a limiting case of summation. We now put that idea together with the notion of integration with respect to time. The object is to extend some of the financial arithmetic of Section 5.3 to the case of continuous time.

Recall from Section 9.1 that if £P is invested at a rate of interest r per annum, compounded continuously, it is worth £Pe^r at the end of one year. If the asset is held for T years with all interest reinvested, its value in £ at the end of T years is $P(e^r)^T = Pe^{rT}$. Since time is being treated continuously and compounding is continuous, this formula for compound value is true whether or not T is a whole number. Similarly, the present value today of a sum M to be received T years from now is Me^{-rT}.

Now suppose that we have a continuous income stream $f(t)$ for $0 \le t \le T$. Then $f(t)$ is a rate of flow, with the interpretation that the amount of money received during the short time interval $[t, t + \Delta t]$ is approximately $f(t)\Delta t$.

Suppose all income is invested (and interest reinvested) at the constant rate of interest r, with continuous compounding. The compounded value at time T of the money received during the time interval $[t, t+\Delta t]$ is therefore approximately equal to

$$e^{r(T-t)} f(t) \Delta t. \tag{19.4}$$

It follows that if we split the time interval $[0, T]$ into a large number of small sub-intervals, the compounded value at time T of the entire stream can be approximated by a sum of terms of the form (19.4). Passing to the limit, we see that the exact expression for the compounded value at time T of the stream $\{f(t) : 0 \le t \le T\}$ is

$$\int_0^T e^{r(T-t)} f(t)\, dt = e^{rT} \int_0^T e^{-rt} f(t)\, dt.$$

The present value at time 0 of the income stream $\{f(t) : 0 \le t \le T\}$ is

$$\int_0^T e^{-rt} f(t)\, dt.$$

This may be demonstrated in either of two ways. One is to proceed from first principles as for compounding, noting that the present value at time 0 of the income received during the short time interval $[t, t + \Delta t]$ is approximately $e^{-rt} f(t)\Delta t$. The other is to start with our final expression for the compounded value of the stream at time T, and discount it back to time 0 by multiplying by e^{-rT}.

Exercises

19.3.1 Suppose a monopolist's marginal revenue is $6 - 2x$ where x denotes sales. Find the total revenue and the demand function faced by the monopolist.

19.3.2 Assuming that net investment at time t is given by $I(t) = 12t^{1/2}$, find the change in the capital stock during the time intervals $[0, 1]$, $[1, 3]$ and $[0, 3]$. If the capital stock is 25 when $t = 0$, find the capital stock at each time $t > 0$.

19.3.3 Suppose a continuous income stream flows at a constant rate Y over the time interval $[0, T]$ and suppose the continuous rate of interest is the constant r. Find

    (a) the compounded value at time T of the income stream;

    (b) the present value at time 0 of the income stream.

19.4 Numerical integration

We remarked at the end of Section 19.2 that it is often not possible to evaluate a definite integral exactly, and numerical approximations have to be used. This happens when we have a functional form for the integrand which is difficult, in the sense that none of the rules given in Sections 19.2 seems to work. Numerical integration is also helpful when one wants to find the area under a curve which does not have a known functional form, for example one obtained by plotting data.

Suppose we attempt to approximate the definite integral $\int_a^b f(x)\,dx$, which we denote by I. We showed in Section 19.1 that I can be approximated by summing areas of rectangles: recall in particular Figure 19.1. This is in fact a rather inefficient method, but it is convenient to start with two very crude approximations to I, each based on the area of a single rectangle: $I \approx (b-a)f(b)$ and $I \approx (b-a)f(a)$.

Our first serious approximation to I is simply the average of the two single-rectangle approximations just given. This is known as the **trapezium rule**:

$$\int_a^b f(x)\,dx \approx \tfrac{1}{2}(b - a)(f(a) + f(b)).$$

The trapezium rule is illustrated in Figure 19.7. The rule approximates I by T, the area of a four-sided figure with two parallel sides. Such a figure is known in geometry as a **trapezium**.

Figure 19.7 shows that the trapezium rule approximates I by $\int_a^b L(x)\,dx$, where L is the unique linear function which takes the same value as f when $x = a$ and when $x = b$. This way of looking at the trapezium rule suggests a more sophisticated alternative. Just as there is exactly one linear function whose graph meets that of f at two given points, there is exactly one quadratic function whose graph meets that of f at three given points. **Simpson's rule** approximates I by $\int_a^b Q(x)\,dx$, where Q is the quadratic function with the property that $Q(x) = f(x)$ at $x = a$, $x = b$ and $x = \tfrac{1}{2}(a + b)$. The rule is illustrated in Figure 19.8.

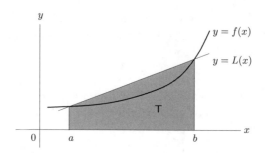

Figure 19.7: **The trapezium rule approximates $\int_a^b f(x)\,dx$ by the area T**

We now give a formula for Simpson's rule. Let $c = \frac{1}{2}(a+b)$. We show in the appendix to this chapter that

$$\int_a^b Q(x)\,dx = \tfrac{1}{6}(b-a)(f(a) + 4f(c) + f(b)). \qquad (19.5)$$

Simpson's rule then consists of approximating I by the right-hand side of (19.5). Summarising, we have

Simpson's rule

$$\int_a^b f(x)\,dx \approx \tfrac{1}{6}(b-a)(f(a) + 4f(c) + f(b)), \quad \text{where } c = \tfrac{1}{2}(a+b).$$

Simpson's rule is not the only sensible way of approximating I, given $f(a)$, $f(b)$ and $f(c)$. An obvious alternative is to approximate each of $\int_a^c f(x)\,dx$ and $\int_c^b f(x)\,dx$ by the trapezium rule, and add. This gives

$$I \approx \tfrac{1}{4}(b-a)(f(a) + 2f(c) + f(b)),$$

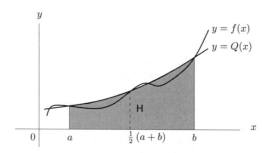

Figure 19.8: **Simpson's rule approximates $\int_a^b f(x)\,dx$ by the area H**

which is clearly different from Simpson's rule. In fact, mathematical analysis and computational experience suggest that for most functions Simpson's rule is a more accurate approximation than this double-trapezium rule.[3] So from now on we concentrate on Simpson's rule and its variants.

A more complicated but typically more accurate version of Simpson's rule works as follows. Letting $c = \frac{1}{2}(a + b)$ as above, we approximate each of $\int_a^c f(x)\,dx$ and $\int_c^b f(x)\,dx$ by Simpson's rule, and add. This gives us the approximation

$$I \approx \tfrac{1}{6}(c - a)(f(a) + 4f(p) + f(c)) + \tfrac{1}{6}(b - c)(f(c) + 4f(q) + f(b)),$$

where $p = \frac{1}{2}(a + c)$ and $q = \frac{1}{2}(c + b)$. Simplifying the right-hand side, and using a more rational notation, we have

$$\int_a^b f(x)\,dx \approx \frac{h}{3}(y_0 + 4y_1 + 2y_2 + 4y_3 + y_4)$$

$$\text{where } h = \tfrac{1}{4}(b - a) \text{ and } y_k = a + kh \text{ for } k = 0, 1, \ldots, 4.$$

This is known as **Simpson's rule with five ordinates**.[4]

A still more elaborate approximation is obtained by splitting the interval $[a, b]$ into three (rather than two) subintervals of equal length and applying the original (3-ordinate) Simpson's rule to each subinterval. This gives us **Simpson's rule with seven ordinates**:

$$\int_a^b f(x)\,dx \approx \frac{h}{3}(y_0 + 4y_1 + 2y_2 + 4y_3 + 2y_4 + 4y_5 + y_6)$$

$$\text{where } h = \tfrac{1}{6}(b - a) \text{ and } y_k = a + kh \text{ for } k = 0, 1, \ldots, 6.$$

Similarly, one can formulate a Simpson-type rule for 9, 11 or any larger odd number of ordinates.

Example We use the rules described above to approximate

$$\int_0^1 \frac{4}{1 + x^2}\,dx.$$

We call the definite integral I and the integrand $f(x)$. According to the trapezium rule, $I \approx \frac{1}{2}(f(0) + f(1)) = 2(1 + \frac{1}{2})$. Thus $I \approx 3$.

---

[3]In the second half of the appendix to this chapter we give a reason why Simpson's rule works well for many functions.

[4]The **ordinate** of a point in the xy–plane is its y–coordinate (the x–coordinate is sometimes called the **abscissa**, pronounced with a silent c as in 'scissors'). Simpson's rule with five ordinates is so called because it uses the ordinates of five points on the graph of the integrand. Similarly, the original Simpson's rule is often referred to as Simpson's rule with three ordinates.

According to Simpson's rule with 3 ordinates,

$$I \approx \tfrac{1}{6}(f(0) + 4f(\tfrac{1}{2}) + f(1)) = \tfrac{2}{3}(1 + \tfrac{16}{5} + \tfrac{1}{2}) = 1 + \tfrac{32}{15}.$$

Thus $I \approx 3.133$.

According to Simpson's rule with 5 ordinates,

$$I \approx \tfrac{1}{12}(f(0) + 4f(\tfrac{1}{4}) + 2f(\tfrac{1}{2}) + 4f(\tfrac{3}{4}) + f(1)) = \tfrac{1}{3}(1 + \tfrac{64}{17} + \tfrac{8}{5} + \tfrac{64}{25} + \tfrac{1}{2}),$$

so $I \approx 3.14157$. We leave it to you to show that according to Simpson's rule with 7 ordinates, $I \approx 3.14159$.

All in all, we can be pretty sure that $I \approx 3.1416$. You may recall from school that π, the ratio of the circumference of a circle to its diameter, is 3.1415927 to 7 decimal places. This is no coincidence: we shall show in the next chapter that the integral I of this example is exactly π. Thus this example demonstrates the accuracy of Simpson's rule.

Lorenz curve and Gini coefficient

As we remarked at the beginning of this section, numerical methods such as Simpson's rule are helpful when one is working with curves of unknown functional form, obtained for example by plotting data. As an example of such a curve, we consider the **Lorenz curve** for the personal distribution of incomes. This curve tells us the proportion of total income received by the poorest $p\%$ of persons,[5] for all p from 0 to 100. Such a curve is illustrated in Figure 19.9.

Figure 19.9 illustrates five general properties of Lorenz curves. The curve is upward-sloping (since the poorest 30% receive more income than the poorest 20%). It passes through the origin, since the aggregate income of zero persons is zero, and the point $(100, 100)$, since all the people receive all the income. Apart from its end-points, the curve lies below the 45° line: the poorest 30% of people receive less than 30% of total income simply because they are the *poorest* 30%.

Finally, Lorenz curves are convex. The reason for this is as follows. Let P and Q be any two points on the Lorenz curve. Suppose we draw a box with P and Q at opposite corners, and scale the sides of the box from 0 to 100: then that part of the original Lorenz curve between P and Q becomes the Lorenz curve for a particular section of the population. Because Lorenz curves, apart from their endpoints, lie below the 45° line, the part of the original Lorenz curve which is strictly between P and Q must lie below the line PQ. Since this is true for any points P and Q on the Lorenz curve, the curve is convex.

---

[5]We use 'poor' to mean 'low-income', though this is a slight abuse of language, since the words 'rich' and 'poor' should really refer to wealth rather than income. Lorenz curves can in fact be drawn not only for income but also for wealth and indeed for non-monetary quantities; for example one could draw a Lorenz curve to depict the proportion of total employment in a large industry accounted for by the smallest 20%, 40% or whatever of firms.

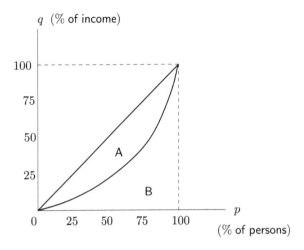

Figure 19.9: **A Lorenz curve for income**

The Lorenz curve for income gives us a useful qualitative picture of how unequally distributed income is. Suppose that everybody had approximately the same income. Then the poorest 30% of persons would receive only a little less than 30% of total income, the poorest 60% of persons would receive nearly 60% of total income and so on. In such a case, the Lorenz curve is close to the 45° line. Conversely, if only a tiny proportion of the population received almost all the income, the Lorenz curve would be _|-shaped. Thus, the more unequal the distribution of income, the more bowed-out is the Lorenz curve.

These ideas lead us to a quantitative measure of inequality, known as the **Gini coefficient**, defined as the ratio

$$G = \frac{\text{area between Lorenz curve and diagonal}}{\text{total area under diagonal}}.$$

This must lie between 0 (complete equality) and 1 (winner takes all).[6]

Given the areas A and B in Figure 19.9, the Gini coefficient is $A/(A+B)$. Since $A + B = \frac{1}{2} \times 100 \times 100 = 5000$,

$$G = 1 - \frac{B}{5000}.$$

Approximating the Gini coefficient

To calculate G from the Lorenz curve, it suffices to compute B using some method of numerical integration. The one we use is Simpson's rule with 5

---

[6]The Gini coefficient may be defined for any statistical distribution for which a Lorenz curve is defined. In the case, mentioned in the preceding footnote, of a Lorenz curve for the distribution of employment across firms in an industry, the Gini coefficient measures the extent to which employment in the industry is concentrated in the largest firms.

ordinates. Let q_1, q_2 and q_3 denote the percentage of total income received by the poorest 25%, 50% and 75% of the population respectively; thus q_1, q_2, q_3 are the vertical co-ordinates of the points on the Lorenz curve whose horizontal co-ordinates are $25, 50, 75$. By Simpson's rule with 5 ordinates,

$$B \approx \frac{25}{3}(0 + 4q_1 + 2q_2 + 4q_3 + 100),$$

whence

$$G = 1 - \frac{B}{5000} \approx 1 - \frac{1}{300}(2q_1 + q_2 + 2q_3 + 50).$$

Summarising, we have the following approximation to the Gini coefficient:

$$G \approx \frac{1}{300}(250 - 2q_1 - q_2 - 2q_3), \tag{19.6}$$

where q_1, q_2 and q_3 are the percentages of total income received by the poorest 25%, 50% and 75% of the population.

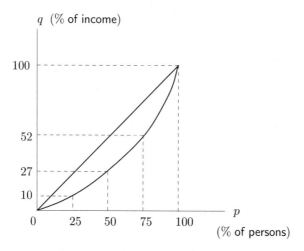

Figure 19.10: **Using Simpson's rule with 5 ordinates to approximate the Gini coefficient**

To see how (19.6) may be applied, consider the Lorenz curve of Figure 19.10. We read from the diagram that $q_1 = 10$, $q_2 = 27$ and $q_3 = 52$. By (19.6),

$$G \approx (250 - 20 - 27 - 104)/300 = 0.33.$$

One general point worth noticing about the approximation (19.6) is that the right-hand side cannot exceed $5/6$ whereas the left-hand side can in principle be anything from 0 to 1. Thus, when the true Gini coefficient is close to 1, (19.6) is a poor approximation to it. But in most examples in applied economics G is sufficiently far below 1 for (19.6) to give a good approximation.

Exercises

19.4.1 Use the trapezium rule with 3 ordinates (the double-trapezium rule) to find an approximation to

$$\int_1^{49} \frac{1}{1 + \sqrt{x}} \, dx.$$

19.4.2 Use Simpson's rule with 5 ordinates to find an approximation to

$$\int_0^1 \frac{1}{1 + x^3} \, dx.$$

19.4.3 Evaluate $\int_1^2 (1/x) \, dx$. Find also the approximations to this integral by using

(a) the trapezium rule with 3 ordinates;

(b) Simpson's rule with 3 ordinates.

Compare the accuracy of the two approximations.

19.4.4 Write down the value of $\int_0^1 x^n \, dx$, where $n \neq -1$. Find also the approximation to the integral obtained by applying Simpson's rule with 3 ordinates. Show that Simpson's rule gives the exact result when n is 0, 1, 2 and 3. Find the percentage error in the cases $n = 4$ and $n = 5$.

19.4.5 The following table gives points on a Lorenz curve for the distribution of employment in a large industry.

Percentage of firms	0	25	50	75	100
Percentage of employment	0	13	32	56	100

Use Simpson's rule to find an approximation to the area under the Lorenz curve. Hence find an approximate value for the Gini coefficient.

19.4.6 Suppose the area under a Lorenz curve is found approximately by using Simpson's rule with 7 instead of 5 ordinates. Find the resulting approximation for the Gini coefficient. What is the maximum value the approximation can take? Comment.

Problems on Chapter 19

19–1. Verify that
$$\frac{1}{x-2} + \frac{2}{x+3} = \frac{3x-1}{(x-2)(x+3)}.$$

Hence find
$$\int_3^4 \frac{3x-1}{x^2+x-6}\,dx.$$

What happens if instead the limits are (i) -5 and -4, (ii) -1 and 1, (iii) 1 and 4, (iv) -4 and 0, (v) -4 and 3?

19–2. Suppose the inverse demand function for a good is $p = f(q)$, where p denotes price and q denotes quantity. Suppose the graph meets the p–axis. If a consumer demands an amount q_0 of the good, the **gross consumer's surplus** is defined to be the area in the qp–plane bounded by the axes, the inverse demand curve and the vertical line $q = q_0$. Write down an expression for this as a definite integral.

The gross consumer's surplus provides a measure of the total benefit the consumer receives from buying amount q_0 of the good. In contrast, the **net consumer's surplus** is defined as the gross consumer's surplus *less* the cost of buying amount q_0. Depict this as an area in the qp–plane and write down an expression for it involving an integral.

Find the gross consumer's surplus and the net consumer's surplus in the case where $f(q) = 30 - q^2$.

19–3. Suppose the rate of flow of a continuous profit stream is $g(t)$ at each time $t \geq 0$; suppose the continuous rate of interest is the constant r. Let $V(T)$ be the present value at time 0 of the profit stream up to time T.

(i) Obtain from first principles an expression for $V(T)$.

(ii) Use the fundamental theorem of calculus to find $V'(T)$.

(iii) In the special case where $g(t) = 60/(1 + \sqrt{t})$ and $r = 0.05$, use Simpson's rule to find an approximate value for $V(12)$.

(iv) Under the assumptions of (iii), use your answers to (ii) and (iii) to find an approximate value for $V(12.5)$.

19–4. Suppose the continuous interest rate at time t is $r(t)$, which we allow to depend continuously on t.

(i) Let £P be invested at time 0, and let the asset be held for T years with all interest reinvested; let the value of the investment after t years ($0 \leq t \leq T$) be £$A(t)$. Explain why the following propositions are true:

(a) if $0 < t < T$ and Δt is a small positive number, then

$$A(t + \Delta t) \approx (1 + r(t)\Delta t)A(t).$$

(b) if $0 < t < T$ then $\dfrac{d}{dt} \ln A(t) = r(t)$.

Hence show that $A(T) = P \exp \displaystyle\int_0^T r(t)\, dt.$

(ii) Show that the the present value at time 0 of the income stream $\{f(t) : 0 \le t \le T\}$ is

$$\int_0^T e^{-R(t)} f(t)\, dt,$$

where $R(t) = \displaystyle\int_0^t r(s)\, ds.$

Appendix to Chapter 19

In this appendix we go more deeply into the theory underlying Simpson's rule. We begin this appendix by tying up a loose end from Section 19.4: we derive the equation (19.5). We then make some remarks about why Simpson's rule works as well as it does.

Quadratic functions

Let $f(x)$ be a continuous function defined when $a \leq x \leq b$, let $c = \frac{1}{2}(a+b)$ and let $Q(x)$ be the quadratic function with the property that $Q(x) = f(x)$ when x is a or b or c. We want to prove that

$$\int_a^b Q(x)\, dx = \tfrac{1}{6}(b-a)(f(a) + 4f(c) + f(b)).$$

Let $h = \frac{1}{2}(b-a)$. Since nothing important depends on where the y–axis enters the picture, we may simplify the proof by assuming that $c = 0$. Then $a = -h$, $b = h$ and Q is the quadratic function which agrees with f when $x = 0$ and when $x = \pm h$. Letting

$$Q(x) = \alpha x^2 + \beta x + \gamma,$$

we have $f(0) = Q(0) = \gamma$ and $f(h) + f(-h) = Q(h) + Q(-h) = 2(\alpha h^2 + \gamma)$. Hence

$$2\alpha h^2 = f(h) + f(-h) - 2f(0), \quad \gamma = f(0). \tag{19.7}$$

But then

$$\begin{aligned}
\int_a^b Q(x)\, dx &= \int_{-h}^h (\alpha x^2 + \beta x + \gamma)\, dx \\
&= \tfrac{2}{3}\alpha h^3 + 2\gamma h \\
&= h(\tfrac{1}{3}[f(h) + f(-h) - 2f(0)] + 2f(0)) \quad \text{by (19.7)} \\
&= \tfrac{1}{3}h(f(-h) + 4f(0) + f(h)) \\
&= \tfrac{1}{6}(b-a)(f(a) + 4f(c) + f(b)) \quad \text{as required.}
\end{aligned}$$

Cubic functions

We now give a generalisation of the result just proved. Again, let $f(x)$ be a continuous function defined when $a \leq x \leq b$. Let $c = \frac{1}{2}(a+b)$, and let S be the approximation to $\int_a^b f(x)\, dx$ given by Simpson's rule with three ordinates.

We show that $S = \int_a^b \phi(x)\,dx$ for any *cubic* function ϕ with the property that $\phi(x) = f(x)$ when x is a or b or c.

As before, we may simplify the proof by assuming that $c = 0$; then for some $h > 0$, $a = -h$, $b = h$ and

$$S = \tfrac{1}{3}h\big(f(-h) + 4f(0) + f(h)\big).$$

Since ϕ is a cubic function we may choose a constant λ and a quadratic function q such that $\phi(x) = \lambda x^3 + q(x)$ for all x. Hence

$$\int_a^b \phi(x)\,dx = \lambda \int_{-h}^h x^3\,dx + \int_{-h}^h q(x)\,dx.$$

It is easy to see that the first integral on the right-hand side is zero. Further, since Simpson's rule is exact for quadratic functions, the second integral is

$$\tfrac{1}{3}h\big(q(-h) + 4q(0) + q(h)\big).$$

But $q(x) = f(x) - \lambda x^3$ when x is 0 or $\pm h$, so

$$\int_a^b \phi(x)\,dx = \tfrac{1}{3}h\big(f(-h) + \lambda h^3 + 4f(0) + f(h) - \lambda h^3\big) = S.$$

The result just proved is interesting because it gives some insight into why Simpson's rule works as well as it does. Suppose $f(x)$ is a differentiable function defined when $a \le x \le b$, and let $c = \tfrac{1}{2}(a + b)$. The there is exactly one cubic function ϕ such that

$$\phi(a) = f(a), \quad \phi(b) = f(b), \quad \phi(c) = f(c) \ \text{ and } \ \phi'(c) = f'(c).$$

Provided $b-a$ is not too big, we would expect ϕ to be a good approximation to f in the interval $[a, b]$. Hence $\int_a^b f(x)\,dx$ will be well approximated by $\int_a^b \phi(x)\,dx$. For reasons explained above, this approximation is Simpson's rule with three ordinates.

Chapter 20

ASPECTS OF INTEGRAL CALCULUS

In this chapter, we consider some more advanced topics in integral calculus. In the first section we return to the problem of calculating integrals, and explain some techniques for doing this. Our aim is not to empower you to integrate any function you might encounter; we pointed out at the end of Section 19.2 that that is an impossible task. All we are attempting to do is to give helpful hints for explicit integration of some functions which are not directly covered by the rules of Section 19.2.

In the remainder of the chapter we extend the notion of integration, by allowing the limits or the integrand to become infinite; we also explain a technique which is sometimes useful in comparative statics.

When you have studied this chapter you will be able to:

- integrate products of functions using integration by parts;

- simplify and evaluate integrals by a change of variable;

- calculate infinite and improper integrals;

- differentiate functions expressed as integrals.

20.1 Methods of integration

Since integration is the reverse of differentiation, it is not surprising that two useful methods of integration consist of running backwards the product rule and the composite function rule of differentiation. These methods are known respectively as integration by parts and integration by substitution, and we discuss them in turn.

Integration by parts

We showed in Section 19.1 that if the function g has a continuous derivative,

$$\int_a^b g'(x)\,dx = g(b) - g(a).$$

Suppose that $g(x)$ can be expressed as a product of two functions, say $g(x) = p(x)q(x)$. Rewriting the equation above, with the $g'(x)$ on the left-hand side expanded by the product rule, we have

$$\int_a^b (p'(x)q(x) + p(x)q'(x))\,dx = p(b)q(b) - p(a)q(a).$$

Rearranging,

$$\int_a^b p'(x)q(x)\,dx = \Big[p(x)q(x) \Big]_a^b - \int_a^b p(x)q'(x)\,dx. \tag{20.1}$$

The technique known as **integration by parts** uses (20.1) as follows. Suppose the integrand $f(x)$ can be written as a product of two functions, of which one is easy to integrate and the other becomes simpler when differentiated. Denote the first function by $p'(x)$, where $p(x)$ is an easily-found primitive, and the second function by $q(x)$. Then $\int_a^b f(x)\,dx$ is equal to the left-hand side of (20.1), and is evaluated as the right-hand side.

The technique of integration by parts may be applied to indefinite as well as definite integrals. The indefinite-integral version of (20.1) is

$$\int p'(x)q(x)\,dx = p(x)q(x) - \int p(x)q'(x)\,dx \tag{20.2}$$

Example 1 Evaluate $\displaystyle\int x^3 \ln x\,dx$.

We begin by noting that an obvious primitive of x^3 is $x^4/4$, while $\ln x$ simplifies on differentiation to $1/x$. We therefore apply (20.2) with $p(x) = x^4/4$ and $q(x) = \ln x$:

$$\int x^3 \ln x\,dx = \frac{x^4}{4}\ln x - \int \frac{x^4}{4}\frac{1}{x}\,dx$$

$$= \frac{1}{4}\left(x^4 \ln x - \int x^3\,dx \right)$$

$$= \left(\frac{4\ln x - 1}{16} \right) x^4 + C,$$

where C is a constant.

The calculations used in Example 1 are easily adapted to integrate $x^\alpha \ln x$, where α is any constant other than -1. The result is

$$\int x^\alpha \ln x \, dx = \left((1+\alpha)^{-1}\ln x - (1+\alpha)^{-2}\right) x^{1+\alpha} + C.$$

In particular this applies when $\alpha = 0$: $\int \ln x \, dx = x(\ln x - 1) + C$.

Some functions can be integrated by repeated integration by parts. Our next example illustrates this.

Example 2 Evaluate $I = \displaystyle\int_0^2 x^2 e^{x/2} \, dx$.

The trick here is to integrate $e^{x/2}$ and differentiate x^2; two rounds of this procedure reduce the problem to integrating a simple exponential. We begin by applying (20.1) with $p'(x) = e^{x/2}$ and $q(x) = x^2$. Evidently we may take $p(x)$ to be $2e^{x/2}$; thus

$$I = \left[2x^2 e^{x/2} \right]_0^2 - 4J, \quad \text{where} \quad J = \int_0^2 xe^{x/2} \, dx.$$

To evaluate J we apply (20.1) again, with $p'(x) = e^{x/2}$ and $q(x) = x$:

$$J = \left[2xe^{x/2} \right]_0^2 - \int_0^2 2e^{x/2} \, dx = \left[(2x - 4)e^{x/2} \right]_0^2.$$

Hence

$$I = \left[(2x^2 - 8x + 16)e^{x/2} \right]_0^2 = 8(e - 2).$$

Integration by substitution

Having run the product rule of differentiation in reverse, we now do something similar with the composite function rule.

Let F, f and g be functions, with F a primitive for f, so that F' and f are the same function. By the composite function rule,

$$\frac{d}{dx}F(g(x)) = f(g(x))g'(x).$$

Integrating from $x = a$ to $x = b$ we have

$$F(g(b)) - F(g(a)) = \int_a^b f(g(x))g'(x) \, dx.$$

Setting $g(a) = r$ and $g(b) = s$, we may write the left-hand side of this equation as $F(s) - F(r)$, which is in turn equal to $\int_r^s f(t) \, dt$. Hence

$$\int_r^s f(t) \, dt = \int_a^b f(g(x)) \, g'(x) \, dx, \quad \text{where } r = g(a) \text{ and } s = g(b). \qquad (20.3)$$

The indefinite-integral form of (20.3) is

$$\int f(t)\,dt = \int f(g(x))\,g'(x)\,dx, \quad \text{where } t = g(x). \qquad (20.4)$$

The use of (20.3) and (20.4) in integration is known as **integration by substitution** or **integration by change of variable**.

To see how the method can be used, suppose we have a situation where the integrand can be written in the form $f(g(x))g'(x)$, and f is easy to integrate. Then we may read (20.3) or (20.4) from right to left and integrate with respect to t rather than x. In the indefinite-integral case we have to convert back to x at the end to get the answer, using the substitution $t = g(x)$. In the definite-integral case there is no need to do this, but it is important to calculate the integral using the proper limits, $r = g(a)$ and $s = g(b)$.

Example 3 Earlier in this section, we explained how to integrate $x^{\alpha} \ln x$, where $\alpha \neq -1$. We now deal with the case where $\alpha = -1$ by calculating

$$\int \frac{\ln x}{x}\,dx.$$

Since the integrand is $(\ln x)\dfrac{d}{dx}(\ln x)$, we may set $t = \ln x$, $f(t) = t$ and read (20.4) from right to left:

$$\int \frac{\ln x}{x}\,dx = \int t\,dt = \tfrac{1}{2}t^2 + C = \tfrac{1}{2}(\ln x)^2 + C,$$

where C is an arbitrary constant.

The procedure adopted in the last example can be made more automatic by the following notational trick. Having made the substitution $t = g(x)$, with the consequence that $dt/dx = g'(x)$, we write the latter equation in the form

$$dt = g'(x)dx.$$

Integration by substitution then amounts to replacing $g(x)$ by t and $g'(x)dx$ by dt.

The reason why we call this a "notational trick" is that our treatment of differential calculus has given no warrant for using dx and dt as free-standing expressions: recall our remarks on differentials in Section 14.2. The trick is best thought of as a way of remembering the rules (20.3) and (20.4), and as a help in simplifying calculations. For instance, Example 3 can be simplified as follows: setting $t = \ln x$ we have $dt = x^{-1}dx$, from which it is immediate that the integral is $\int t\,dt$.

Example 4 Evaluate $\displaystyle\int_0^X xe^{-x^2/2}\,dx$.

We make the substitution $t = \frac{1}{2}x^2$. Then $e^{-x^2/2} = e^{-t}$ and $x\,dx = dt$. Further, when $x = 0$, $t = 0$; and when $x = X$, $t = \frac{1}{2}X^2$, which we denote by T. Thus

$$\int_0^X xe^{-x^2/2}\,dx = \int_0^T e^{-t}\,dt = \left[-e^{-t}\right]_0^T = 1 - e^{-X^2/2}.$$

There is another kind of situation in which (20.3) or (20.4) can be used to evaluate integrals. Suppose we wish to calculate $\int f(x)\,dx$, where $f(x)$ involves some complication such as a square root of a function of x. Then a suitable substitution of the form $x = g(t)$ may enable us to simplify the integrand. Writing (20.4) with the variables x and t interchanged,

$$\int f(x)\,dx = \int f(g(t))\,g'(t)\,dt, \quad \text{where } x = g(t).$$

The hope is that a suitable choice of the function g makes the right-hand side easier to integrate than the left: we therefore find $\int f(x)\,dx$ by reading the equation from left to right. The notational trick introduced above for automating the calculations is also helpful here: writing $x = g(t)$ we have $dx = g'(t)dt$.

Similar arguments apply to definite integrals. As before, we need to be careful to get the limits of integration right; if the required integral is $\int_a^b f(x)\,dx$, then integration with respect to t is from u to v, where $g(u) = a$ and $g(v) = b$. With indefinite integrals, we do not need to bother about limits of integration but we do have the final task of converting the answer into an expression involving x rather than t.

Example 5 Evaluate $\displaystyle\int_1^2 x\sqrt{x-1}\,dx$.

Letting $t = x - 1$, we have $x = t + 1$, whence $dx = dt$. Therefore

$$x\sqrt{x-1}\,dx = (t+1)\sqrt{t}\,dt = \left(t^{3/2} + t^{1/2}\right)\,dt.$$

Further, $t = 0$ when $x = 1$ and $t = 1$ when $x = 2$. Thus

$$\int_1^2 x\sqrt{x-1}\,dx = \int_0^1 \left(t^{3/2} + t^{1/2}\right)\,dt = \left[\tfrac{2}{5}t^{5/2} + \tfrac{2}{3}t^{3/2}\right]_0^1 = \tfrac{16}{15}.$$

A general feature of integration by change of variable there is often some choice of substitution. For instance, Example 5 can also be solved by setting $u = \sqrt{x-1}$: see Exercise 20.1.3.

Our final example brings together most of the techniques of this section.

Example 6 Evaluate $I = \int \ln(1 + \sqrt{x})\, dx$.

Here a convenient substitution is $t = 1 + \sqrt{x}$. Then $x = (t-1)^2$ and $dx = 2(t-1)dt$. Hence $I = \int 2(t-1)\ln t\, dt$, and we integrate by parts:

$$I = (t-1)^2 \ln t - J, \quad \text{where } J = \int (t-1)^2 t^{-1}\, dt.$$

J is easily calculated using the methods of Section 19.2:

$$J = \int (t - 2 + t^{-1})\, dt = \tfrac{1}{2}t^2 - 2t + \ln t + C,$$

where C is a constant. Letting $A = 2 - C$, we have

$$I = [(t-1)^2 - 1]\ln t - \tfrac{1}{2}(t-2)^2 + A = (x-1)\ln(1+\sqrt{x}) - \tfrac{1}{2}(\sqrt{x}-1)^2 + A,$$

where A is an arbitrary constant.

Exercises

20.1.1 Use integration by parts to find:

$$\text{(a) } \int x\sqrt{x+1}\, dx, \quad \text{(b) } \int_0^3 (x+3)(x+2)^{-4}\, dx.$$

20.1.2 (a) If a is a constant, then $\dfrac{d}{dx}(x+a) = 1$. Use this fact and integration by parts to find

$$\int \ln(x+a)\, dx.$$

(b) Let a and b be constants. Using your answer to (a) and the fact that $x + b = (x + a) + (b - a)$, find

$$\int (x+b)\ln(x+a)\, dx.$$

20.1.3 (a) Evaluate the indefinite integral of Exercise 20.1.1, part (a), by making the substitution $t = \sqrt{x+1}$.

(b) Evaluate the definite integral $\displaystyle\int_1^2 x\sqrt{x-1}\, dx$ of Example 5 by making the substitution $u = \sqrt{x-1}$.

20.1.4 Find the following integrals by making a suitable substitution:

$$\text{(a) } \int x(x^2+1)^{10}\, dx, \quad \text{(b) } \int x^3 \exp(x^4+1)\, dx, \quad \text{(c) } \int \frac{6x}{x^2+1}\, dx.$$

20.1.5 Let a and b be constants such that $0 < a < b$. By making a suitable substitution, find

$$\int_a^b x^{-1/3} \exp(-x^{2/3})\, dx.$$

20.1.6 By making a suitable substitution, find

$$\int \frac{e^x}{1 + e^x}\, dx.$$

Hence find $\displaystyle\int_0^2 (1 + e^x)^{-1}\, dx$ and $\displaystyle\int_0^2 (1 + e^{-x})^{-1}\, dx$.

20.2   Infinite integrals

We introduce this topic with an example. Using the rules of Section 19.2, it is easy to show that

$$\int_1^X \frac{1}{x^2}\, dx = 1 - \frac{1}{X}$$

for any positive number X. As $X \to \infty$, $1/X \to 0$. Hence

$$\lim_{X \to \infty} \int_1^X \frac{1}{x^2}\, dx = 1,$$

which we write more concisely as

$$\int_1^\infty \frac{1}{x^2}\, dx = 1. \tag{20.5}$$

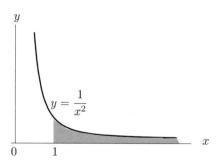

Figure 20.1: **The area of the shaded region is 1**

The left-hand side of (20.5) is called an **infinite integral**: the adjective "infinite" refers not to the value of the integral — which as we have seen is the finite number 1 — but to the fact that integration is taking place over an infinite interval. In geometrical terms, what we are talking about here is the shaded area in Figure 20.1. The crucial point to notice is that the shaded region extends infinitely far to the right, but tapers sufficiently sharply for its area to be finite.

We generalise as follows. Suppose we have a continuous function $f(x)$ defined for all $x \geq a$, and suppose the integral $\int_a^X f(x)\,dx$ approaches a finite limit L as $X \to \infty$; then we write

$$\int_a^\infty f(x)\,dx = L.$$

In this case we say that the infinite integral **exists** or **converges**.

By contrast, if $\int_a^X f(x)\,dx$ does not approaches a finite limit as $X \to \infty$, we say that the infinite integral **does not exist** or **diverges**.

Discounting infinite streams

Infinite integrals occur in economics when we calculate present values of income streams that go on for ever.[1] Suppose the (instantaneous) interest rate is the constant r, and recall from Section 19.3 that the present value at time 0 of the income stream $\{f(t) : 0 \leq t \leq T\}$ is

$$\int_0^T e^{-rt} f(t)\,dt.$$

Now suppose the income stream $f(t)$ flows for all $t \geq 0$, and that the integral above tends to a limit as $T \to \infty$. The limit may then be written

$$\int_0^\infty e^{-rt} f(t)\,dt.$$

An important special case is where we have a constant income stream, so that $f(t) = Y$ for all t, where Y is a constant. Then the present value of the entire stream is

$$\int_0^\infty e^{-rt} Y\,dt = \lim_{T \to \infty} \left[-\frac{Y}{r} e^{-rt} \right]_0^T = \frac{Y}{r} \lim_{T \to \infty} \left(1 - e^{-rT} \right) = \frac{Y}{r}.$$

Notice that this is identical to the formula we derived in Section 5.3 for the present value of a perpetuity in discrete time when income is paid at the end of each year.

---

[1] As an example, think of the "perpetuities" discussed in Section 5.3. Also, the fiction of an infinite stream is often a helpful approximation device for analysing income streams that go on for a long time.

Two-sided infinite integrals

If $f(x)$ is a continuous function defined for all $x \leq a$, and if the definite integral $\int_Y^a f(x)\,dx$ approaches a finite limit as $Y \to -\infty$, we denote the limit by

$$\int_{-\infty}^a f(x)\,dx.$$

If the integrals $\int_{-\infty}^a f(x)\,dx$ and $\int_a^\infty f(x)\,dx$ both exist, we denote their sum by

$$\int_{-\infty}^\infty f(x)\,dx.$$

Example We showed in Example 4 of Section 20.1 that

$$\int_0^X xe^{-x^2/2}\,dx = 1 - e^{-X^2/2}.$$

A similar argument, also using the substitution $t = \frac{1}{2}x^2$, shows that

$$\int_{-Y}^0 xe^{-x^2/2}\,dx = -\left[1 - e^{-Y^2/2}\right].$$

Letting $X \to \infty$ and $Y \to \infty$, we have

$$\int_0^\infty xe^{-x^2/2}\,dx = 1, \qquad \int_{-\infty}^0 xe^{-x^2/2}\,dx = -1$$

and hence

$$\int_{-\infty}^\infty xe^{-x^2/2}\,dx = 1 + (-1) = 0.$$

Improper integrals

Associated with the notion of an infinite integral is that of an **improper integral**, for example

$$I = \int_0^1 x^{-1/2}\,dx.$$

What is "improper" about this integral is that the integrand is not defined at one of the limits of integration. In this case the lower limit causes the problem, since $x^{-1/2} \to \infty$ as $x \to 0$.

Nevertheless, we can define and evaluate I as

$$I = \lim_{\delta \downarrow 0} \int_\delta^1 x^{-1/2}\,dx,$$

where $\downarrow$ means "tends from above" as in Section 8.4. In fact

$$I = \lim_{\delta \downarrow 0} \left[2\sqrt{x}\right]_\delta^1 = \lim_{\delta \downarrow 0}(2 - 2\sqrt{\delta}) = 2.$$

More generally, suppose the function $f(x)$ is defined and continuous for $a < x \le b$, but is not defined for $x = a$. If the integral

$$\int_{a+\delta}^{b} f(x)\,dx$$

tends to a finite limit I as $\delta \downarrow 0$, then we say that the integral $\int_a^b f(x)\,dx$ exists and has the value I. Otherwise, we say that the integral $\int_a^b f(x)\,dx$ diverges.

Similar definitions apply to cases where the integrand behaves badly at the upper limit of integration.

Exercises

20.2.1   (a) Find $\int_1^X x^{-3/2}\,dx$. Hence find $\int_1^{\infty} x^{-3/2}\,dx$.

(b) Show that $\int_1^{\infty} x^{-1}\,dx$ diverges.

(c) Try to formulate a general result concerning the existence or otherwise of $\int_1^{\infty} x^{-\alpha}\,dx$, where α is a constant.

20.2.2   (a) Find $\int_{\delta}^1 x^{-1/3}\,dx$, where $\delta > 0$. Hence find $\int_0^1 x^{-1/3}\,dx$.

(b) Show that $\int_0^1 x^{-1}\,dx$ diverges.

(c) Try to formulate a general result concerning the existence or otherwise of $\int_0^1 x^{-\alpha}\,dx$, where α is a constant.

20.2.3 Show that $\int_0^{\infty} e^{-cx}\,dx$ exists for $c > 0$. If $c > 0$ and the area bounded by the curve $y = Ae^{-cx}$, the x-axis and the y-axis is 1, what is A?

20.2.4 An integral which is both infinite and improper is

$$I = \int_0^{\infty} x^{-1/3} \exp(-x^{2/3})\,dx.$$

This is defined as follows. Given positive numbers δ, X such that $\delta < 1 < X$, let $J(\delta)$ and $K(X)$ be the integrals of $x^{-1/3}\exp(-x^{2/3})$ over the intervals $[\delta, 1]$ and $[1, X]$ respectively. If $\lim_{\delta \to 0} J(\delta)$ and $\lim_{X \to \infty} K(X)$ both exist, we define I to be their sum.

Using your answer to Exercise 20.1.5, find $J(\delta)$ and $K(X)$. Hence show that I exists, and evaluate it.

20.3   Differentiation under the integral sign

Suppose $f(x, y)$ is a function of two variables and a, b are constants. We may then define the function of one variable

$$I(y) = \int_a^b f(x, y)\, dx.$$

If the function f is differentiable,[2] the derivative $I'(y)$ exists and is given by

$$I'(y) = \int_a^b \frac{\partial f}{\partial y}\, dx.$$

To summarise:

$$\frac{d}{dy}\left(\int_a^b f(x, y)\, dx\right) = \int_a^b \frac{\partial}{\partial y} f(x, y)\, dx. \tag{20.6}$$

Without going into a detailed proof of (20.6), we can see how it arises as an extension of the fact that the derivative of a sum is the sum of the derivatives. Using the subscript notation of Section 14.1, we denote $\partial f(x, y)/\partial y$ by $f_2(x, y)$. Let n be a large positive integer. Suppose we split the interval $[a, b]$ into n subintervals of equal length, say $[x_0, x_1], [x_1, x_2], \ldots, [x_{n-1}, x_n]$ where $x_0 = a$ and $x_n = b$. Then $I(y)$ is approximately equal to

$$\frac{b-a}{n} \sum_{i=1}^n f(x_i, y),$$

and the right-hand side of (20.6) is approximately equal to

$$\frac{b-a}{n} \sum_{i=1}^n f_2(x_i, y).$$

The second sum is the derivative with respect to y of the first; the limiting case of this result as $n \to \infty$ is (20.6).

   Equation (20.6) is useful because one sometimes wishes to differentiate an expression which is defined as a definite integral. Finding a derivative in this way is known as **differentiation under the integral sign**.

   As an example of this, we derive a formula for the derivative of the present value of an income stream with respect to the rate of interest. As we noted in Section 19.3, the discounted value at time 0 of the income stream $\{g(t) : 0 \le t \le T\}$, when the rate of interest is held constant at r, is

$$P = \int_0^T e^{-rt} g(t)\, dt.$$

---

[2]Differentiability of functions of two variable was defined in Section 14.2.

Obviously P depends on r, and dP/dr may be found by differentiation under the integral sign:

$$\frac{dP}{dr} = \int_0^T \frac{\partial}{\partial r}\left(e^{-rt}g(t)\right) dt = \int_0^T g(t)\frac{\partial}{\partial r}\left(e^{-rt}\right) dt = -\int_0^T e^{-rt}\, t\, g(t)\, dt.$$

$$(20.7)$$

Extension to infinite integrals

Under appropriate assumptions about the function f, a formula similar to (20.6) holds for infinite integrals. For example, if $g(t)$ does not increase too fast as $t \to \infty$, then (20.7) remains true when T is replaced by ∞. However, the conditions required for such formulae to hold are quite strong: differentiation under the integral sign of infinite or improper integrals is best handled with discretion.

The general case

In (20.6) we assume that the limits of integration a and b are constants. We now build up to a generalisation of (20.6) which is applicable when a and b are allowed to depend on y.

We begin by noting that the definite integral $\int_a^b f(x, y)\, dx$ depends on the three quantities a, b and y. We may therefore define the function of three variables

$$J(a, b, y) = \int_a^b f(x, y)\, dx.$$

We already have expressions for two of the three partial derivatives of J: $\partial J/\partial b = f(b, y)$ by the fundamental theorem of calculus, and

$$\frac{\partial J}{\partial y} = \int_a^b \frac{\partial f}{\partial y}\, dx$$

by differentiation under the integral sign. To find the remaining partial derivative, we use the fact that

$$J(a, b, y) = -\int_b^a f(x, y)\, dx.$$

Hence $\partial J/\partial a = -f(a, y)$ by the fundamental theorem of calculus. Summarising,

$$\frac{\partial J}{\partial a} = -f(a, y), \quad \frac{\partial J}{\partial b} = f(b, y), \quad \frac{\partial J}{\partial y} = \int_a^b \frac{\partial f}{\partial y}\, dx.$$

It is now straightforward to extend differentiation under the integral sign to the case where the limits of integration depend on the variable y. Let $I(y)$

be defined as above, except that a and b now depend on y, say $a = p(y)$ and $b = q(y)$. Then

$$I(y) = J(p(y), q(y), y).$$

By the rules of total differentiation introduced in Chapter 14,

$$I'(y) = \frac{\partial J}{\partial a} p'(y) + \frac{\partial J}{\partial b} q'(y) + \frac{\partial J}{\partial y}.$$

Using the expressions for the partial derivatives of J which we obtained above, we have the following extension of (20.6), known as **Leibniz's formula**:

$$\frac{d}{dy} \left(\int_{p(y)}^{q(y)} f(x, y) \, dx \right) = f(q(y), y) q'(y) - f(p(y), y) p'(y) + \int_{p(y)}^{q(y)} \frac{\partial}{\partial y} f(x, y) \, dx.$$

$$(20.8)$$

Application to consumer demand

Suppose that persons in an economy differ in their taste for Product X, and that t indexes taste: t varies from 0 to 1, with higher–t persons being more disposed to purchase the product.

For each person the demand for Product X depends on the person's taste parameter t, and the price p of the product, in the following way. There is some price $P(t)$, depending on t, such that the person buys no units of the product if $p > P(t)$: $P(t)$ is known as the **reservation price** of X for somebody of taste t. On the other hand, if $p \leq P(t)$ a person with taste t will purchase $h(t, p)$ units of product X, where h is a smooth function such that

$$h(t, P(t)) > 0. \qquad (20.9)$$

Since t is a positive indicator of taste for X, we assume that $P(t)$ is an increasing function of t, and that $h(t, p)$ is increasing in t for given p. We also make the usual law-of-demand assumption that $h(t, p)$ is a decreasing function of p for given t. Indeed, to simplify the mathematics, we make the slightly stronger assumptions that $P'(t) > 0$, $\partial h / \partial t > 0$ and $\partial h / \partial p < 0$ for all t and p.

These assumptions about demand for the product are illustrated in Figure 20.2, which depicts the demand curves for Product X for two persons with taste parameters a, b, with $a < b$. The fact that the quantities $x_a = h(a, P(a))$ and $x_b = h(b, P(b))$ are strictly positive, and the resulting discontinuities in the demand curves,[3] reflect the inequality (20.9).

The underlying economic assumption here is that when the price of X is above a person's reservation price, that person will switch to a rival product;

---

[3]These discontinuities do not contradict the assumption that h is a smooth function; rather, they come from the fact that the smooth function h ceases to describe demand for X when $p > P(t)$.

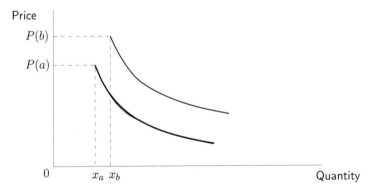

Figure 20.2: **Demand curves for Product X**

on the other hand, the person's demand for the product is not negligible at a price equal to or just below the reservation price. An example (to which models like this have been applied using real data) is the domestic use of natural gas: when the price is sufficiently high, a household will not use this fuel at all but switch to electricity for cooking, heating and so on; however, a household which uses gas at all will do so in non-negligible quantities.

We now consider the distribution of tastes in the population. Let there be N persons in the population, where N is sufficiently large and tastes sufficiently diffuse for t to be treated as a continuous variable. Thus there is a continuous function $f(t)$ with the following property: for any a, b such that $0 < a < b < 1$, the number of people with taste-parameter t between a and b is $\int_a^b f(t)dt$. The function f is illustrated in Figure 20.3 and has the following properties:

(i) $\displaystyle\int_0^1 f(t)\, dt = N.$

(ii) If ε is a small positive number, the number of persons with taste-parameter between t and $t + \varepsilon$ is approximately $\varepsilon f(t)$.

We now find an expression for the total demand for Product X. Since $P(t)$ is a monotonic increasing function, it has an inverse function, which we denote by $T(p)$. Thus

$$p = P(t) \quad \text{if and only if} \quad t = T(p),$$

which in turn implies that

$$p \leq P(t) \quad \text{if and only if} \quad t \leq T(p).$$

What this means in words is that for any given price p, persons with taste parameter $t < T(p)$ will not buy Product X, while those with taste parameter $t \geq T(p)$ will buy positive quantities of Product X.

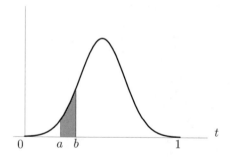

Figure 20.3: **The graph of function f**

If $t \geq T(p)$ and s is a small positive number, the (approximately) $sf(t)$ persons with taste-parameter between t and $t + s$ will each buy approximately $h(t, p)$ units of Product X. Thus, again approximately, the total demand for product X from persons with tastes in this range is $sf(t)h(t, p)$. Summing up and taking limits, we see that the total quantity of Product X that is demanded when the price is p is

$$x = \int_{T(p)}^{1} f(t)h(t, p) \, dt.$$

We can investigate what happens when the price of X changes by calculating dx/dp. By Leibniz's formula (20.8),

$$\frac{dx}{dp} = -f(T(p)) \, h(T(p), p) \, T'(p) + \int_{T(p)}^{1} f(t) \frac{\partial}{\partial p} h(t, p) \, dt. \qquad (20.10)$$

Let $H(p) = f(T(p)) \, h(T(p), p)$; we denote the integral on the right hand side of (20.10) by $K(p)$. Then $H(p) > 0$ by (20.9), $K(p) < 0$ since $\partial h / \partial p < 0$ and $dx/dp = -H(p)T'(p) + K(p)$ by (20.9). Also, T is the inverse function of the function P, whose derivative is always positive, so $T'(p) > 0$.

To summarise, (20.10) expresses dx/dp as the sum of two negative terms, the first of which measures the tendency of consumers to leave the market for X when its price goes up, and the second the tendency of those still in the market to buy less of the product. The relative strength of these effects depends, among other things, on the absolute values of $T'(p)$ and $\partial h / \partial p$.

Exercises

20.3.1 Verify the formula (20.7) for the derivative of the present value of an income stream with respect to the rate of interest in the case of a constant income stream $g(t) = Y$. Show that in this case the formula remains true when T is replaced by ∞.

20.3.2 Differentiate the following expressions with respect to y:

$$\text{(a)} \int_1^5 \frac{f(x)}{x+y}\,dx \qquad \text{(b)} \int_1^{e^y} f(xy)\,dx$$

$$\text{(c)} \int_y^1 f(x-y)\,dx \qquad \text{(d)} \int_{1-y}^1 f(x)\,dx$$

Comment on the relation between your answers to (c) and (d).

Problems on Chapter 20

20–1. By making appropriate substitutions, evaluate the following integrals:

$$\text{(i)} \int_0^1 x\sqrt{1-x^2}\,dx, \quad \text{(ii)} \int_0^1 x\sqrt{1-x}\,dx, \quad \text{(iii)} \int_0^1 x^2\sqrt{1-x}\,dx.$$

20–2. For any non-negative integer n, let

$$I_n = \int_0^\infty x^n e^{-x}\,dx.$$

Use integration by parts to show $I_n = nI_{n-1}$ for $n = 1, 2, \ldots$. Hence evaluate I_n.

20–3. A function f is said to be **even** if

$$f(-x) = f(x) \quad \text{for all } x \in \mathcal{R};$$

a function f is said to be **odd** if

$$f(-x) = f(x) \quad \text{for all } x \in \mathcal{R}.$$

(i) Show that if $A > 0$ and f is even,

$$\int_{-A}^A f(x)\,dx = 2\int_0^A f(x)\,dx.$$

(ii) Show that if $A > 0$ and f is odd,

$$\int_{-A}^A f(x)\,dx = 0.$$

(iii) Use result (i) and Simpson's rule to find an approximation to

$$\int_{-1}^1 e^{-x^2/2}\,dx$$

which is correct to 3 decimal places.

(iv) Use result (ii) to show that

$$\lim_{A \to \infty} \int_{-A}^{A} x e^{-x^2/2} \, dx = 0.$$

Explain why this result is a special case of that of the Example in Section 20.2.

(v) Use result (ii) to show that

$$\lim_{A \to \infty} \int_{-A}^{A} x^3 \, dx = 0.$$

Is it correct to infer that $\int_{-\infty}^{\infty} x^3 \, dx = 0$?

[Hint for (i) and (ii): split the range of integration into the two intervals $[-A, 0]$ and $[0, A]$ and make a suitable substitution on the first interval.]

20–4. A firm wishes to build a plant and must decide on its size. The larger the plant, the longer it takes to build, so we may use building time s as our measure of plant size. Time is measured as a continuous variable, and the instantaneous rate of interest is the constant r.

Suppose that building begins at time $t = 0$. While the plant is being built, the firm incurs cost c per unit time. Once the plant is built, the flow of profit at time t for a plant of size s is $f(s, t)$ ($s \le t \le T$). Here c and T are positive constants, the latter denoting the lifetime of the firm, and f is a smooth function such that $\partial f / \partial s > 0$.

Let $V(s)$ be the present value at time 0 of the profit stream from a plant of size s. Write down an expression for $V(s)$. Also find an equation which must be satisfied by the value of s that maximises $V(s)$.

Chapter 21

INTRODUCTION TO DYNAMICS

Economic dynamics is concerned with the movement of economic variables over time. This chapter is about the two main mathematical tools of economic dynamics: **differential equations** and **difference equations**. As we explained in Section 9.3, there are two ways of treating time in economics: discrete-time analysis and continuous-time analysis. Differential equations belong to continuous-time analysis, difference equations to discrete-time analysis.

We start with the continuous-time case. Suppose the economic variable y varies over time according to the rule $y = f(t)$. As we said in Section 9.3, the rate of change of y is dy/dt: if we know the function f, we can find the rate of change of y at each time t by differentiation. We can also find the higher derivatives d^2y/dt^2, d^3y/dt^3 and so on. However, we often meet the reverse situation. An economic relationship might be expressed in terms of derivatives and we wish to find the original function $y = f(t)$.

In this chapter, we restrict our attention to equations involving only the first derivative. We also give a brief introduction to the analogous difference equations.

When you have studied this chapter you will be able to:

- solve separable first-order differential equations;

- solve linear first-order differential equations;

- solve Bernoulli's equation, and apply the solution in a simple model of economic growth;

- solve linear first-order difference equations with constant coefficients.

21.1   Differential equations

An equation involving derivatives dy/dt, d^2y/dt^2, d^3y/dt^3 and so on, is called a **differential equation**.[1] If only the first derivative dy/dt is present, the differential equation is said to be of the **first order**.

The simplest cases can be solved by integration. For example, if

$$\frac{dy}{dt} = t^2$$

then

$$y = \frac{t^3}{3} + C,$$

where C is an arbitrary constant. For each value of C, we obtain a function which satisfies the differential equation; as C varies, we get all the solutions. Such a formula, giving all possible solutions to the differential equation, is called the **general solution**.

Geometrically, the solution for any particular C is a curve in the ty–plane; the general solution is the family of curves obtained by allowing C to vary. For an example of this, see Exercise 21.1.1.

Sometimes we want to find the solution curve that passes through a particular point. A statement specifying the value of y when $t = 0$ is called an **initial condition**. More generally, a condition of the form

$$y = b \quad \text{when} \quad t = a$$

is called a **boundary condition**. This will fix the constant of integration and select a single solution curve. Thus, in the above example, the initial condition

$$y = 2 \quad \text{when} \quad t = 0$$

gives $2 = 0 + C$, so $C = 2$; the chosen solution is $y = \frac{1}{3}t^3 + 2$.

The next level of complexity is this: suppose we wish to find y as a function of t, given information which relates dy/dt to t *and* y at each time t. In other words, we start with an economic model which describes the rate of change of y as a function not only of time but also of the current level of y, say

$$\frac{dy}{dt} = F(t, y), \tag{21.1}$$

where F is a function of two variables.

Finding the general solution of a differential equation of the form (21.1) means finding a formula which specifies all functions $y = f(t)$ satisfying the equation. In the example above, we saw that the general solution contained an

---

[1]Not all economic applications of differential equations are to situations where the independent variable is time. But most are, which is why in this chapter we usually denote the independent variable by t rather than, say, x.

arbitrary constant. In fact this will always be the case for well-behaved first order differential equations. As in the example, the arbitrary constant can be determined by specifying an initial or boundary condition.

All the differential equations considered in this chapter will be of the form (21.1). The presence of y on the right-hand side means that the general solution cannot be found by integration alone. It is important to be aware from the start that there is *no* general formula for solving (21.1). Our exposition therefore takes the form of introducing various techniques which are suitable for particular kinds of differential equation.

Separable equations

A **separable differential equation** is an equation of the form

$$\frac{dy}{dt} = F(t)G(y).$$

It is convenient to rearrange this as follows:

$$\frac{1}{G(y)} \frac{dy}{dt} = F(t). \tag{21.2}$$

The standard solution method for (21.2) is to find a function $g(y)$ such that $g'(y) = \dfrac{1}{G(y)}$. Then the left-hand side of (21.2) is $g'(y)\dfrac{dy}{dt}$, which is equal to $\dfrac{d}{dt}g(y)$ by the composite function rule. Then (21.2) states that

$$\frac{d}{dt}g(y) = F(t),$$

and integration with respect to t gives

$$g(y) = \int F(t)\, dt$$

One can then perform the integration and solve for y; the general solution involves a constant of integration as a result of the indefinite integral on the right-hand side.

The usual way of setting out the solution of (21.2) is to write the last equation as

$$\int \frac{1}{G(y)}\, dy = \int F(t)\, dt \tag{21.3}$$

and then perform both integrations. Since the left-hand side of (21.3) involves only y and the right-hand side only t, the solution method is known as **separating the variables**. Although two indefinite integrals appear in (21.3), only one constant of integration need appear in the solution.[2]

---

[2]We made a similar point about combining indefinite integrals in Chapter 19, in connection with Example 1 of Section 19.2.

Example 1 Solve the differential equation

$$\frac{dy}{dt} = t^3 y^2.$$

Writing the equation in the form $y^{-2}\dfrac{dy}{dt} = t^3$, we have

$$\int y^{-2}\, dy = \int t^3\, dt.$$

Hence

$$-y^{-1} = \tfrac{1}{4}t^4 + C,$$

where C is a constant of integration. Setting $A = -4C$ to simplify the algebra, we have the general solution

$$y = 4/(A - t^4),$$

where A is an arbitrary constant.

Example 2 Solve the differential equation

$$\frac{dy}{dt} = \frac{e^{2t}}{y},$$

given that $y = 2$ when $t = 0$.

Multiplying the equation by $2y$ and integrating, we have

$$\int 2y\, dy = \int 2e^{2t}\, dt.$$

Thus $y^2 = e^{2t} + C$, where C is a constant of integration. Taking square roots, we obtain the *general* solution

$$y = \pm \left(e^{2t} + C\right)^{1/2}.$$

We now bring into play the boundary condition that $y = 2$ when $t = 0$. This tells us that $C = 2^2 - e^0 = 3$ *and* that the positive square root should be taken. Thus our solution is

$$y = \left(e^{2t} + 3\right)^{1/2}.$$

Example 3 Solve the differential equation

$$\frac{dy}{dt} + ay = 0, \tag{21.4}$$

where a is a nonzero constant.

Separating the variables gives

$$\int y^{-1}\,dy = \int (-a)\,dt.$$

Integrating, we obtain $\ln y = -at + C$, where C is an arbitrary constant. Hence

$$y = e^{C-at} = e^{C}e^{-at}.$$

Setting $A = e^{C}$, we may write the general solution

$$y = Ae^{-at},$$

where A is a constant.

The method we used in Example 3 involved $\ln y$, and therefore requires y to be positive: indeed the arbitrary constant A is positive by construction since it is equal to e^{C}. However, it is easy to see that $y = -e^{-at}$ also satisfies (21.4). The truly general solution to (21.4) is $y = Ae^{-at}$, where the constant A may be any real number.

We now demonstrate that this is so. By the rule for differentiating a product,

$$\frac{d}{dt}\left(ye^{at}\right) = \left[\frac{dy}{dt} + ay\right]e^{at}.$$

Thus the term in square brackets is zero for all t if and only if ye^{at} is equal to a constant, say A. The general solution to (21.4) is therefore $y = Ae^{-at}$, where A is an arbitrary constant. For example, the differential equation

$$\frac{dy}{dt} + 5y = 0$$

has the general solution $y = Ae^{-5t}$.

An important point to notice about the solution to (21.4) is that the behaviour of y as t becomes very large depends strongly on whether a is positive or negative. If $a > 0$ then $y \to 0$ as $t \to \infty$, regardless of the value of A. If $a < 0$ then, as $t \to \infty$, $y \to \infty$ if $A > 0$, while $y \to -\infty$ if $A < 0$.

Exercises

21.1.1 Find the general solution of the differential equation

$$\frac{dy}{dt} = t^3,$$

and sketch the family of solution curves. Also find

(a) the solution which satisfies $y = 4$ when $t = 0$,

(b) the solution which satisfies $y = 0$ when $t = 4$.

21.1.2 Find the general solutions of each of the following differential equations:

$$\text{(a)}\ \frac{dy}{dt} = t^5; \quad \text{(b)}\ \frac{dy}{dt} = y^5.$$

21.1.3 Find the solution of the equation

$$\frac{dy}{dx} = 3yx$$

which satisfies $y = 2$ when $x = 0$.

21.1.4 Find the general solution of each of the following differential equations:

$$\text{(a)}\ \frac{dp}{dt} = t^2 p^2; \quad \text{(b)}\ \frac{dp}{dt} = t^2 p.$$

In each case, find the solution which satisfies $p = 3$ when $t = 0$.

21.1.5 The logistic model of population growth is governed by the differential equation

$$\frac{1}{y}\frac{dy}{dt} = a - by,$$

where a and b are positive constants and y is assumed to be positive. You are asked to find the solution of this equation which satisfies $y = y_0$ when $t = 0$, where $0 < y_0 < a/b$.

By separating the variables and using the fact that

$$\frac{1}{y(a - by)} = \frac{1}{a}\left(\frac{1}{y} + \frac{b}{a - by}\right),$$

show that the solution is

$$y = a \big/ (b + Ce^{-at}),$$

where $C = a/y_0 - b$. What happens to y as $t \to \infty$?

21.2 Linear equations with constant coefficients

In this section, we consider differential equations of the form

$$\frac{dy}{dt} + ay = b, \tag{21.5}$$

where a and b are constants such that $a \neq 0$. After investigating this equation in detail, we will consider briefly the more general case where the right-hand side is allowed to be a simple function of t.

The special case of (21.5) when $b = 0$ was solved in the last section, and we shall use that solution below. When we allow b to be any constant, (21.5) could be solved by separating the variables, and the reader is encouraged to try this. However, this is not the solution method we adopt in this section: instead, we introduce a procedure which can be generalised to the analogous difference equations (see Section 21.4) and to second-order differenctial and difference equations (see Chapter 24).

We start by trying to find some function y^P, containing no arbitrary constant, which satisfies the equation (21.4). Such a function is called a **particular solution**. As a first guess, we look for a solution of the form $y^P = c$, where c is constant. Bearing in mind that the derivative of a constant is zero, this satisfies the equation provided

$$ac = b. \tag{21.6}$$

Thus $y^P = \dfrac{b}{a}$ is a particular solution.

The next stage of the method is to subtract (21.6) from (21.5). Letting $z = y - c$, and again bearing in mind that the derivative of a constant is zero, we see that

$$\frac{dz}{dt} + az = 0. \tag{21.7}$$

We showed in Section 21.1 that the general solution of (21.5) is $z = Ae^{-at}$, where A is an arbitrary constant. Using the definition of z and (21.6), we have as our general solution of (21.5):

$$y = \frac{b}{a} + Ae^{-at}, \tag{21.8}$$

where A is an arbitrary constant.

Equation (21.7) is called the **associated homogeneous equation** of (21.5). It is obtained from (21.5) by using z instead of y as the dependent variable and replacing the right hand side by 0, and gets its name from the fact that all remaining terms are of degree one in z and dz/dt: expressions such as $\ln z$ or $(dz/dt)^2$ do not appear. The general solution for z in the associated homogeneous equation is often called the **complementary solution**. Equation (21.8) tells us that the general solution for y in the original equation is the sum of the particular solution y^P and the complementary solution z.

The following example shows how the method works in practice.

Example 1 Solve the differential equation

$$\frac{dy}{dt} + 5y = 10.$$

We look first for a particular solution of the form $y^P = c$ where c is constant. This satisfies the equation provided $5c = 10$, so $c = 2$: our particular solution is $y^P = 2$.

We now look for the complementary solution. This is the general solution of the associated homogeneous equation

$$\frac{dz}{dt} + 5z = 0,$$

which is of course (21.7) with $a = 5$. The general solution for z is $z = Ae^{-5t}$; the general solution for y is

$$y = y^P + z = 2 + Ae^{-5t},$$

where A is an arbitrary constant.

An important feature of equation (21.5), and Example 1 in particular, is that the coefficient of dy/dt is 1. If instead the coefficient of dy/dt is some non-zero constant k, the constant particular solution is found as before by putting $dy/dt = 0$. To find the complementary solution, we divide the associated homogeneous equation by k and then proceed as above. See Exercise 21.2.3 for an example.

Complicating the right-hand side

The next step is to consider a variant of (21.5) in which the constant b on the right-hand side is replaced by a function of t, say $g(t)$. The differential equation to be solved is

$$\frac{dy}{dt} + ay = g(t). \tag{21.9}$$

Suppose that we have (somehow) found a particular solution y^P: then

$$\frac{dy^P}{dt} + ay^P = g(t).$$

Subtracting this equation from (21.9), and setting $z = y - y^P$, we retrieve the homogeneous equation (21.7). Thus the general solution to (21.9) is

$$y = y^P + z,$$

where z is the familiar complementary solution.

What is *un*familiar about all of this is the procedure for finding the particular solution y^P: notice in particular that if $g(t)$ is not constant, then y^P cannot be a constant.

As we indicated at the beginning of this section, we restrict ourselves to cases where $g(t)$ takes a simple form. In such cases, the following method usually (but not always!) works: *try for a particular solution of the same general form as the right hand side*. For example, if $g(t)$ is a linear function of t, we try for a particular solution which is also a linear function of t; and if $g(t) = be^{rt}$, where b and r are constants, we try for a particular solution of the form Be^{rt} where B is another constant.

Example 2 Solve the differential equation

$$\frac{dy}{dt} + 5y = 4e^{3t}.$$

The first step is to find a particular solution y^P. Following the guideline above, we try for a solution of the form Be^{3t}, where B is a constant. Substituting $y = Be^{3t}$ into our differential equation, we have

$$3Be^{3t} + 5Be^{3t} = 4e^{3t},$$

whence $B = \frac{1}{2}$. Our particular solution is therefore

$$y^P = \frac{1}{2}e^{3t},$$

The complementary solution is the general solution to the homogeneous equation

$$\frac{dz}{dt} + 5z = 0.$$

As in Example 1, $z = Ae^{-5t}$. The general solution for y is therefore

$$y = y^P + z = \frac{1}{2}e^{3t} + Ae^{-5t},$$

where A is an arbitrary constant.

Equations with boundary conditions

For the same reason that the particular solution y^P contains no arbitrary constant, it does not have to satisfy any boundary condition we choose to impose. To solve (21.9) — or its special case (21.5) — subject to a boundary condition, we find first the general solution $y^P + z$, noting that z involves an arbitrary constant A; we then use the boundary condition to solve for A.

Example 3 Solve the differential equation

$$\frac{dy}{dt} + 5y = 4e^{3t},$$

subject to the initial condition that $y = 0$ when $t = 0$.

The general solution to this differential equation was found in Example 2 to be

$$y = \frac{1}{2}e^{3t} + Ae^{-5t}.$$

It remains to choose the constant A so as to satisfy the initial condition. Since $e^0 = 1$, the condition requires that $\frac{1}{2} + A = 0$. Hence $A = -\frac{1}{2}$, and the solution we seek is

$$y = \frac{1}{2}\left(e^{3t} - e^{-5t}\right).$$

An alternative way of handling (21.9) in the case where $g(t)$ is not constant will be discussed in the next section. We now turn to an economic application where the right hand side is constant.

Application to price adjustment

This application concerns an old friend: supply and demand in a competitive market with linear supply and demand schedules. We introduce dynamics by supposing that the market does not clear instantaneously, but that price increases when there is excess demand and decreases when there is excess supply.

These assumptions may be expressed by the three-equation model

$$q^D = a_0 - a_1 p, \quad q^S = b_0 + b_1 p, \quad \frac{dp}{dt} = \lambda(q^D - q^S), \tag{21.10}$$

where p is price, q^D is quantity demanded and q^S is quantity supplied. a_0, b_0, a_1, b_1 and λ are constants, with a_1 and b_1 positive to reflect the usual assumptions about the response of supply and demand to changes in price; λ is also assumed to be positive, for reasons explained below. We assume that $a_0 > b_0$, thereby ensuring that the equilibrium price is positive. It is easy to check that the equilibrium price, at which $q^D = q^S$, is

$$p^* = (a_0 - b_0)/(a_1 + b_1). \tag{21.11}$$

The third equation of the model (21.10) is the price adjustment equation relating the rate of change of price to excess demand. Our assumption that $\lambda > 0$ means that price increases when there is excess demand and decreases when there is excess supply. Observe the economic interpretation of the constant λ: the larger is λ, the faster price responds to excess demand or supply.

Substituting the first two equations of the model into the third, we obtain a differential equation which describes the dynamics of price:

$$dp/dt = \lambda([a_0 - b_0] - [a_1 + b_1]p).$$

Hence by (21.11),

$$dp/dt = \lambda(a_1 + b_1)(p^* - p).$$

Now let $c = \lambda(a_1 + b_1)$. Then $c > 0$, and we have the linear differential equation

$$\frac{dp}{dt} + cp = cp^*, \tag{21.12}$$

which is solved in the usual way. A particular solution is $p = p^*$, the equilibrium price. The complementary solution is Ae^{-ct}, and the general solution is

$$p = p^* + Ae^{-ct},$$

where A is an arbitrary constant.

The most important thing to notice about the solution is that, since $c > 0$, $p \to p^*$ as $t \to \infty$. Thus in this model equilibrium is **stable**, in the sense that price approaches equilibrium price as $t \to \infty$. Notice that this is so for any value of A. The interpretation of A is the deviation of price from equilibrium price at time 0.

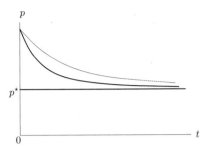

Figure 21.1: **Fast and slow price adjustment**

How quickly p approaches p^* depends on the value of c. A high c implies a rapid approach to equilibrium, as in the solid curve in Figure 21.1, whereas a low c implies a slow approach, as in the broken curve. Since $c = \lambda(a_1 + b_1)$, c will be larger the larger is λ: the faster price responds to excess supply or demand, the faster it approaches equilibrium. Figure 21.1 is drawn on the assumption that $A > 0$; as an exercise, draw the analogous diagram for negative A.

Stationary solutions

When we solved (21.12), our particular solution was the equilibrium price $p = p^*$, and the complementary solution Ae^{-ct} can be interpreted as the deviation of price from equilibrium price at time t. Such an interpretation can always be given to the solution of differential equations of the form (21.5):

$$\frac{dy}{dt} + ay = b \quad (a, b \text{ constant}).$$

The particular solution $y^P = b/a$ is called the **stationary solution**, since it is independent of t: the term 'stationary' comes from the usual interpretation of t as time. The variable z in the associated homogeneous equation (21.7) can be thought of as the deviation of y from the stationary solution.

More generally, any constant solution of a differential equation is called a stationary solution (or **stationary point**, or **stationary state**). In this more general context we speak of a, rather than *the* stationary solution, since there may be more than one of them: see Problem 21–1 for an example.

Exercises

21.2.1 Find the general solutions of each of the following differential equations:

(a) $\dfrac{dy}{dt} + 7y = 14$; (b) $\dfrac{dy}{dt} - 7y = 14$.

In each case, say what happens to y as $t \to \infty$.

21.2.2 Find the general solution of the equation

$$\frac{dy}{dt} + 4y = 12.$$

Find also the solutions satisfying each of the following initial conditions:

(a) $y = 2$ when $t = 0$,   (b) $y = 3$ when $t = 0$,   (c) $y = 4$ when $t = 0$.

Sketch the three solution curves in the same ty–plane.

21.2.3 Find the general solution of the equation

$$7\frac{dy}{dt} + y = 14.$$

Find also the solution which satisfies $y = 5$ when $t = 0$.

21.2.4 Find the general solution of the equation

$$\frac{dy}{dt} + 2y = 3e^{-t}.$$

Find also the solution which satisfies $y = 4$ when $t = 0$.

21.2.5 Find the solution of the equation

$$\frac{dy}{dx} - 3y = 4x - 1$$

which satisfies $y = 1$ when $x = 0$.

21.2.6 In the following market model, p is price, q^D is quantity demanded and q^S is quantity supplied:

$$q^D = 3 - 2p, \quad q^S = -1 + 4p, \quad \frac{dp}{dt} = \tfrac{1}{2}(q^D - q^S).$$

Obtain a first-order differential equation for p and find its general solution. What happens to p as $t \to \infty$?

21.3   Harder first-order equations

We now consider first-order differential equations of the form

$$\frac{dy}{dt} + f(t)y = g(t). \tag{21.13}$$

Like the differential equations of the preceding section, equation (21.13) is linear, in the sense that terms such as $\ln y$ or $(dy/dt)^2$ do not appear. Here, however, neither $f(t)$ nor $g(t)$ is required to be constant.

The standard method of solving equations of the form (21.13) is to multiply the equation by an expression known as an **integrating factor**, chosen so as to make the left-hand side of the resulting equation easy to integrate. Suppose we multiply (21.13) by a function $h(t)$; then

$$h(t)\frac{dy}{dt} + h(t)f(t)y = h(t)g(t). \qquad (21.13')$$

If the function $h(t)$ has the property that

$$h(t)f(t) = h'(t), \qquad (21.14)$$

then the left-hand side of (21.13') is equal to

$$\frac{d}{dt}(h(t)y)$$

by the product rule. We may then integrate both sides of (21.13'):

$$h(t)y = \int h(t)g(t)\,dt.$$

Dividing through by $h(t)$, we have the general solution to (21.13).

What we have not yet explained is how to find an integrating factor $h(t)$ satisfying (21.14). We begin with two special cases, and then say a little about the general case.

Two special cases

(i) Suppose $f(t)$ is a constant, say a. Then, letting $w = h(t)$, we may write (21.14) as

$$\frac{dw}{dt} = aw.$$

Obviously this is satisfied when $w = e^{at}$, so in this case we choose e^{at} to be our integrating factor. Observe that no constant of integration is required: we are only looking for an integrating factor, not a whole family of them.

Example 1 Solve the differential equation

$$\frac{dy}{dt} + 5y = 4e^{3t}.$$

We solved this differential equation as Example 2 of the last section, but now we do so again by the integrating-factor method. Since the coefficient of y is the constant 5, our integrating factor is e^{5t}, and we have

$$e^{5t}\frac{dy}{dt} + 5e^{5t}y = 4e^{8t}.$$

Since the left-hand side of this equation is $\dfrac{d}{dt}(e^{5t}y)$, we have by integration:

$$e^{5t}y = \int 4e^{8t}\,dt = \tfrac{1}{2}e^{8t} + A,$$

where A is an arbitrary constant. Dividing through by e^{5t}, we have the general solution for y:

$$y = \tfrac{1}{2}e^{3t} + Ae^{-5t},$$

as before.

(ii) Suppose $f(t) = c/t$, where c is a constant: then (21.14) becomes

$$h'(t) = \frac{c}{t}h(t).$$

But the power rule of differentiation states that if $w = t^c$, then

$$\frac{dw}{dt} = ct^{c-1} = \frac{cw}{t}.$$

We therefore choose as our integrating factor $h(t) = t^c$.

Example 2 Find the solution of the differential equation

$$\frac{dy}{dt} - \frac{2y}{t} = 4t$$

which satisfies the boundary condition that $y = 2$ when $t = 1$.

This is an equation of the form (21.13), with $f(t) = -2/t$. We therefore multiply by the integrating factor t^{-2}:

$$\frac{1}{t^2}\frac{dy}{dt} - \frac{2y}{t^3} = \frac{4}{t}.$$

The left-hand side of this equation is $\dfrac{d}{dt}\left(\dfrac{y}{t^2}\right)$ and, assuming $t > 0$, the right-hand side is $\dfrac{d}{dt}(4\ln t)$. Hence

$$t^{-2}y = 4\ln t + A,$$

where A is a constant, and the general solution to our differential equation is

$$y = t^2(4\ln t + A).$$

The final step is to use the boundary condition to solve for A. Since $2 = 1\times(0 + A)$, $A = 2$, and the solution we seek is

$$y = 2t^2(2\ln t + 1).$$

The general case

How do we find an integrating factor $h(t)$ satisfying (21.14), when no special conditions are imposed on $f(t)$? If $h(t) > 0$ for all t, (21.14) may be written

$$\frac{d}{dt}(\ln h(t)) = f(t) :$$

so if p is a function such that $p'(t) = f(t)$ for all t, and $h(t) = e^{p(t)}$, then the function h satisfies (21.14).

In principle, therefore, it is a straightforward matter to find an integrating factor for the differential equation (21.13): we choose a function $p(t)$ which is a primitive of $f(t)$, and let $e^{p(t)}$ be our integrating factor.[3] In practice, difficulties may arise when finding explicit expressions for the primitive $p(t)$ and the indefinite integral $\int e^{p(t)}g(t)\,dt$; recall the general remarks on integration at the end of Section 19.2.

Bernoulli's equation

This equation, named after the renowned Swiss mathematician Jacob Bernoulli (1654–1705),[4] is the following variant of (21.13):

$$\frac{dy}{dt} + f(t)y = g(t)y^{\alpha}, \tag{21.15}$$

where α is a constant. We assume that α is neither 0 nor 1.[5]

To solve (21.15), let $x = y^{1-\alpha}$. Then

$$\frac{dx}{dt} = (1-\alpha)y^{-\alpha}\frac{dy}{dt} = (1-\alpha)\left(g(t) - f(t)y^{1-\alpha}\right).$$

Therefore

$$\frac{dx}{dt} + (1-\alpha)f(t)x = (1-\alpha)g(t).$$

This linear differential equation is the same as (21.13) except that x has been substituted for y, and $f(t)$ and $g(t)$ have been multiplied by $1 - \alpha$. We can therefore solve for x in the usual way, and finally transform back to y.

Example 3 Find the general solution of the differential equation

$$\frac{dy}{dt} - \frac{2y}{t} = 4ty^2.$$

---

[3]This is often expressed by saying that the integrating factor is $\exp(\int f(t)\,dt)$. The formula is slightly misleading, since indefinite integrals contain an arbitrary constant, while integrating factors do not.

[4]Many other members of the Bernoulli family were mathematicians, including Daniel Bernoulli (1700–1782), whose work on the measurement of risk has had a major influence on modern economic theory.

[5]Setting $\alpha = 0$ takes us back to the linear equation (21.13); if α were 1 we would have the separable equation $dy/dt = (g(t) - f(t))y$.

This is a Bernoulli equation with $\alpha = 2$, so that $1 - \alpha = -1$. Proceeding as above, we have the linear equation

$$\frac{dx}{dt} + \frac{2x}{t} = -4t,$$

where $x = y^{-1}$. Multiplying through by the integrating factor t^2 (recall special case (ii) above), we see that

$$\frac{d}{dt}(t^2 x) = -4t^3.$$

It follows that

$$t^2 x = -\int 4t^3 \, dt = A - t^4,$$

where A is a constant of integration. Since $y = x^{-1}$, the general solution for y is

$$y = \frac{t^2}{A - t^4}.$$

An application: the Solow–Swan growth model

In the simplest version of this model of economic growth, gross investment is a constant proportion s of output, the depreciation rate of capital is the positive constant δ, and labour input L is constant. Output Q is related to the capital stock K and labour input L by the production function $Q = F(K, L)$; hence gross investment is $sF(K, L)$, and net investment is

$$sF(K, L) - \delta K.$$

Now net investment is the rate of change of the capital stock. When we treat time t as a continuous variable, rates of change are derivatives with respect to t. Hence net investment is dK/dt, and the capital stock K satisfies the differential equation

$$\frac{dK}{dt} + \delta K = sF(K, L). \tag{21.16}$$

We consider the case where the production function has the Cobb–Douglas form:

$$F(K, L) = AK^\alpha L^\beta,$$

where A, α and β are positive constants. Since L is assumed constant, we may choose units such that $L = 1$. Then (21.16) reduces to

$$\frac{dK}{dt} + \delta K = sAK^\alpha. \tag{21.17}$$

The Bernoulli equation (21.17) is solved in the usual way by making the substitution $x = K^{1-\alpha}$. The differential equation for x is

$$\frac{dx}{dt} + (1 - \alpha)\delta x = (1 - \alpha)sA.$$

This is an equation of the type considered in Section 21.2: a particular solution is sA/δ and the complementary solution is $c\exp(-(1-\alpha)\delta t)$, where c is a constant of integration. Hence the general solution for x is

$$sA/\delta + c\exp(-(1-\alpha)\delta t);$$

the general solution for the capital stock is

$$K = \left[\frac{sA}{\delta} + ce^{-(1-\alpha)\delta t}\right]^{\gamma},$$

where $\gamma = (1-\alpha)^{-1}$ and c is an arbitrary constant.

In the solution procedure we have just explained, our particular solution for x is stationary, being the constant sA/δ. The corresponding value of K, namely $K^* = (sA/\delta)^{\gamma}$ is a stationary solution for K: if K happens to be equal to K^* at time 0, then $K = K^*$ for all t. It is not hard to see that sA/δ is the only stationary solution for x, and hence that K^* is the only non-zero stationary solution for K. In the theory of economic grrowth, K^* is called the **steady-state** capital stock.

If $\alpha < 1$, which means that there are diminishing returns to capital,[6] then

$$e^{-(1-\alpha)\delta t} \to 0 \text{ as } t \to \infty.$$

In this case the capital stock tends to K^* and output tends to $A(K^*)^{\alpha}$ as $t \to \infty$, whatever the value of K at time 0.

The result of convergence to a stationary solution suggests that this so-called "growth model" has rather little to do with economic growth. Notice however that the particular version of the model discussed above assumes constant labour input and no technical progress. For the case where labour input grows at a constant positive rate n, see Problem 21–3. The model can be extended to allow for technical progress, by measuring labour input in a way that takes account of improved quality: see for example Olivier Blanchard, *Macroeconomics*, Second Edition (Prentice Hall International, 2000), chapter 12.

Exercises

21.3.1 Find the general solution of the differential equation of Exercise 21.2.4 by the integrating-factor method.

21.3.2 Find the general solutions of the following differential equations:

$$\text{(a) } \frac{dy}{dt} - \frac{y}{2t} = 3t; \quad \text{(b) } \frac{dy}{dt} + \frac{y}{2t} = 3t.$$

Comment on the behaviour of the two general solutions when t is small and positive.

---

[6]Recall the discussion of "diminishing returns and all that" in Section 17.4.

21.3.3 Find the general solution of the differential equation

$$\frac{dy}{dt} + 4y = ty^3.$$

21.3.4 Write the differential equation of Exercise 21.1.5 as a Bernoulli equation and solve it by the method of this section.

21.4   Difference equations

As we noted at the beginning of this chapter, difference equations are the discrete-time analogue of differential equations. Recalling the basic notation of discrete-time analysis introduced in Section 9.3, we assume that the 'time' variable t takes only integer values; thus variables depending on time are now represented by sequences, say $\{y_t\}$. In applications, discrete-tim t often refers to a finite interval of time such as a year or a day; for this reason we shall sometimes use the phrase 'in period t' rather than 'at time t'. The rate of change of y in period t is now $y_{t+1} - y_t$, which we shall often denote by Δy_t; thus we define the **forward difference operator** Δ by

$$\Delta y_t = y_{t+1} - y_t.$$

Application of the operator Δ may be regarded as the discrete-time counterpart of differentiation with respect to time.[7]

Difference equations are like differential equations, except that derivatives are replaced by differences. Thus the discrete-time analogue of the differential equation

$$\frac{dy}{dt} + ay = b,$$

where a and b are constants, is the first-order difference equation

$$\Delta y_t + ay_t = b.$$

Recalling the definition of the operator Δ, we may write this equation as

$$y_{t+1} + cy_t = b, \tag{21.18}$$

where $c = a - 1$. Since (21.18) simply relates the value of y in a period to its value in the previous period, it can be written in the equivalent form

$$y_t + cy_{t-1} = b. \tag{21.18'}$$

---

[7]Δ is called the forward difference operator to distinguish it from the **backward difference operator** D defined by $Dy_t = y_t - y_{t-1}$. We shall not mention the operator D again.

First-order difference equations

In this section we are concerned with difference equations which contain y_t and y_{t+1}, but not y_{t+2} or further terms in the sequence. Since continuous-time analysis is typically easier than discrete-time analysis (as we noted in Section 9.3), our treatment of first-order difference equations will have even less pretention to generality than our discussion of first-order differential equations. We concentrate on equation (21.18) and then, as in Section 21.2, comment briefly on the case where the right-hand side is a simple function of t instead of a constant.

To find the general solution of this difference equation means finding a formula giving all sequences $\{y_t\}$ which satisfy (21.18). As in the differential equation case, this will contain an arbitrary constant which will be tied down if we specify the value of y_t for some particular t.

We start with the very simple case where $b = 0$. Then

$$y_{t+1} = -cy_t \text{ for all } t,$$

and hence

$$y_1 = -cy_0, \quad y_2 = -cy_1 = (-c)^2 y_0, \quad y_3 = (-c)^3 y_0$$

and so on. It follows that

$$y_t = (-c)^t y_0 \quad \text{for } t = 0, 1, 2, \dots.$$

A similar argument shows that $y_t = (-c)^t y_0$ for $t = -1, -2, \dots$. In what follows, however, we shall typically restrict t to non-negative integer values: we 'begin the story' at time 0 and are interested in what happens subsequently.[8]

To summarise: if $b = 0$, the general solution to (21.18) is $y_t = A(-c)^t$, where A is an arbitrary constant, which may be interpreted as y_0.

In the case where $b \neq 0$, we use a method which is very similar to that given in Section 21.2 for the analogous differential equations. We begin by finding a particular solution, defined as a sequence $\{Y_t\}$ such that

$$Y_{t+1} + cY_t = b \text{ for all } t.$$

We then set $z_t = y_t - Y_t$ and subtract the difference equation for $\{Y_t\}$ from (21.18), obtaining

$$z_{t+1} + cz_t = 0.$$

By analogy with the differential-equation case, this equation is called the **associated homogeneous equation** of (21.18), and the general solution for z_t is called the **complementary solution** of (21.18).

---

[8]Under this restriction, (21.18) holds for $t = 0, 1, 2, \dots$, whereas (21.18′) holds for $t = 1, 2, 3, \dots$

We now apply the same argument to the associated homogeneous equation that we used for the special case of (21.18) where $b = 0$: the complementary solution is

$$z_t = A(-c)^t,$$

where A is an arbitrary constant. Notice that A is interpreted as z_0, not y_0. The general solution to (21.18) is then

$$y_t = Y_t + A(-c)^t,$$

the sum of the particular solution and the complementary solution.

It remains to find the particular solution Y_t. Again by analogy with differential equations, we try $Y_t = Y$ where Y is constant: as before, this is known as a stationary solution. Equation (21.18) then requires that $Y + cY = b$. Provided $c \neq -1$, this gives us the particular solution

$$Y_t = b/(1 + c) \quad \text{for all } t.$$

The general solution to (21.18) is

$$y_t = (1 + c)^{-1}b + A(-c)^t.$$

What we do when $c = -1$ will become clear in Example 2 below.

Example 1 Find the solution of the difference equation

$$y_{t+1} - \tfrac{1}{2}y_t = 2$$

which satisfies the boundary condition $y_0 = 2$.

As a particular solution, we try $Y_t = Y$ where Y is constant. This satisfies the equation provided $Y - \tfrac{1}{2}Y = 2$. Hence $Y = 4$.

The associated homogeneous equation is $z_{t+1} = \tfrac{1}{2}z_t$; hence the complementary solution is $A(\tfrac{1}{2})^t$, where A is an arbitrary constant. The general solution to our difference equation is therefore

$$y_t = 4 + 2^{-t}A,$$

where A is a constant.

It remains to use the boundary condition $y_0 = 2$ to find A. Setting $t = 0$ in the general solution we have $2 = 4 + A$; hence $A = -2$, and the solution we seek is

$$y_t = 4 - 2^{1-t}.$$

Example 2 Find the general solution to the difference equation

$$y_{t+1} - y_t = 1.$$

In this case, there is no stationary solution: for if we substituted $y_t = Y$ for all t into our difference equation we would have 0=1, which is absurd. This means that we must seek a non-constant particular solution. A moment's thought shows that the difference equation is satisfied when $y_t = t$ for all t, so we take that as our particular solution. The associated homogeneous equation is $z_{t+1} = z_t$, so the complementary solution is $Z_t = A$, where A is an arbitrary constant. The general solution to our difference equation is therefore

$$y_t = t + A,$$

where A is a constant.

The solution may also be found from first principles. Letting $y_0 = A$ we have

$$y_1 = 1 + y_0 = 1 + A, \quad y_2 = 1 + y_1 = 2 + A, \quad y_3 = 1 + y_2 = 3 + A$$

and so on; thus $y_t = t + A$ for all t.

Extensions

A variant of (21.18) which is easily dealt with is where the coefficient of y_{t+1} is some non-zero constant k, not necessarily equal to 1: in this case we can divide the difference equation by k and proceed as above.

A class of variants which is harder to handle is the case of a *non-constant right-hand side*: b is replaced by u_t, where $\{u_t\}$ is a given sequence. As in the corresponding differential equation, the only difference this makes concerns the search for a particular solution. The basic method is again trial and error, but as in Section 21.2 guidelines can be given. The principle is to try for a sequence $\{Y_t\}$ of the same general form as $\{u_t\}$. Thus, if the right-hand side is of the form ak^t, where a and k are constants, we try a particular solution of the form αk^t, where α is another constant; and if the right-hand side is a linear function of t, we try a particular solution which is also a linear function of t.

As in Section 21.2, the guidelines do not inevitably work. Recall that in Example 2 of this section there was no particular solution of the 'obvious' form, namely a constant, and we had to look for something a little more complicated. Cases with a non-constant right-hand side where the guidelines do not work arise for similar reasons and are dealt with in similar ways.

Qualitative behaviour

We now return to the difference equation (21.18), with a constant right-hand side:

$$y_{t+1} + cy_t = b.$$

To keep things simple, we assume that $c \neq -1$; then the general solution is

$$y_t = Y + A(-c)^t,$$

where A is an arbitrary constant and Y is the constant particular solution, equal to $b/(1+c)$.

The stationary solution Y has the property that if y_0 happens to be equal to Y, then $y_t = Y$ for all t. We say that the stationary solution is stable if $y_t \to Y$ as $t \to \infty$, regardless of initial conditions (and therefore for all A). It is clear from the general solution that this happens if and only if the limit of $(-c)^t$ as $t \to \infty$ is 0. Hence the stationary solution stable if and only if $|c| < 1$.

The picture of the solution path is more complicated than in the case of first-order differential equations. If $c < 0$, so that $-c$ is positive, then y_t always stays on the same side of Y as y_0, moving towards or away from Y according as $-1 < c < 0$ or $c < -1$. On the other hand, if $c > 0$ the complementary solution $A(-c)^t$ changes sign each period. This is known as **alternating behaviour**. The stability condition given above tells us that alternations are explosive or damped according as $c > 1$ or $0 < c < 1$. Alternations are illustrated in the two panels of Figure 21.2, where (as in Figure 5.1) we have depicted each member of a sequence by a bullet.

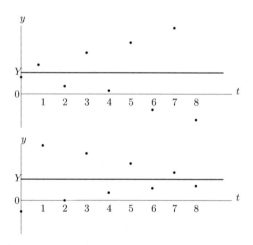

Figure 21.2: **Explosive and damped alternations**

It is very important to note that we encountered nothing like this alternating behaviour when we studied the corresponding first order differential equations. Therefore, changing from continuous to discrete time can significantly change the qualitative behaviour of the solution.

The cobweb model

A well-known economic model leading to alternating behaviour is the **cobweb model** of a market, which has been applied both to agricultural markets and (with somewhat greater empirical success) to markets for educated manpower.

In this model supply q_t in period t is predetermined, depending on the price p_{t-1} that obtained in period $t-1$; this dependence is expressed in the supply function

$$q_t = g(p_{t-1}), \quad \text{where } g' > 0.$$

Quantity demanded in period t depends on that period's price:

$$q_t^D = f(p_t), \quad \text{where } f' < 0.$$

Finally it is assumed that the market clears each period, given the predetermined suuply. Thus p_t always takes the value such that $q_t^D = q_t$. This gives us the difference equation

$$f(p_t) = g(p_{t-1}). \tag{21.19}$$

We solve (21.19) in the constant-elasticity case where

$$f(p) = Ap^{-a}, \quad g(p) = Bp^b,$$

and A, B, a, b are positive constants. Substituting these functions into (21.19) and replacing t by $t+1$ throughout,[9] we have

$$A(p_{t+1})^{-a} = B(p_t)^b.$$

This does not look very like anything we have met so far in this chapter, but we can reach a more familiar kind of difference equation by taking natural logarithms.[10] Doing this, and rearranging, we see that

$$\ln A - \ln B = a \ln p_{t+1} + b \ln p_t.$$

Setting $y_t = \ln p_t$ for all t, we have the difference equation

$$y_{t+1} + cy_t = u,$$

where $c = b/a$ and $u = (\ln A - \ln B)/a$.

The difference equation in y_t has the stationary solution $y_t = Y$, where

$$Y = \frac{u}{1+c} = \frac{1}{a+b} \ln \frac{A}{B},$$

and the general solution

$$y_t = Y + (-c)^t K,$$

where K is a constant. Since a and b are positive, so is c, and we have alternations, which are damped or explosive according as $c < 1$ or $c > 1$.

---

[9] As one does when going from (21.18′) to (21.18).

[10] We could reach a familiar form of difference equation more quickly by assuming the supply and demand functions to be linear rather than log-linear. We do not adopt this alternative assumption since it raises the possibility of the price becoming negative.

In terms of the original variables, the stationary solution for price is

$$P = e^Y = (A/B)^\gamma,$$

where $\gamma = 1/(a + b)$. The corresponding quantity supplied and demanded is

$$Q = AP^{-a} = A^{1-\alpha}B^\alpha,$$

where $\alpha = a/(a + b)$. We can think of the point (Q, P) in the qp–plane as representing the long-eqilibrium of the market. Since $c = b/a$, price and quantity display alternations about (Q, P) which are damped if $a > b$ and explosive if $a < b$. Thus the market tends toward its long-run equilibrium if and only if the absolute value of the elasticity of demand exceeds the elasticity of supply.

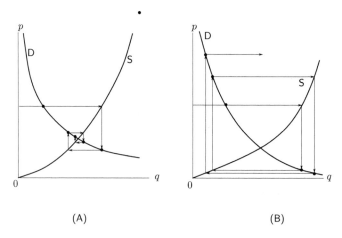

(A)   (B)

Figure 21.3: **The "cobweb" model**

The damped and explosive cases are depicted in the two panels of Figure 21.3. In each panel, D is the demand curve $q = Ap^{-a}$ and S is the supply curve $q = Bp^b$. The reason for the name 'cobweb model' should be obvious from the diagrams. How the name and the diagrams should be interpreted is perhaps less obvious. Recall that in each period actual price and quantity are represented by a point on the demand curve D; thus the successive price-quantity combinations that an observer of the market would record are depicted by the bullets.

Since quantity supplied is determined by the preceding period's price, points on the supply curve do not represent quantity-price combinations in any period. The relevance of the supply curve S is that it indicates what quantity will be supplied next period, given this period's price; this is the meaning of the arrows in Figure 21.3. Thus the 'cobwebs' in the diagram have, to use a rather pretentious phrase, an analytical rather than a temporal significance: the successive price-quantity combinations generated by the model do not cycle around the stationary point but jump along the demand curve from one side of that point

to the other. To model truly cyclical behaviour we need mathematical tools
which will be introduced in the next chapter.

Exercises

21.4.1 Find the constant particular solution of the difference equation

$$\Delta y_t + a y_t = b.$$

How does this relate to the derivation given in the text?

21.4.2 Find the general solution of the equation

$$y_{t+1} + 3y_t = 12.$$

Also find the solution which satisfies $y_0 = 2$.

21.4.3 Which of the following equations is equivalent to that in Exercise 21.4.2?

$$\text{(a) } yt + 3y_{t+1} = 12, \quad \text{(b) } yt + 3y_{t-1} = 12.$$

Find the general solutions of the two equations.

21.4.4 Find the solution of the difference equation

$$3u_{n+1} + 2u_n = 10$$

which satisfies $u_0 = 4$.

21.4.5 Find the general solution of each of the following difference equations:

$$\text{(a) } 3y_{t+1} + 5y_t = 16, \quad \text{(b) } 5y_{t+1} + 3y_t = 16.$$

In each case, find the solution which satisfies $y_0 = 0$ and draw a diagram
sketching this solution.

21.4.6 Write down the discrete time analogue of the market model in Exercise
21.2.6. Obtain a first-order difference equation for p and find its general
solution. What happens to p_t as $t \to \infty$? Comment.

Problems on Chapter 21

21–1. We stated early in this chapter that there is no general formula for solving (21.1). For this reason, one is often forced to find out what one can
about the solutions to a differential equation using elementary calculus
and geometric intuition, without attempting to calculate the general solution. This problem illustrates the techniques involved. As it happens,
the equations of parts (i) and (ii) are quite easy to solve explicitly, but
you are *not* asked to do this.

   (i) Consider the differential equation

$$\frac{dy}{dt} = t(2 - t).$$

   Use the equation to show that all solution curves in the ty–plane have
   a minimum at $t = 0$ and a maximum at $t = 2$. Find the slopes of the
   solution curves when $t = -1, 1, 3$. Show in a diagram the directions
   of the tangents to the curves when $t = -1, 0, 1, 2, 3$. Hence sketch
   the family of solution curves. What happens to each solution (a) as
   t increases, (b) as $t \to \infty$?

   (ii) Now consider the equation

$$\frac{dy}{dt} = y(2 - y).$$

   Explain why the lines $y = 0$ and $y = 2$ in are solution curves in
   the ty–plane. Show in a diagram the directions of the tangents to
   the curves when $y = -1, -0.5, 0.5, 1, 1.5, 2.5, 3$. Hence sketch the
   family of solution curves. What happens to each solution (a) as t
   increases, (b) as $t \to \infty$?

   (iii) Explain how the answer to Exercise 21.1.5 can be used to confirm
   some, but not all, of your results in part (ii) of this problem.

21–2. **Hotelling's rule**[11] for a competitive mining industry states that

$$\frac{1}{z}\frac{dz}{dt} = r,$$

where $z = p - c$, and p and c denote respectively price and marginal cost
of extraction. The interest rate is assumed constant and is denoted by r.

   (i) Find the general solution of this differential equation.

---

[11]Named after the American economist and statistician Harold Hotelling (1895–1973).

(ii) Now suppose that extraction costs are zero and that the inverse demand function for the mineral takes the isoelastic form

$$p = q^{-\alpha} \quad (\alpha > 0)$$

where q is the rate of extraction. Show that the value of q at each time t can be written as

$$Ae^{-rt/\alpha},$$

where A is a constant.

(iii) Let the total amount of mineral to be extracted be S, and suppose extraction begins at $t = 0$. Find the constant A, and write down expressions for the rate of extraction and the price as functions of t.

21–3. Consider the following variant of the Solow–Swan growth model of Section 21.3: instead of being constant, labour input $L(t)$ at time t is $L(0)e^{nt}$, where n is a positive constant.

(i) Suppose the production function is Cobb–Douglas, with $\alpha + \beta = 1$ (constant returns to scale). Obtain a differential equation similar to (21.17), but with K replaced by K/L and δ by $\delta + n$: Write down the solution for $K(t)/L(t)$, and derive the solution for $K(t)$. Sketch graphs of $K(t)/L(t)$ and $\ln K(t)$ as functions of t.

(ii) Let the model be as in (i), except that α and β do not necessarily sum to 1; continue to assume that $0 < \alpha < 1$. By introducing the variable $N = L^{\beta/(1-\alpha)}$ and using the results of (i), derive the solution for $K(t)$.

21–4. Write down the discrete-time analogue of the differential equation

$$\frac{dy}{dt} + ay = b,$$

where a and b are constants; assume that $a \neq 0$. Obtain in terms of a and b the general solutions of both the differential equation and the difference equation. In each case, write down the stationary solution.

For the differential equation, find the condition in terms of a for all solutions to approach the stationary solution as $t \to \infty$.[12] Find the corresponding condition for the difference equation.

Find also the condition in terms of a for the general solution of the difference equation to exhibit alternating behaviour. Comment on the variety of possible behaviours of the two equations.

---

[12]In the example of price adjustment at the end of section 21.2, this corresponds to equilibrium being stable.

Chapter 22

THE CIRCULAR FUNCTIONS

Up to now, we have been getting by with a rather small repertoire of functions. In particular, we have not yet introduced any function which describes oscillatory behaviour. This chapter is concerned with the most common functions with this property; we start with some geometrical motivation, demonstrate the algebraic properties of these functions and then show how they may be differentiated and integrated.

Apart from incidental remarks, this chapter and the next contain no economic applications. The economic relevance of these chapters lies in their use in solving dynamic equations, as will become clear in Chapter 24.

When you have studied this chapter you will be able to:

- calculate sines, cosines and tangents of arbitrary angles, and understand their meaning;

- manipulate expressions involving sines and cosines, using the addition formulae;

- differentiate and integrate expressions involving trigonometric functions;

- convert Cartesian coordinates into polar coordinates, and vice versa.

22.1 Cycles, circles and trigonometry

What we mean by oscillatory behaviour is depicted in the three panels of Figure 22.1.

If we think of x as time and of y as some observable variable, then each of the functions f, g, h of Figure 22.1 describes y oscillating over time. The function f of panel A shows **regular oscillations**, with the waves retaining their height as time goes on; the function g of panel B is said, for obvious reasons, to display **explosive oscillations**; and the function h of panel C displays **damped oscillations**.

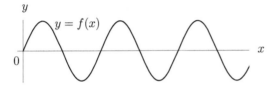

(A) Regular oscillations

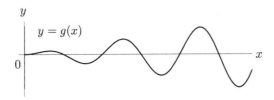

(B) Explosive oscillations

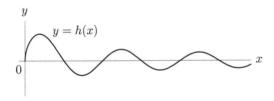

(C) Damped oscillations

Figure 22.1: **Oscillatory behaviour**

What kind of economic variable is represented by y in Figure 22.1? Diagrams such as Figure 22.1 are often useful when describing cyclical behaviour of prices or quantities, with the y measuring the *deviation* of the relevant price or quantity from its equilibrium level or long-term trend: this is consistent with the depicted property of y as being positive half the time and negative the other half. In reality, cycles in commodity prices or GDP do not follow such a predictable up-and-down pattern as in the diagrams, but it is helpful to use such a wave-pattern as a benchmark.

As far as the mathematics is concerned, the really interesting case is panel A. For if we can find a function whose graph displays regular oscillations, it is easy to find functions whose graphs display explosive or damped oscillations. For instance, if $f(x)$ is as in panel A and r is a positive constant, then the graph of $y = e^{rx} f(x)$ is as in panel B and the graph of $y = e^{-rx} f(x)$ is as in panel C.

Thus our main task is to find algebraic formulae for regular oscillations.

Properties of circles

As a first step toward a mathematical description of oscillations, we give some properties of circles. By definition, all points on a circle are equally far from the centre : this distance is called the **radius** of the circle. The **diameter** of a circle is twice the radius.

The **circumference** of a circle is the distance all the way round it. The ratio of the circumference of a circle to its diameter is the same for all circles: it is a number called π between 3 and 4. It may be shown that π is an irrational number: it cannot be expressed as the ratio of two integers. An approximate value of π, correct to 7 decimal places, is 3.1415927; a cruder approximation is $\frac{22}{7}$. By definition of π, the circumference of a circle of radius r is $2\pi r$. Another important property of π, which we shall use but not prove in this book, is that the area of a circle of radius r is πr^2.

Given two points A and B on a circle with centre O, we may define the **arc** AB to be that part of the circle between A and B (the short way round). The angle $A\hat{O}B$ is said to be **subtended** by the arc AB.

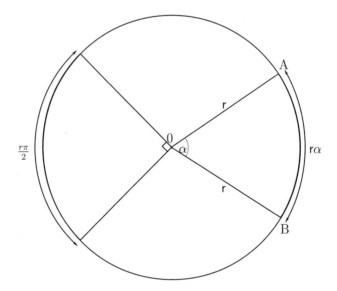

Figure 22.2: **Radian measure**

How do we measure angles? In school geometry, angles are usually measured in degrees: a right angle is 90 degrees (written 90°) and the three angles of any triangle sum to 180°. For our purposes, it is convenient to measure angles another way, known as **circular measure** or **radian measure**. This way of measuring angles will become essential when we return to calculus in Section 22.3; *to ensure that you become familiar with radian measure, we introduce it now and use it for the rest of this book.*

The size of an angle, measured in radians, is the length of the arc which subtends it in a circle of radius 1. Generally, an angle of α radians in a circle of radius r is subtended by an arc of length $r\alpha$: see the arc AB in Figure 22.2. Since a quarter-circle subtends a right angle, the circular measure of a right angle is $\pi/2$ radians: again see Figure 22.2. This gives the conversion factor between radians and degrees: since $\pi/2$ radians is 90 degrees, 1 radian is $180/\pi$ degrees and 1 degree is $\pi/180$ radians. It follows that the sum of all the angles of a triangle is π radians.

Trigonometric functions

We now get closer to the main topic of this chapter by introducing the basic trigonometric functions: sine, cosine and tangent.

Let ABC be a right-angled triangle with the right angle at B, and let $\hat{BAC}$ be α radians. The **sine** of the angle α, written $\sin\alpha$, is the ratio BC/AC; **cosine** of the angle α, written $\cos\alpha$, is the ratio AB/AC; and the **tangent** of the angle α, written $\tan\alpha$, is the ratio BC/AB. The definitions are illustrated in Figure 22.3.

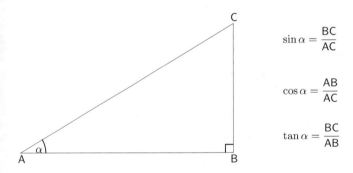

$$\sin\alpha = \frac{BC}{AC}$$

$$\cos\alpha = \frac{AB}{AC}$$

$$\tan\alpha = \frac{BC}{AB}$$

Figure 22.3: **Sine, cosine and tangent**

The trigonometric functions are so called because they are used in trigonometry, the branch of geometry concerned with triangles. The reason for the alternative name **circular functions** will become clear in the next section. Recalling that the side of a right-angled triangle opposite the right angle is called the **hypotenuse**, we may spell out the definitions as follows:

$$\text{sine} = \frac{\text{length of opposite side}}{\text{length of hypotenuse}},$$

$$\text{cosine} = \frac{\text{length of adjacent side}}{\text{length of hypotenuse}},$$

$$\text{tangent} = \frac{\text{length of opposite side}}{\text{length of adjacent side}}.$$

Three important relations between trigonometric functions are the following:

T1 $\tan\alpha = \dfrac{\sin\alpha}{\cos\alpha}$.

T2 $\cos(\frac{\pi}{2} - \alpha) = \sin\alpha$, $\sin(\frac{\pi}{2} - \alpha) = \cos\alpha$.

T3 $(\cos\alpha)^2 + (\sin\alpha)^2 = 1$.

T1 and **T2** are obvious by inspection of Figure 22.3, while **T3** is a consequence of Pythagoras' theorem: by that theorem,

$$AB^2 + BC^2 = AC^2,$$

and division by AC^2 yields **T3**. In what follows, we shall frequently use the phrase "Pythagoras' theorem" to mean the equation **T3**.

If m is a natural number it is common to refer to $(\sin\alpha)^m$ as $\sin^m\alpha$, with similar notation for cosines and tangents. Thus Pythagoras' theorem may be written

$$\cos^2\alpha + \sin^2\alpha = 1.$$

Measurement

We have now defined sines, cosines and tangents for all acute angles (angles smaller than right angles). It is clear from Figure 22.3 that sines, cosines and tangents of acute angles are positive; sines and cosines are less than 1 (since the longest side of a right-angled triangle is the hypotenuse) while tangents may be greater or less than 1.

The functions sin, cos and tan are tabulated on scientific calculators. When using the calculator it is important to press the appropriate key to ensure that you are calculating trigonometric functions of angles measured in radians. Having done this one can check, for example, that $\sin 0.5 = 0.4794$, $\cos 1.0 = 0.5403$ and $\tan 1.5 = 14.1014$, all to 4 decimal places.

Experimenting with the calculator reveals that $\sin\alpha \to 0$ as $\alpha \to 0$ (for example, $\sin 0.05 = 0.050$ and $\sin 0.001 = 0.001$, both to 3 decimal places) and that $\sin \alpha \to 1$ as $\alpha \to \pi/2$ (for example $\sin 1.5 = 0.9975$ to 4 decimal places, and $\sin 1.57 = 0.9999996$ to 7 decimal places). To see why this is so, consider again Figure 22.3. If we keep the side AB of the triangle fixed and move C towards B, then α and $\sin \alpha$ approach 0; while keeping the side BC of the triangle fixed and moving A towards B makes α tend to $\pi/2$ and the length of AC approach that of BC, so that $\sin \alpha \to 1$. For these reasons we define

$$\sin 0 = 0, \quad \sin \tfrac{\pi}{2} = 1.$$

Fractions of π

The sines, cosines and tangents of some particular angles occur sufficiently often in examples to be worth remembering, and are given in Table 22.1.

Table 22.1 Sines, cosines and tangents of selected angles

α	$\sin \alpha$	$\cos \alpha$	$\tan \alpha$
0	0	1	0
$\pi/6$	$1/2$	$\sqrt{3}/2$	$1/\sqrt{3}$
$\pi/4$	$1/\sqrt{2}$	$1/\sqrt{2}$	1
$\pi/3$	$\sqrt{3}/2$	$1/2$	$\sqrt{3}$
$\pi/2$	1	0	∞

The top and bottom rows of the table follow from what happens to $\sin \alpha$ when α becomes very small or approaches a right angle. The remaining rows come from the two panels of Figure 22.4.

Panel I of Figure 22.4 shows a right-angled isosceles triangle.[1] We assume that the two equal sides each have length 1, so the length of the third side is $\sqrt{2}$ by Pythagoras' theorem. The two equal sides of an isosceles triangle meet the third side at the same angle, so the angles of the triangle other than the right angle must each be $\pi/4$. The third row of Table 22.1 can now be read from the diagram.

An equilateral triangle is one whose sides are all equal in length; the angles of such a triangle are all $\pi/3$. In panel II of Figure 22.4 we depict such a triangle, with each side having length 2. In the diagram we have split the triangle in two by joining the vertex A to the midpoint M of the opposite side BC. By symmetry, the line-segment AM is perpendicular to the side BC of the triangle;

---

[1] An isosceles triangle is one with two sides of equal length.

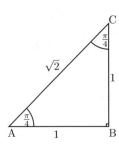 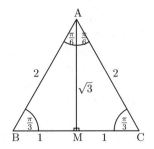

Figure 22.4: **Isosceles and equilateral triangles**

hence by Pythagoras' theorem, the length of AM is $\sqrt{3}$. This gives us the entries of the second and fourth rows of Table 22.1.

Most students find that the easiest way to remember the contents of Table 22.1 is to commit to memory not the table itself but the two panels of Figure 22.4.

Exercises

22.1.1 Convert to radians

(a) $10°$ (b) $85°$ (c) $19°$.

22.1.2 Convert the following angles, given in radians, to degrees:

(a) 1.2 (b) 0.85 (c) $\frac{1}{3}$.

22.1.3 (a) Suppose the straight line $y = 2x - 4$ makes an angle α with the x–axis. By considering the point where the line meets the x–axis and another point on the line to the right of it, find $\tan\alpha$.

(b) As (a), for the line $y = 2x + 1$.

(c) How do the results of (a) and (b) generalise?

22.1.4 Suppose α is an acute angle with $\cos\alpha = 1/\sqrt{10}$. By using Pythagoras' theorem, find $\sin\alpha$ and $\tan\alpha$.

22.2 Extending the definitions

Consider the circle in the xy–plane whose centre is the origin O and whose radius is 1. A particular point on that circle is the point I with coordinates $(1,0)$. Let A be another point on the circle, both of whose coordinates are positive. Then $\hat{\text{IOA}}$ is an acute angle, say α radians. The points I and A are shown in Figure 22.5, from which it is clear that the coordinates of A are $(\cos\alpha, \sin\alpha)$. To summarise: if the line OI is rotated anticlockwise through α radians, we obtain the point $(\cos\alpha, \sin\alpha)$.

The statement just made concerned a real number α, which is between 0 and $\pi/2$. Now let θ be *any* real number. By repeating the statement with α replaced by θ, we may define $\cos\theta$ and $\sin\theta$ as follows.

Definition If the line OI is rotated anticlockwise through θ radians, we obtain the point $(\cos\theta, \sin\theta)$.

Before seeing how this definition is used, we make clear what is meant by an "anticlockwise rotation through θ radians". First, such a rotation has an obvious meaning when $0 < \theta < 2\pi$: for instance, the point C in Figure 22.5 is obtained by an anticlockwise rotation of OI through $\pi + \alpha$ radians. Secondly, a rotation through 2π radians takes you back where you started, and one can then carry on rotating. Thus the point C can obtained by an anticlockwise rotation of OI through $3\pi + \alpha$ or $5\pi + \alpha$ radians. Similarly the point B in Figure 22.5, which is obtained by an anticlockwise rotation of OI through $\pi - \alpha$ radians, is also obtained by a rotation of OI through $3\pi - \alpha$, $7\pi - \alpha$ or $19\pi - \alpha$ radians.

Thirdly, we may consider the case where $\theta < 0$; here, an anticlockwise rotation through θ radians is defined to be a clockwise rotation through $|\theta|$ radians. For example, the point D in Figure 22.5 is obtained by an anticlockwise rotation of OI through $-\alpha$ radians.

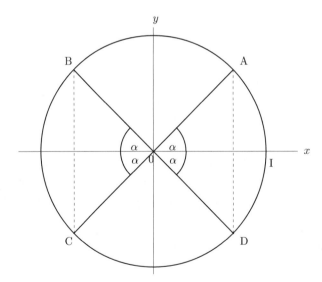

Figure 22.5: **The extended definitions**

The fact that the extended definitions of sines and cosines are in terms of rotations explains why these functions are called 'circular'. We now derive some consequences of the definitions.

Consider first the point B in Figure 22.5. As we noted earlier, B is obtained by an anticlockwise rotation of OI through $\pi - \alpha$ radians, and therefore has coordinates $(\cos(\pi - \alpha), \sin(\pi - \alpha))$. On the other hand, it is clear from Figure 22.5 that the x–coordinate of B is $-\cos\alpha$ and the y–coordinate is $\sin\alpha$. Equating coordinates,

$$\cos(\pi - \alpha) = -\cos\alpha, \quad \sin(\pi - \alpha) = \sin\alpha.$$

Applying similar reasoning to the points C and D of Figure 22.5, we have

$$\cos(\pi + \alpha) = -\cos\alpha, \quad \sin(\pi + \alpha) = -\sin\alpha$$

and

$$\cos(-\alpha) = \cos\alpha, \quad \sin(-\alpha) = -\sin\alpha.$$

Using the general definitions of sine and cosine, one can show that the equations just derived for an acute angle α hold for any angle. For any real number θ,

$$\cos(\pi + \theta) = -\cos\theta, \quad \sin(\pi + \theta) = -\sin\theta; \tag{22.1}$$

$$\cos(-\theta) = \cos\theta, \quad \sin(-\theta) = -\sin\theta. \tag{22.2}$$

Also, rules **T2** and **T3** of the preceding section hold for all angles: for any real number θ,

$$\cos(\tfrac{\pi}{2} - \theta) = \sin\theta, \quad \sin(\tfrac{\pi}{2} - \theta) = \cos\theta; \tag{22.3}$$

$$\cos^2\theta + \sin^2\theta = 1. \tag{22.4}$$

We now show how (22.1)–(22.4) may be applied.

Calculation

Using (22.1) and (22.2), any term of the form $\cos\theta$ may be expressed as $\pm\cos\alpha$, where α is an acute angle; a similar result holds for sines. In the days when students had to compute values of circular functions using tables rather than calculators, use of these facts was necessary for calculating $\sin\theta$ or $\cos\theta$ for any θ outside the closed interval $[0, \pi/2]$. Nowadays any £5 calculator will tell you that, for instance, $\sin 2 = 0.9093$ and $\cos(-10) = -0.8391$, both to 4 decimal places.

However, the technique of reduction to an acute angle is still sometimes helpful in conjunction with the facts about sines and cosines of fractions of π given in Table 22.1. For example,

$$\sin(13\pi/4) = \sin(3\pi + \pi/4) = (-1)^3 \sin\pi/4 = -1/\sqrt{2},$$

where the second equality comes from repeated application of (22.1). Similarly,

$$\cos(23\pi/6) = \cos(4\pi - \pi/6)$$
$$= (-1)^4 \cos(-\pi/6) \quad \text{by (22.1)}$$
$$= \cos\pi/6 \qquad\qquad \text{by (22.2)}$$
$$= \sqrt{3}/2.$$

Tangents

In Section 22.1 we defined $\tan\alpha$ for any acute angle α, and showed that it was equal to $\sin\alpha / \cos\alpha$. We therefore use

$$\tan\theta = \frac{\sin\theta}{\cos\theta}$$

as our general definition of the tangent function. Notice that the denominator $\cos\theta$ is zero when $\theta = \frac{\pi}{2}$ and hence, by (22.1), when $\theta = \frac{\pi}{2} + k\pi$ for any integer k. Thus $\tan\theta$ is defined for all real values of θ *except* $\pm\frac{\pi}{2}$, $\pm\frac{3\pi}{2}$ $\pm\frac{5\pi}{2}$ and so on.
 From (22.1)–(22.3) we have

$$\tan(\pi + \theta) = \tan\theta, \quad \tan(-\theta) = -\tan\theta, \quad \tan(\tfrac{\pi}{2} - \theta) = 1/(\tan\theta).$$

Also, dividing (22.4) by $\cos^2\theta$ yields

$$1 + \tan^2\theta = 1/\cos^2\theta. \tag{22.4$'$}$$

In what follows, both (22.4) and (22.4$'$) will be referred to as Pythagoras' theorem.

Graphing the circular functions

The graphs of the sine and cosine functions are the solid and broken curves in Figure 22.6. Not all the features of the sketch can be inferred from properties of the functions stated above, but many can, and we now explain how.
 We showed in the last section that $\sin x$ increases from 0 to 1 as x increases from 0 to $\pi/2$. Given the part of the curve $y = \sin x$ from $x = 0$ to $x = \pi/2$, the part from $x = 0$ to $x = -\pi/2$ is then determined by the fact that $\sin(-x) = -\sin x$. By (22.1) and (22.2),

$$\sin x = \sin(\pi - x) \quad \text{for all } x,$$

whence

$$\sin(\tfrac{\pi}{2} + \alpha) = \sin(\tfrac{\pi}{2} - \alpha) \quad \text{for all } \alpha;$$

applying (22.2) again, we see that

$$\sin(-\tfrac{\pi}{2} - \alpha) = \sin(-\tfrac{\pi}{2} + \alpha) \quad \text{for all } \alpha.$$

Therefore, if S is the section of the curve $y = \sin x$ from $x = -\pi/2$ to $x = \pi/2$, the section from $x = \pi/2$ to $x = 3\pi/2$ is the reflection of S in the vertical line $x = \pi/2$, and the section from $x = -\pi/2$ to $x = -3\pi/2$ is the reflection of S in the vertical line $x = -\pi/2$. Continuing in this way, we obtain the entire graph.

All of this explains the wave-like behaviour of the function $\sin x$, as depicted by the solid curve in Figure 22.6. The diagram also illustrates properties of the sine function which have not yet been discussed, but will be demonstrated in the next section. The function is smooth, with flat rather than kinked maxima and minima. Further, the curve $y = \sin x$ switches from concave to convex and back again in such a way that d^2y/dx^2 always has the opposite sign to y; the reason for this, as we shall see in the next section, is that $d^2y/dx^2 = -y$. In particular, the curve has a non-stationary point of inflexion at $(k\pi, 0)$ for every integer k; its slope at such a point is in fact 1 if k is even, -1 if k is odd.

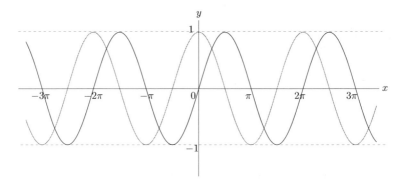

Figure 22.6: **The sine and cosine functions**

Given the graph of $\sin x$, that of $\cos x$ is easily obtained. From (22.2) and (22.3),

$$\cos x = \cos(-x) = \sin(\tfrac{\pi}{2} - (-x)) = \sin(\tfrac{\pi}{2} + x)$$

for all x. Thus the graph of $\cos x$ is obtained from that of $\sin x$ by shifting it leftward by $\pi/2$ units. This is illustrated in Figure 22.6.

The graph of the tangent function is depicted in Figure 22.7: the behaviour of the graph when $-\pi/2 < x < \pi/2$ follows from the behaviour for such x of the sine and cosine functions, and the remainder of the graph now follows from the fact that $\tan(\pi + x) = \tan x$.

Notice three important differences between Figures 22.6 and 22.7. First, $\sin x$ and $\cos x$ are defined for every real number x, whereas $\tan x$ is not defined when $x = (k + \tfrac{1}{2})\pi$ for some integer k. Secondly, the tangent function can take

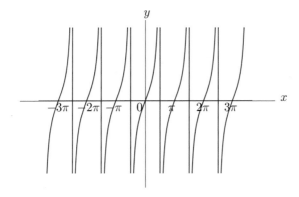

Figure 22.7: **The function** $y = \tan x$

any real value, whereas the sine and cosine functions take values between -1 and 1. Thirdly, the value of the tangent function repeats itself after intervals of π, whereas the values of the sine and cosine functions repeat after intervals of 2π. The technical term for these phenomena is that sin, cos and tan are **periodic functions**: sin and cos each have period 2π, while tan has period π.

Rotations as matrices

At the beginning of this section, we defined the functions sin and cos in terms of rotations. We now show that rotations are a special case of the mappings which can be described by matrices, as in Section 11.2.

Let OPRQ be a rectangle in the xy–plane, two of whose sides lie on the axes. Let the coordinates of P be $(p, 0)$ and let the coordinates of Q be $(0, q)$, so that the coordinates of R are (p, q). Suppose the entire rectangle is rotated about O through α radians, transforming the points P, Q, R into P*, Q*, R* respectively. All of this is depicted in Figure 22.8. In the diagram, p and q are positive numbers and α is an acute angle, but nothing important depends on this.

It is clear from Figure 22.8 that P* has coordinates $(p \cos \alpha, p \sin \alpha)$ and Q* has coordinates $(-q \sin \alpha, q \cos \alpha)$. By the parallelogram law of addition,[2] R* has coordinates

$$(p \cos \alpha - q \sin \alpha, \ p \sin \alpha + q \cos \alpha).$$

Thus the coordinates of R* are obtained from the coordinates (p, q) of R by pre-multiplying the vector $\begin{bmatrix} p \\ q \end{bmatrix}$ by the matrix $\begin{bmatrix} \cos \alpha & -\sin \alpha \\ \sin \alpha & \cos \alpha \end{bmatrix}$. This matrix therefore describes the operation of rotation through α radians.

---

[2]Recall Section 11.1, especially Figure 11.1.

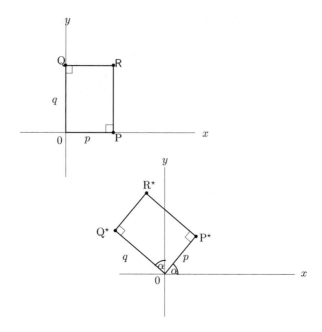

Figure 22.8: **Anatomy of a rotation**

The addition formulae

We now combine the notion of rotations as matrices with the fact, explained in Section 11.3, that multiplication of matrices is composition of mappings. Since rotation through the angle $\alpha + \beta$ is the same as rotation through the angle β followed by rotation through the angle α, we have

$$
\begin{bmatrix} \cos(\alpha + \beta) & -\sin(\alpha + \beta) \\ \sin(\alpha + \beta) & \cos(\alpha + \beta) \end{bmatrix} = \begin{bmatrix} \cos\alpha & -\sin\alpha \\ \sin\alpha & \cos\alpha \end{bmatrix} \begin{bmatrix} \cos\beta & -\sin\beta \\ \sin\beta & \cos\beta \end{bmatrix}.
$$

Working out the matrix multiplication, we see from the off-diagonal entries that

$$\sin(\alpha + \beta) = \sin\alpha\cos\beta + \cos\alpha\sin\beta, \tag{22.5}$$

and from the diagonal entries that

$$\cos(\alpha + \beta) = \cos\alpha\cos\beta - \sin\alpha\sin\beta. \tag{22.6}$$

Equations (22.5) and (22.6) are called the **addition formulae** for sines and cosines respectively. Replacing β by $-\beta$ in the addition formulae, and using (22.2), we have

$$\sin(\alpha - \beta) = \sin\alpha\cos\beta - \cos\alpha\sin\beta, \tag{22.5'}$$

$$\cos(\alpha - \beta) = \cos\alpha\cos\beta + \sin\alpha\sin\beta. \tag{22.6'}$$

Notice that Pythagoras' theorem (22.4) may be derived from (22.6′) by setting $\alpha = \beta = \theta$ and recalling that $\cos 0 = 1$.

Subtracting (22.5′) from (22.5) we have

$$\sin(\alpha + \beta) - \sin(\alpha - \beta) = 2\cos\alpha\sin\beta, \qquad (22.7)$$

a result which will be used at a crucial point in the next section.

Exercises

22.2.1 Evaluate the sine, cosine and tangent of each of the angles

$$\frac{3\pi}{4}, \quad \frac{7\pi}{6}, \quad \frac{5\pi}{3}, \quad \frac{13\pi}{6}, \quad -\frac{\pi}{3}.$$

22.2.2 (a) Sketch the graphs of $\sin 2x$, $\cos 2x$ and $\tan 2x$. State the period of each function.

(b) As (a), but with the number 2 replaced by 3.

(c) Briefly describe the graphs of $\sin nx$, $\cos nx$ and $\tan nx$ when n is an arbitrary natural number.

(d) As (c), but with the arbitrary natural number n replaced by the arbitrary positive real number a.

22.2.3 Let α and β be positive acute angles such that $\tan\alpha = 1/3$ and $\sin\beta = 1/\sqrt{5}$. Without using a calculator, explain why $\alpha + \beta$ is an acute angle, and find $\cos(\alpha + \beta)$ and $\alpha + \beta$.

22.2.4 Use the formulae for $\sin(\alpha + \beta)$ and $\cos(\alpha + \beta)$ to show that

$$\sin 2\alpha = 2\sin\alpha\cos\alpha, \quad \cos 2\alpha = \cos^2\alpha - \sin^2\alpha.$$

Deduce that
$$\sin 3\alpha = 3\sin\alpha - 4\sin^3\alpha.$$

22.3 Calculus with circular functions

Our immediate object in this section is to find the derivatives of the functions $\sin x$, $\cos x$ and $\tan x$.

The key to this comes from an experiment with the calculator which we performed in Section 22.1. In that section, we noted that $\sin 0.05 = 0.050$ and $\sin 0.001 = 0.001$, both to 3 decimal places. These examples were used to make the point that $\sin\theta \to 0$ as $\theta \to 0$, but they also illustrate another important fact: $\sin\theta \approx \theta$ when $|\theta|$ is small. More precisely,

$$\lim_{\theta \to 0} \frac{\sin\theta}{\theta} = 1. \qquad (22.8)$$

We now give a geometrical demonstration of (22.8).[3] In Figure 22.9, the angle θ is subtended by the arc AB of the circle with centre O and radius r; the tangent to the circle at A meets the radius through B at the point T. Let Q_1, Q_2 and Q_3 denote respectively the area of the triangle OAB, the area of the sector (or 'slice of pie') OAB and the area of the triangle OAT. Then Q_2 is $\dfrac{\theta}{2\pi}$ times the area of the circle, and is therefore equal to $r^2\theta/2$. Also, by the half-base-times-height formula for the area of a triangle,

$$Q_1 = \tfrac{1}{2}r \times r \sin\theta, \quad Q_3 = \tfrac{1}{2}r \times r \tan\theta.$$

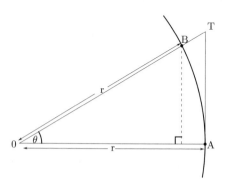

Figure 22.9: **Proof of (22.8)**

It is clear from Figure 22.9 that $Q_1 < Q_2 < Q_3$, whence

$$\tfrac{1}{2}r^2 \sin\theta < \tfrac{1}{2}r^2\theta < \tfrac{1}{2}r^2 \tan\theta.$$

The left-hand inequality tells us that $\sin\theta < \theta$, and the right-hand one that

$$\theta < \frac{\sin\theta}{\cos\theta}.$$

Hence

$$\cos\theta < \frac{\sin\theta}{\theta} < 1.$$

We can now take limits. When θ is small, $\cos\theta$ is close to 1, and hence $(\sin\theta)/\theta$ is squeezed between 1 and something close to 1. Thus (22.8) holds as required.

---

[3]It is crucial for (22.8) that angles be measured in radians. In this respect (22.8) is different from the addition formulae (22.5) and (22.6), which remain true when angles are measured in degrees, and from the other results of Section 22.2, which can easily be translated into degrees by replacing π by 180 where appropriate. We chose to work in radians from the beginning, to keep the notation consistent and to save you the trouble of having to remember which results do and do not depend on (22.8). Notice also that our geometrical argument using Figure 22.9 assumes that θ is positive, whereas the limit (22.8) is equally applicable whether θ approaches 0 from above or below; this is so because $\sin(-\theta) = -\sin\theta$.

Differentiating the circular functions

The rules for this are:

(a) $\dfrac{d}{dx}(\sin x) = \cos x$, (b) $\dfrac{d}{dx}(\cos x) = -\sin x$, (c) $\dfrac{d}{dx}(\tan x) = 1 + \tan^2 x$.

To derive (a) from the fundamental limit formula (22.8), we need to show that

$$\frac{\sin(x+h) - \sin x}{h} \to \cos x \quad \text{as } h \to 0.$$

Applying (22.7) with $\alpha = x + \frac{1}{2}h$ and $\beta = \frac{1}{2}h$, we see that

$$\sin(x+h) - \sin x = 2\cos(x + \tfrac{1}{2}h)\sin(\tfrac{1}{2}h).$$

Therefore

$$\frac{\sin(x+h) - \sin x}{h} = \cos(x + \beta)\,\frac{\sin \beta}{\beta},$$

where $\beta = h/2$. As $h \to 0$, $\beta \to 0$; hence $\cos(x + \beta) \to \cos x$, $(\sin \beta)/\beta \to 1$ by (22.8) and (a) holds as required.

Given (a), it is easy to derive (b) and (c) from the standard rules of differentiation. By (a) and the composite function rule,

$$\frac{d}{dx}\sin\left(\frac{\pi}{2} - x\right) = -\cos\left(\frac{\pi}{2} - x\right),$$

and (b) now follows from (22.3). Also,

$$\frac{d}{dx}(\tan x) = \frac{d}{dx}\left(\frac{\sin x}{\cos x}\right) = \left(\cos x \frac{d}{dx}\sin x - \sin x \frac{d}{dx}\cos x\right)\bigg/\cos^2 x$$

by the quotient rule. Hence by (a) and (b),

$$\frac{d}{dx}(\tan x) = \left(\cos^2 x + \sin^2 x\right)\big/\cos^2 x = 1 + \tan^2 x.$$

By Pythagoras' theorem, an alternative way of writing (c) is

$$\frac{d}{dx}(\tan x) = 1/\cos^2 x.$$

Using the rules (a) and (b), we can verify some properties of the sine function which we mentioned in the last section in connection with the graph of that function. If $y = \sin x$, $dy/dx = \cos x$ and

$$\frac{d^2 y}{dx^2} = \frac{d}{dx}\cos x = -\sin x = -y.$$

Also $dy/dx = \cos 0 = 1$ when $x = 0$, and similarly when $x = \pm 2\pi$, $\pm 4\pi$ and so on; while $dy/dx = \cos \pi = -1$ when when $x = \pi$, and similarly when $x = -\pi$, $\pm 3\pi$ and so on.

Applying the rules

The formulae for differentiating sin, cos and tan may be combined with the rules of earlier chapters, bringing these functions into the main body of calculus.

Example 1 By the composite function rule,

$$\frac{d}{dx}(\sin^4 x) = 4(\sin x)^3 \frac{d}{dx}(\sin x) = 4\sin^3 x \cos x.$$

Example 2 If $y = x^5 \cos 3x$,

$$\frac{dy}{dx} = 5x^4 \cos 3x + [x^5 \times (-\sin 3x) \times 3] = x^4(5\cos 3x - 3x\sin 3x)$$

by the product rule and the composite function rule.

Example 3 By the rule for differentiating $\cos x$,

$$\int \sin x \, dx = C - \cos x,$$

where C is an arbitrary constant.

Higher derivatives and Maclaurin series

We showed above that if $y = \sin x$ then $dy/dx = \cos x$ and $d^2y/dx^2 = -y$. Hence

$$\frac{d^3y}{dx^3} = -\frac{dy}{dx} = -\cos x,$$

and so on. Thus the successive derivatives of $\sin x$ are

$$\cos x, \quad -\sin x, \quad -\cos x, \quad \sin x, \quad \cos x, \quad -\sin x, \quad \ldots$$

Similarly, the successive derivatives of $\cos x$ are

$$-\sin x, \quad -\cos x, \quad \sin x, \quad \cos x, \quad -\sin x, \quad -\cos x, \quad \ldots$$

Since $\sin 0 = 0$ and $\cos 0 = 1$, the values at $x = 0$ of $\sin x$ and its successive derivatives are 0, 1, 0, -1, 0, 1 and so on. Recalling the facts about Maclaurin series given in Section 10.4, we may write the Maclaurin expansion of the sine function as

$$\sin x = x - \frac{x^3}{3!} + \frac{x^5}{5!} - \frac{x^7}{7!} + \ldots$$

It is shown in advanced textbooks that the series on the right hand side converges to $\sin x$ for every real number x. Similarly, the Maclaurin expansion of the cosine function is

$$\cos x = 1 - \frac{x^2}{2!} + \frac{x^4}{4!} - \frac{x^6}{6!} + \ldots$$

and this is also valid for all real x.

What is remarkable about these series expansions is their resemblance to e^x. As we stated in Section 10.4,

$$e^x = 1 + x + \frac{x^2}{2!} + \frac{x^3}{3!} + \frac{x^4}{4!} + \cdots$$

for all real x. Thus the function $\sin x$ is obtained from the series for e^x by retaining only the odd-power terms and replacing every other $+$ by $-$; $\cos x$ is similar, with 'even' replacing 'odd'. We shall say more about the relation between the circular and exponential functions in the next chapter.

The inverse trigonometric functions

The notion of the inverse function of a trigonometric function may seem absurd, since it is clear from Figures 22.6 and 22.7 that the circular functions are not monotonic — indeed we pointed out at the beginning of the chapter that the reason why sines and cosines occur in economics is precisely that these functions are oscillatory, and therefore non-monotonic. But we can make sense of monotonicity and inverse functions in the context of the circular functions if we restrict attention to particular intervals. We deal with sin, cos and tan in turn.

The inverse sine function

Recall from Figure 22.8 that the function $\sin x$ increases monotonically from a value of -1 at $x = -\pi/2$ to a value of 1 at $x = \pi/2$. Thus if $-1 \le y \le 1$, there is exactly one value of x such that $y = \sin x$ **and** $-\pi/2 \le x \le \pi/2$. This value of x is denoted by $\arcsin y$ or $\sin^{-1} y$, and the function arcsin is known as the **inverse sine function**. For example, $\arcsin(1/2) = \pi/6$, and $\arcsin(-1/\sqrt{2}) = -\pi/4$.

The inverse cosine function

The function $\cos x$ decreases monotonically from a value of 1 at $x = 0$ to a value of -1 at $x = \pi$. Thus if $-1 \le y \le 1$, there is exactly one value of x such that $y = \cos x$ **and** $0 \le x \le \pi$. This value of x is denoted by $\arccos y$ or $\cos^{-1} y$, and the function arccos is known as the **inverse cosine function**. For example, $\arccos(1/2) = \pi/3$, and $\arccos(-1/\sqrt{2}) = \pi - \pi/4 = 3\pi/4$.

The inverse tangent function

Recall from Figure 22.9 that for any real number y there is a unique value of x such that $y = \tan x$ and $-\pi/2 < x < \pi/2$. This value of x is denoted by $\arctan y$ or $\tan^{-1} y$, and the function arctan is known as the **inverse tangent function**. For example, $\arctan(\sqrt{3}) = \pi/3$ and $\arctan(-1) = -\pi/4$.

Since the inverse tangent is probably the most commonly used of the three functions just introduced, we give its derivative:

$$\frac{d}{dx}\arctan x = \frac{1}{1+x^2}.$$

The reason for this is as follows. Let $y = \arctan x$; then $x = \tan y$, so $dx/dy = 1 + \tan^2 y$. But then, by the inverse function rule,

$$\frac{dy}{dx} = \frac{1}{dx/dy} = \frac{1}{1+\tan^2 y} = \frac{1}{1+x^2}.$$

In Section 19.4, we approximated the integral

$$I = \int_0^1 \frac{4}{1+x^2}\,dx$$

by Simpson's rule, and stated that the exact value of I was π. We can now explain why this is so. As we have just shown, $\arctan x$ is a primitive for $(1+x^2)^{-1}$. Also, we showed in Section 22.1 that $\tan 0 = 0$ and $\tan(\pi/4) = 1$; hence $\arctan 0 = 0$ and $\arctan 1 = \pi/4$. Therefore

$$I = \Big[\,4\arctan x\,\Big]_0^1 = 4\Big(\frac{\pi}{4} - 0\Big) = \pi.$$

Exercises

22.3.1 Differentiate

(a) $\sin ax$ (b) $\cos ax$ (c) $\tan ax$ (d) $\sin^5 x$

(e) $\sin(x^5)$ (f) $x\sin x$ (g) $x^5\tan 2x$ (h) $(\cos x)/x$

22.3.2 Show that

$$y = A\sin mx + B\cos mx,$$

where A, B and m are constants, satisfies the differential equation

$$\frac{d^2y}{dx^2} + m^2 y = 0.$$

22.3.3 Find the following integrals:

(a) $\displaystyle\int \sin^6 x \cos x\,dx,$ (b) $\displaystyle\int_0^{\pi/4} x\cos x\,dx.$

22.3.4 Use the series for $\sin x$ and $\cos x$ to evaluate $\sin 1$ and $\cos 1$ correct to 3 decimal places.

22.3.5 Write down the values of the following:

(a) $\arcsin \sqrt{3}/2$ (b) $\arccos(-1/2)$ (c) $\arctan 1$ (d) $\arctan(-1/\sqrt{3})$.

22.3.6 Find the derivatives of $\arcsin x$ and $\arccos x$.

22.3.7 Find $\displaystyle\lim_{\theta\to 0}\frac{\tan\theta}{\theta}$. Hence find $\displaystyle\lim_{x\to 0}\frac{\arctan x}{x}$.

22.4 Polar coordinates

Where is Wembley Stadium? One answer is: ten miles North-West of the centre of London. Another way of answering the question would be to give a grid reference on a map of the London area.

The point we are making here is that in ordinary conversation we have two ways of describing the location of a point in a plane. The mathematical version of the grid-reference method is the usual system of x and y coordinates, sometimes called **Cartesian coordinates**.[4] In this section we are concerned with the other, more natural, way of locating points, in terms of distance and direction from a given origin.

Let P be a point in the xy–plane other than the origin, and let r be the distance of P from O. Then we may describe the position of P by two numbers: r itself, and the angle θ which the line OP makes with the x–axis. More precisely, if R is the point with (Cartesian) coordinates $(r, 0)$, θ is the angle through which the line OR must be rotated to transform R into P. We may determine θ uniquely by requiring that $-\pi < \theta \leq \pi$.[5] The numbers r and θ are called the **polar coordinates** of P.

The fact that P is obtained by rotating the line OR through θ radians gives us a simple relation between the Cartesian and polar coordinates:

$$x = r \cos \theta, \quad y = r \sin \theta. \tag{22.9}$$

For example, the point A in Figure 22.10 has polar coordinates $(4, \pi/6)$; its Cartesian coordinates (a_1, a_2) are given by (22.9) as

$$a_1 = 4 \cos \tfrac{\pi}{6} = 2\sqrt{3}, \quad a_2 = 4 \sin \tfrac{\pi}{6} = 2.$$

The point B in Figure 22.10 has polar coordinates $(6, 3\pi/4)$. Since

$$\cos \tfrac{3\pi}{4} = -\cos \tfrac{\pi}{4} = -1/\sqrt{2}, \quad \sin \tfrac{3\pi}{4} = \sin \tfrac{\pi}{4} = 1/\sqrt{2},$$

the Cartesian coordinates of B are $(-3\sqrt{2}, 3\sqrt{2})$.

From Cartesian to polar

We now explain how to obtain the polar coordinates of a point from the Cartesian ones.[6] By (22.9) and Pythagoras' theorem,

$$r = (x^2 + y^2)^{1/2}.$$

---

[4]After the French mathematician and philosopher René Descartes (1596–1650).

[5]This is a common convention which we use for the rest of this book, but it is not universal; some books let $0 \leq \theta < 2\pi$.

[6]Most modern scientific calculators have a routine for this, but it is sometimes helpful to know the 'long-hand' method, using the calculator only for square roots and inverse trigonometric functions.

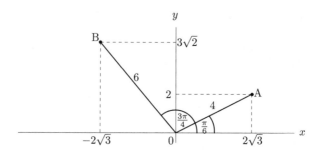

Figure 22.10: **Cartesian and polar coordinates**

Finding θ is a little trickier. This polar coordinate can be found by using the fact that

$$\theta = \pm \arccos(x/r),$$

where the $+$ sign is chosen if $y > 0$ and the $-$ sign if $y < 0$. An alternative, and in our view easier, method is to use the following consequence of (22.9):

$$\tan \theta = y/x \quad \text{if } x \neq 0. \tag{22.10}$$

Notice that (22.10) is not sufficient on its own to determine θ: for example if $y/x = 1$ then θ may be either $\pi/4$ or $-3\pi/4$, depending on whether x is positive or negative. The way to find θ using (22.10) is via a two-stage process. One first finds an acute angle α such that

$$\tan \alpha = |y/x|;$$

θ is then evaluated as α, $-\alpha$, $\alpha - \pi$ or $\pi - \alpha$ according to the signs of x and y. The procedure — usually performed with the aid of a diagram — is illustrated by the two examples below.

Example 1 The point C in Figure 22.11 has Cartesian coordinates $(\sqrt{3}, -3)$. To find its polar coordinates (r, θ), we note first that

$$r = \sqrt{3 + 9} = \sqrt{12} = 2\sqrt{3}.$$

To calculate θ, we find first an acute angle α such that

$$\tan \alpha = 3/\sqrt{3} = \sqrt{3};$$

clearly $\alpha = \pi/3$. But since C has a positive x–coordinate and a negative y–coordinate, θ must be between 0 and $-\pi/2$. Hence $\theta = -\alpha$, and the polar coordinates of C are $(2\sqrt{3}, -\pi/3)$.

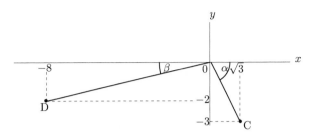

Figure 22.11: **Deriving polar coordinates from cartesian coordinates**

Example 2 The point D in Figure 22.11 has Cartesian coordinates $(-8, -2)$; let its polar coordinates be (s, ϕ). Then $s = \sqrt{64 + 4}$. To find ϕ, we start with an acute angle β such that

$$\tan \beta = |y/x| = 0.25;$$

thus $\beta = \arctan 0.25$. Since both Cartesian coordinates are negative, ϕ must be between $-\pi/2$ and $-\pi$. Hence $\phi = \beta - \pi$, and the polar coordinates of D are $(\sqrt{68}, \arctan 0.25 - \pi)$. Using a calculator, we see that the polar coordinates of D are $(8.25, -2.90)$, both to 2 decimal places.

Exercises

22.4.1 Find the polar coordinates of the points whose Cartesian coordinates are

(a) $(1, \sqrt{3})$ (b) $(-2, 2)$ (c) $(-\frac{1}{2}, -\frac{1}{2}\sqrt{3})$ (d) $(1, -1)$.

22.4.2 Find the Cartesian coordinates of the points whose polar coordinates are

(a) $(1, \pi/3)$ (b) $(2, 3\pi/4)$ (c) $(1/2, -\pi/6)$ (d) $(1, 2)$.

22.4.3 Describe the sets of points in the plane which satisfy the following conditions:

(a) $r = 2$ (b) $\theta = 1$ (c) $r \cos \theta = 4$ (d) $r \sin \theta = 3$.

Problems on Chapter 22

22–1. Let $f(x) = 5 \cos x + 12 \sin x$. Find a positive number R and an acute angle α such that

$$f(x) = R \cos(x - \alpha) \quad \text{for all } x.$$

Hence write down the maximum and minimum values of the function $f(x)$, and sketch its graph.

22-2.   (i) For the function $y = e^{-3x} \sin 4x$,

      (a) find the points where its graph cuts the x-axis;

      (b) find the critical points, and show that the critical values form a geometric progression;

      (c) sketch the graph.

    (ii) As (i), but with $y = e^{3x} \sin 4x$.

22-3.   In the analysis of business cycles, it is a common procedure to decompose the time path of the natural logarithm of national income into the sum of a linear function, known as the trend, and a periodic function. This problem gives an example of this.

    (i) Suppose national income Y depends on time t in the following way:

$$\ln Y = 3t + 1 + 2 \sin 6t.$$

Sketch on the same diagram the graphs of the linear function $3t + 1$ and the periodic function $2 \sin 6t$. Hence sketch the graph of $\ln Y$.

    (ii) Suppose a second economic variable Z can be decomposed similarly, so that

$$\ln Z = 2t + 5 + 3 \sin(6t + \alpha).$$

By considering the periodic components, describe how $\ln Y$ and $\ln Z$ move together in the each of the following cases:

      (a) $\alpha = \pi$ (b) $\alpha = -\pi$ (c) $\alpha = 3\pi$

      (d) $\alpha = -3\pi$ (e) $\alpha = 6\pi$ (f) $\alpha = -6\pi$.

22-4. Let the function G be defined by

$$G(x) = \frac{2}{\pi} \arctan\left(\left[\frac{m}{x}\right]^{\alpha}\right) \qquad (x > 0),$$

where m and α are constants such that $m > 0$ and $\alpha > 1$. For each $x > 0$, let $f(x) = -G'(x)$.

Show that:

    (i) $G(x) \to 1$ as $x \to 0$, $G(x) \to 0$ as $x \to \infty$;

    (ii) $G(m) = \frac{1}{2}$;

    (iii) $x^{\alpha} G(x)$ approaches a positive constant as $x \to \infty$;

    (iv) $f(x) > 0$ for all $x > 0$, and $f(x) \to 0$ as $x \to 0$ and as $x \to \infty$;

    (v) there exists a positive number x^* such that $f'(x^*) = 0$, $f'(x) > 0$ if $0 < x < x^*$ and $f'(x) < 0$ if $x > x^*$.

Find an expression for x^* in terms of m and α.

[Hints: for (iii), use your answer to Exercise 22.3.7; in (v), it makes sense not to try to differentiate $f(x)$ explicitly, but instead to work with the function $\alpha/f(x)$.]

The function G was used by the British economist David Champernowne to give a summary description of the distribution of personal incomes. $G(x)$ denotes the proportion of the population with income greater than x; thus, if x and h are positive numbers and h is small, $hf'(x)$ is approximately equal to proportion of the population with income between x and $x + h$. Property (ii) says that m should be interpreted as median income; (iv) and (v) say that the function f has the properties usually associated with histograms in economic statistics; and (iii) says that the function G possesses a property of real-life income distributions known as the 'Pareto tail'.

Chapter 23

COMPLEX NUMBERS

When discussing quadratic equations in Section 4.1, we said that the equation

$$ax^2 + bx + c = 0$$

has no real solution when $b^2 < 4ac$. As we explained in that section, there is no mystery about this: the geometry of the 'no real roots' case is simply that the relevant parabola lies entirely above or entirely below the x–axis.

However, for some purposes it is helpful to work with a larger number system than $\mathcal{R}$ in which all quadratic equations have solutions. This turns out to have interesting implications concerning the circular functions, which we shall apply to economic dynamics in Chapter 24.

When you have studied this chapter you will be able to:

- add, subtract and multiply complex numbers;

- use conjugacy to find the real and imaginary parts of a ratio of complex numbers;

- compute powers of complex numbers using the trigonometric form;

- perform simple manipulations involving the complex exponential function.

23.1   The complex number system

To construct the **complex number system** $\mathcal{C}$, we introduce a number i such that

$$i^2 = -1$$

and define $\mathcal{C}$ to consist of all expressions of the form

$$z = a + bi,$$

466

where a and b are real numbers. Here a is called the **real part** of z and bi is called the **imaginary part**.

The real numbers form a subset of $\mathcal{C}$: a real number is a complex number with zero imaginary part. Similarly we define an **imaginary number** to be a complex number with zero real part; examples are i, $i/3$ and $-5i$. Two complex numbers are equal if and only if their real parts are equal *and* their imaginary parts are equal.

Complex numbers obey the usual algebraic laws of addition, multiplication and division, remembering that $i^2 = -1$.

Example 1 From the definition of i and the rules of arithmetic,
$$i^3 = i^2 i = -i, \quad i^4 = (i^2)^2 = (-1)^2 = 1, \quad i^5 = i^4 i = i.$$
Also, $(-i)^2 = (-1)^2 i^2 = i^2 = -1$ and similarly
$$(-i)^3 = -i^3 = i, \quad (-i)^4 = i^4 = 1, \quad (-i)^5 = -i^5 = -i.$$

Example 2 Given $z = 3 + 2i$, $w = -1 + 5i$, find the real and imaginary parts of the complex numbers $z + w$, $4z - 3w$ and zw.

Performing the arithmetic in the obvious way, we have
$$z + w = 3 + 2i - 1 + 5i = (3 - 1) + (2 + 5)i = 2 + 7i,$$
$$4z - 3w = 12 + 8i + 3 - 15i = 15 - 7i,$$
$$zw = (3 + 2i)(-1 + 5i) = -3 + 15i - 2i + 10 \times (-1) = -13 + 13i.$$

Finding the real and imaginary parts of the ratio of two complex numbers is slightly harder, and we shall explain how to do this after we have introduced the notion of conjugates. Before that, we show how complex numbers can be used to solve quadratic equations. As in Chapter 4, we often refer to such solutions as 'roots'.

The key here is that $i^2 = (-i)^2 = -1$, so the solutions of the quadratic equation $x^2 = -1$ are $\pm i$. Similarly, if p is any positive real number, the roots of the equation $x^2 = -p$ are $\pm i\sqrt{p}$; we sometimes refer to this pair of imaginary numbers as $\pm\sqrt{-p}$. The following two examples show how these facts may be put together with the usual methods of solving quadratic equations.

Example 3 Solve the equation $x^2 - 4x + 13 = 0$.

By completing the square we see that
$$(x - 2)^2 = 4 - 13 = -9,$$
whence $x - 2 = \pm 3i$. The solutions are therefore $2 + 3i$ and $2 - 3i$.

Example 4 Solve the equation $2x^2 + 3x + 2 = 0$.

This is most easily done by the 'formula method'. The roots are
$$\tfrac{1}{4}(-3 \pm \sqrt{9 - 16}),$$
which simplifies to $(-3 \pm i\sqrt{7})/4$.

Conjugates

If z is a complex number, with real part a and imaginary part bi, the **complex conjugate** of z is the complex number $\bar{z}$, with real part a and imaginary part $-bi$. Notice the connection with quadratic equations: *if a quadratic equation with real coefficients has complex solutions, they must be complex conjugates.* This point is illustrated by Examples 3 and 4: thus, in the former example, the roots are $2 + 3i$ and its conjugate $2 - 3i$. The general proposition follows from the usual formula for the roots.

Modulus

If z is a complex number, with real part a and imaginary part bi, the **modulus** of z is the real number
$$|z| = \sqrt{a^2 + b^2}.$$
For example, if $z = 3 + 4i$, $|z| = \sqrt{3^2 + 4^2} = 5$; if $z = 8 - i$, $|z| = \sqrt{8^2 + 1^2} = \sqrt{65}$.

The modulus is the generalisation to $\mathcal{C}$ of absolute value, in two respects. First, $|z|$ is a *non-negative* real number, which takes the value 0 only if $z = 0$. Secondly, if $b = 0$ the modulus of z reduces to the absolute value of a.

The notion of modulus is intimately related to that of complex conjugate: if $z = a + bi$, then

$$z\bar{z} = (a + bi)(a - bi) = a^2 - (bi)^2 = a^2 + b^2 = |z|^2.$$

Thus, for any complex number z, $z\bar{z}$ is a non-negative real number and

$$|z| = \sqrt{z\bar{z}}.$$

This is the correct generalisation to complex numbers of the fact that $|x| = \sqrt{x^2}$ for all x in $\mathcal{R}$. By contrast, if z is a complex number, $|z|$ is *not* in general equal to $\sqrt{z^2}$. Indeed, z^2 is not necessarily positive (for example, $i^2 = -1$) or even real (for example, $(1 + 2i)^2 = -3 + 4i$).

More on multiplication

For any real numbers a, b, c, d,

$$(a + bi)(c + di) = (ac - bd) + (ad + bc)i$$

and

$$(a - bi)(c - di) = (ac - bd) - (ad + bc)i.$$

Therefore, if z and w are complex numbers and $zw = p$, $\bar{z}\bar{w} = \bar{p}$. But then

$$p\bar{p} = (zw)(\bar{z}\bar{w}) = (z\bar{z})(w\bar{w}).$$

Taking square roots, we see that

$$|zw| = |z|\,|w|.$$

In particular, if neither z nor w is 0, then $|zw|$ is the product of the strictly positive numbers $|z|$ and $|w|$ and is therefore strictly positive. This shows that the product of two nonzero complex numbers is nonzero; this result obviously extends by iteration to products of three, four or more complex numbers.

Division

If z and w are complex numbers, with $w \neq 0$, then

$$\frac{z}{w} = \frac{z\bar{w}}{w\bar{w}} = \frac{z\bar{w}}{|w|^2}.$$

Thus, to calculate the real and imaginary parts of z/w, we compute the complex number $z\bar{w}$ and divide it by the real number $|w|^2$.

Example 5 As in Example 2, let $z = 3 + 2i$, $w = -1 + 5i$. Then

$$\frac{z}{w} = \frac{(3+2i)(-1-5i)}{|w|^2} = -\frac{(3+2i)(1+5i)}{(-1)^2 + 5^2} = -\frac{(3-10) + (2+15)i}{26}.$$

Thus $\dfrac{z}{w}$ has real part $\dfrac{7}{26}$ and imaginary part $-\dfrac{17}{26}i$.

Powers

We have already used the notation z^2 to denote $z \times z$ when z is a complex number, and higher powers of z are defined similarly: $z^3 = z^2 \times z$, $z^4 = z^3 \times z$ and so on. It is easy to see that $(a + bi)^n$ is not in general equal to $a^n + b^n i$. In the next section, we shall explain how the real and imaginary parts of z^n *are* related to the real and imaginary parts of z.

Since a product of nonzero complex numbers is nonzero, we may define

$$z^{-n} = 1/z^n$$

for any nonzero complex number z and any natural number n. If $z \neq 0$, we define $z^0 = 1$.

Notice that we have not yet said anything about fractional powers of complex numbers, such as square roots. For this reason, our discussion of quadratic equations has extended only as far as the case of real coefficients and complex solutions. The reader may conjecture that the usual formula holds when the coefficients are complex; but as we have not yet attached a meaning to the expression $\pm\sqrt{b^2 - 4ac}$ when $b^2 - 4ac$ is a complex number, we are not in a position to confirm or deny the conjecture. All will be revealed in Section 23.3.

General remarks

Given that arithmetic with complex numbers seems fairly simple, you may be tempted to ask the question: why don't we do *all* our algebra with complex numbers? The answer is that there is one very important operation that cannot be performed with complex numbers; they cannot be ordered in any sensible way. In particular, since it takes two real numbers a and b to describe the single complex number $a + bi$, the complex numbers cannot be squeezed into the real line.

The fact that there is no natural way of ordering the complex numbers is a serious limitation, since most interesting quantitative statements, from "my dad's got a bigger car than your dad" to sophisticated arguments about the effect of tax cuts on work incentives, involve some notion of ordering. Thus the number system that is relevant for most applications in economics is $\mathcal{R}$ rather than $\mathcal{C}$. Complex numbers do however have their uses, as we shall see in the next chapter.

For the rest of this chapter we explore further the algebra of complex numbers. It turns out that the circular functions are a great help.

Exercises

23.1.1 Simplify the expressions

$$(-i) \times i, \quad (-2i)^5, \quad i^6, \quad (-i)^7, \quad 1/i.$$

23.1.2 Given $u = -2 + 7i$, $v = 3 - 2i$, find the real and imaginary parts of the complex numbers

$$u + v, \quad -3u - 2v, \quad uv.$$

23.1.3 Solve the equations

$$\text{(a) } x^2 + 4x + 13 = 0, \quad \text{(b) } x^2 - 5x + 9 = 0.$$

23.1.4 Suppose u and v are as in Exercise 23.1.2. Verify that

$$|uv| = |u|\,|v|.$$

Also find the the real and imaginary parts of u/v and v/u.

23.1.5 Show that, for any complex numbers w and z such that $z \neq 0$,

$$|w/z| = |w|/|z|.$$

23.1.6 Let z, w, u, v be complex numbers such that

$$z + w = u, \quad i(z - w) = v.$$

Find z and w in terms of u and v. If u and v are real, what can you say about z and w?

23.2   The trigonometric form

We saw in the last section that it takes two real numbers a and b to describe
a single complex number $a + bi$. This means that we can represent complex
numbers by points in the xy–plane; the point with coordinates (a, b) represents
the complex number $a + bi$. When the coordinate plane is used in this way it is
known as the **Argand diagram**: see Figure 23.1.

We explained in Section 22.4 that there two common ways of describing a
point in the plane by a pair of real numbers, namely the Cartesian coordinates
and the polar coordinates. The Cartesian coordinates of a point in the Argand
diagram represent the real and imaginary parts of a complex number; what do
the polar coordinates represent?

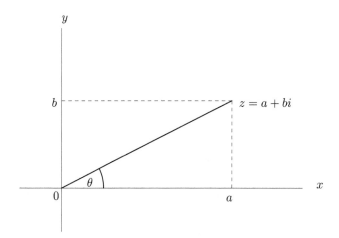

Figure 23.1: **Argand diagram**

To answer this question, we use the relation between Cartesian and polar
coordinates explained in Section 22.4. Let z be the complex number $a + bi$,
where a and b are real numbers; we assume that a and b are not both zero. Let
(r, θ) be the polar coordinates of the point with Cartesian coordinates (a, b).
By (22.9), $a = r \cos \theta$ and $b = r \sin \theta$; thus $z = r \cos \theta + ir \sin \theta$. Summarising,
we see that
$$z = a + bi = r(\cos \theta + i \sin \theta).$$
The expression $a + bi$ is called the **algebraic form** of z and the expression
$r(\cos \theta + i \sin \theta)$ is called the **trigonometric form** of z. In what follows, we
shall frequently write the algebraic form as $a + ib$. We now state some properties
of the trigonometric form.

By a basic relationship between Cartesian and polar coordinates,
$$r = \sqrt{a^2 + b^2} = |z|.$$

Thus the first polar coordinate r is the modulus of z, which is a positive number.[1] The second polar coordinate θ is called the **argument** of z and written $\arg z$; recall from Section 22.4 that this is a real number between $-\pi$ and π.

The modulus and argument of a complex number z are calculated by the usual method for finding polar coordinates. For example, we showed in Section 22.4 that the point with Cartesian coordinates $(\sqrt{3}, -3)$ has polar coordinates $(2\sqrt{3}, -\frac{\pi}{3})$, and the point with Cartesian coordinates $(-8, -2)$ has polar coordinates $(8.25, -2.90)$. Therefore

$$\sqrt{3}-3i = 2\sqrt{3}\left(\cos(-\tfrac{\pi}{3})+i\sin(-\tfrac{\pi}{3})\right), \quad -8-2i = 8.25\left(\cos(-2.9)+i\sin(-2.9)\right).$$

As we stated earlier, the trigonometric form of a complex number $z \neq 0$ is $r(\cos\theta + i\sin\theta)$, where r is the *positive* number $|z|$ and θ is the number $\arg z$, with the property that $-\pi < \arg z \leq \pi$; $|z|$ and $\arg z$ are uniquely determined by z. While this is *the* trigonometric form of z, we shall often write down equations of the form

$$z = c(\cos\alpha + i\sin\alpha),$$

where c and α are *any* real numbers. If this equation holds and $c > 0$, then $c = |z|$ and α is either $\arg z$ or $\arg z \pm 2\pi$ or $\arg z \pm 4\pi$ or ... Similarly, if $c < 0$ then $c = -|z|$ and $\alpha = \arg z \pm k\pi$ for some odd natural number k. These facts follow immediately from the properties of circular functions given in the preceding chapter.

To illustrate these points, let z be the complex number $\sqrt{3} - 3i$, whose trigonometric form we have already shown to be $2\sqrt{3}(\cos(-\pi/3)+i\sin(-\pi/3))$. Then

$$z = 2\sqrt{3}\left(\cos(17\pi/3) + i\sin(17\pi/3)\right) = -2\sqrt{3}\left(\cos(8\pi/3) + i\sin(8\pi/3)\right).$$

Manipulating the trigonometric form

A fact about the trigonometric form which has numerous applications is the following: for any real numbers α and β,

$$\cos(\alpha + \beta) + i\sin(\alpha + \beta) = (\cos\alpha + i\sin\alpha)(\cos\beta + i\sin\beta) \qquad (23.1)$$

This equation follows immediately from the addition formulae of Section 22.2: equality of the real parts of both sides of (23.1) is the addition formula for cosines (22.6), and equality of the imaginary parts is the addition formula for sines (22.5).

Alternatively, one may derive (23.1) from first principles, using the same logic that we used to derive the addition formulae in the last chapter. A sketch similar to Figure 22.6 shows that multiplication by $\cos\alpha + i\sin\alpha$ is represented

---

[1]The fact that $|z|$ is the distance from z to the origin in the Argand diagram is yet another illustration of the principle that modulus is to $\mathcal{C}$ as absolute value is to $\mathcal{R}$.

in the Argand diagram by a rotation through the angle α; (23.1) then follows from the fact that rotation through the angle $\alpha + \beta$ is the same as rotation through the angle β followed by rotation through the angle α.

Powers again

Let θ be any real number: then by (23.1),

$$\cos 2\theta + i \sin 2\theta = (\cos \theta + i \sin \theta)^2,$$
$$\cos 3\theta + i \sin 3\theta = (\cos \theta + i \sin \theta)(\cos 2\theta + i \sin 2\theta)$$
$$= (\cos \theta + i \sin \theta)^3$$

and so on. Thus

$$(\cos \theta + i \sin \theta)^n = \cos n\theta + i \sin n\theta \tag{23.2}$$

for every positive integer n.

We now extend this result to negative powers. Letting $\beta = -\alpha$ in (23.1) and recalling that $\cos 0 = 1$ and $\sin 0 = 0$, we see that

$$1 = (\cos \alpha + i \sin \alpha)(\cos(-\alpha) + i \sin(-\alpha)).$$

Setting $\alpha = n\theta$ and rearranging, we have

$$(\cos n\theta + i \sin n\theta)^{-1} = \cos(-n\theta) + i \sin(-n\theta).$$

By (23.2), the left-hand side of this equation is the reciprocal of $(\cos \theta + i \sin \theta)^n$. Hence

$$(\cos \theta + i \sin \theta)^{-n} = \cos(-n\theta) + i \sin(-n\theta)$$

for every positive integer n.

Another way of stating this result is to say that (23.2) continues to hold when the positive integer n is replaced by the negative integer $-n$. Note also that since $\cos 0 = 1$, $\sin 0 = 0$ and $z^0 = 1$ for every nonzero complex number z, (23.2) holds when n is replaced by 0.

Summarising, we have the following famous theorem of Abraham De Moivre (1667–1754):

De Moivre's theorem For any real number θ and any integer n,

$$(\cos \theta + i \sin \theta)^n = \cos n\theta + i \sin n\theta. \tag{23.2}$$

A useful corollary of De Moivre's theorem is the fact that

$$(\cos \theta - i \sin \theta)^n = \cos n\theta - i \sin n\theta \tag{23.3}$$

for every real number θ and every integer n. To derive (23.3) from De Moivre's theorem, we replace θ by $-\theta$ in (23.2), and apply the rules $\cos(-\alpha) = \cos \alpha$, $\sin(-\alpha) = -\sin \alpha$ to both sides of the resulting equation.

Applying De Moivre's theorem

The reason why De Moivre's theorem is useful is that it gives us an explicit expression for the real and imaginary parts of z^n, given a complex number z and an integer n. If we put z into trigonometric form as $r(\cos\theta + i\sin\theta)$ then

$$z^n = r^n(\cos n\theta + i\sin n\theta)$$

by De Moivre's theorem.

This fact will be used when we return to difference equations in the next chapter. It is also used to calculate powers of complex numbers, though that is more often done electronically these days. We give two examples to show how the method works.

Example 1 Find $(3 + 2i)^7$.

We start by writing $3 + 2i$ in trigonometric form as $r(\cos\theta + i\sin\theta)$, where $r = \sqrt{13}$ and $\theta = \arctan(2/3)$. Hence

$$(3 + 2i)^7 = 13^{7/2}(\cos\alpha + i\sin\alpha),$$

where $\alpha = 7\arctan(2/3)$. Performing the calculations, we see that

$$(3 + 2i)^7 = 13^{3.5}(-0.56164 - 0.82738\,i) = -4449 - 6554i.$$

Example 2 Find $(1 - i)^8$.

Rather than starting with the true trigonometric form of $1 - i$, it is easier to use (23.3). Since $\cos(\pi/4) = \sin(\pi/4) = 1/\sqrt{2}$,

$$1 - i = \sqrt{2}(\cos(\pi/4) - i\sin(\pi/4)).$$

Hence

$$(1 - i)^8 = 2^4(\cos 2\pi - i\sin 2\pi) = 16(1 - 0) = 16.$$

Exercises

23.2.1 Mark the roots of the equations in Exercise 23.1.3 in an Argand diagram.

23.2.2 Suppose the complex number $z = x + yi$ is represented by a point P in an Argand diagram. Obtain the coordinates of the points Q and R representing iz and $\bar{z}$ respectively. Describe how Q and R are related geometrically to P.

23.2.3 In Exercise 22.4.1, we asked you to find the polar coordinates of the points in the plane with Cartesian coordinates

(a) $(1, \sqrt{3})$ (b) $(-2, 2)$ (c) $(-\frac{1}{2}, -\frac{1}{2}\sqrt{3})$ (d) $(1, -1)$.

Now suppose these points are in an Argand diagram. For each point, write down the algebraic form, modulus, argument and trigonometric form of the corresponding complex number.

23.2.4 Obtain the trigonometric form of the complex numbers

$$2, \quad i, \quad -1, \quad 1+i, \quad -1+i, \quad -1-i.$$

23.2.5 Use De Moivre's theorem to evaluate

$$\left(1+i\sqrt{3}\right)^{20} + \left(1-i\sqrt{3}\right)^{20}.$$

23.3   Complex exponentials and polynomials

As we explained in Section 22.3, the sine and cosine functions can be expressed as sums of infinite series. We now explore the implications of this for expressions of the form $\cos\theta + i\sin\theta$, which we introduced in the last section.[2]

Using the Maclaurin series of Section 22.3 we have, for any real number θ,

$$\cos\theta + i\sin\theta = 1 - \frac{\theta^2}{2!} + \frac{\theta^4}{4!} - \frac{\theta^6}{6!} + \dots$$

$$+ i\left[\theta - \frac{\theta^3}{3!} + \frac{\theta^5}{5!} - \frac{\theta^7}{7!} + \dots\right]$$

$$= 1 + \frac{(i\theta)^2}{2!} + \frac{(i\theta)^4}{4!} + \frac{(i\theta)^6}{6!} + \dots$$

$$+ \left[i\theta + \frac{(i\theta)^3}{3!} + \frac{(i\theta)^5}{5!} + \frac{(i\theta)^7}{7!} + \dots\right]$$

$$= 1 + i\theta + \frac{(i\theta)^2}{2!} + \frac{(i\theta)^3}{3!} + \frac{(i\theta)^4}{4!} + \dots.$$

But this is just like the series for the exponential function e^x, except that the real number x has been replaced by the imaginary number $i\theta$.

Because of this development, the exponential function is defined for complex numbers as follows. For any real number θ, we let

$$e^{i\theta} = \cos\theta + i\sin\theta. \tag{23.4}$$

For an arbitrary complex number $z = x + iy$, we let

$$e^z = e^x e^{iy} = e^x(\cos y + i\sin y).$$

To check that this is a reasonable definition of the exponential function, we must show that

$$e^{z+w} = e^z e^w \tag{23.5}$$

---

[2]When we say that a complex number z is the sum of an infinite series, or more generally the limit of a sequence, we mean that the real parts of the relevant sequence converge to the real part of z, and similarly for the imaginary parts.

for every pair of complex numbers z, w. To do this, we recall from Section 9.1 that $e^{a+b} = e^a e^b$ for every pair of real numbers a and b, and from (23.1) that

$$\cos(\alpha + \beta) + i\sin(\alpha + \beta) = (\cos\alpha + i\sin\alpha)(\cos\beta + i\sin\beta)$$

for every pair of real numbers α and β. The latter equation may be written $e^{i(\alpha+\beta)} = e^{i\alpha}e^{i\beta}$. Therefore, if $z = a + i\alpha$ and $w = b + i\beta$ are any two complex numbers,

$$e^{z+w} = e^{a+b}e^{i(\alpha+\beta)} = e^a e^b e^{i\alpha} e^{i\beta} = e^a e^{i\alpha} e^b e^{i\beta} = e^z e^w,$$

proving (23.5).

It is possible to prove that

$$e^z = 1 + z + \frac{z^2}{2!} + \frac{z^3}{3!} + \dots \tag{23.6}$$

for every complex number z. As we showed in Section 10.4, the special case of (23.6) when z is real is just the Maclaurin series of the (real) exponential function. Also, we began this section by defining $e^{i\theta}$ in such a way that (23.6) holds when z is purely imaginary. The general case of (23.6), when z has non-zero real and imaginary parts, is not something we can attempt to prove in this book.

The trigonometric form again

The really important fact about the complex exponential is the defining equation (23.4), sometimes known as **Euler's formula**. Here are four immediate consequences.

(a) We may write the trigonometric form of any complex number z as

$$z = re^{i\theta},$$

where $r = |z|$ and $\theta = \arg z$. Notice that the conjugate of z is

$$\bar{z} = re^{-i\theta}.$$

(b) By (23.4) and Pythagoras' theorem,

$$|e^{i\theta}| = 1$$

for every real number θ.

(c) De Moivre's theorem may be written in the rather obvious-looking form

$$(e^{i\theta})^n = e^{in\theta} \quad \text{for every integer } n.$$

(d) The following special cases of (23.4) are used sufficiently often to be worth remembering:

$$e^{\pi i/2} = i, \quad e^{\pi i} = -1, \quad e^{2\pi i} = 1.$$

Facts (a) and (c) show that the $e^{i\theta}$ notation greatly simplifies the manipulation of trigonometric forms. We now put this notation to work.

Roots

So far in this chapter the word 'root' has been used in the sense of square root, or more generally a solution of a quadratic equation. We now generalise in a different direction by considering nth roots. If n is a natural number and c is a complex number, an nth root of c is a complex number z such that

$$z^n = c.$$

If $c = 0$, the only solution of this equation is $z = 0$. Now suppose that $c \neq 0$; then we may put c into trigonometric form as

$$c = re^{i\theta}.$$

If we now let

$$\lambda = r^{1/n}e^{i\theta/n},$$

then $\lambda^n = re^{i\theta} = c$. Hence $z = \lambda$ is a solution to our equation.

But it is only one of several solutions. For since $e^{2\pi i} = 1$,

$$c = re^{i(\theta + 2\pi)} = re^{i(\theta + 4\pi)} = \ldots .$$

Thus for any natural number k, the complex number λ_k obtained from our expression for λ by replacing θ by $\theta + 2k\pi$ is also a solution to $z^n = c$.

Summarising, we see that if

$$\lambda_k = r^{1/n}e^{i(\theta + 2k\pi)/n} \quad \text{for } k = 0, 1, 2, \ldots,$$

then $\lambda_0, \lambda_1, \lambda_2, \ldots$ are all solutions to the equation $z^n = c$. Not all of these solutions are different: the fact that $e^{2\pi i} = 1$ implies that $\lambda_n = \lambda_0$, $\lambda_{n+1} = \lambda_1$ and so on. But $\lambda_0, \lambda_1, \ldots, \lambda_{n-1}$ are all different, and these are the n solutions of our equation.

Example 1 Find all solutions of the equation $z^6 = 27$.

Since $27 = 3^3 e^0$, the roots are $\lambda_0, \lambda_1, \ldots, \lambda_5$, where

$$\lambda_k = 3^{1/2}e^{i(0+2k\pi)/6} = \sqrt{3}e^{k\pi i/3} \quad (k = 0, 1, \ldots, 5).$$

Then $\lambda_0 = \sqrt{3}$ and

$$\lambda_1 = \sqrt{3}e^{i\pi/3} = \sqrt{3}(\cos\tfrac{\pi}{3} + i\sin\tfrac{\pi}{3}) = \sqrt{3}(\tfrac{1}{2} + \tfrac{1}{2}\sqrt{3}i) = \frac{1}{2}(\sqrt{3} + 3i).$$

Since $e^{\pi i} = -1$, $e^{2\pi i/3} = -e^{\pi i/3}$, so

$$\lambda_2 = -\sqrt{3}e^{-i\pi/3} = -\bar{\lambda}_1 = -\tfrac{1}{2}(\sqrt{3} - 3i).$$

Using again the fact that $e^{\pi i} = -1$, $\lambda_j = -\lambda_{j-3}$ for $j = 3, 4, 5$.

The six solutions of the equation $z^6 = 27$ are therefore $\sqrt{3}, -\sqrt{3}$ and $\pm\tfrac{1}{2}(\sqrt{3} \pm 3i)$, where all four possible combinations of $+$ and $-$ are allowed.

Quadratic equations again

We are now in a position to solve the equation

$$az^2 + bz + c = 0,$$

where a, b and c are complex numbers. The solutions are

$$z = \frac{-b \pm d}{2a}$$

where d is a complex number such that $d^2 = b^2 - 4ac$. d is calculated by expressing $b^2 - 4ac$ in trigonometric form as $re^{i\theta}$, and letting $d = r^{1/2}e^{i\theta/2}$.

In some simple cases one can complete the square rather than using the formula, as the following example shows.

Example 2 Solve the quadratic equation $z^2 + 2z + i = 0$.

Completing the square, we write the equation as

$$(z + 1)^2 = 1 - i.$$

Thus the solutions are $z = -1 \pm w$, where w is a complex number such that

$$w^2 = 1 - i = \sqrt{2}(\cos \tfrac{\pi}{4} - i \sin \tfrac{\pi}{4}) = 2^{1/2}e^{-\pi i/4}.$$

We may therefore set $w = 2^{1/4}e^{-\pi i/8}$. The solutions of the quadratic equation are

$$-1 \pm 2^{1/4}\left(\cos \tfrac{\pi}{8} - i \sin \tfrac{\pi}{8}\right).$$

The fundamental theorem of algebra

Examples 1 and 2 are polynomial equations. The most important fact about such equations is the so-called fundamental theorem of algebra, stated and proved by Gauss in his PhD thesis submitted in 1799 when he was 22 years old. The theorem says in effect that *when complex numbers are allowed, every polynomial may be factorised*. A more precise statement is as follows.

Let $a_1, \ldots, a_n$ be complex numbers. Then there exist complex numbers $\lambda_1, \ldots, \lambda_n$ such that, for every complex number z,

$$z^n + a_1 z^{n-1} + \ldots + a_{n-1}z + a_n = (z - \lambda_1)(z - \lambda_2)\ldots(z - \lambda_n). \qquad (23.7)$$

The relevance of this theorem for equations should be obvious: if we denote the left-hand side of (23.7) by $p(z)$, then the equation $p(z) = 0$ has n solutions, namely $\lambda_1, \ldots, \lambda_n$. These numbers are not necessarily all different, as we know from the case of coincident roots in a quadratic equation.

We now consider what the theorem means. The special case where $n = 2$ and a_1 and a_2 are real is virtually the definition of complex numbers, and we have just discussed the case where $n = 2$ and a_1 and a_2 are complex. For $n > 2$ things are much tougher, and it is not intuitively obvious that the theorem should be true; one might think that having extended the number system from real to complex in order to factorise quadratics, one would have to extend it further to factorise cubics, further still to factorise quartics, and so on. The content of the theorem is that one need not do this: the complex number system is big enough to handle polynomials of any degree.

A brief word about the proof. With some effort, one can prove the theorem for $n = 3$ and $n = 4$ by the same means as for $n = 2$, namely by grinding out a formula for the roots.[3] For $n = 5$, this method is unavailable: no formula exists, for deep reasons that we shall not go into here. Because of this, proofs of the fundamental theorem of algebra are necessarily indirect and tricky, and we shall not attempt one.

Conjugacy again

One useful fact about polynomials is the following: *if, in* (23.7), *the coefficients* $a_1, \ldots, a_n$ *are real numbers, then the roots* $\lambda_1, \ldots, \lambda_n$ *occur in conjugate pairs.* In other words: if p is a polynomial whose coefficients are all real, and λ is a solution of the equation $p(z) = 0$, then so is $\bar{\lambda}$. This has the implication that a polynomial equation with real coefficients cannot have an odd number of solutions with non-zero imaginary parts. In particular, a cubic equation with real coefficients must have at least one real root.

The fact that solutions to polynomial equations with real coefficients occur in conjugate pairs is easily proved. Recall that, for any complex numbers z and w, the conjugate of $z + w$ is $\bar{z} + \bar{w}$ and the conjugate of zw is $\bar{z}\bar{w}$. Repeated application of these facts shows the following: if z is a complex number and p a polynomial with coeffients in $\mathcal{C}$, the conjugate of $p(z)$ is $\bar{p}(\bar{z})$, where $\bar{p}$ is the polynomial whose coefficients are the conjugates of those of p. If all the coefficients of p are real numbers, then p and $\bar{p}$ are the same function, so the conjugate of $p(z)$ is $p(\bar{z})$; but then $p(z) = 0$ if and only if $p(\bar{z}) = 0$, as was to be proved.

Remarks on calculus

The easy case is where we have a function which maps $\mathcal{R}$ into $\mathcal{C}$, say $z = f(t)$ where t is a real variable and z can be complex. Here we simply split f into its real and imaginary parts, say

$$f(t) = g(t) + ih(t).$$

---

[3]The relevant formulae were discovered by Italian mathematicians in the sixteenth century, about 100 years before the invention of complex numbers. The original applications were, of course, to finding real roots of equations with real coefficients.

If g and h are continuous functions, we write

$$\int f(t)\, dt = \int g(t)\, dt + i \int h(t)\, dt,$$

while if g and h are differentiable we write

$$f'(t) = g'(t) + ih'(t).$$

In short, integration and differentiation of complex-valued functions of a real variable are performed part by part. With these definitions,

$$\frac{d}{dt} e^{ct} = ce^{ct}$$

for any complex constant c. This fact will be used in the next chapter.

Extending calculus to functions which map $\mathcal{C}$ into $\mathcal{C}$ is much harder, and we shall have nothing to say about this. The calculus of functions of a complex variable was one of the great achievements of nineteenth-century mathematics, and it is used in some branches of statistics. As far as we know it has no applications in economics.

Exercises

23.3.1 Using your answers to Exercises 23.2.3 and 23.2.4, write each of the following complex numbers in the form $re^{i\theta}$:

$$1+i, \quad -1+i, \quad 1+i\sqrt{3}, \quad -\tfrac{1}{2} - \tfrac{1}{2}\sqrt{3}\, i.$$

23.3.2 Find the real and imaginary parts of the following complex numbers, expressing your answers as simply as you can:

(a) $e^{\pi i/3}$ (b) $2e^{-3\pi i/4}$ (c) $e^{\pi i/6} + e^{-\pi i/6}$ (d) $e^{2\pi i/3} - e^{-2\pi i/3}$.

23.3.3 If $p(z) = (1 - 2i)z^2 + (3 + i)z - 4 + 3i$, write down $\bar{p}(z)$. For this p, and $c = 2 - i$, verify that the conjugate of $p(c)$ is $\bar{p}(\bar{c})$.

23.3.4 Find all the solutions of the equation $z^3 = 1$. Hence find all solutions of the equations $z^3 = -8$ and $z^3 = i$.

23.3.5 Solve the equation

$$z^2 - 6iz - 9 + 4i = 0.$$

23.3.6 Show that

$$y = Pe^{imx} + Qe^{-imx},$$

where P, Q are complex constants and m is a real constant, satisfies the differential equation

$$\frac{d^2y}{dx^2} + m^2 y = 0.$$

Explain the connection of this result with that of Exercise 22.3.2.

Problems on Chapter 23

23–1. Suppose that A and B are complex constants, and

$$y_t = A(1+i)^t + B(1-i)^t$$

for $t = 1, 2, \ldots$ Use De Moivre's theorem to express y_t in terms of trigonometric functions. Hence:

(i) find the real and imaginary parts of y_t in the case where A and B are real;

(ii) show that y_t is real for all t if and only if A and B are conjugates;

(iii) find A, B and a general expression for y_t in the case where $y_0 = 2$ and $y_1 = 5$. The expression for y_t should be the simplest you can find.

23–2. Suppose that A and B are complex constants, and

$$y = Ae^{(-2+5i)t} + Be^{(-2-5i)t}$$

for all real t. Express y in terms of trigonometric functions. Hence:

(i) find the real and imaginary parts of y in the case where A and B are real;

(ii) show that y is real for all t if and only if A and B are conjugates.

(iii) find A, B and a general expression for y in the case where $y = 0$ and $dy/dt = 1$ when $t = 0$. The expression for y should be the simplest you can find.

23–3. (i) Show that 3 is a solution of the equation

$$z^3 - 2z^2 - 2z - 3 = 0.$$

Hence express the left-hand side of the equation as the product of a linear factor and a quadratic factor, and find the other two solutions.

(ii) Show that $1 - 3i$ is a solution of the equation

$$z^3 - 4z^2 + 14z - 20 = 0.$$

Write down the other complex solution. Use these two solutions to express the left-hand side of the equation as the product of a quadratic factor and a linear factor, and find the remaining solution.

23–4. (i) Evaluate

$$\int_0^{\pi/2} e^{it} \, dt.$$

(ii) Using your answer to (i) and integration by parts, evaluate

$$\int_0^{\pi/2} te^{it}\, dt \quad \text{and} \quad \int_0^{\pi/2} t^2 e^{it}\, dt.$$

(iii) Using your answer to (ii), evaluate

$$\int_0^{\pi/2} t \sin t\, dt \quad \text{and} \quad \int_0^{\pi/2} t^2 \cos t\, dt.$$

Chapter 24

FURTHER DYNAMICS

We continue the story we began in Chapter 21, extending our study of dynamics to differential equations involving second derivatives, and their discrete-time counterparts. The techniques of the last two chapters turn out to be very useful here. This is a long but not difficult chapter, and we recommend that you read it in fairly large doses; its length is mainly due to the large number of worked examples illustrating the various possibilities that can arise.

When you have studied this chapter you will be able to:

- solve second-order differential equations and difference equations with constant coefficients;

- test such equations for oscillatory solutions, and describe the main properties of the oscillations when they occur;

- find whether or not a stationary solution to such an equation is stable;

- apply these methods in simple dynamic economic models.

24.1   Second-order differential equations

A second-order differential equation is an equation of the form

$$\frac{d^2y}{dt^2} = F\left(t, y, \frac{dy}{dt}\right), \tag{24.1}$$

where F is a function of three variables.[1]   To solve such an equation means finding all possible functions $y = f(t)$ which satisfy the equation. The general

---

[1] Equation (24.1) is properly described as an "ordinary differential equation of second order and first degree". "Ordinary" means that only ordinary derivatives, as opposed to partial derivatives, are present. The **degree** of a differential equation is the greatest power to which the derivative of highest order is raised. For instance, if we were to replace the left hand side of (24.1) by a cubic function of d^2y/dt^2 we would have a differential equation of second order and third degree. All differential equations discussed in this book are of first degree.

solution of a second-order differential equation typically contains *two* constants of integration, and if we want to tie these down we need two boundary conditions. In most cases encountered in economics, the boundary conditions are either of the form '$y = y_1$ when $t = t_1$ and $y = y_2$ when $t = t_2$', or of the form '$y = y_0$ and $dy/dt = z_0$ when $t = t_0$'.

In this chapter, the only second-order differential equations we discuss are of a particularly simple form, namely **linear equations with constant coefficients**. By this is meant equations of the form

$$\frac{d^2y}{dt^2} + b\frac{dy}{dt} + cy = G(t),$$

where b and c are constants.[2] We begin with an even simpler case, where $G(t) = 0$. Such a linear equation is said to be **homogeneous**. The equation of interest is then

$$\frac{d^2y}{dt^2} + b\frac{dy}{dt} + cy = 0, \tag{24.2}$$

where b and c are constants. We assume throughout that b and c are real numbers.

Some motivation

In economics, rates of change of rates of change are seldom the focus of interest in dynamic analysis.[3] The reader may therefore wonder how equations of the form (24.2), or more generally (24.1), arise in economic applications. We give a brief answer to this before discussing methods of solution.

Suppose we have a mathematical model of some system (economic, biological or whatever) which can be described in terms of two variables y and z: thus in a microeconomic model of a single market y might be price and z quantity, while in a macroeconomic growth model y might be national income and z the capital stock. Suppose the model is a dynamic one, in the sense that its equations specify the rates of change of y and z at time t as functions of their levels at time t, and possibly t itself. The equations are therefore of the form

$$\frac{dy}{dt} = f(y, z, t), \quad \frac{dz}{dt} = g(y, z, t). \tag{24.3}$$

Solving the model means expressing y and z as explicit functions of t.

As a first pass at solving (24.3), one might attempt to do what we have been doing with simultaneous equations since the beginning of this book, namely to eliminate one of the variables. This is often a sensible thing to do, and its cost is almost always the appearance of a second derivative: in other words, eliminating z from (24.3) gives a differential equation in y of the form (24.1).

---

[2] The more general case where the coefficient of d^2y/dt^2 is a non-zero constant a is reduced to the given form by dividing through by a.

[3] A rare instance is mentioned in the next section.

To illustrate this, suppose (24.3) takes the particularly simple form

$$\text{(i)} \quad \frac{dy}{dt} = \alpha y + \beta z, \quad \text{(ii)} \quad \frac{dz}{dt} = \gamma y + \delta z,$$

where $\alpha, \beta, \gamma, \delta$ are constants. Then (ii) may be written

$$\text{(ii')} \quad \frac{dz}{dt} - \delta z = \gamma y.$$

To eliminate z, it suffices to transform (i) in such a way that z appears only in the form of the left-hand side of (ii'). The appropriate transformation is to differentiate (i) with respect to t and subtract δ times (i) from the resulting equation. Doing this, and using (ii'), we have

$$\frac{d^2y}{dt^2} - \delta\frac{dy}{dt} = \alpha\left(\frac{dy}{dt} - \delta y\right) + \beta\gamma y.$$

Rearranging, we obtain (24.2), with $b = -(\alpha + \delta)$ and $c = \alpha\delta - \beta\gamma$.

To summarise, equations such as (24.1) and (24.2) result from eliminating the variable z from a pair of equations such as (24.3). As we shall see in the next chapter, one can often say something about systems of the form (24.3) without doing any elimination; however, such methods build on those used in this chapter to analyse (24.2).

The characteristic equation

We now explain how to solve equations of the form (24.2). Our first step is to look for solutions of the form $y = e^{pt}$ where p is a constant. This is not an entirely wild guess, since (24.2) is the natural second-order generalisation of the equation

$$\frac{dy}{dt} + ay = 0,$$

and we showed in Chapter 21 that this has an exponential solution. If $y = e^{pt}$, the left-hand side of (24.2) is

$$(p^2 + bp + c)e^{pt},$$

which is zero if and only if $p^2 + bp + c = 0$.

All of this suggests that if we want to solve (24.2), we should look at the roots of the quadratic equation

$$x^2 + bx + c = 0. \tag{24.4}$$

This is called the **characteristic equation** of the differential equation (24.2). We have just shown that $y = e^{pt}$ is a solution of (24.2) if and only if $x = p$ is a solution of (24.4).

Distinct real roots

Suppose for the moment that the characteristic equation has two distinct real roots, say p and q. Then (24.2) is satisfied when $y = e^{pt}$ and when $y = e^{qt}$. Now let A and B be any constants and let

$$f(t) = Ae^{pt} + Be^{qt}.$$

Then

$$f'(t) = Ape^{pt} + Bqe^{qt}, \quad f''(t) = Ap^2 e^{pt} + Bq^2 e^{qt}$$

and hence

$$f''(t) + bf'(t) + cf(t) = \left[p^2 + bp + c\right] Ae^{pt} + \left[q^2 + bq + c\right] Be^{qt}.$$

By our choice of p and q, both terms in square brackets are zero, so (24.2) is satisfied when $y = f(t)$.

We have shown that a solution to (24.2) is given by

$$y = Ae^{pt} + Be^{qt}, \tag{24.5}$$

where A and B are constants. Since the general solution of a second-order differential equation typically contains two constants of integration, and A and B can be any constants, it seems reasonable to conclude that (24.5) is the general solution of (24.2). This is actually true, and we shall give a more rigorous demonstration in the appendix to this chapter.

To summarise: *if the characteristic equation* (24.3) *has two distinct real roots* p, q, *the general solution to* (24.2) *is* (24.5).

Example 1 Find the general solution of the differential equation

$$\frac{d^2 y}{dt^2} + \frac{dy}{dt} - 6y = 0.$$

The characteristic equation is $x^2 + x - 6 = 0$, with roots 2 and -3. The general solution of the differential equation is therefore

$$y = Ae^{2t} + Be^{-3t}$$

where A and B are constants.

Complex roots

Now consider the case where the characteristic equation (24.4) has complex roots. Since b and c are real numbers, the roots are complex conjugates: we write

$$p = g + ih, \quad q = g - ih,$$

where g and h are real. Since the derivative with respect to t of e^{pt} is pe^{pt} even when p is complex (a fact stated in Section 23.3), everything we have done up to now remains valid: the general solution to (24.2) is (24.5), where the constants A and B are now complex numbers.

This solution looks peculiar, since for all relevant purposes we are interested only in real solutions for y. But, as we explain in the next paragraph, a simple restriction on the constants A and B ensures that the imaginary part of the right-hand side of (24.5) is zero. Thus (24.5) is a perfectly sensible solution formula. There is however a good reason for rearranging it, which is that we want to use the information that p and q are complex conjugates. Notice that e^{pt} and e^{qt} are also complex conjugates: by the results of Section 23.3,

$$e^{pt} = e^{gt}e^{iht} = e^{gt}(\cos ht + i \sin ht), \quad e^{qt} = e^{gt}e^{-iht} = e^{gt}(\cos ht - i \sin ht).$$

This indicates that the explicitly real solution for y will involve circular functions. Before giving the solution, we attend to the constants A and B.

The restriction on these constants which ensures that y is real is that A and B are complex conjugates. For suppose that $B = \bar{A}$, and let $Y = e^{pt}$. For reasons we have just explained, $\bar{Y} = e^{qt}$; hence (24.5) says that

$$y = AY + \bar{A}\bar{Y}.$$

But $\bar{A}\bar{Y}$ is the conjugate of AY. Hence y is twice the real part of AY. In particular, y is real.

We now turn these facts into a solution formula. Let A be written in trigonometric form as $|A|e^{i\alpha}$, and suppose from now on that $B = \bar{A}$. We have just shown that y is twice the real part of Ae^{pt}. But

$$Ae^{pt} = |A|\,e^{i\alpha}e^{gt+iht} = |A|\,e^{gt}e^{i(ht+\alpha)},$$

which has real part $|A|\,e^{gt}\cos(ht + \alpha)$. Setting $C = 2|A|$, we have

$$y = Ce^{gt}\cos(ht + \alpha). \tag{24.6}$$

To summarise: *if the characteristic equation* (24.4) *has complex conjugate roots* $g \pm ih$, *the general solution to* (24.2) *is* (24.6), *where C and α are constants.*

Another way of writing (24.6) is sometimes useful. Setting $A' = C\cos\alpha$, $B' = -C\sin\alpha$ and applying the addition formula for cosines, we have

$$y = e^{gt}(A'\cos ht + B'\sin ht), \tag{24.6'}$$

where A' and B' are constants. This equation can also be obtained directly from (24.5) and the trigonometric forms of the complex conjugates e^{pt} and e^{qt}: some manipulation yields (24.6'), with $A' = A + B$ and $B' = i(A - B)$; these are real numbers when A and B are complex conjugates.

Example 2 Find the solution of the differential equation

$$\frac{d^2y}{dt^2} - 6\frac{dy}{dt} + 13y = 0$$

which satisfies the boundary conditions

$$y = 1 \text{ and } \frac{dy}{dt} = 2 \text{ when } t = 0.$$

The characteristic equation is $x^2 - 6x + 13 = 0$, which may be written

$$(x - 3)^2 = -4.$$

Thus the roots of the characteristic equation are $3 \pm 2i$, and the general solution of the differential equation is

$$y = Ce^{3t}\cos(2t + \alpha),$$

where C and α are constants.

We now use the boundary conditions. Since $y = 1$ when $t = 0$, $C\cos\alpha = 1$. Differentiating the general solution,

$$dy/dt = Ce^{3t}[3\cos(2t + \alpha) - 2\sin(2t + \alpha)].$$

This, together with the boundary condition that $dy/dt = 2$ when $t = 0$, implies that

$$3C\cos\alpha - 2C\sin\alpha = 2.$$

Our boundary conditions therefore imply that $C\cos\alpha = 1$ and $C\sin\alpha = \frac{1}{2}$. Using the general solution and the addition formula for cosines, we may express the required solution in the form (24.6′) as

$$y = e^{3t}(\cos 2t - \tfrac{1}{2}\sin 2t).$$

Coincident roots

Finally, consider the case where $b^2 = 4c$. Letting $p = -\frac{1}{2}b$, we have $b = -2p$, $c = p^2$, and the characteristic equation has coincident roots at p. Obviously $y = e^{pt}$ is a solution to the differential equation (24.2): hence the general solution is

$$y = Ae^{pt} + Bg(t),$$

where $g(t)$ is some solution that is not a constant multiple of e^{pt}.

It is not hard to verify that a possible choice for $g(t)$ is te^{pt}: see Exercise 24.1.1. Hence the general solution may be written

$$y = (A + Bt)e^{pt} \qquad (24.7)$$

where A and B are constants. Thus *if the characteristic equation (24.4) has coincident roots at p, the general solution to (24.2) is (24.7)*.

Example 3 Find the general solution of the differential equation

$$\frac{d^2y}{dt^2} - 6\frac{dy}{dt} + 9y = 0.$$

Since the characteristic equation may be written $(x-3)^2 = 0$, the general solution of the differential equation is

$$y = (A + Bt)e^{3t},$$

where A and B are constants.

The non-homogeneous case

We return to differential equations of the form

$$\frac{d^2y}{dt^2} + b\frac{dy}{dt} + cy = G(t), \tag{24.8}$$

where b and c are constant and $G(t)$ is not necessarily zero.

The standard method of solution is adapted from the method for linear first order differential equations with constant coefficients introduced in Section 21.2. We start by finding a **particular solution**, defined as a function $H(t)$ such that

$$H''(t) + bH'(t) + cH(t) = G(t). \tag{24.9}$$

Setting $z = y - H(t)$ and subtracting (24.9) from (24.8), we have the **associated homogeneous equation**

$$\frac{d^2z}{dt^2} + b\frac{dz}{dt} + cz = 0.$$

But this equation is just (24.2), with y replaced by z, and we solve it in the usual way; y is then given as $z + H(t)$. The general solution for z is often called the **complementary solution**; the solution for y is therefore the sum of the complementary solution and the particular solution.

The hard part of this is of course finding the particular solution $H(t)$. The method here is essentially trial and error, but a guideline can be given which usually (but not always!) works: *try for a function $H(t)$ of the same general form as $G(t)$.* For example, if $G(t)$ is a constant we try for a constant particular solution, known as a **stationary solution**. If $G(t) = Pe^{at}$, where P and a are constants, we try $H(t) = Qe^{at}$, where Q is another constant. And if $G(t)$ is a linear function of t, we try for an $H(t)$ which is also a linear function of t.

Example 4 Find the general solution of the differential equation

$$\frac{d^2y}{dt^2} + \frac{dy}{dt} - 6y = -3.$$

We start by trying for a stationary solution, say $y = k$. Then

$$0 + 0 - 6k = -3.$$

We may therefore take $y = \frac{1}{2}$ as our particular solution.

To find the general solution, we let $z = y - \frac{1}{2}$. This gives us a homogeneous equation in z which is just the equation of Example 1, with y replaced by z. Hence the complementary solution is

$$z = Ae^{2t} + Be^{-3t},$$

where A and B are constants, and the general solution for y is

$$y = Ae^{2t} + Be^{-3t} + \tfrac{1}{2}.$$

Example 5 Find the general solution of the differential equation

$$\frac{d^2y}{dt^2} - 6\frac{dy}{dt} + 13y = 5e^{4t}.$$

Here we try for a particular solution of the form $y = ke^{4t}$, where k is a constant. Then

$$(16 - 24 + 13)ke^{4t} = 5e^{4t}.$$

Hence $k = 1$, and $y = e^{4t}$ is our particular solution.

To find the general solution for y, we let $z = y - e^{4t}$. Then

$$\frac{d^2z}{dt^2} - 6\frac{dz}{dt} + 13z = 0.$$

From the result of Example 2, the general solution for z is

$$z = Ce^{3t}\cos(2t + \alpha),$$

where C and α are constants. Hence the general solution for y is

$$z = Ce^{3t}\cos(2t + \alpha) + e^{4t}.$$

Example 6 Find the solution of the differential equation

$$\frac{d^2y}{dt^2} - 6\frac{dy}{dt} + 9y = 27t - 63,$$

given that $y = 1$ and $dy/dt = 0$ when $t = 0$.

Trying for a particular solution of the form $y = at + b$, we have

$$0 - 6a + 9at + 9b = 27t - 63.$$

If this is to hold for all t, we must have $9a = 27$ and $-6a + 9b = -63$; hence $a = 3$, $b = -5$ and the particular solution is $y = 3t - 5$.

To obtain the general solution, we let $z = y - 3t + 5$. Then z satisfies the homogeneous equation

$$\frac{d^2z}{dt^2} - 6\frac{dz}{dt} + 9z = 0,$$

which we solved in Example 3. Thus $z = (A + Bt)e^{3t}$, where A and B are constants, and the general solution for y is

$$y = (A + Bt)e^{3t} + 3t - 5.$$

Finally, we use the boundary conditions to evaluate the constants A and B. Since $y = 1$ when $t = 0$, $A - 5 = 1$, so

$$y = (6 + Bt)e^{3t} + 3t - 5.$$

Using the fact that $dy/dt = 0$ when $t = 0$, we see that $B + 3(6+0) + 3 = 0$. Hence $B = -21$, and the solution we seek is

$$y = (6 - 21t)e^{3t} + 3t - 5.$$

Exercises

24.1.1 Suppose the characteristic equation of the differential equation

$$\frac{d^2y}{dt^2} + b\frac{dy}{dt} + cy = 0$$

has equal roots. If each root is equal to p, verify that te^{pt} is a solution to the differential equation.

24.1.2 For each of the following equations, find the general solution:

(a) $\dfrac{d^2y}{dt^2} - \dfrac{dy}{dt} - 6y = 0$ (b) $\dfrac{d^2y}{dt^2} - \dfrac{dy}{dt} - 6y = 3$

(c) $\dfrac{d^2y}{dt^2} + 4\dfrac{dy}{dt} + 5y = 0$ (d) $\dfrac{d^2y}{dt^2} + 4\dfrac{dy}{dt} + 5y = 10$

(e) $\dfrac{d^2y}{dt^2} + 10\dfrac{dy}{dt} + 25y = 0$ (f) $\dfrac{d^2y}{dt^2} + 10\dfrac{dy}{dt} + 25y = 10.$

24.1.3 Find the general solutions of the equations

(a) $3\dfrac{d^2y}{dt^2} + 2\dfrac{dy}{dt} - y = 6$ (b) $\dfrac{d^2y}{dt^2} + 6\dfrac{dy}{dt} + 9y = 1 - t.$

24.1.4 (a) Find the solution of the differential equation

$$\frac{d^2y}{dt^2} + 4y = 20$$

which satisfies $y = 8$ and $\dfrac{dy}{dt} = 8$ when $t = 0$.

(b) Find the solution of the differential equation

$$\frac{d^2y}{dt^2} - 4\frac{dy}{dt} + 3y = e^{2t}$$

which satisfies $y = 0$ and $\dfrac{dy}{dt} = 2$ when $t = 0$.

24.2 Qualitative behaviour

Having explained how to solve some second-order differential equations, we now consider the main *qualitative* features of the solutions: what do their graphs look like, and what happens to y when t becomes large?

To keep things relatively simple we consider differential equations of the form

$$\frac{d^2y}{dt^2} + b\frac{dy}{dt} + cy = u,$$

where b, c and u are constants.[4] We assume that $c \neq 0$, so that there is a constant particular solution $y = Y$, where

$$Y = \frac{u}{c},$$

As we noted above, a constant particular solution is called a stationary solution, and we shall refer to Y as the **stationary value** or **equilibrium value** of y.[5] The commonsense interpretation is that if $y = Y$ and $dy/dt = 0$ when $t = 0$, then $y = Y$ for all t.

As we explained in the preceding section, the general solution for y depends on the roots of the characteristic equation

$$x^2 + bx + c = 0.$$

If $b^2 > 4c$, this equation has two distinct real roots, say p and q, and the general solution to the differential equation is

$$y = Ae^{pt} + Be^{qt} + Y,$$

---

[4]The case where the right-hand side is a linear function of t is considered in Problem 24–3.

[5]In economics, the word 'equilibrium' is almost always used in a model-specific sense. For this reason, we normally avoid using the word in a general mathematical context. We depart from our usual practice when discussing stability because the phrase 'stable equilibrium' is more familiar and less cumbersome than 'stable stationary solution'.

where A and B are constants. If $b^2 = 4c$, the characteristic equation has coincident roots at $p = -\frac{1}{2}b$, and the general solution is

$$y = (A + Bt)e^{pt} + Y,$$

where A and B are constants. Finally, if $b^2 < 4c$, the characteristic equation has complex conjugate roots, say $g \pm hi$; the general solution is then

$$y = Ce^{gt}\cos(ht + \alpha) + Y,$$

where C and α are constants.

The two main questions which concern us in this section are:

(A) Under what circumstances does $y \to Y$ as $t \to \infty$?

(B) Under what circumstances does the solution involve oscillatory behaviour, in the sense of Chapter 22?

We deal with (B) first, as we already have the answer: oscillations occur when the general solution contains sines and/or cosines, and we have just shown that this happens if and only if $b^2 < 4c$. An example, related to Example 2 of the last section, is the differential equation

$$\frac{d^2y}{dt^2} - 6\frac{dy}{dt} + 13y = 52,$$

for which the general solution is

$$y = Ce^{3t}\cos(2t + \alpha) + 4,$$

where C and α are constants. Of course, if C happens to be zero then $y = 4$ for all t, but if $C \neq 0$ there will be oscillations.

In this instance the oscillations are **explosive**, in the sense that the waves get larger and larger as t increases. This is because the cosine term, which oscillates between -1 and 1, is multiplied by something (namely Ce^{3t}) whose absolute value is an increasing function of t, tending to infinity as $t \to \infty$.

The opposite case, that of **damped oscillations**, is where the solution displays oscillations which get smaller and smaller as t increases, with the effect that $y \to Y$ as $t \to \infty$. An example is given by the differential equation

$$\frac{d^2y}{dt^2} + 6\frac{dy}{dt} + 13y = 52,$$

for which the general solution is

$$y = Ce^{-3t}\cos(2t + \alpha) + 4.$$

This solution, and that to the previous example, are sketched in the two panels of Figure 24.1.

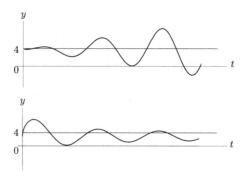

Figure 24.1: **Explosive and damped oscillations**

The main difference between Figure 24.1 and the illustrations of explosive and damped oscillations in Figure 22.1 is that in the earlier diagram the oscillations were about the horizontal axis, whereas the stationary value is now 4. The third case considered in Figure 22.1, that of regular oscillations which were neither damped nor explosive, occurs as the solution to the second-order differential equation in the case where $b = 0 < c$.

Stability

We now turn to question (A). The stationary solution is said to be **stable** if $y \to Y$ as $t \to \infty$, *regardless of initial conditions*. The necessary and sufficient condition for stability in terms of the roots of the characteristic equation is as follows:

> **equilibrium is stable if and only if both roots of the characteristic equation have negative real parts**.

We shall not give a rigorous proof of this proposition: essentially it follows from the fact that, for a real number g, $e^{gt} \to 0$ as $t \to \infty$ if and only if $g < 0$. What we shall do is to spell out the proposition in more detail and illustrate it with examples.

Because the roots of the characteristic equation may be real and distinct, real and coincident or complex conjugates, the stability proposition can be divided into three parts:

1. Let $b^2 > 4c$ and let the roots of the characteristic equation be p and q. Then equilibrium is stable if and only if $p < 0$ and $q < 0$.

2. Let $b^2 = 4c$ and let the characteristic equation have coincident roots at $p \, (= -\frac{1}{2}b)$. Then equilibrium is stable if and only if $p < 0$.

3. Let $b^2 < 4c$ and let the roots of the characteristic equation be $g \pm ih$. Then equilibrium is stable if and only if $g < 0$.

Part 3 of the proposition is the distinction between damped and undamped oscillations, which we have already explained. We now give examples to illustrate parts 1 and 2.

Example 1 In Example 4 of the last section, we showed that the differential equation

$$\frac{d^2y}{dt^2} + \frac{dy}{dt} - 6y = -3$$

has general solution

$$y = Ae^{2t} + Be^{-3t} + \tfrac{1}{2}.$$

Here the stationary value of y is $\tfrac{1}{2}$; equilibrium is *unstable* because $y \to \infty$ as $t \to \infty$ if $A > 0$, and $y \to -\infty$ as $t \to \infty$ if $A < 0$. Notice that if A happens to be zero, then $y \to -\tfrac{1}{2}$ as $t \to \infty$, whatever the value of B. This, however, does not contradict our statement above that equilibrium is unstable: for stability, by definition, means convergence to the stationary value *regardless of initial conditions.*

Example 2 It is easy to show that the differential equation

$$\frac{d^2y}{dt^2} + 4\frac{dy}{dt} + 4y = 8$$

has general solution

$$y = (A + Bt)e^{-2t} + 2.$$

The equilibrium value of y is 2, and equilibrium is *stable*; for as $t \to \infty$, both e^{-2t} and te^{-2t} tend to zero.[6]

A simple stability condition

The following proposition relates stability of equilibrium to the parameters b and c of the differential equation:

equilibrium is stable if and only if $b > 0$ and $c > 0$.

We now explain how this proposition follows from the one stated earlier about the roots of the characteristic equation.

To keep the argument to reasonable length, we ignore cases where either b or c is zero.[7] This leaves us with three possibilities:

$$\text{(i) } c < 0 \qquad \text{(ii) } 4c > b^2 \qquad \text{(iii) } 0 < 4c \le b^2.$$

In case (i), the roots of the characteristic equation are real with opposite signs (their product is $-c$) and hence equilibrium is unstable. In case (ii) the roots

---

[6] Recall Problem 10–3.
[7] see Exercise 24.2.2 for the case $b = 0$.

of the characteristic equation are complex conjugates, with common real part $-\frac{1}{2}b$, so equilibrium is stable if and only if $b > 0$. In case (iii), $(b^2 - 4c)^{1/2}$ is a real number, which is non-negative and less than $|b|$; therefore the roots of the characteristic equation are real, and both have the same sign as $-b$; hence, as in case (ii), equilibrium is stable if and only if $b > 0$.

Figure 24.2 summarises most of the results given above about stability and oscillations, by indicating which regions of the bc–plane correspond to stability and which to oscillations. In the diagram **S** means stable and **U** unstable; thus we have **S** in the positive quadrant, **U** elsewhere. Also, **O** means oscillatory and **N** non-oscillatory; thus we have **O** where $4c > b^2$, **N** elsewhere.

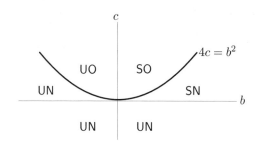

Figure 24.2: **Classification of second-order differential equations**

An economic example: inflation and unemployment

We illustrate the concepts of stability and oscillations with a macroeconomic model of inflation. The model is similar to that of of Chapters 8 and 9 of Olivier Blanchard, *Macroeconomics*, Second Edition (Prentice Hall International, 2000): in what follows we shall refer to this excellent textbook as *OBM*.

Following *OBM*, page 154, we suppose that the *rate of change* of the inflation rate is proportional to the difference between the actual unemployment rate u and the natural rate of unemployment rate u_n; when $u > u_n$ the inflation rate *decreases* and when $u < u_n$ the inflation rate *increases*. We assume that u_n is a constant; we denote the price level by P and the inflation rate by z.[8] In continuous time,[9] $z = \dfrac{1}{P}\dfrac{dP}{dt}$, and the rate of change of the inflation rate is $\dfrac{dz}{dt}$. The assumed relation between this rate of change and the unemployment rate may be written

$$\frac{dz}{dt} = -\alpha(u - u_n), \qquad (24.10)$$

where α is a positive constant.

---

[8]*OBM* and many other books on macroeconomics denote the inflation rate by π; we do not, for obvious reasons.

[9]Blanchard formulates his model in discrete time.

We assume that, at any given time, the unemployment rate u is determined by aggregate demand, which depends on the real value of the money supply. Specifically, we assume that u is a linear, decreasing function of $\ln(M/P)$, where M is the (nominal) money supply.[10] Thus

$$u = \gamma - \beta \ln \frac{M}{P}, \tag{24.11}$$

where β and γ are positive constants.

Our final assumption is that M grows at a constant rate μ. Then

$$\frac{d}{dt} \ln \frac{M}{P} = \frac{1}{M} \frac{dM}{dt} - \frac{1}{P} \frac{dP}{dt} = \mu - z.$$

Hence, by (24.10) and (24.11),

$$\frac{d^2 z}{dt^2} = -\alpha \frac{du}{dt} = \alpha \beta \frac{d}{dt} \ln \frac{M}{P} = \alpha \beta (\mu - z).$$

The behaviour of the inflation rate z is therefore given by the differential equation

$$\frac{d^2 z}{dt^2} + \alpha \beta z = \alpha \beta \mu.$$

It is easy to see that the general solution displays *regular* oscillations about the rate of growth of the money supply; the solution is in fact

$$z = \mu + C \cos(t\sqrt{\alpha\beta} + k),$$

where C and k are constants. It follows from (24.10) that the unemployment rate also displays regular oscillations:

$$u = u_n + C' \sin(t\sqrt{\alpha\beta} + k),$$

where $C' = C\sqrt{\beta/\alpha}$.

Two variants of the model

1. Suppose that the rate of change of the inflation rate is a decreasing function, not only of the level of the unemployment rate, but also of its rate of change.[11] Then (24.10) is replaced by

$$\frac{dz}{dt} = -\alpha(u - u_n) - \theta \frac{du}{dt}, \tag{24.10'}$$

---

[10] The 'semi-logarithmic' functional form may be rationalised as follows. By definition of the unemployment rate, $1 - u = N/L$, where N is employment and L is the labour force. If u is reasonably small, $\ln(1 - u) \approx -u$, so $u \approx \ln L - \ln N$. If we assume that L is constant and N is proportional to some positive power of M/P via a production function and an aggregate demand relation, we obtain an equation like (24.11).

[11] A possible rationale for this invokes the idea of 'hysteresis': see *OBM*, pages 438–442.

where α and θ are positive constants. This, together with (24.11) and our assumption about the money supply, implies that

$$\frac{d^2z}{dt^2} = \alpha\beta(\mu - z) + \theta\beta\frac{d}{dt}(\mu - z).$$

Since μ is constant, the behaviour of the inflation rate z is given by the differential equation

$$\frac{d^2z}{dt^2} + \theta\beta\frac{dz}{dt} + \alpha\beta z = \alpha\beta\mu.$$

The stationary value of z is again μ. Since $\theta\beta$ and $\alpha\beta$ are positive constants, equilibrium is stable.

2. In this variant we assume that (24.10) holds, and retain our assumption that the money supply grows at a constant rate μ. On the other hand, we alter (24.11) by making u a decreasing function, not only of M/P, but also of the inflation rate. Thus we assume that an increase in z, given M/P, increases aggregate demand and therefore lowers unemployment; a justification for this may be based on the distinction between real and nominal rates of interest explained in Chapter 14 of *OBM*. Specifically, we assume that (24.11) is replaced by

$$u = \gamma - \beta\ln\frac{M}{P} - \sigma z, \qquad (24.11')$$

where β, γ, σ are positive constants.[12]

To apply (24.11') in conjunction with our other assumptions we argue as above, with $\beta\ln(M/P)$ replaced by $\beta\ln(M/P) + \sigma z$. Hence $\beta(\mu - z)$ is replaced by

$$\beta(\mu - z) + \sigma\frac{dz}{dt},$$

and the differential equation for z is

$$\frac{d^2z}{dt^2} - \alpha\sigma\frac{dz}{dt} + \alpha\beta z = \alpha\beta\mu.$$

Once again, the stationary value of z is μ. Since $\alpha\sigma$ and $\alpha\beta$ are positive constants, equilibrium is *unstable*.

Exercises

24.2.1 Classify the differential equations in Exercise 24.1.2 as **SO**, **SN**, **UO** or **UN**, where **S**, **U**, **O** and **N** are defined as in the text. In each case, illustrate the main features of the solution in a graph.

---

[12]σ is the lower-case version of the Greek letter sigma, whose upper-case symbol is Σ.

24.2.2 Show directly that the stationary solution of an equation of the form

$$\frac{d^2y}{dt^2} + cy = u,$$

where u and c are constants such that $c \neq 0$, is always unstable.

24.2.3 (a) Show that, in variant 1 of the model of inflation given in the text, we have damped oscillations if θ is sufficiently small. How small is that?

(b) Show that, in variant 2 of the model of inflation given in the text, we have explosive oscillations if σ is sufficiently small. How small is that?

24.3 Second-order difference equations

We now turn to the case where time is measured discretely. In Section 21.4 we defined the forward difference operator Δ, which is the discrete-time counterpart of the operation of differentiation with respect to time:

$$\Delta y_t = y_{t+1} - y_t.$$

Similarly, we define the discrete-time analogue of d^2y/dt^2 as

$$\Delta^2 y_t = \Delta(\Delta y_t) = \Delta(y_{t+1} - y_t) = (y_{t+2} - y_{t+1}) - (y_{t+1} - y_t).$$

Simplifying, we have

$$\Delta^2 y_t = y_{t+2} - 2y_{t+1} + y_t.$$

The discrete-time analogue of the differential equation

$$\frac{d^2y}{dt^2} + b\frac{dy}{dt} + cy = G(t)$$

is the difference equation

$$\Delta^2 y_t + b\Delta y_t + cy_t = d_t,$$

where b and c are constants and $\{d_t\}$ is a given sequence. Using the definitions of the operators Δ and Δ^2, we may write the difference equation as

$$(y_{t+2} - 2y_{t+1} + y_t) + b(y_{t+1} - y_t) + cy_t = d_t.$$

Setting $f = b - 2$, $g = 1 - b + c$, we write the equation in simplified form as

$$y_{t+2} + fy_{t+1} + gy_t = d_t.$$

We now explain how to solve such equations.

We begin by considering the homogeneous case, where $d_t = 0$ for all t: the equation of interest is

$$y_{t+2} + f y_{t+1} + g y_t = 0. \tag{24.12}$$

Given the method of solution of the continuous-time analogue in Section 24.1, it should not be surprising that the solution procedure for (24.12) involves solving a quadratic equation known as the **characteristic equation**. In this case the characteristic equation is

$$x^2 + fx + g = 0. \tag{24.13}$$

Let the roots of the quadratic equation (24.13) be p and q. As in the case of differential equations, we have different forms for the general solution of (24.12), depending on whether the roots are distinct $(p \neq q)$ or coincident $(p = q)$. The solution formulae, which we derive in the appendix to this chapter, are as follows.

(a) If the characteristic equation (24.13) has two distinct roots p and q, the general solution to (24.12) is

$$y_t = A p^t + B q^t, \tag{24.14}$$

where A and B are constants.

(b) If the characteristic equation (24.13) has coincident roots at p, the general solution to (24.12) is

$$y_t = (A + Bt) p^t, \tag{24.15}$$

where A and B are constants.

Example 1 Find the general solution of the difference equation

$$y_{t+2} + 4 y_{t+1} - 5 y_t = 0.$$

The characteristic equation is $x^2 + 4x - 5 = 0$, which may be written

$$(x - 1)(x + 5) = 0.$$

The roots are 1 and -5. Since $1^t = 1$ for all t, the general solution given by (24.14) is

$$y_t = A + B \times (-5)^t,$$

where A and B are constants.

Example 2 Find the general solution to the difference equation

$$y_{t+2} + 6 y_{t+1} + 9 y_t = 0.$$

The characteristic equation is $x^2 + 6x + 9 = 0$ which has coincident roots at $x = -3$. By (24.15), the general solution is

$$z_t = (A + Bt) \times (-3)^t,$$

where A and B are constants.

Complex roots

As in the continuous-time analogue, we have to do more work to put (24.14) into a convenient form in the case where the characteristic equation has complex roots. Suppose the roots p and q of (24.13) are complex numbers. Assuming that f and g are real numbers, the roots are complex conjugates, and we may write them in trigonometric form as

$$p = re^{i\theta} = r(\cos\theta + i\sin\theta), \quad q = re^{-i\theta} = r(\cos\theta - i\sin\theta).$$

Then (24.14) may be written

$$y_t = r^t(Ae^{i\theta t} + Be^{-i\theta t}).$$

To ensure that y_t is real, A and B have to be complex conjugates. Suppose this is so, and let A be written in trigonometric form as $|A|e^{i\alpha}$. Then $B = |A|e^{-i\alpha}$; letting $u = \alpha + \theta t$, we see that

$$y_t = |A|\, r^t(e^{iu} + e^{-iu}) = 2|A|\, r^t \cos u.$$

Letting $C = 2|A|$ and summarising, we have the following result: *if the characteristic equation (24.13) has complex conjugate roots $r(\cos\theta \pm i\sin\theta)$, the general solution to (24.12) is*

$$y_t = Cr^t \cos(\theta t + \alpha), \tag{24.16}$$

where C and α are constants.

Example 3 Solve the difference equation

$$y_{t+2} + \tfrac{1}{2}y_{t+1} + \tfrac{1}{4}y_t = 0.$$

The characteristic equation is

$$x^2 + \tfrac{1}{2}x + \tfrac{1}{4} = 0.$$

The roots of this equation are $\tfrac{1}{2}(-\tfrac{1}{2} \pm i\sqrt{d})$, where

$$d = 4\times\tfrac{1}{4} - (\tfrac{1}{2})^2 = \tfrac{3}{4}.$$

The roots of the characteristic equation are therefore $\tfrac{1}{4}(-1 \pm i\sqrt{3})$. Now

$$\tfrac{1}{2}(-1 + i\sqrt{3}) = -\cos\tfrac{\pi}{3} + i\sin\tfrac{\pi}{3} = \cos(\pi - \tfrac{\pi}{3}) + i\sin(\pi - \tfrac{\pi}{3}),$$

so the roots may be written in trigonometric form as

$$\tfrac{1}{2}(\cos\tfrac{2\pi}{3} \pm i\sin\tfrac{2\pi}{3}).$$

Applying (24.16), we see that the general solution of the difference equation is

$$y_t = \frac{C}{2^t} \cos\left(\frac{2\pi t}{3} + \alpha\right),$$

where C and α are constants.

Points to notice

Three general properties of the solution (24.16) in the case of complex roots are worthy of remark.

1. The solution formula (24.16) uses the *trigonometric* form of the roots of the characteristic equation. This is in contrast to the corresponding formula (24.6) for the continuous-time case, which used the algebraic form of the roots.

2. The common modulus r of the roots of the characteristic equation is given by the equation

$$r = \sqrt{g}.$$

The reason for this is as follows. The real number g is the product of the roots of (24.13), which are the complex conjugates $re^{i\theta}$ and $re^{-i\theta}$. Hence $g = r^2$, which gives us the desired equation.

3. There is an alternative way of writing (24.16). Setting $A' = C\cos\alpha$, $B' = -C\sin\alpha$ and applying the addition formula for cosines, we have

$$y_t = r^t(A'\cos\theta t + B'\sin\theta t),$$

where A' and B' are constants.

The non-homogeneous case

We can now consider difference equations of the form

$$y_{t+2} + fy_{t+1} + gy_t = d_t, \tag{24.17}$$

where $\{d_t\}$ is a general sequence.[13]

The solution procedure is similar to that already explained for second-order differential equations and for first-order difference equations. We consider the associated homogeneous equation

$$z_{t+2} + fz_{t+1} + gz_t = 0,$$

and call *its* general solution the **complementary solution**. The general solution to (24.17) is

$$y_t = Y_t + z_t,$$

where Y_t is a particular solution and z_t the complementary solution.

As usual, the difficult part is finding the particular solution. The basic method is trial and error, guided by the usual principle of trying first for a particular solution of the same general form as the right-hand side.

---

[13]In some circumstances, the dynamics of a variable y are described by a still more general equation in which the coefficient of y_{t+2} is a constant a rather than 1. Such an equation is easily reduced to the form (24.17) by dividing through by a.

Example 4 Find the general solution of the difference equation

$$y_{t+2} + 4y_{t+1} - 5y_t = 2 \times 3^t.$$

First, we first try for a particular solution of the form $Y^t = a \times 3^t$. Then

$$(9a + 12a - 5a)3^t = 2 \times 3^t$$

for all t, so $a = 2/(9 + 12 - 5) = 1/8$. The particular solution is therefore $3^t/8$.

Since the associated homogeneous equation is the difference equation of Example 1, the complementary solution is $z_t = A + B \times (-5)^t$, where A and B are constants. Adding the particular solution to the complementary solution, we have the general solution

$$y_t = A + B \times (-5)^t + \tfrac{1}{8} \times 3^t.$$

Example 5 Solve the difference equation

$$y_{t+2} + 6y_{t+1} + 9y_t = 64,$$

given that $y_0 = 3$ and $y_1 = 7$.

Here we try for a particular solution of the form $Y_t = a$, where a is a constant. Then $16a = 64$, and our particular solution is $Y_t = 4$.

Using the result of Example 2, we see that the complementary solution is

$$z_t = (A + Bt) \times (-3)^t.$$

Thus the general solution to our difference equation is

$$y_t = (A + Bt) \times (-3)^t + 4,$$

and it remains to use the initial conditions ($y_0 = 3$, $y_1 = 7$) to determine the constants A and B. From these conditions, $A = 3-4$ and $-3(A+B) = 7 - 4$. Hence $A = -1$, $B = 0$ and the solution is

$$y_t = 4 - (-3)^t.$$

Qualitative behaviour

Our discussion here is similar to that in Section 24.2. We focus on difference equations of the form

$$y_{t+2} + fy_{t+1} + gy_t = d,$$

where f, g, d are constants. We assume that $1 + f + g \neq 0$, thereby ensuring that there is a constant particular solution

$$Y = d/(1 + f + g).$$

Y is called the stationary value, or equilibrium value, of y.

We say that the equilibrium is **stable** if $y_t \to Y$ as $t \to \infty$, regardless of initial conditions; this is the same as saying that the complementary solution z_t approaches zero as $t \to \infty$. The main general result on stability is that *equilibrium is stable if and only if both roots of the characteristic equation have absolute value (or modulus) less than* 1. This result follows from the solution formulae above, and the fact that the limit of p^t as $t \to \infty$ is 0 if and only if $|p| < 1$, in which case the limit of tp^t is also zero.

We now show how this result may be applied. In Example 3 above, the stationary value Y is 0; equilibrium is stable because the roots of the characteristic equation are complex conjugates with common modulus $\frac{1}{2}$. In Example 5, with coincident roots at -3, equilibrium is unstable.

The solution path may display alternations,[14] oscillations or neither. Oscillations occur when the roots are complex; recall that in this case the common modulus of the roots is $\sqrt{g}$, so the oscillations are explosive if $g > 1$, damped if $g < 1$ and regular if $g = 1$. Alternating behaviour is possible when the roots are real and at least one of them is negative. If the roots are real with opposite signs we have a mixture of alternating and monotonic behaviour, with the dominant mode depending on which root has larger absolute value.

A multiplier-accelerator model

A famous example of a second-order difference equation in macroeconomics occurs in the multiplier-accelerator model, a popular version of which is as follows:

$$C_t = a + cY_{t-1}, \quad I_t = b + v(Y_{t-1} - Y_{t-2}), \quad Y_t = C_t + I_t. \qquad (24.18)$$

Here Y_t denotes national income in period t, C_t is aggregate consumption and I_t is investment: a, b, c (the marginal propensity to consume) and v (the accelerator coefficient) are positive constants, with $c < 1$.

Substituting the first and second equations of (24.18) into the third we have

$$Y_t = a + b + (c + v)Y_{t-1} - vY_{t-2}.$$

Rearranging, and replacing t by $t + 2$ throughout, we have the following difference equation for national income:

$$Y_{t+2} - (c + v)Y_{t+1} + vY_t = a + b. \qquad (24.19)$$

The difference equation (24.19) has the stationary solution $Y = \bar{Y}$, where

$$\bar{Y} = \frac{a + b}{1 - c}.$$

---

[14]Recall Section 21.4 for discussion of alternations.

Notice that $\bar{Y}$ is the product of autonomous spending on consumption and investment $(a + b)$ and the Keynesian multiplier $1/(1 - c)$.

The characteristic equation corresponding to (24.19) is

$$x^2 - (c + v)x + v = 0.$$

This gives us a remarkably simple stability condition: *equilibrium income $\bar{Y}$ is stable if and only if $v < 1$.*

We now explain why the stability condition takes this form. The result is immediate if the roots of the characteristic equation are coincident, in which case they are both equal to $\sqrt{v}$,[15] or if the roots are complex conjugates, in which case they have common modulus $\sqrt{v}$. The non-trivial case is where the roots are real and distinct, say p and q. Then $p + q = c + v > 0$, $pq = v > 0$ and

$$(p - 1)(q - 1) = pq - (p + q) - 1 = v - (c + v) + 1 = 1 - c > 0.$$

Hence p and q are positive numbers which are both on the same side of 1. Using again the fact that $pq = v$, we see that if $v > 1$ then p and q are both greater than 1 and the equilibrium is unstable, while if $v < 1$ then p and q are both between 0 and 1 and the equilibrium is stable. This proves the stability result.

In this model national income cannot display alternating behaviour, but it may oscillate: oscillations happen if and only if $(c + v)^2 < 4v$. Notice that damped or explosive oscillations are compatible with the model: we have damped oscillations if $c = v = 0.8$, explosive oscillations if $c = 0.8$ and $v = 1.2$. More generally, the possibilities are depicted in Figure 24.3, where **S** means stable, **U** unstable, **O** oscillatory, **N** non-oscillatory and the solid curve in the vc–plane has the equation $c = 2\sqrt{v} - v$.

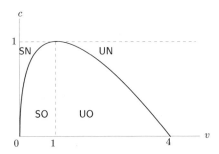

Figure 24.3: **Classification of second-order difference equations**

Regular oscillations (neither damped nor explosive) occur in this model only if v is exactly 1. The fact that regular oscillations arise only in a very special case is one of the many reasons why this simple model does not provide a very satisfactory explanation of business cycles.

---

[15]The case of coincident roots at $-\sqrt{v}$ is *not* possible because $c + v$ is positive.

Exercises

24.3.1 (a) Find the solution of the equation

$$y_{t+2} - y_{t+1} - y_t = 0$$

which satisfies $y_0 = 0$ and $y_1 = 1$. [The solution, for non-negative values of t, is known as the **Fibonacci sequence**, and has many applications in mathematics and biology.]

(b) Find the solution of

$$y_{t+2} + 2y_{t+1} - 8y_t = 0$$

which satisfies $y_0 = 2$ and $y_1 = 0$.

(c) Find the solution of

$$2y_{t+2} - 5y_{t+1} + 2y_t = 0$$

which satisfies $y_0 = 1$ and $y_1 = 3$.

24.3.2 Find the general solution of each of the following difference equations:

(a) $y_{t+2} + 3y_{t+1} - 4y_t = 6$

(b) $y_{t+2} + 2y_{t+1} + 2y_t = 6$

(c) $y_{t+2} - 8y_{t+1} + 16y_t = 6$

Classify each equation as **SO, SN, UO** or **UN**, where **S, U, O** and **N** are defined as in the text. In each case, indicate graphically the main features of the solution. Do any of the solutions exhibit alternating behaviour?

24.3.3 Find the general solution of the equation

$$y_{t+2} + y_{t+1} + y_t = 4t + 1.$$

24.3.4 In the following market model, p_t is price, q_t^D quantity demanded and q_t^S quantity supplied in period t:

$$q_t^D = 3 - 2p_t, \quad q_t^S = -1 + 4p_{t-1}, \quad p_{t+1} - p_t = \tfrac{1}{2}(q_t^D - q_t^S).$$

(a) Obtain a second-order difference equation for p_t and find its general solution. What happens to p_t as $t \to \infty$?

(b) How is this model related to that of Exercise 21.4.6? Comment on any important differences and similarities between the solutions.

24.3.5 In the following macroeconomic model, Y_t is income, C_t is consumption and I_t is investment, each in period t:

$$C_t = \tfrac{1}{2}Y_{t-1}, \quad I_t = 20 + \tfrac{4}{3}(Y_{t-1} - Y_{t-2}), \quad Y_t = C_t + I_t.$$

Obtain a second-order difference equation for Y_6 and find the stationary solution. Find the general solution of the difference equation and say what happens to Y_t as $t \to \infty$.

Problems on Chapter 24

24–1. Given the system of differential equations

$$\frac{dy}{dt} = 4y - 5z, \quad \frac{dz}{dt} = y - 2z,$$

use the method given in Section 24.1 to derive a differential equation for y. Find its general solution and hence find an expression for z.

For each of the following pairs of boundary conditions, find the solutions y and z of the system which satisfy them:

(a) $y = 1$ and $z = -3$ when $t = 0$;

(b) $y = 1$ and $dz/dt = 7$ when $t = 0$;

(c) $y = 1$ and $dy/dt = -1$ when $t = 0$;

(d) $y = 1$ when $t = 0$ and $y \to 0$ as $t \to \infty$.

Comment on the main differences between these solutions. What is the key feature of the characteristic equation which leads to boundary condition (d) completely determining the solution?

24–2. In this problem, the differential equations themselves provide useful information about the solutions.

(i) Find the general solution of each of the following differential equations:

(a) $\dfrac{d^2y}{dx^2} = -(2x - 1)^2$ (b) $\dfrac{d^2y}{dx^2} = 3x^2 - 6x + 4$ (c) $\dfrac{d^2y}{dx^2} = 2x - 1.$

In each case, find the solution which satisfies $y = 1$ and $dy/dx = 0$ when $x = 0$, and sketch its graph.

(ii) Find the general solution of the differential equation

$$\frac{d^2y}{dx^2} + 2a\frac{dy}{dx} + (a^2 + b^2)y = 0,$$

where a and b are nonzero constants. Use the differential equation to show that any solution $y = f(x)$ has the property that all positive critical values are maxima and all negative critical values are minima. Hence show that the two functions of Problem 22–2 have this property.

24–3. Use the classifications **S**, **U**, **O** and **N** given in Section 24–2 to describe the possible forms which can be taken by the general solution of the differential equation

$$\frac{d^2y}{dt^2} + b\frac{dy}{dt} + cy = kt + \ell,$$

where b, c, k and ℓ are constants with $b \neq 0$ and $c \neq 0$. For each form, indicate the main features in a graph.

24–4. Write down the discrete-time analogue of the differential equation

$$\frac{d^2y}{dt^2} + b\frac{dy}{dt} + cy = u,$$

where b, c and u are constants; assume that $b \neq 0$ and $c \neq 0$. In each case, state the stationary solution.

Find the condition in terms of b and c for the general solution of the differential equation to exhibit oscillatory behaviour. Find also the corresponding condition for the difference equation.

For the differential equation, find the condition in terms of b and c for the stationary solution to be stable. Find also the corresponding condition for the difference equation. Comment.

Appendix to Chapter 24

We shall give an alternative derivation of the general solution to

$$\frac{d^2y}{dt^2} + b\frac{dy}{dt} + cy = 0. \tag{24.2}$$

As before, we consider the characteristic equation

$$x^2 + bx + c = 0, \tag{24.4}$$

whose roots we denote by p and q. We distinguish carefully between the distinct-roots case ($p \neq q$) and the coincident-roots case ($p = q$). On the other hand, we are not concerned here with the distinction between real and complex roots, as complex roots may be regarded as a special case of distinct roots. Our object is to derive the solution formulae (24.5) for $p \neq q$ and (24.7) for $p = q$.

We have three reasons for presenting the alternative derivation. First, it is helpful to see how the key results on second-order linear differential equations follow (by deduction, rather than by analogy) from the results of Chapter 21 on first-order equations. Secondly, we owe the reader a more convincing explanation than that given earlier of how the coincident-roots case fits into the overall picture. Thirdly, the method we use is easily adapted to derive the main results on second-order difference equations, as we shall show later in this appendix.

Since p and q are the roots of the quadratic equation (24.4), $b = -(p+q)$ and $c = pq$. The left-hand side of (24.2) is therefore

$$\frac{d^2y}{dt^2} - (p+q)\frac{dy}{dt} + pqy,$$

which may in turn be written

$$\frac{d}{dt}\left[\frac{dy}{dt} - py\right] - q\left[\frac{dy}{dt} - py\right].$$

Let z be the term in square brackets: then (24.2) may be written

$$\frac{dz}{dt} - qz = 0.$$

We showed in Chapter 21 that the general solution to this differential equation is $z = ke^{qt}$, where k is a constant. Substituting this solution into the definition of z,

$$\frac{dy}{dt} - py = ke^{qt}.$$

We now solve differential equation by the integrating-factor method of Section 21.3. Multiplying through by e^{-pt} and integrating,

$$ye^{-pt} = \int ke^{(q-p)t}dt. \tag{24.20}$$

Denote the indefinite integral on the right-hand side of (24.20) by I. Consider first the case where $p \neq q$. Then

$$I = A + Be^{(q-p)t},$$

where $B = k/(q-p)$ and A is another constant. Hence by (24.20),

$$y = Ae^{pt} + Be^{qt}.$$

This shows that the general solution for y is indeed given by (24.5) in the case of distinct roots. Now suppose $p = q$. Then $I = \int k\,dt = A + Bt$, where $B = k$ and A is another constant. Hence from (24.20),

$$y = (A + Bt)e^{pt},$$

which is (24.7).

More on difference equations

Consider the difference equation

$$y_{t+2} + fy_{t+1} + gy_t = 0, \tag{24.12}$$

where f and g are constants. The characteristic equation is

$$x^2 + fx + g = 0, \tag{24.13}$$

and we denote its roots by p and q. We now explain why the general solution to (24.12) is (24.14) in the case of distinct roots $(p \neq q)$ and (24.15) in the case of coincident roots $(p = q)$.

Since p and q are the roots of (24.13), $p + q = -f$ and $pq = g$. Thus (24.12) may be written

$$y_{t+2} - (p + q)y_{t+1} + pqy_t = 0.$$

Setting $z_t = y_{t+1} - py_t$, we have $z_{t+1} = qz_t$ for all t. Therefore $z_t = q^t z_0$, so

$$y_{t+1} - py_t = q^t z_0. \tag{24.21}$$

To solve the first-order difference equation (24.21), we look first for a particular solution of the same form as the right hand side. Substituting $y_t = Bq^t$ into (24.21) and dividing through by q^t we have the equation $(q - p)B = z_0$, which may be solved for B if and only if $p \neq q$. Thus if $p \neq q$, (24.21) has particular solution Bq^t, where $B = z_0/(q - p)$. Since the complementary solution is Ap^t, where A is a constant, the general solution to (24.21) is $y_t = Ap^t + Bq^t$. This shows that, if $p \neq q$, the general solution to (24.12) is (24.14).

Now suppose $p = q$. In this case, dividing (24.21) by p^{t+1} yields $w_{t+1} - w_t = B$, where $w_t = y_t/p^t$ for all t and $B = z_0/p$. Proceeding in the way that we solved Example 2 of Section 21.4, we find that $w_t = A + Bt$, where A is a constant. Thus $y_t = w_t p^t = (A + Bt)p^t$, and the solution to (24.12) is indeed given by (24.15).

Chapter 25

EIGENVALUES AND EIGENVECTORS

This chapter is concerned with an important topic in linear algebra. The first two sections lay the foundations for our discussion of dynamic systems in Chapter 26. The third section explains some properties of symmetric matrices that are useful in statistics and econometrics.

Two general points about this return to linear algebra should be noted. The first concerns notation. As in Chapters 11 and 12, 'vector' will always mean column-vector. To save space, we sometimes write the n–vector with components $x_1, \ldots, x_n$ as $(x_1 \ \ldots \ x_n)^{\mathrm{T}}$: the superscript ^{T} denotes transposition as in Chapter 13. Secondly, the idea of linear independence plays an important role in this chapter: you may find it helpful to refresh your memory of what we said about it in Sections 11.1 and 12.4.

When you have studied this chapter you will be able to:

- calculate the eigenvalues and eigenvectors of a 2×2 matrix;

- use diagonalisability to calculate powers of square matrices;

- perform simple matrix operations when scalars are complex;

- test symmetric matrices for positive definiteness using eigenvalues.

25.1   Diagonalisable matrices

We begin by recalling what we said in Section 11.4 about powers of square matrices. If $\mathbf{A}$ is a square matrix, then

$$\mathbf{A}^2 = \mathbf{A}\mathbf{A}, \quad \mathbf{A}^3 = \mathbf{A}^2\mathbf{A}, \quad \mathbf{A}^4 = \mathbf{A}^3\mathbf{A}$$

and so on. By the associative law of matrix multiplication, $\mathbf{A}^{r+s} = \mathbf{A}^r\mathbf{A}^s$ for any pair of natural numbers r, s. Thus we could calculate $\mathbf{A}^{11}$ by computing $\mathbf{A}^2$

and $\mathbf{A}^3$ using their definitions, then $\mathbf{A}^5$ as $\mathbf{A}^3\mathbf{A}^2$ and $\mathbf{A}^6$ as $\mathbf{A}^3\mathbf{A}^3$ and finally $\mathbf{A}^{11}$ as $\mathbf{A}^6\mathbf{A}^5$.

The fact that we can calculate powers in this way gives no insight into any general relation that may hold between the entries of $\mathbf{A}^k$ and those of $\mathbf{A}$. To investigate such relations, we start by noting how easy it is to calculate powers of a diagonal matrix: if $\mathbf{A} = \begin{bmatrix} b & 0 \\ 0 & c \end{bmatrix}$, then

$$\mathbf{A}^2 = \begin{bmatrix} b & 0 \\ 0 & c \end{bmatrix}\begin{bmatrix} b & 0 \\ 0 & c \end{bmatrix} = \begin{bmatrix} b^2 & 0 \\ 0 & c^2 \end{bmatrix}, \quad \mathbf{A}^3 = \begin{bmatrix} b^2 & 0 \\ 0 & c^2 \end{bmatrix}\begin{bmatrix} b & 0 \\ 0 & c \end{bmatrix} = \begin{bmatrix} b^3 & 0 \\ 0 & c^3 \end{bmatrix}$$

and so on.

To generalise this example, we use the following notation for diagonal matrices: $\mathrm{diag}(d_1, \ldots, d_n)$ is the diagonal matrix whose diagonal entries are $d_1, \ldots, d_n$. For instance

$$\mathrm{diag}(b, c) = \begin{bmatrix} b & 0 \\ 0 & c \end{bmatrix}, \quad \mathrm{diag}(4, 0, -1) = \begin{bmatrix} 4 & 0 & 0 \\ 0 & 0 & 0 \\ 0 & 0 & -1 \end{bmatrix}.$$

Powers of diagonal matrices obey the following rule:

$$\text{if } \mathbf{D} = \mathrm{diag}(d_1, \ldots, d_n) \text{ then } \mathbf{D}^k = \mathrm{diag}(d_1^k, \ldots, d_n^k) \text{ for } k = 1, 2, \ldots \quad (25.1)$$

To generalise further, we define a class of square matrices as follows: we say that a square matrix $\mathbf{A}$ is **diagonalisable** if, for some invertible matrix $\mathbf{S}$, $\mathbf{S}^{-1}\mathbf{A}\mathbf{S}$ is a diagonal matrix. In what follows, we shall often use the phrase 'd–matrix' as a shorthand for 'diagonalisable matrix'. Every diagonal matrix is a d–matrix, as may be seen by letting $\mathbf{S} = \mathbf{I}$; but there are plenty of diagonalisable matrices which are not diagonal matrices, as we explain below.

As we have just noted, the square matrix $\mathbf{A}$ is diagonalisable if and only if $\mathbf{S}^{-1}\mathbf{A}\mathbf{S} = \mathbf{D}$ for some invertible matrix $\mathbf{S}$ and some diagonal matrix $\mathbf{D}$. If this is so, then

$$\mathbf{S}\mathbf{D}\mathbf{S}^{-1} = \mathbf{S}\mathbf{S}^{-1}\mathbf{A}\mathbf{S}\mathbf{S}^{-1} = \mathbf{I}\mathbf{A}\mathbf{I} = \mathbf{A}.$$

It follows that

$$\mathbf{A}^2 = (\mathbf{S}\mathbf{D}\mathbf{S}^{-1})(\mathbf{S}\mathbf{D}\mathbf{S}^{-1}) = \mathbf{S}(\mathbf{D}\mathbf{I}\mathbf{D})\mathbf{S}^{-1} = \mathbf{S}\mathbf{D}^2\mathbf{S}^{-1},$$

$$\mathbf{A}^3 = \mathbf{A}^2\mathbf{A} = (\mathbf{S}\mathbf{D}^2\mathbf{S}^{-1})(\mathbf{S}\mathbf{D}\mathbf{S}^{-1}) = \mathbf{S}(\mathbf{D}^2\mathbf{I}\mathbf{D})\mathbf{S}^{-1} = \mathbf{S}\mathbf{D}^3\mathbf{S}^{-1}$$

and so on. Thus

$$\text{if } \mathbf{A} = \mathbf{S}\mathbf{D}\mathbf{S}^{-1} \text{ then } \mathbf{A}^k = \mathbf{S}\mathbf{D}^k\mathbf{S}^{-1} \text{ for } k = 1, 2, \ldots \quad (25.2)$$

Taken together, (25.1) and (25.2) provide what we are looking for, in the case where $\mathbf{A}$ is a d–matrix: a neat formula relating $\mathbf{A}^k$ to $\mathbf{A}$, for an arbitrary positive integer k. The questions that now arise are: how can we tell if a given matrix is diagonalisable? and if it is, how do we find $\mathbf{S}$ and $\mathbf{D}$? To answer these questions, we introduce the concepts of eigenvalue and eigenvector.

The key definitions

Let $\mathbf{A}$ be a square matrix, λ a scalar. We say that λ is an **eigenvalue** of $\mathbf{A}$ if there exists a vector $\mathbf{x}$ such that $\mathbf{x} \neq \mathbf{0}$ and

$$\mathbf{Ax} = \lambda\mathbf{x}.$$

Such an $\mathbf{x}$ is called an **eigenvector** of $\mathbf{A}$ corresponding to the eigenvalue λ.

To illustrate these definitions, we note two important special cases. First, 0 is an eigenvalue of $\mathbf{A}$ if and only if $\mathbf{A}$ is singular. Secondly, recall from Chapter 11 that an $n \times n$ matrix $\mathbf{A}$ can be regarded as a mapping, transforming any n–vector $\mathbf{x}$ into the n–vector $\mathbf{Ax}$; thus 1 is an eigenvector of $\mathbf{A}$ if and only if $\mathbf{A}$ transforms some non-zero vector into itself.

By definition, the scalar λ is an eigenvalue of the matrix $\mathbf{A}$ if and only if $(\lambda\mathbf{I} - \mathbf{A})\mathbf{x} = \mathbf{0}$ for some non-zero vector $\mathbf{x}$; in other words, λ is an eigenvalue of $\mathbf{A}$ if and only if $\lambda\mathbf{I} - \mathbf{A}$ is a singular matrix. Thus the eigenvalues of $\mathbf{A}$ can in principle be found by solving the equation

$$\det(\lambda\mathbf{I} - \mathbf{A}) = 0. \tag{25.3}$$

The 'in principle' in the last sentence waves aside some serious mathematics which will be dealt with in the next section. For the moment, we note that if $\mathbf{A}$ is a 2×2 matrix then (25.3) is a quadratic equation in λ.

Example 1 Find the eigenvalues and eigenvectors of the matrix

$$\mathbf{A} = \begin{bmatrix} 3 & -1 \\ 4 & -2 \end{bmatrix}.$$

We find the eigenvalues using (25.3). In this case

$$\det(\lambda\mathbf{I} - \mathbf{A}) = \begin{vmatrix} \lambda - 3 & 1 \\ -4 & \lambda + 2 \end{vmatrix} = (\lambda - 3)(\lambda + 2) + 4.$$

Hence the eigenvalues of $\mathbf{A}$ are the roots of the quadratic equation

$$\lambda^2 - \lambda - 2 = 0.$$

The eigenvalues are therefore 2 and -1.

We now find the eigenvectors of $\mathbf{A}$ corresponding to the eigenvalue 2. $\mathbf{Ax} = 2\mathbf{x}$ if and only if

$$3x_1 - x_2 = 2x_1, \quad 4x_1 - 2x_2 = 2x_2.$$

Now each of these equations simplifies to $x_1 = x_2$. [The fact that the two equations collapse to one should not be surprising, since we have just shown that $2\mathbf{I} - \mathbf{A}$ is singular.] Thus the eigenvectors corresponding to the eigenvalue 2 are the non-zero multiples of $\begin{bmatrix} 1 \\ 1 \end{bmatrix}$.

Similarly, $\mathbf{A}\mathbf{x} = -\mathbf{x}$ if and only if $x_2 = 4x_1$; thus the eigenvectors of $\mathbf{A}$ corresponding to the eigenvalue 2 are the non-zero multiples of $\begin{bmatrix} 1 \\ 4 \end{bmatrix}$.

Terminology

Numerous synonyms for 'eigenvalue' appear in books on linear algebra and its applications, including **proper value**, **characteristic root** and **latent root**. Similarly, there are numerous synonyms for eigenvector.

The reason for all these phrases involving 'root' is that the eigenvalues are the solutions ('roots') of a polynomial equation. Much more will be said on this in the next section. For the rest of this section, we return to d–matrices and powers of matrices.

Three propositions

The following propositions connect eigenvalues and eigenvectors with diagonalisability.

Proposition 1 An $n \times n$ matrix $\mathbf{A}$ is diagonalisable if and only if it has n linearly independent eigenvectors.

Proposition 2 If $\mathbf{x}^1, \ldots, \mathbf{x}^k$ are eigenvectors corresponding to k different eigenvalues of the $n \times n$ matrix $\mathbf{A}$, then $\mathbf{x}^1, \ldots, \mathbf{x}^k$ are linearly independent.

Proposition 3 An $n \times n$ matrix $\mathbf{A}$ is diagonalisable if it has has n different eigenvalues.

The proof of Proposition 1 is given below, and deserves careful study because of its implications for calculation. Proposition 2 is proved in the appendix to this chapter. Proposition 3 follows immediately from Propositions 1 and 2.

We now prove Proposition 1. Suppose the $n \times n$ matrix $\mathbf{A}$ has n linearly independent eigenvectors $\mathbf{x}^1, \ldots, \mathbf{x}^n$, corresponding to eigenvalues $\lambda_1, \ldots, \lambda_n$ respectively. Then

$$\mathbf{A}\mathbf{x}^j = \lambda_j \mathbf{x}^j \quad \text{for } j = 1, \ldots, n. \tag{25.4}$$

Define the two $n \times n$ matrices

$$\mathbf{S} = (\mathbf{x}^1 \ \ldots \ \mathbf{x}^n), \quad \mathbf{D} = \text{diag}(\lambda_1, \ldots, \lambda_n) \tag{25.5}$$

Since $\mathbf{x}^1, \ldots, \mathbf{x}^n$ are linearly independent, $\mathbf{S}$ is invertible. By (25.4),

$$\mathbf{A}\mathbf{S} = \mathbf{S}\mathbf{D}. \tag{25.6}$$

Premultiplying (25.6) by $\mathbf{S}^{-1}$ we have $\mathbf{S}^{-1}\mathbf{A}\mathbf{S} = \mathbf{D}$, so $\mathbf{A}$ is indeed a d–matrix.

Conversely, suppose that $\mathbf{A}$ is a d–matrix. Then we may choose an invertible matrix $\mathbf{S}$ and a diagonal matrix $\mathbf{D}$ satisfying (25.6). Given the properties of $\mathbf{S}$ and $\mathbf{D}$, we may define vectors $\mathbf{x}^1, \dots, \mathbf{x}^n$ and scalars $\lambda_1, \dots, \lambda_n$ satisfying (25.5); then (25.6) may be written in the form (25.4). Since $\mathbf{S}$ is invertible the vectors $\mathbf{x}^1, \dots, \mathbf{x}^n$ are linearly independent: in particular none of them is the zero-vector. Hence by (25.4), $\mathbf{x}^1, \dots, \mathbf{x}^n$ are n linearly independent eigenvectors of $\mathbf{A}$.

Applying the propositions

Given the eigenvalues of a square matrix $\mathbf{A}$, Proposition 3 provides an easily-checked sufficient condition for $\mathbf{A}$ to be a d–matrix. If this condition is met, Proposition 2 and the proof of Proposition 1 show how to find $\mathbf{S}$ and $\mathbf{D}$. We may then use (25.1) and (25.2) to find $\mathbf{A}^k$ for any positive integer k. The following example illustrates the procedure.

Example 2 As in Example 1, let

$$\mathbf{A} = \begin{bmatrix} 3 & -1 \\ 4 & -2 \end{bmatrix}.$$

We show that $\mathbf{A}$ is a d–matrix, and find $\mathbf{A}^k$ for any positive integer k.

We know from Example 1 that the eigenvalues are 2 and -1. Thus $\mathbf{A}$ is a 2×2 matrix with two different eigenvalues; by Proposition 3, $\mathbf{A}$ is a d–matrix.

Now let $\mathbf{x}$ and $\mathbf{y}$ be eigenvectors of $\mathbf{A}$ corresponding to the eigenvalues 2 and -1 respectively. By Proposition 2, $\mathbf{x}$ and $\mathbf{y}$ are linearly independent; hence by the proof of Proposition 1 we may write $\mathbf{S}^{-1}\mathbf{A}\mathbf{S} = \mathbf{D}$, where $\mathbf{D} = \mathrm{diag}(2, -1)$, and $\mathbf{S} = (\mathbf{x} \ \mathbf{y})$. Now $\mathbf{x}$ and $\mathbf{y}$ can be any eigenvectors corresponding to the eigenvalues 2 and -1 respectively: so by the results of Example 1 we may let $\mathbf{x} = (1 \ 1)^{\mathrm{T}}$, $\mathbf{y} = (1 \ 4)^{\mathrm{T}}$. Summarising,

$$\mathbf{S} = \begin{bmatrix} 1 & 1 \\ 1 & 4 \end{bmatrix}, \quad \mathbf{D} = \begin{bmatrix} 2 & 0 \\ 0 & -1 \end{bmatrix}.$$

To find $\mathbf{A}^k$ using (25.1) and (25.2), we must first compute $\mathbf{S}^{-1}$. Doing this by the formula for inverting 2×2 matrices given in Section 13.2, we have

$$\mathbf{S}^{-1} = \tfrac{1}{3} \begin{bmatrix} 4 & -1 \\ -1 & 1 \end{bmatrix}.$$

Hence by (25.1) and (25.2),

$$\mathbf{A}^k = \begin{bmatrix} 1 & 1 \\ 1 & 4 \end{bmatrix} \begin{bmatrix} 2^k/3 & 0 \\ 0 & (-1)^k/3 \end{bmatrix} \begin{bmatrix} 4 & -1 \\ -1 & 1 \end{bmatrix} \quad \text{for } k = 1, 2, \dots$$

It would not be difficult to perform the multiplication, but we think that the answer is expressed more clearly in this form.

Two remarks about the propositions and their uses

1. When we write a d–matrix in the form $\mathbf{SDS}^{-1}$, we have some choice as to how to write $\mathbf{S}$ and $\mathbf{D}$. For example, we could have chosen the second column of $\mathbf{S}$ in Example 2 to be $(\frac{1}{2}\ \ 2)^{\mathrm{T}}$ rather than $(1\ \ 4)^{\mathrm{T}}$. The one rule that must be strictly adhered to is the following: having chosen which eigenvalue is to be the first diagonal entry of $\mathbf{D}$, we choose the first column of $\mathbf{S}$ to be an eigenvector *corresponding to that eigenvalue*, and similarly for the other entries of $\mathbf{D}$ and columns of $\mathbf{S}$.

2. Proposition 1 gives a necessary and sufficient condition for a matrix to be diagonalisable. Proposition 3, by contrast, gives a sufficient but not necessary condition for a matrix to be diagonalisable. In other words, any $n \times n$ matrix with n different eigenvalues is a d–matrix, but there exist d–matrices of order n which do not have n different eigenvalues. The simplest example is the $n \times n$ identity matrix, which is obviously diagonalisable (with $\mathbf{S} = \mathbf{D} = \mathbf{I}$) but whose only eigenvalue is 1.

Exercises

25.1.1 Find the eigenvalues and eigenvectors of the matrix

$$\begin{bmatrix} 2 & 4 \\ 5 & 3 \end{bmatrix}.$$

25.1.2 Given a square matrix $\mathbf{A}$ and a scalar θ, how are the eigenvalues and eigenvectors of the matrices $\theta\mathbf{A}$ and $\mathbf{A} + \theta\mathbf{I}$ related to those of $\mathbf{A}$?

25.1.3 Given the matrix

$$\mathbf{A} = \begin{bmatrix} 1 & 1 \\ 1 & 1 \end{bmatrix},$$

find a diagonal matrix $\mathbf{D}$ and an invertible matrix $\mathbf{S}$ such that $\mathbf{A} = \mathbf{SDS}^{-1}$. Hence find $\mathbf{A}^k$ for every positive integer k.

25.2   The characteristic polynomial

We remarked earlier that the eigenvalues of a square matrix $\mathbf{A}$ are the solutions to the equation

$$\det(\lambda\mathbf{I} - \mathbf{A}) = 0. \tag{25.3}$$

This section is mainly concerned with that equation.

We begin with an illustration of a difficulty which we avoided in the last section only by crafty selection of examples.

Example 1 Find the eigenvalues of the matrix

$$\mathbf{A} = \begin{bmatrix} 0 & 1 \\ -1 & 0 \end{bmatrix}.$$

In this case (25.3) is the quadratic equation

$$\lambda^2 + 1 = 0.$$

This equation has no real root. If we allow complex scalars, which seems in this context to be a sensible thing to do, we can say that the eigenvalues of $\mathbf{A}$ are i and $-i$.

Complex linear algebra

Example 1 shows that when we do eigenvalue theory we are led inexorably into the complex number system $\mathcal{C}$. *For the rest of this section, scalars will be allowed to be complex.* Under this convention, all the main results of Chapters 11 and 12 on vectors, matrices and systems of linear equations continue to apply, as do the results on determinants and transposition in Sections 13.1 and 13.2. The set of all n–vectors with complex components is called **complex n–space** and is denoted by $\mathcal{C}^n$.

The results of Section 13.3 on inner products and quadratic forms *do not* go through unchanged to the case of complex scalars. The reason is that much of that section depended on the fact that $\mathbf{x}^T\mathbf{x} > 0$ for any non-zero vector $\mathbf{x}$ in $\mathcal{R}^n$, which in turn depends on the fact that the square of any non-zero real number is positive. By contrast, the square of a non-zero complex number need not be positive or even real. For a sketch of how the material of Section 13.3 may be adapted to deal with complex scalars, see Problem 25–2.

Eigenvectors, eigenvalues and diagonalisable matrices are defined in complex linear algebra in the same way as when scalars are real. Similarly, the three propositions of Section 25.1 remain true when scalars are complex.

Example 2 Consider again the matrix

$$\mathbf{A} = \begin{bmatrix} 0 & 1 \\ -1 & 0 \end{bmatrix},$$

whose eigenvalues we calculated in Example 1. We show that $\mathbf{A}$ is a d–matrix and calculate $\mathbf{A}^k$ for every positive integer k.

We showed in Example 1 that the eigenvalues of $\mathbf{A}$ are i and $-i$. Also, $\mathbf{Az} = i\mathbf{z}$ if and only if $z_2 = iz_1$, and $\mathbf{Az} = -i\mathbf{z}$ if and only if $z_1 = iz_2$.

Thus the eigenvectors corresponding to the eigenvalue i are the non-zero multiples of $\begin{bmatrix} 1 \\ i \end{bmatrix}$, and the eigenvectors corresponding to the eigenvalue $-i$ are the non-zero multiples of $\begin{bmatrix} i \\ 1 \end{bmatrix}$. It follows that

$$\mathbf{S}^{-1}\mathbf{A}\mathbf{S} = \mathbf{D}, \quad \text{where} \quad \mathbf{S} = \begin{bmatrix} 1 & i \\ i & 1 \end{bmatrix} \quad \text{and} \quad \mathbf{D} = \begin{bmatrix} i & 0 \\ 0 & -i \end{bmatrix}.$$

To calculate $\mathbf{A}^k$, we note first that

$$\mathbf{D}^k = i^k \begin{bmatrix} 1 & 0 \\ 0 & (-1)^k \end{bmatrix}, \quad \mathbf{S}^{-1} = \tfrac{1}{2} \begin{bmatrix} 1 & -i \\ -i & 1 \end{bmatrix}.$$

If k is even, say $k = 2m$, then $\mathbf{D}^k = (-1)^m\mathbf{I}$, so

$$\mathbf{A}^k = \mathbf{S}\mathbf{D}^k\mathbf{S}^{-1} = (-1)^m\mathbf{S}\mathbf{I}\mathbf{S}^{-1} = (-1)^m\mathbf{I}.$$

If k is odd, say $k = 2m + 1$, then

$$\mathbf{D}^k = (-1)^m \begin{bmatrix} i & 0 \\ 0 & -i \end{bmatrix}, \quad \mathbf{D}^k\mathbf{S}^{-1} = (-1)^m/2 \begin{bmatrix} i & 1 \\ -1 & -i \end{bmatrix},$$

and

$$\mathbf{A}^k = (-1)^m/2 \begin{bmatrix} 1 & i \\ i & 1 \end{bmatrix} \begin{bmatrix} i & 1 \\ -1 & -i \end{bmatrix} = (-1)^m/2 \begin{bmatrix} 0 & 2 \\ -2 & 0 \end{bmatrix} = (-1)^m\mathbf{A}.$$

Summarising, we see that

$$\mathbf{A}^2 = -\mathbf{I}, \quad \mathbf{A}^3 = -\mathbf{A}, \quad \mathbf{A}^4 = \mathbf{I}, \quad \mathbf{A}^5 = \mathbf{A}$$

and so on.

Two remarks about Example 2

1. In this example, unlike in Example 2 of the last section, we pressed through to the end, multiplying out the product $\mathbf{S}\mathbf{D}^k\mathbf{S}^{-1}$ to get an explicit expression for $\mathbf{A}^k$. The reason for this is that the entries of $\mathbf{A}$, unlike the eigenvalues, are real numbers; hence the entries of $\mathbf{A}^k$ are all real, for any positive integer k, and it is desirable to obtain an answer which exhibits this.

2. In this particular case, the efficient way of calculating $\mathbf{A}^k$, for every positive integer k, is not to compute the eigenvalues but simply to notice that $\mathbf{A}^2 = -\mathbf{I}$. This can be seen either by inspection or by appealing to the facts about rotations which we used to obtain the trigonometric addition formulae in Section 22.2: the matrix $\mathbf{A}$ represents a clockwise rotation through a right-angle. The object of the exercise, however, was to illustrate a method which generalises. Notice that the method requires one to find the real and imaginary parts of λ^k for each eigenvalue λ of $\mathbf{A}$ and each positive integer k. In Example 2, this calculation was trivial: $i^k = (-1)^m$ if $k = 2m$, $i^k = (-1)^m i$ if $k = 2m + 1$. In more complicated cases, the calculation requires the general method of computing powers of complex numbers using the trigonometric form and De Moivre's theorem, as explained in Chapter 23.

Using the fundamental theorem of algebra

We now turn to the general case of an $n \times n$ matrix $\mathbf{A}$. For any complex number λ, let

$$\phi(\lambda) = \det(\lambda \mathbf{I} - \mathbf{A}).$$

By the usual rules for expanding determinants, the function ϕ is an nth-degree polynomial. Thus there are constants $\alpha_1, \alpha_2, \ldots, \alpha_n$, depending on the entries of $\mathbf{A}$, such that

$$\phi(\lambda) = \lambda^n + \alpha_1 \lambda^{n-1} + \ldots + \alpha_{n-1}\lambda + \alpha_n \quad \text{for all } \lambda \in \mathcal{C}. \tag{25.7}$$

The function ϕ is called the **characteristic polynomial** of $\mathbf{A}$.[1]

By the fundamental theorem of algebra, which we stated without proof in Section 23.3, there exist complex numbers $\lambda_1, \lambda_2, \ldots, \lambda_n$ such that

$$\phi(\lambda) = (\lambda - \lambda_1)(\lambda - \lambda_2) \ldots (\lambda - \lambda_n) \quad \text{for all } \lambda \in \mathcal{C}. \tag{25.8}$$

But by definition of the function ϕ, those values of λ for which $\phi(\lambda) = 0$ are the eigenvalues of $\mathbf{A}$. Hence the eigenvalues of $\mathbf{A}$ are the constants $\lambda_1, \lambda_2, \ldots, \lambda_n$ of (25.8).

To summarise: *any $n \times n$ matrix has n eigenvalues, in general complex and not necessarily all different.*

The fact that the eigenvalues may be complex even if the entries of the matrix are real was illustrated above in the case $n = 2$. It is important to note that if all the entries of the $n \times n$ matrix $\mathbf{A}$ are real numbers, then so are the coefficients $\alpha_1, \ldots, \alpha_n$, of (25.7); hence, by a fact about polynomials which we explained in Section 23.3, the eigenvalues of $\mathbf{A}$ occur in conjugate pairs. For instance, if $\mathbf{A}$ is a 3×3 matrix whose entries are all real numbers, then the

---

[1] Some books define the characteristic polynomial to be $\det(\mathbf{A} - \lambda \mathbf{I})$, but it is more convenient to work with an nth degree polynomial in which the coefficient of λ is 1 than with one in which it is $(-1)^n$.

eigenvalues of $\mathbf{A}$ are either all real or of the form $a + ib, a - ib, c$ where a, b, c are real numbers.

We now elaborate on our statement that the n eigenvalues of an $n \times n$ matrix are not necessarily all different. There are two alternative ways of describing the case where they are not all different, each of which has its uses. If we have a 3×3 matrix $\mathbf{A}$ with characteristic polynomial

$$(\lambda - 4)^2 (\lambda - 5),$$

we may say

either that the eigenvalues of $\mathbf{A}$ are $4, 4, 5$;

or that $\mathbf{A}$ has eigenvalues 4 (with **multiplicity** 2) and 5 (with multiplicity 1).

More on diagonalisable matrices

As we stated at the end of the last section, having n distinct eigenvalues is a sufficient but not necessary condition for an $n \times n$ matrix to be diagonalisable. If the $n \times n$ matrix $\mathbf{A}$ does not have n distinct eigenvalues but can be written in the form $\mathbf{SDS}^{-1}$, where $\mathbf{D}$ is a diagonal matrix, *the number of times each eigenvalue occurs on the diagonal of $\mathbf{D}$ is equal to its multiplicity.*

To prove this, let $\mathbf{D} = \operatorname{diag}(\lambda_1, ..., \lambda_n)$; we wish to show that these are the same $\lambda_1, ..., \lambda_n$ that occur on the right-hand side of (25.8). Let λ be any scalar. Since $\mathbf{A} = \mathbf{SDS}^{-1}$ and $\lambda\mathbf{I} = \mathbf{S}(\lambda\mathbf{I})\mathbf{S}^{-1}$,

$$\lambda\mathbf{I} - \mathbf{A} = \mathbf{S}(\lambda\mathbf{I} - \mathbf{D})\mathbf{S}^{-1}.$$

Taking determinants, and recalling that $\det(\mathbf{S}^{-1}) = 1/(\det \mathbf{S})$, we see that

$$\det(\lambda\mathbf{I} - \mathbf{A}) = \det(\lambda\mathbf{I} - \mathbf{D}) = (\lambda - \lambda_1)(\lambda - \lambda_2) \ldots (\lambda - \lambda_n),$$

so (25.8) holds as required.

Example 3 We show that the matrix

$$\mathbf{A} = \begin{bmatrix} 1 & 0 & 2 \\ 0 & 2 & 0 \\ -1 & 0 & 4 \end{bmatrix}$$

is diagonalisable.

Expanding $\det(\lambda\mathbf{I} - \mathbf{A})$ by its second row, we see that

$$\phi(\lambda) = (\lambda - 2)(\lambda^2 - 5\lambda + 6) = (\lambda - 2)^2(\lambda - 3);$$

the eigenvalues are $2, 2, 3$. If A is to be a d–matrix, say $\mathbf{SDS}^{-1}$, then the eigenvalue 2 must occur twice on the diagonal of $\mathbf{D}$, and the corresponding

columns of $\mathbf{S}$ must be two linearly independent eigenvectors corresponding to this eigenvalue. Now the eigenvectors of $\mathbf{A}$ corresponding to the
eigenvalue 2 are those non-zero vectors $\mathbf{x}$ such that $x_1 = 2x_3$; two linearly
independent vectors of this type are

$$\mathbf{s}^1 = \begin{bmatrix} 2 \\ 0 \\ 1 \end{bmatrix}, \quad \mathbf{s}^2 = \begin{bmatrix} 0 \\ 1 \\ 0 \end{bmatrix}.$$

Hence $\mathbf{A}$ is a d–matrix, and we may let $\mathbf{D}$ be $\mathrm{diag}(2, 2, 3)$, and the first two
columns of $\mathbf{S}$ be $\mathbf{s}^1$ and $\mathbf{s}^2$. The third column of $\mathbf{S}$ is then an eigenvector
corresponding to the eigenvalue 3, and it is easy to check that $(1\ 0\ 1)^{\mathrm{T}}$
will do. Summarising, $\mathbf{S}^{-1}\mathbf{A}\mathbf{S} = \mathbf{D}$ where

$$\mathbf{S} = \begin{bmatrix} 2 & 0 & 1 \\ 0 & 1 & 0 \\ 1 & 0 & 1 \end{bmatrix}, \quad \mathbf{D} = \begin{bmatrix} 2 & 0 & 0 \\ 0 & 2 & 0 \\ 0 & 0 & 3 \end{bmatrix}.$$

Trace and determinant

We now look again at the form (25.7) for the characteristic polynomial ϕ of an
$n \times n$ matrix $\mathbf{A}$.

The **trace** of a square matrix $\mathbf{A}$ is defined to be the sum of its diagonal
entries and is written $\mathrm{tr}\,\mathbf{A}$. We show in the appendix to this chapter that α_1,
the coefficient of λ^{n-1} in (25.7), is equal to $-\,\mathrm{tr}\,\mathbf{A}$. Also, setting $\lambda = 0$ in (25.7),

$$\alpha_n = \phi(0) = \det(-\mathbf{A}) = (-1)^n \det \mathbf{A}.$$

Summarising,

$$\alpha_1 = -\,\mathrm{tr}\,\mathbf{A}, \quad \alpha_n = (-1)^n \det \mathbf{A}.$$

But since the right-hand sides of (25.7) and (25.8) are equal for all values of λ,

$$\alpha_1 = -(\lambda_1 + \ldots + \lambda_n), \quad \alpha_n = (-1)^n \lambda_1 \ldots \lambda_n.$$

It follows that

$$\mathrm{tr}\,\mathbf{A} = \lambda_1 + \ldots + \lambda_n, \quad \det \mathbf{A} = \lambda_1 \ldots \lambda_n. \tag{25.9}$$

It is conventional to state (25.9) as follows: *the trace is the sum of the eigenvalues and the determinant is the product of the eigenvalues.* These statements
are true whether or not the matrix is diagonalisable. In interpreting them, each
eigenvalue must be counted as many times as its multiplicity. Thus in Example
3, $\mathrm{tr}\,\mathbf{A} = 1 + 2 + 4 = 7$, which is equal to the sum of the eigenvalues, regarded
as $2 + 2 + 3$. Similarly, expanding by the second row, $\det \mathbf{A} = 2(4 + 2) = 12$;
this is equal to the product of the eigenvalues, regarded as $2 \times 2 \times 3$.

Non-diagonalisable matrices

We have yet to give an example of a square matrix which is not a d–matrix. Here is one. Let

$$\mathbf{A} = \begin{bmatrix} 0 & 1 \\ 0 & 0 \end{bmatrix}.$$

The characteristic polynomial is λ^2, the eigenvalues are $0, 0$ and the eigenvectors are the non-zero multiples of $(1 \; 0)^{\mathrm{T}}$. But then $\mathbf{A}$ is a 2×2 matrix which does not have two linearly independent eigenvectors; so by Proposition 1 of Section 25.1, $\mathbf{A}$ is not diagonalisable.

If in this example we replace the 0 in the bottom-left entry by a positive number δ, we obtain a d–matrix: the eigenvalues are now the two different numbers $\pm\sqrt{\delta}$. This is so for any positive δ, however small. This result generalises: given a square matrix $\mathbf{A}$ which is not diagonalisable, we can always find a d–matrix whose entries are arbitrarily close to those of $\mathbf{A}$.

Actually we can go further, and say that "almost all square matrices are diagonialisable". We will not be able to give this statement a precise meaning in this book, but the following remarks should be helpful.

Consider a quadratic equation with real coefficients, say $x^2 + bx + c = 0$. This may be represented by a point (b, c) in the xy–plane. The equation has two distinct real roots if $b^2 > 4c$, two distinct complex roots if $b^2 < 4c$ and coincident roots if $b^2 = 4c$. In geometrical terms, the last case occurs only when the point (b, c) lies on a particular curve in the plane, the parabola $y = \frac{1}{4}x^2$. In this sense, "almost all" quadratic equations with real coefficients have distinct roots.

Similar remarks apply to quadratic equations with complex coefficients, and to polynomial equations generally. Thus "almost all" $n \times n$ matrices have n distinct eigenvalues and are therefore d–matrices. In this sense, then, non-diagonalisable matrices are special cases and d–matrices are general (the proper mathematical term is **generic**).

Obviously this is a bit vague and you should be wary of arguments from genericity. After all, a similar argument shows that almost all $n \times n$ matrices are invertible,[2] and we know that singular matrices are important. However, it is useful to know that in many practical contexts the assumption that relevant square matrices are diagonalisable does not involve much loss of generality, and we frequently make this assumption in the next chapter.

Remarks on computation

You will probably have noticed that this chapter has adopted a very different approach to computation to that of earlier chapters concerned with matrix algebra, in particular Chapter 12. In Chapter 12 we were concerned with efficient

---

[2]Recall Problems 12–3 and 13–1.

methods for solving systems of equations and inverting matrices, which can in principle be applied to matrices of any size. In practice, software for matrix inversion and solving linear equations supplements the methods of Chapter 12 by tricks to reduce rounding errors and avoid division by very small numbers. But it remains true that Gaussian elimination and the Gauss–Jordan method lie at the heart of actual computation.

In this chapter, by contrast, we have said little about computation, merely noting that the eigenvalues of a 2×2 matrix are the roots of a quadratic equation and finding the eigenvalues by inspection in other simple cases. General numerical methods for finding eigenvalues exist, and are incorporated in standard software packages such as MATLAB, but the underlying theory is complicated and will not be treated in this book.

Exercises

25.2.1 What can be said about the eigenvalues of a triangular matrix?

25.2.2 Let $\mathbf{B}$ be an $m \times n$ matrix, $\mathbf{C}$ an $n \times m$ matrix. Prove that the $m \times m$ matrix $\mathbf{BC}$ and the $n \times n$ matrix $\mathbf{CB}$ have the same trace.

[HINT   Let $\mathbf{P}$ be the $m \times n$ matrix defined by $p_{ij} = b_{ij}c_{ji}$. What is the sum of the entries in the ith row of $\mathbf{P}$? What about the columns?]

25.2.3   (a) Given the matrix
$$\mathbf{A} = \begin{bmatrix} 1 & -1 \\ 3 & 1 \end{bmatrix},$$
find a diagonal matrix $\mathbf{D}$ and an invertible matrix $\mathbf{S}$ such that $\mathbf{A} = \mathbf{SDS}^{-1}$. Hence find $\mathbf{A}^k$ for every positive integer k.

(b) As (a), but with
$$\mathbf{A} = \begin{bmatrix} 1 & -1 \\ 5 & 3 \end{bmatrix}.$$

25.2.4   (a) Suppose the $n \times n$ matrix $\mathbf{A}$ is diagonalisable and has only one eigenvalue α, with multiplicity n. Find $\mathbf{A}$.

(b) In the text, we showed that the matrix
$$\begin{bmatrix} 0 & 1 \\ 0 & 0 \end{bmatrix}$$
is not diagonalisable. Show how to reach the same conclusion by a method that does not involve calculating any eigenvectors.

25.2.5 Show that the matrix $\begin{bmatrix} 0 & -4 \\ 25 & 20 \end{bmatrix}$ is not diagonalisable.

25.3   Eigenvalues of symmetric matrices

By a **real symmetric matrix** we mean a matrix whose entries are all real numbers, and whose transpose is itself. Such matrices were discussed at some length in Section 13.3, and we now discuss properties of their eigenvalues and eigenvectors. These properties may be summarised in two theorems, of which this is the first.

Theorem 1 If $\mathbf{A}$ is a real symmetric matrix,

   (a) all the eigenvalues of $\mathbf{A}$ are real numbers;

   (b) $\mathbf{A}$ is diagonalisable — there exist a diagonal matrix $\mathbf{D}$ and an invertible matrix $\mathbf{S}$, both with entirely real entries, such that $\mathbf{S}^{-1}\mathbf{A}\mathbf{S} = \mathbf{D}$;

   (c) the matrix $\mathbf{S}$ of (b) can be chosen so that $\mathbf{S}^{\mathrm{T}} = \mathbf{S}^{-1}$.

We shall not attempt a full proof of Theorem 1, but the following remarks about why it is true and how it is used should be read with care.

Making scalars real

If all entries and all eigenvalues of a matrix are real numbers, then finding the eigenvectors involves solving systems of linear equations with real coefficients. Thus part (a) of Theorem 1 tells us that, as long as we confine ourselves to symmetric matrices, we can work with eigenvalues and eigenvectors without ever leaving the real number system. *For the rest of this section, all scalars will be assumed to be real.*

Symmetry and real eigenvalues

Having said what part (a) of Theorem 1 implies, we now say a little about why it holds in the case of 2×2 matrices. Let

$$\mathbf{A} = \begin{bmatrix} a_{11} & a_{12} \\ a_{21} & a_{22} \end{bmatrix},$$

a 2×2 matrix. The characteristic polynomial of this matrix is

$$(\lambda - a_{11})(\lambda - a_{22}) - b,$$

where $b = a_{12}a_{21}$. Thus the eigenvalues of $\mathbf{A}$, if real, can be depicted in the xy–plane as the x–coordinates of the points where the parabola $y = (x-a_{11})(x-a_{22})$ intersects the horizontal line $y = b$; the eigenvalues are complex when the line $y = b$ lies below the vertex of the parabola. If $\mathbf{A}$ is symmetric, $b = a_{12}{}^2 \geq 0$, so the line $y = b$ must intersect the parabola; this is illustrated in Figure 25.1. This geometrical argument demonstrates that the eigenvalues of a symmetric 2×2 matrix are indeed real.

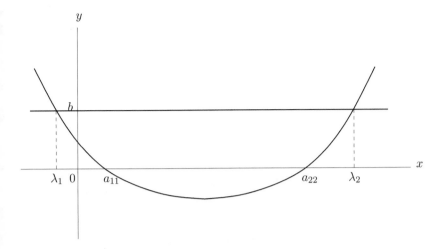

Figure 25.1: **The eigenvalues of a 2x2 symmetric matrix are real**

Orthogonal matrices

Taking part (a) of Theorem 1 as given, we now prove parts (b) and (c) in the case where $\mathbf{A}$ is an $n \times n$ matrix with n different eigenvalues. Then (b) follows immediately from Proposition 1 of Section 25.1, and it remains to show that the matrix $\mathbf{S}$ can be chosen such that $\mathbf{S}^{\mathrm{T}} = \mathbf{S}^{-1}$. An invertible matrix with this property is called an **orthogonal matrix**: recall Exercise 13.2.2. By the properties of the matrix inverse given in Section 12.3, a square matrix $\mathbf{S}$ is orthogonal if and only if $\mathbf{S}^{\mathrm{T}}\mathbf{S} = \mathbf{I}$. This happens if and only if the following two properties are satisfied:

(i) for any column $\mathbf{u}$ of $\mathbf{S}$, $\mathbf{u}^{\mathrm{T}}\mathbf{u} = 1$;

(ii) for any two different columns $\mathbf{u}$ and $\mathbf{v}$ of $\mathbf{S}$, $\mathbf{u}^{\mathrm{T}}\mathbf{v} = 0$.

Given that $\mathbf{A}$ is a symmetric $n \times n$ matrix with n distinct eigenvalues we may, as in Section 25.1, choose $\mathbf{S}$ to be a matrix of eigenvectors of $\mathbf{A}$. Specifically, each column of $\mathbf{S}$ is an eigenvector corresponding to a different eigenvalue of $\mathbf{A}$. Then there is no difficulty in scaling the columns of $\mathbf{S}$ so that property (i) is satisfied: for if $\mathbf{x}$ is an eigenvector of $\mathbf{A}$ and $\mathbf{u} = (\mathbf{x}^{\mathrm{T}}\mathbf{x})^{-1/2}\mathbf{x}$, then $\mathbf{u}$ is an eigenvector corresponding to the same eigenvalue, and $\mathbf{u}^{\mathrm{T}}\mathbf{u} = 1$.[3] Also, *property (ii) is satisfied automatically.* For if $\mathbf{u}, \mathbf{v}$ are eigenvectors of $\mathbf{A}$ corresponding to

---

[3]To see this, let $\theta = (\mathbf{x}^{\mathrm{T}}\mathbf{x})^{-1/2}$; then $(\theta\mathbf{x})^{\mathrm{T}}(\theta\mathbf{x}) = \theta^2\mathbf{x}^{\mathrm{T}}\mathbf{x} = (\mathbf{x}^{\mathrm{T}}\mathbf{x})^{-1}\mathbf{x}^{\mathrm{T}}\mathbf{x} = 1$.

two different eigenvalues λ, μ, then

$$\lambda \mathbf{u}^{\mathrm{T}} \mathbf{v} = (\mathbf{A}\mathbf{u})^{\mathrm{T}} \mathbf{v} \qquad \text{since } \mathbf{A}\mathbf{u} = \lambda \mathbf{u}$$
$$= \mathbf{u}^{\mathrm{T}} \mathbf{A} \mathbf{v} \qquad \text{since } \mathbf{A} \text{ is symmetric}$$
$$= \mu \mathbf{u}^{\mathrm{T}} \mathbf{v} \qquad \text{since } \mathbf{A}\mathbf{v} = \mu \mathbf{v},$$

and the fact that $\mathbf{u}^{\mathrm{T}} \mathbf{v} = 0$ follows from the fact that $\lambda \neq \mu$.

Let us summarise what we have done. In the case where $\mathbf{A}$ is a symmetric $n \times n$ matrix with n different eigenvalues, we have proved parts (b) and (c) of Theorem 1, and we have shown how to find $\mathbf{S}$ and $\mathbf{D}$, given the eigenvalues. The method is as follows. We write the eigenvalues of $\mathbf{A}$ as the diagonal entries of a diagonal matrix $\mathbf{D}$, and find a matrix $\mathbf{X}$ whose columns are eigenvectors, ordered in the same way that the corresponding eigenvalues are ordered in $\mathbf{D}$. We then obtain a matrix $\mathbf{S}$ by multiplying each column $\mathbf{x}$ of $\mathbf{X}$ by $(\mathbf{x}^{\mathrm{T}}\mathbf{x})^{-1/2}$. $\mathbf{S}$ is an orthogonal matrix and $\mathbf{S}^{-1}\mathbf{A}\mathbf{S} = \mathbf{D}$.

Example 1 Given that

$$\mathbf{A} = \begin{bmatrix} 4 & 1 \\ 1 & 4 \end{bmatrix},$$

find a diagonal matrix $\mathbf{D}$ and an orthogonal matrix $\mathbf{S}$ such that $\mathbf{S}^{-1}\mathbf{A}\mathbf{S} = \mathbf{D}$.

The characteristic polynomial is $\lambda^2 - 8\lambda + 15$, so the eigenvalues are 5 and 3, with corresponding eigenvectors $\mathbf{x} = (1 \ 1)^{\mathrm{T}}$ and $\mathbf{y} = (-1 \ 1)^{\mathrm{T}}$. Setting

$$\mathbf{D} = \mathrm{diag}(5, 3),$$

we choose as the first column of $\mathbf{S}$ the vector $(1^2 + 1^2)^{-1/2}\mathbf{x} = (1/\sqrt{2})\mathbf{x}$. Similarly the second column of $\mathbf{S}$ is $(1/\sqrt{2})\mathbf{y}$. It follows that

$$\mathbf{S} = \frac{1}{\sqrt{2}} \begin{bmatrix} 1 & -1 \\ 1 & 1 \end{bmatrix}.$$

Symmetry and diagonalisability

Perhaps the most surprising part of Theorem 1 is (b): a symmetric matrix must be diagonalisable, whatever the multiplicity of its eigenvalues. This is a special case of a result known as **Schur's lemma**, which states the following: if $\mathbf{A}$ is a square matrix, not necessarily symmetric, whose entries and eigenvalues are all real, there is an orthogonal matrix $\mathbf{S}$ and an upper triangular matrix $\mathbf{U}$ such that $\mathbf{S}^{-1}\mathbf{A}\mathbf{S} = \mathbf{U}$. Since $\mathbf{S}$ is an orthogonal matrix, the last equation may be written $\mathbf{S}^{\mathrm{T}}\mathbf{A}\mathbf{S} = \mathbf{U}$. Using the rule for transposing a product and recalling that $(\mathbf{S}^{\mathrm{T}})^{\mathrm{T}} = \mathbf{S}$, we see that $\mathbf{U}^{\mathrm{T}} = \mathbf{S}^{\mathrm{T}}\mathbf{A}^{\mathrm{T}}\mathbf{S}$. In particular, $\mathbf{U}^{\mathrm{T}} = \mathbf{U}$ if $\mathbf{A}^{\mathrm{T}} = \mathbf{A}$; thus if $\mathbf{A}$ is a symmetric matrix, $\mathbf{U}$ is both upper triangular and symmetric, and is therefore a diagonal matrix. This establishes part (b) of Theorem 1, and indeed part (c) since $\mathbf{S}$ is an orthogonal matrix.

Schur's lemma is a very useful result, which can be extended to the case where $\mathbf{A}$ has complex eigenvalues (and indeed entries): see the remarks at the end of Problem 25–2. We shall refer to it in passing in the next chapter, but its proof and its most important implications are beyond the scope of this book.

More on quadratic forms

Let $\mathbf{A}$ be a symmetric matrix. In Section 13.3 we defined $\mathbf{A}$ to be positive semidefinite if the quadratic form $\mathbf{x}^{\mathrm{T}}\mathbf{A}\mathbf{x}$ takes only non-negative values, positive definite if $\mathbf{x}^{\mathrm{T}}\mathbf{A}\mathbf{x} > 0$ whenever $\mathbf{x} \neq \mathbf{0}$. The terms negative semidefinite and negative definite are defined similarly. The second theorem of this section describes such matrices in terms of their eigenvalues.

Theorem 2 A real symmetric matrix $\mathbf{A}$ is

(a) positive definite if and only if all its eigenvalues are positive;

(b) positive semidefinite if and only if all its eigenvalues are non-negative;

(c) negative definite if and only if all its eigenvalues are negative;

(d) negative semidefinite if and only if all its eigenvalues are non-positive.

We prove only part (a): the proofs of the other parts are similar. Suppose $\mathbf{A}$ is positive definite and let λ be any eigenvalue of $\mathbf{A}$: we want to prove that $\lambda > 0$. Since $\mathbf{A}\mathbf{x} = \lambda\mathbf{x}$, $\mathbf{x}^{\mathrm{T}}\mathbf{A}\mathbf{x} = \lambda\mathbf{x}^{\mathrm{T}}\mathbf{x}$; since $\mathbf{A}$ is positive definite and $\mathbf{x} \neq \mathbf{0}$, $\mathbf{x}^{\mathrm{T}}\mathbf{A}\mathbf{x}$ and $\mathbf{x}^{\mathrm{T}}\mathbf{x}$ are positive numbers; hence $\lambda > 0$.

Conversely, suppose that the eigenvalues $\lambda_1, \ldots, \lambda_n$ of $\mathbf{A}$ are all positive, and let $\mathbf{x} \neq \mathbf{0}$; we want to prove that $\mathbf{x}^{\mathrm{T}}\mathbf{A}\mathbf{x} > 0$. Let $\mathbf{D} = \mathrm{diag}(\lambda_1, \ldots, \lambda_n)$; by Theorem 1, there exists an orthogonal matrix $\mathbf{S}$ such that $\mathbf{A} = \mathbf{S}\mathbf{D}\mathbf{S}^{\mathrm{T}}$. Letting $\mathbf{y} = \mathbf{S}^{\mathrm{T}}\mathbf{x}$, we see that

$$\mathbf{x}^{\mathrm{T}}\mathbf{A}\mathbf{x} = \mathbf{y}^{\mathrm{T}}\mathbf{D}\mathbf{y} = \lambda_1 y_1^2 + \ldots + \lambda_n y_n^2.$$

But since $\mathbf{x} \neq \mathbf{0}$ and $\mathbf{S}^{\mathrm{T}}$ is a nonsingular matrix, $\mathbf{y} \neq \mathbf{0}$. This, together with the assumption that $\lambda_1, \ldots, \lambda_n$ are all positive, implies that $\lambda_1 y_1^2, \ldots, \lambda_n y_n^2$ are non-negative numbers, at least one of which is positive. Hence $\mathbf{x}^{\mathrm{T}}\mathbf{A}\mathbf{x} > 0$, and the proof is complete.

Example 2 We showed in Example 1 that the symmetric matrix

$$\mathbf{A} = \begin{bmatrix} 4 & 1 \\ 1 & 4 \end{bmatrix},$$

has eigenvalues are 5 and 3. Since these are positive numbers, $\mathbf{A}$ is positive definite. Of course, this can also be seen using the methods of Section 13.3: the diagonal entries of $\mathbf{A}$ are positive, and $\det \mathbf{A} = 15 > 0$, so $\mathbf{A}$ is positive definite.

Exercises

25.3.1 Given the matrix
$$A = \begin{bmatrix} 1 & -3 \\ -3 & 1 \end{bmatrix},$$
find a diagonal matrix D and an orthogonal matrix S such that $S^{-1}AS = D$.

25.3.2 The geometrical argument which we used to show that the eigenvalues of a 2×2 real symmetric matrix are real applies to a wider class of 2×2 matrices. Which class?

25.3.3 What does Theorem 2 of this section tell us about symmetric matrices that are neither positive semidefinite nor negative semidefinite?

25.3.4 Let A be a positive definite symmetric matrix. By Theorems 1 and 2, we may write $A = SDS^T$, where S is an orthogonal matrix and D is a diagonal matrix whose diagonal entries are all positive. Write a formula, in terms of D and S, for a positive definite symmetric matrix $A^{\frac{1}{2}}$ with the property that $(A^{\frac{1}{2}})^2 = A$. If $B = (A^{\frac{1}{2}})^{-1}$, what can you say about the matrices B and B^2?

Problems on Chapter 25

25-1. (i) Given that
$$A = \begin{bmatrix} 2 & 6 \\ 3 & -1 \end{bmatrix},$$
find all eigenvalues and eigenvectors of A and A^T.

(ii) Which of the following statements are true for every square matrix A?

(a) A and A^T have the same characteristic polynomial.

(b) A and A^T have the same eigenvalues.

(c) A and A^T have the same eigenvectors.

25-2. This problem introduces the most important concepts of linear algebra with complex scalars. Despite appearances, it is not difficult: all it requires is some facility with the algebra of complex conjugates. If you understood Section 23.1, you should have no trouble.

Given an $m \times n$ matrix A with complex entries, we define $\bar{A}$ to be the matrix whose entries are the conjugates of those of A. The **Hermitian transpose** of A is the $n \times m$ matrix $A^H = \bar{A}^T$. The Hermitian transpose z^H of a vector z in C^n is defined similarly. Notice that if z and w are vectors in C^n then $z^H w$ is a scalar.

(i) What is the relation between $\mathbf{z}^H\mathbf{w}$ and $\mathbf{w}^H\mathbf{z}$? Show that if $\mathbf{z} \neq \mathbf{0}$ then $\mathbf{z}^H\mathbf{z} > 0$.

(ii) A **Hermitian matrix** is a square matrix $\mathbf{A}$ such that $\mathbf{A}^H = \mathbf{A}$. Show that all the diagonal entries of such a matrix are real numbers. Explain why a Hermitian matrix whose entries are *all* real numbers is the same thing as a real symmetric matrix.

(iii) Write down general forms for Hermitian matrices of orders 2 and 3.

(iv) If $\mathbf{A}$ is a Hermitian $n \times n$ matrix and $\mathbf{z} \in C^n$, then $\mathbf{z}^H\mathbf{A}\mathbf{z}$ is a real number. Verify this result when $n = 2$, and explain informally why it holds generally.

(v) Using (iv), show that all eigenvalues of a Hermitian matrix are real numbers. [Notice that part (a) of Theorem 1 of Section 25.3 is a special case of this result.]

(vi) A Hermitian matrix $\mathbf{A}$ is said to be positive definite if $\mathbf{z}^H\mathbf{A}\mathbf{z} > 0$ whenever $\mathbf{z} \neq \mathbf{0}$. Show that all the diagonal entries of such a matrix are positive. Show also that the Hermitian matrix

$$\begin{bmatrix} 1 & w \\ \bar{w} & 1 \end{bmatrix}$$

is positive definite if and only if its determinant is positive. How do you think these results generalise?

(vii) A **unitary matrix** is an invertible matrix whose inverse is its Hermitian transpose. Explain why a unitary matrix whose entries are all real numbers is the same thing as an orthogonal matrix. Show also that

$$\begin{bmatrix} 1 & i \\ i & 1 \end{bmatrix}$$

is a unitary matrix.

[If you have got as far as part (vi) you will certainly have realised that the purpose of Hermitian matrices is to generalise the theory of quadratic forms to the complex number system. An important fact about unitary matrices is the complex version of Schur's lemma: if $\mathbf{A}$ is any square matrix, there is a unitary matrix $\mathbf{S}$ and an upper triangular matrix $\mathbf{U}$ such that $\mathbf{S}^{-1}\mathbf{A}\mathbf{S} = \mathbf{U}$.]

25–3. In this problem, all scalars are assumed to be real. We define a **projection matrix** to be a square matrix $\mathbf{P}$ such that $\mathbf{P}^2 = \mathbf{P}^T = \mathbf{P}$.

(i) Show that

$$\frac{1}{3} \begin{bmatrix} 2 & -1 & 1 \\ -1 & 2 & 1 \\ 1 & 1 & 2 \end{bmatrix}$$

is a projection matrix.

(ii) Show that every eigenvalue of a projection matrix is either 1 or 0.

(iii) Let $\mathbf{P}$ be an $n{\times}n$ projection matrix such that $\mathbf{P} \neq \mathbf{O}$. Using the result of (ii), and Theorem 1 of Section 25.3, show that there is an integer r and an $n \times r$ matrix $\mathbf{Z}$ with the following properties: $1 \leq r \leq n$, $\mathbf{Z}^T\mathbf{Z} = \mathbf{I}_r$ and $\mathbf{Z}\mathbf{Z}^T = \mathbf{P}$.

(iv) Prove the following converse to the result of (iii): if $\mathbf{Z}$ is an $n \times r$ matrix such that $\mathbf{Z}^T\mathbf{Z} = \mathbf{I}_r$, then $\mathbf{Z}\mathbf{Z}^T$ is a projection matrix.

25–4. Let $\mathbf{A}$ be the symmetric matrix

$$\begin{bmatrix} 2 & 1 & -2 \\ 1 & 2 & -2 \\ -2 & -2 & 5 \end{bmatrix}.$$

(i) Show that the characteristic polynomial may be written in the form $(\lambda - 1)^2(\lambda - 7)$.

(ii) Show that the vector equation $\mathbf{A}\mathbf{x} = \mathbf{x}$ reduces to a single scalar equation. Hence find eigenvectors $\mathbf{x}$, $\mathbf{y}$ corresponding to the eigenvalue 1 which have the property that $\mathbf{x}^T\mathbf{y} = \mathbf{0}$. [This requires a little algebraic ingenuity but no advanced concepts.]

(iii) Find an eigenvector $\mathbf{z}$ corresponding to the eigenvalue 7.

(iv) Using your answers to (ii) and (iii), find a diagonal matrix $\mathbf{D}$ and an orthogonal matrix $\mathbf{S}$ such that $\mathbf{S}^{-1}\mathbf{A}\mathbf{S} = \mathbf{D}$.

Appendix to Chapter 25

In this appendix we prove two results of the chapter. The first is Proposition 2 of Section 25.1: if $\mathbf{x}^1, \ldots, \mathbf{x}^k$ are eigenvectors corresponding to k different eigenvalues of the $n \times n$ matrix $\mathbf{A}$, then $\mathbf{x}^1, \ldots, \mathbf{x}^k$ are linearly independent.

We prove this proposition in the special case $k = 3$; the general proof is similar but requires messy notation. Let $\mathbf{x}, \mathbf{y}, \mathbf{z}$ be eigenvectors of $\mathbf{A}$ corresponding to three distinct eigenvalues λ, μ, ν: thus

$$\mathbf{Ax} = \lambda \mathbf{x}, \quad \mathbf{Ay} = \mu \mathbf{y}, \quad \mathbf{Az} = \nu \mathbf{z} \tag{25.10}$$

and none of $\mathbf{x}, \mathbf{y}, \mathbf{z}$ is $\mathbf{0}$. Let α, β, γ be scalars such that

$$\alpha \mathbf{x} + \beta \mathbf{y} + \gamma \mathbf{z} = \mathbf{0}. \tag{25.11}$$

We wish to show that $\alpha = \beta = \gamma = 0$.

Premultiplying (25.11) by $\lambda \mathbf{I} - \mathbf{A}$, and using (25.10), we see that

$$\beta(\lambda - \mu)\mathbf{y} + \gamma(\lambda - \nu)\mathbf{z} = \mathbf{0}. \tag{25.12}$$

Premultiplying (25.12) by $\mu \mathbf{I} - \mathbf{A}$, and using (25.10), we see that

$$\gamma(\lambda - \nu)(\mu - \nu)\mathbf{z} = \mathbf{0}.$$

This, together with the facts that $\mathbf{z} \neq \mathbf{0}$ and λ, μ, ν are all different, implies that $\gamma = 0$. Substituting $\gamma = 0$ into (25.12) and using the facts that $\mathbf{y} \neq \mathbf{0}$ and $\lambda \neq \mu$, we see that $\beta = 0$. Substituting $\beta = \gamma = 0$ into (25.10) and using the fact that $\mathbf{x} \neq \mathbf{0}$, we see that $\alpha = 0$.

More on the characteristic polynomial

The other result to be proved in this appendix concerns the interpretation of the coefficient of λ^{n-1} in the characteristic polynomial of an $n \times n$ matrix.

As in Section 25.2, let $\mathbf{A}$ be a square matrix of order n, and let

$$\phi(\lambda) = \det(\lambda \mathbf{I} - \mathbf{A}) = \lambda^n + \alpha_1 \lambda^{n-1} + \ldots + \alpha_{n-1}\lambda + \alpha_n.$$

We wish to show that $\alpha_1 = -\operatorname{tr} \mathbf{A}$.

Expanding the determinant by its first row, we have

$$\phi(\lambda) = (\lambda - a_{11})\det(\lambda \mathbf{I}_{n-1} - \mathbf{B}) + \psi(\lambda),$$

where $\mathbf{B}$ is the matrix obtained by deleting the first row and first column of $\mathbf{A}$ and $\psi(\lambda)$ is a polynomial. Specifically, $\psi(\lambda)$ is the sum of $n - 1$ terms of the form 'constant $\times$ determinant of order $n - 1$', where each of these determinants has only $n-2$ entries which involve λ (one in each column after the first). Hence $\psi(\lambda)$ is a polynomial of degree at most $n - 2$.

We can now expand $\det(\lambda \mathbf{I}_{n-1} - \mathbf{B})$ by its first row, and repeat the process for as long as we can. We end up with an expression for $\phi(\lambda)$ of the form $\phi_1(\lambda) + \phi_2(\lambda)$, where

$$\phi_1(\lambda) = (\lambda - a_{11})(\lambda - a_{22}) \ldots (\lambda - a_{nn})$$

and $\phi_2(\lambda)$ is a polynomial of degree at most $n - 2$. But then the coefficient of λ^{n-1} in $\phi(\lambda)$ is the same as the coefficient of λ^{n-1} in $\phi_1(\lambda)$, so

$$\alpha_1 = -a_{11} - a_{22} - \ldots - a_{nn} = -\operatorname{tr}\mathbf{A}.$$

Chapter 26

DYNAMIC SYSTEMS

In this chapter we generalise the first-order difference equations and differential equations of Chapter 21 to the case where the dependent variable is a vector. It turns out that the resulting framework is sufficiently general to subsume the second-order dynamics of Chapter 24 as another special case.

The main tool used in this chapter is the eigenvalue theory of Chapter 25. Because of this emphasis on algebra rather than calculus, we find it convenient to start with discrete time (difference equations) and then turn to the case of continuous time.

In a single chapter we shall only be able to scratch the surface of a massive body of mathematics, and to give just a few of the many economic applications. We hope to have done enough to give a flavour of what is involved in dynamic analysis. *When you have studied this chapter you will be able to:*

- solve linear systems of difference equations and differential equations in two variables;

- understand the principles of solution of linear dynamic stystems in more than two variables;

- analyse the nature of fixed points of linear systems of differential equations in two variables, using both diagrams and algebra;

- use linearisation to analyse local stability of fixed points of nonlinear systems of differential equations in two variables, and draw the associated phase diagrams.

26.1 Systems of difference equations

The simplest difference equation is

$$y_{t+1} = ay_t, \tag{26.1}$$

where a is a constant and t takes only integer values. The usual interpretation is that we have some scalar quantity y that moves through time, where time is discrete: equation (26.1) shows how the value of y at time $t + 1$ depends on its value at time t. As in Section 21.4, we shall typically restrict t to *non-negative* integer values; thus we can think of the equation as describing a process which begins at time 0.[1] In the spirit of this interpretation, we shall usually work with a specific boundary condition, namely that y_0 is given.

Solving (26.1) means finding y_t explicitly in terms of t and the initial value y_0. This is easily done:

$$y_1 = ay_0, \quad y_2 = ay_1 = a^2 y_0, \quad y_3 = ay_2 = a^3 y_0$$

and so on. Thus the solution is

$$y_t = a^t y_0 \quad (t = 1, 2, \dots).$$

All of this should be familiar from Section 21.4. Our first new step is to generalise (26.1) to the case where the scalar y is replaced by an n–vector $\mathbf{y}$. Our difference equation is now

$$\mathbf{y}(t + 1) = \mathbf{A}\mathbf{y}(t), \tag{26.2}$$

for $t = 0, 1, 2, \dots$; here each $\mathbf{y}(t)$ is an n–vector, with $\mathbf{y}(0)$ given, and $\mathbf{A}$ is a given $n \times n$ matrix. A difference equation in vectors is often referred to as a **system** of (scalar) difference equations. For example, if $\mathbf{y}(t)$ is a 3–vector whose components are v_t, w_t, x_t then (26.2) is a system of three equations relating the values of v, w and x at time $t + 1$ to their values at time t.

We may solve (26.2) in the same way as (26.1): since

$$\mathbf{y}(1) = \mathbf{A}\mathbf{y}(0), \quad \mathbf{y}(2) = \mathbf{A}\mathbf{y}(1) = \mathbf{A}^2 \mathbf{y}(0), \quad \mathbf{y}(3) = \mathbf{A}\mathbf{y}(2) = \mathbf{A}^3 \mathbf{y}(0)$$

and so on, we have

$$\mathbf{y}(t) = \mathbf{A}^t \mathbf{y}(0) \quad (t = 1, 2, \dots). \tag{26.3}$$

To put this solution into a more easily computable form, we focus on the case where $\mathbf{A}$ is diagonalisable. Suppose there exist an invertible matrix $\mathbf{S}$ and a diagonal matrix $\mathbf{D}$ such that $\mathbf{S}^{-1}\mathbf{A}\mathbf{S} = \mathbf{D}$. Then, for reasons explained in section 25.1, $\mathbf{A}^t = \mathbf{S}\mathbf{D}^t\mathbf{S}^{-1}$ for $t = 1, 2, \dots$ Hence (26.3) may be written

$$\mathbf{y}(t) = \mathbf{S}\mathbf{D}^t\mathbf{c} \quad (t = 1, 2, \dots),$$

where $\mathbf{c} = \mathbf{S}^{-1}\mathbf{y}(0)$. If we denote the components of $\mathbf{c}$ by $c_1, \dots, c_n$ and the diagonal entries of $\mathbf{D}$ by $\lambda_1, \dots, \lambda_n$, then the components of $\mathbf{D}^t\mathbf{c}$ are $\lambda_1^t c_1, \dots, \lambda_n^t c_n$. Letting $\mathbf{s}^1, \dots, \mathbf{s}^n$ be the columns of $\mathbf{S}$, we have

$$\mathbf{y}(t) = \lambda_1^t c_1 \mathbf{s}^1 + \dots + \lambda_n^t c_n \mathbf{s}^n \quad (t = 0, 1, 2, \dots) \tag{26.4}$$

---

[1] The notation here is slightly different from that of Section 21.4, with a in (26.1) corresponding to $-c$ in the earlier section.

There are two important points to notice about this result. First, since $\mathbf{y}(0) = \mathbf{Sc}$, (26.4) also holds for $t = 0$.[2] Secondly, the results of Section 25.1 tell us how $\lambda_1, \ldots, \lambda_n$ and $\mathbf{s}^1, \ldots, \mathbf{s}^n$ are related to the matrix $\mathbf{A}$: $\lambda_1, \ldots, \lambda_n$ are the eigenvalues of $\mathbf{A}$ and $\mathbf{s}^1, \ldots, \mathbf{s}^n$ are n linearly independent eigenvectors corresponding respectively to these eigenvalues. We summarise as follows.

Proposition If the matrix $\mathbf{A}$ is diagonalisable, the solution to (26.2) is

$$\mathbf{y}(t) = \lambda_1^t c_1 \mathbf{s}^1 + \ldots + \lambda_n^t c_n \mathbf{s}^n \quad (t = 0, 1, 2, \ldots)$$

where

(a) $\lambda_1, \ldots, \lambda_n$ are the eigenvalues of $\mathbf{A}$;

(b) $\mathbf{s}^1, \ldots, \mathbf{s}^n$ are n linearly independent eigenvectors of $\mathbf{A}$, corresponding to the eigenvalues $\lambda_1, \ldots, \lambda_n$ respectively;

(c) $c_1, \ldots, c_n$ are scalars depending on initial conditions.

Example Solve the difference equation (26.2) in the case where

$$\mathbf{A} = \begin{bmatrix} 3 & -1 \\ 4 & -2 \end{bmatrix}, \quad \mathbf{y}(0) = \begin{bmatrix} 7 \\ 1 \end{bmatrix}.$$

We showed in Example 1 of Section 25.1 that the eigenvalues of $\mathbf{A}$ are 2 and -1, and that $\begin{bmatrix} 1 \\ 1 \end{bmatrix}$ and $\begin{bmatrix} 1 \\ 4 \end{bmatrix}$ are corresponding eigenvectors. Therefore, the solution of the difference equation is

$$\mathbf{y}(t) = 2^t c_1 \begin{bmatrix} 1 \\ 1 \end{bmatrix} + (-1)^t c_2 \begin{bmatrix} 1 \\ 4 \end{bmatrix} \quad (t = 0, 1, 2, \ldots)$$

where c_1, c_2 are constants. We now use our information on $\mathbf{y}(0)$ to find these constants. Setting $t = 0$ in the solution just given, we have

$$c_1 + c_2 = 7, \quad c_1 + 4c_2 = 1.$$

Hence $c_1 = 9$, $c_2 = -2$ and our solution is

$$\mathbf{y}(t) = 2^t \begin{bmatrix} 9 \\ 9 \end{bmatrix} - (-1)^t \begin{bmatrix} 2 \\ 8 \end{bmatrix} \quad (t = 0, 1, 2, \ldots)$$

Qualitative properties of the solution

For the rest of this section, we assume that $\mathbf{A}$ is a d–matrix, so the solution of (26.2) is given by the proposition above. We use that proposition to investigate properties of the solution.

---

[2]Provided that λ_j^0 is interpreted as 1 even when $\lambda_j = 0$. See Problem 26–1.

Eventual behaviour

We consider first what happens to $\mathbf{y}(t)$ as $t \to \infty$. If

$$|\lambda_j| < 1 \quad \text{for } j = 1, \ldots, n \tag{26.5}$$

then all components of $\mathbf{y}(t)$ tend to zero as $t \to \infty$; this is usually written "$\mathbf{y}(t) \to \mathbf{0}$ as $t \to \infty$". Condition (26.5) is sometimes stated in the form: "all eigenvalues of $\mathbf{A}$ lie inside the unit circle": the geometrical analogy refers to the Argand diagram.

We have just stated that if (26.5) holds, then $\mathbf{y}(t) \to \mathbf{0}$ as $t \to \infty$. The converse also holds, in the following sense: $\mathbf{y}(t) \to \mathbf{0}$ as $t \to \infty$ *for all possible initial conditions* only if (26.5) is true.

To see what this means, suppose $n = 2$. Then the solution to (26.2) is

$$\mathbf{y}(t) = \lambda_1^t c_1 \mathbf{s}^1 + \lambda_2^t c_2 \mathbf{s}^2 \quad (t = 0, 1, 2, \ldots)$$

It is clear that if $|\lambda_1| < 1$ and $|\lambda_2| < 1$, then $\mathbf{y}(t) \to \mathbf{0}$ as $t \to \infty$, whatever the values of c_1 and c_2. Now consider what happens if $|\lambda_1| \geq 1 > |\lambda_2|$. Then for large t, the components of $\mathbf{y}(t)$ are close to those of $\lambda_1^t c_1 \mathbf{s}^1$. If initial conditions are such that $c_1 = 0$, $\mathbf{y}(t) \to \mathbf{0}$ as $t \to \infty$; if not, not. Similarly, in the case where $|\lambda_2| \geq 1 > |\lambda_1|$, we have $\lim_{t \to \infty} \mathbf{y}(t) = \mathbf{0}$ if and only if $c_2 = 0$. And if both $|\lambda_1|$ and $|\lambda_2|$ are at least 1, the only case where $\lim_{t \to \infty} \mathbf{y}(t) = \mathbf{0}$ is given by $c_1 = c_2 = 0$. Thus to ensure that both components of $\mathbf{y}(t)$ approach zero as $t \to \infty$ for *any* choice of $\mathbf{y}(0)$, we need $|\lambda_1| < 1$ and $|\lambda_2| < 1$.

Oscillations

Let us assume as usual that all entries of $\mathbf{A}$ and all components of $\mathbf{y}(0)$ are real numbers. It is immediate from (26.3) that $\mathbf{y}(t) \in \mathcal{R}^n$ for all t. Now this does not prevent the scalars $\lambda_1, \ldots, \lambda_n$ and the vectors $\mathbf{s}^1, \ldots, \mathbf{s}^n$ of (26.4) ¿from being complex. What does follow from the fact that all entries of $\mathbf{A}$ are real is that we can apply a result of Section 25.2: the eigenvalues of a matrix whose entries are all real occur in conjugate pairs.

To illustrate this, suppose $n = 3$, λ_1 is real, and λ_2 and λ_3 are complex conjugates. Writing the last two eigenvalues in trigonometric form, we have

$$\lambda_2 = r(\cos\theta + i\sin\theta), \quad \lambda_3 = r(\cos\theta - i\sin\theta),$$

where $r > 0$ and $-\pi < \theta \leq \pi$. By De Moivre's theorem,

$$\lambda_2^t = r^t(\cos\theta t + i\sin\theta t), \quad \lambda_3^t = r^t(\cos\theta t - i\sin\theta t)$$

for $t = 1, 2, \ldots$ We may therefore write the solution (26.4) as

$$\mathbf{y}(t) = \lambda_1^t c_1 \mathbf{s}^1 + (r^t \cos\theta t)\mathbf{u} + (r^t \sin\theta t)\mathbf{v},$$

where $\mathbf{u} = c_2\mathbf{s}^2 + c_3\mathbf{s}^3$ and $\mathbf{v} = i(c_2\mathbf{s}^2 - c_3\mathbf{s}^3)$. The fact that all entries of $\mathbf{A}$ and all components of $\mathbf{y}(0)$ are real numbers ensures that all components of $\mathbf{u}$ and $\mathbf{v}$ are real.

The presence of the sines and cosines means that the components of $\mathbf{y}$ oscillate over time. Indeed, if $|\lambda_1| < r$ then oscillation will be the dominant mode of behaviour. If $r < 1$ the oscillations will be damped, dying away as $t \to \infty$. If $r > 1$ the oscillations will be explosive.

The non-homogeneous case

A generalisation of (26.2) is the difference equation

$$\mathbf{x}(t+1) = \mathbf{A}\mathbf{x}(t) + \mathbf{b}, \qquad (26.6)$$

for $t = 0, 1, 2, \ldots$, where $\mathbf{A}$ is a given $n \times n$ matrix and $\mathbf{b}$ is a given n–vector. The presence of the (generally non-zero) vector $\mathbf{b}$ on the right-hand side of (26.6) is said to make the difference equation **non-homogeneous**, by contrast with the **homogeneous** equation (26.2). Recall that the terms 'homogeneous' and 'non-homogeneous' were used in a similar sense in Section 21.4.

To solve (26.6), assume for simplicity that $\mathbf{I} - \mathbf{A}$ is invertible and let $\mathbf{x}^* = (\mathbf{I} - \mathbf{A})^{-1}\mathbf{b}$. Then

$$\mathbf{x}^* = \mathbf{A}\mathbf{x}^* + \mathbf{b}.$$

Subtracting this equation from (26.6) and setting

$$\mathbf{y}(t) = \mathbf{x}(t) - \mathbf{x}^* \quad (t = 0, 1, 2, \ldots),$$

we obtain (26.2). The solution for $\mathbf{x}(t)$ is therefore

$$\mathbf{x}(t) = \mathbf{x}^* + \mathbf{y}(t) \quad (t = 0, 1, 2, \ldots), \qquad (26.7)$$

where $\mathbf{y}(t)$ is the solution of (26.2). Notice that if $\mathbf{x}(0)$ is given, (26.2) must be solved subject to the initial condition $\mathbf{y}(0) = \mathbf{x}(0) - \mathbf{x}^*$.

The vector $\mathbf{x}^* = (\mathbf{I} - \mathbf{A})^{-1}\mathbf{b}$ is called the **stationary solution** of the difference equation (26.6). The stationary solution is said to be **stable** if $\mathbf{x}(t) \to \mathbf{x}^*$ as $t \to \infty$, for all possible initial conditions. Clearly this happens if and only if $\mathbf{y}(t) \to \mathbf{0}$ as $t \to \infty$, for all possible initial conditions; and we have shown that this occurs if and only if all eigenvalues of $\mathbf{A}$ lie inside the unit circle. Similarly, the general solution $\mathbf{x}(t)$ will display oscillations around $\mathbf{x}^*$ if and only if some eigenvalues of $\mathbf{A}$ are complex.

The method just described of solving (26.6), given the method of solving (26.2), is very similar to our solution of non-homogeneous difference equations in Section 21.4. The solution (26.7) expresses $\mathbf{x}(t)$ as the sum of a particular solution — in this case the stationary one — and the solution of the associated homogeneous equation (26.2). As in the earlier section, the solution method can be extended to cases where the components of $\mathbf{b}$ are not constants but simple functions of t: see Problem 26–2.

Second-order (scalar) difference equations

What we have done so far in this section is reminiscent not only of Section 21.4, to which we have referred many times, but also of Section 24.3. We now make explicit how the material of that section fits into the current picture.

Consider the difference equation

$$y_{t+2} + f y_{t+1} + g y_t = 0, \tag{26.8}$$

where f and g are given scalars. This equation, together with the truism that $y_{t+1} = y_{t+1}$, may be written in the form

$$\begin{bmatrix} y_{t+2} \\ y_{t+1} \end{bmatrix} = \begin{bmatrix} -f & -g \\ 1 & 0 \end{bmatrix} \begin{bmatrix} y_{t+1} \\ y_t \end{bmatrix}.$$

But this is (26.2), with

$$\mathbf{y}(t) = \begin{bmatrix} y_{t+1} \\ y_t \end{bmatrix}, \quad \mathbf{A} = \begin{bmatrix} -f & -g \\ 1 & 0 \end{bmatrix}.$$

Assuming that $\mathbf{A}$ is a d–matrix, and focusing on the second component of $\mathbf{y}(t)$, we see that the solution to (26.8) is

$$y_t = a p^t + b q^t,$$

where a, b are constants depending on initial conditions and p, q are the eigenvalues of $\mathbf{A}$. By definition of $\mathbf{A}$, the scalars p and q are the roots of the quadratic equation

$$\lambda^2 + f\lambda + g = 0. \tag{26.9}$$

In the terminology of Section 24.3, (26.9) is the characteristic equation of the difference equation (26.8). Thus the general solution to (26.8) which we have just derived is almost the one given in the earlier section. The only difference is that we seem to have lost the case of coincident roots, to which we paid considerable attention in Section 24.3. The explanation is that coincident roots in (26.9) are ruled out by our current assumption that $\mathbf{A}$ is a d–matrix. Thus, restricting attention to diagonalisable matrices ignores some mathematically interesting possibilities. For many applications, however, the restriction is fairly innocuous, for reasons stated in Section 25.2.

Our discussion of how second-order scalar difference equations fit into the framework of this section can be generalised in various ways. If we make (26.8) non-homogeneous by replacing the zero on the right-hand side by a non-zero constant, the resulting equation is easily made equivalent to a special case of (26.6). Also, the concepts (if not the computation) are easily extended to equations of third and higher order: see Exercise 26.1.3.

An example: labour force dynamics

We end this section with an example illustrating many of its concepts.

Let the (adult, working-age) population of be divided into three groups: the employed, the unemployed and the 'economically inactive' such as full-time students. The first two groups constitute the labour force. Suppose the population is constant, and that in each month:

(a) 2% of the employed become unemployed and 2% leave the labour force; the remaining 96% stay employed.

(b) 25% of the unemployed become employed and 20% leave the labour force; the remaining 55% stay unemployed.

(c) 8% of the economically inactive join the labour force, of whom half move into employment and half into unemployment.

Let e_t and u_t denote respectively the proportions of the population that are employed and unemployed in month t. We are interested in the movements over time of e_t and u_t.

In each month, the employed consist of those who were employed last month and have remained employed, those who were unemployed last month and have become employed, and employed new entrants to the labour force. Hence by (a)–(c),

$$e_{t+1} = 0.96e_t + 0.25u_t + 0.04(1 - e_t - u_t).$$

A similar argument for the unemployed gives

$$u_{t+1} = 0.02e_t + 0.55u_t + 0.04(1 - e_t - u_t).$$

Simplifying, and setting $\mathbf{x}(t) = \begin{bmatrix} e_t \\ u_t \end{bmatrix}$, we see that

$$\mathbf{x}(t+1) = \mathbf{A}\mathbf{x}(t) + \mathbf{b}, \quad \text{where } \mathbf{A} = \begin{bmatrix} 0.92 & 0.21 \\ -0.02 & 0.51 \end{bmatrix}, \quad \mathbf{b} = \begin{bmatrix} 0.04 \\ 0.04 \end{bmatrix}.$$

The eigenvalues of $\mathbf{A}$ are 0.9095 and 0.5205 to four decimal places; corresponding eigenvalues, to a good approximation, are

$$\mathbf{u} = \begin{bmatrix} 2.0 \\ -0.1 \end{bmatrix}, \quad \mathbf{v} = \begin{bmatrix} 1.0 \\ -1.9 \end{bmatrix}$$

respectively. Further, the stationary solution is $\mathbf{x}^* = (\mathbf{I} - \mathbf{A})^{-1}\mathbf{b}$. Performing the calculations, we see that

$$\mathbf{x}^* = \begin{bmatrix} 0.08 & -0.21 \\ 0.02 & 0.49 \end{bmatrix}^{-1} \begin{bmatrix} 0.04 \\ 0.04 \end{bmatrix} = \frac{0.0400}{0.0434} \begin{bmatrix} 0.49 & 0.21 \\ -0.02 & 0.08 \end{bmatrix} \begin{bmatrix} 1 \\ 1 \end{bmatrix} = \begin{bmatrix} 0.645 \\ 0.055 \end{bmatrix}.$$

The general solution to the difference equation is

$$\mathbf{x}(t) = (0.9095)^t c_1 \mathbf{u} + (0.5205)^t c_2 \mathbf{v} + \mathbf{x}^*,$$

where c_1 and c_2 are constants.

Thus for all t,

$$e_t = 2 (0.9095)^t c_1 + (0.5205)^t c_2 + 0.645,$$

$$u_t = -0.1 (0.9095)^t c_1 - 1.9 (0.5205)^t c_2 + 0.055,$$

where c_1 and c_2 depend on initial conditions. As $t \to \infty$, e_t and u_t tend to their stationary solutions, 0.645 and 0.055 respectively. Thus the labour force participation rate $e_t + u_t$ approaches 70% and the unemployment rate $e_t/(e_t + u_t)$ approaches $8\frac{1}{2}\%$.

This kind of model is known as a **Markov chain**: each member of the population is in one of a finite number of states (in this case 3) and in each period a fixed proportion π_{ij} of the people in state i move into state j. The conclusion above, that the proportions in each state tend to limits independent of the initial proportions, is general for chains in which all the π_{ij} are positive; more complicated behaviour can occur when one allows some of the π_{ij} to be zero. Markov chains are commonly interpreted in terms of probabilities rather than proportions — indeed the π_{ij} are usually called **transition probabilities** — but the general idea is the same.

Exercises

26.1.1 Let

$$\mathbf{A} = \begin{bmatrix} 1.0 & 2.5 \\ -0.25 & -0.75 \end{bmatrix}, \quad \mathbf{b} = \begin{bmatrix} 5 \\ 1 \end{bmatrix}.$$

(a) Find the general solution of the difference equation

$$\mathbf{y}(t+1) = \mathbf{A}\mathbf{y}(t).$$

What happens to $\mathbf{y}(t)$ as $t \to \infty$?

(b) Find the general solution of the difference equation

$$\mathbf{x}(t+1) = \mathbf{A}\mathbf{x}(t) + \mathbf{b}.$$

What happens to $\mathbf{x}(t)$ as $t \to \infty$?

26.1.2 (a) Let

$$\mathbf{A} = \begin{bmatrix} -1 & 3 \\ \frac{1}{2} & -\frac{1}{2} \end{bmatrix}, \quad \mathbf{b} = \begin{bmatrix} -1 \\ 1 \end{bmatrix}.$$

Find the solution of the difference equation

$$\mathbf{x}(t+1) = \mathbf{A}\mathbf{x}(t) + \mathbf{b}$$

which satisfies the initial condition $\mathbf{x}(0) = \begin{bmatrix} 3 \\ 2 \end{bmatrix}$.

What happens to $\mathbf{x}(t)$ as $t \to \infty$?

(b) As (a), except that $\mathbf{x}(0) = \begin{bmatrix} 0 \\ 3 \end{bmatrix}$.

26.1.3 (a) Consider the third-order scalar difference equation

$$y_{t+3} + f y_{t+2} + g y_{t+1} + h y_t = 0,$$

where f, g, h are constants. By defining appropriately the vector $\mathbf{y}(t)$, show how this equation may be expressed in the form (26.2), where $\mathbf{A}$ is a 3×3 matrix.

(b) Now consider the fourth-order scalar difference equation

$$x_{t+4} + b_1 x_{t+3} + b_2 x_{t+2} + b_3 x_{t+1} + b_4 x_t = b_5$$

where $b_1, \ldots, b_5$ are constants. By defining $\mathbf{x}(t)$ appropriately, express this equation in the form (26.6), where $\mathbf{A}$ is a 4×4 matrix and $\mathbf{b}$ is a 4–vector.

26.2 Systems of differential equations

The simplest differential equation is

$$dy/dt = ay, \tag{26.10}$$

where a is a constant. Here t may be thought of as time, now treated continuously, and y denotes some scalar variable which changes over time. To solve the differential equation is to show explicitly how y depends on t. As we explained in Chapter 21,[3] the general solution of (26.10) is

$$y = ce^{at},$$

where c is a constant, which may be interpreted as the value of y at time 0.

The generalisation of (26.10) to vectors is

$$d\mathbf{y}/dt = \mathbf{A}\mathbf{y}. \tag{26.11}$$

---

[3]Our notation here differs from that of Chapter 21: 'a' in (26.10) corresponds to $-a$ in equation (21.4).

Here $\mathbf{y}$ is an n–vector depending on t and $\mathbf{A}$ is a given $n \times n$ matrix. The left-hand side is defined to be the n–vector with components $dy_1/dt, \ldots, dy_n/dt$, where $y_1, \ldots, y_n$ are the components of $\mathbf{y}$: in other words, differentiation with respect to t is done component by component. Thus (26.11) consists of n scalar equations relating the rates of change of $y_1, \ldots, y_n$ to their current values at each time t. For this reason, (26.10) is often referred to as a **system** of (scalar) differential equations.

We now explain how to solve (26.11) when the matrix $\mathbf{A}$ is diagonalisable. Suppose there is an invertible matrix $\mathbf{S}$ and a diagonal matrix $\mathbf{D}$ such that $\mathbf{S}^{-1}\mathbf{A}\mathbf{S} = \mathbf{D}$. Then $\mathbf{S}^{-1}\mathbf{A} = \mathbf{D}\mathbf{S}^{-1}$, so premultiplication of (26.11) by $\mathbf{S}^{-1}$ yields

$$\mathbf{S}^{-1}\frac{d\mathbf{y}}{dt} = \mathbf{D}\mathbf{S}^{-1}\mathbf{y}. \tag{26.11$'$}$$

But by the basic rules of differentiation,[4]

$$\frac{d}{dt}(\mathbf{B}\mathbf{y}) = \mathbf{B}\frac{d\mathbf{y}}{dt}$$

for any constant matrix $\mathbf{B}$ with n columns. Applying this result with $\mathbf{B} = \mathbf{S}^{-1}$, and setting $\mathbf{x} = \mathbf{S}^{-1}\mathbf{y}$, we may write (26.11$'$) as

$$d\mathbf{x}/dt = \mathbf{D}\mathbf{x}. \tag{26.12}$$

Since $\mathbf{D}$ is a diagonal matrix, (26.12) consists of n scalar equations of the form (26.10). Specifically, (26.12) says that

$$dx_j/dt = \lambda_j x_j \quad (j = 1, \ldots, n)$$

where $\lambda_1, \ldots, \lambda_n$ are the diagonal entries of $\mathbf{D}$. The solution to (26.12) is therefore

$$x_j = c_j e^{\lambda_j t} \quad (j = 1, \ldots, n)$$

where $c_1, \ldots, c_n$ are constants. Recalling that $\mathbf{y} = \mathbf{S}\mathbf{x}$ and letting $\mathbf{s}^1, \ldots, \mathbf{s}^n$ be the columns of $\mathbf{S}$, we see that the solution of (26.10) is

$$\mathbf{y} = c_1 e^{\lambda_1 t}\mathbf{s}^1 + \ldots + c_n e^{\lambda_n t}\mathbf{s}^n. \tag{26.13}$$

We now recall the definitions of $\mathbf{S}$ and $\mathbf{D}$, so as to describe the solution in terms of eigenvalues and eigenvectors of $\mathbf{A}$. By the results of Section 25.1, $\lambda_1, \ldots, \lambda_n$ are the eigenvalues of $\mathbf{A}$, and $\mathbf{s}^1, \ldots, \mathbf{s}^n$ are n linearly independent eigenvectors corresponding respectively to these eigenvalues. We summarise as follows.

Proposition If the matrix $\mathbf{A}$ is diagonalisable, the general solution to (26.11) is given by (26.13), where

---

[4]Specifically, the 'combination rule' of Section 6.3.

(a) $\lambda_1, \ldots, \lambda_n$ are the eigenvalues of $\mathbf{A}$;

(b) $\mathbf{s}^1, \ldots, \mathbf{s}^n$ are n linearly independent eigenvectors of $\mathbf{A}$, corresponding to the eigenvalues $\lambda_1, \ldots, \lambda_n$ respectively;

(c) $c_1, \ldots, c_n$ are constants depending on initial conditions.

Example 1 Find the general solution of (26.11) in the case where

$$\mathbf{A} = \begin{bmatrix} -1 & 2 \\ -3 & -8 \end{bmatrix}.$$

Here $\det(\lambda \mathbf{I} - \mathbf{A}) = \lambda^2 + 9\lambda + 14$, so the eigenvalues of $\mathbf{A}$ are -2 and -7. It is easy to show that $\begin{bmatrix} 2 \\ -1 \end{bmatrix}$ and $\begin{bmatrix} -1 \\ 3 \end{bmatrix}$ are corresponding eigenvectors. The general solution of the differential equation is therefore

$$\mathbf{y} = c_1 e^{-2t} \begin{bmatrix} 2 \\ -1 \end{bmatrix} + c_2 e^{-7t} \begin{bmatrix} -1 \\ 3 \end{bmatrix}$$

where c_1, c_2 are constants.

Relation to difference equations

The discrete-time analogue of (26.11) is $\mathbf{y}(t+1) - \mathbf{y}(t) = \mathbf{A}\mathbf{y}(t)$, or

$$\mathbf{y}(t+1) = (\mathbf{I} + \mathbf{A})\mathbf{y}(t).$$

This is similar to (26.2), but with $\mathbf{A}$ replaced by $\mathbf{I} + \mathbf{A}$. This difference in notation between our expositions of difference equations and differential equations should be borne in mind for the rest of this section.

Another difference between this section and the last concerns the treatment of diagonalisability. We explained how to solve the difference equation (26.2) by deriving the solution for general $\mathbf{A}$, namely (26.3), and then specialised to the case where $\mathbf{A}$ is a d–matrix. By contrast, our approach to solving (26.11) was to assume diagonalisability ¿from the start. In the appendix to this chapter, we give a solution formula for (26.11) for general $\mathbf{A}$, using the concept of the matrix exponential.

The 'dot' notation

A common practice in continuous-time dynamics is to place a dot over a variable to denote to denote its rate of change. This applies both to scalars and to vectors: thus

$$\dot{y} = \frac{dy}{dt}, \quad \dot{\mathbf{x}} = \frac{d\mathbf{x}}{dt}$$

and (26.11) may be written

$$\dot{\mathbf{y}} = \mathbf{A}\mathbf{y}.$$

The non-homogeneous case

An important generalisation of (26.11) is the differential equation

$$\dot{\mathbf{x}} = \mathbf{A}\mathbf{x} + \mathbf{b}. \tag{26.14}$$

Here $\mathbf{x}$ is an n–vector depending on t, $\mathbf{A}$ is an $n \times n$ matrix and $\mathbf{b}$ is an n–vector. All entries of $\mathbf{A}$ and components of $\mathbf{b}$ are constants.

To solve (26.14), we look first for a particular solution. Assuming for simplicity that $\mathbf{A}$ is invertible, and letting

$$\mathbf{x}^* = -\mathbf{A}^{-1}\mathbf{b},$$

we see that (26.14) is satisfied when $\mathbf{x} = \mathbf{x}^*$ for all t. For this reason, $\mathbf{x}^*$ is called the **stationary solution** of (26.14). To find the general solution, suppose that $\mathbf{x}$ satisfies (26.14), and let $\mathbf{y} = \mathbf{x} - \mathbf{x}^*$. Then

$$\dot{\mathbf{y}} = \dot{\mathbf{x}} - \mathbf{0} = (\mathbf{A}\mathbf{x} + \mathbf{b}) - (\mathbf{A}\mathbf{x}^* + \mathbf{b}) = \mathbf{A}(\mathbf{x} - \mathbf{x}^*) = \mathbf{A}\mathbf{y},$$

so $\mathbf{y}$ satisfies (26.11). Hence the general solution (26.14) is

$$\mathbf{x} = \mathbf{x}^* + \mathbf{y},$$

where $\mathbf{y}$ is the general solution of (26.11). In the terminology of the last section (and Chapter 21), the general solution of (26.14) is the sum of the stationary particular solution $\mathbf{x}^*$ and the solution of the associated homogeneous equation (26.11).

As an illustration of this solution method, consider the following second-order (scalar) differential equation:

$$\frac{d^2y}{dt^2} + k\frac{dy}{dt} + hy = g,$$

where k, h, g are constants. Setting $z = dy/dt$, we may write our equation in the form

$$dz/dt = g - hy - kz.$$

Setting $\mathbf{x} = \begin{bmatrix} y \\ z \end{bmatrix}$, we have (26.14) with

$$\mathbf{A} = \begin{bmatrix} 0 & 1 \\ -h & -k \end{bmatrix}, \quad \mathbf{b} = \begin{bmatrix} 0 \\ g \end{bmatrix}.$$

The eigenvalues of $\mathbf{A}$ are the roots of the quadratic equation

$$\lambda^2 + k\lambda + h = 0;$$

we denote these roots by p and q. Also, $\mathbf{A}$ is invertible if and only if $h \neq 0$, in which case the stationary solution $\mathbf{x}^*$ has components g/h, 0. Assuming that $\mathbf{A}$ is an invertible d–matrix, the general solution for $\mathbf{x}$ is

$$\mathbf{x} = c_1 e^{pt} \mathbf{u} + c_2 e^{qt} \mathbf{v} + \mathbf{x}^*$$

where $\mathbf{u}$, $\mathbf{v}$ are eigenvectors of $\mathbf{A}$ and c_1, c_2 are constants. Hence the solution for the first component y is

$$y = \alpha e^{pt} + \beta e^{qt} + g/h,$$

where α, β are constants. This is of course the same solution that we obtain from the methods of Section 24.1 in the case where $p \neq q$; equality of p and q is ruled out by our assumption that $\mathbf{A}$ is a d–matrix.

We now turn to a numerical example of (26.14).

Example 2 Find the general solution of (26.14) in the case where

$$\mathbf{A} = \begin{bmatrix} -1 & 2 \\ -3 & -8 \end{bmatrix}, \quad \mathbf{b} = \begin{bmatrix} -1 \\ 25 \end{bmatrix}.$$

It is easy to check that the stationary solution has components 3 and 2, and that the associated homogeneous equation is the differential equation of Example 1. Hence the general solution is

$$\mathbf{x} = c_1 e^{-2t} \begin{bmatrix} 2 \\ -1 \end{bmatrix} + c_2 e^{-7t} \begin{bmatrix} -1 \\ 3 \end{bmatrix} + \begin{bmatrix} 3 \\ 2 \end{bmatrix},$$

where c_1, c_2 are constants.

As in Chapters 21 and 24, we can determine c_1 and c_2 given appropriate boundary conditions. For example, if it is given that $\mathbf{x} = \mathbf{0}$ when $t = 0$, then $2c_1 - c_2 = -3$ and $-c_1 + 3c_2 = -2$; hence $c_1 = -2.2$ and $c_2 = -1.4$.

Exercises

26.2.1 Find the general solution of the differential equation $\dot{\mathbf{y}} = \mathbf{A}\mathbf{y}$, in the case where

$$\mathbf{A} = \begin{bmatrix} 4 & 1 \\ 2 & 3 \end{bmatrix}.$$

Also find the solution such that $\mathbf{y} = \begin{bmatrix} 2 \\ 5 \end{bmatrix}$ when $t = 0$.

26.2.2 Find the general solution of the differential equation $\dot{\mathbf{x}} = \mathbf{A}\mathbf{x} + \mathbf{b}$, in the case where

$$\mathbf{A} = \begin{bmatrix} 4 & 1 \\ 2 & 3 \end{bmatrix}, \quad \mathbf{b} = \begin{bmatrix} 0 \\ 1 \end{bmatrix}.$$

Also find the solution such that $\mathbf{x} = \begin{bmatrix} 7 \\ 1 \end{bmatrix}$ when $t = 0$.

26.3 Qualitative behaviour

We now consider further the differential equation

$$\dot{\mathbf{x}} = \mathbf{A}\mathbf{x} + \mathbf{b}. \tag{26.14}$$

As before, we assume that $\mathbf{A}$ is a nonsingular d–matrix, so that there is a unique stationary solution $\mathbf{x}^* = -\mathbf{A}^{-1}\mathbf{b}$. $\mathbf{x}^*$ is sometimes called the **fixed point** of (26.14).

As we showed in the last section, the general solution of (26.14) is

$$\mathbf{x}(t) = \mathbf{x}^* + c_1 e^{\lambda_1 t}\mathbf{s}^1 + \ldots + c_n e^{\lambda_n t}\mathbf{s}^n. \tag{26.15}$$

Here $\lambda_1, \ldots, \lambda_n$ are the eigenvalues of $\mathbf{A}$, $\mathbf{s}^1, \ldots, \mathbf{s}^n$ are corresponding eigenvectors and $c_1, \ldots, c_n$ are constants. We say that the fixed point $\mathbf{x}^*$ of (26.14) is **stable** if $\mathbf{x}(t) \to \mathbf{x}^*$ as $t \to \infty$, for all possible values of the constants $c_1, \ldots, c_n$; this may be interpreted as saying that the fixed point is approached eventually, regardless of initial conditions.

How is the stability or otherwise of $\mathbf{x}^*$ related to the eigenvalues of $\mathbf{A}$? Consider a particular eigenvalue, say λ_1. We denote the real part of λ_1 by α_1 and the imaginary part by $i\beta_1$ ($\beta_1 = 0$ if λ_1 is a real number). Then

$$e^{\lambda_1 t} = e^{\alpha_1 t} e^{i\beta_1 t}$$

for all t. Since $\alpha_1 t$ and $\beta_1 t$ are real numbers, $e^{\alpha_1 t} > 0$ and $|e^{i\beta_1 t}| = 1$. Hence $|e^{\lambda_1 t}| = e^{\alpha_1 t}$. It follows that

$$\lim_{t \to \infty} |e^{\lambda_1 t}| = 0 \ \text{ if and only if } \ \alpha_1 < 0.$$

A similar result holds for all other eigenvalues. Hence by (26.15), we have the following proposition:

SP1 The stationary solution $\mathbf{x}^*$ is stable if and only if all eigenvalues of $\mathbf{A}$ have negative real part.

The other main result about qualitative behaviour of the solution concerns the presence or otherwise of oscillations. Here the same result holds for systems of differential equations as for systems of difference equations, and for the same reason: *the general solution $\mathbf{x}(t)$ displays oscillations around $\mathbf{x}^*$ if and only if some eigenvalues of $\mathbf{A}$ have non-zero imaginary part.*

Two-dimensional systems

The qualitative behaviour of the equation (26.14) can be analysed in greater detail in the case where $n = 2$. With regard to stability we have the following useful proposition:

SP2 When $n = 2$, the stationary solution $\mathbf{x}^*$ is stable if and only if the matrix $\mathbf{A}$ has negative trace and positive determinant.

To see why this is so, recall from the last chapter that the trace $\operatorname{tr} \mathbf{A}$ of a matrix $\mathbf{A}$ is defined to be the sum of its diagonal entries and is always equal to the sum of its eigenvalues. Also, the determinant is equal to the product of the eigenvalues. Now let $\mathbf{A}$ be a 2×2 matrix with eigenvalues λ_1 and λ_2. In the case where λ_1 and λ_2 are real numbers, they are both negative if and only if $\operatorname{tr} \mathbf{A} < 0 < \det \mathbf{A}$. In the case where λ_1 and λ_2 are complex conjugates, $\det A > 0$ and λ_1 and λ_2 have the same real part, equal to $\frac{1}{2} \operatorname{tr} \mathbf{A}$. Putting the two cases together, we see that both λ_1 and λ_2 have negative real parts if and only if $\operatorname{tr} \mathbf{A} < 0 < \det \mathbf{A}$; **SP2** now follows from **SP1**.

The most helpful aspect of restricting n to be 2 is that we can use diagrams to depict qualitative behaviour. This may seem over-ambitious as we still have three scalar variables, namely t and the two components of $\mathbf{x}$, which we now denote by x and y. However, much can be done by working in the xy–plane — referred to in this context as the **phase plane** — and making appropriate use of arrows to denote the passage of time.

In what follows, we refer to the eigenvalues of the 2×2 matrix $\mathbf{A}$ as the 'roots' of $\mathbf{A}$; we assume for simplicity that these roots are distinct and neither of them is zero. The latter assumption is of course equivalent to invertibility of $\mathbf{A}$, which ensures that there is a unique fixed point. There are then six possible cases.

Positive real roots

In this case the fixed point is unstable, and there are no oscillations. The fixed point is said to be a **source** or **unstable node**.

As an example, consider (26.14) with

$$\mathbf{A} = \begin{bmatrix} 1 & 0 \\ 0 & 2 \end{bmatrix}, \quad \mathbf{b} = \begin{bmatrix} 0 \\ 0 \end{bmatrix}.$$

This gives the pair of equations

$$\dot{x} = x, \quad \dot{y} = 2y.$$

A partial illustration of this system is given in the left panel of Figure 26.1. This is known as a **phase diagram**, and gives the direction of movement of x and y at each point of the phase plane. In this case, x is increasing if $x > 0$ and

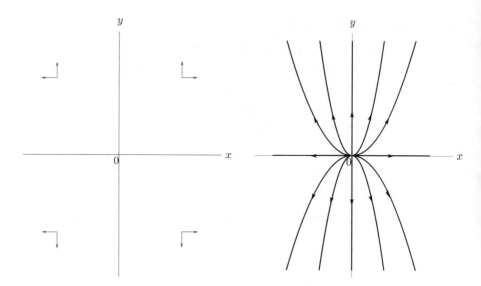

Figure 26.1: **Phase diagram and phase portrait: source**

decreasing if $x < 0$; hence the horizontal arrows pointing away from the y–axis. Similarly, y is increasing if $y > 0$ and decreasing if $y < 0$; hence the vertical arrows pointing away from the x–axis.

The general solution of our system of equations is of course $x = c_1 e^t$, $y = c_2 e^{2t}$ where c_1 and c_2 are constants. Thus the origin is the fixed point. If we start at a point on the y–axis other than the origin we move away from the origin along the y–axis; this is the case where $c_1 = 0$ and $c_2 \neq 0$. All other solution paths consist of movement away from the origin along $y = kx^2$, where k is a constant. The solution paths are depicted in the right panel of Figure 26.1; such a diagram is called a **phase portrait**.

Negative real roots

In this case the fixed point is stable, and there are no oscillations. The fixed point is said to be a **sink** or **stable node**.

To illustrate this, let

$$A = \begin{bmatrix} -1 & 0 \\ 0 & -2 \end{bmatrix}, \quad b = \begin{bmatrix} 0 \\ 0 \end{bmatrix},$$

giving the pair of equations

$$\dot{x} = -x, \quad \dot{y} = -2y;$$

the general solution is $x = c_1 e^{-t}$, $y = c_2 e^{-2t}$, where c_1 and c_2 are constants. The phase diagram and phase portrait are depicted in the two panels of Figure

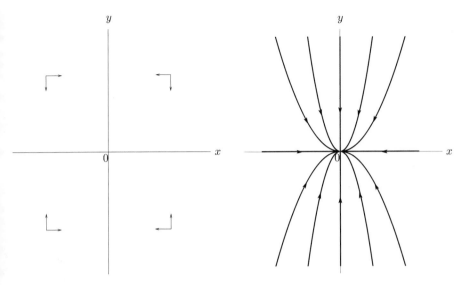

Figure 26.2: **Phase diagram and phase portrait: sink**

26.2: observe that the only difference from Figure 26.1 is that all arrows in both panels point in the opposite direction.

Some points about the phase portrait in Figure 26.2 are worthy of notice. If we start on the y–axis, we remain on it: such paths arise from choosing the constants c_1, c_2 such that $c_1 = 0$. All other paths are tangential to the x–axis, so that $(x(t),\, y(t))$ not only converges to $(0,0)$ but does so along a path that is close to the x–axis for large t; this is so because e^{-2t} is small relative to e^{-t} when t is large.

Real roots of opposite sign

Here, the fixed point is said to be a **saddle point**. The fixed point is unstable, and there are no oscillations. The difference between this case and that of a stable node is that there is now a straight line L with the following property: if $(x(0),\, y(0))$ is on L then $(x(t),\, y(t))$ is on L for all $t > 0$ and approaches the fixed point as $t \to \infty$. L is called the **stable branch**.

The algebra of this is as follows. Consider the general solution (26.15) in the case where $n = 2$, and suppose for definiteness that $\lambda_1 > 0 > \lambda_2$. Then $\mathbf{x}(t) \to \mathbf{x}(0)$ as $t \to \infty$ if and only if $c_1 = 0$. Let the components of the stationary solution $\mathbf{x}^*$ be x^*, y^* and let those of the eigenvector $\mathbf{s}^2$ be u, v. Then the line L in the phase plane consists of all points of the form $(x^* + \mu u,\, y^* + \mu v)$.

Figure 26.3 gives the phase diagram and phase portrait for the system

$$\dot{x} = x, \quad \dot{y} = -y.$$

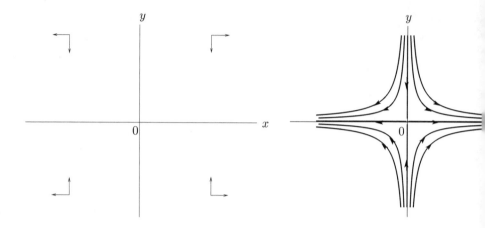

Figure 26.3: **Phase diagram and phase portrait: saddle point**

The fixed point is the origin, which is a saddle point; the stable branch is the y–axis.

Complex roots with positive real part

This case corresponds to the "explosive oscillations" of Chapter 24: in the phase plane, solution paths diverge from the fixed point in spirals of ever-increasing size. The fixed point is said to be a **spiral source** or **unstable focus**.

As an example, consider the pair of equations

$$\dot{x} = x + y, \quad \dot{y} = -x + y.$$

Then $\dot{x}$ is positive to the right of the line $x + y = 0$ and negative to the left of it, while $\dot{y}$ is positive above the line $y = x$ and negative below it. All of this is illustrated in the phase diagram which is the left panel of Figure 26.4.

In this example, the roots are $1 \pm i$ and the general solution is

$$x = (a \cos t + b \sin t)e^t, \quad y = (b \cos t - a \sin t)e^t :$$

see Exercise 26.3.3 for the details. The fixed point is therefore unstable, and the phase portrait is the right panel of Figure 26.4.

A further fact about the phase portrait is worth noting. Since $\dot{y} = 0$ when $y = x$, solution paths cross the line $y = x$ in a horizontal direction. This is illustrated by the shape of the spiral in Figure 26.4, whose slope is zero wherever it crosses $y = x$. Similarly, since $\dot{x} = 0$ when $y = -x$, the spiral is vertical at each intersection with the line $y = -x$.

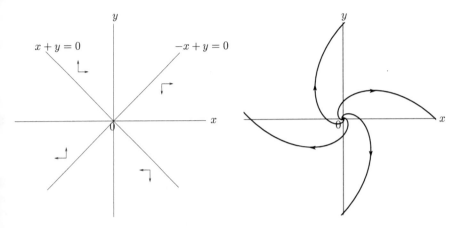

Figure 26.4: **Phase diagram and phase portrait: spiral source**

Complex roots with negative real part

This case corresponds to the "damped oscillations" of Chapter 24: in the phase plane, solution paths converge to the fixed point in spirals of ever-decreasing size. The fixed point is said to be a **spiral sink** or **stable focus**.

An example is the pair of equations

$$\dot{x} = -x - y, \quad \dot{y} = x - y.$$

This is the preceding example with t replaced by $-t$. The roots are $-1 \pm i$. The phase diagram and phase portrait are depicted in Figure 26.5, which is Figure 26.4 with all arrows pointing the opposite way.[5]

Purely imaginary roots

In this case, the fixed point is called a **centre**. Solution paths take the form of concentric circles or ellipses around the fixed point: thus the difference from the two preceding cases is that we have orbits rather than spirals.

Consider for example the pair of differential equations

$$\dot{x} = 4y, \quad \dot{y} = -x.$$

The roots are $\pm 2i$, and the general solution is

$$x = 2a \cos 2t + 2b \sin 2t, \quad y = b \cos 2t - a \sin 2t$$

where a and b are constants.

---

[5]In particular, the divergent clockwise spirals of Figure 26.4 become convergent anti-clockwise spirals in Figure 26.5. Notice however that there is no general connection between stability and direction of rotation: see Exercise 26.3.4.

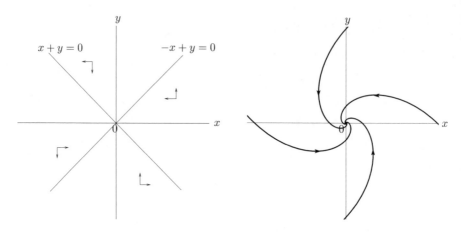

Figure 26.5: **Phase diagram and phase portrait: spiral sink**

The phase diagram and phase portrait are shown in Figure 26.6. The phase portrait reflects the fact that all solution paths are of the form

$$\tfrac{1}{4}x^2 + y^2 = \text{constant}.$$

Phase diagram versus phase portrait

In the examples above, we drew the phase diagram and the phase portrait. You may wonder why we bother with the former, since the latter is typically much more informative. The answer is that in more complicated examples, the extra information comes at the cost of more work.

We illustrate this point by looking again at Example 2 of the preceding section. In the xy–plane notation, the system of differential equations may be written:

$$\dot{x} = -x + 2y - 1, \quad \dot{y} = -3x - 8y + 25.$$

The phase diagram for this system is the left-hand panel of Figure 26.7. The line K consists of the points (x, y) for which $dx/dt = 0$, and the line L consists of

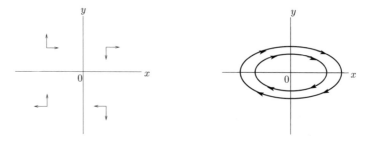

Figure 26.6: **Phase diagram and phase portrait: centre**

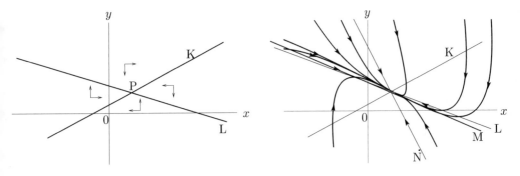

Figure 26.7: **Phase diagram and phase portrait: numerical example**

the points for which $dy/dt = 0$. The lines meet at the point P with coordinates $(3, 2)$, which is therefore the fixed point of the system. Thus K is the line through P with slope $\frac{1}{2}$, and L is the line through P with slope $-\frac{3}{8}$. Now $\dot{x} < 0$ if and only if $x > 2y - 1$, which happens if and only if the point (x, y) is to the right of the line K; similarly $\dot{y} < 0$ if and only if (x, y) is to the left of the line K. Similar reasoning shows that $\dot{y}$ is positive or negative according as the point (x, y) is above or below the line L. This gives the arrows in the phase diagram.

The important point here is that the phase diagram can be obtained without actually solving the system of differential equations it depicts. The bad news is that the phase diagram on its own does not give much information about the shape of solution paths. Indeed the left-hand panel of Figure 26.7 tells us that solution paths may, or may not, be clockwise spirals.

In fact they are not, but to see this we need much more information. We solved this system of equations in Example 2 of the last section: the general solution in our present notation is

$$x = 2c_1 e^{-2t} - c_2 e^{-7t} + 3, \quad y = -c_1 e^{-2t} + 3c_2 e^{-7t} + 2,$$

where c_1 and c_2 are constants. If $c_2 = 0$, then $x = 3 + 2\phi(t)$, $y = 2 - \phi(t)$, where $\phi(t) = c_1 e^{-2t}$: thus in this case the solution path is confined to the line through P of slope $-\frac{1}{2}$, which we denote by M. Similarly, letting N be the line through P of slope -3, we see that N corresponds to solutions for which $c_1 = 0$.[6] Since -2 and -7 are negative real numbers, the fixed point is a stable node. Since e^{-7t} is small relative to e^{-2t} when t is large and positive, all solutions not starting on N are close to M for large t. This gives us the phase portrait in the right-hand panel of Figure 26.7.

---

[6]In the vector notation of the preceding section, M consists of all points of the form $\mathbf{x}^* + \mu \mathbf{s}^1$ and N of all points of the form $\mathbf{x}^* + \mu \mathbf{s}^2$, where $\mathbf{x}^*$ is the fixed point, $\mathbf{s}^1$ is an eigenvector of the matrix $\mathbf{A}$ corresponding to the eigenvalue -2 and $\mathbf{s}^2$ is an eigenvector corresponding to the eigenvalue -7.

An economic example: exchange rate dynamics

We consider a well-known model of exchange rate dynamics due to the economist Rudiger Dornbusch.

Consider a country, which we shall call Home, which is open to a global free market in bonds. Let r be the interest rate in Home and r^* the interest rate in the rest of the world. We refer to the rest of the world as Foreign and treat it as having a common currency (different from that in Home), interest rate and price level. Let q be the natural logarithm of the exchange rate, measured as the Home-money price of a unit of Foreign currency.[7]

In an unrestricted global financial market, a difference between r and r^* can arise only if the exchange rate is expected to change. We assume that expectations are correct, so that differences between r and r^* reflect actual changes in q: specifically,

$$r = r^* + \frac{dq}{dt}. \tag{26.16}$$

This is known as the **interest parity equation**.

Let the price levels at Home and in Foreign be P and P^* respectively, and let their natural logarithms be p and p^*. We assume that the Home price level adjusts gradually after a disturbance: p adjusts to $q + p^*$, the logarithm of the Foreign price level measured in the Home currency. For simplicity we assume that p^* is constant. The adjustment of p is given by the differential equation

$$\frac{dp}{dt} = \sigma(q + p^* - p), \tag{26.17}$$

where σ is a positive constant representing speed of adjustment.

The final component of the model is the Home money market. Let M be the stock of money in Home. The demand for real money balances is a decreasing function of the interest rate, and we assume that this function takes the form

$$\frac{M}{P} = ae^{-\beta r},$$

where a and β are positive constants. It is assumed that the money market clears continuously with the money supply fixed by the Home central bank; thus M is exogenous, and we assume that it is constant. Taking natural logarithms,

$$m - p = \alpha - \beta r, \tag{26.18}$$

where $\alpha = \ln a$.

To see what these assumptions imply, we eliminate r between (26.16) and (26.18), obtaining

$$m - p = \alpha - \beta(r^* + \dot{q}). \tag{26.19}$$

---

[7]Thus *depreciation* of Home's currency means an *increase* in q.

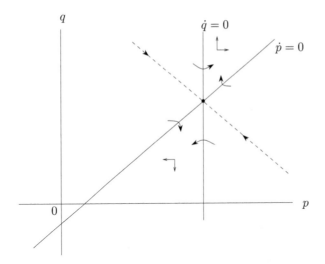

Figure 26.8: **Phase diagram for Dornbusch's model**

(26.17) and (26.19) give us the pair of differential equations

$$\dot{p} = \sigma(-p + q + p^*), \quad \dot{q} = \frac{1}{\beta}(p - m + \gamma),$$

where $\gamma = \alpha - \beta r^*$.

Setting $\dot{p} = \dot{q} = 0$, we see that this system has a unique fixed point in the pq–plane, given by $p = m - \gamma$, $q = m - \gamma - p^*$. The phase diagram is Figure 26.8.[8] It is clear from the directions of the arrows that the fixed point is a saddle point, with the stable branch given by the downward-sloping broken line. Thus if we start on the broken line we converge to the fixed point along it; if not, we move away from it.

To verify the saddle point property algebraically, let $\mathbf{A}$ be the matrix

$$\begin{bmatrix} -\sigma & \sigma \\ 1/\beta & 0 \end{bmatrix}.$$

Then the general solution to our system is

$$\begin{bmatrix} p \\ q \end{bmatrix} = c_1 e^{\lambda t} \mathbf{u} + c_2 e^{\mu t} \mathbf{v} + \begin{bmatrix} m - \gamma \\ m - \gamma - p^* \end{bmatrix},$$

where λ and μ are the eigenvalues of $\mathbf{A}$, $\mathbf{u}$ and $\mathbf{v}$ are corresponding eigenvectors and c_1, c_2 are constants depending on initial conditions. Now

$$\lambda\mu = \det \mathbf{A} = -\sigma/\beta < 0,$$

_____

[8]Since p and q are logarithms, they can can be positive or negative. To avoid clutter, we have assumed in the diagram that parameters are such that the fixed point is in the positive quadrant.

so λ and μ are real numbers of opposite sign. This verifies the saddle point property. Assuming for definiteness that $\lambda < 0 < \mu$, we see that being on the stable branch means that initial conditions are such that $c_2 = 0$.

What is the economic meaning of this solution? Observe first that the domestic price level is assumed to react gradually to changes in conditions, while the exchange rate is not. Therefore, the value of p at time 0 is determined by the economy's previous history, whereas the value of q at time 0 is not. Hence there is nothing in the model to prevent $q(0)$ from taking the value it needs to take to put the economy on the stable branch, given $p(0)$. Most applications of the model assume that precisely this will happen: see Exercise 26.3.6 . However, to say that there is nothing to prevent something ¿from happening does not mean it will happen, and one needs some more positive argument to make instantaneous adjustment to the stable branch convincing. A popular argument is that if everybody believes that everybody believes that ... the price level will not explode or implode, then initial expectations will put the economy on the stable branch, but the theory underlying such arguments is still an active area of research.

The model above is obviously an over-simplified description of exchange-rate dynamics. In particular there is something peculiar about the implicit treatment of Home's real income, which we denote by Y. The model's assumption that Home demand for real money balances depends only on i is most easily justified by assuming that Y is constant; on the other hand, the model allows $q - p$ to change over time, which one would expect to cause changes in Y via changes in the trade balance. The literature of open-economy macroeconomics contains numerous extensions of the model which allow real income to change over time and to affect money demand; most such extensions result in a phase diagram similar to Figure 26.8.

Exercises

26.3.1 For each of the following pairs of differential equations, find the fixed point, and classify it as one of the six cases discussed in the text.

(a) $\dot{x} = x + 2y - 1$, $\dot{y} = 5x + 7y - 2$.

(b) $\dot{x} = 3x + 7y + 2$, $\dot{y} = -2x - 3y + 1$.

(c) $\dot{x} = -3x - 2y + 10$, $\dot{y} = x - 3y - 7$.

(d) $\dot{x} = 9x + 4y$, $\dot{y} = 5x + 3y$.

26.3.2 Sketch the phase portraits for Exercises 26.2.1 and 26.2.2.

26.3.3 Consider again the pair of differential equations

$$\dot{x} = x + y, \quad \dot{y} = -x + y.$$

(a) By calculating the eigenvalues of the matrix

$$\mathbf{A} = \begin{bmatrix} 1 & 1 \\ -1 & 1 \end{bmatrix}$$

and using the results of Section 26.2, show that the general solution for x is

$$x = pe^{(1+i)t} + qe^{(1-i)t},$$

where p and q are (complex) constants.

(b) Using the results of Section 22.3, show that the answer to (a) may be written in the form

$$x = (a\cos t + b\sin t)e^t,$$

where a and b are (real) constants.

(c) Using the answer to (b) and the fact that $y = \dot{x} - x$ [why is this true?], find the general solution to the pair of differential equations.

[This exercise illustrates an important technique. Since the roots of $\mathbf{A}$ are complex, the eigenvectors of $\mathbf{A}$ are rather messy. The steps of the exercise show how the dynamic system may be solved without having to calculate the eigenvectors.]

26.3.4 Consider the pair of differential equations

$$\dot{x} = -x + y, \quad \dot{y} = -x - y.$$

What relation does this system bear to that depicted in Figure 26.5? Without doing any calculations, explain why the origin is a spiral sink, approached via clockwise spirals. Hence give an example of a linear dynamic system whose non-stationary solutions are divergent anti-clockwise spirals.

26.3.5 Show that the pair of differential equations

$$\dot{x} = y - x, \quad \dot{y} = x$$

is a special case of the system depicted in Figure 26.8, with (p, q) replaced by (x, y) and the fixed point shifted to the origin. Draw the phase diagram. Verify algebraically that the origin is a saddle point, find the equation of the stable branch and sketch the phase portrait.

26.3.6 In the model of exchange rate dynamics discussed above, suppose that for $t < 0$ the price level p and exchange rate q are at the fixed point corresponding to a given money supply. At time 0, there is an unanticipated increase in the money supply, which remains constant thereafter at its new level. Using a diagram similar to Figure 26.8, and assuming instantaneous adjustment to the (new) stable branch, describe the time-path of p and q. Why is the behaviour of q in this story known as "exchange-rate overshooting"?

26.4   Nonlinear systems

We begin by considering two-dimensional dynamic systems of the form

$$dx/dt = f(x,y), \quad dy/dt = g(x,y), \tag{26.20}$$

where f and g are smooth functions of two variables.[9] Such a system is said to be **autonomous**, meaning that t does not occur explicitly as an argument of the function f or g. The two-dimensional systems of the last section are special cases of (26.20) for which f and g happen to be linear functions; for example the system depicted in Figure 26.7 is (26.20) with $f(x,y) = -x + 2y - 1$, $g(x,y) = -3x - 8y + 25$.

The point (x^*, y^*) is said to be a **stationary solution** or **fixed point** of the system (26.20) if $f(x^*, y^*) = g(x^*, y^*) = 0$. The interpretation of such a point is as in the last section; if we start at a fixed point we remain there.

Example 1

Suppose that demand for a good depends on its price p, while supply depends on its expected price v. Let quantities demanded and supplied be $D(p)$ and $S(v)$ where D and S are functions such that $D'(p) < 0$ and $S'(v) > 0$. Suppose the price p reacts to market imbalances, rising when there is excess demand and falling when there is excess supply, with its rate of change proportional to the imbalance. Thus

$$dp/dt = \alpha(D(p) - S(v)),$$

where α is a positive constant. We assume that price expectations are formed 'adaptively', which means that v is revised upwards when $p > v$ and downward when $p < v$. Specifically, we assume that

$$dv/dt = \beta(p - v),$$

where β is another positive constant. Letting dots signify rates of change as in the last section, we have the autonomous system

$$\dot{p} = \alpha(D(p) - S(v)), \quad \dot{v} = \beta(p - v).$$

Since D is a decreasing function and S an increasing one, the points for which $D(p) = S(v)$ form a downward-sloping curve in the positive quadrant of the pv–plane.[10] This curve cuts the line $v = p$ at a unique point (p^*, p^*) which is the only fixed point of the system. If we move horizontally to the left of the curve $D(p) = S(v)$, then $D(p)$ increases and $S(v)$ remains the same, so $\alpha(D(p) - S(v))$ becomes and remains positive. Thus $\dot{p} > 0$ to the left of the curve, and similarly $\dot{p} < 0$ to the right of it. Also, $\dot{v} < 0$ when $v > p$ and $\dot{v} > 0$ when $v < p$. The phase diagram for the system is Figure 26.9.

---

[9]The term 'smooth function' is used in the same sense as in Section 14.1.

[10]The equation of the curve is $v = R(D(p))$, where R is the inverse function of S.

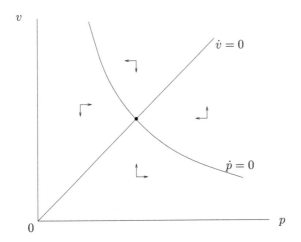

Figure 26.9: **Phase diagram for Example 1**

Example 2

Consider the pair of differential equations

$$\dot{x} = y - x^2, \quad \dot{y} = 1 - xy.$$

In the xy–plane, $\dot{x}$ is positive above the parabola $y = x^2$ and negative below it. $\dot{y} = 0$ on both branches of the curve $xy = 1$; $\dot{y} < 0$ if x and y are both positive and $y > 1/x$, or if x and y are both negative and $y < 1/x$; and $\dot{y} > 0$ at all other points in the plane. This gives us the phase diagram of Figure 26.10; the only fixed point is $(1, 1)$.

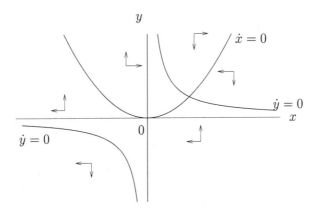

Figure 26.10: **Phase diagram for Example 2**

Example 3

When nonlinearities are allowed, there may be more than one fixed point: thus the system

$$\dot{x} = y, \quad \dot{y} = \sin x$$

has a fixed points at $(k\pi, 0)$ for every integer k.

Linearisation and local stability

Let (x^*, y^*) be a fixed point of the system (26.20), and let (x, y) be a point which is close to (x^*, y^*). By the small increments formula (14.3) and the fact that $f(x^*, y^*) = 0$,

$$f(x, y) \approx f_1(x^*, y^*)(x - x^*) + f_2(x^*, y^*)(y - y^*),$$

where subscripts denote partial derivatives. Similarly, since $g(x^*, y^*) = 0$,

$$g(x, y) \approx g_1(x^*, y^*)(x - x^*) + g_2(x^*, y^*)(y - y^*).$$

Now let

$$\mathbf{x} = \begin{bmatrix} x \\ y \end{bmatrix}, \quad \mathbf{x}^* = \begin{bmatrix} x^* \\ y^* \end{bmatrix}, \quad \mathbf{A} = \begin{bmatrix} f_1(x^*, y^*) & f_2(x^*, y^*) \\ g_1(x^*, y^*) & g_2(x^*, y^*) \end{bmatrix}.$$

We have shown that if $\mathbf{x}$ is close to $\mathbf{x}^*$,

$$\begin{bmatrix} f(x, y) \\ g(x, y) \end{bmatrix} \approx \mathbf{A}(\mathbf{x} - \mathbf{x}^*).$$

Note that, in the terminology of Section 15.3, $\mathbf{A}$ is the Jacobian of the pair of functions (f, g) with respect to (x, y), evaluated at the point (x^*, y^*).

All of this implies that, if (x, y) is close to (x^*, y^*), the nonlinear system (26.20) may be approximated by the linear system

$$\dot{\mathbf{x}} = \mathbf{A}\mathbf{x} + \mathbf{b},$$

where $\mathbf{b} = -\mathbf{A}\mathbf{x}^*$. Such an approximation is known as **linearisation** about the fixed point (x^*, y^*).

What does this approximation tell us about the solutions of the nonlinear system (26.20)? The basic result is as follows: *provided that no eigenvalue of* $\mathbf{A}$ *has zero real part, solution paths of* (26.20) *close to the fixed point* $\mathbf{x}^*$ *are close to those of the linearised system.* In particular,

(a) if both eigenvalues of $\mathbf{A}$ have negative real part, all solutions of (26.20) for which $\mathbf{x}$ is sufficiently close to $\mathbf{x}^*$ when $t = 0$ approach $\mathbf{x}^*$ as $t \to \infty$.

(b) if both eigenvalues of $\mathbf{A}$ have positive real part, *no* solution of (26.20) for which $\mathbf{x} \neq \mathbf{x}^*$ when $t = 0$ approaches $\mathbf{x}^*$ as $t \to \infty$;

The following similar result is more subtle:

(c) if the eigenvalues of $\mathbf{A}$ are real and of opposite signs, the phase portrait of (26.20) close to (x^*, y^*) is similar to that of a linear system whose fixed point is a saddle point at (x^*, y^*). The stable branch is a curve whose tangent at (x^*, y^*) is the stable branch of the linearised system.

In case (a), the fixed point is said to be **locally stable**.[11] In case (c), the fixed point is called a saddle point (or **local saddle**), for obvious reasons. Notice that all of these results assume that no eigenvalue of $\mathbf{A}$ has zero real part; if this assumption holds, (x^*, y^*) is said to be a **hyperbolic fixed point**. The geometry of the non-hyperbolic case may be spelt out as follows:

(d) if the linearised system has a centre at (x^*, y^*), then the behaviour of its solution paths close to (x^*, y^*) gives no information about those of the original system (26.20).

More on Examples 1 and 2

To illustrate the use of linearisation, we consider the first two examples above. In Example 1, concerned with supply and demand, we had the autonomous system

$$\dot{p} = \alpha(D(p) - S(v)), \quad \dot{v} = \beta(p - v).$$

The Jacobian matrix of $(\alpha[D(p) - S(v)], \beta[p - v])$ with respect to (p, v) is

$$\begin{bmatrix} \alpha D'(p) & -\alpha S'(v) \\ \beta & -\beta \end{bmatrix}.$$

Since α and β are positive constants and $D'(p) < 0 < S'(v)$ for all p and v, the entries of the Jacobian matrix are signed

$$\begin{bmatrix} - & - \\ + & - \end{bmatrix}.$$

Let $\mathbf{A}$ be the Jacobian matrix, evaluated at the fixed point (p^*, p^*). Then $\text{tr}\,\mathbf{A} < 0 < \det \mathbf{A}$, so (p^*, p^*) is a stable fixed point for the linearised system. Hence (p^*, p^*) is a locally stable fixed point for the nonlinear system: if p and v both start off sufficiently close to p^*, they both approach p^* as $t \to \infty$. "How

---

[11] The correct mathematical term for what we call local stability is **local asymptotic stability**. A similar remark applies to global stability, defined below. We omit the 'asymptotic' because most economists do.

close is sufficiently close?" is an interesting question, about which we shall say a little more below.

Now consider Example 2, the autonomous system (26.20) in the case where

$$f(x,y) = y - x^2, \quad g(x,y) = 1 - xy.$$

Here

$$\frac{\partial f}{\partial x} = -2x, \quad \frac{\partial f}{\partial y} = 1, \quad \frac{\partial g}{\partial x} = -y, \quad \frac{\partial g}{\partial y} = -x.$$

Thus the Jacobian matrix of (f, g) with respect to (x, y), evaluated at the fixed point $(1, 1)$, is

$$\begin{bmatrix} -2 & 1 \\ -1 & -1 \end{bmatrix}.$$

This matrix has trace -3 and determinant $+3$, so the fixed point is locally stable: if x and y both start off sufficiently close to 1, they both approach 1 as $t \to \infty$. "How close is sufficiently close?" is a difficult question which we shall not attempt to answer. One thing that is clear from the phase diagram, Figure 26.10, is that for some initial conditions (x, y) will not approach $(1, 1)$. In particular, if at time 0 we have $x < 0$, $y < 0$ and $xy \geq 1$, then $x \to -\infty$ and $y \to -\infty$ as $t \to \infty$.

Global stability

Consider again the nonlinear system (26.20) and suppose it has exactly one fixed point, say (x^*, y^*). We say that this fixed point is **globally stable** if all solutions path approach it as $t \to \infty$, regardless of initial conditions.

What conditions ensure global stability? We have just shown (using Example 2) that local stability is *not* enough, even when supplemented by the assumption that (x^*, y^*) is the only fixed point. A theorem which is sometimes useful in this connection was established in 1963 by the Polish mathematician Czesław Olech. To explain what Olech's theorem says, we define the matrix $\mathbf{J}(x, y)$ to be the Jacobian matrix of (f, g) with respect to (x, y). Notice that $\mathbf{J}(x, y)$ depends on x and y: we are concerned with how this matrix behaves for all (x, y), not just at the fixed point. The theorem states that (x^*, y^*) is globally stable if

(i) $\operatorname{tr} \mathbf{J}(x, y) < 0 < \det \mathbf{J}(x, y)$ for all (x, y)

and *at least one* of the following conditions also holds:

(iia) both diagonal entries of $\mathbf{J}(x, y)$ are negative for all (x, y);

(iib) the off-diagonal entries of $\mathbf{J}(x, y)$ are both non-zero and of opposite signs for all (x, y).

Notice in particular that if (iia) and (iib) *both* hold then so does (i), so these two conditions imply global stability of the fixed point.

As a typical application in economics of Olech's theorem, consider Example 1. There is exactly one fixed point (p^*, p^*), and we showed above that the entries of the Jacobian matrix are signed

$$\begin{bmatrix} - & - \\ + & - \end{bmatrix}$$

for all (p, v). Hence conditions (iia) and (iib) both hold, so (p^*, p^*) is globally stable.

Or is it? One important fact about Olech's theorem which we have omitted to mention is that, strictly speaking, it applies only to systems of the form (26.20) defined for all real values of x and y. Our economic example, by contrast, makes sense only when p and v are positive. Therefore, a truly rigorous proof of global stability would have to establish reasons for keeping p and v away from the axes, if necessary by imposing additional assumptions about the functions D and S. We shall not go into this, but instead make the general point that it is safer to apply Olech's theorem when one is working with variables that can take negative as well as positive values. This occurs, for example, when the variables in question are logarithms of economic quantities.

This is as far as we shall go with systems of the form (26.20), except to point out that one may sometimes gain a lot of information simply by looking at the phase diagram. As an example of this, we consider the model of exchange rate dynamics presented at the end of the last section, with the difference that we no longer assume a special functional form for the demand for money. The model is then given by equations (26.16), (26.17) and

$$m - p = f(r), \tag{26.18'}$$

where f is a decreasing function. Proceeding as before, with (26.18) replaced by (26.18'), we obtain the system

$$\dot{p} = \sigma(-p + q + p^*), \quad \dot{q} = r^* - g(m - p),$$

where g is the inverse function of f.

The phase diagram is similar to Figure 26.8. The unique fixed point is given by $p = m - \gamma$, $q = m - \gamma - p^*$, where $\gamma = f(r^*)$; this fixed point is a saddle point. Indeed, the only departure from Figure 26.8 and the ensuing analysis is that the stable branch will typically be a curve rather than a straight line.

More than two dimensions

The n–dimensional generalisation of (26.20) is

$$\dot{x} = F(x), \tag{26.21}$$

where $\mathbf{x} \in \mathcal{R}^n$ and each component of the n–vector $\mathbf{F}(\mathbf{x})$ is a real-valued function of n variables. As in Section 15.3 we may compute the $n \times n$ Jacobian matrix of $\mathbf{F}$ with respect to $\mathbf{x}$.

A fixed point of (26.21) is defined to be a vector $\mathbf{x}^*$ such that $\mathbf{F}(\mathbf{x}^*) = \mathbf{0}$. As in the two-dimensional case, the system (26.21) may be linearised in the neighbourhood of a fixed point $\mathbf{x}^*$; the matrix of coefficients $\mathbf{A}$ in the linearised system is the Jacobian matrix, evaluated at $\mathbf{x}^*$. We say that $\mathbf{A}$ is a hyperbolic fixed point if *no* eigenvalue of $\mathbf{A}$ has zero real part. Again as before, the solutions of the linearised system approximate those of the original system in the neighbourhood of a hyperbolic fixed point; in particular, $\mathbf{x}^*$ is locally stable if all eigenvalues of $\mathbf{A}$ have negative real part.

However, the most important point about systems of the form (26.21) when $n > 2$ is that they are much more complicated than two-dimensional systems. First, checking local stability is harder.[12] Secondly, even simple-looking three-dimensional systems can have very strange solutions. A famous example of this outside economics is the meteorologist Edward Lorenz's model of atmospheric convection, which displays **chaos**, loosely defined as extreme sensitivity of so-lution paths to initial conditions.[13] Models using multidimensional nonlinear dynamics do appear in the literature of economics, but may fairly be described as a specialised taste.

The reader may recall that we started this chapter with a discussion of linear difference equations, but we have said nothing about nonlinear systems in discrete time. This is because their analysis is difficult, and the behaviour of solutions is often quite bizarre. In particular, chaos in continuous time requires $n > 3$, but can occur even in one-dimensional nonlinear difference equations. This fact too has been used in economic theory, but is too far from the standard toolkit for us to discuss it here.

Exercises

26.4.1 Consider the autonomous system

$$\dot{x} = y - ay^2 - x, \quad \dot{y} = x,$$

where a is a non-negative constant. If $a = 0$, this system reduces to that of Exercise 26.3.5. Now suppose that $a > 0$. Show that there are two fixed points and draw the phase diagram. What can you say about the behaviour of solutions near the two fixed points?

26.4.2 For the autonomous system

$$\dot{x} = -3x + y, \quad \dot{y} = 10 - x^2 - y^2,$$

[12]Recall the two propositions about stability in linear systems which we established at the beginning of Section 26.3: **[PS1]** is true for all n, but the very convenient **[PS2]** is applicable only when $n = 2$.

[13]Lorenz's result is often interpreted as saying that long-range weather forecasting is im-possible. Many have disputed this conjecture, and some have made money by doing so.

show that there is exactly one fixed point in the positive quadrant. By linearising the system, show that this fixed point is locally stable. Is there another fixed point? Sketch and comment on the phase diagram.

Problems on Chapter 26

26–1. Let

$$\mathbf{A} = \begin{bmatrix} 1 & -1 & 0 \\ -1 & 2 & -1 \\ 0 & -1 & 1 \end{bmatrix}.$$

(i) Find the general solution of the difference equation $\mathbf{y}(t+1) = \mathbf{A}\mathbf{y}(t)$.

(ii) Find the solution of the difference equation $\mathbf{y}(t+1) = \mathbf{A}\mathbf{y}(t)$, given that

$$\mathbf{y}(0) = \begin{bmatrix} 1 \\ 2 \\ 4 \end{bmatrix}.$$

What happens to the components of $\mathbf{y}(t)$ as $t \to \infty$?

(iii) Find a particular solution of the difference equation

$$\mathbf{x}(t+1) = \mathbf{A}\mathbf{x}(t) + \mathbf{b}, \quad \text{where} \quad \mathbf{b} = \begin{bmatrix} 1 \\ 0 \\ 1 \end{bmatrix}.$$

Hence find the general solution.

(iv) As (iii), except that

$$\mathbf{b} = \begin{bmatrix} 1 \\ 0 \\ 2 \end{bmatrix}.$$

[WARNING. The fact that $\mathbf{A}$ is of order 3 should not cause any trouble, since the characteristic polynomial is easily factorised. Difficulties arise from the fact that two of the eigenvalues of $\mathbf{A}$ turn out to be 0 and 1: they may be surmounted by careful thought, as opposed to mechanical application of formulae in the text.]

26–2. (i) Find the general solution of the difference equation

$$\mathbf{x}(t+1) = \mathbf{A}\mathbf{x}(t) + \mathbf{b}(t),$$

where

$$\mathbf{A} = \begin{bmatrix} 1 & 1/3 \\ 4/3 & 1 \end{bmatrix}, \quad \mathbf{b}(t) = \begin{bmatrix} 2+t \\ 3t \end{bmatrix}.$$

(ii) Let $\mathbf{A} = \begin{bmatrix} -2 & -3 \\ 1 & -6 \end{bmatrix}$. Find the general solution of the difference equation

$$dx/dt = \mathbf{A}x + \mathbf{b}(t)$$

in each of the following cases:

(a) $\mathbf{b}(t) = \begin{bmatrix} e^{-t} \\ 0 \end{bmatrix}$,   (b) $\mathbf{b}(t) = \begin{bmatrix} 0 \\ e^{-2t} \end{bmatrix}$,   (c) $\mathbf{b}(t) = \begin{bmatrix} 4e^{-t} \\ 3e^{-2t} \end{bmatrix}$.

26–3. In an open access fishery, the fish stock x satisfies the differential equation

(I) $$\dot{x} = F(x) - H(x,y),$$

where $F(x)$ is a biological growth function and $H(x,y)$ is a harvest function: y denotes fishing effort. Suppose y responds to profit or loss according to the differential equation

(II) $$\dot{y} = \eta(pH(x,y) - cy),$$

where p is the constant price of harvested fish, c is the constant unit cost of effort and η is a positive adjustment parameter.

Assume that $F(x)$ takes the logistic form

$$F(x) = rx\left(1 - \frac{x}{k}\right),$$

where r and k are positive constants called the intrinsic growth rate and the carrying capacity. Assume also that $H(x,y)$ takes the form

$$H(x,y) = qxy,$$

where q is a positive constant called the catchability coefficient.

Show that, provided $c < kpq$, the system of differential quations (I) and (II) has exactly one fixed point in the positive quadrant. Obtain the associated linearised system and show that the fixed point is locally stable. Show that there is a positive number η_0 such that the fixed point is a stable node of the linearised system if $\eta < \eta_0$ and a spiral sink if $\eta > \eta_0$.

26–4. In this problem we extend the Solow–Swan growth model of Section 21.3 to allow for two types of capital, physical capital K and human capital H. The analogue to equation (21.17) is the pair of equations

$$\frac{dK}{dt} + \delta_1 K = s_1 A K^\alpha H^\gamma, \qquad \frac{dH}{dt} + \delta_2 H = s_2 A K^\alpha H^\gamma.$$

Here $\delta_1, \delta_2, s_1, s_2, A, \alpha, \gamma$ are positive constants with $s_1 + s_2 < 1$ and $\alpha + \gamma < 1$.

(i) Express this pair of equations as an autonomous system in the two variables $k = \ln K$, $h = \ln H$.

(ii) Draw a phase diagram of this system in the kh–plane, and show that there is exactly one fixed point (k^*, h^*).

(iii) Use Olech's theorem to show that (k^*, h^*) is globally stable.

Appendix to Chapter 26

In this appendix we give a solution formula for the vector differential equation (26.11), where $\mathbf{A}$ is a general square matrix. We then show that this formula reduces to the familiar solution (26.13) in the case where $\mathbf{A}$ is a d–matrix.

Recall from the beginning of Section 26.2 that the solution of the scalar differential equation $dy/dt = ay$ is $y = ce^{at}$, where c is the value of y at time 0. Also recall from Section 10.4 that

$$e^x = 1 + x + \frac{x^2}{2!} + \ldots + \frac{x^k}{k!} + \ldots$$

for every real number x: this was extended to complex numbers in Section 23.3. It turns out that these facts have multi-dimensional analogues.

For any square matrix $\mathbf{A}$, we define the **matrix exponential** $e^{\mathbf{A}}$ by the series formula

$$e^{\mathbf{A}} = \mathbf{I} + \mathbf{A} + \frac{1}{2!}\mathbf{A}^2 + \ldots \frac{1}{k!}\mathbf{A}^k + \ldots$$

It may be shown that the right-hand side converges — entry by entry — for every square matrix $\mathbf{A}$. Similarly, if $\mathbf{A}$ is a given square matrix, the series

$$e^{t\mathbf{A}} = \mathbf{I} + t\mathbf{A} + \frac{t^2}{2!}\mathbf{A}^2 + \ldots \frac{t^k}{k!}\mathbf{A}^k + \ldots$$

converges for every real number t.

The matrix exponential has properties similar to the ordinary exponential function: for example $e^{\mathbf{A}+\mathbf{B}} = e^{\mathbf{A}}e^{\mathbf{B}}$, and $e^{m\mathbf{A}} = (e^{\mathbf{A}})^m$ for every positive integer m. More relevantly for our purposes, the general solution of the vector differential equation $d\mathbf{y}/dt = \mathbf{A}\mathbf{y}$ is

$$\mathbf{y} = e^{t\mathbf{A}}\,\mathbf{w}. \tag{26.22}$$

Here $\mathbf{w}$ is a constant vector, which may be interpreted as $\mathbf{y}(0)$.

We now show that (26.22) reduces to the standard solution (26.13) in the case where $\mathbf{A}$ is diagonalisable. To do this, we use two properties of the matrix exponential which are easily derived from its definition:

(i) if $\mathbf{A} = \mathbf{S}\mathbf{D}\mathbf{S}^{-1}$, then $e^{\mathbf{A}} = \mathbf{S}\,e^{\mathbf{D}}\,\mathbf{S}^{-1}$;

(ii) if $\mathbf{D}$ is the diagonal matrix with diagonal entries $\lambda_1, \ldots, \lambda_n$, then $e^{\mathbf{D}}$ is the diagonal matrix with diagonal entries $e^{\lambda_1}, \ldots, e^{\lambda_n}$.

Suppose $\mathbf{A}$ is a d–matrix. Let $\mathbf{D}$ be a diagonal matrix whose diagonal entries (say $\lambda_1, \ldots, \lambda_n$) are the eigenvalues of $\mathbf{A}$; then there is a matrix $\mathbf{S}$ such that $\mathbf{S}^{-1}\mathbf{A}\mathbf{S} = \mathbf{D}$. Multiplying by the scalar t, and rearranging, $t\mathbf{A} = \mathbf{S}(t\mathbf{D})\mathbf{S}^{-1}$. Hence by (i) with $\mathbf{A}$ replaced by $t\mathbf{A}$ and $\mathbf{D}$ by $t\mathbf{D}$,

$$e^{t\mathbf{A}} = \mathbf{S}\,e^{t\mathbf{D}}\,\mathbf{S}^{-1}.$$

We now post-multiply by $\mathbf{w}$ and apply (26.22):

$$\mathbf{y} = \mathbf{S}\, e^{t\mathbf{D}}\, \mathbf{c}, \tag{26.23}$$

where $\mathbf{c} = \mathbf{S}^{-1}\mathbf{w}$. But by (ii), with $\mathbf{D}$ replaced by $t\mathbf{D}$, $e^{t\mathbf{D}}\mathbf{c}$ is the vector whose components are $c_1 e^{\lambda_1 t}, \ldots, c_n e^{\lambda_n t}$. Substituting this into (26.23), we retrieve the standard solution (26.13).

Notes on Further Reading

Most readers of this book will have plentiful sources of advice on further reading in economics. We therefore concentrate on books on mathematics that advanced students in economics find useful, and which can be approached with the preparation we provide.

Many economists find it helpful to own an encyclopaedic calculus textbook and use it as a work of reference. Thomas et al [10] is particularly good, but there are plenty of others. For further reading on differential equations we strongly recommend Kostelich and Armbruster [6], which is easy to read and emphasises the qualitative and geometrical techniques that economist use. Chapter 8 of [6], on nonlinear equations, is especially helpful.

The rigorous foundations of calculus, and their extensions and generalisations, form the mathematical field known as 'analysis'. Real analysis — that part of analysis based on the real rather than the complex number system — is much used in graduate-level microeconomics, and increasingly in macroeconomics as well. Binmore [10] provides a good introduction;[14] the Russian classic by Kolmogorov and Fomin [5] is more advanced.

In linear algebra, further study may proceed along any of three routes: rigour, geometry and computation. Cohn's popular textbook [2] is good on rigour and geometry. Strang [7] is excellent on computation; we also like his populist treatment of the theory, though this is not to everybody's taste.

Turning to books written explicitly for economists, we thoroughly recommend the late Akira Takayama's last book [9], which covers a wide range of material gently and carefully. For students who want to go further in optimisation than our Chapters 17 and 18, we recommend Dixit [3] at the elementary level; Sundaram [8] is more rigorous but very enlightening. Neither of these books says much about computation; Judd [4] is a comprehensive textbook for economists on computational techniques in optimisation and much else besides.

Bibliography

[1] Binmore, K. G., *Mathematical Analysis: A Straightforward Approach*, Second Edition, Cambridge University Press, 1982.

---

[14]This is Ken Binmore the game theorist, but the book was written during his first career as a mathematician.

[2] Cohn, P. M., *Elements of Linear Algebra*, CRC Press, 1994.

[3] Dixit, A. K., *Optimization in Economic Theory*, Second Edition, Oxford University Press, 1990.

[4] Judd, K. L., *Numerical Methods in Economics*, The MIT Press, 1998.

[5] Kolmogorov, A. N. and S. V. Fomin, *Introductory Real Analysis*, Revised English Edition, translated by R. A. Silverman, Dover Publications, 1975.

[6] Kostelich, E. J. and D. Armbruster, *Introductory Differential Equations: From Linearity to Chaos*, Addison-Wesley, 1997.

[7] Strang, G., *Linear Algebra and its Applications*, Third Edition, Harcourt Publishing, 1988.

[8] Sundaram, R. K., *A First Course in Optimization Theory*, Cambridge University Press, 1996.

[9] Takayama, A., *Analytical Methods in Economics*, University of Michigan Press, 1993.

[10] Thomas, G. B., R. L. Finney, M. D. Weir and F. Giordano, *Thomas' Calculus*, Longman, 2000. [The US edition is published by Addison-Wesley.]

Answers

Answers to odd-numbered exercises

Chapter 1

1.1.1 Reflexion in x–axis is $(-2, -3)$, reflexion in y–axis is $(2, 3)$. Fourth vertex of rectangle is $(2, -3)$.

1.1.3 The lines all have slope 1. $y = x + 6$.

1.1.5 The demand schedule is a straight line with slope -3 and intercept 11. The supply schedule is a straight line with slope 2 and intercept 1. Equilibrium price and quantity are 2 and 5 respectively.

With q on the horizontal axis and p on the vertical, the demand schedule is a straight line with slope $-\frac{1}{3}$ and intercept $\frac{11}{3}$; the supply schedule is a straight line with slope $\frac{1}{2}$ and intercept $-\frac{1}{2}$.

1.2.1 $x = 5$, $y = -1$.

1.2.3 $(k - 1)/7$, $(4 + 3k)/7$.

(a) 2/7, 13/7;   (b) 3/7, 16/7;   (c) 1/7, 10/7.

When $k = \frac{1}{2}$ there is no equilibrium.

1.3.1 55 of X, 80 of Y, 80 of Z.

Chapter 2

2.1.1 (a) $x > -\frac{1}{2}$, (b) $x \geq \frac{8}{3}$, (c) $x \geq -12$, (d) $x > -\frac{2}{5}$.

2.2.1 Denoting by x_1 and x_2 the amounts consumed of fish and chips respectively, the budget set consists of the points satisfying $2x_1 + 3x_2 \leq 10$ and $x_1 \geq 0$, $x_2 \geq 0$.

If the prices are reversed, the budget set consists of the points satisfying $3x_1 + 2x_2 \leq 10$ and $x_1 \geq 0$, $x_2 \geq 0$.

2.2.3 Denoting by x and y the amounts produced per day of products X and Y respectively, the feasible set consists of the points satisfying $16x + 8y \leq 240$, $10x + 20y \leq 300$ and $x \geq 0$, $y \geq 0$.

2.3.1 7.5 of X, 12 of Y; 15 of X, 0 of Y.

Chapter 3

3.1.1 (a) $A \subset B$, (b) $B \subset A$, (c) $A \subset B$, (d) neither, (e) $A \subset B$, (f) neither.

3.1.3 (a) $(x - 9)^2$, (b) $(4a - 5b)(4a + 5b)$, (c) $5x(x - 3y)$, (d) $(x - 5)(x + 2)$.

3.1.5 (a) 18, $\mathcal{R}^2$; (b) 2, $\mathcal{R}^{18}$.

3.2.1 $-3, 0, 0, 2a^2 + 5a - 3, 2b^2 - 5b - 3, 2(a - b)^2 + 5(a - b) - 3$ [or $2a^2 - 4ab + 2b^2 + 5a - 5b - 3$].

3.2.3 All are U-shaped with the bottom of the U at the origin. The graph of $y = 2x^2$ rises most steeply, then $y = x^2$ and $y = \frac{1}{2}x^2$ is the least steep.

3.2.5 Original function is $f(x_1, x_2, x_3) = 4x_1 + 2x_2 + x_3$ and new function is $F(x_1, x_2, x_3) = 3x_1 + 3x_2 + 2x_3$.

(a) $f(g_1, g_2, g_3)$, i.e. $4g_1 + 2g_2 + g_3$.

(b) $F(g_1, g_2, g_3)$, i.e. $3g_1 + 3g_2 + 2g_3$.

(c) $F(h_1, h_2, h_3)$, i.e. $3h_1 + 3h_2 + 2h_3$.

(d) $f(h_1, h_2, h_3)$, i.e. $4h_1 + 2h_2 + h_3$.

3.3.1 The image of (x, y) under h is its reflexion in the x–axis.

Points of the form $(x, 0)$ i.e. the x–axis.

Chapter 4

4.1.1 (a) U-shaped with vertex at $(-2, -3)$;

(b) U-shaped with vertex at $(-\frac{1}{3}, -\frac{4}{3})$.

4.1.3 (a) $(-2, 0)$, $(2, 0)$; (b) $x < -2$ or $x > 2$; (c) $-2 < x < 2$.

(a) Graph does not meet x–axis; (b) all x; (c) no x.

4.1.5 (a) $\cap$-shaped with vertex at $(-1, 2)$;

(b) $\cap$-shaped with vertex at $(\frac{1}{2}, 4)$;

(c) ∩-shaped with vertex at $(3, 4)$;

(d) ∩-shaped with vertex at $(-\frac{1}{2}, 2)$;

Maximum values are (a) 2, (b) 4, (c) 4, (d) 2.

When $x \geq 0$ is imposed, maximum values are (a) 1, (b) 4, (c) 4, (d) 1.

4.2.1 (a) Because $(-1)^2 = (-1)^4 = 1$.

(b) $\frac{1}{4}$, 1, 4, $\frac{1}{16}$, 1, 16.

Graphs of $y = x^2$ and $y = x^4$ are both roughly U-shaped, with the vertex at the origin. The graphs meet at the origin and at the points $(\pm 1, 1)$. The graph of $y = x^4$ lies above the graph of $y = x^2$ when $|x| > 1$ and below it when $0 < |x| < 1$. The graph of $y = x^6$ bears the same relationship to that of $y = x^4$ as the graph of $y = x^4$ does to that of $y = x^2$.

4.2.3 (a) 3.728×10^2, (b) 3.728×10^{-3}, (c) 3.728×10^1.

4.2.5 $x = z^{4/3}/2^{1/3}$, $y = 2^{2/3}z^{4/3}$.

If K and L both increase by $s\%$, Y increases by $s\%$.

4.3.1 (a) 3, (b) -3, (c) 2, (d) $\frac{2}{3}$, (e) $\frac{8}{3}$.

4.3.3 $\log Y = \log 2 + \frac{1}{2}\log K + \frac{1}{3}\log L + \frac{1}{6}\log R$.

Chapter 5

5.1.1 (a) 74, 10, 13, arithmetic progression;

(b) -1, -7, -13, arithmetic progression;

(c) 4, 16, 64, geometric progression;

(d) -10, 20, -40, geometric progression;

(e) 3, 18, 81, neither.

5.1.3 (a) No limit ($u_n \to \infty$), (b) no limit ($u_n \to -\infty$), (c) 0, (d) 0.

5.2.1 5050.

5.2.3 (a) No; (b) no; (c) no; (d) yes, $-21/8$.

5.3.1 (a) 196 (Usurian dollars), (b) 214.36, (c) 140, (d) 100.

5.3.3 (a) £563.71, (b) 7.

5.3.5 (a) £839.20, (b) £805.23.

Chapter 6

6.1.1 2, -4, 7, -1; 5, 5, 5, 5. The rate of change of $f(x)$ depends on x whereas the rate of change of the linear function $g(x)$ is constant.

6.1.3 $-1/x_0^2$. $[\frac{1}{h}\left(\frac{1}{x_0+h}-\frac{1}{x_0}\right) = \frac{-1}{x_0(x_0+h)}$, a fraction whose denominator approaches x_0^2 when h becomes very small.]

6.2.1 (a) 0.02, (b) -0.02, (c) 0.04, (d) -0.04.

For $5x-8$ the small increments formula gives the changes as: (a) 0.05, (b) -0.05, (c) 0.05, (d) -0.05. In this case the function is linear: thus the small increments formula is exact and the magnitudes of the changes do not depend on the starting point.

6.2.3 The graph can be drawn without lifting the pencil from the paper, but no linear function can approximate $f(x)$ at $x = 1$.

6.3.1 $-x^{-2}$, always negative. The derivative of $y = x - 2$ is negative for $x > 0$ and positive for $x < 0$.

For $y = x^{-n}$ the derivative is negative if $x > 0$. The sign of the derivative for $x < 0$ depends on whether n is odd or even: it is negative if n is even, positive if n is odd.

Since p is restricted to be positive, the equation $q = p^{-n}$ can serve as a demand schedule for any natural number n.

6.3.3 (a) $16x^3 - 6x^2$, (b) $3x^2 + 6x + 2$, (c) $\frac{3}{2} - \frac{1}{2x^2}$, (d) $2 + x^{-2}$, (e) $2x + a^2x^{-3}$,

(f) $-\frac{2}{bx^3} + \frac{3a}{bx^4}$.

6.4.1 $5x - \frac{1}{2}x^2$, $5 - x$.

6.4.3 2, $\frac{3}{2}$, $\frac{4}{3}$.

6.4.5 $0.2 + 0.1Y$.

Chapter 7

7.1.1 (a) $(4x^3 - 6x)(5x + 1) + 5(x^4 - 3x^2)$,

(b) $(18x^2 + 1)(x^6 - 3x^4 - 2) + (6x^5 - 12x^3)(6x^3 + x)$,

(c) $mx^{m-1}(5x^2 + 2x^{-n}) + (10x - 2nx^{-n-1})(x^m + 8)$,

(d) $(16x^3 + 4x)(x^{n+1} + 5x^n) + ([n+1]x^n + 5nx^{n-1})(4x^4 + 2x^2 - 1)$.

7.1.3 $-5(1+4t)^{-2}$.

7.2.1 $(x^4-2)^3+1$, $(x^3+1)^4-2$; $12x^3(x^4-2)^2$, $12x^2(x^3+1)^3$.

7.2.3 (a) $2x(x^3+1)^5+15x^2(x^3+1)^4(x^2-1)$.

(b) $(30x^4-\frac{44}{3}x^{13/3}-\frac{2}{3}x^{-2/3})(x^5-2)^4$.

7.2.5 $\frac{6}{5}(4+3t)^{-3/5}$.

7.3.1 (a) $\frac{1}{3}y^{-2/3}$, (b) $(3x^2)^{-1}$.

7.3.3 $-\dfrac{1}{2q}$, $\dfrac{q^2-3}{2q^2}$.

Chapter 8

8.1.1 The graph of $y=x^4$ has a minimum point at $(0,0)$. The graph of $y=x^5$ has a critical point of inflexion at $(0,0)$. In general, for any $n \in \mathcal{N}$, the graph of $y=x^{2n}$ has a minimum point at $(0,0)$ and the graph of $y=x^{2n+1}$ has a critical point of inflexion at $(0,0)$.

8.1.3 $3/8$ is a maximum value.

8.2.3 No points of inflexion.

8.3.1 $(1,11)$ is a local maximum; $(7,-97)$ is a local minimum. There are no global maxima and no global minima.

When $x \geq 0$ is imposed, $(1,11)$ is a local maximum, while $(0,1)$ and $(7,-97)$ are local minima. There are no global maxima but $(7,-97)$ is now the global minimum.

8.3.3 (a) Marginal cost is $x^2-12x+160$. By completing the square,
$$\text{MC}=(x-6)^2+124 \geq 124 > 0.$$

(b) 8.

8.4.1 $(2,11)$.

8.4.3 (a) When x is large and negative, y is small and negative.

(b) When x is small and negative, y is large and negative.

Chapter 9

9.1.3 (a) £285.19, (b) £282.16, (c) £281.88. The more frequent the discounting, the smaller is the value.

9.2.1 $\ln(1 + s)$.

9.2.3 (a) Let $y = c^x$, so that $\ln y = x \ln c$. Differentiating, and using the composite function rule on the left-hand side,

$$\frac{1}{y}\frac{dy}{dx} = \ln c, \quad \text{so} \quad \frac{dy}{dx} = y \ln c = c^x \ln c.$$

(b) Let $y = \exp(-\frac{1}{2}x^2)$, so that $\ln y = -\frac{1}{2}x^2$. Differentiating,

$$\frac{1}{y}\frac{dy}{dx} = -x, \quad \text{so} \quad \frac{dy}{dx} = -xy = -x\exp(-\frac{1}{2}x^2).$$

9.2.5 $(Aap^a + Bbp^b)/(Ap^a + Bp^b)$, which $\to b$ when $p \to 0$ and $\to a$ when $p \to \infty$.

9.3.1 (a) $(b + 2ct)/(a + bt + ct^2)$, (b) $(b + c + 2ct)/(a + bt + ct^2)$.

9.3.3 (a) Apply 'the economist's favourite approximation' where x is the rate of growth in discrete time, as usually defined.

(b) With the new definition of the growth rate, the rate of growth of u/v is equal to the rate of growth of u minus the rate of growth of v.

9.3.5 (a) $\ln c$, (b) $c - 1$, (c) $\ln c$.

Chapter 10

10.1.1 (a) $y = 12x - 16$, (b) $y = 27x - 54$.

x	2.1	2.2	2.3	2.4	2.5	2.6	2.7	2.8	2.9
$12x - 16$	9.2	10.4	11.6	12.8	14.0	15.2	16.4	17.6	18.8
$27x - 54$	2.7	5.4	8.1	10.8	13.5	16.2	18.9	21.6	24.3
x^3	9.3	10.7	12.2	13.8	15.6	17.6	19.7	22.0	24.4

As x increases from 2 to 3, the tangent at $x = 2$ becomes a worse approximation to the true function, while the tangent at $x = 3$ becomes a better one.

10.1.3 $\frac{2}{3}$, 0.705.

10.2.1 2.

10.2.3 $(\ln b - \ln a)/(b - a)$.

10.3.1 $4x^3 - 9x^2 + 16x + 5$, $12x^2 - 18x + 16$, $24x - 18$, 24; all derivatives higher than the fourth are zero.

5, 16, -18, 24; the coefficients of x, x^2, x^3, x^4 are these values divided by 1!, 2!, 3!, 4! respectively. The constant term is $f(0)$.

For a polynomial of degree n, the constant term and the coefficients of $x, x^2, \ldots, x^n$ are

$$f(0), \quad \frac{f'(0)}{1!}, \quad \frac{f''(0)}{2!}, \quad \ldots, \quad \frac{f^{(n)}}{n!}$$

respectively.

10.4.1 (a) 2.718, by taking 7 terms; (b) 0.1, 0.095, 0.0953.

True value is 0.0953 to 4 decimal places. The accuracy of the approximation is particularly good because the terms of the expansion alternate in sign.

10.4.3 (a) From the series for e^x,

$$\frac{e^x}{x} = \frac{1}{x} + 1 + \frac{x}{2!} + \frac{x^2}{3!} + \ldots$$

As $x \to \infty$, $x^{-1} + 1 \to 1$ and the terms $x/2!$, $x^2/3!$, $x^3/4!$, ... all $\to \infty$; hence $e^x/x \to \infty$, so $xe^{-x} \to 0$.

(b) A similar argument to (a) shows that as $x \to \infty$, $e^x/x^2 \to \infty$, so $x^2e^{-x} \to 0$. Again by a similar argument, $x^ne^{-x} \to 0$ as $x \to \infty$ for any positive integer n; even more generally, $x^ae^{-x} \to 0$ as $x \to \infty$ for any positive real number a.

10.4.5 (a) $1 + 2x + 2x^2 + \ldots + (2^n/n!)x^n + \ldots$, valid for all x.

(b) $3x - (9/2)x^2 + 9x^3 - \ldots + ([-3]^n/n!)x^n + \ldots$, valid for $-\frac{1}{3} < x \leq \frac{1}{3}$.

(c) $1 + \dfrac{x}{2} - \dfrac{x^2}{8} + \ldots + \dfrac{\frac{1}{2}(\frac{1}{2} - 1) \ldots (\frac{1}{2} - [n-1])x^n}{n!} + \ldots$, valid for $|x| < 1$.

(d) $1 + 5x + 25x^2 + \ldots + 5^nx^n + \ldots$, valid for $|x| < \frac{1}{5}$.

Chapter 11

11.1.1 Components of $\mathbf{a} + \mathbf{b}$ are the sums of Anne's and Bill's weekly expenditures on food, clothing and housing; components of $52\mathbf{a}$ are Anne's annual expenditures on food, clothing and housing.

11.1.3 $p = -\frac{1}{2}$, $q = -5$, $r = 1$.

11.2.1

$$\begin{bmatrix} 6 & 0 & 7 \\ -1 & 7 & 4 \end{bmatrix}, \quad \begin{bmatrix} 10 & -5 & 0 \\ 5 & 15 & 25 \end{bmatrix}, \quad \begin{bmatrix} -8 & 2 & 14 \\ -4 & 8 & -2 \end{bmatrix}, \quad \begin{bmatrix} 2 & -3 & 14 \\ 1 & 23 & 23 \end{bmatrix}.$$

11.2.3 Answers to (a), (b), (c) are respectively

$$\begin{bmatrix} x_1 \\ x_2 \end{bmatrix}, \quad \begin{bmatrix} 3x_1 \\ 3x_2 \end{bmatrix}, \quad \begin{bmatrix} -2x_1 \\ -2x_2 \end{bmatrix}.$$

In (a), **A** maps **x** into its reflexion in the origin. In (b), **A** maps **x** into the end of the line obtained by stretching the line from the origin to **x** by a factor of 3. In (c), **A** maps **x** into the reflexion in the origin of the end of the line obtained by stretching the line from the origin to **x** by a factor of 2.

11.3.1

$$\begin{bmatrix} 5 & 2 & 7 \\ 2 & 0 & -2 \\ -3 & -2 & -9 \\ 1 & -2 & -13 \end{bmatrix}, \quad \begin{bmatrix} 6 & -4 & 1 & 1 \\ 8 & -8 & 6 & 2 \\ 2 & -4 & 5 & 1 \\ 18 & -20 & 17 & 5 \end{bmatrix}, \quad \begin{bmatrix} 4 & 0 \\ 0 & -4 \end{bmatrix}.$$

11.3.3 $\begin{bmatrix} \mathbf{A_1 B_1} & \mathbf{O} \\ \mathbf{O} & \mathbf{A_2 B_2} \end{bmatrix}$

11.4.1 Any square matrices of the same order which satisfy $\mathbf{AB} \neq \mathbf{BA}$ will do.

11.4.3 Any matrix of the form

$$\begin{bmatrix} a & 0 \\ a+d & d \end{bmatrix} \quad \text{or} \quad \begin{bmatrix} a & a+d \\ 0 & d \end{bmatrix}.$$

Chapter 12

12.1.1 Matrices (a) and (b) are respectively

$$\begin{bmatrix} \star & \cdot & 0 & \cdot \\ 0 & \star & 0 & \cdot \\ 0 & 0 & 0 & \cdot \end{bmatrix} \quad \text{and} \quad \begin{bmatrix} 0 & \star & \cdot \\ 0 & 0 & \star \\ 0 & 0 & 0 \\ 0 & 0 & 0 \end{bmatrix},$$

where $\star$ denotes a non-zero number and $\cdot$ denotes a number which may be either zero or non-zero.

In (a), x_3 does not occur in the system of equations. In (b), x_1 does not occur in the system of equations.

12.2.1 (a) $x_1 = -\frac{3}{2}\lambda - \mu - \frac{1}{10}$, $x_2 = \lambda - \mu - \frac{1}{5}$, $x_3 = \lambda$, $x_4 = \mu$.

(b) No solution.

(c) $x_1 = \lambda$, $x_2 = \frac{1}{3} - 2\lambda$, $x_3 = \lambda$.

12.2.3 The left-hand sides of the systems are the same.
(a) $x_1 = 2$, $x_2 = -1$, $x_3 = 5$.   (b) $x_1 = 20$, $x_2 = -5$, $x_3 = 17$.

12.3.1 If $\mathbf{A}$ has a row of zeros, reduction to echelon form will lead to a Type 4 matrix. If $\mathbf{A}$ has a column of zeros, the system $\mathbf{A}\mathbf{x} = 0$ has a solution with the corresponding component equal to 1 and all other components equal to zero.

12.3.3

$$
\begin{bmatrix} 1/5 & 1/5 \\ -2/5 & 3/5 \end{bmatrix},
\quad
\begin{bmatrix} -11/8 & -1/8 & 1/2 \\ -1/4 & 1/4 & 0 \\ 5/8 & -1/8 & -1/10 \end{bmatrix},
\quad
\begin{bmatrix} 3 & -4 & -9 \\ 3 & -4 & -8 \\ -2 & 3 & 6 \end{bmatrix}.
$$

(a) $x_1 = 4$, $x_2 = 7$.   (b) $x_1 = 1$, $x_2 = 3$, $x_3 = -1$.

12.3.5 (a) If $\mathbf{A}$ were invertible we could pre-multiply $\mathbf{AB} = \mathbf{O}$ by $\mathbf{A}^{-1}$; this gives $\mathbf{B} = \mathbf{O}$, contrary to hypothesis. If $\mathbf{B}$ were invertible we could post-multiply $\mathbf{AB} = \mathbf{O}$ by $\mathbf{B}^{-1}$; this gives $\mathbf{A} = \mathbf{O}$, contrary to hypothesis.

(b) $\mathbf{I} + \mathbf{A}$ is invertible with inverse $\mathbf{I} - \mathbf{A}$ and vice versa.

12.4.1 (a) $x_1 = 0$, $x_2 = 0$, $x_3 = 0$. The columns of $\mathbf{A}$ are linearly independent.

(b) $x_1 = 4\lambda$, $x_2 = -4\lambda$, $x_3 = \lambda$ for any λ. The columns of $\mathbf{A}$ are linearly dependent. For example, $\alpha_1 = 4$, $\alpha_2 = -4$, $\alpha_3 = 1$.

12.4.3 (a) 2, (b) 3, (c) 2, (d) 2.

Chapter 13

13.1.1 -40, $1 + abc$, -16.

13.2.1

$$\begin{bmatrix} -1 & 3 & 0 \\ 0 & 2 & -1 \\ 1 & -4 & 1 \end{bmatrix}$$

13.2.5 See the answer to Problem 2–1.

13.3.1 (a) For example

$$\mathbf{p} = \begin{bmatrix} 1 \\ 1 \\ 1 \end{bmatrix}, \quad \mathbf{q} = \begin{bmatrix} -2 \\ 1 \\ 1 \end{bmatrix}.$$

(b) Since $\mathbf{q}^\mathrm{T}\mathbf{p} = \mathbf{p}^\mathrm{T}\mathbf{q} = 0$, $(\mathbf{p}+\mathbf{q})^\mathrm{T}\mathbf{p} = \mathbf{p}^\mathrm{T}\mathbf{p}$ and $(\mathbf{p}+\mathbf{q})^\mathrm{T}\mathbf{q} = \mathbf{q}^\mathrm{T}\mathbf{q}$. The required result follows by addition.

13.3.3 Let $\mathbf{C} = \mathbf{B}^\mathrm{T}\mathbf{A}\mathbf{B}$. Then $\mathbf{C}^\mathrm{T} = \mathbf{B}^\mathrm{T}\mathbf{A}^\mathrm{T}(\mathbf{B}^\mathrm{T})^\mathrm{T}$. $\mathbf{A}^\mathrm{T} = \mathbf{A}$ by assumption and $(\mathbf{B}^\mathrm{T})^\mathrm{T} = \mathbf{B}$ always, so $\mathbf{C}^\mathrm{T} = \mathbf{C}$ as required.

13.3.5 The matrix $\mathbf{A}$ is $\begin{bmatrix} 2 & 2 \\ 2 & 3 \end{bmatrix}$, which has positive diagonal entries and determinant 2.

13.3.7 Positive definite, indefinite, negative semidefinite.

Chapter 14

14.1.1 (a) $\begin{bmatrix} 3 \\ 12y^2 \end{bmatrix}$, $\begin{bmatrix} 0 & 0 \\ 0 & 24y \end{bmatrix}$.

(b) $\begin{bmatrix} 3x^2 \ln y + 12xy^3 + 2e^{2x}y \\ x^3/y + 18x^2y^2 + e^{2x} \end{bmatrix}$,

$$\begin{bmatrix} 6x \ln y + 12y^3 + 4e^{2x}y & 3x^2/y + 36xy^2 + 2e^{2x} \\ 3x^2/y + 36xy^2 + 2e^{2x} & -x^3/y^2 + 36x^2y \end{bmatrix}.$$

(c) $-(x^2+4y^2)^{-3/2}\begin{bmatrix} x \\ 4y \end{bmatrix}$, $2(x^2+4y^2)^{-5/2}\begin{bmatrix} x^2 - 2y^2 & 6xy \\ 6xy & -2x^2 + 16y^2 \end{bmatrix}.$

(d) $\begin{bmatrix} (1 - 2x - 8y)e^{-2x} + e^{3y} \\ 4e^{-2x} + (4 - 3x - 12y)e^{-3y} \end{bmatrix}$,

$$\begin{bmatrix} 4(-1 + x + 4y)e^{-2x} & -8e^{-2x} - 3e^{-3y} \\ -8e^{-2x} - 3e^{-3y} & 3(-8 + 3x + 12y)e^{-3y} \end{bmatrix}.$$

14.1.3 $-2x^2 - y^2 + 2xy + 25x + 20y$, $-4x + 2y + 25$, $-2y + 2x + 20$.

You would have needed first to find p_x and p_y in terms of x and y.

14.2.1 (a) 0.17, (b) 0.36, (c) 0.53, (d) 0.33.

14.2.3

$$\begin{bmatrix} y^2 \\ 2xy + z^2 \\ 2yz \end{bmatrix}, \quad 2\begin{bmatrix} 0 & y & 0 \\ y & x & z \\ 0 & z & y \end{bmatrix}.$$

$$\begin{bmatrix} x_2^2 \\ 2x_1x_2 + x_3^2 \\ 2x_2x_3 + x_4^2 \\ 2x_3x_4 + x_5^2 \\ 2x_4x_5 \end{bmatrix}, \quad 2\begin{bmatrix} 0 & x_2 & 0 & 0 & 0 \\ x_2 & x_1 & x_3 & 0 & 0 \\ 0 & x_3 & x_2 & x_4 & 0 \\ 0 & 0 & x_4 & x_3 & x_5 \\ 0 & 0 & 0 & x_5 & x_4 \end{bmatrix}.$$

14.2.5 $\dfrac{\partial f}{\partial Y} + \dfrac{\partial f}{\partial T} g'(Y)$.

14.3.1 $K/(K + L)$, $K^2/(K + L)^2$.

14.3.3 $\alpha < 1$, $\beta < 1$.

14.4.1 Decreasing if $\alpha + \beta < 1$, constant if $\alpha + \beta = 1$, increasing if $\alpha + \beta > 1$.

$Q = AK^\alpha L^{1-\alpha}$ $(A > 0, 0 < \alpha < 1)$.

14.4.3 Let $x_1 = f_1(p_1, p_2, m)$ and denote the own-price elasticity, the cross-price elasticity and the income elasticity by a, b, c respectively. Then

$$a = \frac{p_1}{x_1}\frac{\partial f_1}{\partial p_1}, \quad \text{so} \quad p_1\frac{\partial f_1}{\partial p_1} = ax_1.$$

Similarly, $p_2\dfrac{\partial f_1}{\partial p_2} = bx_1$ and $m\dfrac{\partial f_1}{\partial m} = cx_1$. Applying Euler's theorem with $r = 0$ we see that $ax_1 + bx_1 + cx_1 = 0$, whence $a + b + c = 0$.

Chapter 15

15.1.1 (a) $-x(4 - x^2)^{-1/2}$, (b) $-x/y$.

15.1.3 $Q^{-2} = aK^{-2} + bL^{-2}$, so $-2Q^{-3}(\partial Q/\partial K) = -2aK^{-3}$, whence $\partial Q/\partial K = a(Q/K)^3$. Similarly $\partial Q/\partial L = b(Q/L)^3$. The slope of an isoquant is therefore given by

$$\frac{dL}{dK} = -\frac{a}{b}\left(\frac{L}{K}\right)^3,$$

which is obviously negative. Notice also that $|dL/dK|$ is an increasing function of L/K: so as we move rightward along an isoquant, increasing K and decreasing L, $|dL/dK|$ falls. Therefore, isoquants are convex. Asymptotes are $K = \tilde{Q}/\sqrt{a}$, $L = \tilde{Q}/\sqrt{b}$.

15.2.1 $Y = m(a + I)$, $C = m(a + bI)$, $\Delta Y = m(I_1 - I_0)$ where $m = 1/(1 - b)$. Assuming $I_1 > I_0$, ΔY is positive and in fact greater than $I_1 - I_0$.

15.2.3 (a) Letting g be the inverse function of f, we may write the equation $x/s = f(p)$ as $p = g(x/s)$. Hence revenue px is equal to $xg(x/s)$. Since f is a decreasing function, so is g. Profit-maximising output x is given by $g(x/s) + (x/s)g'(x/s) = c$. This determines x/s, given c; so when s increases, x increases by the same proportion and p does not change.

(b) It is easiest to work with the variable $z = x/s$. We know from the answer to (a) that MR is $g(z) + zg'(z)$, which we denote by $h(z)$. Hence the first-order condition for a maximum, MR = MC, may be written $h(z) = c_1 + 2c_2sz$.

Suppose s increases. Since $c_2 > 0$, the profit-maximising z decreases, as may be seen from the second-order condition and/or a diagram. Hence p increases. Under the usual assumption that h is a decreasing function, sz increases, so x increases (but by a smaller proportion than s).

15.3.1 $\begin{bmatrix} 2y & -2z \\ 2z & 2y \end{bmatrix}$.

Chapter 16

16.1.1 The contour corresponding to $k = 0$ is the pair of straight lines $y = \frac{1}{2}x$ and $y = 2x$.

The acute angle between the two straight lines contains the directions in which the function is a minimum at $(0, 0, 0)$, and the obtuse angle contains the directions in which the function is a maximum at $(0, 0, 0)$.

16.1.2 [We give this answer because it is relevant to Exercises 16.1.3 and 16.2.1.]

(a) Local minimum, (b) local maximum, (c) saddle point, (d) saddle point. By considering small movements away from $x = 0$, $y = 0$ and using the fact that, for instance, $x^2 > 0$ for $x \neq 0$.

16.1.3 In each case, the Hessian is the zero matrix at $x = 0$, $y = 0$, so the test in terms of the Hessian fails. However, the alternative method of Exercise 16.1.2 gives the following results: (a) local minimum, (b) local maximum, (c) saddle point, (d) saddle point.

16.1.5 (a) Saddle points at $(4, -2, 32)$ and $(12, -6, 0)$;

  (b) saddle point at $(0, 0, 0)$, local minimum points at $(-1, -1, -1)$ and $(1, 1, -1)$;

  (c) local minimum points at $(-1, -1, -2)$ and $(1, 1, -2)$, saddle point at $(0, 0, 0)$.

16.2.1 In Exercises 16.1.2 (a) and 16.1.3 (a), $(0, 0, 0)$ is the global minimum. In Exercises 16.1.2 (b) and 16.1.3 (b), $(0, 0, 0)$ is the global maximum.

16.2.3 9 of X, 6 of Y.

16.2.5 The sum of three convex functions is convex.

Chapter 17

17.1.1 3. The optimum is where the line $3x + 4y = 12$ is tangent to the highest attainable member of the family of curves $xy = k$.

17.1.3 $375/7$.

17.1.5 (a) The circle $x^2 + y^2 = k$ meets the straight line $2x + y = a$ for arbitrarily large k. Hence there is no solution.

  (b) The solution is where the straight line $2x + y = a$ is tangential to the smallest attainable member of the family of circles $x^2 + y^2 = k$.

17.2.1 $3\sqrt{14}$, $-3\sqrt{14}$.

17.2.3 $4/3$.

17.3.1 (a) Maximise $x_1^\alpha x_2^\beta$ subject to $p_1 x_1 + p_2 x_2 = m$.

  (b) $\alpha x_1^{\alpha-1} x_2^\beta = \lambda p_1$, $\beta x_1^\alpha x_2^{\beta-1} = \lambda p_2$. They are sufficient because the indifference curves are negatively sloped and convex.

$$x_1 = \frac{\alpha m}{(\alpha + \beta)p_1}, \quad x_2 = \frac{\beta m}{(\alpha + \beta)p_2}.$$

(c) $\alpha/(\alpha + \beta)$, $\beta/(\alpha + \beta)$.

17.4.1 The isoquants are negatively sloped and convex. The function is concave for $\nu \leq 1$.

Chapter 18

18.1.1 $k^2 y/48$, $k/24$.

(a) 49/48, (b) 4/3, (c) 27/25, (d) 7/24.

The increase in the maximum value when k increases from 7 to 7.2 is approximately 0.2 times the value of the Lagrange multiplier when $k = 7$.

18.1.3 Let a constrained maximum be attained at (x^*, y^*, z^*, w^*). Then the function

$$f(x, y, z, w) - v\big(g(x, y, z, w), h(x, y, z, w)\big)$$

attains its unconstrained maximum at (x^*, y^*, z^*, w^*).

18.2.1 (a) The short-run cost curves are the parts lying in the non-negative quadrant of U-shaped curves with vertices $(0, b/4)$, $(0, b)$ and $(0, 4b)$ respectively.

(b) $C = 2bQ^2$.

18.2.3 Denote the Lagrangian by $L(x_1, \ldots, x_n, \lambda, p_1, \ldots, p_n, m)$. By the envelope theorem,

$$\partial V/\partial p_i = \partial L/\partial p_i = -\lambda x_i, \quad \partial V/\partial m = \partial L/\partial m = \lambda;$$

Roy's identity follows by division.

18.3.1 (a) 40 at $(5, 1)$, (b) 4 at $(1, 0)$.

18.3.3 Let the utility function be U and let $\beta = b_1/(b_1 + b_2)$. When $m > 3p_1 + \dfrac{5\beta}{1 - \beta}p_2$, the demand functions are

$$x_1 = 3 + \frac{\beta}{p_1}(m - 3p_1 + 5p_2), \quad x_2 = -5 + \frac{1 - \beta}{p_2}(m - 3p_1 + 5p_2).$$

When $3p_1 < m \leq 3p_1 + \dfrac{5\beta}{1 - \beta}p_2$, the demand functions are $x_1 = m/p_1$, $x_2 = 0$.

Now let the utility function be $\tilde{U}$. Again let $\beta = b_1/(b_1 + b_2)$; also let

$$a_1 = \frac{3(1-\beta)}{\beta}p_1 - 5p_2, \quad a_2 = \frac{5\beta}{1-\beta}p_2 - 3p_1.$$

Then a_1 and a_2 are of opposite signs. If $m > a_1 > 0 > a_2$ or $m > a_2 > 0 > a_1$, the demand functions are

$$x_1 = -3 + \frac{\beta}{p_1}(m + 3p_1 + 5p_2), \quad x_2 = -5 + \frac{1-\beta}{p_2}(m + 3p_1 + 5p_2).$$

If $a_1 < 0 < m < a_2$, the demand functions are $x_1 = m/p_1$, $x_2 = 0$. If $a_2 < 0 < m < a_1$, the demand functions are $x_1 = 0$, $x_2 = m/p_2$.

Chapter 19

19.1.1 For $0 \leq x \leq 3$, the graph of $y = x$ lies above the x–axis and the area under it is $\frac{9}{2}$. For $-2 \leq x \leq 0$, the graph of $y = x$ lies below the x–axis and the area between the graph and the x–axis is 2. Counting the area below the axis as negative, the value of the integral is $\frac{9}{2} - 2 = \frac{5}{2}$.

19.1.3 For $x \leq 2$, the graph is a straight line of slope -1 and intercept 5. For $x > 2$, it is a straight line parallel to the x–axis, 3 units above the axis. The lines meet at the point $(2,3)$, so the graph of $f(x)$ is continuous at $x = 2$. The value of the integral is 17.

19.2.1 (a) $\dfrac{x^8}{8} + C$, (b) $2\sqrt{x} + C$, (c) $\dfrac{1}{4e^{4t}} + C$.

19.2.3 (a) $\frac{1}{2}x^4 + \frac{3}{2}x^2 - x + C$, (b) $2x^{3/2} - 4\ln|x| - x + C$, (c) $\frac{2}{5}e^{5t} - e^{-5t} - \frac{5}{2}t^2 - x + C$.

19.2.5 (a) $\frac{1}{3}x^3 - x^2 - 3x + C$, (b) $\frac{4}{3}x^{3/4} - 6\ln|x| + C$, (c) $\frac{1}{5}(e^{5x} - e^{-5x}) + e^x - e^{-x} + C$.

19.2.7 $4x + 13\ln|x - 3| + C$.

19.3.1 $6x - x^2$, $p = 6 - x$.

19.3.3 (a) $(Y/r)(e^{rT} - 1)$, (b) $(Y/r)(1 - e^{-rT})$.

19.4.1 15.

19.4.3 $\ln 2$.

(a) 0.708, (b) 0.694. The true value is 0.693 to 3 decimal places, so approximation (b) is much more accurate than (a).

19.4.5 3666.67, 0.27.

Chapter 20

20.1.1 (a) $\frac{2}{3}x(x+1)^{3/2} - \frac{4}{15}(x+1)^{5/2} + C$, (b) $\frac{18}{125}$.

20.1.5 $\frac{3}{2}\left(\exp(-a^{2/3}) - \exp(-b^{2/3})\right)$.

20.2.1 (a) $2(1 - X^{-1/2})$, 2.

(b) $\ln X \to \infty$ as $X \to \infty$.

(c) Integral exists for $\alpha > 1$.

20.2.3 c.

Chapter 21

21.1.1 $y = \frac{1}{4}t^4 + C$. The solution curves are U-shaped with vertex at $(0, C)$.

(a) $y = \frac{1}{4}t^4 + 4$, (b) $y = \frac{1}{4}t^4 - 64$.

21.1.3 $y = 2\exp(\frac{3}{2}x^2)$.

21.1.5 Separating the variables and integrating,

$$at = \int \frac{1}{y}\,dy + \int \frac{b}{a - by}\,dy = \ln y - \ln(a - by) + \text{constant}.$$

Taking exponentials,

$$e^{at} = Cy/(a - by), \qquad (*)$$

where C is a constant. Setting $t = 0$ in $(*)$ gives $C = (a - by_0)/y_0$, and solving $(*)$ for y yields the required solution. Since $C > 0$ by our assumptions on y_0, $0 < y < \frac{a}{b}$.[15] Since $a > 0$, $y \to a/b$ as $t \to \infty$.

21.2.1 (a) $y = 2 + Ae^{-7t}$; $y \to 2$ as $t \to \infty$.

(b) $y = -2 + Ae^{7t}$. When $A > 0$, $y \to \infty$ as $t \to \infty$; when $A < 0$, $y \to -\infty$ as $t \to \infty$, when $A = 0$, $y = -2$ for all t.

21.2.3 $y = 14 + Ae^{-t/7}$, $y = 14 - 9e^{-t/7}$.

21.2.5 $y = \frac{1}{3}(2e^{3x} - 6x + 1)$.

---

[15] Actually this isn't a very good explanation, because we assumed the inequalities in question when we used the expressions $\ln y$ and $\ln(a-by)$. A better answer is to use the 'generalised Rule 2' of Section 19.2 when integrating. The right-hand side of $(*)$ is then replaced by its absolute value. Since the left-hand side is never zero, continuity dictates that $y/(a-by)$ never changes sign, and the rest of the argument is as before.

21.3.1 $y = 3e^{-t} + Ae^{-2t}$.

21.3.3 $y = \left[\dfrac{t}{4} + \dfrac{1}{32} + Ae^{-8t} \right]^{-1/2}$.

21.4.1 Putting $\Delta y_t = 0$ gives the constant particular solution $Y_t = b/a$. In the text the equation is written in the form $y_{t+1} + (a-1)y_t = b$; the constant particular solution is obtained by setting $y_{t+1} = y_t = Y$ and solving for Y. Putting $\Delta y_t = 0$ is equivalent to this but more directly analogous to finding the constant particular solution of a first order differential equation by setting $dy/dt = 0$.

21.4.3   (a) Not equivalent, $y_t = 3 + A(-1/3)^t$.

       (b) Equivalent, $y_t = 3 + A(-3)^t$.

21.4.5   (a) $y_t = 2 + A(-5/3)^t$, $y_t = 2 - 2(-5/3)^t$.

       (b) $y_t = 2 + A(-3/5)^t$, $y_t = 2 - 2(-3/5)^t$.

Chapter 22

22.1.1 (a) 0.175, (b) 1.484, (c) 0.332.

22.1.3 (a) 2, (b) 2.

       (c) If the straight line $y = ax + b$ makes an angle θ with the x–axis, then $\tan \theta = a$.

22.2.1 Sines: $1/\sqrt{2}$, $-1/2$, $-\sqrt{3}/2$, $1/2$, $-\sqrt{3}/2$. Cosines: $-1/\sqrt{2}$, $-\sqrt{3}/2$, $1/2$, $\sqrt{3}/2$, $1/2$.
Tangents: -1, $1/\sqrt{3}$, $-\sqrt{3}$, $1/\sqrt{3}$, $-\sqrt{3}$.

22.2.3 $1/\sqrt{2}$, $\pi/4$.

22.3.1 (a) $a \cos ax$, (b) $-a \sin ax$, (c) $a/\cos^2 ax$, (d) $5 \sin^4 x \cos x$, (e) $5x^4 \cos(x^5)$, (f) $\sin x + x \cos x$, (g) $5x^4 \tan 2x + 2x^5 / \cos^2 2x$, (h) $-(x \sin x + \cos x)/x^2$.

22.3.3 (a) $\dfrac{\sin^7 x}{7} + A$, (b) $\dfrac{\pi + 4}{4\sqrt{2}} - 1$.

22.3.5 (a) $\pi/3$, (b) $2\pi/3$, (c) $\pi/4$, (d) $-\pi/6$.

22.3.7 1, 1.

22.4.1 (a) $(2, \pi/3)$, (b) $(\sqrt{8}, 3\pi/4)$, (c) $(1, -2\pi/3)$, (d) $(\sqrt{2}, -\pi/4)$.

22.4.3 (a) Circle of radius 2 and centre (0,0).

(b) Straight line parallel to y–axis, 4 units to the right of it.

(c) Straight line parallel to x–axis, 3 units above it.

Chapter 23

23.1.1 $1, -32i, -1, i, -i$.

23.1.3 (a) $-2 \pm 3i$, (b) $\frac{1}{2}(5 \pm i\sqrt{11})$.

23.1.5 Let $v = w/z$. Then $vz = w$, so $|v||z| = |w|$, whence $|v| = |w|/|z|$.

23.2.3 (a) $1 + i\sqrt{3}$, 2, $\frac{\pi}{3}$, $2(\cos\frac{\pi}{3} + i\sin\frac{\pi}{3})$.

(b) $-2 + 2i$, $2\sqrt{2}$, $\frac{3\pi}{4}$, $2\sqrt{2}(\cos\frac{3\pi}{4} + i\sin\frac{3\pi}{4})$.

(c) $-\frac{1}{2}(1 + i\sqrt{3})$, 1, $-\frac{2\pi}{3}$, $\cos(-\frac{2\pi}{3}) + i\sin(-\frac{2\pi}{3})$.

(d) $1 - i$, $\sqrt{2}$, $-\frac{\pi}{4}$, $\sqrt{2}\left[\cos(-\frac{\pi}{4}) + i\sin(-\frac{\pi}{4})\right]$.

23.2.5 -2^{20}.

23.3.1 $\sqrt{2}e^{\pi i/4}$, $\sqrt{2}e^{3\pi i/4}$, $2e^{\pi i/3}$, $e^{-2\pi i/3}$.

23.3.3 $(1 + 2i)z^2 + (3 - i)z - 4 - 3i$.

23.3.5 $3i \pm (1 + i)\sqrt{2}$.

Chapter 24

24.1.1 Setting $y = te^{pt}$ we have $dy/dt = (1 + pt)e^{pt}$, whence $d^2y/dt^2 = (2p + p^2t)e^{pt}$. Therefore

$$\frac{d^2y}{dt^2} + b\frac{dy}{dt} + cy = (2p + b)e^{pt} + [p^2 + bp + c]te^{pt}.$$

By definition of p, $b = -2p$ and the term in square brackets is zero; hence the differential equation is satisfied.

24.1.3 (a) $y = Ae^{t/3} + Be^{-t} - 6$, (b) $y = (At + B)e^{-3t} - \dfrac{3t - 5}{27}$.

24.2.1 (a) **UN**, (b) **UN**, (c) **UO**, (d) **UO**, (e) **SN**, (f) **SN**.

24.2.3 (a) $\theta < 2\sqrt{\alpha/\beta}$, (b) $\sigma < 2\sqrt{\beta/\alpha}$.

24.3.1 (a) $y_t = \dfrac{1}{\sqrt{5}}\left[\left(\dfrac{1+\sqrt{5}}{2}\right)^t - \left(\dfrac{1-\sqrt{5}}{2}\right)^t\right]$,

(b) $y_t = \frac{2}{3}((-4)^t + 2^{1+t})$, (c) $y_t = \frac{1}{3}(5\times 2^t - 2^{1-t})$.

24.3.3 $y_t = C\cos(\frac{2}{3}\pi t + \alpha) + \frac{4}{3}t - 1$.

24.3.5 $Y_t - 2Y_{t-1} + \frac{4}{3}Y_{t-2} = 20,\ 60$.

$Y_t = C(\frac{4}{3})^t \cos(\frac{1}{6}\pi t + \alpha) + 60$, $Y_t \to \infty$ as $t \to \infty$.

Chapter 25

25.1.1 $-2, 7$.

The eigenvectors corresponding to -2 are non-zero multiples of $(1\ \ -1)^{\mathrm{T}}$.
The eigenvectors corresponding to 7 are non-zero multiples of $(4\ \ 5)^{\mathrm{T}}$.

25.1.3 Possibilities are $\mathbf{D} = \begin{bmatrix} 2 & 0 \\ 0 & 0 \end{bmatrix}$, $\mathbf{S} = \begin{bmatrix} 1 & 1 \\ 1 & -1 \end{bmatrix}$.

$$\mathbf{A}^k = \begin{bmatrix} 1 & 1 \\ 1 & -1 \end{bmatrix}\begin{bmatrix} 2^{k-1} & 0 \\ 0 & 0 \end{bmatrix}\begin{bmatrix} 1 & 1 \\ 1 & -1 \end{bmatrix} = 2^{k-1}\begin{bmatrix} 1 & 1 \\ 1 & 1 \end{bmatrix}.$$

25.2.1 The eigenvalues are the diagonal entries.

25.2.3 (a) Possibilities are $\mathbf{D} = \begin{bmatrix} 1+i\sqrt{3} & 0 \\ 0 & 1-i\sqrt{3} \end{bmatrix}$, $\mathbf{S} = \begin{bmatrix} 1 & 1 \\ -i\sqrt{3} & i\sqrt{3} \end{bmatrix}$.

$$\mathbf{A}^k = \frac{2^k}{\sqrt{3}}\begin{bmatrix} \sqrt{3}\cos(k\pi/3) & -\sin(k\pi/3) \\ 3\sin(k\pi/3) & \sqrt{3}\cos(k\pi/3) \end{bmatrix}.$$

(b) Possibilities are $\mathbf{D} = \begin{bmatrix} 2+2i & 0 \\ 0 & 2-2i \end{bmatrix}$, $\mathbf{S} = \begin{bmatrix} 1 & 1 \\ -1-2i & -1+2i \end{bmatrix}$.

$$\mathbf{A}^k = 2^{(3k/2)-1}\begin{bmatrix} 2\cos(k\pi/4)-\sin(k\pi/4) & -\sin(k\pi/4) \\ 5\sin(k\pi/4) & 2\cos(k\pi/4)+\sin(k\pi/4) \end{bmatrix}$$

25.2.5 All eigenvectors are multiples of $\begin{bmatrix} 2 \\ -5 \end{bmatrix}$.

25.3.1 Possibilities are $\mathbf{D} = \begin{bmatrix} -2 & 0 \\ 0 & 4 \end{bmatrix}$, $\mathbf{S} = \dfrac{1}{\sqrt{2}}\begin{bmatrix} 1 & 1 \\ 1 & -1 \end{bmatrix}$.

25.3.3 They have at least one positive and one negative eigenvalue.

Chapter 26

6.1.1 (a) $\mathbf{y}(t) = (\frac{1}{2})^t c_1 \begin{bmatrix} 5 \\ -1 \end{bmatrix} + (-\frac{1}{4})^t c_2 \begin{bmatrix} 2 \\ -1 \end{bmatrix}$.

$\mathbf{y}(t) \to \mathbf{0}$ as $t \to \infty$.

(b) $\mathbf{x}(t) = \begin{bmatrix} 18 \\ -2 \end{bmatrix} + (\frac{1}{2})^t c_1 \begin{bmatrix} 5 \\ -1 \end{bmatrix} + (-\frac{1}{4})^t c_2 \begin{bmatrix} 2 \\ -1 \end{bmatrix}$.

$\mathbf{x}(t) \to \begin{bmatrix} 18 \\ -2 \end{bmatrix}$ as $t \to \infty$.

6.1.3 (a)

$$\mathbf{y}(t) = \begin{bmatrix} y_{t+2} \\ y_{t+1} \\ y_t \end{bmatrix}, \quad \mathbf{A} = \begin{bmatrix} -f & -g & -h \\ 1 & 0 & 0 \\ 0 & 1 & 0 \end{bmatrix}.$$

(b)

$$\mathbf{x}(t) = \begin{bmatrix} x_{t+3} \\ x_{t+2} \\ x_{t+1} \\ x_t \end{bmatrix}, \quad \mathbf{A} = \begin{bmatrix} -b_1 & -b_2 & -b_3 & -b_4 \\ 1 & 0 & 0 & 0 \\ 0 & 1 & 0 & 0 \\ 0 & 0 & 1 & 0 \end{bmatrix}, \quad \mathbf{b} = \begin{bmatrix} b_5 \\ 0 \\ 0 \\ 0 \end{bmatrix}.$$

6.2.1 General solution is $\mathbf{y}(t) = c_1 e^{2t} \begin{bmatrix} -1 \\ 2 \end{bmatrix} + c_2 e^{5t} \begin{bmatrix} 1 \\ 1 \end{bmatrix}$. The boundary condition implies that $c_1 = 1$, $c_2 = 3$.

6.3.1 (a) $(-1, 1)$, saddle point. (b) $(2.6, -1.4)$, centre.
(c) $(4, -1)$, spiral sink. (d) $(0, 0)$, source.

6.3.3 (a) The eigenvalues are $1 + i$ and $1 - i$.

(b) $a = p + q$, $b = i(p - q)$.

(c) From the differential equation of the system, $y = \dot{x} - x$. Substituting into the right-hand side of this equation the solution for x given in (b), we obtain

$$y = (-a \sin t + b \cos t)e^t.$$

Hence the general solution is

$$\begin{bmatrix} x \\ y \end{bmatrix} = ae^t \begin{bmatrix} \cos t \\ -\sin t \end{bmatrix} + be^t \begin{bmatrix} \sin t \\ \cos t \end{bmatrix}.$$

26.3.5 The equation of the stable branch is $y = \frac{1}{2}(1 - \sqrt{5})x$.

26.4.1 The fixed points are $(0,0)$ and $(0, 1/a)$. $(0,0)$ is a saddle point; $(0, 1/a)$ is a spiral sink.

Answers to selected problems

Problem 1–1

(i) The equation is of the form $y = sx + c$ where c can be found from the fact that the line passes through $(4, 7)$. The equation is therefore $y = sx + 7 - 4s$, or $y - 7 = s(x - 4)$.

(ii) Since (x_1, y_1) is on the line, $y_1 - 7 = s(x_1 - 4)$; therefore $s = \dfrac{y_1 - 7}{x_1 - 4}$.

(iii) By analogy to (i), the equation of the straight line which has slope s and passes through (x_0, y_0) is $y - y_0 = s(x - x_0)$. By analogy to (ii), the additional information that the line passes through (x_1, y_1) tells us that $s = (y_1 - y_0)/(x_1 - x_0)$. The required equation is therefore

$$y - y_0 = \frac{y_1 - y_0}{x_1 - x_0}(x - x_0).$$

(iv) Taking (x_0, y_0) and (x_1, y_1) to be $(-1, 3)$ and $(1, -5)$ respectively leads to $y = -4x - 1$.

Problem 2–1

Substitute the expression for T into that for C and the resulting expression for C into that for Y. Solving the resulting equation for Y gives
$Y = [c_0 - c_1 t_0 + I + G]/a$,
$C = [c_0 - c_1 t_0 + c_1(1 - t_1)(I + G)]/a$,
$T = [t_0 - c_1 t_0 + t_1 c_0 + t_1(I + G)]/a$,
where $a = 1 - c_1(1 - t_1)$. When G increases by x units, Y increases by x/a units. Since $0 < t_1 < 1$, $0 < 1 - t_1 < 1$; since also $0 < c_1 < 1$, it follows that $0 < c_1(1 - t_1) < 1$; hence $0 < a < 1$, so $\dfrac{1}{a} > 1$. Therefore the change in Y is positive and greater than x. Similarly C increases by $c_1(1 - t_1)(x/a)$ and T by $t_1 x/a$.

Problem 3–3

(i) When $E > P$, $F(X) = \begin{cases} F(X) = X + s(P - X) & \text{if } 0 \le X < P \\ X & \text{if } P \le X < E \\ X - t(X - E) & \text{if } X \ge E \end{cases}$

The graph consists of three line segments: the first has slope $1 - s$ and intercept sP, the second starts at the right end of the first and has slope 1, the third starts at the right end of the second and has slope $1 - t$.

(ii) When $E < P$ and $s + t < 1$,

$$F(X) = \begin{cases} F(X) = X + s(P - X) & \text{if } 0 \le X < E \\ X - t(X - E) + s(P - X) & \text{if } E \le X < P \\ X - t(X - E) & \text{if } X \ge P \end{cases}$$

The graph consists of three line segments: the first has slope $1 - s$ and intercept sP, the second starts at the right end of the first and has slope $1 - s - t$, the third starts at the right end of the second and has slope $1 - t$.

(iii) When $E < P$ and $s + t > 1$, the graph is similar to that in (ii) except that the middle segment now has negative slope.

Problem 4–3

(i) $f(x) = \left(\sqrt{ax} - \sqrt{c/x}\right)^2 + b + 2\sqrt{ac}$. Hence $f(x)$ is minimised when $ax = c/x$, i.e. when $x = \sqrt{c/a}$. The minimum value of $f(x)$ is $b + 2\sqrt{ac}$.

(ii) Average cost is $0.08x + 2 + 50/x$. From (i), this is minimised when $x = \sqrt{50/0.08} = 25$ and its minimum value is $2 + 2\sqrt{50 \times 0.08} = 6$.

Problem 5–4

(i) The profit obtained at time T is $pf(T)$, so the value of the forest at time 0 is $pf(T)/(1 + r)^T$.

(ii) The value of the forest at time 0 is

$$\frac{pf(T)}{(1 + r)^T} + \frac{pf(T)}{(1 + r)^{2T}} + \frac{pf(T)}{(1 + r)^{3T}} + \cdots$$

This is a GP with first term $xpf(T)$ and common ratio x where $x = (1 + r)^{-T}$. Since $0 < x < 1$, the sum is The value of the forest at time 0 is therefore $pf(T)/\left((1 + r)^T - 1\right)$.

Problem 6–3

Revenue $R(x)$ and marginal revenue $R'(x)$ are given by

$$R(x) = px = \tfrac{1}{3}(10 - x)x = \tfrac{1}{3}(10x - x^2)$$

and $R'(x) = \tfrac{2}{3}(5 - x)$. Increase in revenue if sales increase from 3 to 4 is $R(4) - R(3) = 1$, whereas, when $x = 3$, marginal revenue is 4/3. These results are not even approximately equal because, in this case, $h = 1$ is not small enough for the small increments formula to be accurate.

When sales increase from 3 to 3.1, the approximate change in revenue is $\tfrac{2}{3} \times 2 \times 0.01 = 0.13$ to two decimal places.

Problem 7–4

(i) $f'(x) = 5(x+a)^4 - 80 = 5((x+a)^4 - 16)$, which is positive when $|x+a| > 2$ and negative when $|x + a| < 2$. Therefore, f is not monotonic for any value of a.

(ii) Let $x > 0$. Then provided $a \geq 2$, $f'(x) > 0$, so f is monotonic.

(iii) $f'(x) = -2(x + a)^{-3} + 80 = 2(40 - (x + a)^{-3})$. If we restrict x to be positive, f is monotonic provided $a \geq 0.025^{1/3} (\approx 0.2924)$.

Problem 8–4

(i) Differentiating the average revenue function,

$$
\begin{aligned}
\frac{dp}{dx} &= -1800 + 100x - \tfrac{3}{2}x^2 \\
&= -\tfrac{3}{2}\left[\left(x - \tfrac{100}{3}\right)^2 - \left(\tfrac{100}{3}\right)^2 + 1200\right] \quad \text{by completing the square} \\
&\leq 100\left(\tfrac{100}{6} - 18\right) < 0,
\end{aligned}
$$

so AR is monotonic.

(ii) $\text{MR} = \dfrac{d}{dx}(px) = 36000 - 3600x + 150x^2 - 2x^3$, so

$$
\frac{d}{dx}\text{MR} = -3600 + 300x - 6x^2 = -6(x - 20)(x - 30).
$$

Thus MR is not monotonic, being a decreasing function of x for $0 \leq x < 20$ and $x > 30$, and an increasing function for $20 < x < 30$.

(iii) Both graphs meet the vertical axis at 36000. AR is monotonic decreasing with a point of inflexion at $x = 100/3$, where the curve changes from convex to concave. MR has a minimum at $x = 20$ and a maximum at $x = 30$. AR is always above MR: this follows from the fact that $dp/dx < 0$. Both AR and MR are negative for all sufficiently large x: AR $= 0$ when $x = 60$, MR is positive when $x = 40$ but negative when $x = 45$.

Problem 9–3

(i) Let $f(x) = e^{ax}$. Then $f(0) = 1$, so

$$
\lim_{x \to 0} \frac{e^{ax} - 1}{x} = \lim_{x \to 0} \frac{f(x) - f(0)}{x} = f'(0) = ae^{a \times 0} = a.
$$

The second result follows by interchanging a and x.

(ii) $f_a'(x) = e^{ax}$, $f_a''(x) = ae^{ax}$, $f_a(0) = 0$, $f_a'(0) = 1$.

For $a \neq 0$, the curves are all tangential to $y = x$ (i.e. $y = f_0(x)$) at the origin. For $a = 1$ and $a = 5$, the curves are convex and hence lie above $y = x$, the graph of f_5 being more curved than the graph of f_1. For $a = -1$ and $a = -5$, the curves are concave and hence lie below $y = x$, the graph of f_{-5} being more curved than the graph of f_{-1}.

(iii) For $x > 0$, $x^b = e^{b \ln x}$. Hence, by the second result of (i),

$$\lim_{b \to 0} g_b(x) = \lim_{b \to 0} \frac{e^{b \ln x} - 1}{b} = \ln x = g_0(x).$$

$g_b'(x) = x^{b-1}$, $g_b''(x) = (b-1)x^{b-2}$, $g_b(1) = 0$, $g_b'(1) = 1$.

For $b \neq 0$, the curves are all tangential to $y = \ln x$ (i.e. $y = g_0(x)$) at the point $(1,0)$. For $b = \frac{1}{2}$ the curve is concave everywhere but less curved than, and hence above, $y = \ln x$. For $b = 1$ the curve is a straight line; for $b = 2$ the curve is convex. For $b = -1$ and $b = -2$, the curves are concave, the graph of g_{-2} being more curved than the graph of g_{-1}, which in turn is more curved than $y = \ln x$.

Problem 10–4

$D_a = x/(1 - x)$, $D_c = -\ln(1 - x)$. Since $0 < x < 1$, the expressions given for D_a and D_c follow from the power series expansions for $(1 - x)^{-1}$ and $\ln(1 - x)$ respectively. Since $x > 0$, the fact that $D_b < D_c < D_a$ can be read from the coefficients in these series.

Problem 11–2

$A = \begin{bmatrix} 0 & -1 \\ 1 & 0 \end{bmatrix}$, $B = \begin{bmatrix} 1 & 0 \\ 0 & -1 \end{bmatrix}$. A is an anticlockwise rotation through a right angle, B is a reflexion in the x-axis.

$AB = \begin{bmatrix} 0 & 1 \\ 1 & 0 \end{bmatrix}$, $BA = \begin{bmatrix} 0 & -1 \\ -1 & 0 \end{bmatrix}$. AB is the composite mapping consisting of the reflexion B followed by the rotation A; this amounts to interchanging the two coordinates. BA is the composite mapping consisting of the rotation A followed by the reflexion B; this amounts to interchanging the two coordinates and then reflecting in the origin.

Problem 12–2

Suppose A_1 is $k \times k$ and A_2 is $\ell \times \ell$. Then

$$\begin{bmatrix} A_1 & O \\ O & A_2 \end{bmatrix} \begin{bmatrix} A_1^{-1} & O \\ O & A_2^{-1} \end{bmatrix} = \begin{bmatrix} I_k & O \\ O & I_\ell \end{bmatrix} = I.$$

By Fact 4, $\mathbf{A}$ is invertible with inverse as stated.

For the second part, denote the two matrices by $\mathbf{B}$ and $\mathbf{C}$. We may write $\mathbf{B} = \begin{bmatrix} \mathbf{B}_1 & \mathbf{O} \\ \mathbf{O} & \mathbf{B}_2 \end{bmatrix}$ where $\mathbf{B}_1$ and $\mathbf{B}_2$ are 2×2 matrices. Hence $\mathbf{B}^{-1} = \begin{bmatrix} \mathbf{B}_1^{-1} & \mathbf{O} \\ \mathbf{O} & \mathbf{B}_2^{-1} \end{bmatrix}$, where $\mathbf{B}_1^{-1}$ and $\mathbf{B}_2^{-1}$ are calculated by the inversion formula. Also,

$$\mathbf{C} = \begin{bmatrix} \mathbf{C}_1 & \mathbf{0} \\ \mathbf{0} & 2 \end{bmatrix}$$

where $\mathbf{C}_1$ is a 3×3 matrix; hence

$$\mathbf{C}^{-1} = \begin{bmatrix} \mathbf{C}_1^{-1} & \mathbf{0} \\ \mathbf{0} & \frac{1}{2} \end{bmatrix},$$

where $\mathbf{C}_1^{-1}$ is obtained from $\mathbf{C}$ by Gauss–Jordan. Performing the calculations, we have

$$\mathbf{B}^{-1} = \begin{bmatrix} 3/19 & 2/19 & 0 & 0 \\ -2/19 & 5/19 & 0 & 0 \\ 0 & 0 & 1/3 & -2/3 \\ 0 & 0 & 1/6 & 1/6 \end{bmatrix}, \quad \mathbf{C}^{-1} = \begin{bmatrix} -1 & 9 & -4 & 0 \\ 2 & -15 & 7 & 0 \\ 2 & -17 & 8 & 0 \\ 0 & 0 & 0 & \frac{1}{2} \end{bmatrix}.$$

Problem 13–4

(i) The ith component of $\mathbf{y} - \mathbf{Xb}$ is $y_i - b_1 x_{1i} - b_2 x_{2i}$. The result follows.

(ii) $\mathbf{y} - \mathbf{Xb} = \mathbf{y} - \mathbf{Xb}^* + \mathbf{X}(\mathbf{b}^* - \mathbf{b}) = \mathbf{p} + \mathbf{q}$ where $\mathbf{p} = \mathbf{X}(\mathbf{b}^* - \mathbf{b})$, $\mathbf{q} = \mathbf{y} - \mathbf{Xb}^*$ and $\mathbf{p}^T\mathbf{q} = 0$. The result then follows from that of Exercise 13.3.1(b).

(iii) $(*)$ can be written as $\left(\mathbf{X}^T\mathbf{X}\right)\mathbf{b}^* = \mathbf{X}^T\mathbf{y}$. Since $\mathbf{X}^T\mathbf{X}$ is invertible, there is only one vector $\mathbf{b}^*$ which satisfies $(*)$; this is given by $\mathbf{b}^* = \left(\mathbf{X}^T\mathbf{X}\right)^{-1}\mathbf{X}^T\mathbf{y}$.

(iv) The answer to (ii) expresses $Q(\mathbf{b})$ as the sum of two terms, only the second of which depends on $\mathbf{b}$. Since $\mathbf{X}^T\mathbf{X}$ is positive definite, this second term is positve when $\mathbf{b} \neq \mathbf{b}^*$, zero when $\mathbf{b} = \mathbf{b}^*$. Hence $Q(\mathbf{b})$ is minimised when $\mathbf{b} = \mathbf{b}^*$.

Problem 14–3

(i) In this special case,

$$\frac{\partial F}{\partial K} = A(\alpha K^{\alpha-1})L^\beta e^{\mu t} = \frac{\alpha}{K}F(K, L, t) = \frac{\alpha Q}{K}.$$

Similarly, $\dfrac{\partial F}{\partial L} = \dfrac{\beta Q}{L}$ and $\dfrac{\partial F}{\partial t} = \mu Q$. Hence by (14.10),

$$\frac{dQ}{dt} = \frac{\alpha Q}{K}(mK) + \frac{\beta Q}{L}(nL) + \mu Q = (\alpha m + \beta n + \mu)Q,$$

so the rate of growth of output is $\alpha m + \beta n + \mu$.

(ii) In this special case, $dK/dt = nK$, $dL/dt = nL$ and $\partial Q/\partial t = \mu Q$, so by (14.10)

$$\frac{dQ}{dt} = n \left[K \frac{\partial F}{\partial K} + L \frac{\partial F}{\partial L} \right] + \mu Q.$$

By Euler's theorem the term in square brackets is equal to rQ, so the rate of growth of output is $nr + \mu$.

Problem 15–3

(i) $dr/dT = (f(T)f''(T) - [f'(T)]^2)/[f(T)]^2$. So, by the inverse function rule,

$$dT/dr = [f(T)]^2 / \left(f(T)f''(T) - [f'(T)]^2 \right) .$$

So long as the optimal value of T is in the region for which f is concave, then $dT/dr < 0$.

(ii) Define the function $F(r, T) = f'(T)(e^{rT} - 1) - f(T)re^{rT}$. The Faustmann rule can be written in the form $F(r, T) = 0$, so by implicit differentiation

$$\frac{dT}{dr} = -\frac{\partial F}{\partial r} \bigg/ \frac{\partial F}{\partial T} .$$

By definition of the function F,

$$\frac{\partial F}{\partial r} = [Tf'(T) - (1 + rT)f(T)]e^{rT}, \quad \frac{\partial F}{\partial T} = f''(T)(e^{rT} - 1) - r^2 f(T)e^{rT}.$$

It follows that

$$\frac{dT}{dr} = \frac{[Tf'(T)/f(T)] - 1 - rT}{r^2 + [-f''(T)/f(T)](1 - e^{-rT})}. \tag{†}$$

So long as the optimal value of T is in the region for which f is concave, the denominator on the right-hand side of (†) is positive. By the Faustmann rule, the numerator on the right-hand side of (†) can be written as $\dfrac{1 + rT - e^{rT}}{e^{rT} - 1}$, which is easily seen to be negative (use the series for e^x). Hence $dT/dr < 0$.

Part (ii) of this problem could be solved by the method given in the text for comparative statics of optima, which directly exploits the second order condition at the optimum. The above method, which starts by transforming the rule into a form not involving quotients, is simpler in this case.

Problem 16–4

Denote the given utility function by $W(c, y)$. The first-order conditions are

$$\partial W/\partial c = \partial U/\partial c - (1+r)V'(p) = 0, \quad \partial W/\partial y = \partial U/\partial y + (1+r)V'(p) = 0,$$

where $p = (1+r)(y-c)$. [p stands for 'pension', not 'price'!] The Jacobian matrix $\mathbf{J}$ of $(\partial W/\partial c, \partial W/\partial y)$ with respect to (c, y) is the Hessian $D^2 W(c, y)$; therefore

$$\mathbf{J} = \begin{bmatrix} \dfrac{\partial^2 U}{\partial c^2} + s & \dfrac{\partial^2 U}{\partial c\,\partial y} - s \\[3mm] \dfrac{\partial^2 U}{\partial c\,\partial y} - s & \dfrac{\partial^2 U}{\partial y^2} + s \end{bmatrix}, \quad \text{where } s = (1+r)^2 V''(p).$$

Assume that for a given value of r there is a unique pair of optimal values c and y which satisfy the first-order conditions. If in addition $\mathbf{J}$ is invertible at the given optimum, then c and y may be differentiated with respect to r using the implicit function theorem;

$$\begin{bmatrix} dc/dr \\ dy/dr \end{bmatrix} = \mathbf{J}^{-1} \begin{bmatrix} t \\ -t \end{bmatrix},$$

where t is the partial derivative with respect to r of $(1+r)V'((1+r)(y-c))$, considered as a function of c, y, and r. Calculating $\mathbf{J}^{-1}$ by the inversion formula for 2×2 matrices, and t by partial differentiation, we see that

$$\frac{dc}{dr} = \frac{t}{\det \mathbf{J}} \left[\frac{\partial^2 U}{\partial y^2} + \frac{\partial^2 U}{\partial c\,\partial y} \right], \quad \frac{dy}{dr} = -\frac{t}{\det \mathbf{J}} \left[\frac{\partial^2 U}{\partial c^2} + \frac{\partial^2 U}{\partial c\,\partial y} \right],$$

where $t = V''(p) + pV'(p)$.

To discuss the signs of dc/dr and dy/dr, notice that $\det \mathbf{J} \geq 0$ by the second-order conditions for a maximum. These second-order conditions will be met, with $\mathbf{J}$ invertible, if at the optimum $0 < c < y$ (so that $p > 0$), U is concave and $V''(p) < 0$. From now on, assume these further conditions are met. Let

$$\varepsilon = -\frac{V''(p)}{pV'(p)} > 0,$$

and let A, B denote the expressions in square brackets in the solutions just given for dc/dr and dy/dr respectively. Then dc/dr has the sign of $(1 - \varepsilon)A$, and dy/dr has the sign of $(\varepsilon - 1)B$. By the concavity of U, A and B cannot both be positive. If $\dfrac{\partial^2 U}{\partial c\,\partial y} \leq 0$ both A and B will be non-positive; in this case

$$\frac{dc}{dr} \leq 0 \leq \frac{dy}{dr} \text{ if } \varepsilon \leq 1, \quad \frac{dc}{dr} \geq 0 \geq \frac{dy}{dr} \text{ if } \varepsilon \geq 1.$$

If $\dfrac{\partial^2 U}{\partial c\,\partial y} > 0$ it is possible, but not inevitable, that dc/dr and dy/dr have the same sign.

Problem 17–2

(i) w can be interpreted as the wage rate and t as the firm's fixed cost per worker.

(ii) The Lagrangian is

$$L(h, N, \mu) = whN + tN - \mu(F(h, N) - q),$$

so the first-order conditions are

$$wN = \mu \partial F/\partial h, \quad wh + t = \mu \partial F/\partial N.$$

Now $\partial F/\partial h = bN^2(ah+bN)^{-2}$ and $\partial F/\partial N = ah^2(ah+bN)^{-2}$. Substituting these into the first-order conditions and dividing the second condition by the first gives

$$\frac{wh + t}{wN} = \frac{ah^2}{bN^2},$$

whence $\dfrac{ah}{bN} = 1 + \dfrac{t}{wh}$. But $\dfrac{ah}{bN} = \dfrac{h}{bq} - 1$ by the output constraint.

Equating our two expressions for $\dfrac{ah}{bN}$ and rearranging, we see that

$$wh^2 - 2bqwh - bqt = 0.$$

Solving for h by the quadratic formula and taking the positive root gives

$$h = \left(1 + \left[1 + \frac{t}{bqw}\right]^{1/2}\right) bq.$$

N is now found by substituting the solution for h into the output constraint.

(iii) The isoquant $F(h, N) = q$ is a negatively sloped convex curve lying in the positive quadrant with asymptotes $h = bq$ and $N = aq$. The isocost curves have equations of the form $N = k/(wh + t)$ for different values of the total cost k. The economically meaningful parts of these curves lie in the non-negative quadrant, are negatively sloped, convex, have the h–axis as an asymptote and meet the N–axis at $(0, k/t)$. The answer to (ii) lies at the point of tangency of the isoquant and an isocost curve. This isocost curve corresponds to the lowest intercept on the N–axis, and hence the lowest value of k, consistent with being on the isoquant.

Problem 18–2

The Lagrangian for the problem is

$$\mathcal{L}(K_1, K_2, L_1, L_2, \lambda, \mu, p_1, p_2, K, L)$$
$$= p_1 F_1(K_1, L_1) + p_2 F_2(K_2, L_2) - \lambda(K_1 + K_2 - K) - \mu(L_1 + L_2 - L).$$

(i) For $i = 1, 2$, $\partial V/\partial p_i = \partial \mathcal{L}/\partial p_i$ by the envelope theorem, and $\partial \mathcal{L}/\partial p_i = F_i(K_i, L_i)$. The result follows.

(ii) $\partial V/\partial K = \partial \mathcal{L}/\partial K$ by the envelope theorem, and $\partial \mathcal{L}/\partial K = \lambda$. It remains to show that $\lambda = \partial F_i/\partial K_i$ for $i = 1, 2$. But this follows ¿from the first-order conditions $\partial \mathcal{L}/\partial K_i = 0$ for $i = 1, 2$.

(iii) Similar to (ii).

Problem 19–4

(i) (a) The value of the investment at time $t + \Delta t$ is equal to the value at time t plus the interest gained in the time interval $[t, t + \Delta t]$. Approximating this interest by that on $A(t)$ at the rate $r(t)$ gives the result as stated.

(b) Rearranging the result of (a) gives

$$\frac{A(t + \Delta t) - A(t)}{A(t)\, \Delta t} = r(t).$$

Taking the limit as $\Delta t \to 0$, we obtain $A'(t)/A(t) = r(t)$, as required.

Integrating the result of (b) over the interval $[0, T]$ gives

$$\left[\ln A(t) \right]_0^T = \int_0^T r(t)\, dt. \qquad (*)$$

Since $A(0) = P$, the left-hand side of $(*)$ is $\ln(A(T)/P)$, and the result follows.

(ii) Let $P(t, h)$ be the present value at time 0 of the income received during the short time interval $[t, t + h]$. By the final result of (i), with T replaced by t and t by s,

$$f(t)\, h \approx P(t, h) \exp\left[\int_0^t r(s)\, ds \right].$$

Hence $P(t, h) \approx e^{-R(t)} f(t) h$, where $R(t) = \int_0^t r(s)\, ds$. If we split $[0, T]$ into a large number of small sub-intervals, the present value at time 0 of the income stream up to T can be approximated by a sum of terms of the form $P(t, h)$. Passing to the limit as $h \to 0$, the present value of the stream is $\int_0^T e^{-R(t)} f(t)\, dt$.

Problem 20–3

$\int_{-A}^{A} f(x)\, dx = I + J$, where $I = \int_{-A}^{0} f(x)\, dx$ and $J = \int_{0}^{A} f(x)\, dx$. Making the substitution $y = -x$,

$$I = -\int_{A}^{0} f(-y)\, dy = \int_{0}^{A} f(-y)\, dy.$$

In case (i), $I = J$ and the result follows. In case (ii), $I = -J$ and the result follows.

(iii) Denote the required integral by K. By result (i),

$$K = 2 \int_{0}^{1} e^{-x^2/2}\, dx.$$

Using Simpson's rule with 5 ordinates, $K \approx 1.49$ to 2 decimal places.

(iv) The function $y = xe^{-x^2/2}$ is odd. Hence by (ii), $\int_{-A}^{A} xe^{-x^2/2}\, dx = 0$ for all A, and the result follows by letting $A \to \infty$.

This is a special case of the Example in Section 20.2, because we are forcing the limits of integration to tend to infinity together; in the original example, they tend to infinity independently.

(v) By a similar argument to (iv), $\int_{-A}^{A} x^3\, dx = 0$ for all A, so the integral remains zero when we let $A \to \infty$. It is not correct to infer that $\int_{-\infty}^{\infty} x^3\, dx = 0$, because the integrals $\int_{0}^{\infty} x^3\, dx$ and $\int_{-\infty}^{0} x^3\, dx$ diverge.

Problem 21–2

(i) Separating the variables and integrating, $\int z^{-1}\, dz = \int r\, dt$. Hence $\ln z = rt + B$, which can be arranged in the form $z = Ce^{rt}$.

(ii) Since extraction costs are zero, (i) gives $p = Ce^{rt}$. Assuming the market for the resource clears at each instant of time, we have $Ce^{rt} = q^{-\alpha}$, which can be arranged in the form $q = Ae^{(-r/\alpha)t}$.

(iii) Since the total amount of mineral to be extracted is S, $\int_{0}^{\infty} q(t)\, dt = S$. But

$$\int_{0}^{\infty} q(t)\, dt = \lim_{T \to \infty} \int_{0}^{T} Ae^{-\gamma t} dt = \lim_{T \to \infty} \left[(A/\gamma)(1 - e^{-\gamma T}) \right] = A/\gamma,$$

where $\gamma = r/\alpha$. It follows that $A = \gamma S$. Summarising,

$$q(t) = \frac{rS}{\alpha} e^{(-r/\alpha)t}, \qquad p(t) = \left(\frac{\alpha}{rS} \right)^{\alpha} e^{rt}.$$

Problem 22–1

Suppose $R\cos(x - \alpha) = 5\cos x + 12\sin x$ for all x. Then

$$R(\cos x \cos \alpha + \sin x \sin \alpha) = 5\cos x + 12\sin x$$

for all x, so $R\cos\alpha = 5$ and $R\sin\alpha = 12$. Squaring and adding gives $R^2 = 5^2 + 12^2 = 169$; since R is required to be positive, it follows that $R = 13$. Also, $\tan\alpha = 12/5$, so $\alpha = \arctan 2.4 = 1.176$ radians. Thus $f(x) = 13\cos(x-1.176)$.

Since the maximum and minimum values of $\cos(x - \alpha)$ are 1 and -1 for any constant α, the maximum and minimum values of $f(x)$ are ± 13. The graph is like that of $y = \cos x$ but magnified by a factor of 13 and shifted to the right through 1.176 radians.

Problem 23–4

(i) $\displaystyle\int_0^{\pi/2} e^{it}dt = \left[e^{it}/i \right]_0^{\pi/2} = -i(e^{i\pi/2} - 1) = i(1 - i) = 1 + i.$

(ii) Integrating by parts,

$$\int_0^{\pi/2} te^{it}dt = \left[(t/i)e^{it} \right]_0^{\pi/2} - (1/i)\int_0^{\pi/2} e^{it}dt.$$

Hence, using the result of (i),

$$\int_0^{\pi/2} te^{it}dt = (-i\pi/2)e^{i\pi/2} + i(1 + i) = \tfrac{1}{2}(\pi - 2) + i.$$

Again by integration by parts,

$$\int_0^{\pi/2} t^2 e^{it}dt = \left[(t^2/i)e^{it} \right]_0^{\pi/2} - (2/i)\int_0^{\pi/2} te^{it}dt.$$

Hence, using the result above,

$$\int_0^{\pi/2} t^2 e^{it}dt = (-i\pi^2/4)e^{i\pi/2} + 2i(\tfrac{1}{2}[\pi - 2] + i) = \tfrac{1}{4}(\pi^2 - 8) + i(\pi - 2).$$

(iii) Denote the integrals by I and J. Then iI is the imaginary part of the first integral in (ii), so $I = 1$. J is the real part of the second integral in (ii), so $J = \tfrac{1}{4}(\pi^2 - 8)$.

Problem 24–4

The discrete-time analogue of the differential equation is

$$\Delta^2 y_t + b\Delta y_t + cy_t = u,$$

which may be written as

$$(y_{t+2} - 2y_{t+1} + y_t) + b(y_{t+1} - y_t) + cy_t = u,$$

or more simply as

$$y_{t+2} + fy_{t+1} + gy_t = u$$

where $f = b - 2$, $g = 1 - b + c$. For the differential equation, the stationary solution occurs if $d^2y/dt^2 = dy/dt = 0$ and is therefore $y = u/c$. For the difference equation, the stationary solution occurs if $\Delta^2 y_t = \Delta y_t = 0$ and is therefore $y_t = u/c$.

The differential equation exhibits oscillatory behaviour if its characteristic equation has complex roots, i.e. if $b^2 < 4c$. The difference equation exhibits oscillatory behaviour if *its* characteristic equation has complex roots, i.e. if $f^2 < 4g$: this inequality may be written

$$(b - 2)^2 < 4(1 - b + c)$$

and therefore reduces to $b^2 < 4c$.

For the differential equation, the condition for the stationary solution to be stable has been obtained in the text as $b > 0$, $c > 0$. For the difference equation, the condition for the stationary solution to be stable is that the roots of the characteristic equation are are both < 1 in absolute value (or modulus, if the roots are complex). In the case of real roots, it is therefore necessary that $x^2 + fx + g > 0$ at $x = \pm 1$. This ensures that one of the following three cases occurs: (a) both roots between -1 and 1, (b) both roots < -1, (c) both roots > 1. But the product of the roots is g, so if we assume that $g < 1$ then cases (b) and (c) are eliminated and we are left with (a). In the case of complex roots, we have $x^2 + fx + g > 0$ for all x, and in particular at $x = \pm 1$. Also the roots are complex conjugates, so the product of the roots is r^2 where r is the common modulus: to ensure that $r < 1$ we must therefore impose the condition $g < 1$.

To summarise, the criterion ensuring stability in the cases of both real and complex roots is

$$1 + f + g > 0, \quad 1 - f + g > 0, \quad g < 1.$$

In terms of b and c these three conditions may be written respectively as $c > 0$, $c > 2b - 4$, $c < b$ and therefore reduce to the chain of inequalities

$$0 < c < b < 2 + \tfrac{1}{2}c.$$

As in the first-order case, we note that the qualitative behaviour of the discrete-time analogue is not necessarily the same as that of the differential equation for the same parameter values.

Problem 25–3

(i) By inspection, the given matrix is equal to its transpose. By straightforward matrix multiplication, we see that the square of the given matrix is equal to the matrix itself.

(ii) Let λ is an eigenvalue of a projection matrix $\mathbf{P}$, and let $\mathbf{x}$ be a corresponding eigenvectior: $\mathbf{x} \neq \mathbf{0}$ and $\mathbf{Px} = \lambda\mathbf{x}$. Since $\mathbf{P} = \mathbf{P}^2$, $\mathbf{Px} = \mathbf{P}(\mathbf{Px})$: hence

$$\lambda\mathbf{x} = \mathbf{P}(\lambda\mathbf{x}) = \lambda\mathbf{Px} = \lambda^2\mathbf{x}.$$

Since $\mathbf{x} \neq \mathbf{0}$, it follows that $\lambda = \lambda^2$, so λ is either 1 or 0.

(iii) By (ii), the characteristic polynomial of $\mathbf{P}$ is $(\lambda - 1)^r \lambda^{n-r}$ for some r.

Let $\mathbf{D}$ be the diagonal matrix whose first r diagonal entries are equal to 1 and whose remaining diagonal entries are all zero. Hence, by Theorem 1 of Section 25.3, there is an orthogonal matrix $\mathbf{S}$ such that $\mathbf{S}^\mathrm{T}\mathbf{PS} = \mathbf{D}$. Since $\mathbf{S}$ is an orthogonal matrix, $\mathbf{SS}^\mathrm{T} = \mathbf{I}$, whence $\mathbf{P} = \mathbf{SDS}^\mathrm{T}$.

Partition $\mathbf{S}$ as $(\mathbf{Z} \ \mathbf{Y})$, where $\mathbf{Z}$ consists of the first r columns. Then the equation $\mathbf{SS}^\mathrm{T} = \mathbf{I}_n$ may be written

$$\begin{bmatrix} \mathbf{Z}^\mathrm{T}\mathbf{Z} & \mathbf{Z}^\mathrm{T}\mathbf{Y} \\ \mathbf{Y}^\mathrm{T}\mathbf{Z} & \mathbf{Y}^\mathrm{T}\mathbf{Y} \end{bmatrix} \begin{bmatrix} \mathbf{I}_r & \mathbf{O} \\ \mathbf{O} & \mathbf{I}_{n-r} \end{bmatrix}.$$

In particular, $\mathbf{Z}^\mathrm{T}\mathbf{Z} = \mathbf{I}_r$. Also, the equation $\mathbf{P} = \mathbf{SDS}^\mathrm{T}$ may be written

$$\mathbf{P} = \begin{bmatrix} \mathbf{Z} & \mathbf{Y} \end{bmatrix} \begin{bmatrix} \mathbf{I}_r & \mathbf{O} \\ \mathbf{O} & \mathbf{O} \end{bmatrix} \begin{bmatrix} \mathbf{Z}^\mathrm{T} \\ \mathbf{Y}^\mathrm{T} \end{bmatrix}.$$

Hence

$$\mathbf{P} = \begin{bmatrix} \mathbf{Z} & \mathbf{Y} \end{bmatrix} \begin{bmatrix} \mathbf{Z}^\mathrm{T} \\ \mathbf{O} \end{bmatrix} = \mathbf{ZZ}^\mathrm{T},$$

as required.

(iv) Let $\mathbf{Z}$ be an $n \times r$ matrix such that $\mathbf{Z}^\mathrm{T}\mathbf{Z} = \mathbf{I}_r$. Then $\mathbf{ZZ}^\mathrm{T}$ is $n \times n$ and

$$(\mathbf{ZZ}^\mathrm{T})^\mathrm{T} = \mathbf{Z}^\mathrm{TT}\mathbf{Z}^\mathrm{T} = \mathbf{ZZ}^\mathrm{T}.$$

Also

$$(\mathbf{ZZ}^\mathrm{T})^2 = \mathbf{ZZ}^\mathrm{T}\mathbf{ZZ}^\mathrm{T} = \mathbf{ZI}_r\mathbf{Z}^\mathrm{T}.$$

Hence $\mathbf{ZZ}^\mathrm{T}$ is a projection matrix.

Problem 26–4

(i) Writing $k = \ln K$ and $h = \ln H$, we have

$$\frac{dk}{dt} = \frac{1}{K}\frac{dK}{dt} = s_1 A K^{\alpha-1} H^\gamma - \delta_1, \quad \frac{dh}{dt} = \frac{1}{H}\frac{dH}{dt} = s_2 A K^\alpha H^{\gamma-1} - \delta_2.$$

Since $k = \ln K$, $K = e^k$, whence $K^\theta = e^{\theta k}$ for any constant θ. Similarly, $H^\theta = e^{\theta h}$ for any constant θ. We therefore have the following autonomous system in k and h:

$$\dot{k} = s_1 A \exp([\alpha - 1]k + \gamma h) - \delta_1, \quad \dot{h} = s_2 A \exp(\alpha k + [\gamma - 1]h) - \delta_2.$$

(ii) Let $b_i = \ln(s_i A / \delta_i)$ for $i = 1, 2$. Then the set of points in the kh–plane for which $\dot{k} = 0$ is the straight line

$$(\alpha - 1)k + \gamma h + b_1 = 0.$$

Since $\alpha < 1$ and $\gamma > 0$, this is an upward-sloping line of slope $(1 - \alpha)/\gamma$. By a similar argument, the set of points in the kh–plane for which $\dot{h} = 0$ is an upward-sloping straight line of slope $\alpha/(1 - \gamma)$. Since $\alpha + \gamma < 1$,

$$\frac{1 - \alpha}{\gamma} > 1 > \frac{\alpha}{1 - \gamma}.$$

Thus the line $\dot{k} = 0$ is steeper than the line $\dot{h} = 0$, so the two lines intersect at exactly one point (k^*, h^*).

(iii) The Jacobian of the autonomous system is

$$\begin{bmatrix} (\alpha - 1)s_1 e^{-k}Q & \gamma s_1 e^{-k}Q \\ \alpha s_2 e^{-h}Q & (\gamma - 1)s_2 e^{-h}Q \end{bmatrix},$$

where $Q = A\exp(\alpha k + \gamma h)$. For all k and h, both diagonal entries are negative and the determinant is

$$(1 - \alpha - \gamma)s_1 s_2 e^{-(k+h)}Q^2 > 0.$$

Therefore, conditions (i) and (iia) of Olech's theorem hold and (k^*, h^*) is globally stable.

Index

abscissa, 389n
absolute value, 42
addition formulae (for sine
    and cosine), 453–454
adjoint matrix, 233
alternating behaviour, 436
annual percentage rate, 79
antiderivative, *see* primitive
area under a curve, 370–372
Argand diagram, 471
argument of complex number, 472
arithmetic progression, 70
    sum, 75
associative law:
    matrix addition, 191
    matrix multiplication, 196
    vector addition, 187
asymptote, 142
augmented matrix, 207
average product, 257
average revenue, 146

base of logarithm, 66
basic column, *see* echelon matrix
basis, 201
Bernoulli equation, 429–430
binomial:
    series, 178–179
    theorem, 179
boundary condition, 416, 423, 434
boundary maxima and minima, 134
Box–Cox transformation, 161
budget:
    constraint, 24
    line, 25
    set, 25

Cartesian coordinates, 461
centre, 552

CES production function, 181, 289–290
chain rule:
    several variables, 256
    two variables, 253
chaos, 564
characteristic equation:
    and stability of equilibrium, 494–496
    difference equation, 500–502,
        504, 510
    differential equation, 485–487, 509
characteristic polynomial, 520, 531–532
characteristic root, *see* eigenvalue
circular functions, *see* trigonometric
    functions
circular measure, 444
Cobb–Douglas production function, 258
    generalised, 258n
cobweb model, 436–439
cofactor, 228
commutative law:
    matrix addition, 190
    matrix multiplication (failure), 196
    vector addition, 187
comparative statics:
    linear market model, 279–281
    nonlinear market model, 281–283
    of optima, 283–284
    two-market model, 287–288
complementary slackness, 362
complementary solution:
    first-order difference equation, 434
    first-order differential equation, 421
    second-order difference equation, 502
    second-order differential equation, 489
completing the square, 38
complex numbers, 466–470
    conjugate, 468, 479
    trigonometric form, 471–472
composite function, 49

composite mapping, 49
compound interest, 78
concave function of one variable, 142
    global maximum points, 143
concave function of several variables,
        302–305, 308
    global maximum points, 304, 308
conditional demand functions, 335
constant returns to scale, 16
constraint qualification, 328
consumer's surplus, 394
consumption bundle, 39
continuity and differentiability,
        105–106
continuous compounding, 148,
        152, 386
continuous discounting, 152, 386
    infinite streams, 405
continuous function, 93, 104–105
    several variables, 268
contour diagram, 296
convergent series, 77
convex function of one variable, 139
    global minimum points, 140–141
convex function of several variables,
        306, 308
    global minimum points, 306
convex set, 138, 303
coordinates, 1
    Cartesian, 461
    polar, 461–462
cosine, 445, 449
    differentiation, 455–457
    graph, 451–452
cost minimisation, 334–335, 337
Cournot aggregation, 345
Cramer's rule, 233
critical point, 121, 294, 300
    of inflexion, 121
critical value, 121, 295

d–matrix, see diagonalisable matrix
demand and supply, 6–8
    with price adjustment, 424–425
demand function, 264, 331
De Moivre's theorem, 473–474
dependent variable, 48

derivative, 88
    partial, 247
    second, 126, 248
determinant, 225–230
    and eigenvalues, 521
    expansion, 228, 232
    properties, 225–228
diagonal matrix, 196
diagonalisable matrix, 512, 520
difference equation, 432
    boundary condition, 434
    complementary solution,
        433–434, 502
    first-order, 433
    particular solution, 433–434, 502
    qualitative behaviour, 435–436,
        503–504
    second-order, 499
    stationary solutions, 425, 503–504
difference operator:
    backward, 432n
    forward, 432, 499
differentiable, 95, 252
differential, 254, 401
differential coefficient, see derivative
differential equation, 416
    boundary condition, 416, 423
    complementary solution, 421, 489
    first-order, 416
    initial condition, 416
    integrating factor, 427–429
    linear with constant coefficients,
        420–425, 484–489
    particular solution, 421, 489
    qualitative behaviour, 492–496
    second-order, 483
    separable, 417
    stationary solutions, 425, 492
differentiation, 89
    circular functions, 456–458
    combination rule, 97
    composite function rule, 110
    inverse function rule, 114
    power rule, 96, 111
    product rule, 108, 119
    quotient rule, 108, 121
    under the integral sign, 408–412

diminishing returns, 259
discontinuous, 93
distance, 46
distributive laws, 196
divergent series, 77

e, 149, 151
echelon matrix, 204
    basic column, 204
    pivot, 204
economist's favourite approximation,
    154
eigenvalue, 513
    computation, 522–523
eigenvector, 513
elementary operations, 13
    on rows of matrices, 207
ellipse, 323
endogenous variable, 283
Engel aggregation, 345
envelope theorem, 351
    and cost curves, 351–353
equilateral triangle, 447–448
equilibrium, 6
Euler's formula for complex numbers,
    476
Euler's theorem, 261–262, 270
excess demand function, 282
exchange rate dynamics, 554
exogenous variable, 283
exponential function, 148–149
    complex, 475–476
    derivative, 150, 163
    graph, 149

factorial, 44
factorisation, 57
factors of production, 257
Faustmann rule, 162, 290
feasible set, 26
Fibonacci sequence, 506
first-order condition, 131, 298
    constrained optimisation, 319
    utility maximisation, 331
Fisher rule, 162, 290
fixed point, 546
    hyperbolic, 561

flat rate of interest, 79
flow, 385
focus, 550–551
function, 41
    even and odd, 413
    monotonic, 113
fundamental theorem of algebra,
    478, 519
fundamental theorem of calculus, 376

Gauss–Jordan elimination, 211
Gaussian elimination, 14, 207
geometric progression, 70
    sum, 76–77
Gini coefficient, 391
global maxima and minima, 131–133
    constrained, 323–324
    with several variables, 302–306
global stability, 562
gradient, *see* slope
gradient vector, 249
graph, 42
gross output, 15
    vector, 202
growth, 158–159, 264

Hermitian matrix, 529
Hermitian transpose, 528
Hessian matrix, 250
higher derivatives, 174
homogeneous function, 261, 265
Hotelling's rule, 440

i, *see* imaginary number
identity matrix, 199
image, 44
imaginary number, 466–467
implicit differentiation, 274
implicit function theorem, 287
implicit relation, 271
    local solution, 272
independent variable, 48
indeterminate form, 171
indices, 61–64
indifference curve, 278
indirect utility function, 331, 350,
    357

inequality constraints, 360
infinity, 73
inflation, 496–498
inner product, 235
input-output analysis, 15–16, 201,
    223, 242
integer, 36
integral, 372–373
    and area, 370–372
    definite, 380
    improper, 406–407
    indefinite, 378
    infinite, 404–406
integrand, 381
integration, 373
    by change of variable, 400–01
    by parts, 399–400
    by substitution, 400–401
    constant of, 378
    in economics, 384–386
    limits of, 381
    numerical, 387–393
    range of, 381
    rules, 378–381
intercept of straight line, 3
interior maxima and minima, 134
intermediate value theorem, 94
interval, 37
    closed, 371
    open, 371n
inverse function, 114
    derivative, 114
inverse matrix, 214–218
inverse demand function, 251
IS–LM model, 290–291
isoprofit line, 29
isoquant, 110, 275, 278
isosceles triangle, 447–448

Jacobian matrix, 286

Kuhn–Tucker conditions, 363
    sufficiency of, 364–365
Kuhn–Tucker theorem, 363

Lagrange multiplier, 321
    marginal interpretation, 349

Lagrange multiplier rule, 321, 325
    and cost functions, 334–335, 339
    and utility maximisation, 329–332,
        337
    several constraints, 326
Lagrangian function, 321
    behaviour, 327
latent root, *see* eigenvalue
least-squares estimation, 243
Leibniz's formula, 410
l'Hôpital's rule, 171–172
limit:
    of function, 104
    of sequence, 71
    of $\sin\theta/\theta$, 455–456
linear approximations and
    differentiability, 91–92, 166
linear combination, 187
linear dependence and independence,
    187–188
linear function, 41
linear programming, 28–33
linear relation, 2
local maximum and minimum points,
    131–133
    with several variables, 295–301
local stability, 561
logarithm, 66
    change-of-base formula, 66
    common, 66
    natural, 153–154
logistic model, 420
Lorenz curve, 390–391

Maclaurin's theorem, 175
Maclaurin series, 177
    for e^x, 177
    $\ln(1+x)$, 178
    $(1+x)^c$, 178–179
    $\sin x$ and $\cos x$, 458–459
mapping, 49
marginal cost, 135, 336–337
marginal product, 257
marginal rate of substitution,
    274, 276
marginal revenue, 99, 135
marginal utility, 278

Markov chain, 540
matrix, 189
    addition, 190
    adjoint, 233
    as mapping, 191–192
    identity, 199
    inversion, 214–218
    multiplication, 193–195
    multiplication by scalar, 190
    nonsingular, 213
    partitioned, 197
    singular, 213
    square, 198–199
    transpose, 230–231
matrix-vector multiplication, 191
maximum and minimum points:
    general function, 122
    quadratic function, 54–55,
        59–60
mean value theorem, 170
    second, 172–174, 183
minor, 239
mixed derivative theorem, 248, 269
modulus, 42
    of complex number, 472
money base, 82
monotonic function, 114–115
    weakly, 118
monotonic transformations and
        global maxima, 307
multiplier-accelerator model,
        504–505

natural logarithm, 153–154
natural numbers, 36
negative definiteness and
        semidefiniteness, 237
    testing, 237–240
net output, 15
    vector, 202
Newton's method, 168–170
non-negative quadrant, 39
non-negativity restriction:
    one variable, 135, 143
    several variables, 309–312
    together with equation
        constraint, 357

normal good, 281

objective function, 29, 348
Olech's theorem, 562
open access fishery, 562
optimisation, 28, 121, 130
ordered list, 40
ordered pair, 38
ordinate, 389n
orthogonal matrix, 234, 525–526
oscillatory behaviour, 442
    damped and explosive, 442–443,
        493
    systems of differential
        equations, 536–537

parabola, 54
partial derivative, 247
    mixed, 248
    second, 248
particular solution:
    first-order difference equation, 434
    first-order differential equation,
        421
    second-order difference
        equation, 502
    of second-order differential
        equation, 489
periodic function, 452
phase diagram, 547
phase plane, 547
phase portrait, 548
pivot, *see* echelon matrix
point of inflexion, 121, 129
polar coordinates, 463–464
positive definiteness and
        semidefiniteness, 236
    testing, 237–240
price elasticity:
    of demand, 100, 156
    of supply, 100, 156
    own-price and cross-price, 251
primitive, 376
principal minor, 239
production function, 257
    aggregate, 259
profit-maximising monopolist, 134

projection matrix, 529
proper value, *see* eigenvalue
Pythagoras' theorem, 46, 446

quadratic:
  equation, 56
  form, 236
  function, 54
quasi-concave function, 338–339
  and concavity, 339
  and constrained optimisation, 343
  and diminishing returns, 342
  and homogeneity, 341
  in economics, 342
  monotonic transformations,
    339–340

radian, 444
rank of matrix, 220–221
rate of change of:
  function of time, 158
  linear function, 87
rate of growth, 158–159
rational number, 36
returns to scale, 262–263
right-handed system of axes, 246
risk aversion, 161
Rolle's theorem, 170, 182
roots:
  polynomial equation, 478–479
  quadratic equation, 56–58, 478
rotations and matrices, 453
Roy's identity, 356

saddle point:
  of dynamic system, 549
  of function, 296, 299, 316
scalar, 185
Schur's lemma, 526
second derivative, 126
second derivative test, 128
  ambiguous case, 129, 299
  analogue for several variables,
    298
second mean value theorem,
    172–174, 183
second-order conditions, 131, 298

second-order small quantity, 119
sequence, 70
series, 74
set(s):
  elements, 35
  empty set, 36
  intersection, 51
  members, *see* elements
  subset, 36
  union, 51
Shephard's lemma, 355
simultaneous equations, 9–14
sine, 445, 449
  differentiation, 456–458
  graph, 451–452
sink, 548
slope:
  of general function, 88
  straight line, 3
small increments formula, 92, 166
  several variables, 255
  two variables, 252, 269
Solow–Swan growth model, 430–431,
    441, 566
source, 547
spiral sink, 552
spiral source, 550
square matrix, 198–199
  powers, 198, 512
square roots, 45
stable branch, 549
stable focus, 551
stable node, *see* sink
stability, 424, 494–496, 537, 546–547
  local and global, 560–563
stationary point, 121n, 294
stationary solution:
  first-order difference equation, 434
  first-order differential equation,
    425
  second-order difference equation,
    504
  second-order differential equation,
    492
  system of difference equations, 537
  system of differential equations,
    536

stock, 385
Stone–Geary utility function, 332–334
    boundary optima, 359
strict inequality, 20
strictly concave function, 143
strictly convex function, 141
submatrix, 238
supply, 6
symmetric matrix, 236
    eigenvalues, 524–527
systems of difference equations,
    534–537
systems of differential equations,
    541–543, 546–552

tangent line, 88
tangent plane, 252
tangent (trigonometric), 445, 451
    differentiation, 456–458
    graph, 452–453
Taylor approximation, 175–176,
    316–317
Taylor series, 177
Taylor's theorem, 175
technical progress, 263–264
time in economics, 157
    discrete versus continuous,
    157–158, 415
trace, 521
transpose matrix, 230–231
triangular matrix, 198
trigonometric functions, 445–447
    inverse, 458–459
turning points, *see* maximum and
    minimum points
twice differentiable, 126

unemployment, 496–498, 539
unitary matrix, 529
unstable focus, 550
unstable node, 547
utility function, 276
    indirect, 338
    Stone–Geary, 332–334
utility maximisation, 329
    first-order conditions, 337

variable,
    dependent versus independent, 48
    endogenous versus exogenous, 283
    stock versus flow, 385
vector, 186
    addition, 187
    geometric interpretation, 187
    multiplication by scalar, 187
    row versus column, 224–225
velocity, 90

weak inequality, 20

zero matrix, 190
zero vector, 187

3333